Brendan Sainsbury

D0723634

Hiking
IN ITALY

COASTAL SPECTACULARS

1 AMALFI
Depictions of heaven are uncannily reminiscent of the Sentiero degli Dei (Path of the Gods, p253), an aptly named high-level walkway above the elegant cypress trees and whitewashed villages of Campania's precipitous coast.

2 CINQUE TERRE
A twisted network of walking paths trodden down for centuries by hard-working cliff-side farmers, the rugged trails of Cinque Terre are today shared with several thousand tourists who puff their way along the emblematic Sentiero Azzurro (p58).

3 SORRENTO
Once a gathering place for the British literati, Sorrento (p258) has retained its romantic allure on a grassy peninsula where – legend has it – beautiful sirens once lured witless sailors to their deaths. Across the horizon, the idyllic isle of Capri keeps an ever-watchful eye.

4 PORTOFINO
Who knew? Within 5km of Portofino's yacht-filled harbour lies an isolated coastal wilderness where narrow footpaths bisect lonely promontories and paved roads are an ugly 21st-century apparition. Mingle with braying goats and enjoy the serenity for free (p64).

5 GOLFO DI OROSEI
Beyond the beachside glitz of mainland Italy lies what DH Lawrence called 'the savage, dark-bushed, sky-exposed land' of Sardinia (p299) speckled with isolated beaches and lonely coves. Follow the eastern coastal paths, and find out where the real roads lead.

HIKES THROUGH HISTORY

1 TUSCAN TOWERS

Long before Manhattan sprouted skyscrapers, the Ghibellines of medieval San Gimignano (p201) were raising their own lofty towers. Fourteen of them still remain, poking like time-warped beacons above the vine-striped hills of rural Tuscany.

2 VIA FERRATA

Overcome your vertigo, and follow in the footsteps of battle-ravaged WWI soldiers as you cross the Alps on the iconic 'iron ways' – once wartime supply arteries but now fixed protection climbing routes (p46).

3 GREAT ESCAPES

There's no Steve McQueen and no motorbike; however, Parco Nazionale della Majella's trailblazing freedom path across the Apennines (p235) was enough to remind escaping WWII POWs just what they were risking their lives for.

4 LAKESIDE SECRETS

Suspended above Lago Maggiore, the spinach-green Valle Cannobina (p132) hides a cache of mossy secrets beneath its canopy of beech forest. Follow the ancient pilgrims' trails and uncover abandoned medieval hamlets and musty chapels.

5 WALSER HERITAGE

Imagine this. You're in Italy close to the border with France, yet the locals reside in oddly shaped timber-beamed houses and speak a bastardised offshoot of modern German. In the Walser valleys of the Aosta (p106) region, an esoteric 800-year-old culture has survived war, peace, isolation and globalisation.

4

NATIONAL PARKS

1 ABRUZZO

Founded in 1923, Parco Nazionale d'Abruzzo (p238) is the last European refuge of the Marsican bear, and safeguards the nation's valuable haven of wolves and rare woodpeckers.

2 GRAN PARADISO

Italy's first park (p93), which was a present to the nation from King Vittorio Emanuele II, single-handedly saved the endangered ibex from extinction. Protected for over 80 years, it remains one of the country's most unblemished spots.

3 STELVIO

It's hard to compete with the Dolomites for eye-popping beauty, but Stelvio National Park (p142) makes a good stab at it. Order your *prima colazione* (breakfast) in Italian and your *abendessen* (dinner) in German on the culture-transcending Val di Rabbi to Martelltal trek.

4 MONTI SIBILLINI

Imagine *Lord of the Rings* meets *Wuthering Heights* set in the Apennines and you've got a taste of what Parco Nazionale dei Monti Sibillini (p225) has to offer. Coloured by ancient myths and covered with grassy moors, this is the land where Queen Sibilla lived in a cave on her eponymous mountain.

5 GRAN SASSO E MONTI DELLA LAGA

Noted for its 'giant stone' (*gran sasso*) mountains, and expansive national park, Gran Sasso e Monti della Laga (p231) has got wilderness written all over it. Lace up your walking shoes and bring a comprehensive field guide; this is one of most biodiverse areas of Europe.

OFF THE BEATEN TRACK

1 SARDINIA

Almost Italy, but not quite, Sardinia (p289) is the island that everyone aspires to visit but seldom does. Their loss could be your gain. Put your Colosseum plans on hold and head for the less-heralded delights of Dorgali, Oliena and the Gola di Gorropu.

2 MARITIME ALPS

Where have all the people gone? To the coast – most likely leaving this dramatic pocket of the southwestern Alps the preserve of marmots, shepherds and the odd bemused hiker. Climb up onto the Marguareis massif (p82) and savour the taste of solitude.

3 APENNINES

Not considered 'cool' enough for serious skiing, the brooding Apennines (p223) have escaped the resort mayhem of the Alps. Secure inside its lonely valleys, the region stands as a rusty reminder of the Italy that once was – and still is, if you know where to look.

4 JULIAN & CARNIC ALPS

Standing on the cusp of half a dozen ancient cultures, the 'forgotten' Alps were the frenetic front line in two world wars and the tetchy Cold War that followed. These days you can wander across once-disputed borders into Slovenia and Austria without even realising it (p178).

5 SICILY – NEBRODI

In crowded Italy, the opportunities to wander 'as lonely as a cloud' are sometimes dismally thin on the ground; however, claustrophobics can seek solace in unsung Parco Regionale dei Nebrodi (p280), Sicily's so-called 'island within an island'.

PEAK-BAGGERS

1 MONTE PEZ

It's not tall, but it's temptingly traversable and you can reach the summit before lunch if you get up for your porridge early. Not-so-lofty Pez (p159), atop the Sciliar range, is famous for its views of the pink-hued Dolomites clustered like raised daggers around it.

2 MT ETNA

Emperor Hadrian set the pace, hauling himself to the top of Sicily's dozing giant in AD 121. Many have followed since, chancing Etna's better moods in between frequent bursts of volcanic activity. Check out the weather/magma forecast and have a stab at your own historic Etna traverse (p269).

3 CORNO GRANDE

The summit of the Apennines is a straightforward climb starting from the windy plateau of Campo Imperatore (p233) where Mussolini was once snatched by Nazi storm troopers. The greatest escapes these days are by tired tourists heading down the adjacent cable car.

4 APUAN ALPS

King of the Apuan Alps, Pizzo d'Uccello (p211) overlooks the famous Carrera marble mines where Michelangelo hand-picked the stone that he sculpted into the iconic image *David*. The peak itself is an equally dramatic natural sculpture.

5 MONTE BALDO

More a ridge of competing peaks than a stand-alone mountain, Baldo guards the eastern shores of Lago di Garda (p121). Anything but 'bald', the mountain is known as Italy's botanic garden for its rich diversity of plants.

HIKING IN ITALY

Forget Milanese catwalks and supersonic Ferraris. For nearly two millennia Italy's hikers have been the nation's most important trailblazers, from Emperor Hadrian and his epiphanic ascent of Mt Etna in AD 121, to home-grown mountaineer Reinhold Messner and his superhuman scramble up the north face of Everest without oxygen 1959 years later. But there's more to the peninsula's waymarked paths than pure blood and guts. For fresh-air fiends, the monolithic beauty of Italy's *sentieri* (walking trails) is every bit as beguiling as the artistic wizardry of Michelangelo's *David*. Even better, walking along the nation's network of well-organised trails not only enables you to dodge Florentine museum queues, it also provides an excellent excuse to eat copious amounts of ice cream, quaff fine wine, and sink potent shots of grappa en route.

Though Italy's wilderness can't compete size-wise with the boreal forests of North America, its position at the crossroads of feuding empires for over 3000 years has left deep fissures on its landscape. Preserved in ancient pastel-shaded villages and steeply terraced Ligurian vineyards, the imprint of human history is ubiquitous here; yet nowhere has its juxtaposition with the natural environment appeared so harmonious, so finely integrated.

'Looking out of a Gothic window every morning, it seems impossible that the Middle Ages have passed away', wrote EM Forster of Italy in 1905. The implication of the words still resonates. From the lofty *alte vie* of the Dolomites to the ancient pilgrims' routes of pastoral Tuscany, Italy is more than just a titillating art museum for cappuccino-fuelled culture vultures; it is for anyone who has ever ventured wistfully down a rural trail and wondered where the long and winding road might lead.

Contents

THE MAPS

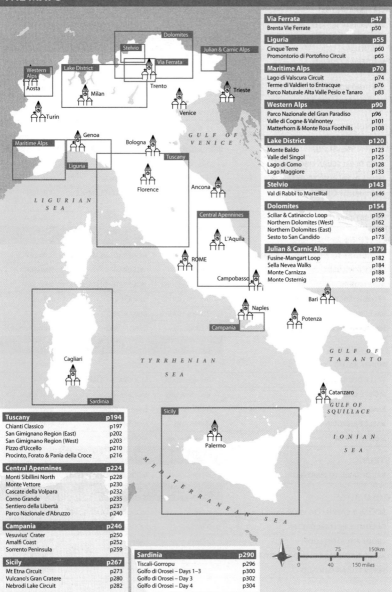

Table of Hikes

VIA FERRATA	DURATION	DIFFICULTY	SEASON
VIA FERRATA SOSAT	2½–3 HOURS	BEGINNER	JUN–OCT
VIA FERRATA ALFREDO BENINI	3½–4½ HOURS	BEGINNER–INTERMEDIATE	JUN–OCT

LIGURIA	DURATION	DIFFICULTY	SEASON
SENTIERO AZZURRO	2½–5 HOURS	EASY–MODERATE	ALL YEAR
SENTIERO ROSSO	9–12 HOURS	MODERATE	ALL YEAR
SANCTUARIO CIRCUIT	5 HOURS	EASY–MODERATE	ALL YEAR
PROMONTORIO DI PORTOFINO CIRCUIT	5–6½ HOURS	MODERATE	ALL YEAR

MARITIME ALPS	DURATION	DIFFICULTY	SEASON
LAGO DI VALSCURA CIRCUIT	5–6 HOURS	MODERATE	JUN–SEP
TERME DI VALDIERI TO ENTRACQUE	4 DAYS	DEMANDING	JUN–SEP
MARGUAREIS CIRCUIT	2 DAYS	MODERATE–DEMANDING	JUN–SEP
RIFUGIO GARELLI	4–5 HOURS	EASY–MODERATE	JUN–SEP

WESTERN ALPS	DURATION	DIFFICULTY	SEASON
VALNONTEY TO RHÊMES NOTRE DAME	2 DAYS	MODERATE–DEMANDING	JUN–SEP
LAKES & WILDLIFE	2 DAYS	MODERATE	JUN–SEP
ALPE MONEY	5¾–6¼ HOURS	MODERATE–DEMANDING	JUN–SEP
SELLA-HERBETET TRAVERSE	6¾–7¼ HOURS	DEMANDING	JUN–SEP
VALLONE DI GRAUSON	7¾–8¼ HOURS	DEMANDING	MAY–SEP
MATTERHORN & MONTE ROSA FOOTHILLS	3 DAYS	DEMANDING	MID-JUN–SEP

THE LAKE DISTRICT	DURATION	DIFFICULTY	SEASON
MONTE BALDO	6½ –7 HOURS	MODERATE	JUN–OCT
VALLE DEL SINGOL	6¼–6½ HOURS	MODERATE–DEMANDING	MAY–OCT
MONTE GRONA	4½ –5 HOURS	MODERATE	MAY–OCT
SASS CORBÉE	3 HOURS	EASY–MODERATE	MAY–OCT
VALLE CANNOBINA	8–9 HOURS	MODERATE	MAY–OCT
MONTE CARZA	5¼ –5¾ HOURS	MODERATE	MAY–OCT

STELVIO	DURATION	DIFFICULTY	SEASON
VAL DI RABBI TO MARTELLTAL	4 DAYS	MODERATE–DEMANDING	JUN–SEP

DOLOMITES	DURATION	DIFFICULTY	SEASON
SCILIAR & CATINACCIO LOOP	4 DAYS	MODERATE–DEMANDING	JUN–OCT
DOLOMITE ROLLERCOASTER	7 DAYS	MODERATE–DEMANDING	JUN–OCT
CRODE FISCALINE LOOP	2 DAYS	EASY	JUN–OCT
PARCO NATURALE DELLE DOLOMITI D'AMPEZZO	2 DAYS	EASY	JUN–OCT
SESTO TO SAN CANDIDO	2½–3 HOURS	EASY	JUN–OCT

JULIAN & CARNIC ALPS	DURATION	DIFFICULTY	SEASON
FUSINE–MANGART LOOP	3–4 HOURS	MODERATE	JUN–SEP
SLOVENIAN TWO-STEP	4–5½ HOURS	MODERATE	JUL–SEP
JÔF FUART	2 DAYS	MODERATE	JUN–SEP
MONTE CARNIZZA	3–4 HOURS	MODERATE	JUN–SEP
MONTE OSTERNIG	3–3½ HOURS	EASY–MODERATE	JUN–SEP

TUSCANY	DURATION	DIFFICULTY	SEASON
CHIANTI CLASSICO	3 DAYS	EASY	APR–MAY, SEP–OCT
MEDIEVAL TOWNS	2 DAYS	EASY	APR–MAY, SEP–OCT
TUSCAN HILL CRESTS	7 HOURS	EASY	APR–MAY, SEP–OCT
PIZZO D'UCCELLO	3 DAYS	MODERATE	JUN–SEP
PROCINTO, FORATO & PANIA DELLA CROCE	2 DAYS	MODERATE	JUN–SEP

CENTRAL APENNINES	DURATION	DIFFICULTY	SEASON
LA GOLA DELL'INFERNACCIO	3 HOURS	EASY	MAY–OCT
SIBILLINI TRAVERSE	6 HOURS	MODERATE–DEMANDING	JUN–OCT
MONTE VETTORE	4–4½ HOURS	EASY–MODERATE	JUN–OCT
CASCATE DELLA VOLPARA	3½–4½ HOURS	MODERATE	JUN–OCT
CORNO GRANDE	5–6 HOURS	MODERATE–DEMANDING	JUN–SEP
SENTIERO DELLA LIBERTÀ	8 HOURS	MODERATE	MAY–OCT
ABOVE PESCASSEROLI	2½–3 HOURS	EASY–MODERATE	MAY–OCT
ROCCA RIDGE	6–7 HOURS	MODERATE	JUN–OCT

CAMPANIA	DURATION	DIFFICULTY	SEASON
VESUVIUS' CRATER	2 HOURS	EASY–MODERATE	APR–JUN
POSITANO CIRCUIT	4–5 HOURS	MODERATE	MAR–MAY
SENTIERO DEGLI DEI	5 HOURS	MODERATE	MAR–MAY
CAPO MURO	6½–7 HOURS	DEMANDING	MAR–MAY
VALLE DELLE FERRIERE	4½–5 HOURS	MODERATE	MAR–MAY
PUNTA PENNA	3–3½ HOURS	EASY–MODERATE	MAR–MAY
PUNTA CAMPANELLA	4–4½ HOURS	MODERATE	MAR–MAY

SICILY	DURATION	DIFFICULTY	SEASON
ETNA'S WESTERN FOOTHILLS	2 DAYS	MODERATE	MAR–NOV
GROTTE D'ETNA	2 DAYS	MODERATE	APR–OCT
VULCANO'S GRAN CRATERE	2½–3 HOURS	EASY	APR–OCT
NEBRODI LAKE CIRCUIT	5–5½ HOURS	EASY–MODERATE	MAR–NOV

SARDINIA	DURATION	DIFFICULTY	SEASON
TISCALI–GORROPU	4 DAYS	EASY	MAR–JUN
GOLFO DI OROSEI	4 DAYS	MODERATE	MAR–JUNE

TRANSPORT	SUMMARY	PAGE
BUS	Delightful forests and natural rock gardens beneath an imposing alpine wall	181
BUS	A striking karst plateau, and two passes on the Slovenian border	182
BUS	A *rifugio* in a rugged mountain setting; great access to vie ferrate	185
PRIVATE	Rustic roads and an airy ridge-top route with one foot in Austria	187
PRIVATE	A climb to wide, open spaces and expansive views on the Austrian border	189

TRANSPORT	SUMMARY	PAGE
BUS	Vineyards, olive groves, medieval villages and beautiful woodlands	196
TRAIN, BUS	Fascinating, beautifully preserved villages and towns	201
BUS	A pretty pastoral meander through the Tuscany of legend	205
BUS	Beech forests, marble quarries and knife-edge ridges, with magnificent views of a sheer alpine face	211
BUS	Glorious panoramic walking to the 'queen' of the Apuan Alps and her spectacular neighbours	215

TRANSPORT	SUMMARY	PAGE
PRIVATE	Popular walk through a deep and twisted limestone gorge	226
PRIVATE	A long, narrow ridge crossing the heart of the Sibillini mountains	227
PRIVATE	Strenuous ascent of the highest mountain in the Sibillini range	229
PRIVATE	Climb through beech woodland to a towering waterfall	232
CABLE CAR	Impressive route to the summit of the highest peak in the Apennines	233
TRAIN	WWII escape route through the middle of Majella national park	236
BUS	Easy stroll through pasture and woodland to an old castle	239
BUS	Beech woodland and a limestone-studded mountain ridge	241

TRANSPORT	SUMMARY	PAGE
BUS, TAXI	A well-trodden walk around the crater rim of Italy's most famous volcano	249
BUS	Stunning vistas of the Amalfi's quintessential town nestled below	251
BUS	A classic walk with superb paths clinging to near-vertical mountainsides	253
BUS	Superb high-level walk beneath soaring limestone cliffs	254
BUS	Timeless villages, cool woodlands, waterfalls, magnficient coast views	256
BUS	Scenic walk to a spectacular headland and beautiful sheltered bay	258
BUS	Panoramic views from the Sorrento Peninsula's southwestern tip and a hilltop chapel	260

TRANSPORT	SUMMARY	PAGE
BUS	A superbly scenic walk around the lava-scarred western foothills of Europe's most active volcano	272
TRAIN	A walk across two partially obscured lava tubes filled with shade, shadows and ice	275
FERRY	A short, steep climb to the rim of a smoking island crater	279
BUS	Shady trail through beech wood to Lago di Biviere, in the heart of the Nebrodi range; a delightful glimpse of rural Sicily	281

TRANSPORT	SUMMARY	PAGE
BUS	Ancient villages and the awesome Gorropu Gorge	294
BUS	A fascinating beach, and spectacular walking along a remote coastline	299

The Author

BRENDAN SAINSBURY

Having been marched across the English Lake District from an early age by his eager parents, Brendan clearly has hiking in his genes. He first arrived in Italy in the late 1980s with an inter-rail ticket and several thousand lire (about £20), and returned in 1992 on a bike to witness Italian cyclist Claudio Chiapucci's heroic stage win at Sestriere in the Tour de France. Hiking and trail running have been perennial hobbies and, in 2008, he successfully completed the infamous Marathon des Sables, a 150-mile (240km) pain-fest across the Moroccan Sahara subtitled the 'toughest footrace on earth'. Brendan now lives in Vancouver, Canada with his wife and three-year-old son.

MY FAVOURITE HIKE

In Italy, I was always running to make the last bus. If I missed it, I felt as if the day was half-ruined. If I caught it, it was like winning a stage of the Giro d'Italia. The closest of many close calls was the Amalfi's Valle delle Ferriere hike (p256). I had precisely four hours to sink lunch, set up the GPS, make notes, do the walk, and get back to flag down the bemused bus driver. Trouble was it was 35°C, there were mountains of steps to climb, and I had my hyperactive two-year-old son strapped to my back.

Somehow we made it; however, the image of tearing through those aromatic lemon groves, the sky turning pink over the Mediterranean, while my two-year-old son whipped me as if I was an under-performing racehorse will remain etched on my mind forever.

Route Descriptions

This book contains route descriptions ranging from day trips to multiday megawalks, plus suggestions for other walks, side trips and alternative routes. Each walk description has a brief introduction outlining the natural and cultural features you may encounter, plus information to help you plan your walk – transport options, level of difficulty, time frame and any permits required.

Day walks are often circular and are located in areas of uncommon beauty. Multiday walks include information on campsites, mountain huts, hostels or other accommodation, and places where you can obtain water and supplies.

TIMES & DISTANCES

Times and distances are provided only as a guide. Times are based on actual walking time and do not include stops for snacks, taking photographs, rests or side trips. Be sure to factor these in when planning your walk. Distances are provided but should be read in conjunction with altitudes. Significant elevation changes can make a greater difference to your walking time than lateral distance.

In most cases, the daily stages are flexible and can be varied. It is important to recognise that short stages are sometimes recommended in order to acclimatise in mountain areas or because there are interesting features to explore en route.

LEVEL OF DIFFICULTY

Grading systems are always arbitrary. However, having an indication of the grade may help you choose between walks. Our authors use the following grading guidelines:

Easy – a walk on flat terrain or with minor elevation changes, usually over short distances on well-travelled routes with no navigational difficulties.
Moderate – a walk with challenging terrain, often involving longer distances and steep climbs.
Demanding – a walk with long daily distances and difficult terrain with significant elevation changes; may involve challenging route-finding and high-altitude or glacier travel.

TRUE LEFT & TRUE RIGHT

The terms 'true left' and 'true right', used to describe the bank of a stream or river, sometimes confuse readers. The 'true left bank' simply means the left bank as you look downstream.

Planning

Hiking is one of Italy's unsung joys. Thanks to the country's privileged EU status, along with its long tradition of recreational hiking overseen by the Club Alpino Italiano (CAI), outdoor-based trips here are easy to arrange and refreshingly low maintenance.

To the surprise of many, Italy has a huge network of efficiently organised trails that are clearly waymarked and lightly trammelled. The almost total lack of dangerous wild animals along with the abundance of towns, villages and *rifugi* (mountain huts) en route mean that point-to-point hiking is safe, easy to plan and anxiety-free. Public transport in Italy is similarly comprehensive and even the most obscure hikes to the most out-of-the-way villages have regular rural bus and/or train connections. Of the 59 hikes in this book only six are inaccessible by public transport (and two of these are doable without a car if you're prepared to walk a few extra kilometres to the start point).

Despite its lack of large-scale wilderness, Italy's countryside can offer plenty of tough technical hikes that will test athletes of Sherpa-like fitness (the Dolomites has long acted as a training ground for Himalaya-bound mountaineers). Advanced walkers can seek out the fixed protection *vie ferrate* (iron ways) in the Dolomites, or consider one of the many long-distance paths that follow ancient pilgrims' routes or circumnavigate glowering mountain massifs such as Monte Rosa. Outside the scope of this book are the rugged summit ascents of illustrious Italian mountains such as Mont Blanc, the Matterhorn, and Gran Paradiso; however, the guide lists some of the peninsula's more hikeable summits including Corno Grande (the highest peak in the Central Apennines), Mt Etna and Pizzo d'Uccello.

At the opposite end of the scale are the more undulating ambles: strolls through quintessential Italian countryside, enlightening (and educational) walks through history, and the scenic coastal treks that criss-cross the Ligurian and Amalfi littorals. Furthermore, many of the multiday walks in this guide have side trips, alternative finishes or short cuts enabling walkers of different abilities to cherry-pick their own itineraries.

While this particular book focuses primarily on hiking routes, the biannual Lonely Planet *Italy* guide provides cultural and factual details for those desiring more background information or a greater choice of sleeping/eating options. If you're focusing your hiking in one specific area, consider checking the more detailed Lonely Planet regional guides to *Tuscany & Umbria, The Italian Lakes, Naples & the Amalfi Coast, Sicily* or *Sardinia*.

DON'T LEAVE HOME WITHOUT...

- A great Italian novel
- GPS
- 'Emergency' power bars
- Water bottle(s)
- Toilet paper
- Lighter
- iPod
- Spork (spoon-fork)
- Lightweight waterproof jacket
- This book
- Ear plugs (for *rifugi*)

TEN REASONS TO GO HIKING IN ITALY

- Its unheralded rural scenery is as stunning as its numerous art treasures are famous.
- Hiking is the greenest and cheapest method of getting around.
- There are over 700 *rifugi* (backcountry hostels) scattered throughout the country offering a cheap overnight bed/meal.
- It is a truly visceral experience.
- There are plenty of clean and efficient methods of public transport offering routes to almost every trailhead.
- It is a wonderful way to meet different people and make friends.
- While Florence heaves and Venice sinks, many of Italy's trails remain surprisingly empty.
- Trails are relatively well marked, and maintained by the CAI (Club Alpino Italiano).
- Hiking provides an excellent excuse to eat more pasta, consume more gelati, and drink more cappuccinos.
- There are no dangerous wild animals.

WHEN TO WALK

Topographical and climatic differences mean that walking in Italy is possible all year round, though the months from April to October are the most reliable.

See Climate (p312) for more information.

Due to snowfall and fickle weather, the hiking season in the Alps, Apennines, Apuane Alps, Julian and Carnic Alps, and the Lake District is relatively short. The best time to tackle these mountainous areas is from late June to late September; the season is a little longer around Lago di Garda, Lago di Como and Lago Maggiore. These months usually have the best weather and longer hours of daylight – it's still light at 9pm. It is also when the nation's comprehensive network of *rifugi* are open for business. Light snow can fall over the highest ground at any time but rarely lies for very long in the high summer.

The cooler months of spring and autumn (Apr, May, Sep & Oct) are good times to consider visiting the coastal and lowland areas of Liguria, Tuscany, Campania, Sicily and Sardinia. Winter is also worth considering in the south if you don't mind the occasional very cold day, but be prepared to adapt to short hours of daylight – darkness can fall as early as 5pm.

August is Italy's most crowded month, when the whole country goes on holiday. Be prepared for more crowded trails and book ahead if you're staying in *rifugi*.

COSTS & MONEY

Italy isn't one of the world's cheap destinations, and a strong local currency doesn't help aspiring visitors arriving from outside the euro-zone. However, by avoiding the expensive tourist hubs of Rome, Venice, Milan and Florence, using public transport (as opposed to hire cars), and staying in *rifugi* whenever possible, hikers can save significant amounts of money.

HOW MUCH?

Rifugio bed €20–25

Pasta dish €6–10

Glass of wine €2–3

Bus ticket per 10km €2.20

Ice cream €1–2

If you're hiking in the summer and staying primarily in *rifugi*, your accommodation budget shouldn't break €30 per night. Food consisting of a picnic lunch and a cheap *rifugi* breakfast and dinner shouldn't exceed €25. Factor in another €20 for unknowns (transport, maps, equipment), and you're looking at a budget of €70 a day. Of course, it may not always be so cheap. *Rifugi* are few and far between in Tuscany where the cheapest hotels are €50 to €80. Similarly you'll need public transport to get you to the start of most walks – this is OK if it's just a short hop on a bus, but a more significant investment if you're taking a train from, say, Rome to Milan.

The long and short of it is, you'll save far more money hiking in Italy than you would visiting the tourist sites in Venice or Rome.

GUIDED & GROUP WALKS

Guided walks, usually with cultural, historical or natural history themes, are organised in many national parks and by some local experts. You can obtain details of these from park and tourist information offices, details of which are given in the walk chapters.

You won't need a professional, qualified mountain guide to do any of the walks described in this book. However, if you want to have a go at one of the major peaks, such as Monte Rosa, Matterhorn, Monviso, Gran Paradiso or Mont Blanc (Monte Bianco), or tackle a high-level trek that includes glacier crossings, then a qualified guide is absolutely essential (unless, of course, you've done that sort of thing before).

The Unione Internazionale Associazione Guide Montagna (UIAGM), the international organisation for mountain guides, operates a qualification system and you should check that the guides you're contacting are entitled to wear the UIAGM's badge.

For contacts in the respective regions, see Guided Walks in the walk chapters or contact the **Guide Alpine Italiane** (☎ 02 2941 4211; www.guidealpine.it; Via Petrella 19/a, Milan).

WALK OPERATORS ABROAD

Many operators offer guided walking holidays in Italy; check outdoor magazines and websites such as www.gorp.com for more information. Trips range from around five to eight days. Prices depend on the standard of accommodation and transport costs. UK midrange operators charge from £600 to £800 for eight days. For luxury operators such as Backroads, bank on up to US$3600 for six days.

UK

ATG (☎ 01865 315678; www.atg-oxford.co.uk; 69–71 Banbury Rd, Oxford OX2 6PJ) This company offers several continuous walking trips (luggage transported), such as eight-day Unknown Umbria and Spoleto, eight-day Montefeltro and Urbino, plus the popular destinations of Cinque Terre, Amalfi Coast and Tuscany.

Exodus Travel (☎ 020 8673 0859; www.exodus.co.uk; 9 Weir Rd, London SW12 0LT) One of the UK's leading soft adventure travel companies, Exodus offers over a dozen Italian hiking trips from negotiating *vie ferrate* (iron ways) in the Dolomites to wine and walking combos in Tuscany.

Continental Europe

Trekking in the Alps (☎ +33 450 54 62 09; www.trekkinginthealps.com; Chemin des Boilles, 74660 Vallorcine, France) Run by an experienced Englishwoman, this company has six-day trips including the Tour of the Matterhorn (€1125), Tour Monte Rosa (€1480) and Aosta Valley summits (€1025).

USA

Backroads (☎ 800 4622848 or 510 527 15 55; www.backroads.com; 801 Cedar St, Berkeley, CA 94710-1800) This company offers walking in style, staying at luxury accommodation – with prices to match. Walks head around Lago di Como (Cernobbio, Lenno, Bellagio), Cinque Terre (Sestri Levante and Portofino), and the Dolomites for eight days between Bolzano and Cortina d'Ampezzo.

Wilderness Travel (☎ 1800 3682794; www.wildernesstravel.com; 1102 Ninth St, Berkeley, CA 94710-1211) This company has an 11-day Sicily trip including Madoine Mountains, Mt Etna and Zingaro Nature Reserve, 10 days in untrammelled Apulia, and numerous Tuscan and Amalfi classics.

BACKGROUND READING
Lonely Planet
For comprehensive and detailed information about the country, use the current Lonely Planet *Italy* guide (updated biannually). For a sharper focus on the individual regions, look out for the city guides to *Rome*, *Venice & the Veneto*, and *Naples & the Amalfi Coast*; or the regional guides to *Sicily*, *Sardinia*, *Tuscany & Umbria*, and *Puglia & Basilicata*. Lonely Planet also produces pocket-sized Encounter guides to Florence, Milan, Rome and Venice. The *Italian Phrasebook* contains all the words and phrases you're likely to need in almost any conceivable situation in Italy. You might also want to consider bringing the *German Phrasebook* if you're hiking in the Dolomites. *Cycling Italy* gives a different perspective on Italy's byways, from Sicily to the Alps.

Non-fiction
Three 'Grand Tour' classics are Johann Wolfgang von Goethe's *Italian Journey*, Charles Dickens' *Pictures from Italy* and Henry James' *Italian Hours*. DH Lawrence wrote three short travel books while living in Italy, combined in one volume, *DH Lawrence & Italy*. A decent antidote to the gushing reams written by foreign expats living in Tuscany, Tobias Jones' *The Dark Heart of Italy* turns the spotlight on football corruption, politics and the shenanigans of Silvio Berlusconi.

For a fascinating insight into the early history of mountaineering in the Alps, hunt for a copy of *Scrambles Among the Alps*, by Edward Whymper, including details of his triumphant but tragic battle to the summit of the Matterhorn in 1865.

Fiction
The love of seemingly every romantic writer since Byron, Italy is well-covered in English literary fiction. British novelist EM Forster skilfully contrasted British Edwardian stuffiness with raw Italian passion in his two early-20th-century Tuscan classics *A Room with a View* and *Where Angels Fear to Tread*. It wouldn't be a holiday without Hemingway. Ernest Hemingway's definitive take on Italy during and after WWI is chronicled in *A Farewell to Arms* and *Across the River and into the Trees*.

Real Italia-philes can spend stormy *rifugi* nights deciphering translations of Boccaccio's *The Decameron* or Dante's *Divine Comedy*. Just as classic but more digestible is *Il Gattopardo* (The Leopard), Giuseppe di Lampedusa's historical novel about the quandaries of the Sicilian aristocracy during the tumult of the Risorgimento.

INTERNET RESOURCES
Most local and regional tourist office websites, and those maintained by the national parks, have some information specifically about walking in their areas. Other sites to try:

Lonely Planet (www.lonelyplanet.com) The official Lonely Planet site with lots of country specific information and a special Walking, Trekking and Mountaineering branch on the Thorn Tree.
Club Alpino Italiano (www.cai.it) Follow the *rifugi* link for an amazing number of links to regional, local, business and activity sites.
Ente Nazionale Italiano per il Turismo (www.enit.it) The official Italian tourist body's website with information on art, nature, discount cards, and festivals/events.

A SHORT HISTORY OF HIKING IN ITALY

When Roman emperor Hadrian trudged his way to the summit of Sicily's Mt Etna in AD 121 to watch the sun rise he, arguably, became the world's first true hiker. It wasn't long before his fellow countrymen were tramping reverently in his footsteps. Utilising the empire's well-organised network of *vie* (roads), Roman citizens regularly travelled on foot around the Italian peninsula, stopping off at various *mansiones* (large villas offering refreshment and accommodation) en route. One of the oldest surviving *vie* in Italy is the Appian Way or *regina viarum* (queen of roads) begun by Roman censor, Appius Claudius Caecus in 312 BC to link Rome with Brindisi in the southeast. Frequented by such biblical luminaries as St Peter and St Paul, this sturdily built highway was constructed to support numerous Roman legions marching south towards the Adriatic and Greece.

Another path with its roots in antiquity was the Via Francigena, a long-distance pilgrims' route that joined Canterbury in England to the religious sites of Rome. A 1700km walking path that zigzagged between various way stations and abbeys, the Via Francigena was first mentioned in the 6th century by an Anglo-German bishop. By the Middle Ages it had become – along with the Camino de Santiago in Spain – one of the most heavily trammelled pilgrims' paths in Europe.

In the days before mass train travel and annual holidays for workers, hiking was more a necessity than a hobby, though there were some notable exceptions. In 1336 Tuscan poet Francesco Petrarch climbed to the top of Mt Ventoux in southeast France and recorded the event in his diary. A century and a half later, Leonardo da Vinci is known to have ascended to a snowfield on Monte Rosa to undertake some scientific experiments. The mountain with the world's earliest recorded ascent date is Monte Rochemelon in Piedmont, scaled by Bonifacius Rotarius in 1358; Rotarius carried a metal replica of the Virgin Mary to the summit, which he offered as thanks for having survived the crusades.

By most reckonings, the modern era of hiking was inaugurated in 1786 when two Frenchmen, Jacques Balmat and Michel-Gabriel Paccard, became the first climbers to conquer Mont Blanc. But it wasn't until 70 years later – in 1857 – that the founding of the Alpine Club of London ushered in what became known as 'the golden age of alpinism'. It was during this period that parties of mainly British climbers undertook successful first ascents of numerous Italian peaks including Gran Paradiso (1860), Marmolata (1864) and the Matterhorn (1865).

Italy's home-grown alpine club, the CAI, was founded in Turin in 1863 and quickly adopted an all-inclusive policy that opened membership to all. By 1913 the club had expanded to 7500 members and by 1939 this figure had increased ten-fold to 75,000 making it the second-largest alpine club in Europe (a position it still enjoys).

By the 1980s, the Himalayan heroics of Italy's greatest mountaineering icon, Reinhold Messner, had woken many ordinary Italians to the joys and possibilities of outdoor hiking. In 1983, with the backing of the CAI, an inspired group of outdoor enthusiasts proposed the development of Italy's first cross-country footpath, the Sentiero Italia (Grand Italian Trail). The idea became reality in 1995 when a reconnaissance group set out from Trieste in the northeast to walk the 6166km to Santa Teresa Gallura in northern Sardinia. For the first time in its history, Italy could call itself a hiking heavyweight, with a network of interconnecting trails that could match anywhere in Europe.

The Italian Parks Portal (www.parks.it) Detailed information on all of the country's 24 national parks along with updates on regional parks, marine parks and other protected areas.

Stanfords (www.stanfords.co.uk) The ultimate travel book/map shop based in London's Covent Garden is a particularly good source for some of the more obscure maps and guides that are listed in this book, most of which can be ordered online.

Environment

Few people visit Italy with the sole intention of watching wildlife. But, despite a dearth of big fauna and a sketchy background in environmental protection, the peninsula continues to harbour around 500 types of birds, 90 mammals and 5560 plant species. A great array of protective legislation and a growing list of protected areas have come to the country relatively late – too late, often, to compensate for the impacts of land clearance and drainage and the predations of hunters on habitats and species.

National and natural parks, and natural reserves are the best places to see wildlife, and several parks and reserves are featured in this book.

This section provides brief descriptions of the species you are most likely to see on the walks described, along with information on protected areas and environmental issues. Some books, which will help with the identification of flora and fauna, are listed below.

Italy is divided into 20 regions. The largest by area is Sicily and the largest by population is Lombardy.

BACKGROUND READING
Natural History Books
Wild Italy (2005) by Tim Jepson fills a gap in the market and is the best umbrella guide for the country's natural history. *Mediterranean Wildflowers* by Neil Fletcher is good for the basics on Italian flora.

For birds, check out the succinct, easy-to-use *RSPB Birds of Britain & Europe* (2009) by Rob Hume, or the beautifully illustrated *Birds of Europe* (2005) by Lars Jonsson. Paul Sterry is the author of both *Complete Mediterranean Wildlife* (2000) and *Birds of the Mediterranean: A Photographic Guide* (2004).

Keith Rushforth, meanwhile, has penned *The Easy Tree Guide: Britain & Europe* (2001). *Mammals of Britain & Europe* (1993), by David MacDonald and Priscilla Barrett is still a seller and still relevant, despite its age.

Kompass do some pocket-sized guides covering flora, animals and birds with Italian text and full-colour photos. Other book recommendations for specific areas can be found on the www.parks.it websites under the individual park pages.

THE LAND
Geography
The distinctive Italian boot that juggles the dual 'footballs' of Sicily and Sardinia embraces a total land area of 301,245 sq km, making it the world's 71st largest country.

Five of Italy's regions are semi-autonomous. They are Sicily, Sardinia, The Valle d'Aosta, Trentino-Alto Adige and Friuli-Venezia Giulia.

Surrounded on three sides by the Mediterranean, Italy is distinctly mountainous – 35% of its territory lies above 702m, in two major ranges, the Alps and the Apennines (Appennini). The highest mountain entirely within Italy is Gran Paradiso (4061m) in Valle d'Aosta; although higher, both Mont Blanc (4807m) and Monte Rosa (4634m) straddle Italy's borders with France and Switzerland respectively. The Apennines are Italy's 1220km-long backbone, extending from Liguria south to the tip of Calabria, with an extension in Sicily. Their highest peak is Corno Grande (2914m) in Abruzzo's Gran Sasso d'Italia group. Several smaller mountain ranges extend east and west from the Apennines; these include the Apuane Alps (Alpi Apuane) in northwest Tuscany, the volcanoes in the south, and the limestone uplands on the Amalfi Coast–Sorrento Peninsula.

Sardinia has its own mountain ranges in the island's southwest and central east; the highest peak is Punta La Marmora (1834m) in the Gennargentu

THE ALPS – CLASSIFYING THE RANGES

The Alps are immense, straddling seven countries and dominating a continent. To simplify things, geographers split the mountains into western and eastern sections along a line that runs from Lake Constance in the north to Lago di Como in the south. For even greater precision, the Italian portions can be further split into the following subregions:

WESTERN ALPS

Ligurian At the eastern end of the Maritimes, this diminutive range runs from Colle di Tenda on the French-Italian border to the Colle di Cadibona where Liguria folds into Piedmont; beyond this lie the Apennines.

Maritime Form the border with France, southwest of Cuneo, and include (on the Italian side) the Parco Naturale delle Alpi Marittime and the Parco Naturale Alta Valle Pesio e Tanaro. Half a dozen of its peaks exceed 3000m.

Cottian Taller still, these mountains west of Turin include the popular ski resort of Sestriere (used in the 2006 Winter Olympics) and the Col du Mt Cenis, an important cross-border transport route.

Graian Home of the Western Europe's highest peak, Mt Blanc (4810m), along with Italy's first national park, Gran Paradiso, sprawled on their eastern slopes. The Italian part of the range stretches across the western edges of Piedmont and the southern Valle d'Aosta.

Pennine Not to be confused with the smaller English hills, this mighty range is dominated by the Matterhorn (4478m), and straddles the Swiss-Italian border in the north of the Valle d'Aosta.

Lepontine Back in Piedmont, this Swiss-Italian range extends south to the western shores of Lago Maggiore.

EASTERN ALPS

Ortles-Cevedale Home of Parco Nazionale dello Stelvio and 3769m-high Mt Cevedale, these mountains stretch across Switzerland's far eastern corner and into the Italian provinces of Lombardy and Trentino-Alto Adige.

Dolomites Though not the highest mountains in the Alps, the Dolomites are undoubtedly the most dramatic, and are a haven for Italian alpinists. Part of Austria until 1919, German is still the dominant language

Carnic Sandwiched between the Dolomites and the Julians, the Carnics usually get lumped with the latter, although they are greener, more rounded and less hostile.

Julian Named for Julius Caesar, this craggy limestone range delineates the Italian border with Slovenia north of Trieste.

massif. Sicily is even more mountainous – 83% of the island in fact; its three ranges include Europe's highest active volcano, Mt Etna (3350m).

The Italian coastline is often precipitous, a feature best seen in the coastal cliffs of Liguria, and the rugged Amalfi Coast and Sorrento Peninsula. Most of Italy's islands lie in the Tyrrhenian Sea: Sicily and the scattered Aeolian Islands (Isole Eolie) off its north coast, a small group near Naples including Capri, Sardinia, and the handful between Corsica and the coast – notably Elba.

Italy has around 1500 lakes, the majority of which are small and high in the mountains. The largest are the glacier-carved Lago di Garda (with an area of 370 sq km), followed by Lago Maggiore (212 sq km) and Lago di Como (146 sq km).

Geology

The area now occupied by the Italian peninsula was once covered by the vast Tethys Sea, between 60 and 245 million years ago. Debris underneath this sea was transformed into layers of limestone, sandstone, clay, shale and the extensive coral reefs from which the Dolomites ultimately emerged.

Around 40 million years ago the massive European and African continental plates collided, pushing up the edges of the plates and, with them, the layers of rock on the sea bed. This prolonged, cataclysmic event marked the emergence of the Alps and, later, the Apennines. The strata were wrapped around the levelled remnant of the ancient mountain mass and pushed up to Himalayan heights; these ranges were subsequently worn down to their present elevations. The Apennines, comprising many rock types but predominantly limestone and sandstone, finally took shape only about 1.6 million years ago. In the meantime, the Tethys Sea had largely dried up when the Strait of Gibraltar closed; when it reopened about two million years ago the Mediterranean basin was flooded and the present shape of the Italian peninsula was settled.

During a succession of ice ages spanning more than a million years, glaciers blanketed the mountains, resulting in the landscape seen today. Outstanding examples of moraine lakes are Lago di Garda and its neighbours, Como and Maggiore. In places, ice trapped in the valleys overflowed across mountain ridges, cutting deep incisions, which later became high passes. Numerous glaciers survive in the mountains today, notably along the borders with France, Switzerland and Austria, in the Ortler Range in Parco Nazionale dello Stelvio and in Parco Nazionale del Gran Paradiso. However, the glaciers are presently retreating, possibly partly as a result of climate change.

WILDLIFE

Italy's wildlife – or what's left of it – will never match the Serengeti, though, thanks to the paucity of sizeable mammals, when you actually 'do' see something, it's often doubly rewarding.

Animals
MAMMALS

Italy's mammals have fought a long and largely unsuccessful battle against their biggest natural enemy – humans. The outcome hasn't always been positive. Italy is a crowded country and the country's fauna is nowhere near as well protected as the nation's many architectural riches. Many species are critically endangered. Others have disappeared altogether.

Apart from the big five (see p30), the peninsula exhibits two important species of deer. **Red deer** range up to 2800m in forests and alpine meadows. In the absence of their natural predators (bears, wolves and lynx) and despite the activities of hunters, the number of red deer in Italy has increased. Adult males stand up to 1.5m tall and display reddish-brown summer coats. Their impressive antlers are shed during spring.

The **roe deer** stand to 90cm tall and have a red-brown coat with a yellowish-white spot under the tail during summer. Their antlers are straight or very slightly curved with a few points towards the top. The species is now protected.

You're likely to see the **red fox** almost anywhere except high in the mountains. With their sleek, doglike profile, pointed ears and long dark bushy tail and rich red-brown coat, they're easy to recognise bounding away to shelter. They prefer to hunt at night, for carrion, small rodents, and even insects and fruit.

The shy **red squirrel**, a protected species, rarely leaves the trees in which it lives, feeding on pine or beech nuts. During autumn red squirrels bury a store of nuts to last through winter as they do not hibernate. Their

Earthquake- and volcano-prone Italy has suffered many natural disasters since Vesuvius buried Pompeii. The worst quake of the last century was in 1908 when Messina (Sicily) and Reggio di Calabria were hit by a sea-quake and tsunami that killed 86,000 people.

The noble ibex has become the symbol of Italy's oldest national park, Gran Paradiso, whose establishment in 1922 was integral in saving the species from extinction.

fur is greyish-red to almost black. The red squirrel is quite common in coniferous forests up to an altitude of 1800m.

REPTILES

Italy is home to two poisonous snakes – the **adder** and the **common viper** – both of which are found in the Alps. They are dangerous only if disturbed, and fatalities are extremely unusual. They feed on frogs, lizards and small insects.

The attractive **green lizard** is a common sight in woodlands, on rocky ground, in stone walls, and along the margins of paths and tracks. Growing to 40cm in length, it is bright green or yellow-green with a faint black stipple pattern and an obvious white patch on the throat.

BIRDS

Italy's more than 500 species of bird are a welcome distraction for budding ornithologists, and the nation's hiking trails provide an ideal habitat in which to view some of the rarer and more colourful varieties.

The magnificent **golden eagle** has a wingspan exceeding 2m, which it holds in a V-shape during its awesome gliding and soaring displays high in mountainous areas – the Alps and Sardinia. It dives with wings folded to catch small rodents, marmots or carrion, including animals trapped in snowdrifts or injured in falls. It is generally dark brown if seen from below, with white wing patches. It prefers areas with steep cliffs and ravines, which provide ideal nesting sites. Once harshly persecuted in the lowlands, it took refuge in the mountains and is now fully protected.

With a wing span up to 2.8m and a body length exceeding 1m, the **lammergeier** is Europe's largest raptor. It was mercilessly hunted as a supposed predator of sheep and, in Italy, became extinct early in the 20th century. It has been successfully reintroduced to Parco Nazionale

ITALY'S BIG FIVE

Italy is more famous for its heavyweight historical monuments than its fearsome fauna, but, while lions and elephants may be restricted to the peninsula's zoos, a more innocuous quintet of wild animals can be found roaming in numerous national and regional parks.

Marsican Bears Critically endangered and critically misunderstood, the Marsican bear has always trodden a shaky line with the vastly more territorial human species. The 40 or so remaining Marsicans are concentrated in Abruzzo in the Apennines and, aside from small pockets in the Pyrenees and Cantabrian Mountains in France and Spain, they are the only bears left in Western Europe.

Wolves A protected species in Italy, current reports suggest that there are 500 to 800 individuals living in the wild, primarily in the Apennines. While the population is increasing overall, wolves still regularly fall prey to poachers and road accidents.

Ibex On the verge of extinction in the early 19th century, the Alpine ibex's survival was assured after the inauguration of the Parco Nazionale Gran Paradiso in 1922 and its installation of a vigorous ibex revival programme. Characterised by their large curved ridged horns, the animals have spread to numerous other alpine locations as far south as the Maritimes.

Chamois The goat-like chamois are extremely agile and can ascend 1000m in 15 minutes over mountainous terrain if disturbed. Well-established populations can be found in the Alps and around the Corno Grande region in the Apennines.

Marmots You'll hear the whistles of these noisy but highly sociable wild rodents all over Italy's northern mountains warning their brethren of your imminent approach. Marmots are essentially large squirrels that live in burrows like rabbits and hibernate during the winter months.

del Gran Paradiso; 60 pairs were released in the park between 1978 and 1995, and the survival rate appears to be strong. The lammergeier, like all vultures, is a scavenger and finds plenty to eat during the winter when animals are killed by avalanches or in falls. They live in strongly bonded pairs, and generally nest on exposed cliff ledges. A lammergeier will vigorously defend its large territory against intruding birds, and territorial fights are common. It is generally slate-black in colour, with a darker stripe across the eyes, and buff-coloured head and underparts.

The **ptarmigan**, or snow grouse, lives year-round on rocky ground at altitudes of 2000m to 2800m. It adapts superbly to its environment by changing colours at least three times during the year, from spotted grey in summer to pure white in winter. Its legs are protected by a special layer of insulating feathers. During winter it digs a hole in the snow for shelter, and during the day it potters about the slopes searching for food. As the spring thaw progresses, it moves to snow-free ground in search of insects and new shoots on emerging plants.

The small **snowfinch** adapts to its changing surroundings in the mountains; its brown back and black throat become paler during colder months. It is strictly an alpine species, never venturing below the limit of tree growth. Snowfinches will nest in sheltered crannies in buildings and in tiny crevices on rock faces. They lives on insects and seeds, but will scavenge around sites frequented by humans.

Though not particularly easy to spot, the small, sparrowlike **Alpine accentor** is seen in the mountains, usually in open, rocky areas. It has a greyish head, dark-brown streaks on its back, reddish stripes on the side and a distinctive row of white dots on its wings.

The pitch-black **Alpine chough**, with its long tail, yellow beak and red feet, is found at very high altitudes. It's very acrobatic in flight and likes to soar on updrafts around peaks and crags. A hardy opportunist, it will swoop around *rifugi* (mountain huts) in search of food scraps, but normally feeds on worms, insects or berries.

In the 20th century, 14 species of animals became extinct in Italy, including the Alpine lynx, the sea eagle, the black vulture and the osprey.

Plants
TREES

The **beech** is one of the most plentiful broad-leaved trees in Italy. Almost pure forests of beech are found throughout the mountains, particularly on limestone. The tree often reaches a height of 45m and can live for more than 300 years. Oil-rich beech nuts are an important food for many birds, squirrels and wild boar.

Beautiful **silver birch** woods occur widely in mountain areas up to about 1800m. The tree, which grows to about 30m high, is white with large black, diamond-shaped markings in mature trees. The small roughly triangular leaves are shiny green with rough edges.

The sweet **chestnut** can be found throughout Italy between 300m and 1000m. It is a vigorous grower, making it suitable for coppicing (regular harvesting) to provide timber for various agricultural uses. For centuries the nuts were a staple food for people in remote areas, and are still valued as the basis of luxurious desserts.

Not surprisingly in a country where wine is so important, the **cork oak** is widely grown, mainly in the Apennines. Its spongy, fissured, light-grey bark, about 5cm thick, can be stripped every six to 12 years.

The **holm oak**, typical of the Mediterranean *macchia* (scrub) vegetation, grows along the coast and up to 600m. It is an evergreen with glossy black-green leaves, which contrast attractively with the new silver-white and pale-yellow foliage during spring.

There are three indigenous types of pine tree in Italy – the hardy Aleppo pine, the domestic pine (most common in Tuscany) and the maritime pine (which despite its name is normally found inland).

Italy is also home to numerous conifers including the deciduous **European larch**, the hardy **Austrian pine**. The very elegant **Italian cypress**, common along Mediterranean coasts and a signature sight in any classic rural Tuscan postcard, has a slender tapered profile. The dense, dark -green foliage is a mass of tiny shoots growing in all directions and the oval cone is shiny green when young then dark reddish-brown.

Higher up, the Christmas tree–shaped **Norway spruce** dominates commercial plantations up to about 1800m with the tough hardy **dwarf mountain pine**, which grows up to 2m in broad dense thickets just below the tree line.

SHRUBS & FLOWERS

The Alps are famous for their high meadows that are bedizened with vibrant carpets of flowers during a short but intense summer season.

Embellishing this colourful spectacle is the pretty **harebell**, which grows in single or small clusters of light-blue, bell-shaped flowers, and wave about in the wind in meadows up to 2200m. The rounded leaves form a mat at the base of the stem.

The seemingly fragile **Alpine pansy** also prefers meadows and stony sites no higher than 2200m. Its long-stemmed, oval leaves are shiny green, and its violet flowers bloom for a short season – June and July.

Prolific in damper, grassier mountain meadows, the **bistort** has dense, elongated clusters of bright pink flowers, which look like a single flower spike from a distance. The rather narrow leaves are darkish green on short stalks from the long, straight stem.

The distinctive **bladder campion** is easily identified – the five white petals of its flower are deeply notched and spray out from a greenish, inflated, bladder-like tube. The roughly oval leaves are light green and set well down the stem. It stands to 60cm tall, and blooms from May to September.

The **common columbine** is widespread in both meadows and wooded areas. The violet-blue or purple flowers hang down; the outer petals, with long, backward-pointing and slightly hooked spurs, surround the inner bell-shaped cluster of petals. The small leaves are dull green. It blooms from May to July.

With a striking, bright yellow, rounded flower, the tall **globeflower** grows in damp sites and along stream margins in upland meadows. It blooms during summer. The dark-green, palm-shaped leaves cluster round the base of the 60cm-long stem.

Up to as high an altitude as 3000m, and visible in rockier terrain are dense thickets of **alpenrose**, which are scattered among rocky outcrops and clumps of grass. The small clusters of bell-shaped, deep pinkish-red flowers last through summer. An evergreen, it has deep-green, shiny leaves with reddish undersides and curled edges.

The daisy-like violet-blue **Alpine aster** is found only in limestone country, commonly on cliffs or well-drained mountain slopes, up to an altitude of 3000m. It blooms throughout summer.

Higher still is the protected **moss campion,** a dense, bright-green cushion of tiny leaves with clusters of equally small pink flowers dotted about the surface. It likes damp, rocky places and scree slopes up to 3700m.

The much sought-after **edelweiss** is a protected species. The small plant prefers grassy or rocky slopes up to 3400m, and flowers between July and September. It is generally white or greyish-white in appearance with longish leaves.

Flowers that prefer damp ground include the **Alpine buttercup**, a white flower usually found in small clusters whose shiny green leaves are generally round with small lobes. It prefers stream margins, and it flowers between June and October.

With deep-green roundish leaves, and violet bell-shaped and fringed flowers, the **Alpine snowbell** makes a seemingly miraculous appearance on the edge of melting snow. The delicate flowers on extremely slender stems (to 15cm long) move gently with the breeze. The plant develops thick mats on stony ground at altitudes up to 3000m.

Another plant that thrives around melting snow is the hardy **white crocus** whose white, violet-tinged flowers poke out as early as March. Until other species come into flower, carpets of crocuses dominate the scene, creeping up with the snow line as high as 2700m.

The striking **trumpet gentian** has erect, deep-blue or purplish blooms with tiny green dots inside; each measures up to 70mm long and seems to weigh down its short stem. It flowers from May to August and likes to keep its roots damp on rocky ground up to 3000m. It is fully protected.

Broom occurs widely, is very adaptable, and has masses of bright yellow, strongly scented flowers that bloom from May to August. It is an evergreen shrub with long, thin branchlets. It is often used to consolidate areas that are subject to landslides.

More forest-based plants include the fast-growing, prickly **common hawthorn**, which can grow up to 900m altitude and is often found in woods dominated by oaks. Elsewhere, on dry soils, this bush is rather stunted and is often found with broom and rockrose, forming the classic Mediterranean *macchia* type of vegetation. The spiny branches offer a safe haven for nesting birds.

The **spring heath** grows to 40cm high and has urn-shaped, bright-pink flowers and darkish-green leaves. It is found in conifer woodlands and rocky places up to 2700m, and blooms from March to June.

More than a dozen species of **orchid** are found in mountainous areas and many more elsewhere. Many are threatened with extinction, being very vulnerable to disturbance of their habitats. Orchids are perennial herbs with simple stems and longish leaves. A common species in the Alps is early purple orchid. It is found in grassy meadows and woodlands up to 2600m.

Pasque flowers, members of the buttercup family, are common in mountain areas from 1200m to 2700m. They generally flower throughout

---

COUNTRY CODE

○ Respect those who live and work in the countryside.

○ Light fires only in fireplaces provided at picnic and camping areas.

○ Leave gates as you find them – open or closed.

○ Keep to defined paths and resist the temptation to take short cuts.

○ Use gates and stiles to cross fences and walls; if necessary, climb a gate at the hinged end.

○ Steer clear of livestock and machinery.

○ Take your rubbish home or to the nearest disposal point.

○ Avoid polluting water sources.

○ Leave all wild creatures and plants as your find them.

○ Drive and park considerately on country roads.

spring and summer. Pasque flowers are poisonous. The common pasque flower has large purple or mauve, bell-shaped flowers with bright-yellow centres (anthers) and feathery leaves. It is found mainly in dry meadows up to 1500m.

One of the most colourful plants on cultivated ground up to 1800m is the bright-red **common poppy**, which brings huge splashes of colour to the fields between May and July. Each long hairy stem has a single four-petalled flower with a darkish centre.

Away from the mountains, **lentisk** is found throughout the Mediterranean basin, mainly in coastal areas, as one of the species of the hardy *macchia* vegetation. An evergreen bush, it has dark green, leathery leaves and exudes a strong, resinous perfume. The yellow or reddish-brown flowers appear from March to June.

The **myrtle** is an integral component of the Mediterranean *macchia*. It grows mainly on the coast in hot dry areas. Both the leaves and flowers are intensely perfumed, and its essential oil is extracted for use in perfume-making. The aromatic fruit is a vital ingredient in grappa.

The low, bushy **white rockrose** is another abundant and colourful plant in Mediterranean areas, especially in exposed, dry sites on limestone. It is often found together with a close relative – pink rockrose.

> Italy's largest national park, Pollino, straddles the border between the regions of Basilicata and Calabria and measures 1960 sq km.

PROTECTED AREAS

Italy's environmental stewardship has improved exponentially in recent years although, starting from such a poor base, there's still a long way to go. The most obvious sign of the sea change is the growth of the national park system. In 1990, the country boasted just four national parks: Gran Paradiso, Abruzzo, Stelvio and Circeo, all established before WWII. Today there are 22 with two more on the way (see boxed text, Italian National Parks – An Overview, p35).

The national parks you will encounter directly in the course of this book are Gran Paradiso, Stelvio, Vesuvio, Cinque Terre, Abruzzo, Gran Sasso e Monti della Laga, Majella, Monti Sibillini, and Gennargentu in Sardinia (park status still pending).

Italy contains many other protected areas. There are over 130 regional parks. Most of these fall under the category of natural parks (*parchi naturali*), areas of land, rivers or wetlands of environmental importance that are endowed with natural assets such as lakes, or harbour traditional cultural settlements. The parks often extend across more than one region. Regional parks are heavily weighted towards the northern regions, most notably Piedmont (Piemonte) and Lombardy, though the south is playing catch-up.

Many of the walks in this book pass through important natural parks. There are half-a-dozen in the Dolomites including Sciliar, Dolomiti Ampezzane, Puez-Odle and Dolomiti di Sesto. Further south is the Alpi Apuane in Tuscany, Parco Regionale di Portofino in Liguri, Parco Regionale dell'Etna and Parco dei Nebrodi in Sicily, and Parco Naturale delle Alpi Marittime and Parco Naturale dell'Alta Valle Pesio e Tamaro in the Maritime Alps.

> The total area of land now protected by Italy's fast-growing national park system is 1.5 million hectares, or 5% of the land mass, and environmentalists are still campaigning for more to be set aside.

There are more than 400 national and regional natural reserves. These are more evenly spread across the country, with several in Calabria, Basilicata, and on Sardinia and Sicily, as well as in the north. They are defined as biodiverse natural areas that contain at least one important species of plant or animal, or at least one unique ecosystem. Whether they are designated national or regional reserves depends on the significance of their individual features.

ITALIAN NATIONAL PARKS – AN OVERVIEW

Italy's 22 national parks now cover nearly 5% of the country's total land mass. The oldest is Gran Paradiso in the Valle d'Aosta established in 1922, while the largest is Stelvio, which encompasses vast swathes of both Lombardy and Trentino-Alto Adige in the northeast. Other gems include Cinque Terre, which protects five fishing villages on the Ligurian coast, Vesuvius containing the eponymous volcano east of Naples, and Abruzzo, Lazio and Molise in the Apennines revered for its expansive beech forests and handful of Marsican bears.

The national park system has had a checkered modern history. During the Mussolini era some of the early parks actually lost their protected status – albeit temporarily – at the expense of dubious development projects while, in the lean financial years of the 1950s, deforestation and the construction of ski resorts regularly infringed upon biodiversity and wildlife.

Miraculously, the 1990s heralded a new beginning in Italy's approach to environmental management and, over the course of the last 17 years, the park system has more than quadrupled in size with notable new editions in the Apennines and Sardinia.

Many of today's parks boast extensive trail networks including Gran Paradiso and Stelvio in the Alps, Cinque Terre in Liguria, Vesuvius near Naples and the four interconnecting parks – Majella, Monti Sibillini, Gran Sasso and Abruzzo – that cover the Apennines.

The nation's 26 marine reserves include the aquatically rich Cinque Terre coast and the sea area off Punta Campanella near Sorrento. Back on land, Italy lists 51 important wetland areas protected as international Ramsar Convention sites.

General information about all Italy's protected areas can be found at the informative website www.parks.it.

Italy has 44 Unesco World Heritage sites; 42 are listed as cultural sites while two – the Aeolian Islands and the Dolomites – are deemed to be of natural scenic importance. Designated by Unesco, these historic or environmentally unique swathes of land are earmarked as places of world significance that would constitute an irreplaceable loss to the planet if they were altered. National governments are obliged to ensure that nothing is done to compromise the qualities of the sites (or risk a de-listing). A sizeable proportion of Italy's Unesco sites are in the great historic cities and towns such as Florence, Naples and San Gimignano. Others include individual buildings and archaeological sites – most notably Pompeii. The Cinque Terre on the Ligurian coast and the Amalfi Coast in Campania are the two main cultural sites you will encounter while using this book. The other protected area of interest to walkers is the Dolomites, a natural Unesco site designated in 2009 for its geomorphology, glacial landforms, fossil records and all-round spectacular beauty.

Since protective measures were introduced in the late 20th century, a handful of animal species have been making a tentative comeback. These include the Marsican bear, the wolf, the otter and the golden eagle.

ENVIRONMENTAL ISSUES

The Italian government's record on environmental issues is less than admirable. Although the Ministry for the Environment was established in 1986, environmental laws are not always stringently enforced. Nonetheless, environmental organisations have had some success in arousing awareness about a wide range of issues, although their membership remains small by comparison with similar organisations in some other European countries. Rubbish is a besetting problem almost wherever you go in Italy, and the well-documented problems in Naples and its hinterland have received international attention recently. Recycling, however, is starting to be taken seriously, partly due to a campaign led by the organisation Legambiente.

RESPONSIBLE WALKING

Italy's countryside has been altered by the impact of many different human activities for thousands of years. However, the invasion by walkers (and other outdoors enthusiasts) during the past 30 years is probably unprecedented in scale.

Italy's rules for national and other parks serve to protect the environment and wildlife while allowing low-impact recreational use, and have been summarised in the boxed text Country Code (p33). Rubbish and human waste disposal are two unsightly problems in Italy and there's little evidence of any concerted attack to reduce this. By following the guidelines below for minimal impact while walking and camping, we can all help to fulfil the responsibilities that go with the rights and privileges of walking in the Italian countryside.

ACCESS

- Although it may not be obvious at the time, many of the walks in this book pass through private property, along recognised routes where access is freely permitted. If there seems to be some doubt about this, ask someone nearby if it's OK to walk through – you'll rarely have any problems.

CAMPING

- If camping near a farm or house, seek permission first.
- In remote areas, use a recognised site rather than create a new one. Keep at least 30m from watercourses and paths. Move on after a night or two.
- If your tent is carefully sited away from hollows where water is likely to accumulate, it won't be necessary to dig damaging trenches if it rains heavily.
- Leave your site as you found it – with minimal or no trace of your use.

WASHING

- Don't use detergents or toothpaste in or near streams or lakes; even it they are biodegradable they can harm fish and wildlife.
- To wash yourself, use biodegradable soap and a water container at least 50m from the watercourse. Disperse the waste water widely so it filters through the soil before returning to the stream.
- Wash cooking utensils 50m from streams, using a scourer instead of detergent.

Atmospheric pollution can make life very unpleasant in many cities, as Italians persist in using their cars, despite good public transport services. Car-free days in city centres have gained widespread support and many towns and cities in the north have introduced bike-sharing schemes similar to the groundbreaking Vélib project in Paris.

Over the years, referenda to impose stricter controls on hunting of wild animals (especially birds) have met stiff resistance because of the strength and determination of the hunting lobby. However, with increasingly large areas of the countryside being given national park protection, the pendulum seems at last to be swinging in favour of the beleaguered animals.

With an eye on trail erosion and high human traffic in the mountains, the CAI has instigated an effective moratorium on building new trails, *rifugi* or *vie ferrate*.

In addition to the CAI (see the boxed text Club Alpino Italiano, p43), Italy's leading environmental organisations include the following:

Greenpeace Italia (www.greenpeace.org/italy) Italian branch of the Canadian-founded world environmental watchdog.

Legambiente (www.legambiente.it) Italy's largest and most dynamic

HUMAN WASTE DISPOSAL

- Bury your waste. Dig a small hole 15cm deep and at least 30m from any watercourse, 50m from paths and 200m from any buildings. Take a lightweight trowel or large tent peg for the purpose. Cover the waste with a good layer of soil and leaf mould.

- Do not contaminate water sources – contamination of water by human faeces can lead to the transmission of Giardia, a human bacterial parasite; gastroenteritis is probably caused by exposed human faecal waste.

- Toilet paper should be carried out. It can be burned, but this is not recommended in a forest, above the tree line or in dry grassland. Burying is a last resort – ideally use biodegradable paper.

- Sanitary napkins, tampons and condoms don't burn or decompose readily, so carry them out, whatever the inconvenience.

RUBBISH

- If you've carried it in, carry it out – everything, including wrappers, citrus peel, cigarette butts and empty packaging, stowed in a dedicated rubbish bag. Make an effort to pick up rubbish left by others.

- Don't bury rubbish – this disturbs soil and ground cover, and encourages erosion and weed growth. Buried rubbish takes years to decompose and will probably be dug up by wild animals who may be injured or poisoned by it.

- If you're camping, remove all surplus food packaging and put small-portion packages in a single container before leaving.

OTHER WALKERS

- It's the custom and polite practice to greet other walkers on mountain paths. A simple *buongiorno*, *giorno* or *salve* (among aficionados) is fine. Germans you meet will usually greet you with a brisk *Grüss Gott* and most others settle for hello. This can become a little tiring when you meet a group of 30 walkers!

- It's usually a toss-up about who should give way on a steep path – walkers ascending or descending. It all comes down to common sense and courtesy, rather than asserting some imagined right.

environmental organisation that manages numerous nature conservation areas throughout the country, and leads campaigns on a wide range of issues including sustainable transport, waste recycling and biodiversity in Italy's parks and reserves.

The Lega Italiana Protezione Uccelli (LIPU; www.lipu.it) Italian League for the Protection of Birds, which manages small natural areas to protect bird habitats and to enable people to see wildlife in natural settings

World Wide Fund for Nature Italia (www.wwf.it) A group that fosters protection of native forests, safe transport and a ban on new autostrade (motorways). It also alerts members to, and organises petitions against, proposals for inappropriate developments in parks and reserves.

Long Distance Hikes

You could study for a PhD, climb the world's 'Seven Summits', and wear out at least half a dozen pairs of walking boots in the time it would take you to cover all of Italy's long-distance trails. In a country where hiking often takes fourth place to food, Ferraris and fashion, the nation's comprehensive network of paths and hiking routes is quite an achievement – and one that few average tourists or Italians know about.

Some of the nation's multifarious paths follow ancient pilgrim routes; others circumnavigate huge mountain massifs, while just one – the marathon Sentiero Italia (SI) – tackles the whole elongated peninsula knee to toe. While the trails themselves are generally old, their amalgamation into various routes and circuits is usually a more modern creation. The *alte vie* (high routes) in the Dolomites were first charted in the 1960s, the SI is a 1990s invention, while the magnificent Tour du Cervino (Matterhorn) is less than a decade old.

This being Italy, history is never far from the agenda and your hours spent tramping the trails won't just lower your blood pressure, they'll also offer fleeting insights into antiquity, the Renaissance, WWI battlefields, and the kind of romantic Tuscan sunsets that made 19th-century English aesthetes weep.

Of the following hikes, four pursue circuitous routes while the other twelve are point-to-points. Some paths combine with other long-distance trails for part of their route, and three – the GTA, GEA and the Via dei Monti Lariani – make up lengthy segments of the all-encompassing SI.

GRAND TRAVERSATA DELLE ALPI (GTA)

Some have labelled the Grande Traversata delle Alpi (GTA) as Italy's grandest long-distance hiking trail, and measuring 640km in length and crossing the entire western swathe of the Italian Alps, it is certainly a

SENTIERO ITALIA – THE LONG & WINDING ROAD

Most countries have at least one definitive long-distance hiking path. In Britain it's the Pennine Way; in Spain, the ancient Camino de Santiago; in the USA, the 5000km Continental Divide trail.

Italy's grand hiking epic, the Sentiero Italia (SI, or Grand Italian Trail) is – in contrast to the rest of the country's ancient relics – a relatively new creation. Dreamt up in 1983 with the help of the Club Alpino Italiano (CAI), the dots of the original 6166km route were first joined together in 1995 by an enthusiastic group of hikers who traversed the length of the peninsula north to south over a period of eight months.

In the years since, subsequent excursions along the Sentiero in its entirety have been rare, although individual walkers regularly enjoy smaller segments of the trail – often without realising it.

Created from a varied collection of shorter paths, the official SI route runs from Trieste on the Adriatic to Santa Teresa Gallura in northern Sardinia over 368 designated legs. While generic information on the trail is scant, individual provinces list more detailed facts on their local SI segments in brochures and online.

To avoid confusion with other numbered trails in Italy, the SI is labelled on rocks, trees and signposts with a distinctive red, white and red motif and emblazoned with the black letters 'SI'.

definite contender. Starting in the small, obscure village of Viozene not far from the Italian Riviera, the route tracks north/north-east as it shadows the border of Piedmont, passing France, the Valle d'Aosta and finally Switzerland where it ends near the foot of Monte Rosa. In its course, the GTA crosses five definitive alpine ranges: the Ligurian, the Maritimes, the Cottian, the Graian and Pennines, and checks in with numerous cultural affiliations – Francophone, Valdostan and Walser, to name but three.

Thanks to a concerted effort by groups of German walkers who have been carefully maintaining the route since the 1970s, the GTA is one of the most well-trammelled and best waymarked long-distance footpaths on the peninsula. Nonetheless, there are some notoriously vague sections and, with a recommended 45 days required to complete the walk in its entirety, few hikers attempt it in one go. Another formidable obstacle is the total elevation which, at 45,000m, is the equivalent of five Mount Everests.

Some of the most spectacular and well-marked segments of the GTA are in the Maritime Alps around the Marguareis range (see p82) and are highlighted in this book. The hike in its entirety forms an impressive 640km segment of the SI (see boxed text Sentiero Italia – The Long & Winding Road, p38).

DOLOMITES: ALTE VIE 1 & 2

Today, there are over half a dozen multi-stage *alte vie* in the Dolomites, but the ever-popular paths 1 and 2 remain the blueprints. Pioneered by Italian climber Piero Rossi in the late 1960s, these two groundbreaking routes have since become Dolomiti rites of passage that showcase the best vistas this dramatic pocket of the Alps has to offer.

Considered the shorter and easier of the two routes, the Alta Via 1 is usually tackled over nine to 10 days with walkers bedding down in a network of strategically placed *rifugi*. Widely known as the 'Classic High Route', the trek begins at Lago di Braies in the German-speaking Val di Pusteria and forges 120km south through the Ladin heartland to Belluno in Italian-speaking Veneto. Highlights of Via 1 include the ethereal Alpe di Fanes, the Parco Nazionale Dolomiti Bellunesi, and the evocative open-air museum surrounding the WWI Lagazuoi tunnels. Perennially popular during July and August, it is best to book ahead for a *rifugi* bed (camping is forbidden). The Via is well waymarked; signs are denoted with a number 1 encased in a blue triangle.

The longer, harder Alta Via 2 is an 11 to 12 day, 180km jaunt that begins in the Alto Adige town of Bressanone (Brixen) before trekking south to Feltre in the Veneto. Nicknamed the 'Route of Legends', the route passes through the Puez-Odle, Sella and Marmolada mountain ranges before traversing the expansive Pale di Martino plateau originally charted by British climber Francis Fox Tuckett in 1864 (see box, p52). Unlike Alta Via 1, Alta Via 2 incorporates some trickier *vie ferrate* sections. Come prepared.

VIA FRANCIGENA

In the Middle Ages, all roads led to Rome, and none were more trafficked than the legendary Via Francigena, an epic pilgrims' path that cut across Europe from Canterbury in Southern England to the venerated burial sites of St Peter and St Paul in the ancient Roman capital. One of three great medieval pilgrims' routes (the others were the Camino de Santiago in Northern Spain and the long route east to Jerusalem), the Via Francigena was first documented in the year 725 by a German bishop named Saint Willibald. In the 990s, English Archbishop of Canterbury, Sigeric the Serious, traversed the 'Via' on foot on his way to visit Pope John XV in Rome. Sigeric is thought to have covered the 1700km journey in 80 days and, in the course of his trip, helped establish a network of abbeys and way stations that subsequently came to characterise the route.

In 1994, following the unearthing of Sigeric's 1000-year-old travel notes in the British Library, the Council of Europe declared the Via Francigena a 'European Cultural Itinerary', granting it the same status as the Camino de Santiago in Spain. Starting on the steps of Canterbury cathedral and progressing southeast through France and Switzerland, the Italian leg of the route can be picked up in the Aosta Mountains. Slicing through Piedmont and Emilia-Romagna, the 'Via' then crosses into Tuscany near Lucca. From here it heads south through San Gimignano and Siena to

LONG DISTANCE HIKES

1 Anello dei Sibillini (GAS)	
2 Grande Traversata delle Alpi (GTA)	
3 Via Francigena	
4 Alta Via dei Monti Liguri	
5 Grande Escursione Appenninica (GEA)	
6 Via Alpina	
7 Sentiero Italia (SI)	

Rome. The Tuscan Hill Crests and Medieval Towns hikes (see p205 & p201) both touch on parts of the Via Francigena, which is marked by distinctive brown signposts.

SENTIERO WALSER

Multiculturalism is never far from the surface in this meandering alpine hike along Europe's culturally porous borders, which juxtaposes Swiss Walser heritage with flavours of Italian Valdostan and the French Savoie. The path follows an ancient Walser migration route across three valleys – the Valtournenche, Val d'Ayas and Val di Gressoney – just north of the main Valle d'Aosta and is designed to be both evocative and educational. The Walsers were a German-speaking clan who migrated south through the Graian Alps in the 12th and 13th centuries from the Valais region of Switzerland and set up home in the still nascent Kingdom of Savoy (see box, p78, for more details).

Well signposted and scattered liberally with interpretive panels, the historic path has some of Europe's tallest mountains – most spectacularly the Matterhorn – as a dramatic backdrop. Day 2 of the Matterhorn & Monte Rosa Foothills walk in the Western Alps chapter follows part of the route. For more information, see p110.

VALLE D'AOSTA: ALTE VIE 1 & 2

The Gaelic-tinged Valle d'Aosta safeguards its own two high-altitude trails, the Alte Vie 1 & 2, which between them circumnavigate almost the entire region. Trail 1, the 13-stage 'Path of the Giants' traverses the north side of the Valle d'Aosta from the Walser village of Gressoney St Jean to French-flavoured Courmayeur and passes in the shadow of Europe's highest peaks, including the Matterhorn and Monte Rosa, on its journey west.

Descending into the Val Ferrat on the penultimate day (Day 12) the 'Via' intersects with the Tour du Mont Blanc (TMB) at the Rifugio Walter Bonatti where the intrepid – or perhaps just plain insane – can swing off for 173km more of scenic but often savage walking. Your second possible temptation dangles in Courmayeur, Alta Via 1's finish point but also the start/finish of the 12-stage Alta Via 2, the so-called high-altitude 'nature trail' which clings to the Valle d'Aosta's southern flanks between Courmayeur and Champorcher taking in large swathes of the wild and rugged Parco Nazionale del Gran Paradiso. Its high point is 3300m Col Lauson, and its highlight is the surprisingly rich array of wildlife, which characterises northern Italy's most unspoiled region. The Valnontey–Rhêmes

Notre Dame walk tackles part of the route (see p94).

GRANDE ESCURSIONE APPENNINICA (GEA)

Solitude comes amid wooded serenity on this rollercoaster trail conceived in the 1980s by a couple of Florentine walking enthusiasts. Tracking along Italy's hilly vertebrae and incorporating stretches of the Sentiero Italia (SI), the European Walking Trail (E1) and the Via Francigena, the Grande Escursione Appenninica (GEA on signs) starts at Bocca Trabaria at the nexus of Tuscany, Umbria and La Marche before tracking northwest along the cusp of Tuscany and Emilia Romagna to Montelungo near the border with Liguria. Although 375km long, the GEA only takes in a small northern portion of the Apennines range and steers refreshingly clear of Tuscany's famously crowded hinterland. Among its many highlights are two of the nation's 24 national parks, the Parco Nazionale dell'Appennino Tosco-Emiliano, a haven for wolves and bald eagles, and the Parco Nazionale delle Foreste Casentinesi, Monte Falterona, Campigna replete with ancient beech and chestnut woods.

The GEA is usually tackled south to north over a period of three weeks or more. Although it crosses some mountainous terrain, the gradients are far easier than the steep ascents and exposed *vie ferrate* more common in the Alps.

TOUR DU MONT BLANC

The first documented circumnavigation of Mont Blanc was by Swiss botanist Horace-Benedict de Saussure in 1758. Twenty-eight years later in 1786 the mountain was finally conquered vertically by daring French climbers Jacques Balmat and Michel-Gabriel Paccard.

Officially waymarked since 1952, the modern Tour du Mont Blanc – also known as the TMB – is a 173km romp around the base of Western Europe's highest mountain through Italy, France and Switzerland. Over time it has become one of the continent's most iconic walks and incorporates some truly breathtaking scenery. The nexus for the hike in Italy is the Valle d'Aosta town of Courmayeur, though many hikers begin the seven to 10 day excursion in

Chamonix in France before proceeding to walk in an anticlockwise direction up 12,000m of combined ascent.

Upping the stakes in what is already a difficult walk, the TMB now hosts Europe's most prestigious mass-participation trail run, the Ultra-Trail du Mont Blanc (UTMB) which takes place every August starting in Chamonix (see box p94).

TOUR MONTE ROSA

The Tour Monte Rosa is a 150km hiking extravaganza around the base of the colossal 4634m Monte Rosa massif (containing the second-highest peak in the Alps). Four of this rather arduous trek's official nine stages are in Italy, while the other five traverse Switzerland with hubs in Sass Fee, Grächen and Zermatt. Zermatt is usually considered the 'classic' start for the hike which then proceeds in a clockwise direction entering Italy at the end of Day 1 at the Theodulpass (3301m). From here it ascends and descends through the Gressoney, Ayas and Valtournenche valleys, enters Piedmont at the Colle d'Olen (2881m), rollercoasters through Alagna Valsesia and the village of Macugnaga, before rising steeply one more time to the Monte Moro pass (2868m) where it reenters Switzerland. From Grächen in Switzerland to the Theodulpass on the Italian border, the Tour Monte Rosa and Tour du Cervino (see right) essentially share the same path for three days of tough hiking, although the latter tour is usually tackled in the opposite direction.

Tour Monte Rosa is a challenging hike with some relatively easy glacier travel in its higher reaches; however, it can be safely completed by experienced hikers who have done their homework. Don't attempt the tour before late June and be sure to check local weather conditions before embarking. There are many scenic highlights, not least the views of Monte Rosa and the Matterhorn (Cervino) en route, both infamous mountains with markedly different features and personalities.

As with the Cervino circuit, sections of the Tour Monte Rosa can be cherry-picked to make up shorter hikes. Similarly, the tired can duck out via numerous escape routes, while the inexperienced can bypass steeper sections by cable car.

A good resource for this hike is the website www.tour-monte-rosa.ch, which contains maps, accommodation options, weather reports and current trail conditions.

TOUR DU CERVINO (MATTERHORN)

Only experienced climbers scale the pyramidal Matterhorn, but you can admire the stark, sometimes deadly, beauty of Europe's 'noble rock' in a 145km circuitous trail inaugurated in 2002 on the 50th anniversary of the Tour du Mount Blanc. Incorporating numerous ancient paths that interconnect the Valais region of Switzerland with the Valle d'Aosta in Italy, this tour embraces three different cultures (Walser, Francophone and Italian) and crosses two waymarked glaciers – at Arolla near Col Collon, and on the lofty Theodulpass. The latter, on the border of Italy and Switzerland, is the walk's high point (3301m) and has been a crucial alpine crossing since Roman times.

The Tour du Cervino passes through six valleys, two of which are in Italy – Valpelline and Valtournenche. The section from the ski resort of Breuil-Cervina to Grächen (Switzerland) runs on the same paths as the adjacent Tour Monte Rosa (see previous column). Due to the short sections of glacier travel, this is considered an advanced trek. Rookies should consider hiring a guide.

GRANDE ANELLO DEI SIBILLINI (GAS)

The Grande Anello (great ring) retains enough misty legends to compete with *Lord of the Rings* for surrealism. An easy six to nine day, 120km tramp around the little-visited Parco Nazionale dei Monti Sibillini in the Central Apennines, the hike crosses a region made infamous by the ancient oracle of Queen Sibilla, an evil prophetess who lived in a cave beneath Monte Sibilla and lured gallant knights to their deaths. Even cynics will be impressed by the ethereal scenery: myriad Mediterranean-meets-alpine flora, the odd howling wolf, and nary a ski resort or tourist-packed cable car to break the natural vista!

The official start of the walk is the attractive town of Visso in Umbria – also the park's HQ – which has good transport links to Rome. Most walkers then proceed

CLUB ALPINO ITALIANO

Walkers visiting Italy can't help but be aware of the presence of the **Club Alpino Italiano** (CAI; ☎ 02 205 72 31; www.cai.it; Via E Petrella 19, 20124 Milan), as owner and manager of mountain *rifugi*, and as the energetic waymarker of paths. The CAI is also the major player in the world of Italian walking, mountaineering, trekking and kindred winter activities.

The club was founded in October 1863 in Turin, following the example set a few years earlier by the establishment of The Alpine Club in London. However, from the outset there was a basic difference between the two organisations: would-be members of The Alpine Club had to demonstrate their competence in alpinism, whereas no such requirement applies in Italy – the club is open to all. On the eve of WWI, when the club celebrated its 50th anniversary with an ascent of Gran Paradiso, Italy's highest mountain, it had 7500 members. At the same time there were only 730 people in The Alpine Club. During the inter-war years, the CAI continued to grow, and by 1939 had 75,000 members. Numbers were halved during WWII but the club quickly recovered and in its centenary year had reached 89,000. Growth after 1970 was phenomenal; the 300,000 mark was passed in 1993. The total was 305,306 in 2009. Only the German Alpine Club is larger; the French equivalent has about 100,000.

The average age of CAI members is in the late 30s, with the largest geographical concentration in Lombardy (Lombardia). The greatest strength is among younger people who make up nearly half the total membership. The club is decentralised from its head office in Turin, with 498 area groups, which are further organised into six regions. This arrangement has enabled closer cooperation with local government authorities. Volunteers are the foundation and strength of the CAI, and enable it to run many different activities.

The CAI has more than 1000 national instructors in mountaineering, ski mountaineering and touring, climbing, trekking and activities specifically for young people. The club's success in sustaining the commitment of its volunteer members is the object of some admiration.

---

in a clockwise direction through Fiastra, Rubbiano, Montemonaco (see p243), Forca di Presta and Forca Canapine. In terms of difficulty, the GAS is not comparable to the Western Alps and Dolomite long-distance circuits, and most of the route hovers between modest elevations of 1000m and 1500m. Similarly there are no technical climbs or *vie ferrate*. For those looking for a bigger challenge you can easily break off the main ring to sniff out more difficult paths, including the Sibillini Traverse and LA Gola dell'Infernaccio hikes listed in this guide (p226).

The GAS is a newish hike and is pretty well waymarked throughout with the standard CAI red and white stripes highlighted with a green letter 'G'. Cosy *rifugi* await at the end of each of the official nine day segments.

For more information see the official park website, www.sibillini.net.

VIA DEI MONTI LARIANI

In an already crowded country, the region of Lombardy packs them in like no other (nine million Italians live here), yet – amazingly – there is still enough space to walk in relative seclusion on a 125km hiking trail that tracks the entire western shoreline of magnificent Lago di Como.

The Via dei Monti Lariani is another path with its roots in antiquity. The name is derived from the words 'Lario' (*Larius* in Latin), the original name of Lake Como; and 'monti', the high pastures criss-crossed by interconnecting footpaths, which the local people used (and in some cases still use) to take their cattle up and down the mountains. Combining the trails into a walkable whole, the CAI has created a four-stage hike that runs from Cernobbio near the town of Como to Sorico at the lake's northern tip. Waymarked with standard red and white CAI signposts complemented by the corresponding segment number, the Monti Lariani is, despite its four-stage layout, usually done as a six-day excursion. While the terrain is hilly verging on the mountainous, elevations rarely exceed 1000m and there are plenty of opportunities to branch off and explore the glittering lakeshore.

Speckled with rustic accommodation options (either in small villages or *rifugi*),

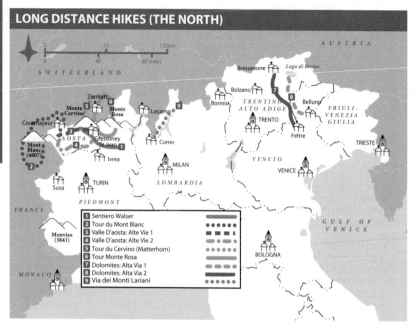

LONG DISTANCE HIKES (THE NORTH)

the Via is clearly summarised in a locally produced brochure called *Hiking on the Via dei Monti Lariani* available in the IAT office in Menaggio (p140). Two maps cover the walk in its entirety: Kompass 1:50,000 map No 91 *Lago di Como-Lugano* and No 92 *Chiavenna-Val Bregaglio*. If you only attempt one stage, base yourself in Menaggio and try the 22km section from Breglia (start of the Monte Grona walk p127) and Garzeno.

The Via dei Monti Lariani represents the Lombardy section of the cross-peninsula Sentiero Italia.

ALTA VIA DEI MONTI LIGURI

Imagine hiking through Cinque Terre and Portofino, and not stopping…until France. The 44-day, 440km Alta Via dei Monti Liguri is the result of an ambitious project to connect the entire length of Liguria from Ventimiglia, in the west, to Ceparana, near La Spezia, in the east. Joining the dots between the southern end of the Grande Traversate delle Alpi (GTA) and the northern end of the Grande Escursione Alpino (GEA), the *alta via* passes through Nervia, Argentina and Arroscea valleys, rising to a high point of 2200m at Monte

Saccarello. Details of the trail have been published in the *Guide Alta Via dei Monti Liguri*, which includes a detailed walk description, and plenty of colour photos and maps at 1:50,000. There's an online version at www.altaviadeimontiliguri.it. If you cannot find a copy in Ligurian bookshops, contact Unioncamere Liguri (☎ 010 2485 2200; Via San Lorenzo 15/1, Genoa). For more information, Associazione Alta Via dei Monti Liguri can be contacted on the same telephone number.

VIA ALPINA

Looked at on Google Earth, the Via Alpina's crusading 'Red Trail' resembles the jagged line of Italy's northern frontier. Yet on closer inspection this 161-stage, 1500km trail veers across an international border an astounding 44 times, taking in the countries of Italy, Slovenia, Austria, Germany, Liechtenstein, Switzerland, France and Monaco.

The breadth of the Red Trail's scenery is so vast it's hard to quantify. Starting in melancholy Trieste, the route forges west through the Julian and Carnic Alps, the Dolomites, the Austrian Tyrol, large tracts of Switzerland, Mont Blanc, the Aosta

Valley and parts of the Franco-Italian Maritimes before docking in glittery Monaco. Throw in multiple languages, a plethora of ancient cultures, war history, national parks, archaeological remains, and some of the most dramatic and varied landscapes in Europe, and it's hard to think of a more 'complete' high-level hike on the planet.

The Via Alpina was conceived in 2000 and tentatively initiated in 2002. Full signage was completed in 2005 on five different colour-coded trails: blue, green, yellow, purple and red; the last making up the all-encompassing Trieste–Monaco route. The brainchild of Frenchman Noël Lebel, director of the Alpine Convention, the US$6.3 million plan aimed to protect important centuries-old Alpine culture from the rapid encroachment of traffic, tourism and climate change.

The biggest dilemma for aspiring hikers is how to traverse the whole 161-stage trail in one snow-free season, though the monster hike has been done. Despite the challenges of some of the terrain, the majority of the trail stays between 1000m and 3000m, and doesn't involve any glacier crossings or technical climbing. It has also been organised so that accommodation and food are a day's walk apart. Existing paths form a continuous chain with established signposts embellished with a distinctive Via Alpina logo.

For more information, check the Via Alpina's website at www.via-alpina.org.

Via Ferrata

During WWI while the British and French were drowning in the mud of Flanders, their Italian allies were engaged in an equally terrifying conflict against their Austrian foes along a battlefront that cut across the Dolomites from Passo di Monte Croce in the east to Marmolada in the west. But, hidden in the swirling mountain mist were two far more foreboding enemies: the freezing winter weather and the precipitous terrain.

In order to maximise ease of movement across the rugged, fickle peaks, the two armies attached ropes and ladders across seemingly impregnable crags in a series of fixed-protection climbing paths known as 'via ferrata' (plural 'vie ferrate') or 'iron ways'. Renovated with steel rungs, bridges and heavy-duty wires after the war, using the vie ferrate evolved into a cross between standard hiking and full-blown rock-climbing and allowed non mountaineers access to areas otherwise out of bounds.

To tackle one of these exhilarating trails you'll first need to don basic climbing equipment (helmet, pads and gloves) and carry a special Y-shaped harness fitted with two karabiners. Faced with technical difficulties and high levels of exposure on many vie ferrate, hikers lock themselves onto fixed metal supports grafted into the rock with the karabiners to assure their safety and arrest potential falls.

Vie ferrate exist all over the Dolomites and you don't have to be a Himalayan Sherpa to enjoy them (Note: Via Ferrata routes are graded separately from the other walks in this book into beginner, intermediate and advanced levels; see Degrees of Difficulty box, p49). Madonna di Campiglio and Cortina d'Ampezzo are the gateways to some of the more spectacular routes. Aside from offering a vertigo-inducing adrenalin rush, the trails also have an important historical value and remain closely associated with their WWI origins. Indeed, the scars of this

TECHNIQUE & SAFETY

You don't need mountaineering experience to use via ferrata equipment, though proper attention to safety and technique is essential. Before even setting out you should familiarise yourself with your harness and equipment. Always check to make sure that your harness waist strap is doubled back through the buckle. Use a specifically designed energy-absorbing device – most belaying devices or figure-of-eight abseil devices are not sufficient. In the event of a fall this device will hugely reduce the impact on your equipment and body.

Once on the route you must ensure that you are clipped into the wire cables with one of your two karabiners at all times. When you come to a bracket, use your free karabiner to clip into the cable on the other side of the bracket before unclipping the first karabiner and continuing. On ladders it makes life easier to loop your lanyard over your forearm while climbing. On vertical sections of cable and on ladders, always unclip one of the karabiners after you have 'leapfrogged' a bracket. Falling with both karabiners attached will prevent your energy absorber from working.

More experienced and confident walkers only clip into the cable on the most difficult sections and can therefore move extremely quickly. The decision whether to clip in or not on any given section is ultimately your own.

VIA FERRATA

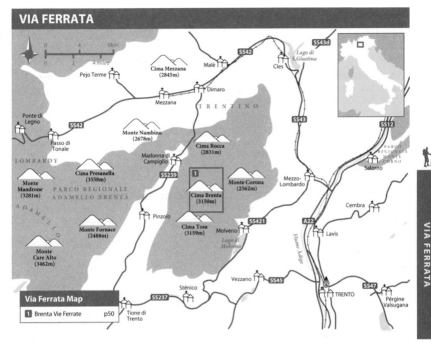

Via Ferrata Map

1 Brenta Vie Ferrate   p50

brutal and lengthy conflict are still etched indelibly over a mountain landscape littered with ingeniously sculpted tunnels, trenches and emplacements. History buffs can visit the large open-air museums at Lagazuoi and Cinque Torri (on the popular Alta Via 1 long-distance path; see p39), which showcases tunnels, battlements and restored forts.

While maintenance of *vie ferrate* continues, the CAI has placed a ban on the construction of any new routes.

EQUIPMENT

The core of the *via ferrata* system is a climbing harness and a *via ferrata* kit. The kit has two specially designed karabiners tied on either end of a length of dynamic (shock-absorbing) rope, commonly referred to as a lanyard. This rope passes through a simple, but extremely important, energy-absorbing device, which in turn is attached to the harness with a locking karabiner. See the Technique & Safety boxed text (p46) for more on the energy absorber.

You can use a straightforward 'sit' harness for a *via ferrata*, but many people use a waist and chest harness combination. This is especially recommended for children and for climbers with heavy packs, so that in the event of a fall they are prevented from flipping upside down (with the associated risk of head injuries). Although not essential, a helmet is strongly recommended. *Via ferrata* kits can be rented from most equipment shops in the Dolomites for less than €5 per day.

If you want to buy your own gear, it's best to do so in Italy; expect to pay at least €50 for the full kit. Alternatively, it should be possible for gear shops in other countries

WARNING

Vie ferrate can never be guaranteed to be safe. Rockfall, lightning, avalanche, sudden weather changes, ice on the rock and cables, and inattention while clipping the cable are all factors that can lead to serious accidents. While the equipment on popular *vie ferrate* is generally sound, it is not fail-safe. Above all you need to remain alert and use your judgement.

to order kits from the manufacturers; **Petzl** (www.petzl.com) and **Camp** (www.camp .it) are two of the biggest.

INFORMATION
Maps & Books
Cicerone's *Via Ferratas of the Italian Dolomites: Vol 1 and Vol 2* by John Smith and Graham Fletcher are the best English-language guides available. Volume 1 covers the Northern Dolomites from Sesto to the Val di Fassa, and Volume 2 tackles the southwestern zone in and around Trentino, including the classic Brenta group.

Walking maps (normally 1:25,000) of areas where *vie ferrate* are common usually have the routes marked, and it is advisable to carry a map with you just as you would on a normal walk.

See the Planning sections of individual *vie ferrate* in this chapter for specific map requirements.

THE BRENTA DOLOMITES

The spectacular Brenta group, just north of Lake Garda are the Dolomites that don't really belong. Comprising an island of dolomite rock surrounded by granite, they are the only segment of the distinctive range that lies to the west of the Adige River wholly in Trentino province. Characterised by a sharp spinal ridge of peaks running north to south, the area is part of the Parco Naturale Adamello Brenta, last bastion of the alpine brown bear. Detailed here are two easier sections of the Bocchette *via ferrata* – one of the most famous routes ever constructed.

The Brenta Dolomites are set back from the WWI front line, and *vie ferrate* were never constructed there for military purposes. However, the dramatic beauty and tricky rock faces attracted the attention of local and foreign climbers, and during the 1930s the construction of a *via ferrata* to the base of difficult climbs began. Work on what was to become the famous Bocchette continued after WWII, and this eventually developed into one of Italy's classic *vie ferrate*. Multiple sections of ladders and narrow ledges now wind along the base of

some of the most impressive rock peaks in Europe.

PLANNING
When to Walk
The routes described here should be snow-free by early June. Late September sees the *rifugi* (mountain huts) shut and the first snows of winter are normally not far behind.

Maps
Use the Kompass 1:25,000 map No 688 *Gruppo di Brenta*.

Information Sources
Weather forecasts for the Brenta are posted daily at many camping grounds, *rifugi* and walking equipment stores.

Contact **Parco Naturale Adamello Brenta** (☎ 0465 67 49 89; www.parcoada mellobrenta.tn.it) for park information.

ACCESS TOWN
For access to these two classic routes in the Brenta Dolomites look no further than the attractive and popular ski resort of Madonna di Campiglio (see Towns & Facilities, p53).

VIA FERRATA SOSAT

Duration 2½–3 hours
Distance 4.5km
Difficulty beginner
Start Rifugio Tuckett
Finish Rifugio Alimonta or Rifugio Brentei
Nearest Town Madonna di Campiglio (p53)
Transport cable car

Summary A good first-timer's route, offering a taste of most *via ferrata* techniques and including an exciting crux section.

Built in 1961, the SOSAT is mainly a high-level walking path, with just one concentrated and relatively short section of *via ferrata*. It offers a well-protected and relatively easy introduction for confident first- timers. The protected section is interesting and varied, involving gullies, ladders and ledges, and the crux (most difficult part of a climb) is an exposed vertical ladder that is enough to set most people's blood coursing. The route is well marked throughout.

DEGREES OF DIFFICULTY

Whether or not you'll enjoy a *via ferrata* is likely to be determined by your reaction to 'exposure' (proximity to a large vertical drop). A well-maintained *via ferrata* is normally a thrilling but safe outing for a properly equipped and suitably experienced walker. However, many routes feature vertical ladders and sections along narrow ledges with several hundred metres of vertical drop beneath. The psychological demands are significant, and walkers prone to even mild vertigo will find an average *via ferrata* terrifying. Most people do find this uncomfortable to begin with, but it is possible to develop your comfort levels by starting on easier routes and progressing onto more challenging and exposed routes. There is no recognised grading standard for *vie ferrate* but the following is a general guide applied to the *via ferrata* descriptions in this book:

- Beginner – suitable for confident walkers with a sound general awareness of mountain conditions and safety. The route will feature exposed sections and perhaps some ladders, but difficult sections will be short. Much of the route may simply be a rugged walk.
- Intermediate – may feature several sustained sections on ladders, cables and artificial footholds. Narrow ledges and significant exposure are common. Will only suit those who are confident.
- Advanced – these routes may be complicated by snow gullies, glaciers and tremendous exposure. Generally mountaineering experience is required.

GETTING TO/FROM THE ROUTE

Rifugio Tuckett (start)

To reach the start of the walk at Rifugio Tuckett, take the **Grostè cable car** (☎ 0465 44 77 44), 1km northwest of Madonna di Campiglio on the main road to Dimaro, to the top station. The first car leaves at 8.30am and the last one leaves the top station at 5pm (return €7.50). From the top station, head southwest along Path No 316, which is signed to the Rifugio Tuckett. The hut is reached after one hour of walking.

Rifugio Alimonta or Rifugio Brentei (finish)

You'll have to hike back down to Madonna di Campiglio, initially on Path No 318 (Il Sentiero Bogani) to Rifugio Casinei, followed by Path No 317 to Rifugio Vallesinella. From here it's a 5km walk along a rough road to back to Madonna. Bank on three to 3½ hours. For those staying at Rifugio Alimonta, take Path No 323 beneath Cima Mondron to link up with Rifugio Brentei.

THE ROUTE

Follow the well-marked Path No 303 east from **Rifugio Tuckett** (see p53) and keep right at two junctions. About 700m from the *rifugio* a third junction is reached, and a sign indicates the SOSAT to the right. Descend south and cross the moraine beneath the **Vendretta di Tuckett** to reach a plaque marking the official start of the Via Ferrata SOSAT. A series of low rock ledges lead around the northwest side of the Punta di Campiglio; wire cables are in place to protect several steps and ledges early on, though many people don't clip on here. The route is then essentially a rough walking path for 1.5km, with paint splashes marking the way through the jumble of boulders.

The descent of an easy, unprotected gully is an indication of the onset of a difficult section. After another 200m you round a corner and the route disappears into a second gully, this time protected. Metal staples provide footholds. The cable then leads along the steep western face of the Punte di Campiglio, descending several ladders and crossing short ledges as it makes its way towards a corner where two cliff faces meet. A large boulder lies wedged in the gully between these cliffs, providing a natural bridge from one to the other. One ladder descends to the boulder, then another, longer ladder (with 51 rungs!) climbs vertically up to a narrow ledge on the opposite cliff wall. This is the crux of the route. The cable continues to protect the ledge for a short distance until the cliff gives way to easier ground, and a path leads around and into the Val Brenta Alta, with wonderful views of the Brenta ridge opening up at the head of the valley.

VIA FERRATA

BRENTA VIE FERRATE

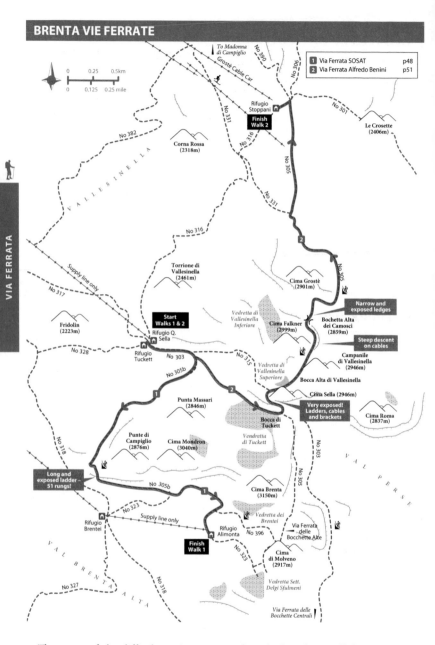

The worst of the difficult sections are now over. Pass a low overhang and then descend two short ladders through a gully, after which a short walk brings you to a trail junction. The orange-roofed **Rifugio Brentei** (☎ 0465 44 12 44; half-board €35;

Jun-Sep) is about 15 minutes down the valley to the southwest, while the **Rifugio Alimonta** (☎ 0465 44 03 66; half-board €35; Jun-Sep) lies a 30-minute climb away to the east. Both *rifugi* are well signed.

VIA FERRATA ALFREDO BENINI

Duration 3½–4½ hours
Distance 7km
Difficulty beginner–intermediate
Start Rifugio Tuckett
Finish Grostè cable car
Nearest Town Madonna di Campiglio (p53)
Transport cable car

Summary An sustained initial section leads through a wide variety of terrain before reaching easier ground in a wonderful high-level situation.

The Benini forms the northern section of the Via Ferrata delle Bocchette Alte and provides more challenging and exposed *via ferrata* sections than the SOSAT. However, it is well within the capabilities of most confident *via ferrata* first-timers given good weather, plenty of time and the prerequisite of freedom from vertigo. It is also an excellent route to try after the SOSAT. It is possible to follow straight onto the Benini from the SOSAT if you start the SOSAT from the Rifugio Alimonta or Rifugio Brentei (see p49).

The Benini is described travelling south to north, because this is arguably the easiest direction for a beginner. From the southern end of the Benini at the Bocca del Tuckett you can see the most difficult section of the route climbing diagonally above the Vendretta di Tuckett on a series of ladders, brackets and airy ledges. If this all proves too much it is easy to turn back, and if you get through you can continue in the knowledge that the other sections will be no more difficult. The majority of traffic comes north to south, with the Rifugio Tuckett often the intended destination.

PLANNING
What to Bring
It is possible, though unlikely, that an ice axe and crampons may be necessary to climb the Vendretta di Tuckett to the Bocca di Tuckett; check at **Rifugio Tuckett** (☎ 0465 44 12 26).

GETTING TO/FROM THE ROUTE
See Getting to/from the Route (p49) for Via Ferrata SOSAT.

THE ROUTE
Follow Path No 303 (well marked) east from the **Rifugio Tuckett** towards the **Vendretta di Tuckett**. Ignore an unmarked path running off to the right and then pass another path heading left towards a prominent gully. This second path (the Sentiero Attrezzato Dallagiacoma, 315) provides rather tortuous walking access onto the Benini just west of Cima Sella, cutting out the initial section of *via ferrata* from the Bocca del Tuckett. However, this path is normally only used when the Vendretta di Tuckett is icy. Continue on Path No 303 past a sign-posted turn-off for the SOSAT, and climb steadily across rock shelves to reach the foot of the glacier (30 minutes from the Rifugio Tuckett). The glacier is not crevassed and is gently angled, providing a 20-minute climb to the **Bocca di Tuckett** (ice axe and/or crampons are not usually needed).

The Benini sets off up the imposing cliffs to the north, immediately using ladders to connect narrow and exposed ledges. You're soon above the glacier and after climbing a high, vertical ladder you drop down onto several brackets leading to a short traverse along a tiny foot ledge. This section is tremendously exposed, but well protected, with each search for a new foothold also forcing you to contemplate the vertical space beneath. Climb a short ladder and onto another exposed ledge before reaching less exposed ground in a wide gully. Scramble up to the base of some easy ladders and climb these to reach the end of this section on the west shoulder of **Cima Sella** (2946m). There is a marked junction here with Trail No 315.

Walk up to the **Bocca Alta di Vallesinella** and cross over to the east side of **Campanile di Vallesinella** (2946m), where a stunning view opens up encompassing from right to left: the summit of Cima Brenta (3150m), the dark depths of the Val Perse, the castellation of Cima Roma and, in the distance on a clear day, the rest of the Dolomites. Easy ledges lead down into a gully from where another well-protected scrambling section leads up a rocky nose in a tremendously exposed situation (two hours from the Rifugio Tuckett). The ledge at the top of this marks the high point of the route (2900m) and the end of the difficult section. Descend steeply using cables and narrow ledges to reach a long traverse on ledges round the east face of Cima Falkner (2999m) to the Bochetta Alta dei Camosci, and then a similar section around Cima Grostè to the end of the Benini. The **Grostè cable car** is then within sight, 45 minutes easy walking away. The ledge sections (around Cima Falkner and Cima Grostè) are only protected where they are particularly narrow, so stay alert on the wider ledges, which are still very exposed.

MORE ROUTES

There are literally hundreds of *via ferrata* routes in Italy, most of which are concentrated in the Dolomites. The following is a very small selection.

BRENTA DOLOMITES
Via Ferrata delle Bocchette Alte
An advanced *via ferrata*, the Bocchette Alte is probably the hardest route in the Brenta and requires basic alpine skills to cope with crossing steep snow gullies. It begins at the Bocca del Tuckett (continuing south from

the Benini) and is sustained and exposed for most of the way to the Rifugio Alimonta. Its height means that ice is a common problem towards the end of the season.

Via Ferrata delle Bocchette Centrali
An excellent intermediate route, the Centrali links the Rifugio Alimonta (and the Bocchette Alte) with the Rifugio Pedrotti. It is well protected and very popular, featuring spectacularly exposed ledges and ladders.

NORTHERN DOLOMITES
Sass Rigais
This 3025m peak can be climbed using a well-maintained *via ferrata* on the south face. Rated beginner to intermediate, this route can be accessed from Ortisei (p177) or Santa Cristina. An exposed ridge leads to the summit, where views extend right across the Dolomites.

Via Ferrata Ivano Dibona
Approached from Cortina, this spectacular but technically straightforward route takes you to the summit of Monte Cristallo. This mountain saw extended and fierce fighting between Italian and Austrian troops during WWI and *vie ferrate* were

---

FRANCIS FOX TUCKETT & THE BRITISH INVASION

For a country whose highest point measures only 978m above sea level (1344m if you include Scotland), the British were enthusiastic participants in the Golden Age of Alpinism. Founded in 1857, the Alpine Club of London was the world's first organised mountaineering body, and its fearless inaugural members audaciously set about clocking first ascents on some of Europe's most notorious peaks, including Monte Rosa (1855), Gran Paradiso (1860) and the Matterhorn (1865).

Born in Bristol in 1834, Francis Fox Tuckett was considered the most daring explorer in a climbing fraternity not known for its shrinking violets. Eschewing the lure of Europe's highest peaks, Tuckett focused his attention on Italy's spectacular northeast, homing in on the still uncharted Dolomites, which in the 1860s was still half-controlled by the Austro-Hungarian Empire.

In less than two decades, Tuckett 'bagged' an astounding 269 Alpine peaks using no maps (there weren't any until he drew them!) and only basic equipment. He was a major player in an expedition that traversed and charted the Pale di San Martino group in 1864 undertaking scientific experiments, but his greatest legacy was cemented in 1871 in the jagged Brenta group where he pioneered a first ascent of 3150m Cima Brenta along ridges subsequently anchored with *vie ferrate*. For single-handedly putting the Dolomites (quite literally) on the map, Tuckett was made a Knight of the Order of St Lazarus by Italian king Victor Emanuele II in 1865, and served as vice-president of London's Alpine Club from 1866 to 1868. Rising above the ski resort of Madonna di Campiglio; Rifugio Tuckett and the Bocca di Tuckett pay testament to a feisty Dolomiti legend.

constructed to move troops and equipment. The Ivano Dibona, however, is a relatively new construction featuring cables, ladders and bridges. The route should suit those wanting easy to moderate walks, but this route becomes very crowded on summer weekends.

TOWN & FACILITIES

MADONNA DI CAMPIGLIO
☎ 0465 / pop 600
This small village is the Dolomites' 'Gucci resort' where the rich and glamorous come to quaff fine wines and hit some formidable downhill ski runs. Austrian emperor Franz Joseph and his wife set the tone in the 19th century – an era relived each February when fireworks blaze and costumed pageants waltz through town during the annual Habsburg Carnival.

Fortunately Madonna di Campiglio has retained its essence, enshrined in a pretty village square overlooked by the castle-like battlements of the Brenta Dolomites.

Information
The **APT office** (☎ 44 75 01; www.campig lio.to; Via Pradalago 4; 9am-12.30pm & 3-7pm Mon-Sat, 10am-1pm Sun) is off Piazza Brenta Alte, in the village centre. Staff at the **Casa delle Guide Alpine** (☎ 44 26 34; Via Cima 3) can provide up-to-date reports on popular *via ferrata* routes.

Supplies & Equipment
There are numerous gear shops in the centre, and **Olimpionico Sport** (☎ 44 12 59; Piazza Righi 15) hires *via ferrata* equipment.

Sleeping & Eating
Accommodation in Madonna is not cheap; near the centre of town the quite adequate **Hotel Palù** (☎ 44 16 95; www.hotelpalu .com; Via Vallesinella 4; half-board per person €45-50) is one of the cheaper options.

Hotel Crozzon (☎ 44 22 22; www.hotel crozzon.com; Viale Dolomiti di Brenta 96, Madonna; per person half-board €55-90) offers bright, clean rooms – some with mountain views. Full board at the on-site restaurant costs just an extra €10 per person. In high summer, guests can dine at the hotel's little chalet in the mountains.

The closest camping ground to the *vie ferrate*, 5km down the valley towards Trento, is **Camping Faè** (☎ 50 71 78; adult/ site €9.50/12.50) with hot showers and a mini-market.

To get an early start, you may want to sleep over in **Rifugio Tuckett** (☎ 44 12 26; per person €22, incl breakfast €26; Jun-Sep) up in the Brenta Dolomites. Take the cable car from Madonna di Campiglio to Passo Grostè followed by Trail No 316.

There are plenty of good places to eat; try **Ristorante/Pizzeria Le Roi** (☎ 44 30 75; Via Cima Tosa 40). For *panini* (bread roll with filling) and other snacks the **L'Azzurro bar** (☎ 44 14 77; Viale Dolomiti di Brenta 118) is excellent. There are several well-stocked supermarkets in the centre of town.

Getting There & Away
Madonna di Campiglio is accessible year-round by buses from Trento (€8, 1½ hours, five daily) run by **Trentino Trasporti** (☎ 0461 82 10 00; www.ttspa.it, in Italian). There are also buses to Milan (€12, 3¾ hours, one daily) and Brescia.

Trento is on the popular and always busy Verona–Bolzano–Brennero train line.

Liguria

HIGHLIGHTS

○ 'Take five' in **Cinque Terre** (p56) on the Sentiero Azzurro between Monterosso al Mare and Riomaggiore

○ Take the high road and find relative solitude on the **Sentiero Rosso** (p60) on the hills above Cinque Terre

○ See how the richest 1% live amid the yachts and Ferraris of ritzy **Portofino** (p64)

Signature food: *Pesto al genovese*	Celebrated native: Christopher Coloumbus	Famous for... Swanky beach resorts

With the five towns of Unesco-listed Cinque Terre grafted like diamond crystals onto its rocky cliffs, the Ligurian coastline contains one of the most popular – and hence, busiest – hikes in Italy. The Sentiero Azzurro (Blue Trail) links the five classic coastal settlements of Riomaggiore, Manarola, Corniglia, Vernazza and Monterosso al Mare via a steep, scenic, coastal trail that winds for 12 precipitous kilometres among terraced escarpments replete with ecstatic views.

For centuries an eastern outpost of the Most Serene Republic of Genoa, Liguria's history is written all over its steep-sided cliffs in diminutive chapels, hidden coves, and deftly terraced olive groves. It is also preserved underfoot on an intricate network of narrow paths that have been trodden down by generations of farmers, monks, sailors, townsfolk and – more recently – tourists.

Aside from the insanely popular Sentiero Azzurro, Liguria harbours plenty of other trails, including the Sentiero Rosso, a longer, higher-altitude version of the Azzurro that gets about one-tenth of the traffic. Countless small paths link the two, some skirting farmland, others visiting half-forgotten sanctuaries or faded Stations of the Cross. Further along the coast the intensely varied Portofino promontory is a surreal mix of deserted coves and sheltered harbours where expensive yachts act as floating homes to holidaying millionaires.

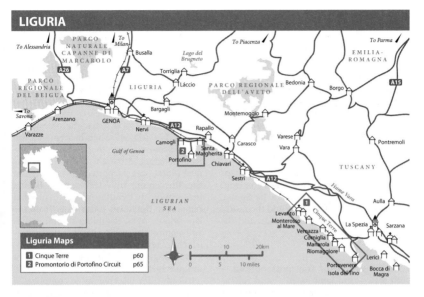

HISTORY

In its turbulent history marked by successive conquests and sea raids, the province of Liguria has been ruled by Greeks, Saracens, Romans, Venetians, Lombards and French, with strong early trade influences from as far afield as Sicily (Sicilia), North Africa and Spain. The many fortified buildings that dot the coast are a reminder that trade and prosperity came at a cost.

Liguria's fortunes have been closely tied to those of Genoa (Genova) since the town gained independence in 1162 and began to extend its influence along the coastline. Successful expansion by the mercantile powers between the 13th and 18th centuries transformed Liguria into a prosperous region of considerable maritime importance. Genoa reached its peak in the 16th century under the rule of imperial admiral Andrea Dora, and managed to benefit from Spain's American fortunes by financing Spanish exploration. However, as the importance of the Mediterranean declined, so too did the region's influence.

In 1796 Napoleon Bonaparte captured Genoa and in 1805 the Republic of Liguria became part of the French Empire. After 1814, with the defeat of Napoleon at Waterloo, Liguria was absorbed into the kingdom of Sardinia-Piedmont (Sardegna-Piemonte). In 1861 Vittorio Emanuele II, king of Sardinia, became the first king of a still fragmented Italy. Genoa played a leading role in the process of Italian unification during the remaining decades of the 19th century, and was the first northern city to rise against the German and Italian fascists towards the close of WWII.

In more recent times Genoa has become Italy's most important port, attracting a massive influx of workers from outlying regional areas and further abroad. Liguria itself has prospered from the postwar industrial expansion of the north and enjoys a good standard of living.

CLIMATE

Protected by both the Alps and the Apennines (Apennini) from cold northerly weather patterns, Liguria enjoys a mild, Mediterranean climate, with average daily maximum temperatures ranging between 10°C in winter and 28°C in summer. The annual rainfall is between 1000mm and 1250mm.

PLANNING
When to Walk

With a pleasant climate year-round, walking in Liguria is recommended at any time. Come in the spring and autumn if you want to avoid the summer crowds and heat.

Maps

The Touring Club Italiano's 1:200,000 map *Liguria* is helpful for planning your visit to the region.

Emergency

In the event of an accident while walking in Liguria, contact the *carabinieri* (police) on the **national emergency** number (☎ 112) or medical assistance on the **national ambulance emergency** number (☎ 118).

GETTING THERE & AROUND

The walks in this chapter are all within steps of the coastal railway line that runs from Ventimiglia through Genoa to La Spezia. Connect in Genoa for Turin and the north, and La Spezia for Florence, Milan and the south and east.

GATEWAY

With its variety of transport options – both water- and land-based – and role as a cheaper, less inundated entry point for Cinque Terre traffic, the Ligurian port town of La Spezia (p67) is the best gateway for the following walks.

CINQUE TERRE

A film director aiming to shoot an authentic period drama set in 17th-century Italy need look no further than Cinque Terre. Bar an overabundance of ogling tourists and a busy 19th-century railway line that burrows through a series of coastal tunnels, barely anything about these five crazily constructed Ligurian villages has changed in over three centuries. Even cars – those most ubiquitous of modern interferences – are missing, thanks to a 1997 Unesco ban.

Rooted in antiquity, Cinque Terre's five towns date from the early medieval period. Monterosso al Mare, the oldest, was founded in AD 643 when beleaguered hill dwellers moved down to the coast to escape from invading barbarians. Riomaggiore, the next oldest, was purportedly established in the 8th century by Greek settlers fleeing persecution in Byzantium. Much of what remains in the towns today dates from the late Middle Ages, including several castles and a quintet of architecturally eclectic parish churches.

Buildings aside, Cinque Terre's most unique historical feature is the steeply terraced cliffs bisected by a complicated system of fields and gardens that has been hacked, chiselled, shaped and layered over the course of nearly two millennia. So marked are these man-made contours that some scholars have compared the extensive *muretti* (low stone walls), to the Great Wall of China in their grandeur and scope.

Inseparable from the sea, the history of Cinque Terre is intrinsically linked to the story of the Italian kitchen. Aside from the ubiquitous prawns, octopus and anchovies, numerous land-reared products

LIGURIAN GASTRONOMY

You could fill a prime-time mini-series on the Food Network with delicious Ligurian recipes. The region is internationally famous for its focaccia, a dimpled rustic bread doused with herbs and olive oil that the local bakers have kneaded into a number of intra-regional varieties, from the crunchy biscuits of Camogli, to the oily cheese breads popular in and around Genoa.

Farinata is another bread-like concoction made from chick-pea flour mixed with water and olive oil. The resulting batter is baked in an oven and seasoned with fresh herbs such as rosemary or pepper. It is sold in bakeries or small take-out pizzerias and makes for an excellent mid-hike snack.

If the region has a signature dish, it is the classic *pesto alla genovese*, a fragrant sauce made from fresh basil blended with garlic, pine nuts, olive oil and hard cheese, and typically served over home-made *trofie* pasta.

Other hard to resist home-grown products include seafood – particularly salty anchovies from Monterosso – extra virgin olive oil processed from the cliff-top olive groves of Cinque Terre, and *limoncello*, a sweet lemon liqueur. You can round off most Ligurian feasts off with a glass (or three) of sweet, white Sciacchetrà wine fabricated in the vine-strafed Cinque Terre village of Manarola.

are also nurtured on these lovingly farmed cliff terraces including vines, olives and fruit trees.

ENVIRONMENT

The Cinque Terre is part of the northwestern extremity of the Apennines. The hillsides of the Cinque Terre have been terraced and intensively cultivated for centuries, and little remains of the original coastal vegetation except at the southeastern extreme, towards Portovenere, and on Punta Mesco, between Monterosso al Mare and Levanto. Here there are extensive stands of Aleppo pine and patches of coastal *macchia* (scrub) – a well-established mixture of species such as myrtle, broom, arboreal heather and juniper. A little further inland, higher up on the ridge traversed by the Sentiero Rosso, cluster pines and broad-leaved trees, such as chestnuts, form almost pure forests, although walkers will also see the occasional cork oak.

There's not much large terrestrial fauna about – occasional signs that warn of hunting activities may explain the lack of mammals. However, a little birdlife survives and there's quite a variety of marine species along some stretches of the coast, in particular Punta Mesco and surrounds.

PLANNING
When to Walk

The crowd-shy would be wise to avoid the Cinque Terre during the peak summer months of July and August, when the area becomes inundated with hordes of tourists keen to experience its much-famed beauty first hand.

Maps

The Cinque Terre is well covered by maps, widely available in bookshops throughout the Cinque Terre and in surrounding towns. The Club Alpino Italiano (CAI) produces a good 1:40,000 map *Cinque Terre e Parco di Montemarcello*, with track notes (in Italian and German), and profiles on the back for the Sentiero Azzurro and Sentiero Rosso.

Occasionally more accurate, but more difficult to read, is the Kompass 1:50,000 map No 644 *Cinque Terre*, which has inset street maps of all five villages, plus Levanto and Portovenere, and comes with a slender, illustrated guide (in Italian and German)

CINQUE TERRE CARD

Easily the best way to get around the Cinque Terre is with a **Cinque Terre card**.

Two versions of the card are available: either with or without train travel. Both include unlimited use of walking paths (which otherwise cost €5) and electric village buses, as well as the elevator in Riomaggiore, and cultural exhibitions. Without train travel, a basic one-/two-/three-/seven-day card for everyone over the age of four costs €5/8/10/20. A card that also includes unlimited train trips between the towns costs €8.50/14.70/19.50/36.50.

Both versions of the card are sold at all Cinque Terre park information offices.

---

to the region. The Edizioni Multigraphic 1:25,000 map *Cinque Terre, Golfo della Spezia, Montemarcello* has a guide in Italian printed on the reverse side.

Books

Shops in the Cinque Terre sell a range of publications in different languages. Recommended is the *Guide to the Cinque Terre*, by Alberto Girani, with an accompanying map at 1:30,000.

Information Sources

The **national park website** (www.parconazionale5terre.it) has lots of up-to-date information, including descriptions and maps of all of the trails. Also handy is the official **Consorzio Turistico Cinque Terre website** (www.cinqueterre.it).

Leaving Luggage

You can leave excess gear at any train station while you do an overnight walk, but at €2.60 for every 12 hours or part thereof, this is an expensive business. Your hotel in town may store a spare bag for a day or two.

GETTING THERE & AWAY

All five Cinque Terre villages, plus Levanto, are served at less than hourly intervals between 6am and 11pm by La Spezia–Genoa trains. A trip anywhere within the Cinque Terre costs €1.40. Train travel is included in the pricier version of the Cinque Terre card (see box, above).

By car, the Cinque Terre is accessible from the A12 and the S1, which passes through La Spezia. Cars are banned from the villages themselves; you must park at the perimeter.

For a more romantic entry to the Cinque Terre, from June to September **Golfo Paradiso** (☎ 0185 77 20 91; www.golfoparadiso .it) runs a ferry service from a quay in the Mandraccio quarter of Genoa's Porto Antico to towns along the Riviera di Levante, including the Cinque Terre and Porto venere (one-way/return €20/30).

There is also a ferry service operated by **Golfo dei Poeti** (☎ 0187 77 77 27; www .navigazionegolfodeipoeti.it) between all the villages (except Corniglia), Portovenere and La Spezia (€11, three a day). Passengers have the option of paying for only a section of the trip on the legs between Monterosso and Vernazza, and Manarola and Riomaggiore. **Servizio Marittimo del Tigullio** (☎ 0185 28 46 70; www.traghettiportofino. it; Via Palestro 8/1b) runs seasonal ferries to/from Cinque Terre from Santa Margherita (one-way/return €17/24.50).

ACCESS TOWNS

With the start and finish of all three walks in this section easily accessed by train or boat from all the Cinque Terre, you can base yourself in any of the five villages. Riomaggiore (p67) is the largest village and the headquarters of the national park. The only hostel accommodation is in Manarola.

SENTIERO AZZURRO

Duration 2½–5 hours
Distance 12km
Difficulty easy–moderate
Start Riomaggiore (p67)
Finish Monterosso al Mare (p57)
Transport train, ferry, car

Summary The classic way to explore the extraordinary villages and cultivated hillsides of the Cinque Terre, while enjoying delightful coastal scenery.

There's a reason why the Sentiero Azzurro is one of Italy's most crowded trails, and the only one you'll have to pay cash to enter. Arguably the most gorgeous coastal hike in the country (although fans of the Amalfi

might agree to differ), the route follows an ancient network of walking paths that has linked the five Cinque Terre villages together for over a millennium. Studded with panoramic vistas, it traverses windswept olive groves and seemingly impregnable vineyards, before dipping serendipitously into each of the flavourful maritime villages where a bundle of historical distractions can quickly turn this moderate 12km hike into an elongated all-day marathon.

While not as flat or straightforward as some Italian paths, the Azzurro is not a difficult hike, and people of all shapes and sizes complete it every day, year-round. The most popular direction of traffic is east to west starting in Riomaggiore and finishing in Monterosso, and this is how it is described below. If you're not up for going the full distance, try hiking as far as the middle village, Corniglia, and getting a train back. Keep your Cinque Terre card (p57) handy at all times as local park wardens often set up spontaneous checkpoints in order to regulate trail traffic.

HISTORY

Hugging the coast, the 12km Sentiero Azzurro consists of a one-time mule path which linked all five oceanside villages by foot. Today's protected trail dates back to the early days of the Republic of Genoa in the 12th and 13th centuries, and until the opening of the railway line in 1874, it was the most practical means of getting from village to village. For thousands of visitors, it still is.

PLANNING
Permits & Regulations

To undertake this walk you will need to purchase a Cinque Terre card (see box, p57). Park wardens make regular checks.

GETTING TO/FROM THE WALK
Riomaggiore (start)

For information on getting to/from Riomaggiore see p67.

Monterosso al Mare (finish)

Monterosso is 10 to 15 minutes from Riomaggiore on thrice-hourly trains (€1.40). There are also good direct connections to La Spezia (€1.90, 15 minutes) and Santa Margherita (€3.30, 45 minutes).

THE WALK

Although it's possible to walk out of the train station at Riomaggiore and head immediately up the coast towards Manarola, it's worth first exploring the most interesting part of this, the easternmost of the five villages of the Cinque Terre. To do so, turn right outside the station entrance and follow the footpath beside the railway line through a tunnel for 150m. Once you emerge into daylight, passages lead down to the right to the waterfront, where small fishing boats are stacked in a tiny piazza, while the pedestrian main street leads left up the steep-sided Valle di Riomaggiore.

The Sentiero Azzurro proper, also known as Trail No 2, begins back at the piazza outside the train station, where a staircase (left) leads over the railway line to the beginning of the excessively famous **Via dell'Amore**. This cliffside path between Riomaggiore and Manarola passes through a roofed gallery, something of a shrine on the theme of *l'amore* (love), which also serves the more practical purpose of protecting walkers from falling rocks. At the end of Via dell'Amore – which is the shortest of the four segments – a 150m tunnel leads from the **Manarola** train station into the village, about 30 minutes from Riomaggiore.

If you plan to stay in the village, **Ostello Cinque Terre** (☎ 0187 92 02 15, fax 92 02 18; www.cinqueterre.net/ostello; Via Riccobaldi 21, Manarola; dm/d €23/65), roughly 300m north of the train station, is a well-run, popular choice, so you'll need to book ahead. They rent out bikes, kayaks and Nordic walking sticks.

From the end of the tunnel, head left, down towards the picturesque waterfront with its rocky boat landing and tiny harbour protected by a breakwater. From here follow the marked and rerouted footpath round the small headland. The way ahead, carved into the steep hillside, is clear. The path soon joins the route once followed by the old railway line, now colonised along some of its length by the low-key holiday resort **Villaggio Marino Europa**, then passes under the present-day line and alongside the platforms of the Corniglia train station. A 365-step brick staircase zigzags up to the ridge top where the village of **Corniglia** is perched above the sea, roughly 3km and one hour from Manarola. Go left at the top of the steps and right in front of the nearby car park. Turning left on the Via Serra by the 14th-century Chiesa di San Pietro will bring you to the sealed road to San Bernardino which you cross and continue on the path on the other side.

Two small bridges mark the beginning of the climb to Prevo. The hillside above the tiny grey-sand beach of **Guvano** is steep and somewhat unstable. Even so, the buildings of **Prevo** soon come and go, and the track proceeds more gently again through olive groves. As **Vernazza** nears, the views across the village and along the coast to Monterosso are truly grand.

The buildings of Vernazza, about 1½ hours from Corniglia, cluster improbably on a dramatic headland, dominated by the tower of the Castello Belforte, and a breakwater extends across the entrance of a small harbour where colourful boats are moored in rows. The Sentiero Azzurro winds down through narrow lanes and crosses the main pedestrian street, which runs from east to west, between the waterfront piazza – well worth a detour – and the train station. By now it's likely to be lunchtime, and you'll find a variety of fairly pricey cafés to choose from.

Leave the village on the narrow Via E Vernazza which becomes a well-formed track beside the church, Chiesa di Santa Margherita d'Antiochia. The track climbs away steeply and gives excellent views as far back, eventually, as Corniglia and Riomaggiore. It levels out and becomes narrower and not as well maintained, but remains generally well marked and is not difficult to follow all the way to **Monterosso al Mare**, about 1½ hours from Vernazza. Once in Monterosso, after skirting the seaward side of the upmarket Porta Roca Hotel, you come to a sheltered **beach** separated by the railway line from Piazza Garibaldi in the old village, where the Sentiero Azzurro officially ends.

Boat services leaves from the western end of the beach. To reach the train station, continue round the waterfront and through a tunnel under the headland to another, longer beach. The train station is upstairs in buildings that face the sea, approximately halfway along.

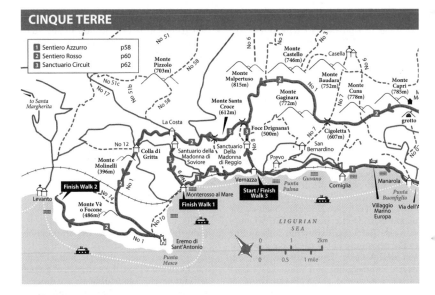

CINQUE TERRE

1 Sentiero Azzurro   p58
2 Sentiero Rosso   p60
3 Sanctuario Circuit   p62

SENTIERO ROSSO

Duration 9–12 hours
Distance 38km
Difficulty moderate
Start Portovenere
Finish Levanto
Nearest Town La Spezia (p67)
Transport bus, train, ferry
Summary An end-to-end, ridge-top traverse of the Cinque Terre along shady woodland paths with sweeping coastal views.

The longest day in this book is just a few kilometres shy of a full marathon and dangles a tempting challenge to energetic hikers, who aim to complete it in under twelve hours. It's an accomplishment you won't forget, especially when you hit the swanky, but undeniably beautiful, beach resort of Levanto and settle down for that long-dreamt-about gelato and/or glass of cold beer.

The other benefit is (relative) solitude. For every 100 people you see on the Sentiero Azzurro, there are fewer than a dozen up here plying their way along a route that is mainly flat, tree-covered and punctuated with plenty of short cuts. An early start is assured by an efficient train and bus connection to Portovenere (via La Spezia), while refreshments en route are possible in a liberal smattering of welcoming bars, restaurants and delis.

Labelled as Trail No 1 on maps and on the ground, the Sentiero Rosso is well signposted throughout making it difficult to get lost.

GETTING TO/FROM THE WALK
Portovenere (start)
From La Spezia's Piazza Giuseppi Verdi, near the waterfront (a 1km walk from the train station), you can catch an **ATC** (☎ 0187 52 25 22) bus to the beginning of the walk at Piazza Bastreri (where the bus turns around) in Portovenere (€0.80, 30 minutes, every half-hour); the service starts at 4.45am (5.45am Sun).

Levanto (finish)
Trains from Levanto can deliver you quickly back to Cinque Terre or La Spezia (€2.40, 20 minutes)

THE WALK
From Piazza Bastreri in **Portovenere**, the Sentiero Rosso begins with a brisk climb up a staircase beside the town's 16th-century castle. On days when the air above the Gulf of La Spezia sheds its characteristic brown haze, there is a magnificent view across the water to the Alpi Apuane in northern Tuscany. The 13th-century **Chiesa di San**

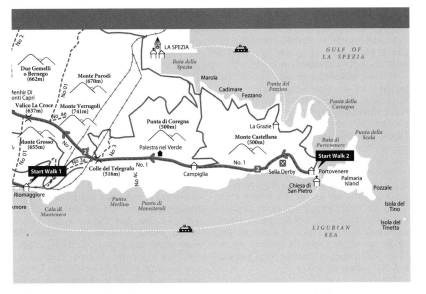

Pietro, perched dramatically at the seaward end of the promontory in Portovenere, also appears to good advantage as the track climbs past the castle. Fork right on the main track at the junction with Track No 1a and ignore a turn-off for Rifugio Muzzorone. You'll join a paved road where you turn right and follow it down, past a **marble quarry**, and take a marked track on the right (red and white marker on a rock), which cuts off one of the road's numerous switchbacks. The path soon joins the road again. Ignore a marked path immediately to the right and follow the road down for approximately 300m turning left at a sign for 'Campiglia'. In a couple of minutes you'll touch another road at a lovely viewpoint with a picnic table and park board. For the next half-hour the Sentiero Rosso is a narrow footpath that hugs the coastal cliffs. This is the toughest and most rugged part of the hike, but the path is well marked and never fully exposed.

Eventually you'll touch a further hairpin bend, where the Alta Via del Golfo (AVG; see p66) heads off to the right along the road, then continues up the crest of the ridge. Continue on the track until you reach another road where you turn left towards Campiglia. At a scruffy soccer pitch on the left on the outskirts of the village, the track detours left through pines and climbs gently into the little piazza beside the Chiesa di Santa Caterina in **Campiglia**.

Follow signs through the village (there's a good **shop** on the right for coffee, focaccia, cheese, fruit etc), then left up stairs at a junction (signposted). Track No 1 climbs quite steeply up a ridge, then levels out and proceeds along the crest, passing an array of curious-looking sculptures: the exercise stations of **Palestra nel Verde** (Gymnasium in the Forest). **La Pineta bar** emerges suddenly out of the forest. There's a spring here and a small booth where you can grab refreshments. The track joins, then leaves, a paved road on the way to **Colle del Telegrafo** (516m), where several roads and tracks meet, two to three hours from Portovenere. From here, Track No 3 descends left to Riomaggiore. **Bar Trattoria Da Natale** offers a last opportunity to replenish supplies before the Santuario della Madonna di Soviore, another four to six hours away.

From Colle del Telegrafo, cross the road and head back into the trees up the foot track labelled No '1'. This soon gives characteristic Cinque Terre views all the way along the coast to Monterosso al Mare. After 10 minutes a telegraph tower appears ahead atop Monte Verrugoli, while down to the left Riomaggiore clings impressively to the sides of a canyon. The route follows

LIGURIA

a pleasantly shady vehicular track through chestnut forest, past Track No 4e on the right, and into the small saddle of **Valico La Croce**, where track 01 (not to be confused with Track No 1) crosses the ridge.

Heading to the left here, away from the vehicular track, continue along the crest of the main ridge, passing a **grotto**, then the junction with Track No 2 and, a few minutes later, a sign that points to the **Menhir di Monte Capri**. This standing stone lies, rather than stands, 50m off to the right. Some 15 minutes later the track switches back to the west side of the ridge and the first significant descent of the day begins. The track drops steadily into a saddle where it meets Track No 6, then continues more levelly into a grassy clearing that makes a pleasant spot for lunch. A few minutes further on, signposts announce the saddle known as **Cigoletta** (607m), where Track No 7 comes in from the right. You are roughly halfway to Levanto.

Tracks No 1 and No 7 merge for a short distance; then Track No 1 doubles back to the right and heads uphill, with brief glimpses of the coast below. The trail swings north for a way, then west again, in a wide arc round the head of the drainage basin that feeds Rio Vernazzola. Paths Nos 5 and 6 go off to the right by a picnic table and a solar-powered emergency call station before the Sentiero Rosso reaches its highest point on the ridge of **Monte Malpertuso** (815m). Descend, on a vehicular track briefly before diverging to the left on a path that emerges again onto the road. Follow it down to a three-way intersection of sealed roads. The markers point down to a larger road at **Foce Drignana** with a sign on the left for Track No 8. This track leads down to Vernazza, for an early end to the day.

If continuing on, cross the road and head up to a spur on a marked path. The foot track rounds Monte Santa Croce (a path to the summit branches off to the left) on its north side, continues through a saddle and along the ridge, then descends to meet a major sealed road. A sign points left down the road towards Genoa, Levanto and Monterosso. This road is the route for the next 3.5km with the exception of a brief detour (keep an eye out for the red and white marker), after 1.5km, through the grounds of the **Santuario della Madonna di Soviore**, the oldest sanctuary in Liguria. The

bar on the terrace (with views as far as Corsica on the right day) serves drinks, snacks and meals until 10.45pm. For the weary traveller, the bar is a good point at which to leave the Sentiero Rosso and follow Path No 9 down to Monterosso al Mare.

Another 2km down the road at **Colla di Gritta**, cross the road ahead, enter the car park beside Ristorante Albergo Il Bivio and go left to find Track No 1 as it leaves the car park by a set of stairs. The track climbs a pine-clad ridge with occasional views back along the coast. It traverses some minor peaks, including Monte Molinelli, then descends into a saddle, 2.8km from Colla di Gritta, where Track No 14 heads right (poorly marked). Straight ahead is Monte Vè o Focone, but the track swings left (south) round it towards Punta Mesco. Just short of the promontory, Track No 1 doubles back to the right towards Levanto. It's worth continuing for five minutes (100m) along Track No 10 to the ruins of an old hermitage, **Eremo di Sant'Antonio** (dating from the 11th century), and an old *semaforo* (beacon), with an uninterrupted view back along the Cinque Terre coast.

Back at the sharp bend in Track No 1, go left and make the gradual 5km descent, through pine forest and then cultivated land, briefly joining a sealed road (for 300m) along the way, to **Levanto**. A final staircase below the 13th-century walls of a Malaspina family castle leads down to the grey-sand beach. To reach the train station, head north along the waterfront for 500m, then follow the main street, Corso Roma, away from the beach for 1km.

SANTUARIO CIRCUIT

Duration 5 hours
Distance 9km
Difficulty easy–moderate
Start/Finish Vernazza
Nearest Town Riomaggiore (p67)
Transport train
Summary An undemanding circuit on some of Cinque Terre's quieter trails to a couple of strategically perched sanctuaries.

Unbeknown to many, the Parco Nazionale Cinque Terre hides a whole network of well-marked walking paths, and not all of them are as crowded as the Sentiero Azzurro, or as arduous as the Sentiero Rosso. The following sojourn links Path Nos 8, 1 and 9, with an optional return leg along a section of the Sentiero Azzurro, to make up a subtle but rewarding walk. It incorporates two Cinque Terre villages – Vernazzo and Monterosso al Mare – and two ancient but often ignored Ligurian chapels.

GETTING TO/FROM THE WALK

Vernazza is connected by regular trains to Riomaggiore (€1.40, 15 minutes) and La Spezia (€1.70, 20 minutes)

THE WALK

This walk starts in the Cinque Terre village of **Vernazza** where you can fuel up on pizza next to the pretty harbour. Head up arterial Via Roma and proceed under the railway arch next to the station. On the other side, a flight of stairs on the left takes you up to a good stone path that zigzags up the terraced hillside following the sculpted Stations of the Cross. After approximately 15 minutes you'll pass a larger shrine and 10 minutes further on, a white house on your right. Soon after, the path meets a paved road at a gatepost; turn sharp left here and continue through the trees to the **Sanctuario della Madonna di Reggio**. Behind the sanctuary, the path cuts up to a paved road; cross it and take a steep overgrown path through the bushes (signposted 'Foce Drignana 30 mins'). Soon the path widens and connects with another paved road. Turn right and then in about 200m turn left at a T-junction, signposted 'Monterosso'. Within another 200m turn right onto another road that doubles back. After a couple of minutes you'll reach a junction where the Sentiero Rosso (Trail No 1) crosses the road.

Turn left onto Trail No 1 and follow the marked path up to a spur. From here the path tracks around the (hidden) summit of Monte Santa Croce (a path to the summit branches off to the left) on its north side, continues through a saddle and along the ridge, then descends to meet a major sealed road. A sign points left down the road towards Genoa, Levanto and Monterosso. Follow this road carefully for 1.5km until you see a small red and white marker on the left directing you down a small side road and into the grounds of the **Santuario della**

Madonna di Soviore, the oldest sanctuary in Liguria. The bar on the terrace (with views as far as Corsica on the right day) serves drinks, snacks and meals until 10.45pm.

The descent to Monterosso al Mare begins on an easy, paved mule track (Trail No 9), still used by pilgrims to the Santuario della Madonna di Soviore. Leaving from the edge of the terrace outside the sanctuary bar, follow the track as it descends steeply through forest, past the ruins of a hexagonal chapel, and across the main access road to Monterosso al Mare. A little further on, the trail joins a small sealed road for a short distance. The road peters out but the trail continues its descent to **Monterosso al Mare**. It finally emerges at Via Roma just past the Casa del Limon. Follow the Via Roma down to Monterosso al Mare's eastern beach accessed by walking under the tunnel from the main square. To return to Vernazza via the Sentiero Azzurro turn left here and pick up the path at the end of the small beach. To reach the train station, turn right and continue around the waterfront and through a tunnel under the headland to another, longer beach. The train station is upstairs in buildings that face the sea, approximately halfway along.

PARCO REGIONALE DI PORTOFINO

A byword for refined luxury, stately Portofino is beyond the wallet-stretching capabilities of most budget-minded travellers. That's not to say you can't linger over an expensive post-hike coffee in its yacht-filled harbour logging the ubiquity of the Gucci handbags and Prada sunglasses.

Backed by shapely cypress trees and characterised by an extravagant array of pastel-shaded villas, Portofino sits on a small promontory of protected land – the Parco Naturale Regionale di Portofino – that juts out into the azure Mediterranean. Unbeknown to the plethora of soft-top sports car drivers who zoom in via the sinuous road from Santa Margherita, the promontory is criss-crossed with copious trails, many of them surprisingly remote and all of them refreshingly free.

LIGURIA

ENVIRONMENT

The Portofino promontory rises to a high point of 610m at Monte di Portofino, and its limestone and conglomerate soils support a wide variety of plant species. The southern slopes of the promontory experience a predominantly Mediterranean climate, and the vegetation is dominated by pine, oak and other species of the coastal *macchia*. North of the ridge of hills that cross from west to east, however, the hours of sunlight are reduced, the prevailing winds are continental ones, and the plant species that thrive are those usually associated with cooler climates further north.

Many bird species are found here, including a number of migratory ones that call in twice a year on their way back and forth between continental Europe and Africa. The waters off the promontory are one of the richest marine habitats in the Mediterranean and are protected in a marine reserve.

ACCESS TOWN

At the end of the walk, Santa Margherita (p68) is a viable overnight stop that mixes Riviera swank with more affordable prices. Alternatively the walk can be done in a day from Cinque Terre.

PROMONTORIO DI PORTOFINO CIRCUIT

Duration 5–6½ hours
Distance 18km
Difficulty moderate
Start Camogli
Finish Santa Margherita (p68)
Transport train, bus, ferry

Summary Walk through a picturesque, unspoiled coastal park to the tiny, remote settlement of San Fruttuoso and its historic abbey, finishing on a trail through luxury resorts.

The compact Portofino peninsula is a colourful melange of improbable juxtapositions. In the course of this 18km hike, you'll roam from well-defined village paths, to precarious rock scrambles (with fixed hand chains for support), to an isolated boat-access-only fishing village, to a favourite millionaire yachters' retreat. At times it feels more like 'Around the World in 80 Days' than around the promontory in 18km.

Overall the hike isn't tough, but the rocky coastal section makes it unsuitable for young children and the unsure of foot. There's a steep ascent/descent before the gorgeous village of San Fruttuoso hidden in a tiny cove, and plenty of steps during the end section into Santa Margherita. Portofino is one of Italy's swankiest spots and a great place to stop for a snack or reviving drink.

PLANNING
What to Bring

The walk crosses terrain with little shade, so bring plenty of water, sunscreen and a hat with a brim. Weather permitting, don't forget to pack a swimming costume.

Maps

The Sagep 1:10,000 map *Guida al Parco di Portofino* is sold with a detailed guidebook to all the marked tracks in the park. If you can't find it, the Edizione Multigraphic 1:25,000 map No 6 *Portofino, Golfo di Tigullio, Golfo Paradiso* also covers the walk.

Books

Sagep's guide to the promontory, *Guida al Parco di Portofino*, by Alberto Girani, now translated into English, provides a good introduction to the park and contains all the official walk itineraries. It was reprinted in 2008.

GETTING TO/FROM THE WALK
Camogli (start)

Camogli can be accessed by road from the A12 (take the exit at Recca). Not all La Spezia–Genoa trains stop in Camogli but if you get off in Santa Margherita, where most do stop, it's possible to swap to a local train for the short hop across the promontory to Camogli. Trains of both varieties run frequently.

Santa Margherita (finish)

For access details to Santa Margherita see p68.

THE WALK

From the station in **Camogli**, cross the road and turn left (south) down Via Nicolò Cuneo. At the first hairpin bend take the left turn into a lane, Via San Bartolomeo, between two buildings. Within 200m the

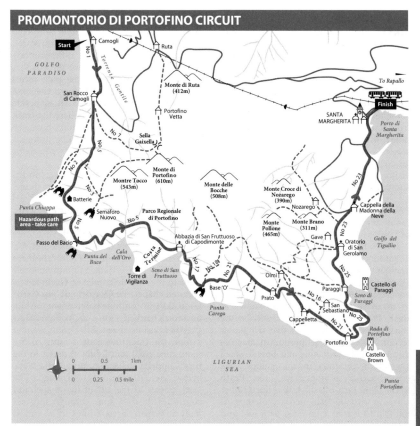

PROMONTORIO DI PORTOFINO CIRCUIT

lane comes to the Torrente Gentile and crosses to its west bank. A gentle 1km ascent up successive flights of steps between old houses and stone walls following trail markers (two red-painted dots), leads to the **San Rocco di Camogli** chapel, 30 minutes from the start of the walk. There's a good deli here with delicious pizza. Around to the right of the parish church, which is decorated in the trompe l'oeil style seen in many Ligurian towns, is a paved path marked Via Mortola. Follow it along a reasonably level walkway (Track No 5), marked periodically with the two red dots, through some houses and a patio, and into some trees. Ignore Track No 3, marked with two red triangles, which goes off to the left towards Semaforo Nuovo (1km from San Rocco). After another 1km Track No 5 comes to a grotto

on a headland with good views of rocky Punta Chiappa below and, on a clear day, back up the coast to Camogli and beyond. Just round the bend, the remains of a WWII German anti-aircraft gun emplacement sit beside the track in an area known, simply, as **Batterie**.

Conglomerate cliffs now rise above the track, and the walk gets tougher with five or six exposed sections that offer a wire cable fixed to the rock as hand support (not suitable for children or those unsure of foot). **Passo del Bacio** gives more fine views. Across the steep-sided Cala dell'Oro to the southeast is a rocky headland topped by a 16th-century **torre di vigilanza** (watchtower), built for defence against raiders from North Africa. The track follows the contours into and out of several gullies, and into the valley at the head of the Cala dell'Oro, then climbs steeply to the crest of the Costa Termine ridge.

It's a straightforward descent from here, with occasional glimpses of the Seno di San Fruttuoso and the *torre di vigilanza*, to the tiny and very picturesque settlement of **San Fruttuoso**, nestled among olive trees and some magnificent pines. Three to 3½ hours from Camogli, this is roughly the halfway point of the walk, yet it feels like another world. Ferries from Portofino and Camogli dock regularly at the tiny quay, while visitors to the **Abbazia di San Fruttuoso di Capodimonte** (☎ 0185 77 27 03; admission €9; 10am-5.45pm, closed Mon Nov-Feb), a Benedictine abbey that houses the Doria family crypt and a small museum. A couple of small eateries overlook the tiny beach.

Follow the two red dots (signposted 'Base O') around a small promontory and through another small group of waterfront buildings. Starting to climb, the path passes a rough concrete helipad and, in another 20 minutes or so arrives at a track junction known as **Base 'O'**. From here, go east, still on the track marked by two red dots on flatter terrain. Pines and Mediterranean *macchia* dominate the headlands, and broad-leaved vegetation abounds in the gullies. The coastal scenery is impressive. From **Prato** to the Olmi turn-off, the trail is lined rather surreally with old-fashioned street lamps. At the Olmi turn-off follow the path east and then turn left in front of a house (following two red dots). At a junction with a picnic table and a park noticeboard turn right on a paved track and head downhill (signposted 'Portofino al Mare'). The scenery quickly takes on a swankier sheen and you'll pass some tennis courts and a rather posh-looking hotel on the left. Within 20 minutes the route will lead you down to the main road in **Portofino** town opposite the parish church. It's worth diverting briefly to the harbourside to soak up a bit of the Mediterranean decadence.

From Portofino it's a pleasant walk to Santa Margherita. The official time of one hour and 50 minutes is generous, but if you're tired of walking, there's a bus stop beside the parish church (on the south side of the main road). Directly over the road from here, steps lead up to the beginning of the path to Paraggi and Santa Margherita.

The path almost immediately forks. Ignore the left fork to San Sebastiano and keep following the trail signed with three red dots as it heads roughly east at first, among elegant residences just above the road. A short distance further on the path meets a sealed road. Turn right down the road then almost immediately veer left, up beside an imposing gateway. From here the track proceeds without fuss, staying above the road but within sight of it, until it descends to meet the road at the attractive harbour at **Paraggi**.

When you reach the road go left (north) for just one short block to Hotel Argentina. Turn left here, then right behind the hotel and up narrow stairs between stone walls, sometimes roofed by greenery. The going is again straightforward and there is only the odd track junction to watch out for. Track marking is adequate. Follow the three dots arranged in a triangle up innumerable steps to the hillside hamlet of **Gave** and its restored chapel, the **Oratorio di San Gerolamo**. As you continue north down the hill, on a track marked with '+' signs, Santa Margherita is visible ahead. After going right at a fork, the track descends a ramp to the road; turn right and follow it down to the tiny **Cappella della Madonna della Neve** below the settlement of Nozarego. The track passes to the left of the chapel and continues down a spur through increasingly suburban surroundings to its end at the southern corner of the boat harbour in **Santa Margherita**. The train station is on the north side of the port. To reach it, walk the entire length of the seaside promenade to the Via della Stazione at the far end. This small alley will take you, via a flight of steps, up to the station terminal.

MORE WALKS

LIGURIA
For details on the long-distance Alta Via dei Monti Liguri that runs the breadth of the province, see p45.

GULF OF LA SPEZIA
Alta Via del Golfo
Beginning at Bocca di Magra, southeast of La Spezia, the Alta Via del Golfo (AVG) follows ridge tops around the Gulf of La

Spezia only a kilometre or two from the coast, avoiding La Spezia and finally meeting the Sentiero Rosso at Campiglia and descending to Portovenere. The route is shown on the CAI 1:40,000 *Cinque Terre e Parco di Montemarcello* map but not on the Kompass 1:50,000 *Cinque Terre* map. The 'official' walking time of just over 15 hours, while likely to be well on the conservative side, suggests that the AVG might best be done over two days. Finding somewhere to stay in Buonviaggio or Sarbia might not be easy; check with the APT or CAI in La Spezia before you set off.

PORTOFINO PROMONTORY
Portofino Hinterland

This is a challenging, nine-hour walk through the heart of the Portofino hinterland, beginning in Ruta and finishing in Chiavari, on the coast to the east of the promontory. En route it takes in several hill sanctuaries, some magnificent coastal panoramas and pockets of coastal *macchia*. The walk climbs to a high point of 801m at the summit of Monte Manico del Lume; landmarks along the way include Passo dei Quattro Pini, Passo del Gallo, Passo della Serra, the small village of Chignero, Monte Lasagna and Monte Pegge. A detailed route description is in *The Park of Portofino Quick Guide*, by Fabrizio Calzia and Alberto Girani, available from bookshops in the area. The Euro Cart 1:25,000 *Tigullio* map shows the route, but as it combines several different tracks, you'll need the Sagep guide to follow the walk accurately.

TOWNS & FACILITIES

LA SPEZIA
☎ 0187 / pop 90,000

To most nonresidents, the hard-working port town of La Spezia is little more than a gateway to Cinque Terre. But, though not as attractive as its famous Unesco neighbour, Italy's largest naval base has its architectural merits. Echoes of Genoa ring through the narrow winding streets of the Old Town capped by the medieval Castello di San Giorgio and demarcated by pedestrianised Via del Prione.

Information

Cinque Terre Park Office (☎ 74 35 00; open 7am-8pm) is handily situated inside La Spezia's train station. There's internet access for €0.80 per 10 minutes.

Sleeping & Eating

There are a number of cheap hotels around the train station, but many tend to be scruffy. **Albergo Birillo** (☎ 73 26 66; Via Dei Mille 11/13; s €30-50, d €55-75) is a homey haven where rather tight-fitting rooms are made up for by the ultra-friendly owners.

The waterfront has plenty of relaxed places to wine and dine. Also good is **Vicolo Intherno** (☎ 2 39 98; Via della Canonica 22; meals around €20; Tue-Sat) a Slow Fish-affiliated restaurant, or the rarely empty **Zanzibar Café** (☎ 334 8045941; Via Prione 289; snacks €5-10; 6.30am-8.30pm Tue-Thu, Fri & Sat till 1am) where zebra-striped seats and mood lighting suggest delusions of trendiness.

Getting There & Away

La Spezia is on the Genoa–Rome railway line and is also connected to Milan (€21, three hours, four daily), Turin (€24, three hours, several daily) and Pisa (€5, 50 minutes, almost hourly). The Cinque Terre and other coastal towns are easily accessible by train. **Consorzio Marittimo Turistico Cinque Terre Golfo dei Poeti** (☎ 96 76 76; www.navigazionegolfodeipoeti.it; Passeggiata Constantino Morin) runs boat services to Genoa and Lerici, as well as coastal towns including all Cinque Terre towns except Camogli.

RIOMAGGIORE
☎ 0187 / pop 1800

Cinque Terre's easternmost village, Riomaggiore, is the largest of the five, and acts as its unoffical headquarters (the main park office is based here). Its peeling pastel buildings that tumble like faded chocolate boxes down a steep ravine to a tiny harbour have become the region's favourite postcard view and glow romantically at sunset. The Sentiero Azzurro starts here.

Information

Parco Nazionale office (☎ 92 06 33; www.parconazionale5terre.it, in Italian; Piazza Rio Finale 26; internet access per 10 min

€0.80; 6.30am-8pm Oct-May, to 10pm Jun-Sep) is right next to the train station.

Sleeping & Eating

B&Bs and a handful of hotels are situated in the village, as well as room and apartment rental agencies such as **Edi** (☎ 92 03 25; Via Colombo 111) and **La Dolce Vita** (☎ 76 00 44; Via Colombo 120).

Some of the cheapest harbourside rooms are with **La Casa di Venere** (☎ 349 0753140; www.lacasadi-venere.com; Via Sant'Antonio 114; s without bathroom €30-50, d without bathroom €40-60, d with bathroom €50-70), just off the upper stretch of the main street.

Places to eat and drink line arterial Via Colombo including **Bar Centrale** (☎ 76 00 75; Via Columbo 144; snacks from €5; 7.30am-midnight), the liveliest late-night and early-morning spot, and **La Lampara** (☎ 92 01 20; Via Malborghetto 2; meals €25; 7am-midnight) with pizza and *pasta al pesto*.

Getting There & Away

Riomaggiore is easily accessible by regular trains that run along the coastal line connecting it with the other four Cinque Terre towns (€1.40, five to 20 minutes), La Spezia (€1.40, 10 minutes), Santa Margherita (€3.90, one hour) and Genoa (€4.80; 1½ hours).

Servizio Marittimo del Tigullio (☎ 0185 28 46 70; www.traghettiportofino .it) provides direct summer boat services to Vernazza, Monterosso al Mare and Santa Margherita.

SANTA MARGHERITA

☎ 0185 / pop 10,200

Elegant hotels with Liberty facades overlook million-dollar yachts in this fishing-village-turned-wealthy-retirement-spot that looks like a museum to art nouveau. The good news is you don't have to be a millionaire to stay here.

Information

Pop into the headquarters of the **Parco Naturale Regionale di Portofino** (☎ 28 94 79; www.parks.it/parco.portofino; Viale Rainusso 1) to pick up walking maps and information.

Sleeping & Eating

Hotel Fasce (☎ 28 64 35; www.hotelfasce .it; Via Luigi Bozzo 3; s/d €98/108) is one of Santa Margherita's cheaper options, with a rooftop sun deck, 16 decent-size rooms (though bathrooms are tiny) and a limited breakfast.

Lido Palace Hotel (☎ 28 58 21; www .lidopalacehotel.com; Via Doria 3; s €105-187, d €130-210) right on the waterfront is a Liberty-style grande dame offering the quintessential Santa Margherita experience.

Trattoria dei Pescatori (☎ 28 67 47; Via Bottaro 43-44; meals around €35; Wed-Mon Sep-Jun, daily Jul & Aug), which opened in 1910, serves *moscardini affogati* (spicy stewed baby octopus) in the summertime, wild mushrooms in the autumn and oven-baked fish and handmade pastas year-round.

For a coffee and snack hit resplendent art-nouveau **Bar Colombo** (☎ 28 70 58; Via Pescino 13; open until late Tue-Sun), a former hang-out of silver-screen stars such as Burton and Taylor.

Getting There & Away

ATP Tigullio Trasporti (☎ 28 88 34; www .tigulliotrasporti.it, in Italian) runs buses to/from Portofino (every 20 minutes) and Camogli (every 30 minutes).

By train, there are hourly services to/from Genoa (€2.40, 35 minutes) and La Spezia (€4.40, 1½ hours).

Servizio Marittimo del Tigullio (☎ 28 46 70; www.traghettiportofino.it; Via Palestro 8/1b) runs seasonal ferries to/from Cinque Terre (one-way/return €17/24.50), Porto Venere (€21/32), San Fruttuoso (€9.50/14.50) and Portofino (€5.50/8.50).

Maritime Alps

HIGHLIGHTS

- Meeting nothing but marmots between **Terme di Valdieri** and **Entracque** (p75)
- Playing cards and sinking grappa in the **Rifugio Garelli** (p86)
- Watching aggressive ibex mating rituals by the **Lago di Valscura** (p73)
- Dipping your hiking boot into a 4km portion of France during the two-day **Marguareis Circuit** (p82)

Signature food: *Risotto alla Piemontese*	Celebrated native: Michele Ferrero (chocolate magnate)	Famous for... Rum-filled chocolates

Northern Italy, crowded? Not if you bring your hiking boots. Shoehorned between the rice-growing plains of Piedmont and the sparkling coastline of Liguria lie the brooding Maritime Alps – a small pocket of dramatically sculpted mountains that rise like stony-faced border guards along the frontier of Italy and France. Smaller, yet no less majestic than their alpine cousins to the north, the Maritimes are speckled with mirror-like lakes, foraging ibex, and a hybrid cultural heritage that is as much southern French as northern Italian.

Despite their diminutive size, there's a palpable wilderness feel to be found among these glowering peaks. Get out of the populated valleys and onto the imposing central massif and you'll quickly be projected into a high-altitude Shangri-La. Whistling marmots scurry under rocky crags doused in mist above a well-marked network of mountain trails where the sight of another hiker – even in peak season – is about as rare as an empty piazza in Rome. This is Italy at its most serene and serendipitous. Not 20km to the south are the fancy resort towns of Portofino and San Remo; yet up here in the high country that straddles the invisible border between Italy and France all you need is a map, a decent pair of shoes, and enough cheese and ciabatta to keep you going until dinnertime.

The main trailheads lie to the south of the town of Cuneo in a couple of recently inaugurated regional parks, fanning out from the small ski centre of Limone Piemonte and the airy spa of Terme di Valdieri. Flush up against the frontier with France (the epic Marguareis Circuit actually crosses the border for approximately 4km), the Maritimes retain a notable Alpine flavour in both their architecture and their terrain. But, whether it's *bonjours* or *buongiornos* you're offering, the welcomes are always warm and the hiking positively sublime.

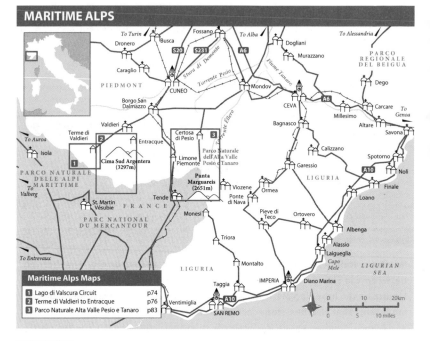

MARITIME ALPS

Maritime Alps Maps

1	Lago di Valscura Circuit	p74
2	Terme di Valdieri to Entracque	p76
3	Parco Naturale Alta Valle Pesio e Tanaro	p83

HISTORY

Recent archaeological discoveries point to the occupation of the Vei del Bouc Valley, southeast of San Giacomo, by shepherds during the Bronze Age. A better known site from the same period is Vallée des Merveilles (Valley of the Marvels), south of the border in France's Parc National du Mercantour, where there is an extensive collection of rock engravings that date from about 1800 BC to 1500 BC. The practice of grazing livestock in the valleys and high meadows of the Maritime Alps continues today, though many of the *gias*, or herders camps, that walkers come across are now abandoned.

The profusion of walking routes across the Maritime Alps from north to south testifies to the centuries-old commerce between southern Piedmont and France. People, ideas and goods for trade have crossed the Alps freely here since before the days of the Roman Empire. Even the dominant language on both sides of the Alps was for a long time the same – *l'occitano* or *langue d'oc*. Track M11 over Colle di Finestra, for example, is sometimes referred

to as the Sentiero del Sale or 'Salt Route' in reference to its former status as the thoroughfare between Cuneo and the coast.

Colle di Finestra has more recent, tragic historical resonances. In September 1943 several hundred Jews fleeing the Nazi occupation of southern France crossed the Alps here on foot in search of a safe haven in Italy. Most were captured and first interned in a concentration camp at Borgo San Dalmazzo, then transported to camps in Germany and never seen again.

All the walks in this chapter have stages in common with the Grand Traversata delle Alpi (GTA). Some of these date from the mid-19th century, when the Argentera was a huge royal hunting reserve, and follow hunting trails built for Vittorio Emanuele II, king of Sardinia-Piedmont and the first king of a united Italy. Lodges occupied by the king's hunting parties can be seen at Terme di Valdieri, on Piano del Valasco (p73) and near San Giacomo (p80). Other sections of the GTA follow roads that were built, or enlarged, for military purposes between the world wars, especially in the 1930s – the wide, stone-paved track between Lago Inferiore di Valscura and Lago delle Portette on the Lago di Valscura Circuit (p73) is a good example. For more information on the GTA, see Long Distance Hikes, p38.

CLIMATE

The position of the Maritime Alps exposes them to Mediterranean as well as continental weather patterns. This, combined with their somewhat lower altitude, means that the weather here is generally milder than in the mountains further north. They become free of snow somewhat earlier than more northerly parts of the Alps, though heavy snow cover in winter is a certainty.

PLANNING

Maps

Although the Maritime Alps are in southern Piedmont, the Touring Club Italiano (TCI) 1:200,000 *Liguria* map, widely sold in bookshops, is good for planning and access information. See the Planning sections of individual walks for details on specific map requirements.

PLACE NAMES

Place names in Italian, French and local dialects are at times used interchangeably. The local word *gias*, found on signposts and maps throughout the region, refers to a summer pasture where a herder brings livestock to graze. A *gias* will usually consist of a stone building or two in better or worse repair, and perhaps a pen or corral, in a relatively flat, grassy area. There's generally water nearby, but don't rely on a *gias* for shelter as some of the buildings are roofless, and those that keep the weather out may be occupied.

The Parco Naturale delle Alpi Marittime used to be known as the Parco Naturale dell'Argentera. Both names may appear on maps of the region, in books and, rarely now, on signposts.

Books

Wild Italy, by Tim Jepson (2005), has a good section on Maritime Alps plants and animals. Two attractive new park guides in Italian are widely sold in the region – see the individual park sections later in this chapter for details. The Club Alpino Italiano (CAI) guide to the area is called

Valli Cuneesi: Pesio, Gesso e Stura. Larger bookshops in the region should carry these titles.

Weather Information

A regional **weather report** in Italian is available on ☎ 011 318 55 55.

Emergency

For medical assistance the **national emergency** number (☎ 118) can be contacted 24 hours a day.

GETTING THERE & AROUND

The region is easily accessed from Turin and southern France. The gateway town of Cuneo is on the main Turin–Nice railway line from where there are connections to the rest of Italy and France. Local bus connections in Cuneo province are relatively good although there are some limitations outside the peak summer months (Jul & Aug).

GATEWAY

The provincial capital, Cuneo (p87), makes a good base for all the walks described.

PARCO NATURALE DELLE ALPI MARITTIME

Though strictly a regional park, the Alpi Marittime promotes conservation efforts – particularly with regard to the ibex – that would put many national parks in the shade. The key is in its special cross-border relationship with the Parc National du Mercantour in France, one of only five national parks on the French mainland (see boxed text, p35). Both parks have their origin in a huge hunting reserve created in 1857 for Vittorio Emanuele II (see p93).

The current park was established in 1995, combining the former Parco Naturale dell'Argentera and the Riserva del Bosco e dei Laghi del Palanfrè.

Two walks are described, one of a day's duration and the other of four or five days. Both visit lakes and waterfalls and give superb views of the highest peaks in the Maritime Alps.

ENVIRONMENT

The park is dominated by a number of granite massifs with peaks over 3000m, in particular the Argentera group, which gave the park its previous name and whose highest point is Argentera Cima Sud (3297m). To the northwest, separated from the Argentera group by Vallone del Valasco and Valle Gesso della Valetta, is the massif topped by Monte Matto (3097m). To the southeast, on the French border and accessible from both countries, is the Gelas group, which includes Monte Gelas (3143m), Cima della Maledia (3061m) and the southernmost 3000m mountain in the Alps, Monte Clapier (3045m).

The park also harbours the most southerly glaciers in the Alps. These persist high on the north-facing slopes of the peaks along the French border. They are much reduced in extent, and consist of little more than a névé, where the falling snow collects and lies permanently.

The dominant vegetation types above the tree line are peat bogs, grasses, abundant wildflowers and low, wiry Alpine heathland plants including the dwarf pine and bilberry. Most of the forests on the lower slopes of the park are almost pure stands of beech. Many of the rest consist of conifers such as the silver fir, red spruce, arolla pine and European larch.

There are a number of smaller plants endemic, or nearly so, to the park, including a species of gentian, a violet found only here and on Corsica, and the so-called ancient king, a rare plant that grows slowly in cracks in the rock high in the mountains, takes decades to reach maturity, flowers once and then dies.

More than 400 of the park's plant species, and their habitats, are represented in the Giardino Botanico Valderia in Terme di Valdieri (p75).

The open higher slopes and ridges of the Maritime Alps are home to the ibex – reintroduced earlier this century – and the more numerous chamois. Walkers can sometimes approach both species quite closely as they graze, though they'll often keep their distance. The rarer mountain sheep cross into the area from Parc National du Mercantour in France but are seldom seen.

Alpine marmots are both seen and heard here. Foxes, badgers, martens, squirrels, ermine and snow hares are also found, and wolves have recently returned after an absence of several decades.

PARKS WITHOUT BORDERS

In practical recognition of the fact that wildlife does not respect national frontiers, the erstwhile Parco Naturale dell'Argentera (now delle Alpi Marittime), and France's Parc National du Mercantour joined forces in 1987 to cooperate in their natural and cultural conservation work. The link was formalised in 1998 when a three-fold charter was signed to improve the understanding and preservation of the area's heritage, and to bring people together. The ultimate aim is to create a single large European park under European law.

Back in 1993 the parks' efforts had been rewarded with the Council of Europe's coveted Diploma Europeo, given to internationally important reserves for their nature conservation achievements. The Diploma was renewed in 1998, testimony to the parks' successes in involving the forestry and pastoral sectors and in preparing management plans.

Among the most notable successes has been the reintroduction of species long absent from the Maritime Alps. The handsome ibex was hunted virtually to extinction in Italy in the 19th century, and fared little better in France. It was first reintroduced to the Valle Gesso between 1920 and 1932. From the descendants of that group a number were released, between 1987 and 1995, at several other sites in the Alpi Marittime and Mercantour parks. Breeding has been successful and numbers are steadily increasing. Since 1986, 80 gipeti (bearded vultures) have also been released. Some have formed breeding pairs, and in the last few years a small number of young have hatched.

For walkers, the Italian-French guide Montagne Senza Frontiere comprises a guidebook and four 1:50,000 maps. A great deal of background information sets the scene for descriptions of a variety of walks, the routes of which ignore the dotted Italy-France border line on maps.

Flocks of choughs wheel and whistle overhead in the higher parts of the park, and you may spot an golden eagle. Reintroduction of the lammergeier or bearded vulture, once hunted to extinction in the Alps, is still in progress. At lower altitudes, forest birds include the black woodpecker and eagle owl.

Animal life on a smaller scale is abundant, and includes butterflies of all shades, from drab through to conspicuous blue, that flit about the grassy valley floors and slopes.

PLANNING
Maps
The best map for both walks is the Blu Edizioni 1:25,000 map *Parco Naturale delle Alpi Marittime*, available in bigger bookshops in the region. On the back are extensive park notes in Italian and useful information such as telephone numbers of *rifugi*.

There are also the older Istituto Geografico Centrale (IGC) maps – the 1:25,000 No 113 *Argentera Regional Park – Entracque – Valdieri*, and the 1:50,000 No 8 *Alpi Marittime e Liguri*, which covers a larger area, including the Marguareis group.

Books
Blu Edizioni and the park authorities publish an attractive guidebook in Italian, *La guida del Parco Alpi Marittime* (2000), with information on flora, fauna and human history, and track notes to 20 short walks. Similar and more up to date is *Atlante del Patrimonio Naturale e Culturale* (2006). Both are available from the bookshops in Cuneo (p87).

Information Sources
Administrative and technical functions are spread between the towns of Valdieri and Entracque at the **park headquarters** (☎ 0171 9 73 97; Piazza Regina Elena, Valdieri). The park also has a website (www .parks.it/parco.alpi.marittime). More useful and more conveniently placed for walkers using public transport are **visitor centres** (opposite Albergo Turismo, Terme di Valdieri); (☎ 0171 97 86 16; Piazza Giustizia e Libertà 2, Entracque).

ACCESS TOWN
From June to September you can use the gateway town of Cuneo (p87) as a base for both walks and catch the regular local buses to Terme di Valdieri.

LAGO DI VALSCURA CIRCUIT

Duration 5–6 hours
Distance 21km
Difficulty moderate
Start/Finish Terme di Valdieri
Nearest Town Cuneo (p87)
Transport bus
Summary A superb day walk, with mountain views and a historic track, to glacial lakes at the head of a picturesque alpine valley.

The main quirk of this hike lies in the quality of its sturdy stone-paved paths. A military road built on the eve of WWII, the historic trail is good enough to be traversed by park vehicles as far as the Piano del Valasco, an improbably verdant alpine meadow that appears like a green mirage after the ruggedness of valley below.

Beyond this the path gets narrower and steeper with the odd rockfall requiring more careful negotiation. Nearer the lakes, snow lingers until late June and majestic ibex are a common sight (the park is a former royal hunting ground). The lakes themselves stand on a lonely section of the French-Italian border and protect the friendly Rifugio Questa. But, with a steep, short cut back down to the lush 'Piano', you won't need a full two days to complete this relatively straightforward out-and-back hike.

PLANNING
When to Walk
From mid-September to mid-June, Terme is accessible only by private transport meaning this walk is best done in high summer. During July and August a second daily bus to Cuneo leaves Terme at 6:15pm meaning it is possible to complete the walk in a day from Cuneo (if you catch the 8.10am bus to Terme). Outside these months, you may prefer to bed down at the Albergo Turismo in Terme (p75) – take your pick.

If you arrive early in the season you can save time by staying in Terme at the economical **Albergo Turismo** (☎ 0171 973 34; r €45-55; mid-May–late Oct) right at the start of the Lago di Valscura circuit. It offers half-board and the heartiest meals in the village.

GETTING TO/FROM THE WALK

Terme di Valdieri is served by **Nuova Benese** (☎ 0171 69 29 29; www.benese.it) buses from Cuneo from mid-June to mid-September (€2.50, one per day at 8.10am Mon-Sat). During July and August there's an extra bus at 2.30pm. Buses leave the west side of Cuneo's Piazza Galimberti and also call at the train station. In Terme the return bus leaves at 12.05pm from an area between the Grande Albergo Royal and the upper village. There's a second bus at 6.15pm in July and August. By car, take Corso Francia to Borgo San Dalmazzo, then follow the signs to Terme.

THE WALK

From the southwestern end of Terme di Valdieri, just uphill from the park visitor centre, follow the rocky road southwest, then west. The road bends up and away from the river on a manageable incline for several kilometres to the lower end of the beautiful **Piano del Valasco**, an hour or so from Terme.

The rebuilt **Reale Casa di Caccia** (Royal Hunting Lodge) is visible further up the plain, a short detour from the main track. The lodge was restored a couple of years ago after being damaged by fire.

At a signpost marking the upper end of Piano del Valasco (1814m), cross a bridge over a stream. On the opposite side another track goes southeast towards Colletto del Valasco. Ignore this and stay beside the stream on its west side, following signs towards Rifugio Questa, and rejoin the old road after a few hundred metres. About 30 minutes from the lower end of the plain, the *rifugio* is signposted off to the left on a steep uphill path (this is your return route). Keep right on the well-built military path, which leads north past some small waterfalls, doubles back through a tunnel in the rock, and then winds generally northwest up a glacial valley, past rocks scored by an ancient glacier and **ruined military buildings**, to **Lago Inferiore di Valscura** (2274m), in a pretty cirque, after another 50 minutes or so.

From the lake, ignore a signposted track which leads around its north side towards Bassa del Druos (2628m). Follow the GTA to the left as it climbs out of the valley

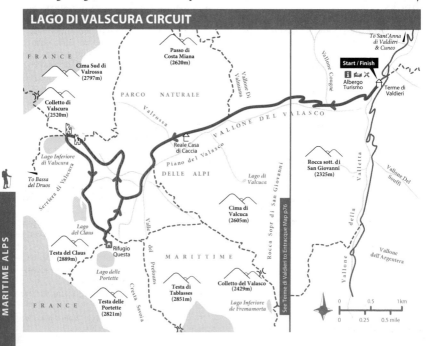

LAGO DI VALSCURA CIRCUIT

and heads roughly south towards Lago del Claus. The partly paved track – a military road built between the world wars – is wide and level as it crosses a large jumble of scree. There are fine views of the Argentera massif away to the east and, closer at hand, back down Vallone del Valasco.

Around 40 minutes from Lago Inferiore di Valscura, the track passes by some lakelets and into a glacial basin where cliffs surround the deep, clear waters of **Lago del Claus** (2344m). After another 20 minutes south, a zigzagging descent leads to a track junction where a signpost points up the hill to **Rifugio Questa** (☎ 0171 9 73 38; www .rifugioquesta.it; half-board €35, dinner €18; mid-Jun–mid-Sep), perched above the steep-sided **Lago delle Portette**. The *rifugio* sleeps 45 people and serves drinks and food, including hot lunches.

Back at the signpost below Rifugio Questa, head down to the north on the GTA, leaving the more substantial track which heads east. The GTA is always adequately marked with red-and-white squares as it descends in 45 minutes back to the three-way junction you passed through earlier on the route. Go right, and in less than two hours, returning by the way you came, you will be back in Terme di Valdieri.

TERME DI VALDIERI TO ENTRACQUE

Duration 4 days
Distance 45km
Difficulty demanding
Start Terme di Valdieri
Finish Entracque
Nearest Town Cuneo (p87)
Transport bus
Summary Pass crossings and an easy summit on the French border among 3000m-plus peaks and retreating glaciers, home to chamois and ibex. The challenging Passo dei Ghiacciai requires experience and caution, but can be avoided.

Because of the rugged nature of the ridges in the Argentera region, most walking routes follow valleys, or link valleys by means of pass crossings. This walk could be dubbed 'the five passes route'. It crosses three significant passes and makes side trips

WARNING

Consult *rifugio* staff about current conditions before attempting to cross Passo dei Ghiacciai (see Day 3, p79). Snow slopes may make it hazardous unless you're equipped with crampons and an ice axe and are familiar with their use. The crossing should not be attempted in poor visibility. If in doubt, take the longer but more straightforward Alternative Route: via San Giacomo (p80), or complete the walk in three days by descending from Rifugio Soria-Ellena through San Giacomo to Entracque.

to another two, and crosses an easy peak of nearly 3000m, on the border with France. Of the five passes, only one is technically challenging, and we describe an alternative route that avoids it should weather or snow conditions dictate.

The walk begins in the tiny spa village of Terme di Valdieri and ends in the somewhat larger centre of Entracque. There is no wild camping in the park, and overnight accommodation is in *rifugi*. Additional stops, at Rifugio Morelli-Buzzi and the Foresteria in San Giacomo, could extend the walk by a day each and shorten the first and last days respectively.

PLANNING
When to Walk

The best period in which to do this walk is from mid-June until mid-September, when all *rifugi* are open, and especially July and August, when regular public transport reaches Terme di Valdieri. These months also tend to have the best weather. Buses operate to a restricted timetable at other times, and much of the accommodation closes down.

It's impossible to predict when conditions will be best for the Passo dei Ghiacciai crossing (see the boxed text, Warning). Late in the summer, the snow slopes that render it *una cosa alpinistica* (one for the alpinists) may be dangerously firm but relatively narrow. Earlier in the season, while there's likely to be more snow, the crossing may be easier because the snow slopes receive more sun and are therefore softer. Always approach the crossing with respect.

TERME DI VALDIERI TO ENTRACQUE

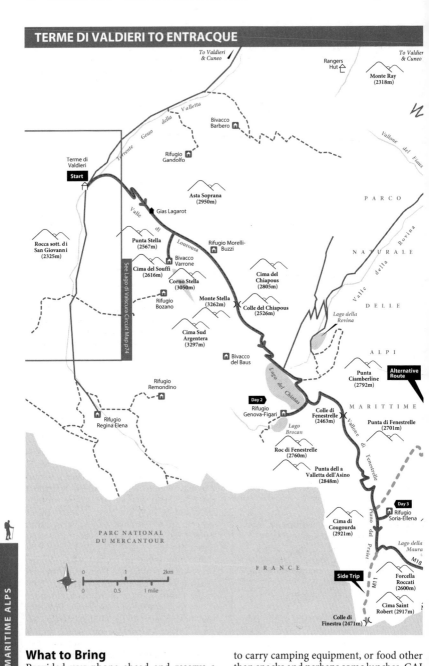

What to Bring

Provided you phone ahead and reserve a place at each night's *rifugio*, there's no need to carry camping equipment, or food other than snacks and perhaps some lunches. CAI regulations require that you use a sleeping

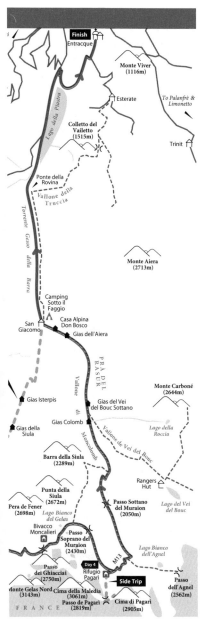

Rifugio staff will usually ask to see your passport (or CAI membership card) when you arrive, and may keep it overnight.

See the boxed text Warning (p75) regarding Passo dei Ghiacciai. Bring crampons and an ice axe – and make sure you know how to use them – if you intend to cross the pass.

GETTING TO/FROM THE WALK
Terme di Valdieri (start)
See Lago di Valscura Circuit p73.

Entracque (finish)
Nuova Benese (€2.20, up to five per day, year-round) buses return to Cuneo from Entracque. The last one leaves at 6.45pm (7.15pm on Sun).

THE WALK
Day 1: Terme di Valdieri to Rifugio Genova-Figari
5½–6½ hours, 11.5km, 1160m ascent, 510m descent
The start of the track is well signposted where it leaves the main road on the southeast (true right) bank of the Torrente Gesso della Valletta, about 50m downhill from the Grande Albergo Royal in Terme di Valdieri. Within a few minutes the track crosses on a footbridge the stream that enters from the southeast, turns up the northeast (true right) bank of the stream and begins to climb on switchbacks. Deciduous forest, with occasional clearings that offer views back to Terme, gives way to pines. After about an hour, there are views across the valley to Monte Stella (3262m) and to the dramatic couloir of Canalone di Lourousa.

Another 25 minutes of straightforward walking leads to **Gias Lagarot**, a stone-walled, tin-roofed hut and a stockyard. After a further 10 minutes, near a memorial cross beside a beautiful stream, a track branches off to the right, across the valley and up to Bivacco Varrone, now visible near the foot of the couloir. Ignore this and continue up the valley to surmount a big moraine wall which brings Colle del Chiapous into view, then at 2351m, you reach **Rifugio Morelli-Buzzi** (☎ 0171 9 73 94; dm incl half-board €35; mid-Jun–late Sep). The *rifugio* serves hot meals and drinks – including coffee, of course – and makes a good spot for lunch or to stay overnight. A set of switchbacks up a moraine

sheet and pillowcase at *rifugi*. Light footwear to put on at the day's end is optional as most *rifugi* have a supply of 'hut slippers'.

A HUNTING GROUND FOR THE SAVOY KINGS

Before claiming the throne of the newly unified Italy in 1861, Savoy's reigning king, Victor Emmanuel II, spent much of his leisure time in his native Piedmont indulging in one of his favourite hobbies – hunting. The main focus for his passion was the Maritime Alps, or more specifically the fabled Valle Gesso, centred today on the small spa of Terme di Valdieri. The monarchy first fell in love with the region during the 1850s and promptly declared it a Royal Hunting Reserve. Within 15 years they had built a summer residence at Sant'Anna, a thermal spa at Terme, and two hunting lodges at San Giacomo and the Casa di Caccia (p74) on the Piano del Valasco.

Victor Emanuel II passed his love of hunting on to his son, Umberto I, and his grandson Victor Emmanuel III, and the latter re-introduced the elegant ibex into a revitalised ecosystem in the 1920s. When Italy became a republic in 1946, the wildlife in the former reserve continued to prosper, and in 1995 the region was further protected by the inauguration of the Parco Naturale delle Alpi Marittime. With over 4500 chamois, 500 ibex and copious marmots, roe deer and mountain goats, it still exhibits some of the richest fauna in Italy.

wall comes into view 20 minutes further on. The ascent is less strenuous than it looks, and from the top it's only a short distance to the signpost that marks the top of the grassy **Colle del Chiapous** (2526m). From the pass the track crosses a mass of moraine, then zigzags down below cliffs, first on the west side of the valley, then on the east. **Lago del Chiotas**, nearly 550m below the pass, is artificial but still spectacular. The track drops down the valley until almost level with the top of the dam wall, then makes its way southeastwards around to the wall and crosses it.

Once across, follow the occasional red-and-white GTA markers down a short stretch of road, through a tunnel, then up and around the southeastern end of Lago del Chiotas on a rough road, to **Rifugio Genova-Figari** (☎ 0171 97 81 38; www.rifugio genova.it; dm incl half-board €35; mid-Jun–mid-Sep), at 2015m, between Lago del Chiotas and the naturally occurring Lago Brocan. Phone ahead to be sure of a bed and a place at the table. (Note the signpost, halfway round the lake, indicating the start of the following day's route over Colle di Fenestrelle.)

Day 2: Rifugio Genova-Figari to Rifugio Soria-Ellena

3–3½ hours, 7km, 490m ascent, 660m descent

From the *rifugio* return to the signpost that points towards Colle di Fenestrelle, and follow that track as it climbs gently, then somewhat more steeply, to the east. After about 90 minutes of zigzagging ascent

around the north and east sides of the Vallone di Fenestrelle, the track crosses a false pass over a spur, descends to cross a gully where there may be some snow, then climbs for another 20 minutes to the signposted **Colle di Fenestrelle** (2463m).

The descent from the pass is well defined and adequately marked. Ibex and chamois often graze in this open, grassy valley. Lower down towards Piano del Praiet you may hear the piercing alarm cries of marmots and spot them scampering for cover. Cowbells are another common sound here. On the valley floor a signpost points the way to **Rifugio Soria-Ellena** (☎ 0171 97 83 82; www.rifugiosoriaellena.com; half-board €35; mid-Jun–mid-Sep), which looms atop a knoll at 1840m, on the east side of the stream. Phone ahead to reserve a spot. The 40m climb from the river bank to the *rifugio* is the steepest ascent of the day.

SIDE TRIP: COLLE DI FINESTRA
2½–3 hours, 6km, 690m ascent

On a clear day it's well worth following the track that leads south, up the valley beyond Rifugio Soria-Ellena, to Colle di Finestra (2471m) on the French border. From the *rifugio*, return to the valley floor and follow the well-defined track south, which soon begins to climb and, after a couple of switchbacks, reaches a signposted junction where track M18 goes left towards Pera de Fener. This is the Day 3 route to Passo dei Ghiacciai and Rifugio Pagarì (p79). Take the right fork (M11) and ascend gradually south for 20 minutes to the remains of a building (2090m) on the east side of the track, then for perhaps another hour to **Colle di Finestra**. Beyond lies France. The track continues south through Parc National du Mercantour past Lac de Fenestre, visible less than 1km away, to the GR52 long-distance track and Refuge Madone de Fenestre.

Retrace your steps from the col to Rifugio Soria-Ellena.

Day 3: Rifugio Soria-Ellena to Rifugio Pagarì

4½–6 hours, 7.5km, 1160m ascent, 350m descent

From the *rifugio* drop to the valley floor and follow the track south towards Colle di Finestra for 20 minutes, as far as the signpost to Pera de Fener. Go left here, and follow the well-defined track M18, marked with occasional cairns, red-paint stripes and arrows, as it zigzags up a spur, keeping a series of rocky cascades on its left (north) side. About an hour from the *rifugio* the track crosses, then twice recrosses, a stream tumbling from a wide, scree-filled gully below Monte Gelas Nord (3143m), which dominates the skyline above. Continue to zigzag up the true right bank of the stream, and sidle into the wide gully, which may contain some snow. Pass a faint track on the right (at spot height 2441m on the Blu map), which climbs towards the spectacular Forcella Roccati. As you climb eastwards, views open of Lago della Maura down on the left side and, further back to the northwest, the Argentera massif. The track remains clear and well marked, and continues to the remains of a stone building on a grassy area.

On a good day the Passo dei Ghiacciai is visible from here, only a few hundred metres away to the northeast. Note that there is a lower, more precipitous notch further north on the same ridge; the route does not go through it. Cairns now lead up and around unstable slopes of scree to the top of the knoll above the ruined building. From this knoll, rocky terraces lead below cliffs towards the pass. Depending on the season, the cairned and marked route may be interrupted by several quite steep tongues of snow. Late in summer, these remain in shade for much of the day and consequently may be too firm to cross safely unless you are equipped with crampons and/or an ice

axe. An alternative route can sometimes be found by descending on rocky ground, skirting below the snow and scrambling up below the pass to rejoin the marked route. Cairns and red-paint markers lead around to the left and finally up to a dip in the narrow, rocky ridge top where marker flags on a cable have been fixed to the rock. Below and to the left (north) is Bivacco Moncalieri, and below it are two lakes, Lago Bianco del Gelas and a smaller, unnamed one. Far below to the northeast, beyond the lakes, a walking track can be seen snaking up the side of Vallone del Vei del Bouc.

To cross **Passo dei Ghiacciai** (2750m), follow cairns and red markers north along the crest until a straightforward, well-marked descent leads directly to **Bivacco Moncalieri** (2710m) in a splendid setting. This basic 11-bed hut remains open during summer. Ibex often graze nearby.

From here the track is indistinct at times, though marked with cairns and splashes of red paint, as it leads down from the uphill side of the *bivacco* across the loose moraine below Ghiacciaio Nord-Est del Gelas, then down to cross the outlet from Lago Bianco del Gelas. The remains of Rifugio Moncalieri, destroyed by avalanche in 1975, are visible on the north side of the lake. The route towards Rifugio Pagarì leads to the right, between the two lakes, on the downhill side of the smaller, unnamed one and along the moraine wall which dams it. Follow cairns and paint markers left (north), over the lip of the moraine and across the outlet stream from the unnamed lake, which vanishes under rocks here for a short distance. Alternating patches of grass and rocky ground lead generally east across a couple of stream gullies and around the base of a big bluff. At a prominent red-paint marker, the track veers northwest for a short way, down the toe of a spur through scrubby alpine vegetation. It then doubles back to the east at more markers and traverses into a big, scree-filled basin, where it stays high below cliffs, avoiding the worst of the scree. A climb of 15 to 20 minutes leads to a ridge top and **Passo Soprano del Muraion** (2430m). The Vallone del Muraion and the track from Rifugio Pagarì down the valley to San Giacomo now appear below, and across to the east is Lago Bianco dell'Agnel.

A winding, ascending traverse leads across a broad gully to another ridge, where the *rifugio* comes into view. Ten minutes later the main track down the valley goes off to the left. Go right, and just over the brow of the hill, with the impressive north-east face of Cima della Maledia (3061m) behind it, is **Rifugio Pagarì** (☎ 0171 97 83 98; www.rifugiopagari.com; dm €26; mid-Jun–mid-Sep). Also known as Rifugio Federici-Marchesini, this *rifugio* is the highest in the Maritime Alps at 2650m.

ALTERNATIVE ROUTE: VIA SAN GIACOMO
6½–7½ hours, 15km, 1435m ascent, 625m descent

To avoid Passo dei Ghiacciai, take this route. From the **Rifugio Soria-Ellena**, retrace your steps back to the Piano del Praiet signpost. From here head northeast on a wide, rocky track above the true left side of the river. Punta della Siula (2672m) comes into view above a wide valley on the right, and after 30 minutes a signpost indicates that you are passing **Gias della Siula** (1480m). A further 15 minutes down the valley is **Gias Isterpis**, recently rebuilt, where you can sometimes buy cheese. The deep Vallone di Moncolomb soon appears on the right, coming in from the east. The track, which is now an unsealed road, zigzags down through lovely beech forest, past a waterfall on the Torrente Gesso della Barra and into **San Giacomo** (1213m).

The park **information centre** (☎ 0171 97 84 44; daily Jun–early Sep) is on the left as you enter the village. Baita Monte Gelas, on the right, serves meals, snacks and drinks. **Camping Sotto il Faggio** (☎ 0171 97 87 04; site €16-20) is across the bridge just below the village. There's also a *posto tappa* with accommodation by the info centre.

At the bridge in San Giacomo turn east across the river, past the camping ground, and reverse the route description given for the start of Day 4 (next column) to reach **Rifugio Pagarì** in 4½ to 5½ hours. From the *rifugio* you can tackle Cima di Pagarì.

SIDE TRIP: CIMA DI PAGARÌ
2–3 hours, 2.5km, 255m ascent

On a good day, this makes a fine farewell to the high Maritime Alps. For the best chance of clear views, do it first thing in the morning before descending to Entracque – and go during autumn. From the flagpole in front of the *rifugio*, follow red markers and cairns south to **Passo di Pagarì** (2819m) and the international border. There may be some low-angled snow to cross. A path of military origin leads towards the top from the north side of the pass, but it's not essential you find it. Just head up to the northeast over rocky but easy terrain, and the summit (2905m) with its many cairns will appear before long. Just above the col, a dry-stone battlement in excellent condition overlooks the valley on the French side. During WWII this position was held first by German troops, then Italian Fascists, and finally partisans, all of whom sheltered in the *rifugio*. The summit offers views in all directions – north over the *rifugio*, northwest to the Argentera massif, southeast to Monte Clapier and south over France's Parc National du Mercantour. On a really clear day, look for the coast and Corsica.

To return, you just retrace your steps to the *rifugio*.

Day 4: Rifugio Pagarì to Entracque
5–6 hours, 19km, 1750m descent

From the *rifugio* the well-marked track M13 zigzags in a northeasterly direction at first, down a rocky spur with good views towards Passo dell'Agnel and the peaks that surround it, away to the east. The track then swings a little west of north and follows the side of Valle Muraion for a couple of kilometres, winding without difficulty through **Passo Sottano del Muraion** (2050m) and finally dropping to the valley floor, and a signpost, about 1½ hours' walk from the *rifugio*. A couple of minutes on from the signpost is a lovely pool where a stream cascades across the track from the southwest.

Proceed roughly north down the valley, here referred to as Vallone di Moncolomb, and cross to the east side and Gias del Vei del Bouc Sottano. Here a signpost indicates the start of the track up Valle del Vei del Bouc that is visible from Passo dei Ghiacciai. Continue north along a grassy plain, **Prà del Rasur**, which extends for 1km or more, to the *gias* at its northern end. The track then enters the first patches of beech forest and soon passes **Gias dell'Aiera**.

The main track, now a little-used road, winds along the north bank of the river, which twists and cascades below. Several pedestrian short cuts avoid bends, though the distance saved is not great. The road passes through a former royal hunting lodge, now the **Casa Alpina Don Bosco**, among tall pines and beeches, and five minutes later crosses a bridge over the Torrente Gesso della Barra just below **San Giacomo** (see p80).

From here continue along the road down the west side of the river to Entracque. It's 4km from San Giacomo to **Ponte della Rovina**, where there's a trough and running water. A further 3km takes you the length of **Lago della Piastra** and brings you to a signposted turn-off down to the right towards Entracque. Follow this road back towards the base of the dam that holds back the lake, then north through a peaceful rural setting to **Entracque**, which should take another 30 minutes or so.

PARCO NATURALE ALTA VALLE PESIO E TANARO

This park, only 10km east of Parco Naturale Alpi Marittime, might almost be in another mountain range, so different is its landscape – thanks mainly to its distinct underlying geology. The peaks of the Argentera and Gelas massifs are clearly visible from the summit of Punta Marguareis (2651m), the highest point in the park and the highlight of the Marguareis Circuit (p82), which begins and ends in the popular winter resort of Limone Piemonte.

The 66-sq-km park was founded in 1978, but the valley's environment has been carefully managed since the 12th century, when Carthusian monks founded the Certosa di Santa Maria (Certosa di Pesio) charterhouse, now near the northern edge of the park, where the Rifugio Garelli walk (p86) begins and ends.

ENVIRONMENT

Whereas the Argentera and Gelas mountain groups are granite formations, the Pesio Valley is limestone country. The north-facing ramparts of Punta Marguareis and its satellite peaks are the most impressive of many cliffs in the area, and the surrounding valleys and plateaus are riddled with caves. Some of these, below the Conca delle Carsene karstic basin to the west of Punta Marguareis, have been plumbed to depths in excess of 600m. In all, more than 150km of caves have been explored in the region. Rainfall is abundant but, instead of forming streams and clear deep lakes, surface water here tends to disappear underground. Sometimes it reappears later in spectacular fashion, as in the Piscio del Pesio waterfall, where an underground river gushes from a cliff.

Though robbed by the porous terrain of much of the rain, the upper slopes of the park harbour a wide variety of plant species, including lilies, gentians and alpine pasque flowers. By contrast, the deep valleys are well watered and densely wooded. There are extensive pure stands of silver fir, sweet chestnut, beech and European larch as well as mixed broad-leaved forests.

Some Alpine animals are found here too, in particular the Alpine marmot, the chamois and, at lower altitudes, wild boar, roe deer and red deer. You may spot a golden eagle riding the thermals from Rifugio Garelli.

PLANNING

Maps

The best map for all walks in the park is the Blu Edizioni 1:25,000 map *Alpi Liguri – Parco Naturale Alta Valle Pesio e Tanaro*, available in bigger bookshops in the region.

Also useful is the older IGC 1:25,000 map No 114 *Limone Piemonte – Valle delle Meraviglie – St Dalmas de Tende*. The IGC 1:50,000 map No 8 *Alpi Marittime e Liguri* covers a larger area, including the Argentera group. Neither of these shows the route from Porta Sestrera to Lago Rataira or the track through Colle Palù to Punta Marguareis.

Books

Blu Edizioni and the park authorities publish a guidebook in Italian, *La Guida del Parco Alta Valle Pesio e Tanaro*, with information on natural and human history, and track notes to 16 short walks. You'll find it at bookshops.

Information Sources

The **park headquarters** (Ente di Gestione dei Parchi e delle Riserve Cuneesi; ☎ 0171 73 40 21; www.parks.it/parchi.cuneesi; Via Sant'Anna 34, Chiusa di Pesio) has some basic information. The **APT office** (☎ 0171 9 21 01; Via Roma 30) in Limone Piemonte has more information of use to walkers.

ACCESS TOWN

With train links to Limone Piemonte and buses to Certosa di Pesio, Cuneo (p87), the region's gateway town, makes a good access town for these two walks.

MARGUAREIS CIRCUIT

Duration 2 days
Distance 35km
Difficulty moderate–demanding
Start/Finish Limone Piemonte
Nearest Town Cuneo (p87)
Transport train

Summary Climb above ski slopes to the karst country of the Alta Valle Pesio and a fascinating mountain *rifugio* with grand-stand views of the limestone cliffs of Punta Marguareis, and enjoy further sweeping views from the top.

Climb steeply out of Limone onto the lonely ridges above the local ski station and all falls silent, save for the ripples of wind in your rain jacket and the whistling of watching marmots. The high country around the French-Italian border, bisected by a well-marked section of the GTA, is dramatic and isolated, but with enough well-placed *rifugi* to break the hiking into doable segments. The Marguareis is a true multinational hike with 4km of Day 2 passing through a mountainous nodule of France. While the path peters out in places, you're never out of sight of the next red and white CAI marker. Keep your eyes peeled, be prepared to bid the odd *bonjour*, and bask in your new-found solitude.

PLANNING
When to Walk

In conjunction with the weather, the factor that determines the best time for this walk is the availability of accommodation at Rifugio Garelli (p84).

Walkers embarking on the Marguareis Circuit looking for an early start may want to overnight at the central three-star **Hotel Marguareis** (☎ 0171 92 75 67; Via Genova 30; s/d €48/96) in the ski resort of Limone.

What to Bring

Camping gear is not required provided you reserve a place at Rifugio Garelli, but a sleeping sheet and pillowcase are. You'll also need your passport or other identity document.

If you want to cover every contingency, and are a citizen of a country whose nationals require a visa to enter France, you might obtain one for this walk. In practice, the walk traverses 4km of a remote corner of France, crossing the border from Italy and back again within a couple of hours, at two windswept cols far from human habitation.

GETTING TO/FROM THE WALK

Limone Piemonte lies on the train line from Cuneo to Ventimiglia and Nice (France). Numerous trains make the journey from Cuneo every day (€2.50, 40 minutes).

THE WALK
Day 1: Limone Piemonte to Rifugio Garelli

5–6 hours, 14km, 1560m ascent, 595m descent

From Piazza Risorgimento, in front of the train station in Limone Piemonte, head under the railway bridge on Via Vialeggia and go quite steeply uphill to the east. The paved road bends left and becomes Via Almellina. This dwindles to an unsealed road as it climbs up the Valle Almellina for 2km or so to a cluster of disused buildings, **Casali Braia**.

Follow the road as it bends back to the south and zigzags up the slope through patches of beech forest to the **Rifugio Capana Chiara**, at the bottom of a ski lift. There is a spring with drinking water outside the lodge. From here, take a faint track that leads uphill, roughly parallel to a small stream, to a clearer path that traverses the slope 200m above (this main path can be clearly seen from the bottom of the ski lift).

Turn left when you reach the main path and traverse the slope beneath a rocky crag, ascending slightly. The path is marked clearly by red and white CAI markers.

PARCO NATURALE ALTA VALLE PESIO E TANARO

1 Marguareis Circuit   p82
2 Rifugio Garelli   p86

The track rounds a spur and becomes more easterly, passing through an eroded gully system, where the trickle emitted by Fonte del Carlaccio may be the only water. Continue to the northeast up this gully system and into a grassy hollow where a signpost denotes the time and distance to the Rifugio Garelli. Follow the spaced markers out of the hollow and up 200m on very faint tracks to a more prominent track just below the ridge top south of Punta Melasso (2076m).

Turn south (right) on this track. Despite the presence of Limone in the valley to the west, the walk now retains a palpable feeling of isolation, thanks to the imposing formations of Rocce del Cros straight ahead and Roccia il Pulpito across Valle Pesio to the northeast. The track passes the sheep-trodden **Fonte Paciot**, and skirts the wilds of

Cima Baban (2102m) marked by a wooden post. Before reaching the ominous hump of **Monte Jurin** (2192m), the path drops off the ridge and sidles down the mountain's eastern slopes. To the southeast, through a low saddle and across the limestone plain of Conca delle Carsene, Punta Marguareis looms. The track winds easily down to a boggy hollow containing a cattle trough before bearing right and climbing briefly, below a set of cliffs, to the saddle of **Colle del Carbone** (2019m).

A faint route now continues down through the col, roughly southeast, to meet the GTA with its reassuring red-and-white markers. After passing the new **Gias dell'Ortica** hut, and the remains of the old one, two junctions are marked with signposts denoting the GTA and the route to Rifugio Garelli. Follow the GTA as it swings down to the valley floor, then climbs to a small pass south of Testa di Murtel. It follows a scenic, pine-clad ridge top and passes a scantily fenced-off sinkhole before a final switchback leads to **Passo del Duca** (1989m) and a small shrine – 50 minutes from Colle del Carbone.

The track drops into a small saddle, **Colle del Prel** (1925m), where track H11 heads north. Stick to the GTA as it swings spectacularly around to the south below Testa del Duca, then tends gradually east and descends for half an hour to the bottom of Vallone del Marguareis and a gushing river. Head southeast and follow the river uphill for 40 minutes to the pretty **Laghetto di Marguareis**. This lakelet was becoming shallower each year as the flow of water from melting snow scoured the bed of its outlet stream deeper, but some discreet engineering works now maintain the level. Here the track nearly doubles back on itself and sidles to the northwest across the north side of the valley. Just around a ridge, at 1965m, sits the palatial **Rifugio Garelli** (☎ 0171 73 80 78; half-board €36; 15 Jun-15 Sep, weekends only mid-May–mid-Jun & mid-Sep–mid-Oct with accommodation Sat night only). While you can obtain a key and let yourself in at other times (☎ 0174 4 47 30) the opening periods give a fair indication of when the weather is likely to be good. With its steeply pitched roofs mirroring the shape of the limestone cliffs opposite, this modern structure sleeps up to 94 people and has excellent facilities, including hot showers.

Day 2: Rifugio Garelli to Limone Piemonte

6–7½ hours, 21km, 1145m ascent, 2110m descent

From a signpost on the edge of Pian del Lupo, the tiny plain behind the *rifugio*, follow red-and-white GTA markers uphill to the east. They lead up the left (north) side of a valley to **Porta Sestrera** (2225m) after 30 minutes. Proceed for a few minutes down the broad, grassy valley ahead, until a well-defined but less clearly marked track diverges to the right towards a cairn in a saddle. From here the very broad Colle del Pas is visible to the south. Cairns and occasional red-paint markers persist as the track contours a little east of south. If you get off route, continue south and don't lose too

much height. Head for a standing stone on the lip of the depression which hides **Lago Rataira** (Lago Ratauoloira on the Blu map). In poor visibility it would be not too inconvenient a detour to follow the GTA as far as **Lago Biecai** and then head back to Lago Rataira along track G5. At Lago Rataira you join track G5, and paint markers lead south over a little spur and up to **Colle del Pas** (2340m), 45 minutes from Porta Sestrera.

Head through the pass and down towards a grassy plain, just west of **Rifugio Saracco Volante**, and the dark entrance to one of this region's many deep caves. Descend from the pass for 10 minutes, passing an indistinct fork on the left, which leads to the *rifugio*, until signs prominently painted on two large rocks point the way to 'Marguareis'. Follow a minor track west, in the direction indicated by the signs, up grassy slopes, then cunningly through some bands of rock to **Colle Palù** (2485m) after 30 minutes.

The mighty whaleback of Punta Marguareis, with its prominent summit cross, is 1km to the west. After negotiating a short section of steeper, rocky ground to the right (north) of the pass, a well-defined track leads across rounded, grassy slopes, up and across a broad rocky spur, across a gully and up to the summit of **Punta Marguareis** (2651m). From here on a clear day you'll see the Argentera group to the west and solitary Monviso (3841m), source of the river Po, further away to the northwest.

From the summit, follow the open crest south until it drops steeply into **Col de la Galine** (2358m). Here a well-defined, marked track crosses the ridge. Follow it to the right (southwest), around a knoll and down into a gully, then through a maze of limestone formations, to reach **Colle dei Signori** (2108m) about an hour from the summit. **Rifugio Don Barbera** is tucked away to the northeast, below the col, and has water – but may be closed.

The route now ducks across French territory for a few kilometres. A road leads through Colle dei Signori and circuitously towards Col della Boaria. Leave this road a few metres north of Colle dei Signori, and drop to the west on a rough track onto the grassy Plan Chevolail. The walking is easy but yellow-paint markers are few until the track passes through a narrowing at the western end of the plain, then up through a gap to the right of a plug of rock. Continue west above bluffs and around the head of a succession of gullies which drain to the south – look for markers, and don't lose height too soon. About 40 minutes after leaving the col, the track finally descends to the floor of Vallon de Malabergue to meet a track that comes up the valley from Rèfrei and Tende. Follow this, still on the north side of the stream bed, until a tributary gully enters from the north. Cross here to the south side of the main gully and continue slightly to the north of west, past a *gias* on the opposite bank, until a signpost points back down the valley to Rèfrei and Tende.

Head west from the signpost for 50m, along a tributary gully that leads towards Col della Boaria, then follow yellow markers up onto a small rocky spur on the south side of the gully. The track leads deviously up and emerges on grassy slopes within sight of the road from Colle dei Signori. Ten minutes further west, the track rejoins the road, and some ruined buildings and a signpost indicate that you've reached **Col della Boaria** (2102m).

In Italy once more, leave the road again and follow a marked track northwest from the col, down Vallone la Boaria. The track drops quite steeply at times and eventually swings west into the broader Valle San Giovanni about 30 minutes from the col. The track swings north again and remains above the river as it tumbles through a short gorge, then 100m further downstream winds down to the river and crosses to the true left (west) bank. Signs of civilisation become more frequent as the track leaves the river and winds through pastures on the north side of the craggy Bec Valletta to a T-junction above a cluster of buildings at **Maire Valletta**.

Go left for 50m, then right at another junction, following yellow markers down the hill to the northwest on a very rustic track. This soon joins a dirt road, which continues down Valle San Giovanni. It's a pleasant walk down the road, which is sealed below **Casali Brick**, to a tiny church in the tumbledown village of **San Giovanni**. From here it's a further couple of kilometres back to the bright lights of Limone.

SLOW FOOD FOR FAST WALKERS

In a country where food is a second religion, the northwest is a symbolic Rome. Aping the yin-yang of Italy's traditional north–south divide, the well-endowed region of Piedmont differs significantly from its less rain-lashed southern counterparts. You'll find more rice here, a penchant for cheese sauces over tomato, and as much butter as olive oil. With the Po River valley comprising the nation's biggest rice-growing area, risotto (using Arborio rice produced in the eponymous Piedmontese town) is a popular signature dish. Additional flavour-enhancing ingredients include nuts, garlic, a wide variety of local cheeses, and one of two indigenous wild *funghi* – porcini mushrooms and the much sought after white truffles.

Other Piedmontese inventions are less heralded but no less enticing. Turin introduced the planet to tic-tacs, breadsticks and solid chocolate, Cuneo answered with some exquisite rum-filled chocolates of its own, while diminutive Bra was where the emblematic Slow Food movement was inauspiciously born in 1986.

Slow Food was the brainchild of a group of disenchanted Italian journalists who, united by their taste buds, successfully ignited a global crusade against the fast-food juggernaut whose plastic tentacles were threatening to engulf Italy's centuries-old gastronomic heritage. Their mantra was pleasure over speed, and taste over convenience in a manifesto that promoted sustainability, local production and the protection of long-standing epicurean traditions. Paradoxically, Slow Food grew quickly and by the 2000s they were sponsoring more restaurants in Piedmont than McDonald's. If you're hiking in the Maritime Alps check out the Slow Food-sponsored Osteria della Chiocciola in Cuneo (p87).

Piedmont also produces some formidable wines. Vintages worth popping a cork for are the legendary Barolo, the so-called 'wine of kings', and its younger, more elegantly flavoured 'queen', Barbaresco, both of which are concocted from Nebbiolo grapes grown in a fertile triangle of land shoehorned between the two formerly feuding fiefdoms of Alba and Asti.

ALTERNATIVE ROUTE: PUNTA MARGUA-REIS VIA CANALONE DIE TORINESI
1½–3 hours, 3km

There's a more challenging and direct route up Punta Marguareis from Rifugio Garelli than the one described via Porta Sestrera and Colle Palù. The Canalone dei Torinesi, a deep gully to the west of Marguareis' subsidiary summit Cima Pareto, is the *via normale* (normal route) to the top from the north side. In good conditions, this option might save you an hour or more on Day 2 of the Marguareis Circuit; if snow-filled, however, it can be all but impassable without crampons and an ice axe. Check with *rifugio* staff what condition the route is in before you attempt it.

It's 50 minutes to an hour's walk from the *rifugio*, via Laghetto di Marguareis and then a faint track up the valley to the southeast, to the scree fan at the foot of the Canalone. Here paint markers on a big boulder indicate the way, unmistakably, up. The route steepens from this point, the ground underfoot is loose, and the narrow confines of the upper part quite often hold snow until at least early summer. Rockfall is another potential hazard.

In short, don't underestimate the seriousness of the *via normale*. If you're ready for it, though, another 50 minutes should bring you to **Colle dei Torinesi** (2448m) at the top of the gully. From here, a faint, cairned track leads south and skirts around the west side of some depressions to meet the track from Colle Palù. From Colle dei Torinesi to the summit of Punta Marguareis is less than 1km and takes 30 minutes or so.

RIFUGIO GARELLI

Duration 4–5 hours
Distance 18km
Difficulty easy–moderate
Start/Finish Certosa di Pesio
Nearest Town Cuneo (p87)
Transport bus
Summary A return trip from an ancient but still functioning charterhouse, to a fascinating *rifugio* with great mountain views.

If you want to get an insider's view of a *rifugio* – without staying at one – and experience the primeval essence of the Marguareis range on a day hike, head south for the Rifugio Garelli. This fleeting taste of the Maritime Alpine wilderness gets you up and back in four to five hours along a not-too-taxing route, and enables you to complete a small section of the Marguareis Circuit in reverse.

It's a climb of just over 1100m from Certosa di Pesio to the *rifugio* at 1965m.

PLANNING
When to Walk

As for the Marguareis Circuit, a major factor in planning an overnight, or longer, trip is the opening period of Rifugio Garelli (see p84) The day walk can, however, be done earlier or later provided you can reach Certosa di Pesio.

What to Bring

If staying at the *rifugio*, you won't need a tent or sleeping bag, but you will need a sleeping sheet and pillowcase, and your passport or other identity document. Outside Rifugio Garelli's opening season you'll need to carry all food for the walk.

GETTING TO/FROM THE WALK

Certosa di Pesio is accessible via the buses of **Autolinee Valle Pesio** (☎ 0171 73 44 96) from Cuneo (mid-Jun–mid-Sep, three per day). Buses leave the west side of Cuneo's Piazza Galimberti at 8.25am, 12.10pm and 2.45pm (though several more daily go as far as Chiusa di Pesio). The last bus out of Certosa on the return trip leaves at 5.30pm (6.20pm on Sun). From September to June buses will take you as far as San Bartolomeo, 3km north of Certosa di Pesio.

THE WALK

From the car park where the bus from Cuneo turns around by the church in Certosa di Pesio, follow the paved road for 3km in a southerly direction beside the Pesio River to the **Rifugio Pian delle Gorre**. It's a straightforward tramp on a quiet, shaded road that should take about 45 minutes.

From Pian delle Gorre, at a barrier and information board, a substantial, drivable track (the left fork if you've followed the east bank of the Pesio) leads roughly southeast for a kilometre or so, and ends at a small turning area labelled 'Il Salto'. Here turn left by another park noticeboard. This time it's a foot track, which soon gives the first views of the Marguareis massif ahead, and climbs rather more steeply through fine mixed forest before it emerges in a clearing at **Gias Sottano di Sestrera**, a stone hut where there's a water trough and another parting of ways.

Yet another left fork now leads up Vallone di Sestrera, and climbs steadily, with views of the *gias* across the valley to the east, then of the cliffs and gullies of the Marguareis group. Climbing above the trees, the next major landmark is **Gias Soprano di Sestrera**, another stone hut characterised by its solar panels. Once you're here, after about two hours of climbing from Pian delle Gorre, the **Rifugio Garelli** (p84) is within view, only a few hundred metres further on. You can either make the *rifugio* your lunch stop, or a base for the night.

The return journey begins by reversing part of the Marguareis Circuit – following the GTA, first to **Laghetto di Marguareis**, then down the valley to the foot of the descent from Passo del Duca. From here, continue down the true left bank of the Marguareis (though the Blu map shows the track on the right bank for a short distance). Eventually the track enters beech forest, then crosses the pretty stream on a bridge shortly before returning you to Gias Sottano di Sestrera. From here, retrace your steps past Rifugio Pian delle Gorre to Certosa.

MORE WALKS

More walk options, both long and short, abound in the Maritime Alps, especially from mid-July to mid-September. As long as transport services run and accommodation remains open, the GTA and its network of *rifugi* and other places to stay, known as *posti tappa* (staging posts), are an excellent basis for walks of almost any length. For example, three stages of the GTA connect Trinità, near Entracque at the end of the Terme di Valdieri to Entracque walk, via the villages of Palanfrè and Limonetto, to Rifugio Garelli. Further east beyond Rifugio Garelli, two more stages reach the end of the GTA at Viozene. It would thus be possible, for example, to follow the GTA for eight days, from Viozene to Terme di

Valdieri or vice versa, linking much of the territory covered by the walks in this chapter. In addition, minor tracks make many variations possible. And just over the border on the French side of the range, linked via a number of passes to the Italian system, is a comparable network of French tracks and huts. For more information on the GTA see the Long Distance Hikes chapter, p38.

TOWN & FACILITIES

CUNEO
☎ 0171 / pop 50,000
Cuneo is the region's main entry town. Rarely frequented by international visitors, this understated provincial capital retains a Napoleonic grandiosity in its broad tree-lined avenues and gargantuan main piazza, a feature that sets it markedly apart from other more quintessential Italian cities. In a region where gastronomy is king (the Slow Food movement was born in Piedmont), Cuneo is a noted culinary hot spot – an added bonus for pasta-craving hikers in need of some energy replenishment.

Information
Cuneo's tourist office (☎ 69 32 58; www.comune.cuneo.it; Via Roma 28; 9.30am-12.30pm & 3-6.30pm Mon-Sat) has information on the town.

Region-wide information is provided by **Azienda Turistica Locale del Cuneese** (ATL; ☎ 69 02 17; www.cuneoholiday.com; Via Vittorio Amedeo II 8a; 8.30am-1pm & 2.30-6pm Mon-Fri), also stocks excellent free hiking/biking booklets with maps.

Supplies & Equipment
There's a plethora of good bookshops in Cuneo. Reliable sources for local walking maps and guidebooks are **ICAP** (☎ 69 89 89; Piazza Galimberti 10) and **Antica Libreria Salomone** (☎ 69 25 62; Via Roma 64d). Park visitor centres and *rifugi* (mountain huts) also sell them.

A range of books and outdoor gear, including everything for *vie ferrate* (iron ways) is available at **Ravaschietto Sport** (☎ 69 20 81; Via Roma 39).

MARITIME ALPS

Sleeping & Eating

Hotel Ligure (☎ 63 45 45; www.ligurehotel
.com; Via Savigliano 11; s €55-65, d €70-
80, apt for longer stays from €40) In the
heart of the old town, this two-star hotel
has a handful of apartments with their own
kitchens (minimum seven-night stay; no
breakfast). If you're just passing through,
its freshly spruced-up hotel rooms (with
breakfast) are simple but spotless. Call
ahead to reserve a parking space.

Hotel Royal Superga (☎ 69 32 23; www
.hotelroyalsuperga.com; Via Pascal 3;
s €55-70, d €75-95) For Superga, read superb. This appealing, old-fashioned hotel in
a corner of Piazza Galimberti has all mod
cons including a free internet point (still
all too rare in Italy), free DVDs to watch
in your room, free *apéritif* if you linger in
the lobby between 5pm and 9pm and free
city bikes for guests. Breakfast is a delicious
spread made from organic produce.

Osteria della Chiocciola (☎ 6 62 77;
Via Fossano 1; lunch menus €17.20, dinner menus €28-33; Mon-Sat) You can
stop by for a glass of wine (from €6) with
cheese and salami on the ground floor of
this acclaimed Slow Food restaurant. Upstairs, in a buttercup dining room, choose
from the handwritten menu's alchemy of
flavours.

Bar Corso (☎ 60 20 14; Corso Nizza 16;
7am-1am Thu-Tue) makes Cuneo's best gelati, and is a popular spot for a drink.

Getting There & Away

Regular trains run from Cuneo's central
train station, at Piazzale Libertà, to Saluzzo
(€2.70, 35 minutes, up to six daily), Turin
(€5.30, 1¼ hours, up to eight daily), San
Remo (€6.50, 2¼ hours, three daily) and
Ventimiglia (€5.40, two hours, around four
daily), as well as Nice (2¾ hours, at least six
daily) in France.

Western Alps

HIGHLIGHTS

- Enjoying the dearth of ski lifts in the wildlife-packed **Parco Nazionale del Gran Paradiso** (p93)
- Sampling esoteric Walser culture in the **Val d'Ayas**, **Val di Gressoney** and **Valsesia** (p107)
- Walking amid colourful carpets of wildflowers in alpine meadows on the **Lakes & Wildlife** walk (p98)
- Feeling the dominating presence of the mighty mountain massifs of the **Matterhorn & Monte Rosa** (p106)

Signature food: Polenta with Fontina cheese	Celebrated native: Jean-Antoine Carrel (climber)	Famous for... Mont Blanc tunnel

Western Europe's highest peaks rise like stark white sentinels above the semi-autonomous Valle d'Aosta, the smallest and least populous of Italy's regions, which remained a virtual cul de sac until the opening of the Mont Blanc tunnel in 1965. At 4810m, Mont Blanc (Monte Bianco) is the tallest giant, but it is matched for Tolkeinesque beauty by the pyramidal Matterhorn (Monte Cervino), grandiose Monte Rosa and wilderness-flecked Gran Paradiso.

Comprising one large glacial valley running east–west which is bisected by several smaller valleys, the Valle d'Aosta's Western Alps offer some spectacular hiking with access to numerous long-distance walking paths such as the 165km Tour du Mont Blanc and Aosta's two blue riband high-altitude trails, the Alte Vie 1 & 2.

Despite an overabundance of modern and often incongruous ski resorts, Aosta has managed to protect a significant portion of its ancient ecosystem in the Parco Nazionale del Gran Paradiso (PNGP), a 700-sq-km swathe of the Graian Alps that makes up Italy's oldest and most revered national park and provides a grand paradise for walkers.

Bordered by France and Switzerland on two sides, Aosta's cultural nuances are Valdostan – a historical mix of French-Provençal and northern Italian – and over 50% of the local population still speak an esoteric local language known as Valdôtain. Even more curious is the Swiss-influenced Walser heritage prevalent in a trio of the region's northern valleys.

WESTERN ALPS

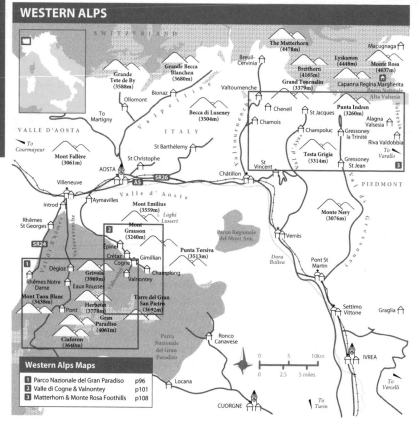

Western Alps Maps

HISTORY

Valle d'Aosta's roots are Roman – the eponymous regional capital boasts significant ruins – while annexation by the House of Savoy in the 11th century led to the building of numerous medieval castles. In the 12th- and 13th-centuries German-speaking Walsers from Switzerland migrated into the Val de Gressoney and a few villages still preserve the language and architecture.

With the opening of the Mont Blanc tunnel in 1965, life in the Valle d'Aosta changed exponentially with tourists flocking in to ski the high Alps in the two popular resort towns of Courmayeur and Cervinia. Transformed from rural backwater to 21st-century success story, the Aostan economy now revolves around tourism and high quality cheese and wine production.

ENVIRONMENT

Within the vast chain of the Western Alps, stretching from the far southwest corner of mountainous northern Italy to Lago Maggiore, Valle d'Aosta separates the Graian Alps to the south from the Pennine Alps to the north. The Gran Paradiso massif – the heart of PNGP – is the most significant range in the Graian Alps, with 15 glaciers and 10 major summits, topped by Gran Paradiso (4061m). The park consists essentially of deep lateral valleys and their separating ridges extending south from Valle d'Aosta. These valleys were cut by glaciers pushing north towards Valle d'Aosta where they dumped huge masses of moraine. The Pennine Alps are dominated by the chain of peaks between the Matterhorn (Monte Cervino; 4478m) and Monte

Rosa (4637m). Long, deep, glaciated valleys extend generally southwards from the range to Valle d'Aosta; Valsesia to the east is oriented southeast in its upper reaches. The Dora Baltea, Valle d'Aosta's river, and Fiume Sesia are both tributaries of the Po, Italy's longest river. Granitic gneiss is the most common rock type throughout; there are relatively small outcrops of other rocks, notably the distinctive greenstone, and compass-distorting magnetite near Cogne.

The patterns of trees and flowering plants change with altitude. In the valleys are fields (some still used for crops) and mixed woodlands. The lower reaches of the mountainsides' meadows, rich in wildflowers, may be grazed by cattle and sheep, and are separated by woodlands of oak and chestnut. Further up, between 800m and 1000m, woodlands of beech, larch and spruce are widespread. In the subalpine zone – between 1600m and 2000m – spruce, larch, Arolla pine and mountain pine mark the tree line.

Above the tree line, alpenrose, dwarf juniper and bilberry are easiest to identify. In the grasslands up to 2400m you'll find gentians, arnica, primulas, pasque flowers and tormentil. On the cliffs and screes in marginal growing conditions, many of the species are dwarf, cushion-forming perennials. In the high alpine zones, yellow genipi,

VALDOSTANE GASTRONOMY

Valdostane (ie peculiar to the Valle d'Aosta) wine, spirits, cheese, game, fruit and honey are excellent reasons for an extended visit to Valle d'Aosta; these delights are best appreciated – or justified – after the energy-burning walks in the Parco Nazionale del Gran Paradiso (PNGP) and its surrounds.

Valdostane wines enjoy Italy's first *denominazione di origine controllata* authentication system; labels bear the letters DOC, which can be used for at least 20 wines produced in the region. Most of the vineyards are in the main valley; the principal varieties of white grapes are Chardonnay and Müller-Thurgau and the reds include Pinot noir, Torrette, Chambave Muscat and Pinot gris. Enfer d'Arvier is a particularly fine wine, which should appeal to anyone keen on robust, full-flavoured Australian reds. A very drinkable bottle costs up to €5 and you can pay up to €30 for a well-aged wine.

Genepy (or *genepi*) is a Valdostane speciality and once tasted, becomes an indispensable conclusion (with a good espresso) to a day in the mountains. This herb-rich nectar is an infusion of an alpine plant *Artemesia glacialis* which grows on moraine edges. For around €3 you can savour a generous nip in the bar; a bottle of the delectable Herbetet brand costs around €18.

Fontina cheese is also protected against imitations by the *denominazione* system, using the distinctive motif of the silhouette of the Matterhorn and the words *Consorzioni Produttori Fontina*. It's made by traditional methods, with unpasteurised milk and no colouring agents. After a long maturation process, this full-fat cheese has a unique flavour, which must owe a lot to the diet of the local cows that graze the flower-rich meadows where artificial fertilisers seem to be unknown. *Fontina* pops up all over the place on restaurant menus. It's basic to *zuppa Valdostane* (slices of dark bread soaked in stock and thick *Fontina* sauce) and *polenta Valdostane*.

Two common items on restaurant menus are *camoscio* (chamois) and *cervo* (venison).

Apples and pears are grown locally; look out for bottles of *Puro succo di mele Renetta e Golden*, a delicious fruit juice. Each 1L bottle is made from 2kg of apples and is additive-free.

Local honey is derived from various flowers, including rhododendron (recommended), clover, acacia, thyme, eucalyptus and mixtures of whatever the bees found, called *millefiori*, *bosco* and *montagna*.

Caffe alla Valdostane is a trap for the unwary. It's a heady concoction of strong, sweet black coffee, orange curacao and local grappa, which can give you a flying start after lunch or put all thought of further activity beyond comprehension.

For further gastronomic exploration look for a copy of *Valle d'Aosta Gastronomica*, by Bovo, Sanguinetti and Vola. It is an excellent guide (in Italian) to the history and traditions of local wines and other delights, with about 100 recipes.

saxifrages and moss campion survive; algae and mosses occur on the snow line.

Its fauna population is what makes PNGP special among Italy's national parks. There are about 3700 ibex and 8400 chamois, greater numbers of marmots, and small populations of ermine, weasels, badgers, voles and white hares. However, in the valleys of the Pennine Alps it's unusual to see anything more than marmots. Among the 100 species of nesting birds recorded, you're most likely to see royal eagles, ptarmigan, alpine choughs and alpine accentors.

CLIMATE

Conditions in the valleys to the north and south of Valle d'Aosta and in upper Valsesia are markedly cooler than at lower altitudes, though in summer, temperatures well into the 20s°C are common. Even so, the mean annual temperature at Aosta is just 10°C. Overnight frost is likely above 1800m at any time. Rainfall is concentrated in the summer; May and September are usually comparatively dry. Each valley experiences its own daytime pattern of prevailing winds, and the Gran Paradiso and Monte Rosa massifs create their own climates. Snow can fall at any time of the year, although it is uncommon during July and August.

PLANNING
When to Walk

Conditions vary widely from year to year, but walks reaching 2500m should be accessible, without the use of ice axe or crampons, from late May to late September. Snow usually lies above 2500m until mid-June, or even later. From about mid-July until late August the area is very busy and accommodation is at a premium. Public transport services are more frequent during summer; camping areas are generally open from late May to mid-September. A few *rifugi* are open in April; most are open during May (at least at weekends), and all should be open from early June until mid-September.

Maps

For access to and within the area, the Touring Club Italiano's 1:200,000 map *Piemonte e Valle d'Aosta* is very good. Studio FMB's 1:100,000 map *Valle d'Aosta* in its Eurocart series is also adequate. Both are available at newsagents and bookshops. See the Planning sections of individual walks for specific map requirements.

PLACE NAMES

French and Italian versions of place names are used throughout the area, with a tendency for French to be favoured the further west you travel, eg Colle della Finestra and Col Fenêtre between Val di Rhêmes and Valgrisenche are one and the same place.

Books

Cicerone publish the English language *Gran Paradiso: Alta Via 2 Trek and Day Walks* (2008) by Gillian Price focusing on 28 walks along the south side of the Valle d'Aosta.

Numerous Italian-language guides to walks and climbs throughout the area are available. *A Piedi in Valle d'Aosta* by Stefano Ardito comes in two volumes, each describing more than 90 walks.

Information Sources

Information on the PNGP can be found on the generic Italian parks website (www .parks.it/parco.nazionale.gran.paradiso) or on its own independent website (www .pngp.it). There are numerous visitor centres. The newest and the easiest to reach if you are doing the Gran Paradiso walks is the interactive **Tutel-Attiva Laboratorio Parco** (☎ 0165 74 92 64; Villaggio Minatori; 2-6pm, closed Wed) in Cogne, which opened in 2007.

Emergency

In Valle d'Aosta, call **mountain rescue** (☎ 0165 23 02 53). For medical assistance call the **national emergency** number (☎ 118).

GETTING THERE & AROUND

The Valle d'Aosta – home of all of this chapter's walks – is easily accessed by trains and buses from the major northern Italian cities of Milan and Turin. From France you can cut through the famous Mont Blanc tunnel. All of the Valle d'Aosta's main tributary valleys are served by frequent local buses. The train line runs the course of the valley from Pont-St-Martin on the border with Piedmont to Prè-St-Didier a few kilometres southwest of Courmayeur.

GATEWAY

The busy, sprawling town of Aosta (p114) is the capital of the autonomous region of Valle d'Aosta. It's the hub of the excellent bus services and the train terminus, and it has all the facilities you're likely to need.

PARCO NAZIONALE DEL GRAN PARADISO

Italy's oldest national park is also one its most diverse – and aptly named. Gran Paradiso, formed in 1922 after Vittorio Emanuele II gave his hunting reserve to the state (ostensibly to protect the endangered ibex), is a veritable 'grand paradise'. What makes it special is a tangible wilderness feel (rare in Italy). The park's early establishment preceded the rise of the modern ski resort and, as a result,

the area has, so far, resisted the lucrative lure of the tourist trade with all its chairlifts, dodgy architecture and *après* ski shenanigans.

Gran Paradiso incorporates the valleys around the eponymous 4061m peak (Italy's 7th highest), three of which are in the Valle d'Aosta: the Valsavarenche, Val di Rhêmes and the beautiful Valle di Cogne. On the Piedmont side of the mountain, the park includes the valleys of Soana and Orco.

This section describes two flexible, linked two- to three-day walks within the park, and three day walks from Cogne (on the edge of the park) and the nearby village of Valnontey. The Vallone di Grauson walk is just outside the park but is no less scenic and offers superb views of the central Gran Paradiso massif.

PLANNING

Maps

Kompass' 1:50,000 map No 86 *Gran Paradiso, Valle d'Aosta* is useful for general

---

ITALY'S FIRST NATIONAL PARK

The ibex, Europe's largest alpine wild animal, is at the heart of the history of PNGP. Desire for its preservation motivated the park's creation and it has been the focus of a long-term conservation project there.

Climate change and hunting drove ibex into the mountainous areas in prehistoric times. The first attempt to protect it was a hunting ban in the early 19th century but the ruling House of Savoy was exempt. King Vittorio Emanuele II of Piedmont (Piemonte) – later the first king of Italy – regularly visited the Gran Paradiso area. A royal hunting reserve of 22 sq km was created in 1856 for his exclusive use. Some say his motive was to protect the ibex, others that it was pure selfishness. However, local people benefited. To create the reserve, locals had forfeited their hunting rights to the king, and in return could join special new corps of wardens whose job it was to curtail poaching, or become porters or gamekeepers who were paid to get rid of the lynx and bearded vulture, regarded as predators.

Mulattiere (or paths) were built to hunting lodges and across mountain passes. Of the former hunting lodges, Lauson is now Rifugio Sella (above Valnontey) and Nivolet is Rifugio Savoia (near Col del Nivolet, above Valsavarenche).

In 1919, faced with rising maintenance costs, the revival of poaching during WWI and the consequent decline of the ibex population, King Vittorio Emanuele III surrendered his hunting rights and gave the property to the state so that a national park could be established. This eventually happened on 3 December 1922. The park's purpose was to preserve flora, fauna and natural beauty.

The PNGP's area is around 700 sq km, of which about 90% belongs to small landowners and *comunes* (town councils). The park's administrative council must approve all building work and land-use changes within the park, so new developments generally harmonise with traditional architectural styles. Park staff aim to instil an understanding of how people, wildlife and the landscape are interrelated, through guided walks within the park.

In 1972, PNGP was twinned with neighbouring Parc Nationale de la Vanoise in France, making a truly European park of 1230 sq km. As far as possible, the two parks are managed as one – as *uno parco senza frontiere* (one park without borders).

orientation, but the depiction of paths is not always accurate; the accompanying booklet (in Italian and German) is very informative.

IGC's 1:50,000 map No 3 *Il Parco Nazionale del Gran Paradiso* is easy to read and reliable enough. It has a companion two-volume guide with the same title.

Guided Walks

There are some good options for guided walks in PNGP including trips to the summit of Gran Paradiso – a long day trip if tackled via the classic route. Società **Guide Alpine di Cogne** (☎ 0165 7 48 35; www .guidealpinecogne.it; Via Bourgeois 33, Cogne) offer this and other treks. Check their website for prices. Gentler guided nature walks in the park from July to September are organised by the **Associazione Guide della Nature** (☎ 0165 7 42 82; Piazza Chanoux 36, Cogne; 9am-noon Mon, Wed & Sat).

The **Società delle Guide Alpine di Courmayeur** (☎ 0165 84 20 64; www.guide courmayeur.com; Strada del Villair), founded in 1859, is Italy's oldest guiding association and offers trips in and around Mont Blanc for all abilities, including children.

ACCESS TOWN

Far from the madding crowd, dreamy Cogne (p115) is the best access point for the Gran Paradiso national park. There are regular and relatively quick bus links with the town of Aosta and the main valley.

VALNONTEY TO RHÊMES NOTRE DAME

Duration 2 days
Distance 30.5km
Difficulty moderate–demanding
Start Valnontey
Finish Rhêmes Notre Dame
Nearest Town Cogne (p115)
Transport bus

Summary The two most dramatic and spectacular days of the Alta Via 2, over the highest and most challenging pass, with scores of ibex, chamois and marmots for company, in the heart of the national park.

This is an outstandingly varied and challenging walk, with 3030m of ascent. From Valnontey, the route crosses Col Lauson (3296m) on the Grivola–Gran Paradiso Range, the highest pass accessible to walkers in the park, then descends into more isolated Valsavarenche at Eaux Rousses. From there it's over the easier – or less demanding – Col di Entrelor and down into Val di Rhêmes and the tiny village of Rhêmes Notre Dame-Bruil. Each of the two days can be self-contained; with public transport available.

The route is described from east to west, because it's potentially less unnerving to climb to Col Lauson from the east than to descend that way.

When the seasonal bus service from Cogne to Valnontey isn't operating, it is possible to start the walk in Cogne (see the Day 1 Alternative Start, p97).

KINGS OF THE WILD FRONTIER

Most sane people complete the famous 173km hiking circuit of Mont Blanc in seven to 10 days; but for a few resolute 'loonies' – around 2000 of them annually to be more precise – mere walking is not enough. Since 2003 a significant contingent of willowy-framed ultra-runners has been competing in an event known as the Ultra Trail Tour du Mont Blanc, or UTMB. Considered one of the most arduous single stage foot races in the world, this masochistic mountain romp starts in Chamonix, France and follows the traditional Tour de Mont Blanc hiking route in an anti-clockwise circuit through Italy and Switzerland. Aside from the crippling distance, runners must also cross approximately 15 alpine passes and log a total elevation gain of nearly 9000m (that's nine vertical kilometres!). The top competitors usually complete the course in a mind-boggling 21 hours, though times of 30 to 45 hours are more normal. The nexus for the race in Italy is the Valle d'Aosta town of Courmayeur.

If none of the above fazes you, check out the official race website at www.ultratrailmb.com. But beware, race qualification rules are stringent.

The walk follows part of the Alta Via 2 (AV2, see p41) and there's a good case for claiming they are the best two days for scenery, wildlife and ease of access. Much of it follows paths built in the 1860s to make ibex hunting easier for royal parties (see p93). Waymarking and signposting of the paths is generally reliable. Ibex are now back in force and you can expect to see them in many places, together with chamois and marmots.

It's possible to vary the route of this walk, and spread the long ascent to Col di Entrelor over a couple of days; see the Day 2 Alternative Route, Pont to Laghi Djouan (p97).

PLANNING
Maps
The IGC 1:25,000 maps Nos 101 *Gran Paradiso, La Grivola, Cogne* and 102 *Valsavarenche, Val di Rhêmes, Valgrisenche* are at the ideal scale though path information is not universally accurate.

GETTING TO/FROM THE WALK
Valnontey (start)
A frequent bus service travels between Via Bourgeois in Cogne (p115) and Valnontey (€1.10, 10 minutes) daily from late June to mid-September. A timetable is available from the AIAT office in Cogne. When the bus service isn't operating it is possible to walk the 3km from Cogne. The road to Valnontey branches from Via Bourgeois in the centre of Cogne.

Rhêmes Notre Dame (finish)
A bus service is operated by **SAVDA** (☎ 0165 26 20 27; www.savda.it) between Aosta and Rhêmes Notre Dame-Bruil (€2.50, one hour, 7.50am, 1.35pm, 5.45pm; from Sep-Jun the 7.50am bus runs Sat & Sun only and the 5.45pm bus runs Mon-Fri).

By road from Valle d'Aosta, turn off S26 to Villeneuve, 11km southwest of Aosta and follow SR23 west then south through Introd; a couple of kilometres further on, turn off along SR24 to Rhêmes Notre Dame-Bruil (19km from Villeneuve).

THE WALK
Day 1: Valnontey to Eaux Rousses
7½–8 hours, 17km, 1630m ascent
From the far side of the bridge over Torrente Valnontey in Valnontey village, follow the broad path waymarked 2 for the

AV2. The path winds up through forests and its comfortably graded zigzags take you deeper into Vallone del Lauson and past numerous waterfalls on Torrente Lauson. It gradually leaves the trees behind and leads into open ground, bare but for innumerable wildflowers. When **Alpe Gran Lauson**, across the *torrente*, is occupied and the cows are busily grazing, it's possible to buy milk, cream, butter and cheese there. The ascent to **Rifugio Sella** (☎ 0165 743 10; www.rifugiosella.com; half-board €35; early Apr-late Sep, takes two to 2½ hours); drinks and snacks are served either in the smallest building or the main one. The *rifugio* is an extremely popular day's outing from Valnontey. Snacks and drinks are available all day and a substantial lunch is served. To spend a night in this magnificent location it's essential to book well ahead. The website has an online booking service.

From the signposted path junction close to the PNGP's **Casotto del Lauson**, continue in the direction of Col Lauson and shortly bear right with a 2 waymarker, which may seem like the wrong direction, but the old path soon swings round to make a fine traverse of the mountainside above the *rifugio*. The path then leads into an impressively huge amphitheatre walled with rugged colourful peaks and glaciers to the south. Next you cross a classic hidden valley, gaining height comfortably towards the seemingly impregnable cliffs. A bridge crosses the *torrente;* the path then bears leftish (west), up and across the steep slope. Continue past the turnoff to the right for Route No 26b (to Col de la Rousse and Col de la Noire) and into a silent world of scree, rock and sparse vegetation. The route leads on through a long, narrow valley then zigzags up the ever-steepening boulder-scree slope at the valley head.

Having exhausted the scope for zigzags, the path narrows and rises steeply to a false col, and the exciting part of the ascent comes into view. There's a series of built-up lengths of path, between small bluffs, around which the exceedingly narrow path creeps; then a steep section over fine scree and you can collapse with relief at small **Col Lauson** (3296m; two hours from Rifugio Sella). The magnificent prospect westwards is filled with peaks and glaciers in layers separating the depths of Valsavarenche and Val di Rhêmes. The most striking peak to the southeast is Torre

PARCO NAZIONALE DEL GRAN PARADISO

| 1 Valnontey to Rhêmes Notre Dame | p94 |
| 2 Lakes & Wildlife | p98 |

del Gran San Pietro (3692m), crowning the ridge along Valnontey's eastern side.

The descent starts steeply – follow the yellow (and occasionally red) waymarkers for the safest route, though small landslips can occasionally blur its line. The route heads down towards the towering cliffs of Grivola (3969m), crosses reddish boulders and scree and soon starts a series of zigzags. Then comes a steep bit and another section through boulders; from the first patch of grass, the old path, with its comfortable gradient, becomes consistently easy to follow. Around here, to the left (south) are good views of Gran Paradiso's glaciers and snowfields and the spiky peaks of Becca di Montandayne (3838m) and Herbetet

(3778m). The path soon starts to work its way towards Torrente Levionaz.

The path winds down in long zigzags across broad spurs, then steepens, winds in and out of a rock-filled gully, and into the main valley, passing the signposted turn-off for a route to Rifugio Chabod on the left. A bit further on, you may find the ground around the path unusually bare of vegetation and the path itself more eroded – this is a favourite grazing area for a herd of ibex. Continue down and cross the bridge over Torrente Levionaz (1¼ to 1½ hours from Col Lauson) and go on down to riverbank level. About 1.5km further on there's a short climb to the PNGP base at **Levionaz** (30 minutes from the bridge). Skirt the buildings and shortly pass a tiny *oratorio* (oratory) on the right.

Then come a few hundred eroded metres of path. Beyond the turnoff for Route No 10 (to the right) the path contours a boulder field then leads into woodland. Further down, the path has been carefully rebuilt where it crosses a very long landslip several times. About an hour from Levionaz you cross a massively gouged-out stream, then

WARNING – COL LAUSON

Check in the information office in Cogne about conditions at Col Lauson. The steep and unstable ascent is sometimes snow-bound early in the season and not passable or safe for inexperienced walkers.

stay in the open for the last 30 minutes of descent, latterly on a walled path between fields to the main road through the valley. The bus stop is 50m to the right, at the junction of the road leading to the hotel at **Eaux Rousses** (p116). There is also accommodation at **Pont** about 5km up the road; at **Bien**, about 1km down the road; and at **Dégioz** (day-gosh) a couple more kilometres down the valley. Details are available from the accommodation list available from the AIAT in Aosta (p114). If you want to abandon the hike here, there's a **SAVDA** (☎ 0165 26 20 27; www.savda.it) bus service between Aosta and Eaux Rousses (€2.80, one hour, three a day mid-Jun–mid-Sep, three a day Mon-Sat at other times).

ALTERNATIVE START: COGNE TO VALNONTEY
40 minutes, 3km, 130m ascent

Walk across Piazza Chanoux (with the AIAT office on your left) in **Cogne** and follow a well-used path across the spacious meadows between the town and Torrente Valnontey to a bridge over the river, and turn left. Follow the wide vehicle track upstream to the bridge over the stream on the western edge of **Valnontey**. The path to Rifugio Sella leads off to the right.

Day 2: Eaux Rousses to Rhêmes Notre Dame
6½–7 hours, 13.5km, 1400m ascent

Follow the AV2 from the L'Hostellerie du Paradis which takes you north across some terraces and into a conifer wood. This part of the Alta Via 2 is also a *sentiero natura* (nature path/walk) running from Eaux Rousses to Champlanaz (above Montagna Djouan) and is characterised by its iron-rich mineral spring, forest trees, glacial features and alpine grazing settlements. A descriptive leaflet is usually available at the PNGP visitor centre at Dégioz.

After joining a path that comes up from the village of Creton, a steep section takes you to PNGP's **Casa Reale at Orveille** (see the boxed text Italy's First National Park, p93), which was a favourite royal hunting lodge in the late 19th century. Skirt this and continue gaining height. The views from here are spectacular in all directions, but particularly of the soaring spires of Grand Nomenon (3488m) and Grivola (3969m), above the opposite side

of Valsavarenche. Continue up to **Montagna Djouan**, occupied in summer.

Go on to a deserted stone building at **Champlanaz** (Alp Tsoplanaz on the 1:25,000 map). The path leads on into the valley with Col di Entrelor at its head. Continue steadily upwards on the narrow path traversing the steep valley side. Almost an hour from Casa Reale you come to a path junction beside the largest of the Laghi Djouan; Route No 9 from Valle delle Meyes comes in on the left. The path leads on up the valley (not up to the stone building as the 1:25,000 and 1:50,000 maps show) to sombre **Lac Noire**. From here it rises in zigzags up a broad spur, overlooked by massive cliffs of Pointe Gollien to the northwest, towards which the path narrows determinedly. It keeps close to the cliffs to the final steep ascent through a boulder field to **Col di Entrelor** (3007m; 1¼ to 1½ hours from Laghi Djouan). The inspiring view includes the great peaks on the opposite side of Val di Rhêmes, topped by Grande Rousse (3607m).

To start the descent, bear right through boulders, carefully following the yellow waymarkers; soon there's a short, slightly exposed bit to negotiate, then it's down again through boulders, towards the cliffs on the northern side of Vallone di Entrelor. A longish stretch down over scree brings you to the start of the clearly defined path. It keeps as close as possible to the cliffs until the valley starts to widen, then heads more towards the middle of the valley. At a path junction by the ruinous **Alpe Plan des Feyes** (Alp Plan de la Feya), bear left with the AV2 and Route No 10 (Route No 7 goes to the right). A little further down, keep to the path on the northeast side of the valley, descending past the neat, extensive fields of **Alpages d'Entrelor** on the left. At the bottom of these fields, where there's a large timber crucifix, the wide path swings to the right (north) to descend through larch woodland. After approximately 1km, bear right along a narrower waymarked path, which continues to lose height steadily. It reaches a vehicle track (not on the 1:25,000 map) – follow this for just 10m then drop down to the right along a path. Cross the bridge almost opposite the end of the path and you've reached **Rhêmes Notre Dame** (2¾ to three hours from Col di Entrelor).

LAKES & WILDLIFE

Duration 2 days
Distance 22km
Difficulty moderate
Start/Finish Pont
Nearest Town Cogne (p115)
Transport bus

Summary Lakes, wildflowers and wildlife are the highlights of this magnificently scenic walk, with the chance to stay at a historic *rifugio* and a choice of routes to minimise the degree of ascent.

There's much more to walking in PNGP than crossing high passes with long ascents and descents. Numerous tarns and high valleys, amazingly rich in wildflowers can be linked by good paths, and the views of the highest peaks are unfailingly spectacular.

This walk starts and finishes in upper Valsavarenche and offers a choice of routes from Pont up to the beautiful alpine meadows of Piano del Nivolet. The main route does involve 1785m of ascent and a fairly high pass – Grand Collet (2832m) – but the amount of ascent is less than the daily stages on the previous walk (p94), and importantly for your knees, involves a great deal less descent. The vistas of the Gran Paradiso Range from this ascent are magnificent.

A side trip covers most of the lakes sitting in a hanging valley above Rifugio Savoia and Laghi del Nivolet. This is just one possible route around this fascinating area, where you can follow paths or find a way across country. The return is via the beautiful Valle delle Meyes where you're almost certain to see herds of ibex and chamois.

If time is short, it's possible to go direct to Rifugio Savoia from Pont, do the side trip and then return to Pont in one day. The walk also offers an alternative approach to Laghi Djouan on the route of the previous walk.

Paths are generally good, apart from the odd rockfall; signposts are extremely minimal, though waymarking is adequate.

PLANNING
What to Bring
You'll need to carry food and drink for both days – there are no settlements between Pont and Rifugio Savoia.

Maps
The IGC 1:25,000 map No 102 *Valsavarenche, Val di Rhêmes, Valgrisenche* is best, though its depiction of paths and other features isn't entirely accurate. For orientation and identification of features outside the scope of the 1:25,000, try the Kompass 1:50,000 map No 86 *Gran Paradiso, Valle d'Aosta*.

GETTING TO/FROM THE WALK
A bus service operated by **SAVDA** (☎ 0165 26 20 27; www.savda.it) runs between Aosta and Pont (€2.70, 1¼ hours, 7.15am, 12.30pm, 4.50pm mid-Jun–mid-Sep). From late September to early June, the bus terminates at Eaux Rousses, 5km down the road.

By road from Valle d'Aosta, turn off S26 to Villeneuve, 11km southwest of Aosta and follow SR23 west then south through Introd. A couple of kilometres further on at a junction, continue along SR23 to Pont, 25km from Villeneuve.

THE WALK
Day 1: Pont to Rifugio Savoia via Grand Collet
3½–3¾ hours, 9km, 1015m ascent
From the large car park at **Pont**, skirt the camping ground and follow the riverbank path upstream for about 15 minutes to a signpost pointing to Grand Collet along Route No 2a. The narrow, rocky path rises steeply and directly for a few hundred metres then starts to traverse the precipitous slope through scattered boulders, thickets of alpenrose and across grass. At length, an easy stretch along a grassed slope brings you to the deserted **Alpe de Seyvaz** (an hour from the riverbank path). This spectacular viewpoint affords perhaps the most impressive views of all of the Gran Paradiso Range, seemingly at arm's length across the valley.

From the wooden crucifix just north of the Alp, bear slightly right along a faintish path which soon becomes clearer and ascends straight up the steep mountainside, through a few shallow valleys; waymarkers are sparse so follow cairns, more or less in line of sight, for the best way up. If in doubt, remember that the route tends to the right (north). Cross a shallow valley with a large scree slope sprawled across its northern side; bear up to the right to another partly grassed area and then edge right across it.

From here, either continue up a grassy ramp and bend to the right at the top of the crag to rejoin the cairns, or climb through a small cliff to a bare, flat area at the foot of the final ascent. This is a zigzag path up the steep, gravel slope to the relatively wide **Grand Collet** (an hour from Alpe de Seyvaz).

From the northern end of the col descend along the edge of a gravel slope then follow a clear, cairned path through scree and boulders down to the valley floor. Keep to its right (northern) side for about 200m then bear left, following cairns. The views of the massive peaks, along the Italian-French border west of Col del Nivolet, are superb. The main part of the descent then falls into two sections: initially across grassy slopes, then much more steeply via a rocky path down to **Alpe du Grand Collet** (45 minutes from the col).

Follow the well-used path leading southwest across Piano del Nivolet, where most of the stream crossings are bridged. The path draws you towards the road on the right, passing beneath power lines and along the shore of the larger of the **Laghi del Nivolet**, to reach the road close to the *rifugio* (about an hour from Alpe du Grand Collet).

The main building of **Rifugio Savoia** (☎ 0165 9 41 41; half-board €36; mid-Jun–late Sep) is an original 19th-century hunting lodge. More luxurious accommodation in a modern annexe is available in midsummer only. Be prepared for enormous servings at the three-course evening meal.

Rifugio Città di Chivasso (☎ 0124 95 31 50; dm €20; Apr-May & Jun-Sep), a CAI establishment near Rifugio Savoia, is an alternative.

ALTERNATIVE ROUTE: VIA LA CROIX D'AROLLEY
2¾–3 hours, 8km, 580m ascent
Follow the signposted path starting behind Hotel Gran Paradiso at **Pont**, up to **La Croix d'Arolley** (Cross of Arolley; 55 minutes). Continue along the well-used path into a broad valley, across a sheltered basin then up through a series of rock slabs and meadows, and eventually into the broad expanses of Piano del Nivolet. The path can be boggy in places until you reach ruinous **Alpe du Grand Collet** (45 minutes from the cross). From here follow the main route to **Rifugio Savoia**.

SIDE TRIP: LAGHI ROSSET, CHANAVEY & TRE BECCHI
3–3½ hours, 8km, 470m ascent
The dissected plateau sitting high above Rifugio Savoia and the Laghi Nivolet cradles several lakes, ranging from the relatively large Lago Rosset to Lacs Chanavey, a chain of ponds overlooked by a rugged array of peaks and a glacier or two. Several paths crossing the plateau en route to two difficult cols (Rosset & Leynir) can be linked by lesser paths and some cross-country walking to make a scenic tour. The IGC 1:25,000 map isn't much help with the location of the paths.

On the northern side of **Rifugio Savoia** head along a well-used path which angles generally north up the slope above the *rifugio*. Then follow a path up to **Alpe Riva**. Bear left, contour the slope on the right and cross a stream (with difficulty after heavy rain) and gain some height. The path then bends to the right and crosses a stream. Follow the path marked with yellow arrows, recross the stream and ascend to the shore of **Lago Rosset**. Continue along the shore but bear left shortly to pass above **Lago Leità** (an hour from the *rifugio*). Cross the slope above its feeder stream, ascend for a few minutes then turn sharp right across the slope. The path zigzags up, with a small lake below on the left, then crosses a flat, broad spur to the foot of the final steep climb to **Col Rosset** – a strange, barren and quiet place (45 minutes from Lago Leità).

Then head eastwards cross-country, above Lacs Chanavey in a deep basin on the right, and along the crest above its eastern side. Descend this spur, and rejoin the path followed earler. On the next steep descent you can see a narrow path leading east; follow it until it fades, then descend and cross a shallow valley. Continue along the base of the slope on the right and the path reappears on the left; follow it up to a shallow gap. Cross the gap and follow the path, now above Lago Rosset, to meet a well-defined path. For a good view of Laghi Tre Becchi, just continue east for about 100m. Return to the clear path and follow it above Lago Rosset. After a while it bends to the right; a path joins it from the left, then almost immediately, a lesser path diverges to the right; ignore it and follow the main path to Alpe Riva and on down to Rifugio Savoia (about 30 minutes from the point above Laghi Tre Becchi).

Day 2: Rifugio Savoia to Pont

4¾–5 hours, 13km, 100m ascent, 670m descent

Walk northeast from the *rifugio* along the scenic, almost-level road to a signpost on the right with faint lettering 'Pont'. Turn left here following a 3a waymarker and yellow arrows (an hour from the *rifugio*). Ascend to a junction marked by large cairns and bear right (another 20 minutes). Fairly soon the path forks; normally you'd go right to cross a nearby stream; if the water is high, bear left for an easier crossing. Then comes a vague stretch across a potentially boggy area, beyond which the path is clear. After about 30 minutes, Valle delle Meyes comes into view. Descend to a path junction beside a huge boulder encrusted with red-orange lichen.

Bear right here (Path No 9a), soon passing beside a tarn. As the path starts to drop sharply watch for a waymarked path on the right and follow it; about 10 minutes further, on a bend, follow a path to the left to reach the stone buildings of **Meyes d'en Haut**, a favourite ibex haunt. The path then drops steeply past a lone stone building to another cluster of stone buildings, **Meyes d'en Bas**, complete with a tiny chapel. Follow triangular waymarkers for Route No 4 down to the end of a gravel road, which makes easy walking, through a 400m long-tunnel (you can see each end in the middle) and down to the main road beside Hotel Genzianella (2½ hours from Valle delle Meyes).

ALPE MONEY

Duration 5¾–6¼ hours
Distance 15km
Difficulty moderate–demanding
Start/Finish Valnontey
Nearest Town Cogne (p115)
Transport bus

Summary An outstandingly scenic walk to traditional alpine grazing huts below the edge of a glacier, and around the glacier-ringed head of Valnontey; ibex encounters almost guaranteed.

On good paths almost all the way, this walk is a dramatic introduction to Valnontey and the magnificent Gran Paradiso Range. It is best walked in the direction described so that you're heading towards the best views. The ascent from Valnontey is steep (750m for the day) but the path, narrow in places, is well graded, adequately signposted and waymarked.

It is quite common for places to be named 'Money' around Valle d'Aosta; this is of ancient origin and believed to mean shared, or perhaps common, pasture.

PLANNING
When to Walk

Several stream crossings could make the walk extremely hazardous, if not impossible, during the spring thaw and after heavy rain. The simple bridge over the youthful Torrente Valnontey regularly falls victim to its turbulent waters – check locally that it exists before setting out. If there's any doubt, the walk to the village of Alpe Money and back is well worthwhile; allow about five hours. Until about late June, snow drifts may linger on the route from Alpe Money to the head of the valley.

GETTING TO/FROM THE WALK

See Valnontey to Rhêmes Notre Dame walk (p94).

THE WALK

From the cluster of signposts by the Valnontey village bridge, set out along the broad vehicle track (following Route No 23). On the eastern side of the river pass Camping Gran Paradiso, then head through conifer woodland. Soon you pass the miniscule settlement of Valmianaz where a restored house on the right displays some fine timberwork. About 45 minutes from Valnontey the track narrows to path width, and 10 minutes further on you reach a junction. Turn left up the path marked 20. It rises steeply to a line of cliffs, with magnificent views of the valley and enclosing peaks, then finds an ingenious route up through the cliffs, across open ground, above another cliff line and into a wide valley with the leading edge of Ghiacciaio di Patri looming almost overhead. On a broad platform breaking the steepness of the mountainside, the path then crosses huge rock slabs to **Alpe Money** (one hour from the path

VALLE DI COGNE & VALNONTEY

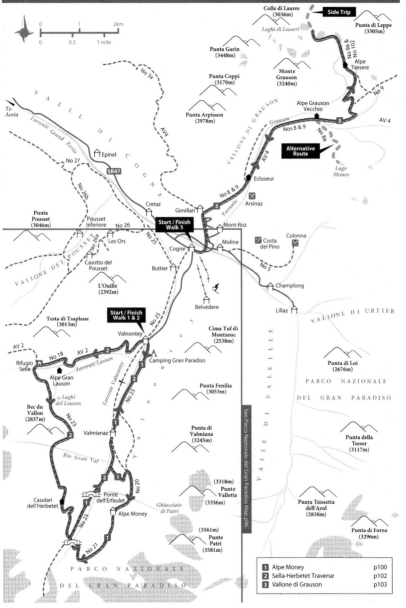

1	Alpe Money	p100
2	Sella–Herbetet Traverse	p102
3	Vallone di Grauson	p103

junction). At an altitude of 2325m, there are at least five recognisable structures, one

roofed and seemingly liveable. The view across the valley to Gran Paradiso and its spectacular satellites and glaciers dictates a lunch stop here.

The path onwards (Route No 21) is easy to follow, with cairns and yellow waymarkers, southwards over narrow spurs and across the intervening streams (with the bridges, hopefully, intact). Patches of dwarf willow and crimson-flowering alpenrose bring colour to a landscape of greys and whites. About an hour from Alpe Money, descend the narrow crest of a long spur northwestwards, cross two streams and more moraine to the **bridge** over Torrente Valnontey (two hours from Alpe Money).

Head downstream close to the river for about 50m then go through a patch of larches and continue boulder-hopping downstream for about 100m. The route then gradually swings away from the river; about 25 minutes from the bridge, at a prominent path junction, keep to the right along Path No 23. It makes for relatively easy walking down the valley, with mighty cliffs soaring above. About 30 minutes |from the path junction, cross substantial **Ponte dell'Erfaulet** over Torrente Valnontey; it's then just on an hour to Valnontey village.

SELLA-HERBETET TRAVERSE

Duration 6¾–7¼ hours
Distance 15km
Difficulty demanding
Start/Finish Valnontey
Nearest Town Cogne (p115)
Transport bus

Summary An incredibly exhilarating and scenic traverse high on the precipitous western side of Valnontey, along a narrow path, exposed in places, with plenty of wildlife for company.

This is one of the classic walks in PNGP, and all Valle d'Aosta for that matter. It starts with an ascent to popular Rifugio Sella (see p95); between there and Casolari dell'Herbetet (a park rangers base to the south) there's a short, airy traverse with a length of chain for protection, where you need a good head for heights. The day's ascent is 1180m. From the *casolari*, it's downhill virtually all the way back to Valnontey village.

The views across the valley to the spiky peaks and small glaciers lining the eastern skyline and around to the mighty Ghiacciaio Tribolazione below Gran Paradiso itself, are awesome indeed. Herds of ibex and chamois graze peacefully on steep patches of grass and you should also hear and see marmots.

PLANNING
Maps

The IGC 1:25,000 map No 101 *Gran Paradiso, La Grivola, Cogne* has a somewhat fanciful depiction of Route No 23 (Rifugio Sella to Casolari dell'Herbetet) but is useful for identification of features. The FMB 1:50,000 map *Gran Paradiso* is satisfactory.

GETTING TO/FROM THE WALK

See Valnontey to Rhêmes Notre Dame walk (p94).

THE WALK

The first stage of the walk up to **Rifugio Sella** is straightforward and is described in Day 1 of the Valnontey to Rhêmes Notre Dame walk (p94), where full details of the *rifugio* are also given.

To continue from Rifugio Sella, go to the left (south) of the main building, cross a bridge over Torrente Lauson and follow the wide path (waymarked 23). The rather broken-up path goes directly up and across the slope, over the crest of a spur and down a bit as Valnontey opens up ahead. Then it's up steadily, through massive rock outcrops and on into a wide valley, passing a small pond on the left – the main **Lago del Lauson**. The path then skirts a small valley and rises to a large cairn where it ends on the crest of a spur of **Bec du Vallon** (2837m), 35 to 40 minutes from the *rifugio*. It's worth pausing here, before tackling the serious stuff ahead, to absorb the magnificence of the view: the peaks lining the eastern side of Valnontey and the depths of Vallone di Grauson beyond Cogne.

The traverse starts with several metres across awkwardly angled rock, then you can cling to a firmly anchored, head-height chain, where handholds are scarce and footholds only a little more plentiful, until you reach a wooden ramp. Then the narrow and much less exposed path zigzags across the folds of Bec du Vallon's southern slopes. The path contours easily across steep grassed slopes and crosses two streams (the second of which could present a slight problem after heavy rain). Then it's across a boulder field to the welcome flatness of **Pian di Ressello** (about two hours from the *rifugio*). This is an extraordinary balcony with cliffs above, precipitous slopes below and truly awesome views to the head of Valnontey.

Follow the path southwest and down from the edge of Pian di Ressello. Beyond a small stream, the path narrows and the nothingness to the left is momentarily apparent. Soon enough you reach **Casolari dell'Herbetet**, another magnificent lookout (30 minutes from Pian di Ressello). Then the path twists and turns down to a junction – bear left; it eventually reaches **Ponte dell'Erfaulet** (locally known as Ponte Erfollet) over Torrente Valnontey. From here it's easy going back to the village of Valnontey (2¼ hours from Casolari dell'Herbetet).

VALLONE DI GRAUSON

Duration 7¾–8¼ hours
Distance 20km
Difficulty demanding
Start/Finish Cogne (p115)
Transport bus
Summary A choice of beautiful alpine lakes, high above meadows carpeted with wildflowers, and with awesome views of peaks above Valnontey and Valle di Cogne.

Vallone di Grauson reaches deep into the range of peaks northeast of Cogne and is just outside PNGP. Its lower reaches are rugged and precipitous, with small meadows and patches of larch woodland between the cliffs; Torrente Grauson thunders down in waterfalls and cascades. Higher up, the valley widens and looks relatively benign with its grassy expanses divided by low moraine ridges and streams, and dotted with stone huts, some still used by herdsmen during midsummer cattle grazing.

Laghi di Lussert, a chain of three tarns, the highest at 2907m, lies below the colourful cliffs of Punta di Laures (3367m) and Punta di Leppe (3305m) and is the objective for this longish, exceptionally scenic day. The daunting amount of ascent (1400m)

comes in stages and is generally on good paths. The route is waymarked and signposted, though you need to be aware of the local geography to interpret some of the signs. Route No 4 (in a triangle) is the long distance Route AV4.

The walk can start in either Cogne or the village of Gimillan, about 2km to the north.

PLANNING
What to Bring
Carry some water; there's a *sorgente* (spring) at Alpe Grauson Vecchio (1¼ hours from Cogne), which produces delicious water almost too cold to drink.

Maps
There's no 1:25,000 coverage of this walk; use the Kompass 1:50,000 map *Il Parco Nazionale del Gran Paradiso* instead (see Maps, p317). You may be able to procure extra information from the AIAT at Cogne (p115) on this walk.

GETTING TO/FROM THE WALK
See Getting There & Away (p116) under Cogne. You can save at least 45 minutes and 250m of ascent by catching the bus to Gimillan (€0.90, 12 minutes, frequent daily service late Jun–mid-Sep, once a day Tue & Fri mornings at other times). By car, the Gimillan road winds up from a crossroads immediately over the bridge at the eastern end of Cogne. There is a large car park on the left of the road at the edge of the village, about 2.5km from Cogne.

THE WALK
To reach Gimillan on foot, head east along the road through Cogne and follow it across the bridge over Torrente Grand Eyvia. Cross the main Cogne–Lillaz road to the corner of the Gimillan road and walk up a path signposted to Gimillan. Turn left at a road by an old hospital and follow it for about 250m to a path on the left waymarked 8. Go up beside some conifers on the right and on to the road. Turn left for about 20m, cross the road and ascend a path with a field on the left, to the road again. Then it's left for just 20m; cross and continue up a path ahead to the road; cross it once more and go straight up to meet the road close to a large car park on the left at the edge of **Gimillan**.

Walk past the car park and bus stop and on up the road to a clutch of footpath signs on the right. Bear right between houses, pass a small car park, cross the road and follow the signposted path (Routes No 8 and 9) up through fields. At a T-junction, it's right, the path quickly taking you into the embrace of Vallone di Grauson. Keep right at a fork then descend to a bridge over Torrente Grauson (1¼ hours from Cogne).

Cross the bridge and turn left along a path, bypassing the old buildings of **Ecloseur**, up the valley. A line of cliffs ahead across the valley is easily surmounted. Then you cross a small meadow, skirt the southeast end of low cliffs, traverse another meadow and continue along the steep mountainside. Just over an hour from the Torrente Grauson bridge, you reach a large crucifix and then a path junction. This is the parting of the ways if you're heading for Lago Money (see the Alternative Route, right).

For Laghi di Lussert, head down into the spacious valley towards the neat group of stone buildings that is **Alpe Grauson Vecchio**. Shortly before a bridge, a small sign points to the *sorgente* on the right. Head upstream beside Torrente Grauson (on your left) to another bridge; cross it to a sheltered meadow then ascend beside a stream to a signposted path junction. Following Path Nos 9 and 9a go up (generally north), over flowery meadows. Where the path divides, go left, soon passing a lone stone building, and up to another junction on the edge of a basin. Here, bear left towards Colle di Laures along the route numbered both Path Nos 9 and 102. The path takes you up to the row of well-maintained stone buildings that is **Alpe Tsesere** (an hour from Alpe Grauson Vecchio).

Continue on Path No 9a/102; having crossed two small streams, go right at a path junction with a 9a waymarker. This takes you up into a spacious valley; cross its wide expanses, passing the rather amorphous lowermost **Lago di Lussert**. The middle lake is about 300m further west; go up the left hand (southern) slope, then head northwest to reach the upper lake (an hour from Alpe Tsesere), from where Colle di Laures is easy to pick on the skyline to the northeast (see the Side Trip, next column).

Retracing your steps to return; it takes about 3½ hours to reach Cogne. Views of the Gran Paradiso Range spread across the skyline constantly seize your attention.

ALTERNATIVE ROUTE: LAGO MONEY
5½–6 hours, 16km, 1000m ascent

On the southern side of Vallone di Grauson, Lago Money, cradled below an arc of peaks (topped by Penne Blanche, 3254m), is a less taxing objective than Laghi di Lussert. Follow the main route to the path junction near the crucifix above **Alpe Grauson Vecchio**, then take Path No 8a, gaining height quickly to a wide valley. Just around a bend leave the wide path and go right, up a spur, and follow yellow arrows along a narrower path. This leads up to a split level basin, divided by a massive moraine bank. Continue across the basin, and go up the bank to the shore of the tarn, **Lago Money**. Retrace your steps back to Gimillan and Cogne.

SIDE TRIP: COLLE DI LAURES
1 hour, 2km, 130m ascent

In midsummer, very fit walkers should be able to climb from the topmost lake of Laghi di Lussert, over snow-free but rather steep and rocky ground to Colle di Laures (3036m), for great views into Valle d'Aosta.

VALLE D'AOSTA TO VALSESIA

This section takes in four valleys – Valtournenche, Val d'Ayas, Valle di Gressoney – on the northern side of Valle d'Aosta, and upper Valsesia in Piedmont, all reaching down from the long mountainous chain forming the border with Switzerland and dominated by the Matterhorn and Monte Rosa. This area is not in a national park – as is obvious from the multifarious and incongruous developments for skiing, epitomised in the artificial town of Breuil-Cervinia at the head of Valtournenche. Yet the scenery is truly magnificent in scale, diversity and extent: *pics*, *puntas* and *testas* (mountain peaks of subtly differing shapes), dominated by the Matterhorn and Monte Rosa. Wildlife is scarce, apart from ubiquitous marmots, but the countless meadows are exceptionally rich in wildflowers.

In three of the four valleys – Ayas, Gressoney and Sesia – the history and traditions

THE CURSE OF THE MATTERHORN

Placed like an upturned arrowhead above the border of Switzerland and Italy, the Matterhorn is the world's sixth-deadliest mountain (one place ahead of Everest) and has claimed the lives of over 500 alpinists since it was first conquered in 1865.

Casting a powerful spell on wide-eyed mountaineers during the Golden Age of Alpinism, Europe's 'noble rock', as Byron eloquently coined it, had thwarted over a dozen climbers when precocious English engraver Edward Whymper arrived in the Italian village of Breuil in the summer of 1860.

No climbing novice, the 20-year-old Whymper was a young and talented alpinist who had already hauled himself to the top of numerous European peaks, logging a handful of first ascents in the process.

Teaming up with local Italian guide Jean-Antoine Carrel, Whymper's initial forays up the Matterhorn via the southeast ridge were wholly unsuccessful. By 1864 he had made seven abortive attempts on the precipitous pyramid and was beginning to radically re-think his strategy.

Whymper concluded that the key to conquering the mountain lay not on the south face but on the steep northeast Hörnli ridge; Carrel was less convinced. Readying for an eighth summit attempt in July 1865, Whymper arrived in Breuil only to find that Carrel had set off for the peak without him with an exclusively Italian climbing group. Enraged, the Englishman raced to Zermatt where he teamed up with the boyish Lord Francis Douglas, brother of the Marquess of Queensberry, under the stewardship of Swiss guide Peter Taugwalder and his son Peter Jnr.

Congregating in the Monte Rosa Hotel, the party encountered another mountaineering trio: Douglas Hadow, Charles Hudson and their French guide Michel Croz, also setting out for the summit. At 19, the baby-faced Hadow was fresh from a fast ascent of Mont Blanc while the more experienced Hudson had been part of the first team to ascend Monte Rosa in 1855.

Finding strength in numbers, the two teams agreed to combine and set out for the Hörnli ridge on 14 July 1865 just as Carrel's group began mounting their own challenge on the southeast ridge. A race ensued, but better conditions and an earlier start in the morning of the final day meant that Whymper's party of seven got to the top first, leaving Carrel still flailing on the steep slopes 600m below. But the story wasn't over. The fast ascent and rushed preparations had taken their toll on Whymper's group – particularly on Hadow.

Roping up for the descent, Croz was instructed to go first followed by Hadow, Hudson, Douglas, the Taugwaders and lastly, Whymper. Not far below the summit the exhausted Hadow, who had to be helped every step of the way by Croz, slipped and careered feet first into the French guide. Croz plunged headlong to his death off the Matterhorn's steep north face taking Hadow, Hudson and Douglas with him. The other three were saved when the rope between Douglas and Taugwader snapped as the latter tried to arrest the fall.

The Matterhorn incident had huge repercussions on the nascent climbing fraternity and was debated vociferously in the British newspapers of the day. Queen Victoria even discussed banning the sport, and numerous conspiracy theories circulated speculating whether Whymper and the Taugwaders had cut the rope to save their own skins. Realistically, there is little doubt that the tragedy was accidental; the first of many misadventures on a mountain that still harbours a silent curse.

---

of the Walser people are an integral part of the landscape and proudly upheld. They offer many fascinating insights into a tough, enduring way of life now rare in Western Europe (see p107).

This section is devoted to a flexible three-day walk from Valtournenche to Riva Valdobbia or Alagna Valsesia; for suggestions for further walking in Valtournenche and from Alagna Valsesia see p113.

GETTING THERE & AROUND

All three Aosta valleys are penetrated by regular SAVDA buses that stop at most points of interest. The buses interconnect with the main Valle d'Aosta bus/train services at Chatillon (for Valtournenche), Verrés (for Val d'Ayas), and Pont St Martin (for the Valle di Gressoney). Alagna Valsesia in Piedmont is best accessed by a train/bus combo via Vercelli.

ACCESS TOWN

You can base yourself in Aosta (p114) and still get to the trailhead of this walk for an early start. Alternatively there are plenty of hotels/guesthouses in the small village of Valtournenche. Ask at the **tourist office** (☎ 0166 9 20 29; valtournenche @montecervino.it; Via Roma 45; 9am-noon & 3-6.30pm) for details.

MATTERHORN & MONTE ROSA FOOTHILLS

Duration 3 days
Distance 50km
Difficulty demanding
Start Valtournenche
Finish Alagna Valsesia
Nearest Town Aosta (p114)
Transport bus

Summary An exceptionally scenic walk linking four contrasting valleys, in the presence of two Alpine giants: the Matterhorn and Monte Rosa; the Walser people's history and culture provide a unifying theme.

This is essentially a valley-to-valley walk, crossing one of the passes between each of three valleys, none of which is above 3000m. It is *not* an ascent of the two Alpine giants!

The walk starts in the town of Valtournenche, in the valley of the same name (with the Matterhorn at its head) and finishes in either Riva Valdobbia or Alagna Valsesia, in upper Valsesia, below Monte Rosa's southeast faces. Total ascent is 3725m. The route follows part of the AV1 (see p41), from Valtournenche to Gressoney St Jean, then follows the Sentiero Walser (p40) from St Jacques to Colle di Valdobbia. The walk then follows a waymarked route to Riva Valdobbia and up to Alagna Valsesia.

Waymarking and signposting of the routes varies from excessive to rare, along paths, tracks and short stretches of quiet road. Point-to-point times given on signposts seem to match those taken by fit walkers. Landslides sometimes remove sizeable chunks of path. Some sections of path are more like scree slopes than paths.

If you're interested in adapting the route, each of the three days of walking is self-contained, with public transport available.

A more leisurely itinerary could be spread over as many as six days.

In each of the valleys, there's a choice of accommodation, in *rifugi* or hotels. Camping would be a heroic option, considering the amount of ascent.

PLANNING
When to Walk

The passes on the route of this walk should be clear of snow from mid-June until late September. The *rifugi* are open for approximately the same period.

What to Bring

Before mid-June an ice axe may be necessary and gaiters are recommended. During summer, it can be unbelievably hot, so a hat, sunglasses and sunscreen are essential.

Maps

On all but the local maps, path numbers shown may differ from those on the ground. You'll be able to find at least some of the following maps in the villages and towns en route.

For positive identification of features, the IGC 1:25,000 series is superior: maps 108 *Cervino-Breuil Cervinia-Champoluc* and 109 *Monte Rosa-Alagna V-Macugnaga-Gressoney*.

In the Kompass 1:50,000 series, the sheets are No 87 *Breuil-Cervinia-Zermatt* and No 88 *Monte Rosa*. These include detailed notes in German and Italian.

In IGC's 1:50,000 series, easier to read than Kompass, the maps are No 5 *Cervino-Matterhorn e Monte Rosa* and No 10 *Monte Rosa, Alagna e Macugnaga*.

There are also some free local maps distributed by the **tourist office** (☎ 0166 9 20 29; Via Roma 45; 9am-noon & 3-6.30pm) in Valtournenche. Check also with the tourist office about damaged paths.

PLACE NAMES

Many places have dual Italian-French or Italian-German identities. The Italian names are used here, except where another name is better known to English-language speakers, ie, the Matterhorn rather than Il Cervino. Some variations exist between the spelling of names in the maps quoted and local signposts; the local spelling is given here as far as possible.

WALSER HERITAGE

Between the 12th and 15th centuries, Walser people migrated south from Switzerland and settled the more intractable and remote reaches of Val d'Ayas, Valle di Gressoney and Valsesia. At that time the climate was mild enough to make high-level settlement possible. Until the climate cooled in the 18th century, a settlement in Val d'Ayas was among the highest in Europe, at 2072m.

Many Walser villages survive and the landscape still bears the mark of their activities. Walser hamlets were clusters of two-storey timber-and-stone houses, each with the dwelling, storage and animal shelter under one roof and with ingenious design features allowing ventilation and heat conservation. Most hamlets had a communal oven and forge, and a chapel. Forests were cleared to provide timber for building and space for grazing and cultivation on terraces. Canals were laboriously dug; some are still used.

Colle di Valdobbia and Colle Pinter were on frequently used routes between the valleys; sections of the paths were lined with upended stones or timber fences – some are still intact.

As the Industrial Revolution progressed during the 19th century, the people left the valleys and agriculture began a long decline, only halted recently. Tourism began to bring back some prosperity to the valleys from the 1950s, but at the price of attrition of Walser traditions. In Valle d'Aosta the traditions live on in Valle di Gressoney, while Alagna Valsesia is the stronghold in Valsesia. Houses are being restored, relatively remote villages remain inhabited and the Walser heritage has become a tourist attraction.

The Sentiero Walser (SW) draws much of this together. It's a long-distance route from Colle di San Teodulo, northeast of Valtournenche, to St Jacques, over Colle Pinter to Gressoney La Trinité and Gressoney St Jean and up to Colle di Valdobbia. The route, signposted at crucial junctions, is easy enough to follow and there are elaborate information boards at many interesting features along the way. A booklet, *Il Grande Sentiero Walser*, is available from local tourist offices. The excellent **Museo Walser** (☎ 0163 92 29 35; admission €2; afternoon daily in midsummer, afternoon Sat, Sun & holidays only at other times) in the village of Pedemonte, close to Alagna, houses a vast number of artefacts in a typical Walser building and is worth a visit.

Information Sources

Each valley has a tourist office, and most are useful for accommodation information; contact details are listed with town information. Alternatively, the accommodation guides available from the UIT at Aosta (see p114) cover all but Valsesia.

Guided Walks

The **Corpo Guide Alagna** (☎ 0163 9 13 10; www.guidealagna.com; Piazza Grober 1) in Alagna Valsesia has a long and honourable history of guiding on Monte Rosa. You can join a group of four to climb to Capanna Margherita (p110).

GETTING TO/FROM THE WALK

Valtournenche (start)

From Aosta (p114) there are hourly trains to Chatillon (€2.20, 20 minutes) from where **SAVDA** (☎ 0165 26 20 27; www .savda.it) buses go to Valtournenche (€2.20, 40 minutes, seven a day). If you leave Aosta at 8.30am you can be on the trail soon after

10am. Chatillon also provides good access to Milan and Turin by train or **SADEM** (☎ 011 300 06 06; www.sadem.it) buses.

By car, Chatillon is 24km east of Aosta via S26 or the A5; from there SR406 takes you the 19km to Valtournenche.

Alagna Valsesia (finish)

Five daily **ATAP** (☎ 0158 40 81 17; www .atapspa.it) buses link Alagna Valsesia with Varallo (50 minutes) and Vercelli (2½ hours) both of which are connected by train with Turin and Milan. In August there's a direct Alagna–Milan bus run once a day by **Baranzelli** (www.baranzelli.it) leaving Alagna at 5.25pm and arriving in Milan at 8.35pm.

THE WALK

Day 1: Valtournenche to St Jacques

5¾–6¼ hours, 15km, 1275m ascent

Towards the southern end of Valtournenche village, join the AV1 at a junction

MATTERHORN & MONTE ROSA FOOTHILLS

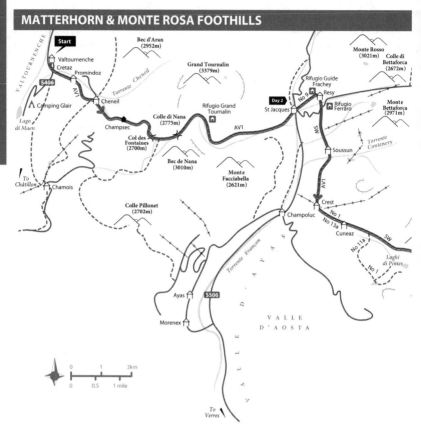

of the main road with a road signposted to Cretaz. A few metres along this road take the first right, signposted to Cheneil. Follow this minor road for about 250m, then go left up steps between houses in Cretaz and shortly turn right along a narrow lane; 150m along continue ahead at a junction. The path crosses Torrente Cheneil and soon leads into forest; bear left at a Y-junction. It's a steep climb; follow waymarkers at the next two junctions. About 45 minutes from Valtournenche, cross a gravel road and go up to the gently sloping meadows and scattered houses of **Promindoz**. Cross the gravel road diagonally left and go up a wide path signposted to Cheneil. About 50m further on, the path swings right across a field; then on the edge of a forest ascend steeply left beside a stream. Shortly, ignore

a path left and continue up to the edge of spacious meadows and on to the signposted path junction at **Cheneil** (40 minutes from Promindoz). Have a drink on the terrace at **Hotel Panorama Bich** (☎ 0166 9 20 19; www.hotelpanoramalbich.it; half-board per person €40) and contemplate the Matterhorn in all its glory. In this tall, traditional stone building some rooms have Cervino-gazing balconies; facilities are shared. The evening meal is first-rate, and may include genuine minestrone. There's sometimes a three-night minimum. Cheneil comprises a few chalets, the hotel and a small chapel.

Continue straight (southeast) on a wide path that soon leads into the beautiful upper reaches of the valley, dotted with larches and alpenrose. At **Champsec**, a long, low deserted building set into the slope, go

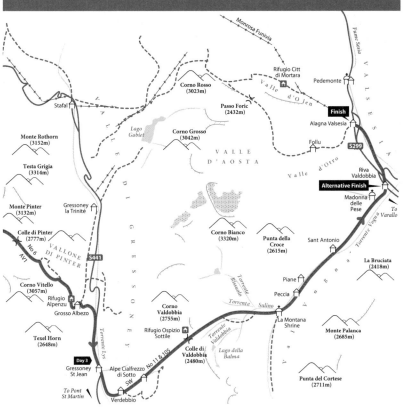

up to the left; the path continues to gain height, skirting a small basin – good marmot country – and on to **Col des Fontaines** (2700m, one to 1½ hours from Cheneil). On a good day, the magnificent view takes in the multitudinous peaks of PNGP to the southwest.

Then it's east down the path towards the head of the valley below. The path soon starts to regain height and reaches **Colle di Nana** (2775m), 40 minutes from Col des Fontaines. The outlook is eternally memorable – the sprawling glaciers, snowfields and cliffs of the Monte Rosa massif, nearby to the northeast, and the mountains south of Valle d'Aosta's depths in the opposite direction.

The descent starts with the path worming through boulders and down a narrow cleft. It's then slightly exposed for about 100m across a precipitous slope; the rest of the descent to a gravel road is straightforward (40 minutes from Colle di Nana).

Rifugio Grand Tournalin (☎ 0125 30 70 03; www.rifugiograndtournalin.com; beds €30, half-board €40), built in the late 1990s, is a few minutes up to the left. At lunchtime, it offers pasta, minestrone, *torta* (cake) and drinks.

Continue down the gravel road; from the second derelict stone building on the right, follow a waymarked diversion. Further down, cross the road and go on down through fields. When you reach the road again, go right for a few metres and take another waymarked short-cut, then another down towards a mountain pasture to a grassed vehicle track. Turn left and

CAPANNA REGINA MARGHERITA

Imagine gazing down at the Matterhorn, browsing myriad books in a high-altitude library, and drinking water made from a giant snow-melting machine. All of these fantasies can be realised at the Capanna Regina Margherita, Europe's highest mountain hut, that sits atop the exposed summit of Punta Gnifetti (German: Signalkuppe) at an incredible 4559m.

As the sixth-tallest peak in the Monte Rosa massif, Punta Gnifetti is one of the highest points in Europe and was named after the sturdy Italian pastor who first climbed it in 1842. In 1893, the CAI, overcoming precipitous topography, built a small *rifugio* on top naming it after the then Italian queen, Margherita, who tore up royal protocol and traversed several glaciers to attend the opening ceremony in a heavy 19th-century ankle-length dress with half a dozen ladies-in-waiting in tow.

In the century since its inauguration, the Capanna has evolved into an important meteorological and scientific observatory that collects weather data and studies the effects of high altitude on human physiology. In 1979, the original *rifugio* was replaced with a more modern building equipped with 70 beds, a 350-volume library, plus the aforementioned snow-making machine.

Reaching the Capanna is no 'walk in the park' and glacier travelling skills are required if you intend to tackle it alone. Ascending independently or in an organised group, you'll likely take a cable car from Alagna Valsesia or Gressoney La Trinitè to Punta Indren and then hike for two hours up to the Rifugio Gnifetti. From here it's four more hours of tough ascent across the Lys glacier to the Capanna *rifugio*.

Climbers rarely regret the toil in getting there. High above the clouds, the Matterhorn, and almost everywhere else in Europe, the jaw-dropping views defy written description. The most ethereal sight is the 'Spectre of Brocken' when the shapes of the Capanna and the surrounding mountains cast giant shadows onto the screen of mist that hangs beneath the snow-capped peaks just before sunset.

Dorm beds at the Capanna are €80 a night; book ahead. Non-expert climbers can organise guides for two-day trips (late Jun–mid-Sep) through the Corpo Guide Alagna (p107) in Alagna Valsesia from €100 to €200 depending on group size.

---

after 20m, bear right down a path which descends through conifers to a road. Then it's left for about 25m and down to the right to another house. Descend past a tiny shrine on the left, on a clear path across fields, past a wooden crucifix and back into forest briefly. Then, via more fields, you reach some houses; go between two on the left and one on the right and follow the path down to a bitumen road. Cross the bridge here and you've reached **St Jacques** (1½ hours from Rifugio Tournalin; p117). The nearest camping, **Sole e Neve** (☎ 0125 30 66 10; www.campingsoleneve.com; per person/site €7.50/6.50) is at **Morenex** (Ayas), about 10km southwest of town. **Champoluc** is a low-key winter ski resort with a far greater choice of accommodation and you can join the route for Day 2 there – the price of Champoluc's comforts is 120m extra ascent. **VITA** (☎ 0125 96 65 46; www.vitagroup.it) buses operate services between St Jacques and Verrès in Valle

d'Aosta (€3.20, one hour, nine a day), from where there are bus and train connections to Aosta, Milan and Turin.

Day 2: St Jacques to Gressoney St Jean
7½–8 hours, 17km, 1350m ascent
If you're starting from **Champoluc**, it's best to locate waymarked Route No 13 to Crest in the town centre.

In St Jacques, a few steps downhill from the bridge, turn left along Chemin de Resy (with a waymarker for Route No 9 and sign for Rifugio Frachey). Beyond the small cluster of traditional houses, follow Route No 9 up towards Resy (as signposted). The wide path gains height in conifer forest, crosses a meadow below a lone house, then goes above it and past two older buildings. The steep ascent persists to the settlement of **Resy** from where there are excellent views down Val d'Ayas (50 minutes from St Jacques).

At Resy, the **Rifugio Guide Frachey** (☎ 0125 30 74 68; www.rifugioguide frachey.it; half-board per person €38) offers a possible alternative to staying in St Jacques. Nearby there's also **Rifugio Ferraro** (☎ 0125 30 76 12; www.rifugioferraro .com)

To continue, head south and about 50m beyond Rifugio Ferraro, follow the sign-posted Sentiero Walser (SW; destination Crest), down fields to a narrow path which contours a small valley, then leads to a very shaky bridge. Cross it and continue along a vehicle track. About 15 minutes from Resy, turn right and go down a wide track; about 150m beyond the end of a ski lift, turn right at a junction and descend to a gravel road. Here a SW signpost points you ahead towards Crest. Beyond various skiing in-stallations, the road ascends to a junction; bear right here with the SW. A few minutes further on, stay above the traditional build-ings of the hamlet of **Soussun** and contour to a gravel road. Shortly you pass the re-mains of a water mill where you can make out the date 1601 on a timber beam. The vehicle track descends to cross Torrente Contenery, then regains the height fitfully. Around a bend, you come to a SW sign directing you down to the right towards Crest; the path may be overgrown but can be bypassed in the adjacent field. Turn right at a gravel road for 60m then go left, indicated by a signpost to Colle Pinter, and you will soon reach a chapel. From here go down through the old village of **Crest** to a water trough liberally decorated with waymarkers (1½ hours from Resy).

Continue on the path up Valle di Cuneaz (waymarked 13a and 1); cross a gravel road a few hundred metres further on and stay on the path ahead up to a vehicle track. Turn right and follow a path past a house to a small stream, easily crossed. Ascend to the village of **Cuneaz** (30 minutes from Crest) which contains the best examples of traditional Walser buildings seen on this walk, some of which may date from the 15th century. Go up between the houses, then along a wide path; several minutes beyond Cuneaz, bear left at a junction on a narrower path which leads into an im-pressive amphitheatre, enclosed by sharp peaks and cliffs with long waterfalls. Con-tinue ahead at a path junction (with Route

Nos 11a and 1) and up steeply through a gap in the cliff line. The clear path takes you straight up these uppermost reaches of Valle di Cuneaz. A miraculous notch through which the route passes becomes clearly visible between a massive bluff on the left and a flat-topped mountain on the right. Follow the yellow waymarkers up the extremely steep, zigzagging path, across loose scree to the notch on the edge of a hidden valley. Continue upwards past SW signposts to nearby **Laghi di Pinter** and steeply up to **Colle di Pinter** (2777m; 2¼ hours from Cuneaz).

From the col, the rocky path, most promi-nently waymarked as 6, drops very steeply for a few hundred metres to a succession of meadows, dotted with stone buildings and overlooked by the rugged heights of Monte Pinter (north) and Corno Vitello (south). From a well-preserved building behind a sky-scraping flagpole, the path works its way down the centre of steep-sided Vallone di Pinter. About an hour from Colle di Pinter, the floor of Valle di Gressoney comes into view as the path drops across a small stream and down the southern side of the valley to an *alpe*. Head straight down the slope (east–southeast) and make for a rectangu-lar stone ruin, from where the way onwards along Path No 6 becomes clear. Descend across flowery meadows to stone and timber buildings and continue to the right with a SW signpost to **Grosso Albezo** – the Walser name for the next hamlet. Here you can find **Rifugio Alpenzu** (www.rifugioalpenzu.it; dm/s €20/25) a good place for some refresh-ment (1¾ hours from Colle di Pinter).

Continue with Path No 6; a short dis-tance beyond Grosso Albezo you may come to a 'path closed' sign. Follow the alterna-tive path steeply down the mountainside to rejoin the main path about 50m from the reason for the closure – a comparatively minor landslide in a stream. Continue down to a strip of bitumen beside the main road in the valley and turn right. Roadside paths make the last 2km to **Gressoney St Jean** (see p116) easy enough (45 minutes from Grosso Albezo). **VITA** (☎ 0125 96 65 46; www.vitagroup.it) buses leave Gres-soney St Jean for Pont St Martin in Valle d'Aosta (55 minutes, 12 a day) where you can pick up trains or SADEM's buses to Aosta, Turin or Milan.

Day 3: Gressoney St Jean to Alagna Valsesia

6½–6¾ hours, 18km, 1100m ascent

Cross the bridge over Torrente Lys in Gressoney St Jean and walk south down the main road; on the far side of ornate Villa Margherita turn left along a path with a SW sign. It leads across a stone bridge and through the hamlet of **Verdebbio**. About 800m from the Villa, at Ondro Verdebbio, turn left up a path with a SW signpost to Colle di Valdobbia (for centuries an important trade and smuggling route), with waymarkers for Route Nos 11 and 105. The path winds up the steep, wooded mountainside with some good views down the valley. About 1¼ hours from Gressoney St Jean, the path swings around to the east and into a deep valley. Within 10 minutes you should catch sight of the Colle – the pronounced dip between the skyline peaks, with a large building (Rifugio Ospizio Sottile), squatting in the middle.

Soon the route passes below **Alpe Cialfrezzo di Sotto** (where you could buy fresh butter and cheese) and then a simple footbridge takes you over the east branch of the torrente (river). Turn sharp right on the far side. The path zigzags up meadows and passes above Alpe Cialfrezzo di Sopra, then goes up the middle of the valley. In the upper reaches of the stream, where the path has been swallowed by a small landslip, it may be safer to cross downstream. Then it's straightforward, although steep, up to **Colle Valdobbia** (2480m; 1½ hours from Alpe Cialfrezzo di Sotto). **Rifugio Ospizio Sottile** (☎ 0163 9 19 65; www.rifugio sottile.com; dm €13) is a great place to stay, with superb mountain-filled views east and west. A signpost here suggests it takes 2¾ hours to Riva Valdobbia, but this would necessitate seriously fast walking.

The path dives down from the edge of the col into the hanging valley below, then leads above Torrente Valdobbia thundering through a gorge. Beyond a boulder slope it winds down, and about 45 minutes from the col, comes to a junction. Ignore the narrow path ahead across a grassy spur and bear left – there are faint red and yellow waymarkers – soon alongside a stream, then down through cliffs and trees and on to a meadow with stone buildings. Go straight down to the right of the original line of the path, overgrown but marked by two rows of boulders. Here you can pause to take in the spectacular setting – long waterfalls on Torrente Rissuolo to the north and other streams framed by spiky peaks.

Continue a short distance and cross a bridge. Pass a small shrine; the path soon crosses a meadow between lines of boulders. Watch out for overgrowing nettles on the next stretch through woodland. Pass **La Montana shrine** (dated 1678) and go down to the dramatic merging of Torrente Sulino on the left and Torrente Vogna in the deep main valley (about two hours from the col). The wide path soon passes a chapel, then the village of Peccia with many fine Walser-style buildings. About 15 minutes from the confluence, the path becomes a vehicle track and another 30 minutes brings you to the start of a bitumen road at the village of **Sant'Antonio** with refreshments available.

The quiet road steadily descends Val Vogna, past a couple more hamlets. About 2.2km from Sant'Antonio, just past the church of **Madonna delle Pese**, take the path to the right signposted 'Via delle Capelle', to cut off a wide bend. Back on the road, go downhill for 50m and diverge again for another short cut, and continue down to a road junction at the northwest end of **Riva Valdobbia** (45 minutes from Sant'Antonio), an alternative finish for the walk. With luck you'll be greeted by an awesome view of Monte Rosa presiding over upper Valsesia. This largish but compact village of mainly traditional-style buildings at the meeting of Val Vogna and Valsesia has a bar, *tabaccheria* and two small *alimentari*. The bus serving Alagna Valsesia (see Getting There & Around, p105) stops here, but on the main road, not in the town.

To reach **Alagna Valsesia**, 2km further on, cross the road and go down to the main road (S299). Cross a footbridge over Fiume Sesia then turn left with a sign 'Sentiero per Alagna'. This road soon becomes a vehicle track and leads to the river bank. Follow this up to a footbridge; on the far side, turn right along the main road for about 250m to a side road next to the *municipio* building. This minor road leads to Via Centro (30 minutes from Riva); turn right to find the Pro Loco office and accommodation, or left to reach the *campeggio*.

MORE WALKS

PARCO NAZIONALE DEL GRAN PARADISO

Colonna

The earliest recorded mine was operating in Val di Cogne in 1679, but full-scale exploitation lasted for barely a century until 1979. The Colonna mine (at 2400m) was the centre of underground operations and the main output was magnetite, a source of iron ore. Innovations in transport, especially a *funivia* (cable car), overcame most of the problems of high-level operations, but the mine finally closed in 1979.

An informative brochure *Discovering Colonna's Mines* from the AIAT at Cogne describes the history of the mine at Colonna and outlines a circular walk from the **museum** (☎ 0165 74 92 64), set to re-open along with restored mine buildings in 2003, to the mine site and back to Moline, near Cogne. However, this walk contains an extremely hazardous section across a precipitous rocky gully near the mine buildings and is not recommended.

Fortunately you should be able to reach Colonna from Moline, just across the bridge beyond the eastern end of Cogne. The path has yellow waymarkers – ignore occasional outbreaks of red-and-white stripes. Allow about four hours for the 8km return walk, which involves 860m ascent; it's well worth the effort for the superb views of Cogne and Valnontey. Use the IGC 1:25,000 map No 101 *Gran Paradiso, La Grivola, Cogne*. The mine buildings are an anticlimax – they're too fragile for safe access. But the views and the experience of visiting a place that must have demanded nothing short of heroism to develop and maintain are good reasons for doing the walk.

Pousset

Punta Pousset's extraordinary tower of rock (3046m) is an attention-riveting feature of the view westwards from Cogne. Below its formidable slopes is a network of paths, along which a medium day walk from Cogne (or the downstream villages of Cretaz and Epinel) can take you through the woodlands on the southwest side of Val di Cogne up to the beautiful Vallone del Pousset, right below the Punta. The route is shown on the *Try the Trails* leaflet, available from the AIAT office in Cogne (p115).

The best map to use is the FMB 1:50,000 *Parco Nazionale Gran Paradiso*, though it doesn't show all the paths.

Allow about 5¾ hours from Cogne for the 13km walk; 850m of ascent is involved. Between the end of July and mid-August, the walk can be shortened by about 1½ hours by catching the bus from Cogne to Cretaz at the start, and from Epinel to Cogne at the finish.

Rifugio Walk

Rifugio Frederico Chabod and Rifugio Vittorio Emanuele II (a former royal hunting lodge) are perched high above Valsavarenche in the shadow of Gran Paradiso and are popular bases for summit ascents. It is possible to visit them without any aspirations for the big climb, on a fine 14km high-level walk with 1250m of ascent; allow 6½ to seven hours. The walk also offers spectacular views of the glaciers of Gran Paradiso and crosses moraine ridges and boulder fields. It can fit into a fairly strenuous day, or be spread over two days by staying at one of the *rifugi*. Booking is essential during July and August, and highly advisable at other times at both **Rifugio Chabod** (☎ 0165 9 55 74; www .rifugiochabod.com; beds €20; late Mar-early May & late Jun–mid-Sep) and **Rifugio Vittorio Emanuele** (☎ 0165 9 59 20; beds €20; late Mar-late Sep). The morning bus from Aosta to Pont drops you at the start of the path to Rifugio Chabod; and a bus leaves Pont early in the evening. The IGC 1:25,000 map No 102 *Valsavarenche, Val di Rhêmes, Valgrisenche* is the one to take.

VALLE D'AOSTA TO VALSESIA

Valtournenche's Gran Balconata

The Gran Balconata is a circular way-marked route with Breuil-Cervinia and Torgnon as its northernmost and southernmost points respectively. It keeps well above the floor of the valley, passes through a few villages and hamlets, and is extremely scenic with the Matterhorn as a constant presence. There are also views of Monte

Rosa, and a variety of terrain from steep mountainsides to meadows and grassland. It takes at least three days to go the full 40km distance; alternatively, it's easy to join and leave the route at several places and to return to your base by bus. There isn't much to choose between a clockwise direction or the reverse – the views are great either way.

The Kompass 1:50,000 map No 87 *Breuil-Cervinia-Zermatt* covers the whole route. The locally produced Comune di Valtournenche 1:25,000 map *Alta Valle* (available from the tourist office in Valtournenche) gives more detail, but cuts off a few kilometres north of Torgnon.

Valle di Otro & Valle D'Olen

Extending west from Alagna Valsesia, these two magnificently scenic valleys provide striking contrasts between Valsesia's past and present. In Valle di Otro are reputedly the finest Walser villages in the Alps, including Follu with its beautifully decorated church; Valle d'Olen shelters the Monrosa *funivia* and chairlifts, kept busy carrying skiers and climbers to Punta Indren (3260m) on Monte Rosa. The two valleys can be linked by crossing Passo Foric (2432m) from where, on a fine day, the heights of Monte Rosa and the arc of peaks, passes and snowfields above upper Valsesia are in full view. This 13km circular walk from Alagna takes about seven hours and involves 1290m of ascent. You could take two hours off this by returning on the *funivia* from Alpe Pianalunga in Valle d'Olen.

For refreshments (and accommodation), there are **Ristoro Alpino zar Senni** (☎ 0163 92 29 52) in Valle di Otro, a traditional Walser house; and **Rifugio Città di Mortara** (☎ 0163 9 11 04; 29 Jun-30 Sep) not far below the *funivia* station.

The map of local walks from the Pro Loco office at Alagna is more up to date than the IGC 1:25,000 map No 109 *Monte Rosa-Alagna V-Macugnaga-Gressoney*, although the latter is far better for identifying landmarks. Waymarking (red and yellow plus a number) is erratic; there are also a few signposts. The paths and tracks are not unduly rough, although they may be overgrown in places; the route includes about 1km of road walking.

TOWNS & FACILITIES

AOSTA
☎ 0165 / pop 34,100

Jagged Alpine peaks tower spectacularly above sprawling Aosta looking down on a settlement that has honoured them since Roman times. Bounced around between the kingdoms of Burgundy and Savoy in the Middle Ages, the modern town remains bi-lingual with a culture that claims Valdostan roots, a factor best reflected in its musical local dialect and simple but hearty cuisine.

Information

Aosta **tourist office** (☎ 23 66 27; www .regione.vda.it/turismo; Piazza Chanoux 2; 9am-1pm & 3-8pm Jun-Sep, 9.30am-1pm & 3-6.30pm Mon-Sat, 9am-1pm Sun Oct-May) has region-wide information including accommodation lists.

Aosta Web (☎ 06 00 15; Ave Pere Laurent cnr XXVI Febbraio; 9.30am-12.30pm, 2.30-8.30pm, closed Sun morning) has internet for €2 per hour.

Supplies & Equipment

You can stock up on stove fuel, buy maps and replace worn-out socks at **Meinardi Sport** (Via Edouard Albert 23; closed Mon morning), five minutes' walk west from Piazza Chanoux.

Many newsagents and bookshops stock maps. **Libreria Aubert** (Via E Aubert 46) and **Minerva** (Rue de Tillier 24) have plenty of Italian-language books about walks, and natural and cultural history.

For supplies there are two **Standa supermarkets** (Piazza Plouves & Via Chambery; closed Sun siesta). There are many smaller *alimentari* (grocery shops) in Via San Anselmo east of Piazza Chanoux.

Sleeping

Hotel Turin (☎ 4 45 93; www.hotelturin .it; Via Torino 14; s €34-60, d €58-84) A modern, boxy glass-and-steel affair, the three-star Hotel Turin has good facilities and is a handy suitcase-drag from the train station.

Albergo Mancuso (☎3 45 26; www .albergomancuso.com; Via Voison 32; s/d €45/55) This budget place is a little old-fashioned (check out the old 1970s concert photos on the stairway) and certainly not luxury but, to its credit, the Mancuso is friendly, family-run and incredibly cheap. The rooms are all different so ask for a preview before you decide (some are small). They also offer discounts in a couple of local restaurants including the Ulisse (see below).

Hotel Milleluci (☎4 42 74; www.hotel milleluci.com; Loc Porossan Roppoz 15; s €110-130, d €130-240) Old wooden skis, traditionally carved wooden shoes, clawfoot baths, indoor and outdoor pools, a jacuzzi, sauna and gym make this large, family-run converted farmhouse seem more like a palace. Set on a hillside above town, the balconied rooms look out to the so-titled 'thousand lights' twinkling from Aosta below.

Eating

Ristorante – Pizzeria Ulisse (☎4 11 80; Via Aubert Edouard 58; meals €15-18; lunch Mon-Sun, dinner Thu-Mon) This is the sort of place where food can be brought to your table personally by the hardworking chef, and the cooked-to-perfection €5 pizzas margheritas are the best!

Ad Forum (☎4 00 11; Via Mons de Sales 11; meals €22-30; Tue-Sun) Another fantastic restaurant setting; this time in a stylish garden (and interior rooms) built on part of the remains of the Roman Forum. Conceptual dishes such as risotto with strawberries and *spumante*, or *lasagnetta* with pear and blue cheese, come in generous portions, and you get an equally tasty complimentary *apéritif* while you wait.

Vecchia Aosta (☎36 11 86; Piazza Porte Pretoriane 4; set menus €27; lunch Tue-Sun, dinner Tue-Sat) Maybe it's the French influence, but Aosta restaurants such as the Vecchia score consistently highly when it comes to culinary creativity. Grafted onto a section of the old Roman wall, the setting is sublime and the waiters highly knowledgeable (and congenial).

Open-air café terraces spring up on Piazza Chanoux in summer.

Getting There & Away

Buses operated by **SAVDA** (www.savda.it) run to Milan (1½ to 3½ hours, two daily),

Turin (two hours, up to 10 daily) and Courmayeur (one hour, up to eight daily), as well as French destinations including Chamonix. Services leave from Aosta's **bus station** (☎26 20 27; Via Giorgio Carrel), virtually opposite the train station. To get to Valtournenche, take a Turin-bound bus to Châtillon (30 minutes, eight daily), then a connecting bus (one hour, seven daily) up the valley. Direct buses to Cogne run seven times daily (50 minutes).

Aosta's train station, on Piazza Manzetti, is served by trains from most parts of Italy via Turin (€7.55, two to 2½ hours, more than 10 daily).

Aosta is on the A5, which connects Turin with the Mont Blanc Tunnel and France. Another exit road north of the city leads to the Great St Bernard Tunnel and on to Switzerland.

COGNE

☎0165 / pop 1500

The main stepping stone into PNGP, tranquil Cogne (elevation 1534m) provides a refreshing antidote to the overdeveloped ski resorts on the opposite side of the Valle d'Aosta.

Aside from its plethora of outdoor opportunities, Cogne is known for its lacemaking; you can buy the local fabrics at the charming craft and antique shop, **Le Marché Aux Puces** (☎74 96 66; Rue Grand Paradis 4; closed Wed).

Information

Cogne's **tourist office** (☎7 40 40; www .cogne.org; Piazza Chanoux 36; 9am-12.30pm & 2.30-5.30pm Mon-Sat) has stacks of information on the park and a list of emergency contact numbers.

Guided nature walks from July to September are organised by the **Associazione Guide della Nature** (☎7 42 82; Piazza Chanoux 36, Cogne; 9am-noon Mon, Wed & Sat).

For guided ascents of Gran Paradiso contact the **Società Guide Alpine di Cogne** (☎7 48 35; Via Bourgeois 33, Cogne).

Supplies & Equipment

The place to go for stove fuel, outdoor equipment and clothing is **Ezio Sport** (Via Mines de Cogne 66).

WESTERN ALPS

In Cogne, several shops along Via Bourgeois sell maps. Two good bookshops (which also sell maps) are **Montagne di Carta** (Via Dr Grappein 56) and **Cavallo** (Viale Cavagnet 51), with shelves of Italian titles about walks, and natural and cultural history.

Pick up supplies at the smallish **Despar supermarket** (Via Bourgeois) and, 250m east from there, two *alimentari* and a fruit and vegetable shop.

Sleeping & Eating

Wilderness camping is forbidden in the park, but there are 11 *rifugi;* the tourist office has a list.

Camping Lo Stambecco (☎ 7 41 52; www .campinglostambecco.com; Valnontey; person/tent/car €7/3/6; May-Sep) Pitch up under the pine trees in the heart of the park at this well-run and friendly site. Its sister hotel, La Barme, rents bikes to explore the mountains.

Hotel Sant'Orso (☎ 7 48 21; Via Bourgeois 2; Cogne; s/d €46/92, half-board €71/142; spring & autumn closures vary) Cogne personified – ie tranquil, courteous, and understated – the Sant'Orso is nonetheless equipped with plenty of hidden extras. Check out the restaurant, small cinema, sauna, kids' room and terrace. Further kudos is gained by the fact that you can start your cross-country skiing pretty much from the front door. The owners also run the Hotel du Gran Paradis nearby.

Hotel Ristorante Petit Dahu (☎ 7 41 46; www.hotelpetitdahu.com; Valnontey; s €36-50, d €72-100, restaurant menus €35; closed May & Oct) Straddling two traditional stone-and-wood buildings, this friendly, family-run spot has a wonderful restaurant (also open to non-guests; advance bookings essential) whipping up rustic mountain cooking using wild Alpine herbs.

Getting There & Away

There are up to seven **SAVDA** (www.savda .it) buses daily to/from Cogne and Aosta (50 minutes). Cogne can also be reached by cable car from Pila.

Valley buses (up to 10 daily) link Cogne with Valnontey (€0.90, five minutes) in high summer.

By car, take the Aymavilles exit from the S26, 6km southwest of Aosta; continue on SR47 from Aymavilles village to Cogne, 20km further on.

EAUX ROUSSES
☎ 0165 / pop 60

Eaux Rousses is a handful of buildings right on the normal route of the AV2, just above the main valley road. Its name comes from the iron deposit in the cliffs down which the local waterfall cascades.

Information

At Dégioz (day-gosh), a couple more kilometres down the valley, there is a PNGP **visitor centre** (☎ 90 58 08; open daily Jul-Aug, Sun only Jun & Sept); the display features predators.

Supplies & Equipment

At Dégioz there is a small shop, a *tabaccheria* (tobacconist and all-purpose shop).

Sleeping & Eating

L'Hostellerie du Paradis (☎ 90 59 72; www.hostellerieduparadis.it; r €40-80) is a curious place of split-level floors and rooms covered in paintings and photos, but it's just off the AV2. The food is excellent.

There is also accommodation at Pont about 5km up the road; at Bien, about 1km down the road; and at Dégioz. Details are available from the accommodation list available from the AIAT in Aosta (p114).

Getting There & Away

There is a **SAVDA** (☎ 26 20 27; www.savda .it) bus service between Aosta and Eaux Rousses (€2.80, one hour, three a day mid-Jun–mid-Sep, three a day Mon-Sat at other times).

GRESSONEY ST JEAN
☎ 0125 / pop 790

A Walser village that acts as the hub of the Val di Gressoney, Gressoney St Jean was once a favoured retreat for the Italian royal family. There are plenty of places to overnight.

Information

The **tourist office** (☎ 35 51 85; www.aiatmon terosawalser.it; Villa Deslex; 9am-12.30pm & 2.30-6.30pm Mon-Sat, till 6pm Sun) has information.

Sleeping & Eating

Camping Margherita (☎ 35 53 70; www
.campingmargherita.com; Via Schnacke 15;
per person/site €6/12.50) is close to the
village centre. It has wi-fi, bike rental,
barbecue facilities and five-person chalets
for rent.

Hotel Lyskamm (☎ 35 54 36; www.lys
kammhotel.com; Gressoney St Jean; s €40-
60 d €80-120), of 1887 vintage, still wears
its 'Grande Albergo' badge with pride and
has clean rooms, sharp service and a good
restaurant.

There are also several slightly overpriced
restaurants from which to choose, all focusing on local dishes.

There are two well-stocked *alimentari* on
and near the central Obre Platz.

Getting There & Away

VITA (☎ 96 65 46; www.vitagroup.it) buses
leave Gressoney St Jean for Pont St Martin
in Valle d'Aosta (55 minutes, 12 a day)
where you can pick up trains or SADEM's
buses to Aosta, Turin or Milan.

ST JACQUES

☎ 0125 / pop 90

Tiny St Jacques at the head of the Val
d'Ayas is where time seems to have stood
still. There are many fascinating old buildings of Walser origin and it's well worth

a wander after dinner, if your feet have
recovered from the ardours of the hike.

Information

Tourist information for Valle d'Ayas is at
the Champoluc **AIAT** (☎ 30 71 13; www
.aiatmonterosa.com; Via Varasc 16; 9am-
12.30pm & 3-6pm), a five-minute bus ride
down the valley.

Sleeping & Eating

The nearest camping, **Sole e Neve** (☎ 0125
30 66 10; www.campingsoleneve.com; per
person/site €7.50/6.50) is at **Morenex**
(Ayas), about 10km southwest of town.

Hotel Genzianella (☎ 30 71 56; www
.hotelgenzianella.it; Place de la Grotte 5;
s/d €52/104) is a simple 20-room mountain
inn. In summer, hikers sit out in the garden
and contemplate whether to walk west (AV
1) or east (Grande Sentiero Walser).

Various bars in the village offer snacks
and light meals. There's also a small *alimentari*, which sells phone-cards and maps.

Getting There & Away

VITA (☎ 96 65 46; www.vitagroup.it)
buses operate services between St Jacques
and Verrès in Valle d'Aosta (€3.20, one
hour, nine a day), from where there are
bus and train connections to Aosta, Milan
and Turin.

Lake District

LAKE DISTRICT

HIGHLIGHTS

- Walking through a vast array of exquisite Renaissance mansions at the start of the **Sass Corbée** hike (p130)
- Enjoying exceptionally rich displays of wildflowers during spring and early summer on **Monte Baldo** (p121)
- Uncovering half-forgotten hamlets amid the ancient beech woods of the **Valle Cannobina** (p132)
- Tackling the precarious high paths around the craggy peak of Monte Grona that towers over **Lago di Como** (p126)

Signature food: *Costoletta alla Milanese*	Celebrated native: Pliny the Younger (Roman philosopher)	Famous for... Palatial villas

On first impressions, the personality of the Italian Lakes comes across as refined, swanky, and smooth around the edges; imagine a genetic melange of George Clooney and Pierce Brosnan, with a dash of Marcello Mastroianni thrown in for good measure. But, the good news is that, despite the paparazzi-drawing presence of various Hollywood *glitterati* (Clooney, for one, has a home on the shores of Lake Como), you don't need to have a Zurich-based bank account to enjoy these watery havens and their surrounding attractions. The hiking trails are free, the accommodation is surprisingly economical, and the views that extend as far as Switzerland in the north are likely to remain imprinted on your retinas for months, if not years.

The hikes in this region are split between the three main lakes – Maggiore, Como and Garda. Of the three, Garda is the domineering older sibling, once hailed by artists such as Klimt and DH Lawrence, but today host to Italy's largest theme park – the garish Gardaland. Next comes Como, the attractive, popular, but sometimes wayward middle child, that glistens flirtatiously beneath its Alpine peaks but is sometimes drowned by its own beauty. Finally there's Maggiore, the quiet underrated one that often takes a while to get to know, but is well worth the emotional investment.

While the lakes themselves are large, and their picturesque shorelines heavily populated, the actual hiking tends to be centred in specific activity areas. In Maggiore the focus is Cannobio, in Como it's Menaggio, while Garda has a couple of starting points: Limone and Malescine.

CLIMATE

The lakes generally enjoy warm, sunny summers (up to nine hours of sunshine daily) and cold winters. Summer is the wettest season, with frequent thunderstorms. July is the warmest month, with an average maximum temperature of 20°C, and daily maximums in the low 30s being quite common.

Föhn winds, blowing from the north, usually during the morning, are common, attracting hordes of windsurfers, but often shrouding the mountains in fog.

Snow can lie on sheltered slopes of Monte Baldo (above Lago di Garda) and on the mountains northwest of Lago di Como until early June. However, it is not usually very deep.

PLANNING

Maps

Touring Club Italiano's 1:200,000 *Lombardia* map covers the entire Lake District and is ideal for finding your way round.

Emergency

For urgent medical assistance in the Lake District, call the **national emergency number** (☎ 118).

GETTING THERE & AROUND

Most lake-bound traffic passes through Italy's largest city, Milan, which has the best transport connections in the country.

Trains and buses fan out from here to the three different lakes. It is possible to travel between Lakes Maggiore and Como by bus. To get from Lakes Como to Garda, it is quicker to pass through Milan.

GATEWAYS

Spread out across three Italian regions (Piedmont, Lombardy and Trentino-Alto Adige), the Italian Lakes cover a large and diverse area. Geographically, Milan is the most obvious gateway but, with its noise, crowds and big city hassle, it might not be the best preparation for a day or three of sublime hiking. As a result, you may prefer to base yourself in the less frenetic and relatively central lakeside town of Como (p139).

LAGO DI GARDA

Italy's largest lake lies to the east of Lago di Como and Lago Maggiore, meaning its cultural, geological and geographical affinities are closer to southern Austria and the Dolomites than to the Alps. The walks described in this section are based in two areas: around the Monte Baldo Range, rising to 2000m above the eastern shores of the lake, and at Limone sul Garda close to rugged Valle del Singol and surrounding peaks on the western side.

MUSSOLINI'S IGNOMINIOUS END

Stolen like a fugitive from Gran Sasso by the daring German commando Otto Skorzeny in 1943 (see p234), the increasingly pathetic-looking figure of Mussolini seemed to be imminently doomed. Installed briefly as a German puppet of the ill-fated Italian Social Republic, the aptly named *Sawdust Caesar* spent the last 18 months of the war earnestly writing his memoirs and kowtowing to Hitler.

The end came in April 1945 a few days after Italy finally fell from the Nazi's slippery grasp. With the Allies advancing north across the Po River, Mussolini, who had been living on the shores of Lake Garda, attempted to escape to Switzerland with his mistress, Clara Petacci, and several Fascist loyalists dressed as German army privates. His convoy was stopped in Dongo, near Menaggio, on the west coast of Lake Como by Italian partisans where he was quickly unmasked.

The details of Mussolini's execution are murky. Historical testimonies suggest that he was driven to the small lakeside village of Giulino di Mezzegra the next day (28 April) and shot – along with his mistress – by Italian partisan and subsequent Communist Party politician Walter Audisio.

Mussolini's and Petacci's bodies were later taken to Milan where they were strung up at a petrol station in the Piazzale Loreto and stoned by an angry crowd.

LAKE DISTRICT

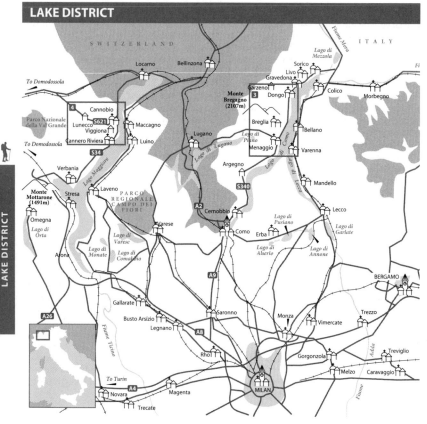

ENVIRONMENT

With an area of 370 sq km, Lago di Garda is the largest of the three lakes. About 40% of its depth (346m at its deepest) is made up of moraine deposits, the legacy of its glacial origins. This massive deposit pushed the lake south beyond its confining valley, out into the Po Valley. The surrounding peaks may be lower than those around Lago di Como and Lago Maggiore, but they lack little in grandeur. Monte Carone (1621m) above Valle del Singol dominates the complex topography of ridges, spurs and valleys in the northwestern corner. Monte Baldo's elegantly simple long sweep, with steep western slopes and more gentle gradients in the east, stands in striking contrast. Geologically, Garda is dominated by limestone formations.

PLANNING
When to Walk

May and September are the best times, when the weather is mild to warm and most likely to be settled. July and August are usually hot, and the area is very crowded with tourists.

GETTING THERE & AROUND

Garda is easily accessed by train on the Milan–Venice line that passes through Desenzano and Peschiera on the southern shores from where buses and ferries connect with the lakeside towns to the north.

ACCESS TOWN

Malcesine (p139) on the eastern shores of Lago di Garda is the best access town for the two walks; one starts in town (or just outside if you use the alternative start).

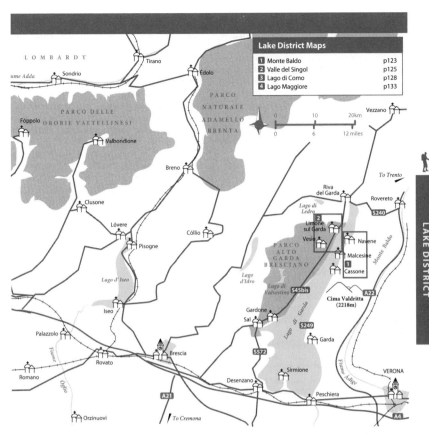

LAKE DISTRICT

The second walk starts a short ferry ride across the lake near Limone sul Garda.

MONTE BALDO

Duration 6½–7 hours
Distance 13km
Difficulty moderate
Start/Finish Monte Baldo cable-car station
Nearest Town Malcesine (p139)
Transport cable car
Summary An outstanding mountain ridge walk with far-ranging lake and alpine views, and abundant wildflowers.

Monte Baldo is a long, rugged ridge paralleling the middle part of Lago di Garda's eastern shore. From its extremities, the ridge narrows dramatically to a knife-edge crest, punctuated by several precipitous peaks, the highest being Cima Valdritta (2218m). Popular with skiers in winter and mountain-bike riders in summer, Monte Baldo is also a magnet for walkers, and a well-used path traverses the ridge. The extensive network of waymarked paths, in conjunction with the *funivia* (cable car) and local buses, provide many opportunities to explore the mountain. Signposts at path junctions give times to destinations; fit, younger walkers should find it easy to better them. Waymarking, with CAI (Club Alpino Italiano) red and white stripes, is reasonably reliable. The main path followed in the walk described here is Path No 651.

The route described is an out-and-back walk, with a total ascent of 750m, but variations are possible. The approach from lakeshore level at Navene (see Alternative Start, p123) gives a much better sense of actually arriving on the mountain than you feel by taking the *funivia* up to the main ridge – but it's a very long climb. If you take the *funivia* up the mountain, you could return to the lakeside on foot, via either Col di Piombi or Val Dritta (p136).

Baldo's exposed upper ridges and fickle weather need to be treated with respect by walkers of all standards.

ENVIRONMENT
The range is composed of a layer of limestone laid down between 135 and 220 million years ago and later folded by upheavals in the earth's crust. Although Lago di Garda was formed by glacial action, the Monte Baldo Range escaped any direct impact of the ice age. This has contributed to its ecological importance.

Up to 350m, olive and citrus groves and oak woodlands are widespread. Sweet chestnuts take over between 350m and 900m; next come beech and conifers in more open woodland. These give way above 1400m to grassy alpine meadows, thickets of mountain pine (spreading as wide as they are high) and alpenrose with small, deep-pink bell-shaped clusters of flowers.

Monte Baldo is popularly known as Italy's botanic garden. Three of the most striking species you're likely to see are the deep-blue trumpet gentian; its more delicate relative, spring gentian; and the bright yellow globeflower. Two small *riserve statali* (state reserves) – Gardesana Orientale on the lower slopes above Navene, and Lastoni Selva Pezzi extending right along the ridge crest – are intended to protect fauna and flora.

PLANNING
What to Bring
Walking poles, or even an ice axe, are essential in May as sections of the paths may be under snow. Large snow drifts can lie on Monte Baldo until early June.

German is widely spoken around the lake, and you're quite likely to have prices in shops quoted in German, even if you've used Italian to start the transaction, so Lonely Planet's *German Phrasebook* will be as useful as the *Italian Phrasebook*.

Maps
The Kompass 1:25,000 map No 690 *Alto Garda e Ledro* is the best of the bunch, although it contains some errors in the location of paths and junctions. The locally produced 1:20,000 Walks Map, *Monte Baldo, Malcesine* has notes in English, German and Italian on about seven walks in the area and is OK.

PLACE NAMES
There are some differences between names signposted along the paths and those on the maps listed; the maps also differ in some spellings. The signposted names are given here, with the more common map name in brackets at the first mention.

Weather Information
You can call for local **weather forecasts** (☎ 1678 603 45).

WARNING – MOUNTAIN BIKES
The tracks criss-crossing the slopes of Monte Baldo, from the main ridge to the lake shore, and the old tracks (and even some paths) around Valle del Singol on the western side of the lake are extremely popular with mountain-bike riders.

Many of these tracks are wide enough to allow riders to pass walkers safely, but many are not. Some riders even take to paths barely wide enough for one person on foot, let alone a bike.

Many riders religiously stick to a 'good riding code' – on catching sight of walkers ahead the leader calls out to following riders to either move to one side to continue, or to stop and wait until the approaching walkers have passed. Other cyclists are not so inclined and clearly believe that their speed and weight justify their headlong descent, regardless of walkers on the path.

A more menacing hinderance is the appearance of the odd motorbike on the narrower, steeper paths of the Valle del Singol, manoeuvring down fragile slopes susceptible to erosion.

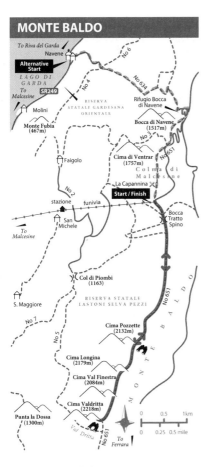

GETTING TO/FROM THE WALK

A tourist bus runs hourly from Malcesine to Navene (€1, 17 minutes, 8am-2pm & 5pm-1am daily) for the alternative start (next column). It also stops at the **Monte Baldo funivia** (☎ 0457 40 02 06; Malcesine–Monte Baldo one way/return €12/18; every 30 minutes 8am-6.45pm, until 5.45pm Sep-Apr). A new *funivia* with rotating glass cabins was installed in 2002.

THE WALK

From the *funivia* station in Monte Baldo, head down a wide track, following the red and white signs (including Route No 651), past Baita dei Forti restaurant to **Bocca Tratto Spino** (Bocca Tredespin). Keep

going up, still following Route No 651, generally along a rocky ridge to the tops of two ski tows, where you keep to the right of a large building. About 100m further on you enter the Riserva Statale Lastoni Selva Pezzi. Gently rising alpine meadows soon give way to low mountain pine and heather. The ridge narrows and the ascent steepens. About 1¼ hours from the start, you pass a sign 'Cima Pozzetta' pointing up to Cima Pozzette (2132m), not a particularly prominent feature. The path then narrows and steepens and is slightly exposed in places. Another steep climb takes you past a sign to Cima Longina (Cima del Longino). The summit of **Cima Longina** (2179m) is a bit further up, topped by a crucifix (about 30 minutes from the Pozzetta sign). It's a stupendous view – mountains near and far with Malcesine directly below.

Continue down to a gap then regain most of this lost elevation through pines. Follow along to the start of the traverse of the extremely steep, eastern flank, below Cima Val Finestra. The narrow, mildly exposed path is even more fun with a covering of snow. It then continues to contour the precipitous, craggy slopes, clad with clumps of low mountain pine, crosses a gully and a spur, then a mighty view of huge rock walls rising from Val Dritta opens up ahead. Descend slightly to the unmarked junction of the path to the summit; it's easy enough along a narrow spur to reach crucifix-topped **Cima Valdritta** (2218m, 1½ to two hours from Cima Longina). With luck you can enjoy the magnificently dramatic views of deep valleys and towering cliffs nearby and the great expanses of the lake framed by ranges of alpine peaks to the north and northwest.

Retrace your steps to return to the *funivia* (2½ to three hours)

ALTERNATIVE START: NAVENE TO FUNIVIA STATION
4¼–5 hours, 7km, 1690m ascent

From between **Bar Navene** and the main church follow waymarked Path No 634 (which shares the road then well-used vehicle track with Route Nos 4 and 6). Once you pass the turn-offs from Path Nos 4 and 6, Route No 634 is bike-free, as it climbs through forest to Bocca di Navene (1517m; three to 3½ hours). Here you'll find **Rifugio Bocca di Navene** (☎ 0457 40 17 94) and can sample their excellent *torta* (cake) or something more filling, with hot or cold drinks.

Walk up the road for a short distance to an unmarked path on the right (not shown on the Kompass 1:25,000 map), which leads up to a wide gravel road. Follow this to a point about 40m beyond a large information board welcoming you to Monte Baldo. Take signposted Route No 3, (which is also Route No 651); ignore a path to the right where Route No 3 leads to Cima di Ventrar and ascend the steep slope to an unnamed point (1751m). Continue south on a broad path across open **Colma di Malcesine**, where wildflowers are very plentiful, to **La Capannina** where you can have drinks and sandwiches, or more substantial polenta and pasta. Descend slightly, past ski lifts and buildings, to the *funivia* station (1¼ to 1½ hours from Bocca di Navene).

VALLE DEL SINGOL

Duration 6¼–6½ hours
Distance 21km
Difficulty moderate–demanding
Start Vesio
Finish Limone sul Garda
Nearest Town Malcesine (p139)
Transport bus, ferry

Summary A superbly scenic walk around the rim of spectacular Valle del Singol, following old tracks and paths past many WWI historic sites.

On the northwestern shore of Lago di Garda, Limone sul Garda (Limone) is an ideal base for exploring an extensive network of paths and roads built during WWI. You can feel you are deep in the mountains, even though the vast expanses of Lago di Garda aren't far away. Valle del Singol provides the ideal mountain walk – following the rim of a valley right around its watershed. This particular valley reaches deeply into the mountains, a vast amphitheatre of limestone crags and towers, and narrow ledges with precariously perched trees.

Both Limone and Valle del Singol are in the northeast corner of Parco Alto Garda Bresciano, a large reserve (383 sq km) extending for around 40km along the western shore of Lago di Garda and west into the mountains. It protects a wide variety of ecosystems from lakeside to alpine, extensive woodlands, traditional mountain settlements and 18th-century villas.

This walk, with its 900m of ascent, could be spread over two days by staying overnight in Baita Bonaventura Segala. The highly recommended ascent of Monte Carone (p137), an alternative rim-hugging route around Valle del Singol (see Valle del Singol Alternative, p137), and an exhilarating excursion through Val Pura (see Valle del Singol & Val Pura, p136) offer further options in this area.

PLANNING
What to Bring
If you plan to stay at Baita Bonaventura Segala, bring a sleeping bag and food. Carry plenty of water as there are no natural sources; you may find bottled drinks at Baita Segala.

Maps
The Kompass 1:25,000 map No 690 *Alto Garda e Ledro* has some useful notes on the reverse side and is better than the same publisher's 1:50,000 map No 102 *Lago di Garda/Monte Baldo*.

The best place to look for maps is the **tabaccheria** (Piazza Garibaldi) near the Limone ferry port.

GETTING TO/FROM THE WALK
Vesio (start)
Regular ferries link Malcesine with Limone sul Garda. The walk starts near Vesio, a village 9km southwest of Limone. There are two morning **SIA** (www.sia-autoservizi .it) buses from Limone to Vesio at 7.15am (Mon-Sat) and 9am (daily). If you miss these there's another at noon on Sunday or 1.15pm during the week. Alight at the stop on the southeastern edge of the village or in the village itself. If you need to stay over in Limone to make the earlier bus, try **Hotel Sole** (☎ 0365 95 40 55; Via Lungolago Marconi 36; per person €42) with tastefully decorated, spacious rooms, many with a lake view and buffet breakfast.

Limone sul Garda (finish)
Regular **ferries** (www.navigazionelaghi.it) link Limone with Malcesine. Check the time of the final crossing before you start the walk. Ferries also run to Desenzano and Peschiera.

VALLE DEL SINGOL

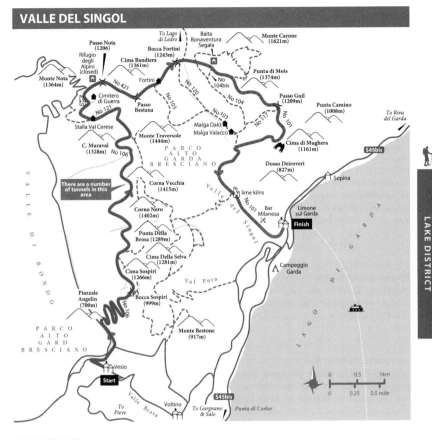

THE WALK

From the southeastern (lower) edge of Vesio, walk northwest for about 600m to a T-junction, then right along Via Orsino to a major junction where a road leads north (to Passo Nota) and where there is a car park and picnic area. Follow Via Dalvra northeast for 100m to a bend and continue on a gravel road signposted Sentiero Angelini. About 50m further along, turn left between stables and fields, a red and white sign reassuringly indicating that you are on Route No 106 to Passo Nota, now a wide gravel road through forest. The road gains height in a stack of tight bends; once it levels out (below Bocca Sospiri) you can begin to appreciate the dramatic views of rugged mountains surrounding Valle di Bondo to the west. After about two hours of generally

very scenic walking, with some fine views of Valle di Bondo and the surrounding rugged peaks, the road burrows through six tunnels in quick succession, all between 20m and 30m long.

About 30 minutes' walk from the last tunnel brings you to a point about 800m north of the point where the path from Monte Traversole meets the track on the right, and a junction. Bear left (west) downhill along Route No 121 (Path No 102 to the right bypasses the wartime cemetery ahead). Pass **Stalla Val Cerese** on the left, used to shelter grazing animals. About 700m from the junction, opposite some ruined stone buildings and beside a picnic site with an enormous barbecue fireplace, is a path on the right, discreetly signed to **Cimitero di Guerra**. The cemetery is about 200m from the road, at one side of a peaceful meadow, and contains graves and memorials to officers and men who died during WWI (25 minutes from the junction).

Return to the main track and continue northwards. A few hundred metres further on you come to a major junction; bear right on Route No 421 towards Bocca Fortini. The wide gravel road soon crosses **Passo Nota**, site of the now closed Rifugio degli Alpini. Continue steeply up over **Passo di Bestana** and bear right on Route No 421. The road descends gently past scattered *fortini* (barracks, gun emplacements and other wartime paraphernalia), remnants of WWI defences. Continue past a signposted junction to Lago di Ledro at **Bocca Fortini**; about 300m further on, Sentiero Tosi Agostino, Route No 105 to Monte Carone, takes off to the left. This is a *via ferrata* (iron way).

After another 250m you reach **Baita Bonaventura Segala** (an hour from the cimitero). Built by the local ANA in the shadow of Monte Carone, this is a smallish place in the style of a *rifugio* (mountain hut), open to walkers on a first-come, first-served basis. Visitors are asked to stay for one night only and to leave a donation in an honesty box. It has a gas cooker and lighting; bottled water, beer and wine are provided (payment goes into the honesty box). Contact the tourist office in Limone for up-to-date information about the water supply.

Continue along the road generally southeast, beneath the towering cliffs of Punta di Mois, across **Passo Guil** and on to Route No 101. This path winds down through cliffs and woodland into Valle del Singol, past some ruins of **old lime kilns**, to **Bar Milanesa**, a pleasant place for a drink and excellent apple strudel (1¾ hours from Baita Segala). Continue down the road, which becomes Via Caldogno, to the junction with the main road (Via IV Novembre) in **Limone** (another 30 or so minutes).

LAGO DI COMO

Lago di Como is where the rich and famous spend their holidays reclining beside stunning Italianate villas. Meanwhile, away from the lakeside shenanighans, the not-so-rich ply a network of not-so-famous hiking paths that contour the lake's sparkling shoreline and its surrounding mountains.

In terms of trail organisation, Como trumps its two watery neighbours with an emblematic long-distance hike, the 125km Via dei Monti Lariani (p137) which parallels the lake's western shore. On its journey north it bisects two distinct areas separated by Val Menaggio which extends from the head of Lago di Lugano (partly in Switzerland) to Como's shore. South of this valley the topography is quite complex; to the north, a mighty horseshoe-shaped ridge rises from Menaggio and sweeps north, via Monte Cardinello (2521m) and eastwards down to the head of the lake.

The small town of Menaggio is the base for the walks described here. Its accessible hinterland offers perhaps the widest variety of walks in any one compact area around Lago di Como. All the walks, from a leisurely stroll along Torrente Sanagra to an ascent of one of the peaks, share scenic landscapes replete with evidence of a long history of settlement, with striking, mostly harmonious contrasts between old and new. The paths and mule tracks surviving from centuries of high-level summer grazing, and still used for this purpose, are ideal for walking – for pleasure rather than necessity.

ENVIRONMENT

Lago di Como's origins are glacial; a few million years ago, the Adda glacier carved out the upper lake basin, then split on either side of a promontory to cut the two arms which give the lake its inverted-Y shape. Two rivers flow into the lake in the north – the Mera and the Adda. The latter is the sole outlet from Lago di Lecco, the eastern arm. The stem of the Y is sometimes called Lago di Colico; the name Como commonly applies to the western arm, and to the lake as a whole, though Lario (the older name, from the Roman Lacus Larionus) is also used. Como has the longest shoreline of the three lakes – more than 270km – and enters the record book as Italy's deepest lake with a depth of 410m near **Argegno** on the western arm.

Geologically, the Como basin is an area of both limestone and crystalline (gneiss) rocks. Monte Grona, above Menaggio, is the northernmost of the dolomitic (limestone) peaks in the southern pre-Alps.

The Como basin's mild climate is ideal for the cultivation of olives and vines and of colourful flowering shrubs in many towns around the shores. In the extensive deciduous woodlands on the steep mountainsides, sweet chestnut and oaks are prominent, many of massive proportions; there are also hazel, silver birch and beech.

The limestone country supports a colourful variety of flora. In early spring, trumpet gentians, spring heath and rock mezereon brighten the rocky ground. In summer, clusters of the well-named yellow globeflower, the orange lily and columbine stand out among dozens of species readily seen.

PLANNING
When to Walk
Spring and autumn are the best times to visit the area; snow lingers on the highest peaks until early June. Thunderstorms and heavy rain are likely from June until September. During July and August, the warmest months, the lakeside towns are very crowded.

What to Bring
If you're camping, bring plenty of fuel for your stove as it can be difficult to source locally.

Maps
The best available map is the Kompass 1:50,000 map No 91 *Lago di Como, Lago di Lugano*, which comes with a booklet in Italian and German. It's useful for general orientation but unreliable for the location of paths, showing many which do not exist.

The marking of paths can be infuriatingly inconsistent. You can find markers lavishly and unnecessarily painted on trees, rocks and walls, but entirely lacking, obscurely placed or overgrown at crucial junctions, in a maze of village alleys or around featureless meadows. Even so, it's better to stick to the marked paths, rather than hope that a beguiling line on a map will lead to where you want to go.

Weather Information
Phone the **Swiss Meteorological Service** (☎ 0041 91 162) for local weather forecasts in Italian and German.

ACCESS TOWN
Menaggio (p140), a small but elegant town on the shores of Lake Como, makes an excellent base for both of the following hikes.

MONTE GRONA

Duration 4½–5 hours
Distance 9km
Difficulty moderate
Start/Finish Breglia
Nearest Town Menaggio (p140)
Transport bus
Summary A steep climb to a rocky summit is rewarded by magnificent panoramic views of Lago di Como and the surrounding mountains.

Steep-sided Monte Grona glowers like a craggy faced old man above the town of Menaggio and Lake Como. While its tree-filled lower reaches are innocuous enough, the stony upper sections are precipitous and narrow, and probably best avoided by those with unsure feet or a real fear of heights. Lower down, the walk to the idyllically located Rifugio Menaggio is relatively straightforward, while easy passage to the surreal Sant'Amate chapel can be made by branching right on a path lower down. If you're a part-time mountain goat eager to escape from another day of lazy Como villa–gazing, challenging Grona could be just the antidote you've been searching for.

The Alternative Finish to Menaggio (p129) is a pleasantly varied alternative to catching the bus and is not unduly strenuous.

PLANNING
What to Bring
Water is available at *sorgenti* (drinking fountains) between Breglia and the Rifugio Menaggio, and at the *rifugio* itself.

GETTING TO/FROM THE WALK
The **SPT** (☎ 031 24 71 11; www.sptlinea .it) bus route C13 links Menaggio (Piazza Garibaldi) and Breglia (1.40, 25 minutes, nine daily). Buy tickets in Menaggio at the newsagent in Piazza Garibaldi.

THE WALK
From the bus stop in Breglia, walk up the road signposted to Rifugio Menaggio. After

LAKE DISTRICT

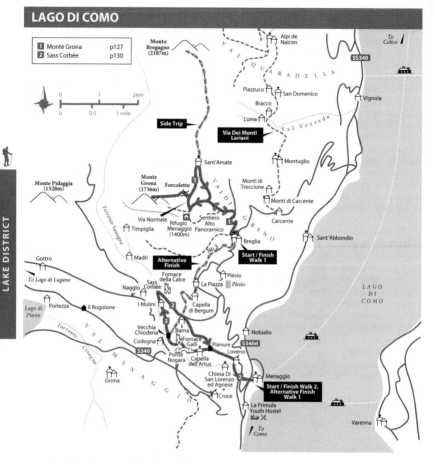

LAGO DI COMO

1	Monte Grona	p127
2	Sass Corbée	p130

a couple of bends, turn right up a path sign-posted to the *rifugio*. The path soon crosses a paved road and ascends a track for 50m or so before turning right by a white house with a large gate. In a couple of minutes you'll join the road again. Follow it up for approximately 200m before turning left by a red and white marker. This takes you up past some small houses and meets the road twice more. On the first occasion cross it; on the second turn right to a *sorgente* (spring) and picnic tables in a more open area. A sign behind the *sorgente* directs you up on a path that crosses the contact zone between greyish crystalline rocks and the smooth, grey-white limestone (dolomite). After crossing the now narrow road a

couple more times the path to the *rifugio* leads off to the left. Within 20 minutes you come to a junction where the return path from Sant'Amate rejoins the main route. Keep left and the path will soon leave the spur and make a fine rising contour around a valley, up to the *rifugio* (1¼ to 1½ hours from Breglia).

Rifugio Menaggio (☎ 0344 372 82; www.rifugiomenaggio.eu; B&B/half-board/full board €25/40/50; open mid-Jun–mid-Sep plus weekends & holidays year-round) offers lunch, snacks and drinks during the day.

Directly above the *rifugio*, prominent red and yellow signs indicate the way to the Forcoletto and Monte Grona, via two routes: the Via Direttissima (which ascends very steeply) and the Via Normale. Fork right on the Via Normale, a steep but manageable push up to **Forcoletto**, the saddle on the ridge linking Monte Grona and Monte Bregagno. Turn left on the ridge and scramble over some small crags. After several minutes the path divides to cross Monte Grona's northern face. The upper and lower paths are both very narrow and exposed and offer no hand support. If the weather is bad, or if you are not extremely sure of foot, do not attempt this last section. The two paths reunite at a small gap just short of the summit's rock tower. A firmly anchored wire cable provides some assistance for the final climb to the top of **Monte Grona** (an hour from the *rifugio*). A topographic plate marks out the surrounding peaks.

Return to Forcoletto and head northeast and north towards **Sant'Amate**, along a clear path on or just below the ridge crest. From the old chapel, take on the Side Trip to Monte Bregagno, or take the descent path, signposted to Breglia. It crosses the steep grassy eastern flank of the ridge. About 30 minutes walk brings you back to the path you took up to the *rifugio*. Breglia is 50 minutes to an hour further on. If you're walking all the way to Menaggio (see Alternative Finish), you need to turn off southwest just before you reach the main road in Breglia.

SIDE TRIP: MONTE BREGAGNO
1½ hours, 6km, 600m ascent

From **Sant'Amate chapel**, follow the way-marked path up the grassy ridge north to the crucifix-topped summit. The highlights of the stunning view are Lago di Como, almost at your feet, and Monte Rosa on the western skyline.

ALTERNATIVE FINISH: MENAGGIO
2 hours, 7.5km, 100m ascent, 650m descent

This alternative to catching a bus back to Menaggio starts at a path junction on the road from Rifugio Menaggio. Just above the main road in **Breglia**, beside a large tree, turn southwest down a lane with a red and white Route No 3 waymarker (Via dei Monti Lariani). After a few minutes, bear left where there's a sign to Sorgente Chiarella; the path soon leads into woodland. Cross a stream, then don't be tempted to go down to the left at a junction but ascend on the main path. About 150m past a *sorgente* bear left to pass below a white, two-storey stone house. A wide track then leads into woodland and descends to a road. Turn left and go down to **La Piazza**, a scattering of mostly old stone houses fringing some meadows.

GRAND VILLAS & RUINED MILLS

The elegant shorelines of Lake Como glisten with architectural masterpieces from multiple eras; but it is the baroque and neoclassical periods that define it best.

At centre stage lie the large stash of palatial villas that embellish towns such as Bellagio; a haul that dates back to days of Roman sage, Pliny the Younger. Pliny built his mythic mansion *Tragedia* in the 1st century AD on a promontory now occupied by the 17th-century Villa Serbelloni. If you're ferrying north from Como en route for the Menaggio hikes, the resplendence of the assembled *palazzi* on this stretch of the lake shore is positively dazzling.

With most of the walking paths emanating from the town of Menaggio, villa-admiring hikers have ample opportunity to cast an eye over some early modern Italian classics. The pick of the bunch reside in Loveno, a Menaggio suburb stacked up like a jewel box on a leafy hill overlooking the lake. The Villa Vigoni near the start of the Sass Corbée hike is now a German-Italian cultural centre. Meanwhile, down on the lakeside, the Gran Hotel Menaggio recalls a gentler more refined era when well-to-do travellers with parasols and Baedeker guides strolled on its manicured waterside lawns.

Further up the valley, history takes a less grandiose turn alongside the Sanagra River, where old water mills, blast furnaces and lime kilns hark back to a short-lived industrial renaissance in the early part of the 20th century. The popular Sass Corbée hike has a number of interactive information boards that provide history buffs with a lowdown on the erstwhile milling industry.

Next, pass the roadside **Capella di Bergum**. About eight minutes further on, go left around a bend (not straight ahead) and up. Only 12m further on, drop down to the right, with a house on the left, on a narrow path that drops to the edge of the village of **Barna**. At a T-junction turn right and descend. Below a gushing fountain, turn left to reach the church piazza. Cross this, passing a small war memorial, and go right along a path (with Casa del Padre Mio on the left), down between houses then diagonally right across a small piazza and along a cobbled lane for about 30m. Take the second turn left, down to a stream, but don't cross it. Instead, turn left and continue down to a wide track which drops to a road at **La Chioderia Vecchia** where you can stop for a beer inside the well-preserved old building (once a nail factory) or outside under trees. Then follow the path beside Torrente Sanagra to a bridge and go up to the left along a vehicle track which eventually takes you to the open expanses of **Pianure**. Continue down the road from here. Beyond the sports centre, turn right down Piazza Wacks Mylius, past the large **Chiesa di San Lorenzo ed Agnese** and on to a junction with an *alimentari* on the left. Walk down Via N Sauro for about 30m then go right, down a steep path. At the bottom turn right along the road, and take the first left beyond the bridge over Torrente Sanagra, up a path (Via Castellino), now in **Menaggio**, which takes you down to Via Calvi – at the far end of which is Piazza Garibaldi.

SASS CORBÉE

Duration 10km
Distance 3 hours
Difficulty easy–moderate
Start/Finish Menaggio (p140)
Transport bus, ferry

Summary A short interactive walk through the attractive suburb of Loveno up into a secluded river valley characterised by its ruined 19th-century industrial mills.

A short hike with a surprising number of historical twists, this easy-ish urban/rural ramble off Lake Como incorporates the popular resort of Menaggio, the villa-sprinkled domain of Loveno, plus a brief foray into the Senagra River valley with its broad-leafed deciduous foliage and rather interesting milling history.

The walk is relatively straightforward save for an energetic (and sometimes wet) scramble up a small gorge on the north side of Sass Corbée (steps and some handrails are provided). The section along the river is well-trammelled and furnished with a number of interactive signs that provide explanations on the various local sights, including a mill, a chapel, an old lime kiln and a former nail-making factory. To avoid the gorge climb and earn the hike an easy rating, try doing it as a straight out and back from Menaggio with a turn around at Sass Corbée.

PLANNING
Maps
The Kompass 1:50,000 No 91 *Lago di Como* shows the route in very generalised fashion. Back it up with the *A Piedi nei Dintorni di Menaggio* booklet from Menaggio's IAT office (p140) which has an alternative description of the walk along with a trail map of the local area, including Sass Corbée.

GETTING TO/FROM THE WALK
The walk starts in Menaggio on the shores of Lake Como. For access information see p139.

THE WALK
From the attractive Piazza Garibaldi in **Menaggio**, take Via Calvi inland from the lake. Cross a road, and head up Via Caronti to the left of the parish church of Santo Stefano. After 150m turn right and then, almost immediately, left into Via Castelino da Castello, an old cobbled street that bends uphill past some beautiful portals. Go under an archway and past the 17th-century church of San Carlo, before turning right at a main road. The road bends back briefly before crossing the Sanagra River on a modern bridge. A little further on you can cut off another bend by taking the steps up to the right of the Hotel Loveno. On rejoining the road turn left and follow it for another 150m before turning left again into a lane, signposted 'Pianure'. The lane becomes cobbled and passes some villas before joining a paved road, where

you turn left once more. This wider road winds up through the affluent neighbourhood of **Loveno** with its sparkling villas and postcard Lake Como views. After about 10 minutes you'll spy the **Chiesa di San Lorenzo ed Agnese** (1641) on the left, luring you inside with its shade, silence, and stunning ceiling frescoes.

A little further on the buildings give way to **Pianure** (also known as Piamuro) a large pasture with a noticeboard and small parking area. Continue straight ahead on the dirt track and cut through some trees to the **Capella dell'Artus**. From here the track heads downhill to the Sanagra River and the hump-back **Ponte Nogara** and mill. Do not cross the bridge, but take the path on the near side of the river past the **Fornace Galli** (an old lime kiln) to the **Vecchia Chioderia**, a former mill and nail-making factory that is now an *agriturismo* (farm-stay accommodation) and trout farm. Continue on the path to the right of the building past the trout ponds, and head towards the *borgo* (old town) of **Mulini**, an old milling settlement of about 10 small houses. Cross the bridge here and follow the path on the other side of the water to **Sass Corbée** where giant boulders lie strewn across the river. After crossing the river, a ladder and steps provide some aid in climbing up the boulders on the other side. It's a bit of a scramble on a narrow path after this (take care if the rocks are wet), but you'll quickly find yourself back on firmer ground at a junction next to the **Fornace della Calce** (another old lime kiln). Turn right here, along a path through trees that cuts along the side of the river gulley getting progressively wider as it descends. After about 30 minutes walking from the **fornace** you'll reach the village of **Barna** entering by the Via della Terragna. Take the steps down to the right by a house and *sorgente* (highlighted by a green marker). Follow the red and white markers around the parish church and, after 150m, go right on Via Belvedere by a noticeboard with a large trail map. Keep straight on this road until it bends right at a sign saying 'Azienda Agricola'. Ignore the road and turn left onto a grassy track. After approximately 300m veer left onto a narrow path that runs parallel with the wider track. The path passes a shrine on the left and becomes cobbled as it starts to zigzag downhill. It will eventually bring you out at Pianure,

from where you can retrace your steps back down to Piazza Garibaldi in Menaggio.

LAGO MAGGIORE

Lago Maggiore is the most demure of the three lakes. While Lago di Garda hosts Gardaland and Como breeds billionaires, tourism is much less pervasive here – you'll see people going about their everyday lives, growing vegetables, cutting grass, and coppicing chestnut trees. There are mountains too, less dramatic than Como's stash, but eye-catching all the same with their steep tree-covered slopes extending well into Switzerland on the lake's northern shores. The walks in this section centre on the old Piedmontese town of Cannobio, at the entrance to Valle Cannobina where a network of age-old paths offers many opportunities for both easy and strenuous walks. Make sure you take a ferry ride on the lake, to fully appreciate the town's superb setting at the end of its long wooded valley.

ENVIRONMENT

At 65km, Lago Maggiore is the longest of the three lakes, but it is also deceptively slender – no more than 4km at its widest point.

Glacial in origin, its main feeders are Fiume Ticino, coming in from the north and carrying through to become the only outflow at Sesto Calende; Fiume Toce, flowing from the west to a bay between Verbania and Stresa; and Fiume Tresa to the east, which arrives at Luino via Lago di Lugano. The highest and most rugged peaks are in the north and northwest, set well back from the lake: Limidario (2187m) on the Swiss border, flanked by the towering rock walls of the Gridone, and Monte Zeda (2156m) in Parco Nazionale della Val Grande, well west of the small town of Cannero Riviera. Elsewhere, the ranges around the lake are much lower and make for less dramatic, though still very attractive, landscape.

Chestnuts dominate the extensive woodlands on the mountainsides, accompanied by oaks, beech, European larch and rhododendrons. For centuries chestnuts were a valuable resource in the valleys although an immense amount of effort was involved in harvesting them, removing the husks, drying them in special buildings, then

WAYSIDE SHRINES

Throughout the mountains around Lago Maggiore (and in many other parts of the country), in villages and at roadsides, wayside shrines testify to the importance of religious belief in people's lives. Some are simple – just a crucifix on a stone base. Others are elaborate structures the size of a small room, with altar and cloth, frescoes, statues, flowers and candles.

In Valle Cannobina, numerous shrines were built on the orders of San Carlo, Archbishop of Milan (1564–1584). A great reformer, he devised a hierarchy of shrines (or sanctuaries), churches, chapels and crosses to bear witness to the divine presence in people's lives.

Near the old settlement of Bronte, high above the valley, is a particularly interesting shrine, visited on the Valle Cannobina walk (see below). Timber-roofed, it spans the path and protects a weather-beaten wooden crucifix. A sign explains that this was once carried in processions between the Monday and Wednesday before Pentecost (a Christian festival 50 days after Easter). On the Tuesday, the route followed was from a church high in the valley of Rio di Orasso, a tributary of Torrente Cannobina, a few kilometres northwest of the shrine. The procession then moved towards La Piazza (east of Olzeno above Rio Cavaglio), then to two other localities and back to the shrine, whereupon celebrations began.

removing an outer skin and finally an inner skin protecting the precious kernel. This was then pounded into a fine flour.

Around the lake shores, the mild climate fosters the cultivation of citrus groves and the widespread growth of palms and oleanders in public gardens and along promenades.

PLANNING
When to Walk

None of the walks described here goes above 1800m, so the best times to visit are May to early July, and September to early October; July and August are the busiest and warmest months.

Many of the signposts at junctions and other crucial places along the paths in the area show the average time to the named destination. The pace is often inconsistent – it's easy to match or better some and difficult to match others.

Maps

The locally published 1:25,000 map *Valle Cannobina, Itinerari Escursionistici* shows the routes of numerous waymarked paths and is the best one for this area.

The Kompass 1:50,000 map No 90 *Lago Maggiore, Lago di Varese* is useful for general orientation.

These maps and others can be purchased at the APT office in Cannobio (p138) and at various shops in the town, notably the *libreria* at the southern end of Piazza Indipendenza.

PLACE NAMES

There are differences between the spelling of many names on the various maps and the signposts on the ground. Here the signpost version is given first, followed by the *Valle Cannobina, Itinerari Escursionistici* map version.

ACCESS TOWN

Clustered at the mouth of the Valle Cannobina beneath the misty knoll of Monte Carza, Cannobio (p138) is the starting point for both of the following walks and is a charming place to stay.

VALLE CANNOBINA

Duration 8–9 hours
Distance 25km
Difficulty moderate
Start/Finish Cannobio (p138)
Transport bus, ferry

Summary An ancient network of superbly built paths winding up the valley, past timeless villages, delicate shrines and remains of old settlements in extensive woodlands.

The tree-covered slopes of the mountains around Cannobio present a dark and mysterious veneer. To find out what's underneath (and there's plenty) you need to venture off into the lush Valle Cannobina on ancient, winding paths at one time frequented by medieval friars and archbishops.

Hidden beneath a seemingly endless canopy of rustling beeches is the ruined Santo Miracolo chapel with its 16th-century frescoes, a smattering of mossy war memorials, and the somnolent communes of Gurrone, Spoccia and Cavaglio.

The walk has a total elevation of 1340m and the wooded stony paths can be slippery after rain. To take it at a more leisurely pace, it's possible to do it in two stages, breaking at Spoccia, which isn't too far from a bus route to/from Cannobio. The bus stops at Ponte Spoccia, which is reached by a path (800m in distance and 200m in descent) that starts just west of the village. There is an early afternoon bus to Cannobio (Mon-Fri) and from Cannobio to Ponte Spoccia (Thu mornings).

GETTING TO/FROM THE WALK

For Cannobio's access information see p138.

THE WALK

From **Cannobio** set out from the southern end of the bridge on the main road over Torrente Cannobino and follow a riverside path to a footbridge; cross it and bear diagonally to right, along Casali Masserecci, a paved lane through the houses. At an intersection with Via Madonna delle Grazie turn left. At the next T-junction turn right and follow Via Vitt Emanuele around to a church and small roundabout. Turn left here along Via alle Parrocchia and left again at a fork to bring you into the diminutive Piazza Municipale with its war memorial. Follow Via Sant'Anna at the far end to the car park where some CAI signs point up a cobbled tree-covered footpath by a large shrine (about 30 minutes from Cannobio).

The path leads up into woodland and soon settles down to contour above the gorge of Torrente Cannobino passing the mossy **Capella del Santo Miracolo** with its 16th-century frescoes. Eventually it descends to cross Rio Cavaglio then zigzags up to a road; turn right to reach **Cavaglio** (two hours from Cannobio). Signposts opposite a small war memorial indicate the direction to Gurrone, initially along a lane then up a very quiet road. **Gurrone** is a compact village of traditional stone and timber houses, 30 minutes from Cavaglio.

LAGO MAGGIORE

| 1 | Valle Cannobina | p132 |
| 2 | Monte Carza | p134 |

Follow a sign to Spoccia, then bear left along a narrow grassy path (not signposted) at the edge of the village by an old building with an overhanging wooden balcony. A few hundred metres further on fork left at a junction, then, after 30m, go right towards Spoccia (signposted). The path wanders up and down and contours past scattered stone buildings. Nearly an hour from Gurrone you come to a topographic plate naming the prominent features in the view, including Monte Zeda to the southwest and the village of Orasso to the northwest. Further on, beyond a few stream crossings, go up to a road; cross diagonally and ascend a bit more to emerge by **Spoccia's** war memorial (nearly two hours from Gurrone) and a *sorgente* (spring).

Nearby signs point the way onwards – head for Bronte, and again at the next junction, and soon you're above the village car park. Continue up steps and along the path above the car park. The broad path leads on across a stream and up, soon past a beautifully kept shrine associated with a traditional Pentecost procession (see p132). At the next junction continue left towards Bronte up a steep climb. Further on, skirt a meadow and continue to gain height to the hamlet of **Bronte** (an hour from Spoccia).

Follow a narrow path up, behind a building housing an aerial cableway (signposted Tre Confini), then pass below some stone houses and turn left behind another disused stone house. Contour the slope just above some trees; cross a stream and continue briefly through trees, then go up to a path junction. Continue more or less ahead towards **Tre Confini** (a path junction in the trees). It's up most of the way to this saddle on a long timbered spur (about 45 minutes from Bronte). From here follow the widest path to the right towards **Le Biuse**. The path becomes a vehicle track at this scattered settlement, where most of the houses have been restored – complete with solar heating panels! Contine down on the vehicle track which becomes paved. About 300m after the paving starts head right (no sign) by a triangular fenced enclosure along a grassy path towards the restored village of **Olzeno** visible in front of you (40 minutes from Tre Confini). Follow waymarkers between houses and at a small building with a sloping roof (the one-time washing place),

turn sharp right, pass a small chapel and some vegetable gardens, before making for a cableway building (actually a public toilet), from where a clear path descends to a road. Cross the road and set out on a long descent, via stone steps, to **Cavaglio** (an hour from Olzeno). Here, take the narrow paved road as it zigzags down to a bridge over the Torrente Cannobino. Turn left onto the Valle Cannobina road and follow it to a point approximately 300m past the 'Cannobio 3km' marker (45 minutes from Cavaglio). Go through the gap in the guard rail (red and white marker) down some steps and left on the paved road at the bottom. This road leads to the **Chiesa di Sant'Anna** where it crosses the river and leads back up to the car park. From here retrace your steps to the start.

MONTE CARZA

Duration 5½–5¾ hours
Distance 11km
Difficulty moderate
Start/Finish Cannobio (p138)
Transport bus, ferry

Summary An age-old church and somnolent village, long lake views with a fine mountain summit, meadows and magnificent chestnut woodlands.

Carza (1116m) is no Mont Blanc, or Marmolada for that matter, but if you want to bag a modest peak and get down in time for lunch, it's a highly satisfying substitute. Starting handily from downtown Cannobio, most of the mountain's well-marked paths are under tree cover, though you'll emerge briefly to spy the antiquated façade of the Carmine Superiore pilgrim's village and the stately plaza in Vigione. The view from the summit is surprisingly vast thanks to Carza's imposing lakeside location and well worth the energy expenditure.

GETTING TO/FROM THE WALK

For information on how to get to Cannobio see p138.

THE WALK

From the southern end of the centre of Cannobio set out along the main Valle Cannobina road (S631); about 200m along, turn left along signposted Via Cuserina then shortly left up Casali Bagnara to a sharp bend, where it's left again towards Viggiona (avoiding the sign for Mt Carza via the more direct return route). The path ascends into chestnut woodland. About 25 minutes from Cannobio, bear right along a wider track and go up to a road. Walk up past a house surrounded by a high fence and turn left along a lane signposted to Trarego-Viggiona. The ascent continues, past restored farmhouses, to the hamlet of **Mulinesc** (Molineggi). A fine path then takes you up to a junction – continue straight on towards Carmine Superiore (or turn right here for the Alternative Route, p136). Then it's mostly down until you reach **Carmine Superiore** (see boxed text below). Cross a small stream to a path junction. To visit the church go left here, up steps to the piazza in front of the 14th-century building (about one to 1½ hours from Cannobio).

From the junction, walk up a cobbled alley; then turn right at the next two junctions. (At the second junction continue straight if you're descending to Cannero Riviera on the Alternative Finish, p136) A steep and initially overgrown ascent through trees brings you, after 50 minutes, to a cobbled lane; turn left to Piazza Pasque in **Viggiona**. To reach the shop and bar in Piazza Vittorio Veneto, walk up Via Tarchetti and take the first left (Via Luigi Canones), which leads to the piazza.

Return to Via Tarchetti and follow it for about 200m, then bear right in front of a three-storey house. Go up a few steps then left around the back of some stone buildings to pick up the path. It's vague at first but you'll soon spot the red and white markers. Ascend to a house with a narrow driveway. Turn right, progressing around the house and pick up the path again heading uphill. At a junction where a small sign points right to Madonnina, turn left. A narrow path gains height through trees, crosses a small meadow and brings you to a junction where you bear right towards **Pro Redond** (about 45 minutes from Viggiona). A superb path leads on across a deep gorge to Pro Redond's open spaces and a large farmhouse. Follow a prominently waymarked path (signposted

---

HIDDEN FRESCOES & HIGH CHAPELS

In the crowded Italian Lakes region you're never far from the bold mark of civilisation, even on the myriad of hiking trails. But, while the human ubiquity may sometimes infringe upon the area's budding wilderness credentials, it throws up some serendipitous historical surprises.

With its lower slopes covered in broccoli-like beech forest, the mountainous terrain around Cannobio on Lake Maggiore hides many man-made secrets. Beneath the thick canopy of the Valle Cannobina, an old stone path trail-blazed by erstwhile Archbishop of Milan, San Carlo Borromeo, in 1574 meanders quietly past the ruined Capella del Santo Miracolo (p133) where faded 16th-century frescoes glimmer mysteriously in the dark wood.

Higher up, soporific villages, such as Cavaglio, Gurrone, and Spoccia, emerge like medieval mirages out of the dense foliage; their narrow alleyways silent save for the meows of slinking cats, their piazzas like microcosms of another era.

Perhaps the most quintessential settlement is the tiny village of Carmine Superiore on the Monte Carza walk that overlooks Lago Maggiore from an unrivalled perch between Cannobio and Cannero Riviera. Solidly built houses, separated by tight passageways, cluster intimately around a large church. Some of the houses are empty and decaying; many more have been faithfully restored. This renaissance has helped to reverse the seemingly terminal decline of the village after many residents left during the interwar years. Superiore refers to the village's location above Carmine Inferiore, not to its alleged status.

Carmine and its church of San Gottardo stand on a site first occupied more than 1000 years ago. Construction of the church began in 1300 and was completed a century or more later. The church was the heart of the village and a safe haven for the inhabitants in times of strife. Frescoes by Lombard artisans dating from the late 14th century still adorn the outside and interior of the church. Those outside are now very faded but the faint colours of the images on the cream walls still convey much of their beauty.

Mt Carza) steeply up to the left to a vehicle track on a wide ridge. The grassy summit of **Monte Carza** isn't much further on, to the left (45 minutes from Pro Redond). It's a magnificent view – the vastness of Lago Maggiore, mountains in most directions, and high-level villages punctuating the deep green woodlands clothing the slopes.

Return to Pro Redond then head down the path signposted to Cannobio. Turn right below the lone house on a wide path, and then, after a couple of minutes, go sharp left downhill (not signposted) keeping a river and gulley to your left. About 30 minutes from Pro Redond, turn left at a junction and sign 'Cannobio 40mins'. At the next junction the 'Sorgente' spring is signposted off to the left. Fork right and descend, still in woodland, keeping a fence to your left. You will soon hit a vehicle track; turn right on it for 40m, then left down a path. Cross another vehicle track and keep to the path down to it again; this time turn right along it for 250m. Bear left on a wide path that, within 50m, delivers you to **Il Laghetto** (474m) where a signposted path points down to Cannobio. Turn left on the vehicle track one more time and then left on a marked trail down to **Piate** (345m). From here signs point down to your start point just above the Valle Cannobina road, on the edge of **Cannobio**, nearly 1½ hours from Pro Redond.

ALTERNATIVE ROUTE: MULINESC TO VIGGIONA
45 minutes–1 hour, 2km, 240m ascent
If time is short or you'd prefer a less strenuous route, you can bypass Carmine Superiore and go direct from Mulinesc to Viggiona. At the junction above **Mulinesc** turn right. Follow the path up through woodland and eventually past Viggiona's 13th-century church and the adjacent cemetery, and along a lane lined with small shrines to Piazza Pasque in **Viggiona**, where you can rejoin the main walk.

ALTERNATIVE FINISH: CANNERO RIVIERA
1 hour, 3.75km
For an easier day out and to reach Cannero Riviera, worth a look in its own right, head generally south from Carmine Superiore. Follow the waymarked path from the northern edge of the hamlet, down through

trees to the main lakeside road, just east of Cannero Riviera. Cross diagonally, descend steps to a lane and go on to the lakeside. The **ASPAN** (☎ 0323 51 87 11) bus service from Verbania Intra to Brissago passes through Cannero Riviera and will take you back to Cannobio (€0.85, 12 minutes, about hourly). Alternatively, catch the **ferry** (€3.70; 1.55pm, 4.55pm and 6.20pm).

MORE WALKS

LAGO DI GARDA
Val Dritta
From above Lago di Garda, the connoisseur's approach to Cima Valdritta on the Monte Baldo Range must surely be via the awesome Val Dritta immediately to the west of the peak. The valley could also provide the descent route from the peak, having climbed it via the ridge route from the Monte Baldo *funivia*, as described in the Monte Baldo walk (p121). The 16km (six to 6½ hour) walk offers beautiful beech woods and stupendous views across Lago di Garda. The amount of ascent involved, even by starting from the San Michele *funivia* station, is formidable: 1270m to La Guardiola overlooking Val Dritta and another 270m to the main ridge. The Kompass 1:25,000 map No 690 *Alto Garda e Ledro* covers this walk.

This is definitely a route for experienced and confident walkers; the valley holds snow late, so walking poles or an ice axe are essential. If you don't have the experience or the equipment, it would be a beautiful walk just up to the valley and back – a real sense of wildness and unspoiled beauty, no power lines, roads or ski tows.

Valle del Singol & Val Pura
Though it doesn't reach any high points, this is a magnificently scenic loop from Limone, into an awesome valley with the most amazing and improbable path in the area. It involves a couple of minor scrambles, one of which bypasses the crossing of a cliff face where a cable is insecurely fixed to the rock, and a steep descent on a scree-covered path into Val Pura. Allow about four hours for the 8.5km walk; the ascent totals 950m. Carry either the Kompass 1:25,000 No 690 *Alto Garda e Ledro* or

the local 1:12,500 *Limone sul Garda* map; neither shows the junction of Path Nos 110 and 109 correctly.

Valle del Singol Alternative

Another highly scenic route around the rim of Valle del Singol is possible. It is more strenuous, but takes less time, than the Valle del Singol walk (p124). Starting and finishing at Limone, it covers 16km and involves about 1500m ascent; allow at least 6½ hours. The paths are well waymarked; carry either the local 1:12,500 *Limone sul Garda* map or the Kompass 1:25,000 No 690 *Alto Garda e Ledro*, though the latter's path numbers and junctions are inaccurate. The route takes you to the foot of Mt Traversole (worth climbing for the magnificent view), to the saddle between Corna Vecchia and Corno Nero, to Baita Segala and back to Limone via the meadows of Malga Dalo and Malgo Valacco.

Monte Carone

The highest peak overlooking Valle Singol, Monte Carone (1621m), can be reached on a 13km day walk from Limone. Allow about seven hours return; it involves about 1600m ascent. From the summit, with its crucifix and flag pole, the views of the Monte Baldo Range are superb. The Kompass 1:25,000 No 690 *Alto Garda e Ledro* map gives an idea of what's involved but the locally produced 1:12,500 *Limone sul Garda* map is more useful.

LAGO DI COMO
Il Rogolone

This walk tracks the same route as the Sass Corbée hike (p130) until the Nogara bridge where, rather than follow the river, you cross the bridge and follow the mule track up to Codogna. Cross the Naggio road and pick up a walled track that passes the 17th-century Villa Camozzi. The trail then leads into woods, crosses several streams and climbs up to Il Rogolone, a large regal oak in a clearing. Next, take the trail uphill signposted Vezlo. Follow to the right and after 30 minutes a car track will usher you into Vezlo village. Cross the road and follow the track into the centre of the settlement where you veer right along Via Gottro. In the small piazza take Via Leopardi and merge into a mule track that will deliver

you to the church of San Siro. Nearby is Villa Camozzi from where you can retrace your steps to Menaggio.

The route is described in the *A Piedi nei Dintorni di Menaggio* booklet available from the IAT in Menaggio (p140).

Via dei Monti Lariani (Section 3)

Section 3 of the 125km Via dei Monti Lariani begins in Menaggio, but to attempt a decent-sized chunk in a day get the SPT bus from Menaggio out to the village of Breglia (see p127). From the bus stop take the road signposted to Rifugio Menaggio but after 30m turn right along a lane. This soon descends into Val di Greno and takes you to the hamlet of Carcente where a well-graded path leads up through woodland. The rollercoaster trail continues, traversing the mighty eastern and northeastern flanks of Monte Bregagno, before descending into the Val Dongana. Measuring 22.5km in total, this is a long day's walking (bank on eight hours or more) and you'll need to get an early start in order to catch the last bus (6.25pm) back to Menaggio via Dongo from the end point at Garzeno.

The route is relatively well way-marked with red and white markers highlighted with the number '3'. Take Kompass 1:50,000 map 91 *Lago di Como* for a generalised overview along with the special *Via dei Monti Lariani* booklet available at the IAT in Menaggio (p140). It's worth checking trail conditions before you set out as the area is prone to landslides.

LAGO MAGGIORE
Monte Faierone & Monte Giove

Towering over the lower reaches of Valle Cannobina, Monte Faierone (1706m) affords excellent views of Lago Maggiore and the surrounding mountains, and a rare opportunity in the area to enjoy walking through open grassland. Starting from Lignago and finishing in Cannobio, the 14km walk involves 1500m ascent and should take 7½ to eight hours. Take the local 1:25,000 *Valle Cannobina, Itinerari Escursionistici* map, available from the APT office in Cannobio (p138). The route follows waymarked and signposted paths. The bus from Cannobio to Sant'Agata (€0.85, Tue & Fri only) saves you 270m ascent and about 45 minutes.

Monte Giove (1298m) is an outlier of Monte Faierone to the southeast and rises directly from lowermost Valle Cannobina. It also provides excellent panoramic views and a shorter, less strenuous walk than that to Monte Faierone. Allow about six hours; 1100m ascent is involved. It is reached by starting out on the Monte Faierone route, and turning off near Rombiago. Return via Biessen, Sant'Agata and Traffiume.

Crealla & Monti Sommalemna

There are many very well-preserved stone buildings among the chestnut woodlands between Gurrone and Lunecco on the northern side of Valle Cannobina. On the opposite side of the valley, from Crealla to Socraggio, there are also many beautiful shrines, plus superb views of the upper valley. East from Socraggio, paths link several high meadows – reminders of another aspect of the valley's history – affording magnificent views. All this can be linked in a long, 20km day's walk starting and finishing at Traffiume; allow 7¾ to 8¼ hours; 1410m ascent is involved.

The paths are well signposted and waymarked. Though not entirely accurate, the 1:25,000 *Valle Cannobina, Itinerari Escursionistici* map is the one to carry. The walk could also be divided into stages by using the infrequent bus services in Valle Cannobina. Visit the APT office in Cannobio (see below) to buy the map or inquire about bus services to/from Traffiume, Lunecco and Socraggio.

Walk from Cannobio to Cavaglio and Gurrone as per the Valle Cannobina walk (p132). Continue through Lunecco, Crealla (with its beautifully preserved church and shrines), Luena (a deserted hamlet with superb views), Corte and on to peaceful Socraggio. The route then takes in Voiasc (Aurasco), Voia (Monti Voja), the spacious meadows of Monti Sommalemna, and Pianoni before returning to Traffiume.

TOWNS & FACILITIES

CANNOBIO

☎ 0323 / pop 5000

Free of Lake Como's glitz, Cannobio nestles quietly at the mouth of the heavily–wooded Valle Cannobina on the shores of tranquil Lake Maggiore. The historic town centre is heavy with historic ambience but light on tourist tittle-tattle. Both walks in this chapter start from Cannobio within football-kicking distance of the atmospheric lakeshore walkway.

Information

The **IAT office** (☎ 7 12 12; Via Giovanola 25; 9am-noon, 4-7pm Mon-Sat, 9am-noon Sun) is where you can buy maps and bus tickets, and obtain an accommodation brochure and bus timetable.

Supplies & Equipment

For self-catering there's a centrally located **supermarket** (Viale Vittorio Veneto) and a larger **Conad supermarket** (Via Al Lago). There are also several speciality **alimentari** (Via Antonio Giovanola), a good **fruit and vegetable shop** (Via Umberto I) and a deservedly popular **bakery** (Piazza San Vittore).

Sleeping & Eating

On the peninsula between Torrente Cannobino and the lake shore, **Camping Riviera** (☎ 713 60; Via Casali Darbedo; sites €9-13, plus per person €6-8.50, bungalows €77-125) has grassed, shady pitches and excellent facilities. There's an on-site shop (open daily), useful for drinks and bread, and Ristorante Riviera with good pizza. A substantial breakfast is also served.

Hotel del Fiume (☎ 73 91 21; www.hotel delfiume.net; Via Darbedo 26; s/d €54/92), surrounded by a camping ground, has reasonably priced (by local standards) double rooms with terraces giving good views. The Valle Cannobina walk (p132) starts from just outside the entrance.

Other hotels are typically expensive but gorgeous, notably **Hotel Pironi** (☎ 7 06 24; www.pironihotel.it; Via Marconi 35; s €100, d €130-170), centrally located and heavy on antiques, frescoes and medieval columns (the building dates from the 15th century).

Ristorante da Nuccia (☎ 722 93; Via Magistris 43) enjoys perhaps the best views of the several lakeside restaurants. Pizzas laced with garlic go for €8; top up with a generous serve of pasta and finish with an excellent espresso.

Getting There & Away

The easiest way to get to Cannobio is to catch a train from Milan Piazza Garibaldi to Luino (€6, one hour 35 minutes); you have to change at Gallarate. From Luino, **Navigazione Lago Maggiore** (☎ 800 551801; www.navigazione.it) operates a ferry service to Cannobio (€3.40, 17 minutes, 7.45am-6.35pm).

Alternatively, use the Milan Central–Domodossola train service to Stresa (€4.95, one hour 20 minutes, frequent) and then catch a ferry to Cannobio (€8.60, 1½ hours, 10am Wed & Sun, 11.15am, 3.30pm Thu-Tue).

By car, follow the A8/26, which skirts the southern end of Lago Maggiore, and the A8 towards Domodossola. Take the Arona exit to the S34; continue for 27km to Cannobio.

COMO
☎ 031 / pop 78,700

By far the largest settlement on the Italian Lakes, Como makes an elegant alternative to Milan. There's easy ferry access to Menaggio and reasonable trains via Milan to Lakes Maggiore and Garda. The walled city has an interesting cache of historical sights including a striking marble-clad cathedral.

Information
The **tourist office** (☎ 26 97 12; www.lakecomo.org; Piazza Cavour 17; 9am-1pm & 2.30-6pm Mon-Sat, plus 9.30am-1pm Sun Jun-Sep) has good information on both the town and the lake, including ferry schedules. There's a smaller **Info Point** at the bus station.

Sleeping & Eating
Ostello Villa Olmo (☎ 57 38 00; Via di Bellinzona 6; dm incl breakfast €15; meals €10. reception 7-10am & 4pm-midnight, closed Dec-Feb) In a rambling garden right on the lakefront, Como's HI hostel is two doors up from the heritage-listed villa of the same name. There's a midnight curfew but a fun night-time bar.

In Riva al Lago (☎ 30 23 33; www.inrivaallago.com; Piazza di Giaccomo Matteotti 4; s/d without bathroom €38/47, s/d with bathroom €45/63, two-person apt from €70) An unassuming exterior, but pleasing rooms with tile floors and original wood beams make this hotel behind the bus station a decent bargain. There are a handful of apartments for up to five people.

Albergo Posta (☎ 26 60 12; www.hotelposta.net; Via Giuseppe Garibaldi 2; s €52-60, d €68-94;) Basic but clean, Posta's advantages are its central position, economical price and hearty breakfast in a glass panelled downstairs restaurant.

For a dinner treat try **Trattoria dei Combattenti** (☎ 27 05 74; Via Balestra 5/9; meals €20; Wed-Mon) set in the Italian retired servicemen's association, with seating inside or in a sunny gravel yard at the front. Simple but irresistible dishes include an *insalatone* (€9) or the €14 set meal.

Self-caterers can stock up on supplies at **Granmercato** (Piazza Matteotti 3; 8.30am-1pm Sun-Mon, 8.30am-1.30pm & 3.30-7.30pm Tue-Fri, 8am-7.30pm Sat). Fresh fruit, vegetables and delicacies abound at Como's **food market** (8.30am-1pm Tue & Thu, 8.30am-7pm Sat) outside Porta Torre.

Getting There & Away
Trains from Milan's Stazione Centrale and Porta Garibaldi station (€3.60-8.50, 40 minutes to one hour, at least hourly) use Como's main train station (Como San Giovanni) and some continue on into Switzerland. Trains from Milan's Stazione Nord (€3.60, one hour, hourly) use Como's lakeside Stazione FNM (listed on timetables as Como Nord Lago). Change in Milan for trains to Lakes Maggiore and Garda.

Navigazione Lago di Como (☎ 800 551801; www.navigazionelaghi.it; Piazza Cavour) ferries and hydrofoils criss-cross the lake, departing year-round from the jetty at the northern end of Piazza Cavour. Single fares range from €1.90 (Como–Cernobbio) to €10 (Como–Lecco). Return tickets are double the price.

The Como-based **ASF Autolinee** (☎ 24 72 47; www.sptlinea.it, in Italian) operates regular buses along the western lake shore departing from the bus station. Use the Como–Colico service for Menaggio.

MALCESINE
☎ 0457 / pop 3400

This busy lakeside town, wedged between the lower mountain slopes of Monte Baldo and the glittering shores of Lago di Garda, has an old centre and a modern periphery. It may have sold its soul to pizza producers and gelato (ice cream) manufacturers, but it's a convenient base for the area.

Information

The **IAT office** (☎ 40 00 44; Via Capitanato 6-8; Mon-Sat) issues a town map and accommodation guide. The website also has plenty of information, including transport timetables.

Various shops in Malcesine sell maps but the best source is **Klaus Giornali e Libri** (Via Statuto 19, Malcesine); it also stocks local history and natural history guides and foreign-language newspapers.

Sleeping & Eating

Centrally located **Camping Priori** (☎ 4 00 50; Via Navene 31; per person/site (€5.50/5.50) is rather small and cramped.

Albergo Aurora (☎ 40 01 14; www.aurora-malcesine.com; Piazza Matteotti 10; d €50) is a one-star family-run inn in the heart of the village. Neat rooms have parquet floors and for €43 per person you can upgrade to half-board.

Malcesine has numerous rather un-Italian pizza and pasta restaurants catering to the numerous German visitors. The choice comes down to outlook as much as anything else.

There's a large **supermarket** (Piazza Statuto; Mon-Sat) and a **Despar supermarket** (Via Navene; Mon-Sat). Opposite the latter is a fruit and vegetable shop. A good bakery is **Il Fornaio** (Via Antonio Bottura), off Piazza Statuto.

Getting There & Away

APTV (☎ 045 805 79 11) run buses from Peschiera to Verona (€2.80, 30 minutes) and Malcesine (€3.20, one hour 20 minutes); they continue on to Riva del Garda. APTV buses also connect Desenzano train station with Riva.

There are two train stations on the lake: Desenzano on the Milan–Venice line for a ferry connection, and Peschiera where you can connect with the APT bus (Verona–Riva del Garda) or the ferry to Malcesine. From the Rome–Bologna–Verona–Trento (and beyond) train line, buses depart from near Verona station. Coming from the north, you could alight at Trento to connect with **SPA** (www.ttesercizio.it) buses to Riva (one hour 15 minutes).

Ferry services to many lakeside towns are operated by **Navigazione Lago di Garda** (☎ 800 551801; www.navigazionelaghi.it).

You can reach Malcesine from Desenzano (ferry/hydrofoil €10.20/13.80, two hours, seven per day) or Peschiera (ferry/hydrofoil €10.20/13.80, two per day). You can also reach Malcesine from Riva del Garda at the northern end of the lake (ferry/hydrofoil €7.30/10.30, one hour and five minutes by hydrofoil, 21 per day).

By car, from the A4 (Milan–Venice) along the southern shore of Lago di Garda, take the Peschiera exit to the S249, which hugs the eastern shore of the lake, to Malcesine (45km). The A22 (Modena–Brennero) parallels the eastern shore, at a distance; take the Lago di Garda Sud exit a few kilometres northwest of Verona, or the Lago di Garda Nord exit near Rovereto, then follow signs to Malcesine (48km/23km).

MENAGGIO
☎ 0344 / pop 3100

Sliding up the Lago di Como towards the ever more precipitous mountains, you'll fall upon Menaggio, a slightly more affordable diamond in Como's vast collection of jewels. This beautiful lakeside town is in a superb location, overlooked by towering peaks; it boasts fine views of the rugged mountains across the water. Its many handsome old buildings are well preserved and the concessions to modern tourism that rob many other towns of their Italian character are absent.

Information

The **IAT office** (☎ 3 29 24; www.menaggio.com; Piazza Garbaldi 3; 9am-12.30pm, & 2.30-6pm Mon-Sat) is where you can obtain detailed information about a range of local walks and a list of local accommodation offers (posted outside after office hours).

Il Ritrovo (Via Calvi 10), is a good source of maps and Italian- and German-language guidebooks.

Sleeping & Eating

At the northern end of town, **Camping Europa** (☎ 3 11 87; Via Cipressi 12; per tent €13) is right on the lake. There's a small shop on-site and a supermarket round the corner. The centre of town is a five-minute walk. The site is open until late September.

Ostello La Primula (☎ 323 56; www.lake comohostel.com; Via IV Novembre 106; dm incl breakfast €16) is a youth hostel 100m uphill from the ferry wharf with a lovely view of the lake. An excellent three-course evening meal costs €13. You can also rent bikes and kayaks for €14.50 per day.

For food shopping, there are two supermarkets: **CompraBene** off Via Roma at the northern end of town and **Consorso Agrario** (Via Lusardi) near the ferry port. **Clerici** (Via Loveno) is an excellent fruit and vegetable shop and almost opposite is **Il Fornaio**, a first-class bakery. Possibly the best gelato in Italy comes from **Panne e Cioccolato** (Via Calvi). Only fresh ingredients and fruit in season are used; the *limoncello* is delicious.

Plenty of scenic restaurants congregate around the lakeside. **Trattoria Le Sorelle** (☎ 323 90; Via Camozzi 16; dishes €6-10), in a narrow lane off Piazza Garibaldi, is an informal, family-run place. It specialises in pasta and fish dishes including trout.

Getting There & Away

Navigazione Lago di Como (☎ 800 551801; www.navigazionelaghi.it) runs ferries from Como to Menaggio (€8.20, frequent). The Servizi Rapidi takes 50 minutes whereas the Motonavi takes a slow but beguiling 2½ hours. Ferries also connect with trains that stop in Colico and Varenna (see below).

Como is on the Milan–Chiasso line (€7.75, 55 minutes). The Milan–Sondrio/ Tirano train service goes through Varenna (€5.10, one hour) and Colico (€5.55, 1½ hours) on Como's eastern shore; both are ports on the lake's ferry network. There are plenty of trains daily on both lines.

From Como train station **SPT** (☎ 031 24 71 11; www.sptlinea.it) bus No 10 leaves for Menaggio (€2.65, one hour and 10 minutes, 13 per day). Buy tickets at the *tabaccheria* at the station.

By car, leave the A9 Milan–Passo Sant'Gottardo at the Como Nord exit to join the S340 along the western shore of the lake. Menaggio is 34km from Como.

LAKE DISTRICT

Stelvio

HIGHLIGHTS

- Juggle your German and Italian phrasebooks and get ready to intersperse *guten tag*s with *salve*s as you criss-cross the unmarked border between **Trentino** and **Alto Adige** (p143)
- Explore fine paths over high passes on the **Val di Rabbi to Martelltal** walk (p144)
- Wander through beautiful cool pine and larch woodlands with peek-a-boo mountain vistas above the **Val di Rabbi** (p144)
- Look out for chamois and red deer in the German-speaking **Martelltal** (p144) – famous for its summer strawberries and winter cross-country skiing

Signature food: Sauerkraut and sausages	Celebrated native: Andreas Hofer (Tyrolean patriot)	Famous for... Spas

It's not quite Yellowstone, but 1346-sq-km Parco Nazionale dello Stelvio is northern Italy's (and the Alps') largest national park, straddling the regions of Trentino-Alto Adige and Lombardy and bordering with the Parco Nazionale Svizzero in neighbouring Switzerland.

The park is primarily the preserve of walkers who come here to enjoy the extensive network of well-organised *rifugi* and marked trails which, while often challenging, don't generally require the mountaineering expertise necessary in the nearby Dolomites. Stelvio's central massif is guarded by Monte Cevedale (3769m) and Ortles (3905m) protecting glaciers, forests, numerous wildlife species and myriad cultural traditions, both Italian and South Tyrolean. Fewer than 100 years ago, this majestic land served as the front line in WWI and remnants of old defences along with a small museum bear testament to the slaughter.

Less blemished with ski facilities than other regions, Stelvio's primary run is at the Passo dello Stelvio (2757m), the second-highest road pass in the Alps. The pass is approached from the north from the hamlet of Trafoi (1543m) on one of Europe's most spectacular strips of asphalt, a series of tight switchbacks covering 15km, with some *very* steep gradients. The road is also famous among cyclists, who train all winter to prepare for its gut-wrenching ascent (it has often featured in the Giro d'Italia).

Stelvio can be approached from Merano (from where you have easy access to the Val d'Ultimo, Val Martello, Val di Solda and the Passo Stelvio), or from the Val di Sole in Trentino.

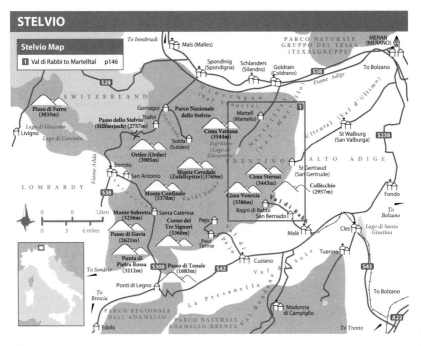

CLIMATE

Stelvio's climate is predominantly alpine in character. July and August are the wettest months (around 100mm each month). Afternoon thunderstorms are common, presaged by towering cumulus then lower, flatter nimbus clouds. The rainfall for May and September is considerably lower – as little as half that of the summer months. Heavy snowfalls typify winter, although snow can fall at any time of the year.

In summer the average temperature is into the 20s°C in the valleys but decreases markedly with altitude. It's not uncommon for summer days to dawn fine and clear, but become cloudy over the mountains during the warmest part of the day.

During April and May, in particular, the föhn, a warm, dry wind, can affect the area. The temperature rises rapidly, possibly triggering avalanches and accelerating the thaw of winter snow.

PLANNING
When to Walk

In most years snow should have retreated from all but the highest ground by mid-June,

and heavy and persistent snow shouldn't return until early October. Lower-level walks in the valleys should be accessible from May to October.

Maps

The Touring Club Italiano's 1:200,000 *Trentino-Alto Adige* is ideal for general planning and access.

PLACE NAMES

Italian names are either used exclusively or given precedence over German names in Trentino and Lombardy, but German is preferred over Italian names in Alto Adige/South Tyrol (eg Martelltal/Val Martello). However, in Stelvio you'll find some path signposts with both or only one (commonly German) version, and even with different spellings in the one language of the same place (eg Passo Soy and Forcella di Soi). The locally preferred version is given precedence in this chapter.

Books

Among the Italian-language titles, *Escursioni Parco dello Stelvio Trentino e Alto*

ITALY'S HIKING HEROES

Ever since Roman Emperor Hadrian stood on top of Mt Etna in AD 121, Italy has been supplying the world with a steady stream of tenacious hikers and mountaineers. Here's a formidable top five.

Reinhold Messner – the king of hiking. Messner was the first person to ascend Everest without oxygen, the first to do it solo, and the first person to climb all 14 eight-thousanders (world peaks over 8000m). Unsatisfied by his jaw-dropping feats, in 1986 he became part of a team that made the first unassisted crossing of Antarctica – on foot.

Sergio Martini – the seventh of 15 people to join the exclusive 8000 club completing the last of his 14 ascents in 2000.

Hans Kammerlander – Messner's protégé held Everest's fastest ascent record (17 hours from Camp 3) for 11 years before it was surpassed in 2007. In 1992 he went up and down the Matterhorn four times – yes FOUR times – in less than 24 hours.

Achille Compagnoni & Lino Lachedelli – the first humans to stand atop the world's second-tallest mountain, K2, in July 1954. Technically a far harder ascent than Everest; only 250 people have successfully summited K2 (as opposed to the 2700 who have climbed Everest).

Jean-Antoine Carrel – Carrel, the man Edward Whymper raced and beat to the top of the Matterhorn in 1865, was nonetheless a legendary climber who accompanied Whymper to the summit of 6268m Chimborazo in Ecuador in 1880 (the furthest point from the earth's centre). He died 10 years later in a blizzard on his beloved Matterhorn.

Adige (1999), by Paolo Turetti and Tiziano Mochan, and *Escursioni Parco dello Stelvio Alta Valcamonica e Alta Valtellina* (1997), by Paolo Turetti, have planimetric maps and lots of background information, plus walk descriptions. They're available at national park visitor centres.

Emergency

If you need emergency assistance in the Malè area, you can contact the local **mountain rescue** (☎ 0339 630 51 33). If on the west side of the park, you can contact the Bormio-based **mountain rescue** (☎ 0342 90 46 86). In South Tyrol you can also contact the regional search and rescue branch of the **Corpo Nazionale Soccorso Alpino e Speleologico** (☎ 0471 79 71 71). Otherwise, for medical assistance contact the **national emergency** number (☎ 118).

GETTING THERE & AROUND

An excellent private train line connects Malè with Trento and the south. From here regular buses ply the Val di Rabbi and the park's main southern entry. The northern entry is similarly served by a reliable bus/train combo connecting Martello with Coldrano, Merano and Bolzano.

GATEWAYS

The aptly named Vale di Sole (Sun valley) is Stelvio's southern gateway. It's main town Malè (p151) is 11km from the start of the walk in Bagni di Rabbi. Thanks to regular inter-valley train connections on the privately run Ferrovia Trento-Malè, the regional capital of Trento (p152) can also act as a viable base for hikers embarking on this walk.

VAL DI RABBI TO MARTELLTAL

Duration 4 days
Distance 55km
Difficulty moderate–demanding
Start Bagni di Rabbi
Finish Martell (Martello)
Nearest Towns San Bernardo, Bagni di Rabbi, Martell
Transport bus

Summary An exceptionally scenic and varied tour on excellent paths and tracks, through valleys and over high mountain passes with several possible variations.

This walk traverses valleys and intervening ridges in the east part of the park, within the Trentino and South Tyrol sections. It's a wonderfully varied excursion; cultivated valleys dotted with well-tended farms and Tyrolean-style villages, pine woodlands, open mountainsides and ridges with fantastic views of peaks and glaciers, and mountain tarns.

Reservoirs in Ultental (Grünsee and Weissbrunnsee) and Martelltal (Zufrittsee) may seem out of place in a national park, but the abundant waters from the glaciers and streams are an invaluable resource for the low-lying, intensively cultivated Vinschgau (Val Venosta) to the north. Geologically, metamorphic rocks are the most widespread type – mica schists to the west of Val di Rabbi, quartz-phyllite extending from Monte Cevedale along the Ultental-Martelltal ridge, with limestone and dolomite further west. Apart from marmots, wildlife is elusive; domestic grazing animals are far more common up to high levels in the valleys.

The valleys are deep and the linking passes high, so this is an energetic walk, with a total of 3640m ascent. The paths and minor vehicle tracks followed are almost all well maintained, so the walking is never difficult; waymarking, using a numbering system, and signposting are excellent throughout.

Day 4, not essential to completing the overall tour, is a highly recommended, comparatively easy walk from Enzianhütte, high up in Martelltal, down the valley to Martell; a fascinating bus journey links the end of Day 3 and Day 4.

You can vary the described route to make easier days. Some alternatives are included in the route description, and you can easily enter or exit the walk from San Gertraud at the end of Day 2.

PLANNING
When to Walk
Those parts of the route above 2600m should normally be free of snow between June and late September, although at high altitudes unseasonable snow can fall at any time.

What to Bring
No special equipment is required during the recommended season but gaiters and an ice axe would probably be welcome, if not necessary, at other times. You'll find refreshment places during the course of each day's walk, but it would still be wise to carry some food and drink to tide you over.

Maps
Unfortunately, complete coverage of the walk at the ideal scale of 1:25,000 isn't available. The best map, the Tabacco 1:25,000 sheet No 08 *Ortles-Cevedale/Ortlergebiet*, covers the earlier and middle parts of Day 1, the end of Day 3 and Day 4; some path junctions are incorrect.

The Kompass 1:50,000 map No 072 *Parco Nazionale dello Stelvio* covers the entire area but isn't always accurate. Some of its place names are, well, unique; with a 1:500,000 map and notes in Italian and German on the reverse, it's good for planning and general orientation.

The Kompass 1:25,000 map No 637 *Cevedale-Valle di Pejo-Alta Valfurva* covers Day 1 as far as the peak Gleck (Collècchio).

Books
Guida Escursionistica Val di Sole, published by Kompass, is an Italian-language guide describing 49 outings, of which 10 are in Val di Rabbi. It has reduced 1:50,000 maps on which the route is superimposed.

GETTING TO/FROM THE WALK
Bagni di Rabbi (start)
Private company **Ferrovia Trento-Malè** (☎ 0463 90 11 50) operates a daily bus service from Malè to Bagni di Rabbi (€1.55), via San Bernardo, with at least five buses each way. Buy tickets at the Malè bus station or on board. By road, SP86 branches off S42 about 2km northeast of Malè; Bagni di Rabbi is 11km up the valley.

Martell/Martello (finish)
SAD (☎ 800 84 60 47; www.sad.it) operates eight daily buses to Coldrano station (20 minutes) where you can catch trains to Merano (50 minutes) and Bolzano (1½ hours).

By road, turn off the busy S38 at Goldrain (Coldrano; 24km west of Meran, 28km southeast of Mals); it's 12km to Martell. To reach Premstlhof from Martell, follow roads to Ennetal (Valdene) and Walderg (Selva).

THE WALK
Day 1: Bagni di Rabbi to Rifugio Stella Alpina
7–7¼ hours, 16km, 1600m ascent
From the bus stop at **Bagni di Rabbi**, set off along the bitumen road up the valley.

VAL DI RABBI TO MARTELLTAL

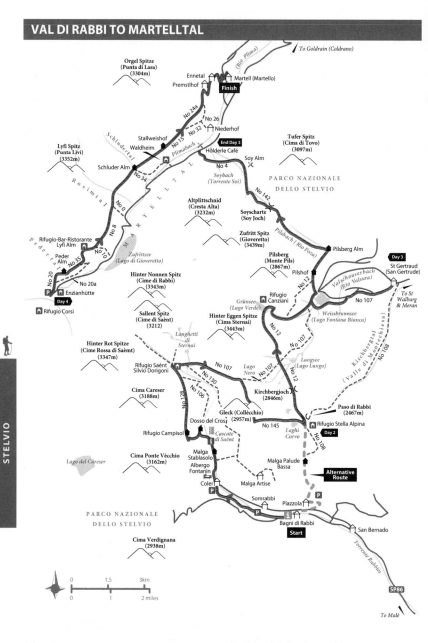

After about 25 minutes you come to a sign-posted junction on the left for a *percorso alternativo* (alternative route) to 'Coler',

'Stablasolo' (Malga Stablasol) and 'Saènt' (Cascate di Saènt). Cross Torrente Rabbiès on a footbridge and follow this path for about 1km, then as it peters out, bear right to the valley road. Go to the right of the road, cross the bridge over the stream and take a path to the left, signposted to 'Malga Stablasolo' and 'Cascate di Saent'; there's a large car park nearby. Continue up the road, past **Albergo Fontanin** (☎ 0463 90 20 80), then follow a riverbank path for 20 minutes to a signposted junction; cross a bridge and head towards **Malga Stablasolo**, via slabs through a boulder field and a track up to the *malga* (herders' summer hut), where you can enjoy a drink overlooking the depths of the narrow valley.

Press on, up the vehicle track signposted to Rifugio Dorigoni; the valley is wider now and unrelentingly rugged with extremely steep cliffs separated by precipitous grassy slopes on which are glued clumps of pines. A short distance along the track, follow a path signposted 106 and you soon come to a small **national park visitor centre**. This houses a wonderful (free) display starring marmots, the most numerous wildlife in this part of the park – 7000 of them at last count. Rejoin the path behind the visitor centre; it climbs steeply to 'Dosso dell'Cros' (Dosso del Cros), 30 minutes from Malga Stablasol. **Dosso del Cros** is a national park outstation where there's a spring and a superb view of Cascate di Saènt.

Go through a gate above Dosso del Cros and bear left at a path junction, towards Rifugio Campisol. (The path to the right, Route No 106, descends to Val Saènt, then continues up to Rifugio Dorigoni.) The narrow path rises steeply though open larch forest with occasional views of the cascade and the peaks above. About 45 minutes from Dosso del Cros, you reach **Rifugio Campisol**, locked but with picnic tables outside. The path to Rifugio Dorigoni (now No 128), leads on across boulders, through a narrow gap and across a steam. It then sets out on a superb, undulating traverse across scree, boulders and grass. Beyond a small stream with stepping stones, the path rises steeply through crags to a grassy basin. Cross it, then go up the slope on the right, across a broad spur, and down into the main valley. Continue to a signposted junction; the path on the right is No 106, the alternative route from near Dosso del Cros. Turn left, soon cross a stream then climb to **Rifugio Saènt Silvio Dorigoni**

(☎ 0463 98 51 07; dm €20; 20 Jun–20 Sep), which charges extra for a shower. A filling three-course dinner is approximately €18. The *rifugio* is perched on a shelf below a massive crag-covered hill (1½ hours from Rifugio Campisol).

Follow a waymarked path from the valley side of the *rifugio*, across the slope (eastwards), past a pond, across a stream and then a grassy, flat area. You soon come to a junction; signposts point right for Route No 130 (Malga Artise) and left for Route No 107 pointing towards Rifugio Lago Corvo [sic]; this is the route to take. The clear path leads towards dark cliffs, then over scree and up across a very steep, boulder-strewn slope. Nearly two hours from the *rifugio*, you reach the crest of the ridge (at 2833m) enclosing Val di Rabbi to the northeast and east; signposts indicate the way onwards, following Route No 145 along the ridge. For a direct route to Rifugio Canziani from here, drop down to the east with Route No 107. This descends steeply past Lago Nero in the valley of Valschauser Bach (Rio Valsura) and meets the route of Day 2 of this walk near Langsee (Lago Lungo).

To continue to Rifugio Stella Alpina, head higher along the ridge, gaining some height. If the weather is fine, diverge to **Gleck** (Collècchio; 2957m), signed as 'Cima Collècchio', for even wider views; the way up is marked by large cairns and the destination painted on a boulder. The main path continues along the ridge for a shortish distance, then bears down left, below a minor summit on the right; the steep descent now starts in earnest. Eventually, you pass one of the larger of the **Laghi Corvo** near its outlet; continue down past a path junction, across a stream, to the *rifugio* (1½ to 1¾ hours from the ridge).

Rifugio Stella Alpina (☎ 0463 98 51 75; dm €20; 20 Jun–20 Sep) is a friendly, homely place; bedrooms have two, four or five beds; facilities, including a hot shower, are shared. The three-course evening meal is substantial and filling.

ALTERNATIVE ROUTE: VIA MALGA PALUDE BASSA
2¾–3 hours, 5km, 1230m ascent

From the upstream side of the **national park visitor centre** in **Bagni di Rabbi**, follow a path signposted 'Piazzola' up to a road; turn right and walk along the road, through a small piazza (where there's a bus stop for the Malè service) and Bar Rosa delle Alpi; 50m further on there's a supermarket. Continue to a road junction where there are signs to various places, including 'Laghi Corvo' via Route No 108. Walk left along this road for a few hundred metres to a junction and go left again with Route No 108. The road gains height between meadows; continue along a vehicle track from the end of the bitumen and, further up, pass the car park for the *rifugio* on the right. A few minutes further on, diverge left up a waymarked path, which ascends steeply through two crossroads to a gravel road; keep following the red and white waymarkers.

About 1½ hours from the start, you come to a gravel road more or less in the open; turn right and you soon reach the ruinous buildings of **Malga Palude Bassa**. A couple of minutes further on, turn up to the left, as waymarked, through trees; at the next gravel road, go right for a short distance then bear left again up a path. About 25 minutes from the *malga* cross a stream to a path junction where Route No 108 goes both ways. The route to the right is longer, slightly less steep, and, in its upper reaches, eroded and bare. The path to the left goes straight up the valley to the **Rifugio Stella Alpina**, another 45 minutes.

Day 2: Rifugio Stella Alpina to St Gertraud

5¼–5¾ hours, 12km,1540m descent, 640m ascent

There are two routes to St Gertraud (San Gertrude) from the *rifugio*. The one described is the longer, more scenic route. The direct approach follows Route No 108 down Kirchbergtal (Valle di Montechiesa) on a vehicle track most of the way. This leads you to a road near the centre of the village; the bus stop is down to the right. To reach the accommodation listed, follow small signs marked 'Kirche' (church) up to the left.

From **Rifugio Stella Alpina**, retrace the previous day's steps for about 250m to a path junction by a stream crossing and follow Path No 12 to the right (north). This route now follows a different line from that shown on the Kompass 1:50,000 map. The faintish path crosses a sheep-cropped meadow towards the cliffs of the Kirchbergjoch ridge,

then makes a rising traverse through crags and across grass, below the cliffs. About 45 minutes from the *rifugio*, on a rocky spur, the path turns sharply left (don't be seduced by the clear onward path) and ascends to a **pass** at 2846m (one to 1¼ hours from the *rifugio*). The fine view northwards is painted in greens, dull red and greenish grey: the lakes in the valley below, artificial Grünsee (Lago Verde) beyond, overlooked by the soaring heights of Hinter Eggen Spitze (Cima Sternai; 3443m) to the west and Pilsberg (Monte Pils; 2867m) to the east, with Rifugio Canziani sitting quietly on the shore of Grünsee.

The well-made path makes relatively easy work of the descent through scree, then it's across rocky meadows to a succession of easy stream crossings. The fourth, however, may dictate a minor diversion of about 30m downstream to keep your boots dry. About 45 minutes from the pass, you meet Route No 107 at a path junction. A few metres further on, the path divides; bear left (Route No 12). The path to the right is No 107, which can be followed down to the valley of Valschauserbach (Rio Valsura), bypassing Rifugio Canziani and joining the main route above Weissbrunnsee; not as the Kompass 1:50,000 maps shows it, with Route No 107 skirting the lake.

Continuing towards Rifugio Canziani, ascend to overlook **Grünsee** and a substantial slice of Ultental (Val d'Ultimo) stretching away northeastwards. Then descend slightly and continue on an extraordinary path of huge flat slabs up to the reservoir wall. Cross the wall and go up to a path junction; the *rifugio* is nearby to the left (1¾ to two hours from the pass).

Rifugio Canziani (Höchsterhütte; ☎ 0473 79 81 20; 39010 St Gertraud, Ultental; dm €20-26), a CAI establishment, is elegant by *rifugio* standards. The bright dining room is very tempting; the modern bedrooms have from three to 10 beds.

To continue, pass the electricity authority installations and descend a wide track, which soon becomes a well-used path (Route No 140), zigzagging down the steep slope. About 45 minutes from the *rifugio*, pass the turn-off to the left for Route No 12 to Pilsberg Alm. If you're following this route to Soyscharte (Soy Joch), pick up the main route in the description of Day 3 at a junction above Weissbrunnsee; allow 1¼ to 1½ hours to reach this junction.

Continue east down through larch woodland, passing a junction where Route No 107 comes in on the right, past the bar-restaurant Zur Knödelmoidl close to **Weissbrunnsee** (Lago Fontana Bianca).

To reach St Gertraud, follow the gravel road just above the southern shore of Weissbrunnsee, signposted as Route No 107, which provides the novelty of level walking for a while. After 10 minutes bear right with No 107 and soon cross a vehicle track. Continue to a T-junction and go to the right, down to another T-junction and again bear right along a forest road for about 250m. Then it's left down a path (still Route No 107) and the real descent starts, through pine forest, eventually to a T-junction on the edge of fields. Turn right along the vehicle track and follow it to a bitumen road with beautiful white, red-spired St Gertraud church above. Accommodation is about 200m up and slightly to the right (1¼ to 1½ hours from Weissbrunnsee). To reach the centre of the village, shop and bus stop, follow the path below Pension Ulternhof down, past stations of the cross, to a minor road then descend steeply between houses to the main Ultental road. **St Gertraud (San Gertrude)** is a typical Tyrolean village, picturesquely scattered around the head of the Ulten valley. Here German is the language of first choice – Italian is either unknown or not readily used. With valley or mountain views, **Pension Ulternhof** (☎ 0473 79 81 17; 114 Ulten; r €38-60) offers spacious, fairly plain rooms. Breakfast is a substantial affair and the evening meal likewise. The village shop has a good range of supplies. The **SAD** (☎ 800 84 60 47) bus service from Meran in Vinschgau provides at least four buses daily, more on workdays.

Day 3: St Gertraud to Martelltal

7–7½ hours, 15km, 1400m ascent

Follow Route No 108 and signs to 'Kirche' up to Pension Ulternhof, then go down the bitumen road below the church. On a sharp bend continue down a vehicle track for about 200m to a signposted turn-off to the left into pine forest. The well-graded path ascends to a vehicle track; turn right for about 250m then left with a sign for Route No 107. At the next junction turn

right along a level track. Continue straight on at the next intersection and follow the level track around the shores of Weissbrunnsee to the road near the former Berggasthaus Enzian (1¼ to 1½ hours from St Gertraud).

Continue up the vehicle track on the uphill side of the hotel, signposted as Route No 12. About 40m along, bear left up steps with route 12 waymarkers. The narrow rocky path gains height readily. After about 20 minutes a path (from the direction of Rifugio Canziani) merges from the left. Nearly an hour from Weissbrunnsee you emerge into the open meadows at **Pilshof** and come to a timber cabin with a picnic table inside. The path leads on, back into forest; two stream crossings on stepping stones could be slightly difficult after heavy rain. The next stream, Pilsbach (Rio Poza), is bridged. Soon the path traverses a rugged, forested slope to **Pilsberg Alm** (30 minutes from Pilshof). Fresh water is available here; the isolated, superbly sited place is usually occupied. A sign points the way to Passo Soy/Soy Joch [sic] and to San Gertraud [sic] down to the right, via an extremely steep route.

Head north up to a prominent signpost on a spur and turn left towards the pass following Route No 142. The path, faint in places, leads up over a stony meadow and keeps to the left (south) of a huge hill of scree and boulders, ascending to a grassy shoulder. This marks a dramatic transition from the open meadows to a wild, cliff-enclosed valley. The path goes up the right side, and ascends scree and boulders in a series of longish zigzags, to the flat pass, mapped as **Soyscharte** (two hours from Pilsberg Alm).

The route descends steeply through boulders; watch the waymarkers (No 142) carefully as they're not always in line of sight. Then drop down a steep, gravel slope to the slightly easier ground of a long moraine spur. Descend the spur and, after a while, cut across to the left to another spur, following it down on a now clear, waymarked path. Reach a small stream on the right and cross it, then another and follow a spur down, past a path junction on the right, to another junction. Bear right here and follow clear paths on to **Soy Alm**, usually open for refreshments (two hours from Soyscharte).

From here the path (now Route No 4) drops down into forest, crosses a bridge over Soybach and descends steeply. Well down, just past a stream crossing, bear right and descend a path to the main road through Martelltal (Val Martello), next to the **Hölderle Café** (45 minutes from Soy Alm). The bus stop is about 200m to the left; there is a bus at about 5pm down the valley to Martell (see Day 4 below) but the last one going up passes here in the early afternoon.

Day 4: Martelltal – Enzianhütte to Martell (Martello)

4¾–5¼ hours, 12km, 300m ascent, 750m descent

It's worth noting that none of the available maps show all the paths and junctions on this section accurately.

First of all, you need to reach **Enzianhütte** (Hotel Enzian); there's a bus from Martell (€1.80) at around 9.30am that takes you to the hotel on an amazing journey up a series of very tight hairpin bends.

From the hotel, walk down the road for about 100m to a signposted vehicle track on the left. Go up past deserted buildings and on the far side of the last one on the left, turn left up a path (Route No 20; Pedertal). The path gains height quickly through open pine woodland. About 25 minutes from the start, cross a bridge over the main stream in Pedertal, then a few minutes further on, at a junction, bear right (No 20a) towards 'Malga Lifi' (the same place as Lyfi Alm and Malga Livi on other signposts). Then it's only a short distance to the open spaces of **Peder Alm** and another junction; continue ahead on a path marked 20a and 35. A small hut here is locked but there are seats under the wide eaves. The route then descends to another junction; stay with 35, crossing a meadow then generally descending to scenically located **Rifugio-Bar-Ristorante Lyfi Alm** (☎ 0473 74 47 08), about an hour from the start. Stop for some local cheese or strudel.

Continue along Route No 8 across a stream, past the turn-off for Route No 10 (to the road by Zufrittsee) then through meadows. The path soon descends in pine forest, negotiating a small cliff via timber steps, across a stream and down past a junction (where Route No 0 would take you down to the valley road). Cross an open stretch of path preceded by a sign warning

you to hurry across here if it's raining, as rockfalls are likely. From a junction further on (about an hour from Lyfi Alm) the path climbs to a bridge over the main stream in Rosimtal. Continue up, past a small hut; another larger hut nearby is firmly locked. Ascend steeply to a path junction with fine views up Rosimtal. The path (Route No 8) rises steeply from here for several hundred metres, then descends via steps and timber ramps into Schludertal and across the valley's stream. A little further on, at **Schluder Alm**, Route No 34 on the right leads down to Waldheim. Continue ahead with Route No 8, generally losing height across slopes where signs warn of falling stones, and down to **Stallwieshof** (about 1¼ hours from Rosimtal) – a possible refreshment stop.

Walk along the road for about 100m, cross a stream with an old water mill nearby, and turn left along a vehicle track with Route Nos 15 and 32. The track, evidently extended since the maps were published, has annihilated chunks of the waymarked path. Just past the turn-off to the right for Route No 32 (to Niederhof), bear right along a path (No 15), which generally descends in pine forest. Forty minutes from Stallwieshof, you reach a path junction, the configuration of which is quite different from that on the maps. Turn left for Premstlhof and follow a well-graded path down to a junction just above a road. A short path on the right towards Premstlhof avoids a bit of road walking. Then continue down the road; just before a gate across it, take a short cut on the left down to **Premstlhof** (about 1¼ hours from Stallwieshof).

To reach **Martell**, walk down the road; take a couple of steep short cuts signposted as Route Nos 8 and 11. The last one lands you in the courtyard of the Gasthof Edelweiss; the bus stop is about 150m up the road to the right (30 to 35 minutes from Premstlhof).

MORE WALKS

VAL DEI FORNI

The vast Forni glacier, in the heart of the Lombardy section of the park, is the largest glacier in the entire Central Alps. This awesome mass of ice, plus two of the park's three highest peaks (Monte Cevedale and Gran Zebrù) are the stunning highlights of walks in Val dei Forni and its upper reaches, Val di Cedec. A good network of well-waymarked paths and tracks provides opportunities for not too strenuous excursions through the valleys with the glacier and the peaks and their impressive satellites almost constantly in view. The best map to use is the Tabacco 1:25,000 sheet No 08 *Ortles Cevedale*.

From the bus stop in **Santa Caterina**, the direct route to **Rifugio-Albergo Ghiacciaio dei Forni** (☎ 0342 93 53 65; www.forni2000 .com; Santa Caterina; half-board per person €48), high up Valle dei Forni, is 4.5km along a bitumen road all the way. This involves 450m ascent and takes 1¼ to 1½ hours.

A moderate 11km circuit from Albergo Forni takes in **Rifugio Branca** (☎ 0342 93 55 01; www.rifugiobranca.it; half-board from €40), which has an unrivalled view of Forni glacier, following Path Nos 28a, then 28c most of the way up Val di Cedec to **Rifugio Pizzini Frattola** (☎ 0342 93 55 13; dm €20), which crouches at the foot of Gran Zebrù. The return is by an unnumbered but signposted path along the western side of Val di Cedec, past Rovine Caserma (ruins of WWI barracks) and down to Albergo Forni. This takes 3¾ to 4¼ hours with 620m ascent. A 3.5km return side trip (400m ascent) from Rifugio Pizzini Frattola up to Passo Zebrù following Path No 30, to overlook spectacular Val Zebrù, is highly recommended; allow 1¼ to 1½ hours.

To vary the return to Santa Caterina, you could choose the relatively straightforward route on the northern side of Val dei Forni, along Path No 27a from above Albergo Forni to Ables, then down Route No 34 to Santa Caterina. This 7.5km route takes 2¼ to 2½ hours and involves 350m ascent.

TOWNS & FACILITIES

MALÈ
☎ 0463 / pop 2200

The hub of the Val di Sole, the small town of Malè is close to the threshold of Val di Rabbi and outside the park. Additional facilities can be found in the various villages that speckle the Val di Rabbi, closer to the start of the walk.

Information

The well-organised **APT office** (☎ 90 12 80; www.valdisole.net; Piazza Regina Elena; 9am-noon & 3.30-6.30pm Mon-Sat, 10am-noon Sun) issues an information booklet in several languages, as well as a trekking booklet for Stelvio and nearby Parco Naturale Adamello-Brenta, outlining walks between *rifugi*. Accommodation information is also available. There's a small **visitors centre** (☎ 98 51 90) in Bagni di Rabbi right at the start of the walk. Maps can be purchased from the **tabaccheria** (Via E Bezzi) near the large church.

Sleeping & Eating

Conveniently close to the train and bus station, **Hotel Alle Alpi** (☎ 90 11 45; www .hotelallealpi.com; Via Garibaldi 12; d half- board per person €42-55) has simply furnished rooms. The rate represents good value and includes a substantial three-course evening meal of unpretentious fare. An altogether different place is **La Segosta** (☎ 0463 90 13 90; www.segosta.com; Via Trento 59; s/d with breakfast €40/€80), with modern, tastefully decorated rooms. Local specialities are prominent on the menu.

Dolomiti Camping Village (☎ 97 43 32; www.campingdolomiti.com; Via Gole 105; 2 adults, tent & car €21-29, two-person bungalow €45-65; mid-May–mid-Oct & Dec-Easter), riverside and adjacent to the rafting centre, is surely the camping ground that has everything including wi-fi'd campsites, new bungalows, apartments in a timber chalet, a wellness centre, indoor and outdoor pools, volleyball courts and restaurant (meals from €15).

For supplies, there's a **supermarket** (closed afternoon Sun) at the western end of town.

Getting There & Away

A private company, **Ferrovia Trento-Malè** (☎ 90 11 50; www.ttesercizio.it), operates a train service between Trento (on the FS Verona–Bolzano–Brennero line) and Malè (€3.90, 1½ hours, hourly); Trento station is about 250m from the FS platforms. The train also connects with the FS line at Mezzocorno, between Trento and Bolzano.

STELVIO

By road from the east, turn west off the A22 at the San Michele junction (between Trento and Bolzano) and follow S43 and then S42 north and west respectively to Malè, a distance of 41km.

TRENTO

☎ 0461 / pop 105,000

Trento often gets rudely ignored. Set in a wide glacial valley guarded by the crenellated peaks of the Brenta Dolomites, this left-leaning but proudly Catholic regional capital has long stood at an important geographical and historical crossroads and is a romantic place to spend to enjoy some pre- or post-hike relaxation.

Information

The **tourist office** (☎ 21 60 00; www.apt .trento.it; Via Manci 2; 9am-7pm year-round) has information on the city and surrounds as well as hikes in the Brenta Group and Stelvio. For walking information, including itineraries and *rifugi* in Trentino, contact the local **Società degli Alpinisti Tridentini** (SAT; ☎ 98 18 71; Via Manci 57; 8am-noon & 3-7pm Mon-Fri).

Supplies & Equipment

Liberia Ancora (Via Santa Croce 35) stocks quality walking maps.

If you're hitting the hills, pick up picnic supplies at **Supermercato Trentino** (Corso III Novembre 4-6).

Sleeping & Eating

Ostello Giovane Europa (☎ 26 34 84; info@gayaproject.org; Via Torre Vanga 9; dm incl breakfast €16-20, s/d incl breakfast €28/50; reception 7.30am-11am & 3-11pm) Spelling out the word 'Welcome' in 32 different languages you're pretty much guaranteed a warm one at this squeaky-clean place bang in the middle of town and just a few minutes' walk from the main

train station. Some rooms have balconies and mountain views.

Hotel Venezia (☎ 23 41 14; www.hotel veneziatn.it; Piazza del Duomo 45; s/d without bathroom €38/55, s/d with bathroom €49/69) The Venezia is a comfortable two-star with a gorgeous location right in happening Piazza del Duomo. Rooms with whitewashed walls and dark timber furniture are plain but not without character, and there's a substantial Teutonic-meets-Roman breakfast.

Due Giganti (☎ 23 75 15; Via Simonino 14; buffets from €7) It sounds like an oxymoron, but it isn't. A 'fast-food' restaurant that's tasty and not conducive to heart-attacks. Come here to fill up on fresh pizzas, buffet salads and regularly topped-up pastas.

Patelli (☎ 23 52 36; Via Dietro le Mura 45; set menus €20-28, mains €8-12; noon-2:15pm & 7-10:30pm) A long cavernous restaurant with waiters in waistcoats and delicately folded napkins, Patelli still feels like the kind of place where you can wear hiking boots and get away with it. Traditional trattoria fare includes fresh gnocchi with chestnuts accompanied by fruity red wines.

Getting There & Away

The town is well connected. Regular trains leave the main train station (Piazza Dante) for Verona (€5.40, one hour), Venice (€8.40, 2½ hours), Bologna (€11.30, 3¼ hours) and Bolzano (€3.35, 30 minutes). Next door to the main station, the Trento–Malè train line connects the city with Malè and the Val di Sole.

From the intercity bus station (Via Andrea Pozzo), local bus company **Trentino Trasporti** (☎ 82 10 00; www.ttesercizio.it, in Italian) runs buses to and from various destinations, including Madonna di Campiglio in the Brenta Group (p53).

Dolomites

HIGHLIGHTS

- Walking in the undulating pastures of the Alpe di Siusi high plain, juxtaposed against the vertiginous **Sciliar** (p158).
- Getting to grips with three different languages (German, Italian and Ladin), multiple cultural traditions, and a curious culinary tradition stuck somewhere between Vienna and Venice (p165)
- Early morning cloud lifting like a theatre curtain to reveal the rugged magnificence of the Tre Cime di Lavaredo on the **Crode Fiscaline Loop** (p170)
- Taking in the full spectacular sweep of one of Unesco's newest 'natural' World Heritage sites in the seven-day **Dolomite Rollercoaster** hike (p161)

Signature food: Apple strudel	Celebrated native: Reinhold Messner	Famous for... *Vie ferrate* (iron ways)

The Western Alps may be taller and the Sicilian volcanoes more explosive; but, for pure, untamed beauty, the monumental Dolomites have no earthly counterpart. Famous for their huge gothic crags and sharp saw-toothed ridges, these distinctive peaks stand like rugged works of art carved by a celestial Michelangelo guarding over the grey borders of the culturally ambiguous South Tyrol.

Renowned for their technically demanding climbing routes and more accessible *vie ferrate*, the Dolomites have long served as an important training ground for Himalayan mountaineers such as Reinhold Messner and Hans Kammerlander. For much of the 19th century they were disputed border territory between Italy and the Austro-Hungarian Empire while, in the second decade of the 20th century, the mountains became a high-altitude battle-front during WWI. Today the Dolomites are a more peaceful, but no less popular, mountain escape that are criss-crossed by numerous trails and overlaid with a hybrid Austro-Italian-Ladin culture. Skiing is the modern wintertime passion while, in the summer, mountain hiking has been popular since Victorian times. This chapter outlines five hikes, including a seven-day Dolomite Rollercoaster that rivals the region's signature *alte vie* (high trails) Nos 1 & 2 for scope.

In July 2009, the Dolomites' unique ecology was recognised by Unesco, who named it a World Heritage site – only the second 'natural' area in Italy to achieve this status.

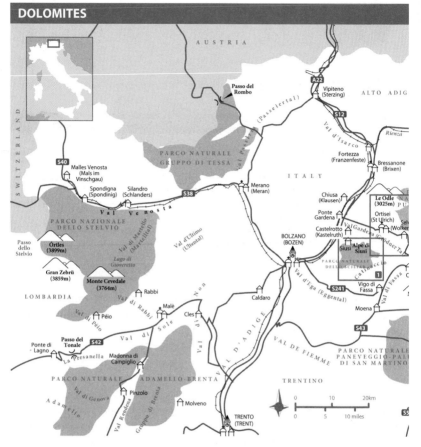

HISTORY

Archaeological finds dating back to the Neolithic period including the mummified remains of Otzi (see boxed text p166) indicate that humans have frequented this area for over 5000 years.

By the time the region was absorbed into the ancient Roman Empire, it had already developed a long history of intense intercultural and commercial exchange. Then, as today, the area's cultural diversity created an unusual backdrop. The Ladin ethnic group, which developed over the centuries in the Badia (Gadertal), Gardena (Grödnertal) and Fassa valleys in Trentino-Alto Adige, and in the Ampezzana and Livinallongo valleys in the Veneto, are descendants of the Celts. Romanised under the Emperors

Augustus and Claudius, they still maintain their own Romance language, as well as a social system founded on the model of *viles* – clusters of family houses where several agricultural activities were carried out in common.

In the northernmost valleys, the original South Tyrol populations, Germanic in language and culture, preserve to this day the system of *maso chiuso* – single-family farms and land that, each generation, are passed down to the first-born son. The South Tyrol territories were administered in the Middle Ages by Germanic bishops or feudal lords. They were subsequently made part of the Kingdom of Bavaria and finally of the Austro-Hungarian Empire of the Hapsburgs. In 1919, with the defeat of the Hapsburgs

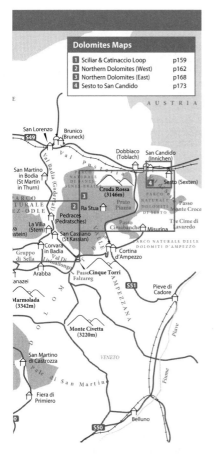

at the end of WWI, South Tyrol was annexed by Italy. The population, after suffering a forced attempt at integration under Mussolini, today enjoys an autonomous government status along with Trentino.

At the beginning of the 19th century, the Dolomites figured prominently in the first explorations and early triumphs in Alpine mountaineering, which laid the foundations of the region's current tourism.

ENVIRONMENT

The area of the Dolomites forms an 80km-long rocky strip that extends east–west between Val d'Isarco (Eisacktal), northeast of Bolzano, and Val di Sesto (Sextental), southeast of San Candido, and defined to the north by Val Pusteria (Pustertal). The

mountains encompass two Italian regions the Veneto and the semi-autonomous Trentino-Alto Adige; the latter consists of the two provinces of Trento and Bolzano (often referred to as the South Tyrol).

To the explorers of the 19th century, influenced by a romantic and heroic vision, these mountains were especially atmospheric. The bizarre, vertical shapes – steeples, pinnacles and towers of white rock – standing out among brilliant green forests and grassy slopes, dotted here and there with tidy farms, captured their imaginations.

The Dolomites owe their name to the French geologist Deodat de Dolomieu, who first described their composition in 1788. De Dolomieu found that the Dolomites were largely made up of extensive stratification of calcium and magnesium rock – all that remained of trillions of sponges and coral of an ancient tropical sea.

One of the most obvious qualities of the Dolomites is their colour; the great vertical peaks are softened by the pale shades of the minerals of which they are composed. In the sunlight they go from whitish to blue-grey, and then turn rose and purple as the sun sets. A series of natural habitats, determined principally by altitude, can be distinguished in horizontal strips on the slopes.

Typical Alpine carnivores like the bear, lynx, wolf and lammergeier (bearded vulture) have been extinct in the area since the beginning of this century. Projects are now underway to reintroduce these animals to their natural habitats, although you are unlikely to see any. Minor carnivores, hoofed herbivores (some of which have been reintroduced), rodents, mustelids, reptiles and many bird species inhabit the high-altitude woods and prairies. You are most likely to encounter them in the early morning or at sunset.

TIME VERSUS DISTANCE

Distances are deceptive in the Dolomites where walking one or 2km can quickly turn into an hour-long slog thanks to a mixture of fickle weather, rocky terrain, steep ascents and exposed paths. Most signposts, *rifugi* and hiking guides thus quote their routes in time (hours and minutes) rather than distance (kilometres).

DOLOMITES

DOLOMITE LINGUISTICS

One of the most idiosyncratic aspects of modern Europe is its grey areas, the once-disputed borderlands where two completely different cultures overlap and mix. Take the bilingual North Italian region of Trentino-Alto Adige (also known as South Tyrol). On paper, its two linguistic groups, the Italians and the Germans, are polar opposites: the former, exuberant, artistic and definitively Mediterranean; the latter well-ordered, diligent and Nordic. Yet, in the isolated valleys of the Dolomite Mountains, the two cultures happily coexist, as do their respective languages.

Of course, this wasn't always the case. Until 1920, the provinces of Trentino and Alto Adige were part of the German-speaking Austro-Hungarian Empire ruled from Vienna. Following Austro-Hungary's defeat in WWI, the region was ceded to Italy and rapidly Italianised under Mussolini who banned the use of the German language in schools and public offices.

Such rulings were fiercely antagonistic to the German-speaking South Tyroleans. In Alto Adige, the more northerly of the two provinces, nearly 70% of the people speak German as a mother tongue and are culturally more at home in Lederhosen than Gucci.

To further confuse phrasebook-wielding visitors, the Dolomites are home to another language, Ladin, a romance tongue related to Swiss Romansh with approximately 20,000 speakers concentrated in five main valleys, namely the Val di Fassa in Trentino, Val Badia and Val Gardena in Alto Adige, and the Arabba and Ampezzo regions in Veneto.

Despite its historical complexity, the South Tyrol has evolved into a model of peaceful coexistence. Rather than using bombs and belligerence to solve their cultural differences, cities such as Trento and Bolzano have blossomed into efficient and artistically rich enclaves that exhibit the best of both worlds. Imagine the rationalism of Kant married with the spontaneous passion of the Renaissance. Intrigued? You will be.

CLIMATE

The dominant climate is typically continental alpine, with long, harsh winters and short, temperate summers. As a general rule, precipitation levels increase with altitude. Snow falls between October and December and begins to melt between March and April; depending on the exposure of the slope, it can last until July or August. January is the coldest month, with an average temperature of below 0°C; the warmest period is usually July to August, which has an average temperature around 20°C.

Be aware, after the middle of August the temperature can drop suddenly. The climate in the Dolomites can be unpredictable, with sunny mornings giving way to sudden, violent thunderstorms in the afternoon.

PLANNING
When to Walk

The walking season is from June to September/October. *Rifugi* offer food, lodging and assistance to walkers from around mid-June to mid-September (depending on the weather). This is the best period for low-risk walking. August is more stable than June weather-wise, but the *rifugi* are usually full and the area can get extremely crowded. September is more tranquil, while in October the days begin to shorten.

Maps

The Touring Club Italiano's 1:200,000 *Trentino-Alto Adige* map is ideal for route planning and general orientation.

PLACE NAMES

Many places in the Dolomites are referred to in German and Ladin (see p165), as well as Italian. Some maps use all three, some use two, others only use one. In this chapter, where appropriate, we have included the German or Ladin spelling for place names.

Books

Gillian Price's *Walking in the Dolomites* (2003) and *Shorter Walks in the Dolomites* (2002) are useful references for other walks in the area. For the harder stuff try *Via Ferratas in the Italian Dolomites* (2002) by John Smith and Graham Fletcher. All three books are published by Cicerone.

Information Sources

The **Regional Agency for Environmental Protection & Prevention in the Veneto** (Arpav; ☎ 0436 792 21; www.arpa.veneto .it; 15 Jun-15 Sep) provides a Dolomites weather forecast, which is available in English.

Permits & Regulations

Within the protected park territory it is prohibited to remove certain plant and animal species (including seeds, insects, butterflies, larvae, chrysalises, nests and eggs of any species), as well as fossils and minerals.

Emergency

In South Tyrol, contact the **mountain rescue service** (☎ 0471 79 71 71) or, in all areas, for medical assistance call the **national emergency** number (☎ 118).

GETTING THERE & AROUND

The Dolomites are easily accessed by train, road or bus with routes from the Po Valley, the Veneto plains and Austria converging on the cultural capitals of Trento and Bolzano. Numerous local bus companies penetrate the remote valleys on winding, alpine roads. Equally spectacular cable cars serve the higher altitudes.

GATEWAY

Combining the best elements of Austro-German and Italian culture, the South Tyrolean city of Bolzano (p174) makes an ideal gateway to the Dolomite region.

A CONFEDERATION OF VALLEYS

The culturally schizophrenic Dolomite region holds many fascinations, not least the potent lure of its Mediterranean-meets-*Mitteleuropa* heritage. But the real ambiguities lie in its deep-cut valleys; sheltered havens that don't just demarcate different drainage basins, but support radically different cultures (and languages). Here's a breakdown of some of their key characteristics.

Val d'Adige – a vine-flecked glacial valley that connects the two regional capitals of Bolzano and Trento and tracks the course of the Adige River. All of the Dolomite ranges, save for the outlying Brenta group, lie to the east.

Val di Non – an Italian-speaking valley northwest of Trento that skirts the Brenta Group, the Non is accessible by private train and famous for its apple orchards and storybook castles.

Val di Sole – the 'sun valley' lives up to its name enabling visitors to pursue numerous outdoor activities such as rafting and cycling. It's biggest town, Malè, makes a good headquarters for the nearby Stelvio National Park (p142) and excursions into the Brenta Dolomites (p48) to the south.

Val di Livinallongo – dominated by the Sella range to the west and Marmolada to the south, the Livinallongo (Buchenstein in German) lies in the Veneto region and mixes its Ladin culture with Italian inflections. It's nexus is the small but popular ski resort of Arabba.

Val Pusteria – wide, pastoral and refreshingly green in its western extremities, the Pusteria culminates in the dramatic turrets of the Sesto Dolomites that lure hikers with challenging *vie ferrate* trails and historians with outdoor WWI memorabilia.

Val Badia – the most mysterious and spiritual of the region's five Ladin-speaking valleys, Badia is the starting point for the Alta Via 1 hiking trail (summer) and a hop-on point for the Sella Ronda ski circuit (winter).

Val Gardena – celebrated for its woodcarvers, esoteric Ladin museum and onion-domed churches, Gardena's nexus is the small town of Ortisei, starting point for this book's seven-day Dolomite Rollercoaster hike.

Val di Fassa – Trentino's only Ladin valley spins on two hubs, the diminutive towns of Canazei and Moena, the latter of which plays host to the annual Marcialonga cross-country ski marathon.

Val de Fiemme – the independently minded Fiemme once set up its own quasi-republic and still fosters a strong community spirit.

Valle Ampezzana – the spiritual capital of the Ladin community, this pivotal Dolomite valley is centred on Cortina D'Ampezzo, a ritzy ski resort that hosted the 1956 Winter Olympics and swings culturally closer to Trentino than its native Veneto.

SCILIAR & CATINACCIO LOOP

Duration 4 days
Distance 37km
Difficulty moderate–demanding
Start/Finish Compaccio
Nearest Town Castelrotto (p175)
Transport bus, cable car

Summary A scenic walk, from the undulating pastures of the Alpe di Siusi to
the jagged peaks of Torri del Vajolet and
Catinaccio.

In mainland Europe, there are few more
jarring or beautiful juxtapositions than the
undulating green pastures of the Alpe di
Siusi – the continent's largest plateau –
ending dramatically at the base of the
towering Sciliar Mountains. To the southeast lies the more jagged Catinaccio range,
best described by its German name 'Rosen-
garten' for the eerie pink hue given off by
the mountain's dolomite rock at sunset.
The two areas are protected in the Parco
Naturale dello Sciliar established in 1974.
Other quirks include the region's distinctive onion-domed churches and curative
hay-baths.

Hiking is a joy here, and you don't need
to be a mountaineer to reach great heights.
The gentle slopes of the Alpe di Siusi are
perfect for families with kids, and average
stamina will get you to the Rifugio Bolzano
(p159) one of the Alps' oldest mountain
huts, which rests at 2457m, just under
Monte Pez (2563m), the Sciliar's summit.

The jagged peaks of the Catinaccio group
provide many more challenging walks, including the popular *via ferrata* (iron way)
Santner.

PLANNING
Maps
The excellent Kompass 1:25,000 map No
629 *Rosengarten-Catinaccio-Latemar* covers the walk, except the starting point from
Compaccio to the Hotel Panorama, usually
covered by chairlift. The Tabacco 1:25,000
map No 5 *Val Gardena-Alpe di Siusi* covers
only the northern section.

GETTING TO/FROM THE WALK
The world's longest **aerial cableway**
(http://seiseralmbahn.it; one-way/return

€9/12; 8am-7pm mid-Dec–Mar & mid-
May–Oct) is a dizzying 4300m 15-minute
trip (800m ascent) from Siusi to Compaccio.
The road linking the two towns is closed to
normal traffic when the cableway is open;
visitors with a hotel booking in the zone can
obtain a permit from Compaccio's tourist office, allowing them to drive between
4pm and 10am. Organise your pass before
arriving in the area. Regular buses operated by **Silbernagl** (☎ 0471 70 74 00; www
.silbernagl.it) serve the area from Castelrotto and Siusi.

THE WALK
Day 1: Compaccio to Rifugio Alpe di Tires
5–7 hours, 12km, 957m ascent, 378m descent

You can walk from Compaccio, heading
southeast along No S-10 and then turn
right (southwest) onto Trail No 10. Continue until it intersects with a dirt road
(No 5) on the left (southeast), which you
follow to Malga Saltner. However, the best
option is to use the **Panorama chairlift**
(€3.10; 8.30am-5.30pm). From the upper
station near the Hotel Panorama, walk
right (southwest) on the dirt road, marked
as Trail S, reaching **Malga Laurinhütte**,
where the proper Trail S starts on your
left (south). Follow it downhill to reach
the dirt road (No 5) where you turn left
(south), cross a bridge and continue to
the evocative **Malga Saltner** (one hour
from the top of the chairlift). Enjoy an
apple strudel with whipped cream before
continuing.

From Malga Saltner continue along Trail
No 5, known as Sentiero dei Turisti, which
joins Trail No 1. Follow this trail west as
it snakes its way up to the Monte Sciliar
(Schlern) high plain. Once you arrive at
the plateau (two hours), you'll find Nos 3
to 4 on your left. To continue to Rifugio
Alpe di Tires, turn left (southeast) on Trail
Nos 3 to 4, which crosses the Monte Sciliar
high plain. Walk across the south face of
Cima di Terrarossa, descending into a deep
valley. At a junction make sure you stick to
Trail No 4 on your left (don't take No 3,
which goes down to Val Ciamin) until you
reach **Rifugio Alpe di Tires** (☎ 0471 72
79 58, 70 74 60; www.tierseralpl.com; dm/r
€19.50/28.90); two hours from the junction
of Trail Nos 1 and 3 to 4.

SCILIAR & CATINACCIO LOOP

ALTERNATIVE DAY 1: VIA FORCELLA DENTI DI TERRAROSSA

1–2½ hours, 4km, 669m ascent, 59m descent

If time is limited, take this shorter route. From Hotel Panorama head west on the dirt road and after a few metres you'll find Trail No 2 on your left (south). Cross a peat meadow, until you reach a trail junction (just before a dirt road, about 10 minutes) where you'll turn right (south) on Trail No 2. Following this trail you'll ascend to **Forcella Denti di Terrarossa** (an excellent sunset lookout) and, in 15 minutes, you'll descend to the **Rifugio Alpe di Tires**.

SIDE TRIP: MONTE PEZ

1¼ hours, 2km, 156m ascent

From the junction of Trail Nos 1 and 3 to 4, continue southwest and, in 10 minutes,

you'll reach the old **Rifugio Bolzano** (☎ 0471 61 20 24; dm/d €18/30), which dates from 1885. From here it's an easy walk up to nearby Monte Pez. Take the trail north of the *rifugio*. From the summit of Monte Pez (2563m) you have a 360-degree view: to the north you can see the Alps stretching into Austria; to the northeast you see Le Odle, Puez (2913m) and Sassongher (2665m); to the east is the Sella group, Sasso Lungo and Sasso Piatto (2964m); southeast you can see the Catinaccio (2981m).

Day 2: Rifugio Alpe di Tires to Rifugio Passo Santner

5–7 hours, 7km, 905m ascent, 606m descent

Head south along a rocky trail (No 3a-554), ascending to **Passo Alpe di Tires** and

REINHOLD MESSNER

While the Germans make up the lion's share of the hikers in the Dolomites, the man invariably venerated as the greatest hiker of them all, the distinctly Teutonic-sounding Reinhold Messner, was actually an Italian (albeit a German-speaking one) from the Alto Adige town of Bressanone (Brixen).

Born in 1944 at the end of WWII Messner grew up surrounded by the sharp, crennellated peaks of the Dolomites. Scaling his first alpine summit at the age of five, he quickly took the Alps by storm and, by his early 20s, was recognised as a rising star in the tough world of mountaineering. Derisive of the siege tactics employed by traditional Himalayan expeditions in the 1960s, Messner advocated a simpler alpine-style approach to climbing that emphasised fast ascents with minimal equipment. By the 1970s he had set his sights on Everest, confidently announcing his ambition to climb the mountain 'by fair means', without the use of supplementary oxygen.

The prophecy was heroically fulfilled in 1978 when Messner, and Austrian Peter Habeler, became the first men to summit the world's tallest peak without oxygen – a feat that was considered physically impossible, if not suicidal, at the time. Unsatisfied with his team effort, Messner returned two years later, and hacked his way up the mountain's north face to the summit, alone, again without oxygen – a superhuman achievement that many have put on a par with the moon landing.

Messner's position as the Tiger Woods of mountaineering has long intrigued his fellow climbers. Not only is his aerobic capacity relatively average for a man of his age, but he also spent the bulk of his climbing career hampered by the loss of three fingers and seven toes following an ill-fated Himalayan expedition in 1970 (that also tragically claimed the life of his younger brother Gunther).

Undaunted by the ageing process, the iron-willed Messner logged another record in 1986 when he became the first person to scale all 'eight-thousanders' (the 14 mountains in the world over 8000m). Shunning a well-earned retirement, he also partook in the first unassisted crossing of Antarctica by foot.

These days Messner treks at a gentler pace, mainly in the Dolomites. Recently retired as a Euro MP for the Italian Green Party, he tends to his quintet of **Messner Mountain Museums** (MMM; ☎ 0471 63 31 45; www.messner-mountain-museum.it, in Italian; adult/student €8/6; 10am-6pm Tue-Sun Mar-Nov), the centrepiece of which is located in Castel Firmiano 6km south of Bolzano.

nearby Passo Molignon (2598m). From here you start the steep descent on a scree slope into a rocky alpine valley. Before reaching the valley floor, the trail forks. Keep to the left (southeast) and stay on Trail No 554, which in two hours will take you up to **Rifugio Passo Principe** (☎ 0462 76 42 44, www.rifugiopassoprincipe.com; dm/half-board €15/38; late May-late Oct) under Monte Catinaccio d'Antermoia (3002m). It is worth taking a break at this tiny *rifugio*.

From here, descend south into the valley along the large Trail No 584. You'll arrive at **Rifugio Vajolet** (☎ 0462 76 32 92, 76 90 45; www.rifugiovajolet.com; dm €20) and **Rifugio Preuss** (☎ 0462 76 48 47), the latter being a bar-restaurant open during the day only. From here you go right (west), up the steep and rocky Trail No 542s to the Catinaccio hidden valley. Those without mountaineering experience will find this part of the walk challenging, but it is equipped with an iron cord for security. You will arrive in an evocative rocky world with a tiny lake and **Rifugio Re Alberto** (☎ 0462 76 34 28, 76 35 48; www.rifugiore alberto.com; dm €22), just in front of three sharp pinnacles called Torri del Vajolet, famous among climbers. Walkers who have booked for the night can call Rifugio Re Alberto from the Rifugio Vajolet and send their backpack up on the cableway.

Follow Trail No 542s up to **Rifugio Passo Santner** (☎ 0471 64 22 30, 0462 57 35 13), 2¾ hours from Rifugio Passo Principe. Rifugio Passo Santner is one of the most spectacularly located *rifugi* in the Alps. It is perched on a precipice under the Catinaccio and on the edge of an almost sheer drop into the valley. The *rifugio* itself is tiny, with only two rooms, each containing four beds. Climbers flock here in summer to tackle the Torri del Vajolet and Catinaccio.

Day 3: Rifugio Passo Santner to Rifugio Antermoia

4–5 hours, 7km, 529m ascent, 766m descent

Retrace your steps to the junction with Trail No 554, where Trail No 584 veers to the right (east). Follow this trail to the high **Passo d'Antermoia** (2770m) and then descend steeply to **Lago d'Antermoia** (2495m). Shortly afterwards you'll reach **Rifugio Antermoia** (☎ 0462 60 22 72, 75 04 80; dm €22-24; 20 Jun-20 Sep).

Day 4: Rifugio Antermoia to Compaccio

3½–4½ hours, 11km, 225m ascent, 890m descent

The trail becomes No 580, which heads east to **Passo di Dona** (2516m) and then descends as Trail No 578. Walking downhill, ignore deviations on your right (east) for Campitello-Mazzin, and you will reach another saddle, **Passo Duron** (2282m, one hour), also known as Passo Ciarégole depending on the map.

Walk straight ahead from this saddle along the mountainside and, while Trail No 578 veers down to the right (east) for Valle di Duron-Campitello, continue left on the narrow and wild Trail No 555. This trail will take you in a northwesterly, slippery descent along the northern slopes of the Croda del Lago group. Before the trail joins a dirt road (Trail No 532), near the group of herders' shelters known as **Malga Dòcoldaura** (2046m), you have to ford the (usually easy) Rivo Duron. Follow Trail No 532 north to the **Sella di Cresta Nera** (2204m) and descend to the hotel **Albergo Dialer** (☎ 0471 72 79 22; www.gasthof-dialer.com) at 2145m, about two hours from Passo Duron. Walk north along the dirt road for 10 minutes and turn left (west) on Trail No 7, veering north after a small creek. This trail will take you down then up to **Rifugio Mahlknechthütte** (☎ 0471 72 79 12; www.mahlknechthuette.com; dm €35, d from €47), 30 minutes from Albergo Dialer. The *rifugio* and the hotel are good alternatives for an overnight stop.

From Rifugio Mahlknechthütte the trail becomes dirt road No 7 (in some sections corresponding to No 12). It will take you to the Hotel Panorama and chairlift, about an hour from the *rifugio*, and then to Compaccio, another 40 minutes' walk.

DOLOMITE ROLLERCOASTER

Duration 7 days
Distance 70km
Difficulty moderate–demanding
Start Ortisei
Finish Hotel Dolomitenhof
Nearest Towns Ortisei (p177), San Candido (p177)
Transport bus

Summary An alternative west–east *alta via* that dips in and out of German-, Italian- and Ladin-speaking valleys. It takes in the whole dramatic sweep of the Northern Dolomites in seven spectacular days.

Most of the official long-distance *alte vie* cross the Dolomites north–south, making this west–east excursion something of a novelty. Stepping aboard the rollercoaster in the Ladin Val Gardena you get dramatic insights into the whole Dolomite range from the wide meadows of Prato Piazza to the celestially sculpted peaks of the Tre Cime di Lavaredo, one of the most striking scenes in the Alps.

The walk has been described as a seven-day trip, with a maximum of six hours' walking per day. For strong walkers happy to spend up to eight hours on the trail, the walk can be done in six days, but this leaves little or no time for side trips. While none of the sections require real technical skills, some have exposed passages.

PLANNING

Maps

Make sure you carry good maps – the Tabacco 1:25,000 No 05 *Val Gardena*, No 07 *Alta Badia*, 03 *Cortina D'Ampezzo* and No 010 *Dolomiti di Sesto* are recommended.

WARNING

Some sections of the following walk are equipped with steel cables or chains to assist walkers with little experience in alpine mountaineering, especially those who have trouble crossing exposed passages. While none of these sections require real technical skills, you might feel more confident wearing proper *via ferrata* equipment (see Equipment, p47).

NORTHERN DOLOMITES (WEST)

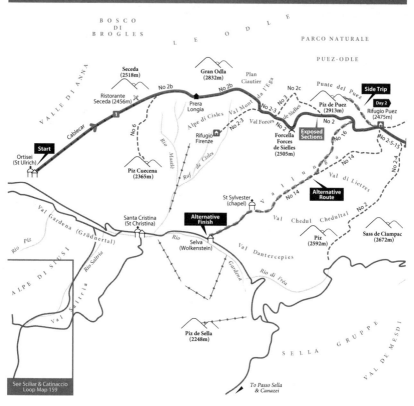

GETTING TO/FROM THE WALK
Ortisei (start)
The walk starts at the base of the cable car in Via Roma in Ortisei, see p177 for information on getting to and from the town.

Hotel Dolomitenhof (finish)
From the end of the walk at Hotel Dolomitenhof, you can walk the 3km to Sesto; buses run from Sesto to San Candido (hourly in high season, from 8.30am to 6pm).

THE WALK
Day 1: Ortisei to Rifugio Puez
4–6 hours, 10km, 450m ascent, 431m descent
The initial climb from Ortisei is easy and spectacular, thanks to the two-section **Seceda cable car** (☎ 0471 79 65 31; €18; 8.30am-12.15pm & 1.45pm-5.30pm

3 Sep–21 Jul; 8.30am-5.30pm 22 Jul–2 Sep). The view from the gondola is memorable, taking in the spiky pinnacles of the Odle group and Sass Rigais (3025m) to the northeast; the massive Sella group and Sasso Lungo (3181m) to the southeast; and the high plain of the Alpe di Siusi at the foot of Monte Sciliar (2563m) to the southwest.

From **Ristorante Seceda** at the top station of the cable car, take Trail No 2b, which heads east at mid-slope through lush green, sloping pastures dotted with wooden *malghe* (herders' hut). Keep to the descending Trail No 2b, which is brick-paved in some slippery sections. It takes you, avoiding numerous deviations, to a lovely area known as **Prera Longia**, where you'll find a romantic *malga* selling milk in a surreal landscape dotted with huge boulders. In

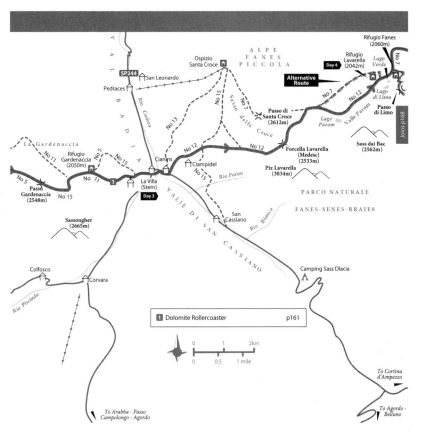

the early morning it is likely that you'll see marmots, roe deer and lots of small birds, such as the alpine finch. Stay on Trail No 2b until you arrive at **Plan Ciautier**, where a number of trails ascend north towards canyons where there are several *vie ferrate*. From here Trail No 2b descends to cross a small riverbed and then to the convergence of Val Mont da l'Ega and **Val Forces de Sielles**, 1½ hours from Ristorante Seceda. The convergence forms the beginning of the large riverbed of the Ruf de Cisles, where water flows only when it rains. Cross the riverbed and climb up Val Forces de Sielles. On the way to the Forcella Forces de Sielles, the trail changes from Trail No 2b to Nos 2 to 3 and then No 2; it is a tough, semi-vertical walk. Don't take the trail that descends southwest (the western branch of Nos 2-3) for Rifugio

Firenze (20 minutes). At **Forcella Forces de Sielles** (one hour from the convergence of the valleys) you will see a section of picturesque Vallunga to the southeast and there is a spectacular view over the Odle group to the northwest. By this time you will probably be ready for a rest, so save your snacks and drinks for this scenic spot!

Return to Trail No 2 and follow it to the left (north). You will come to several short sections of exposed trail, equipped with iron cords, but don't panic – you don't need any equipment. Just hold on to the cord if you need help crossing any of these sections. Turning east with the trail, you'll pass a crest (2600m), the highest point of the day, and then descend to a rocky green balcony above the U-shaped glacial valley of Vallunga. Descending again, Trail No 2c, from Forcella Nivea, comes in from the left. The trails merge in a wide flat grassy area, inhabited by sheep and horses. Continue east along the trail. If you plan to make this walk a one-day loop, you can take Trail No 16, which descends on the right (southwest) to the Vallunga (see Alternative Finish, see below). Otherwise, remaining on Trail No 2, you'll soon reach **Rifugio Puez** (☎ 0471 79 53 65, 84 70 59; dm €20-26; 15 Jun-1 Oct), 2¾ hours from Forcella Forces de Sielles, which lies on the Alta Via 2. At the *rifugio* you can take a well-earned hot shower (coin-operated) and rest.

If you are feeling energetic and daylight is on your side, you can finish the day with the Side Trip to Piz de Puez.

SIDE TRIP: PIZ DE PUEZ
2–2½ hours, 3km, 438m ascent/descent
From Rifugio Puez take the unnumbered steep trail that heads northwest, passing to the left of Col de Puez. Climb uphill to the small saddle below the Puez peak. In a few minutes you'll reach the summit (2913m), from where you can enjoy panoramic views.

ALTERNATIVE FINISH: SELVA
2–2½ hours, 7km, 886m descent
If you plan to complete this walk as a one-day loop, follow No 16, which descends steeply (southwest), eventually reaching the bottom of the Vallunga, where it joins a small dirt road marked as No 14. Turn right (southwest) and meander down the pretty Vallunga with its alpine vegetation. If you walk quietly you should come across small animals such as fawns, squirrels, roe deer and many birds. The contrast between the majesty of the high mountains and the gentle environment of the valley creates a memorable effect and provides a fitting end to the walk. Once at the **St Sylvester** chapel, it takes about 15 minutes to reach the town of **Selva**, from where you can catch a bus back to Ortisei.

Day 2: Rifugio Puez to La Villa/ Stern
4–5 hours, 7.5km, 73m ascent, 1116m descent
Follow No 2-4-15 southeast, crossing an arid high plain inhabited by white partridges to Passo Gardenaccia (2548m). The trail then merges with No 11 and descends

east to the old style **Rifugio Gardenaccia** (☎ 0471 84 92 82), two hours from Rifugio Puez.

From Rifugio Gardenaccia descend southeast along Trail No 11 into the Gardenaccia valley. Walk through a forest, coming out near Maso Ploten, from where you descend to a church on the outskirts of **La Villa** (1433m, 1½ to two hours). From the church take the paved road, curving downhill to reach the provincial road No 244 and the helpful tourist information office. Many of northern Italy's most renowned restaurants and hotels can be found in the area.

La Villa is easily accessible from Bolzano (2½ hours) and Brunico (1¼ hours) on hourly **SAD** (☎ 800 846 047; www.sad .it) buses. Buses run less frequently outside of the summer season.

Day 3: La Villa to Rifugio Lavarella (Lavarela)
5–7 hours, 11km, 1100m ascent, 491m descent
Head east on Trail No 12, which starts across the road from the **La Villa** information office and to the left of Hotel Aurora. Go downhill and cross a bridge (1420m) over a stream. When you reach the asphalt road, turn right and follow it up the slope for a few metres until you find the sign indicating where Trail Nos 12 to 13 head left. Ascend on Trail No 12 to the right (east), passing nearby **Cianins** and **Ciampidel**. Cross over Trail No 15, which ascends from San Cassiano (south) to the Ospizio Santa Croce (north), and continue east on Trail No 12 (well marked), through an enchanting forest, rich in birdlife, until you reach mountain pines. Here, avoid the deviation off to the left (it connects with Trail No 15 to the north) and continue your ascent on Trail No 12, which becomes increasingly steep over a section of scree. After a zigzagging stretch, you reach **Forcella Lavarella** (2533m) – called Medesc on the Tabacco map – about three to four hours from La Villa. Take a break here and enjoy the incredible view with La Villa (west) and the Sella group (southwest).

Continue descending northeast on Trail No 12, avoiding deviations, until this trail merges in a flat meadow with Trail No 7, which comes from Passo di Santa Croce. Turn right (east) and follow Trail Nos 7 to 12 for about 100m to another

THE LADIN TRADITION

The Ladin language and culture can be traced to around 15 BC, when the people of the Central Alps were forcibly united into the Roman province of Rhaetia. The Romans introduced Latin to the province, but the original inhabitants of the area, with their diverse linguistic and cultural backgrounds, modified the language to such an extent that, by around AD 450, it had evolved into an independent Romance language, known as Raeto-Romanic. Today the language and culture are confined mainly to the Val Gardena and Val Badia areas, where about 90% of the locals declared in the 1981 census that they belonged to the Ladin language group. Along with German and Italian, Ladin is taught in schools, and the survival of Ladin cultural and linguistic identity is protected by law.

The Ladin culture is rich in vibrant poetry and legends, set amid the jagged peaks of the Dolomites, and peopled by fairies, gnomes, elves, giants, princesses and heroes. Passed on by word of mouth for centuries, and often heavily influenced by Germanic myths, many of these legends were in danger of being lost. In the first decade of this century, journalist Carlo Felice Wolff spent 10 years gathering and researching the local legends, listening as the old people, farmers and shepherds recounted the stories and fairy-tales. Instead of simply writing down what he was told, Wolff reconstructed the tales from the many different versions and recollections he gathered.

There are a handful of Ladin museums in the area including the **Museo Ladin Ortisei** (☎ 0471 79 75 54; Piazza San Antonio; admission free; 10am-noon & 3-7pm Jul & Aug, 3-6.30pm at other times) in Val Gardena, and **Museo Ladin San Martino** (☎ 0474 52 40 20; www .museumladin.it; Via Tor 72, San Martino, Val Badia; adult/child €6/4.50; 10am-6pm Tue-Sat, 2-6pm Sun mid-Mar–Oct) atmospherically set in a castle 15km south of Brunico in Val Badia.

Y-junction (30 minutes from Forcella Lavarella). Here you have a choice; the more difficult option is Trail No 7 on the left (see Alternative Route, next column). Otherwise, on the right (southeast) is Trail No 12, which is the main, well-marked route. Follow this trail past **Lago Parom** (which is sometimes there and sometimes not). You are likely to see carpets of edelweiss along here. The trail descends along a strange, silent riverbed through a landscape of plume-shaped rocks that, when tapped, emit glassy sounds. These were once part of the coral reef of a tropical sea. Further on, sparse arolla pines grow high among the rocks in a kind of twisted and inhospitable, surreal garden. The trail meanders down, sometimes through slippery arolla pine roots, and when you can hear the roar of water surging from the numerous springs that feed Lago Verde you will be just above positively luxurious **Rifugio Lavarella** (☎ 0474 50 10 79; www.lavarella.it; bed/half-board from €20/38; 15 Jun-10 Oct), 1½ to two hours from the Y-junction. A short distance away, on the other side of the stream, is the recently rebuilt **Rifugio Fanes** (☎ 0474 50 10 97; www.rifugiofanes.com; dm/d €20/28; 15 Jun–5 Oct).

ALTERNATIVE ROUTE: VIA ALPES FANES PICCOLA
1½–2½ hours, 2.5km

If you have time and good weather, a more difficult route offers a spectacular panoramic descent along open rocky hills and secluded meadows inhabited by marmots. At the Y-junction, heading left (northeast) is Trail No 7. Follow cairns and unclear red-and-white marks, but take care – inexperienced walkers could find these difficult to follow, especially with darkness or bad weather (fog could create a real problem for orientation). At the end of this trail, at the junction (2150m) with Trail No 13 coming from Passo San Antonio (north), turn right (south) and, in a few minutes, reach **Rifugio Lavarella**.

ALTERNATIVE FINISH: PODESTAGNO
3–3½ hours, 9km, 132m ascent, 760m descent

If you wish to finish your walk at this point, it is possible to head to Cortina d'Ampezzo or Dobbiaco. From Rifugio Fanes, take the dirt road No 10 up to **Passo di Limo** and then down into the gorgeous Valle di Fanes, taking a short cut to avoid the hairpin bends of the road. Continue along the road and pass a deep gorge at **Ponte Alto**. A brief

DOLOMITES

ÖTZI – THE WORLD'S FIRST HIGH-ALTITUDE HIKER?

When two Austrian students stumbled upon a human corpse wedged into a melting glacier on Hauslabjoch Pass in 1991, they assumed they had found the remains of an unfortunate fellow hiker caught in a killer winter storm. But, when the mummified body was removed and taken to a morgue in Innsbruck a few days later, it was discovered to be over 5300 years old. The male corpse – subsequently nicknamed Ötzi, or 'the Iceman' – is the oldest mummified remains ever found in Europe, dating from an ancient Copper Age civilisation that lived in the Dolomites 150 years before the founding of Ancient Egypt.

Though initially claimed by the Austrian government, it was later ascertained that Ötzi had been unearthed 100m inside the Italian border on the Schnalstal glacier. After a brief diplomatic dispute, the mummy was returned to Italy where it has been on display in the **Museo Archeologico dell'Alto Adige** (☎ 0471 32 01 00; www.iceman.it; Via Museo 43; adult/child under 6yr €8/free; 10am-6pm Tue-Sun) in Bolzano since 1998.

What Ötzi was actually doing 3200m up a glaciated mountainside 52 centuries before alpinism became a serious sport is still a matter of some debate. Some maintain he was a wandering shepherd killed in a violent confrontation; others prefer to merely think of him as the world's first high-altitude hiker.

---

detour for a visit to the impressive **Fanes Falls** is recommended. Follow the road to the S51 road at Podestagno, where you can catch a bus south to Cortina (9km) or north to Dobbiaco (23km). Turning right (south) on the S51, in 20 minutes you reach Hotel Fiames (see p176) 150m north of the shuttle- bus stop. A further 1km south is Camping Olympia (p176).

Day 4: Rifugio Lavarella to Rifugio Biella
5–7 hours, 13km, 809m ascent, 534m descent

Follow the dirt road (northeast), which corresponds with Trail No 7 (also marked with the blue, triangular Alta Via No 1 signs). These roads are occasionally used by 4WD vehicles ferrying customers between the *rifugi*. The road descends steeply into the small valley of Rio San Vigilio and, after a wide curve on the right (east), you come across the first of three shortcuts on the left, which cut across hairpin bends. However, it is just as easy to stick to the road, especially if it is raining, all the way to **Rifugio Pederù** (☎ 0474 50 10 86; www.pederu.it; r with private bathroom per person €36-45; 15 Jun–10 Oct), about 1½ to two hours. Following this route you also pass the start of the Alternative Route via Banc dal Sè (p167). It is possible to exit from the walk at Rifugio Pederù. A road descends into the beautiful Valle di Rudo, reaching San Viglio di Marebbe in two to three hours.

Alternatively, take a shuttle bus from the *rifugio*. In San Viglio you can connect with a bus to Alta Badia or Brunico.

From Rifugio Pederù, take the road (east) that climbs in a series of sharp hairpin bends to a plateau. Once at the top you'll find a short cut (left), indicated by signs. From here you can also continue along No 9 (right fork) to reach Rifugio Fodara Vedla, and do the Side Trip to Malga Ra Stua (p167). Otherwise, follow the short cut to **Rifugio Sennes** (☎ 0474 50 10 92; www .sennes.com; dm €25, r with private bathroom €35; 9 Jun-20 Oct), about two to 2½ hours away. The *rifugio* is beside Lago di Sennes and surrounded by *malghe*. There is a 4WD for customers only from Rifugio Pederù.

From Rifugio Sennes you can either head east following the dirt road Alta Via No 1 (this is the longer route but affords great views) or cut northeast on Trail No 6, to rejoin the Alta Via in sight of the old **Rifugio Biella** (☎ 0436 86 69 91; dm €20-26; 20 Jun-30 Sep), set in an unforgettable lunar landscape. If you take Trail No 6, Rifugio Biella is about an hour from Rifugio Sennes.

SIDE TRIP: CRODA DEL BECCO PEAK
2–3 hours, 4km, 483m ascent

From Rifugio Biella head north up the technically easy, steep trail to Croda del Becco (2810m). Sections of the trail are equipped with iron cord.

ALTERNATIVE ROUTE: VIA BANC DAL SÈ
4–5 hours, 5.5km, 751m ascent, 491m descent

This alternative trail ascends northeast into the heart of the semi-wilderness of the Bancdalsè group. It's an atmospheric route that saves as least an hour, but is a bit exposed.

Following the dirt road from Rifugio Lavarella, about 10 minutes past Lago Piciodèl (right) you will see a huge boulder (1814m). Shortly after the road begins to descend, look to your right (northeast) for a cairn. This marks the turn-off for the unmarked trail called Banc dal Sè, which ascends steeply northeast through the scree. It's marked on some maps with black dots and dashes. Do not attempt this trail in poor weather or fading light (see Warning, below). There are several steep ascents and descents before arriving at the picturesque **Rifugio Fodara Vedla** (☎ 0474 50 15 38; www.fodara.it; 13 Jun-11 Oct), two to 2½ hours from the turn-off. The *rifugio* is surrounded by a village of traditional *malghe* with a tiny wooden chapel. It offers comfortable rooms and a great terrace where you can relax and enjoy the magnificent scenery. If you have time you can spend an extra day here and visit Rifugio Malga Ra Stua (see below).

To continue on to Rifugio Sennes, from Rifugio Fodara Vedla head north on dirt road No 7-1. After a few hundred metres it comes to a fork, where you head right. This way you avoid the busy road and cross a high plain where it is not uncommon to encounter chamois. Eventually you rejoin the dirt road No 7-1 and the main route to **Rifugio Sennes** (one hour from Rifugio Fodara Vedla).

SIDE TRIP: TO RIFUGIO MALGA RA STUA
3½–4 hours, 8km, 448m ascent

From Rifugio Fodara Vedla, take Trail No 9 (east), which follows an old WWI military road down into the Val Salata. When you reach an intersection, turn right (southeast) along a dirt road to reach **Rifugio Malga Ra Stua** (☎ 0436 57 53; www.malgarastua.it; 10 Jun-20 Oct), about one to 1½ hours from Rifugio Fodara Vedla. It is possible to sleep here or just enjoy a pleasant lunch on the deck before heading back to Rifugio Fodara Vedla. At the least, try a marvellous hot chocolate topped with fresh whipped cream.

From the *rifugio* walk back (northwest) along the dirt road No 6 through the beautiful Val Salata. Continue to just before Rifugio Sennes (1½-2 hours), cut across (southwest) on Trail No 7 and then head south to reach Rifugio Fodara Vedla (one hour from Rifugio Sennes).

You can link this loop with the Parco Naturale delle Dolomiti d'Ampezzo route (p171).

Day 5: Rifugio Biella to Rifugio Vallandro
5½–6½ hours, 11km, 323m ascent, 600m descent

Head southeast up No 28, with great views of Lago Grande di Fosses. The trail follows the mountain crest towards the Croda Rossa, a majestic mountain inhabited by golden eagles and ibex. Once you reach **Forcella Cocodain** (one hour), descend left (north) on No 28, a difficult, slippery and rocky route, to a junction (2195m, one hour) where you pick up No 3. The area offers an amazing landscape. From the junction ascend north along combined Trail Nos 3 and 28 until you reach another junction with Trail No 4, coming from the northwest. Ascend to the right on Trail Nos 3-4-28 and then turn right (east) again on Trail Nos 3 to 4. Walking through pastures, you will reach a junction (2260m). From here descend southeast to **Malga Cavalli di Sopra** (also called Casera Cavallo di Sopra), about an hour from Forcella Cocodain, where you can enjoy refreshments from the rustic café while enjoying a fabulous view of the imposing Croda Rossa.

Continue along No 3, ascending southeast along the north face of the Croda Rossa. The trail narrows and there is a sheer drop, but there are fixed iron cords to hold onto for safety. This section is quite exposed and might pose some difficulty for

---

WARNING

The Banc dal Sè route is definitely not recommended in darkness or during bad weather conditions. It is a narrow and slippery mountain route that requires a safe step. The route is at the base of a vertical mountain face and is crossed by several water courses. When it rains, there can be rockfalls and landslides.

DOLOMITES

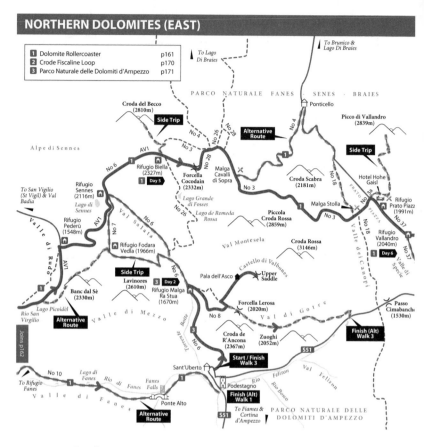

NORTHERN DOLOMITES (EAST)

1 Dolomite Rollercoaster	p161
2 Crode Fiscaline Loop	p170
3 Parco Naturale delle Dolomiti d'Ampezzo	p171

inexperienced walkers. It requires a careful step and, during storms, is not advisable (see Alternative Route). Trail No 3 continues to its highest point (2300m), about an hour from the *malga*, and then descends towards the valley.

When you reach a junction (1965m), where Trail No 18 descends to the left (northwest) towards Ponticello, continue ascending northeast along Trail No 3. You will pass nearby **Malga Stolla**, a rustic wayside café offering a delicious yoghurt and myrtle berry drink, and Trail No 18 heading right (southeast) to Passo Cimabanche on the S51, where there is a bar and bus stops for Cortina (15km) and Dobbiaco.

Taking Trail No 3a, you will soon reach the wide meadows of **Prato Piazza** in front of **Hotel Hohe Gaisl** (☎ 0474 74 86 06; www.hohegaisl.com; d from €56), one hour from the high point, and the nearby **Rifugio Prato Piazza** (☎ 0474 74 86 50; www.pratopiazza.com; d with breakfast €32-38). Turn right and take the road up to **Rifugio Vallandro** (☎ 0474 97 25 05; dm €20; 1 Jun-1 Oct), about 40 minutes. The small, old-style *rifugio* has great views of the Croda Rossa (west) and Cristallo (south), and is still 'guarded' by the ruins of a WWI Austrian fort. Try to get up before dawn to see how the Croda Rossa earned its name.

SIDE TRIP: PICCO DI VALLANDRO
4 hours, 5.5km, 848m ascent/descent
It is worth making the ascent to the summit of Picco di Vallandro (2839m) on Trail No 40, which starts from the chapel next to Rifugio Prato Piazza.

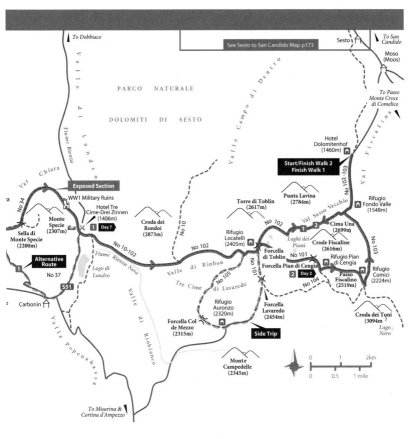

ALTERNATIVE ROUTE: VIA HOTEL PONTICELLO

2½–3 hours, 9km, 500m ascent, 700m descent

From Malga Cavalli di Sopra, descend along the steep dirt road to **Hotel Ponticello** (☎ 0474 74 86 13; www.hotel-brueckele .it), for 1½ hours. To exit from the walk at this point, take the bus from Ponticello to Lago di Braies or Villabassa–Monguelfo–Brunico (seven a day from 10.40am to 5.30pm).

To continue, from the hotel walk south up the road and take Trail No 18 (right) to a junction (1965m) with Trail No 3. Heading left (northeast) you rejoin the main route across Prato Piazza to **Rifugio Vallandro**. To avoid the steep ascent from Hotel Ponticello, the shuttle bus up to Prato Piazza (€1.20, seven a day from 10am to 4.25pm) might be a better bet.

Day 6: Rifugio Vallandro to Hotel Tre Cime-Drei Zinnen

2–2½ hours, 5.5km, 172m ascent, 794m descent

There are some very exposed sections, which are equipped with iron cords, along this route. If this worries you try the Alternative Route via Carbonin (p170).

From Rifugio Vallandro take the dirt road No 34, which ascends north, or the trail, also numbered 34, that heads uphill (east) from just behind the *rifugio*, cutting up to a ruined fort and **Sella di Monte Specie** (2200m, 40 minutes). Avoid the trail on the right, which heads up to the summit of Monte Specie (2307m, 30 minutes); this trail is signed 'Heimkehrer Kreuz' after the war memorial *kreuz* (cross) at the summit. Make the steep descent on No 34, dug into rocks by Austrian soldiers as a strategic military road during

DOLOMITES

WWI and offering breathtaking views. Along the trail there is a very exposed section, with a narrow ledge with a sheer drop to one side. These sections are equipped with iron cord for security. Interesting features along the trail include a ruined military cableway station, a rough-hewn short tunnel, fortifications in the rock face and caves.

At the S51 cross the stream and turn left (north) to **Hotel Tre Cime-Drei Zinnen** (☎ 0474 97 26 33; www.hoteltrecime .com; d with breakfast from €80), two hours from Sella di Monte Specie. From the car park there are good views of the summits of the Tre Cime di Lavaredo to the east. Here you can have a pleasant walk around nearby Lago di Landro. From Hotel Tre Cime buses connect with Dobbiaco (10km) or with Cortina (24km).

ALTERNATIVE ROUTE: VIA CARBONIN
3–4 hours, 6km, 622m descent
From Rifugio Vallandro, descend southeast on the dirt road, shortened by Trail No 37. You'll reach **Carbonin** (one hour) on the S51, and the bus stops for Cortina and Dobbiaco. To rejoin the main trail, turn left on the road and walk 3km north to Hotel Tre Cime. There is a parallel trail following the east side of Lago di Landro.

Day 7: Hotel Tre Cime-Drei Zinnen to Hotel Dolomitenhof
5–7 hours, 12km, 999m ascent, 1105m descent
Cross the road and from the car park take the dirt road No 10-102 east for a long pleasant walk along Fiume Rienza Nera. The trail climbs steeply along the Valle di Rinbon, up to the high plain with great views of the northern faces of Tre Cime di Lavaredo (Cima Grande, 2999m) to the south. A number of trails depart along here; continue to follow No 102 northeast to **Rifugio Locatelli** (☎ 0474 97 20 02; dm €20-26; 1 Jul-30 Sep), for three to five hours. This is one of the most beautiful and most visited places in the Dolomites. The *rifugio*, in operation since 1886, has 60 beds and 100 bunks, but is popular with large groups. Book in advance.

If you decide to stop at Rifugio Locatelli, use your extra day for the Tre Cime di Lavaredo Side Trip (see next column) or link with the Crode Fiscaline Loop (see opposite).

From Rifugio Locatelli continue northeast along No 102, which descends into the steep Val Sasso Vecchio. On the way down you'll pass the picturesque **Laghi dei Piani**. Note the pinnacles of Monte Paterno to the south, particularly the profile of the Frankfurter Würstel, a rocky spur shaped like a sausage! Once you get to **Rifugio Fondo Valle** (☎ 0474 71 06 06; www.rifugio fondovalle.com; bed €15), 1½ to two hours from Rifugio Locatelli, you can take a break and enjoy the views of Croda dei Toni to the south. From the *rifugio* follow the forest road north and after about 30 minutes, you'll reach **Hotel Dolomitenhof**.

SIDE TRIP: TRE CIME DI LAVAREDO LOOP
2–3 hours, 10km, 271m ascent/descent
If you want to finish up the day by taking a closer look at the Tre Cime, remember that crowds of people arrive daily, ferried up by buses on the controversial, paved toll road from Misurina. Early in the morning this loop is definitely more enjoyable and could be perfect as an addition to Day 7.

From Rifugio Locatelli take Trail No 105 southwest, passing a series of lovely small lakes under the north face of the Tre Cime and then heading further up to **Forcella Col de Mezzo** (2315m). From here you can descend to **Rifugio Auronzo** (☎ 0435 3 90 02; www .rifugioauronzo.it; dm/r €14/24; Jun-Sep) and return to Rifugio Locatelli on trail 101, via **Forcella Lavaredo** (2454m).

From Forcella Lavaredo saddle you can also take Trail No 104 east to the romantic **Rifugio Pian di Cengia** and link with the Crode Fiscaline Loop (see below).

CRODE FISCALINE LOOP

Duration 2 days
Distance 17km
Difficulty easy
Start/Finish Hotel Dolomitenhof
Nearest Town San Candido (p177)
Transport bus
Summary A high-altitude loop to the amazing pinnacles of Crode Fiscaline.

This walk starts in Val Fiscalina, one of the most impressive approaches to Tre Cime di Lavaredo. It takes in some amazing rock formations, passes some WWI trenches and includes a night in the lovely, tiny Rifugio Pian di Cengia.

This loop can easily be combined with the Dolomite Rollercoaster walk (p161) or the Side Trip to Tre Cime di Lavaredo (p170) for truly spectacular, longer alternatives.

PLANNING
Maps
The Tabacco 1:25,000 No 010 *Dolomiti di Sesto* is recommended for this walk.

GETTING TO/FROM THE WALK
From San Candido, head southeast on S52 passing through Sesto (7km). In the village of Moso (Moos), turn right onto the Val Fiscalina road heading southwest. Hotel Dolomitenhof is at the end of this road. Regular buses run between San Candido, Sesto and the hotel (hourly in high season from 8.30am to 6pm).

THE WALK
Day 1: Hotel Dolomitenhof to Rifugio Pian di Cengia
4–5 hours, 9km, 1124m ascent, 47m descent
Take the dirt road No 102-103 south towards the spires of Croda dei Toni. As you set out near the hotel, note the unusual fresco on the wall of a house depicting the giants Huno and Hauno, who figure in several ancient legends about the founding of San Candido.

You'll reach **Rifugio Fondo Valle** (see p170) after 30 minutes. From here the trail ascends to a fork; head right on Trail No 102 ascending 850m over the rocky ledges of Val Sasso Vecchio before reaching the **Forcella di Toblin** and **Rifugio Locatelli** (see p170), about two hours from Rifugio Fondo Valle. Rifugio Locatelli is in a large, 1950s-style building with the disconcerting look of an army barracks, but a marvellous terrace view. To the south are the Tre Cime di Lavaredo (which, on closer inspection, prove to be four peaks, not three), dominating a vast, heavily furrowed limestone high plain. The place is very special and everyone knows this. If you're not fortunate enough to arrive in a moment of calm, the chaos is worth enduring for the sake of the view, and the afternoon light all but guarantees outstanding photos.

From the *rifugio* descend southeast on Trail No 101, passing above **Laghi dei Piani**, then ascend among loose rock to **Forcella Pian di Cengia** (2522m). From the saddle continue left (east) along Trail No 101, past old military trenches, to reach **Rifugio Pian di Cengia** (☎ 337 45 15 17; dm €20; 15 Jun–30 Sep), 1½ hours from Rifugio Locatelli. The 15-bunk dorm on the upper floor is accessible through a trapdoor at the top of a ladder.

Day 2: Rifugio Pian di Cengia to Hotel Dolomitenhof
4–5 hours, 8km, 1218m descent
Follow Trail No 101 east among more WWI trenches to **Passo Fiscalino** (2519m), where you find great views. From here it is a short walk left (north, blind alley) to the amazing pinnacles of **Crode Fiscaline**, about 1½ hours return. To continue, from Passo Fiscalino descend east to a fork where you go left (northeast) to **Rifugio Comici** (☎ 0474 71 03 58; 20 Jun-15 Sep), one hour from the saddle and set at the gravelly base of the crag. From here go north, descending the steep Trail No 103 to Rifugio Fondo Valle, 1½ hours, with the Cima Undici on your right and the wonderful Croda dei Toni behind you. On the dirt road again, return to the Hotel Dolomitenhof (30 minutes).

PARCO NATURALE DELLE DOLOMITI D'AMPEZZO

Duration 2 days
Distance 16km
Difficulty easy
Start/Finish Sant'Uberto
Nearest Town Cortina d'Ampezzo (p176)
Transport bus

Summary A return loop taking in Rifugio Malga Ra Stua, Forcella Lerosa and an upper outlook at Pala dell'Asco.

An easy walk, ideal for families, through the grassy expanses of the Parco Naturale delle Dolomiti d'Ampezzo, once the Austrian front line in WWI, but since 1990, a protected area replete with high-altitude grazing meadows and forests dotted with Norway Spruce. Doable over either one or two days (accommodation is available in an easily accessible *rifugio*), the hike provides a good introduction to some of the Dolomites' more scenic peaks, notably Croda Rossa.

DOLOMITES

PLANNING
Maps
The Tabacco 1:25,000 map No 03 *Cortina d'Ampezzo e Dolomiti Ampezzane* is recommended.

Information Sources
Check out the **official park website** (www .dolomitiparco.com) for more details on *rifugi*, walks and general background information.

GETTING TO/FROM THE WALK
From the Cortina bus station, regular local buses stop at both the Fiames International Camping Olympia (4km north of Cortina) and the Sant Uberto car park at a switchback on S51 (3½km north of Fiames) where the minor road to Rifugio Malga Ra Stua branches off. From 9 July to 9 September the road up to Rifugio Malga Ra Stua is closed to normal traffic and a shuttle service (€3.65, 8am-7pm) runs from the car park in Fiames (former airstrip).

THE WALK
Day 1: Sant'Uberto to Rifugio Malga Ra Stua
1 hour, 4km, 247m ascent

If you decide to walk up to Rifugio Malga Ra Stua and prefer to avoid the small busy road, from the eastern side of the S51 switchback, in an area known as Sant'Uberto, take the unnumbered trail that heads uphill and follow the southern slope of Croda de R'Ancona. In one hour you'll arrive at **Rifugio Malga Ra Stua** (☎ 0436 57 53; www.malgarastua .it; 10 Jun-20 Oct), at the beginning of Val Salata, where it's worth staying overnight. This lovely alpine valley is perfect for spending the rest of the day with a relaxing walk northwest to the nearby Campo Croce. More serious walkers can continue to the end of Val Salata, ascend to Rifugio Sennes and pick up sections of the Dolomite Rollercoaster walk (p161), notably the Rifugio Fodara Vedla to Malga Ra Stua loop.

Day 2: Rifugio Malga Ra Stua to Sant'Uberto via Pala Dell'Asco
4–5 hours, 12km, 606m ascent/descent

From Rifugio Malga Ra Stua continue ascending along Val Salata for about 150m and take the dirt road to your right (east), which ascends for about 250m. At the fork

take the branch of Trail No 8 that heads to the right (southeast) – it's longer but easier and far more scenic. Pass a wooden bridge with a gate and follow the series of switchbacks winding uphill past ancient fir trees – at certain points there are panoramic views across the Fanes high plain. You will reach a small, flat valley where, if you approach quietly, you might see the resident chamois and squirrels. Follow the trail around the valley, avoiding the deviations, which head off to the right. In front of you now is the majestic Croda Rossa, one of the most beautiful peaks in the Dolomites. The trail will bring you to a little wooden house with a water fountain at the edge of a dirt road in a wide valley called Valbones, west of Forcella Lerosa (one hour).

If you want more adventure head north across the pastures, rich in marmot dens, to reach another small wooden house (2039m). From here ascend north, progressively turning east, with an easy climb on the fascinating slope of **Pala dell'Asco**, made up by rocky stripes dotted by Arolla pines. You will soon reach the **upper saddle** (2274m, 40 minutes) above an inner rocky basin called Castello di Valbones, at the foot of the imposing reddish peak of Croda Rossa (3146m), usually inhabited by a herd of chamois. Enjoy the astonishing view southwest and descend the slippery grassy slopes in a southwesterly direction in order to return to the Forcella Lerosa dirt road.

At this point you have three options. The first is to turn right (northwest) and follow the dirt road No 8 back down to Rifugio Malga Ra Stua (one hour). This route is a slippery short cut and less attractive than the ascent so, if you're in no hurry, you can return the way you came. Otherwise, see Alternative Finish via Val di Gotres (see below).

ALTERNATIVE FINISH: VIA VAL DI GOTRES
1 hour, 5km

A third option is to turn left (southeast), still following No 8, to **Forcella Lerosa** and descend the picturesque walk along the Val di Gotres. After about 5km you will reach the S51, just 1km southwest of Passo Cimabanche, 14km from Cortina.

At the time of writing, buses passed Passo Cimabanche for Cortina at 8.15am and 10.35am and 4.05pm and 6.25pm. Buy tickets on board.

SESTO TO SAN CANDIDO

Duration 2½–3 hours
Distance 7km
Difficulty easy
Start Sesto
Finish San Candido (p177)
Transport bus, train
Summary A low-altitude, pleasant forest stroll with spectacular Dolomites views.

This delightful walk starts in Sesto in Val di Sesto, in the heart of Parco Naturale Dolomiti di Sesto, and ends in San Candido in Val Pusteria, on the northern edge of the Dolomites. The trail winds through verdant forest and opens to reveal amazing views. The present-day Austrian border is only 8km east of San Candido, which developed at the meeting point of Val di Sesto and the Fiume Drava.

PLANNING
Maps
The Tabacco 1:25,000 No 010 *Dolomiti di Sesto* is recommended for this walk.

GETTING TO/FROM THE WALK
Sesto (start)
From San Candido head southeast on S52 to reach Sesto (7km). Regular SAD buses run between San Candido and Sesto (hourly in high season, from 8.30am to 6pm).

San Candido (finish)
See San Candido Getting There & Away, p177.

THE WALK
From Sesto's *municipio* (town hall), take Via San Vito uphill. At the church entrance turn right (east). After about 30m you come to a wide intersection where there is a sign indicating numerous different trails. Take Trail No 4d for Cappella del Bosco (Waldkapelle). Follow the sign on the paved road that, after a house, becomes a grassy trail heading to a wooden bridge. Before the bridge turn left (north) ascending alongside a stream. When you reach the asphalt, cross the road and take northwest Via Hosler. It ascends gently, affording magnificent views over gentle pastures dotted with wooden *fienili* (haysheds).

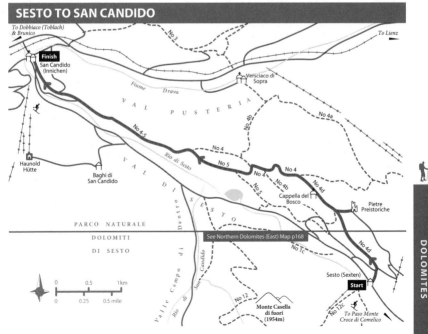

SESTO TO SAN CANDIDO

In a few minutes you come to a farm where Via Hosler ends. Following the 4d trail signs, you'll pass under the ramp of a hayshed and find the frescoed facade of a house. Pass along the right side of the house and pick up the path that heads into the woods. Climbing a steep incline among fir trees and moss-covered boulders, you'll pass two of the numerous wooden sculptures that mark the meditation stops along the way. When you reach a hayshed, ascend right, take a break (1470m, 50 minutes) and enjoy the spectacular panorama of Croda Rossa di Sesto, Croda dei Toni, Tre Scarperi and Rocca dei Baranci in the background.

Take up the trail that heads northwest through the wood. After about 20m you'll find a path on the right marked 'Pietre Preistoriche'. It's a 30-minute return deviation to the **Pietre Preistoriche** site, a one-time prehistoric place of worship – two stone slabs with strange incisions typical of Neolithic rock-carving in the Alps.

Continuing northwest, the main trail climbs a small, rocky valley, until it reaches the **Cappella del Bosco** (10 minutes), a log chapel built in 1917, after locals had to be evacuated from the valley due to the Italian bombing of what was then Austria. From the chapel continue up the path until you come to a fork where you descend to the left onto a dirt road, following the sign for Trail No 4 to San Candido. It's a pleasant descent through the lush woods of the crest all the way to San Candido. Descend first through the firs and then, after a sharp curve to the right, some Scots pines. If you proceed quietly, you might even surprise a fawn or a squirrel or two skipping among the branches. Still walking along Trail No 4, ignore the fork to the left for Trail No 5 to Sesto. You'll come to another little table (1400m) with a fantastic view over Val Campo di Dentro, with the Torre dei Scarperi to the left (south) and the Croda dei Rondoi to the right. Continuing on you will come to a fork without signs – go straight ahead downhill, avoiding the dirt road that ascends to the right. After 30 minutes you'll come to another fork where the road ascends to the right. At this point head downhill on a short cut, which will bring you to a playground, from where a short zig-zagging ramp on the left (west) leads down to the northern side of San Candido.

TOWNS & FACILITIES

BOLZANO (BOZEN)
☎ 0471 / pop 100,000

Biergartens, pizzerias, hearty *guten morgens* and flirtatious *ciao bellas*; where the heck are you? It doesn't take long to decipher that standard cultural generalisations don't apply in Bolzano – a prosperous Alpine settlement of South Tyroleans hemmed in by the steep-sided Dolomites that often feels more like a small town than a provincial capital.

Information
The **tourist office** (☎ 30 70 00; www.bolzano-bozen.it; Piazza Walther 8; 9am-1pm & 2-7pm Mon-Fri, 9am-2pm Sat) is slap bang in the main square.

Supplies & Equipment
The best equipped of Bolzano's outdoor shops, **Sportler** (☎ 97 40 33; www.sportler.it; Via Portici 37) specialises in climbing and mountain technical gear, including clothing and maps.

The bookshop **Athesia** (☎ 92 71 11; www.athesialibri.it; Via Portici 41) offers a good selection of mountain books and maps.

Sleeping
Ostello della Gioventù Bolzano (☎ 30 08 65; www.jugendherberge.it; Via Renon 23; dm incl breakfast €19.50-21.50, s incl breakfast €22-24) Close to the train station, the three- and four-bed dorms in this new independent hostel have partially screened bunks for added privacy. Best of all, there's no daytime lockout.

Hotel Figl (☎ 97 84 12; www.figl.net; Piazza del Grano 9; s €80-100, d €100-110) This is a well-priced and really stylish hotel, with chic, contemporary rooms with glass-partitioned bathrooms, chocolate, caramel and white tones, geometric furniture, and a streamlined ground-floor bar.

Stadt Hotel Città (☎ 97 52 21; www.hotelcitta.info; Piazza Walther 21; s €94-110, d €135-180) Taking price, location, ambience and facilities into account the Stadt Città is the best hotel in town – no contest. Mixing Italian dynamism with German efficiency, the rooms blend funky with traditional, while the on-site café materialises like a dreamy Viennese apparition. Then there's the basement spa (free to guests), an oasis of Teutonic charm.

Eating

Fischbänke Pic-Nic Bar (☎ 97 17 14; Via Dott Streiter 26a; dishes €5-10; 9am-7pm Mon-Fri, 9am-12.30pm Sat) Run by an artist on the site of the old fish market, the eccentric Fischbänke serves alfresco glasses of Tyrolean wine, and quite possibly northern Italy's most beautiful bruschetta. Hours can vary with the whim of the owner.

Hopfen & Co (☎ 30 07 88; Piazza delle Erbe 17; meals €15-20; 9.30am-1am Mon-Sat) Step back into the Habsburg era at this venerable 800-year-old inn that serves up filling portions of traditional dishes including sauerkraut and sausages cooked in beer.

Vögele (☎ 97 39 38; Via Goethe 3; meals €19-24; 9am-1am) Dating back to 1277 and owned by the same family since 1840, this antique-filled pub and restaurant serves hearty Tyrolean fare such as schnitzels in candlelight surrounds; otherwise you can just come by for a drink.

Stadt Caffé Cittá (☎ 97 52 51; Piazza Walther 21; snacks €7-15; 8am-1am Mon-Sat, 8am-7pm Sun) Ah, grand Viennese hospitality transplanted to within spitting distance of the dreamy Dolomites. Where do you start? The glittering *fin de siècle* decor, the well-groomed but cheerful waiters, the creamy coffee, the 'free' buffet snacks or – wait for it – the choice of 32 different daily newspapers in over a dozen languages. Now that's service!

Pick up fruit, vegetables, bread, cheese and meats from the **morning market** (Piazza delle Erbe; Mon-Sat).

Getting There & Away

Bolzano airport (Aeroporto di Bolzano; ☎ 25 52 55; www.abd-airport.it) is served by flights to Rome, Olbia and Cagliari.

Buses run by **SAD** (www.sad.it) leave from the bus station (☎ 840 000 471; Via Perathoner) for destinations throughout the province, including all the walks in this chapter. SAD buses also head for resorts outside the province, including Cortina d'Ampezzo. Updated timetables are on the SAD website.

Regular trains connect Bolzano with Merano (€2.40, 40 minutes), Trento (€3.35, 30 minutes), Verona (€8, 1½ hours), Milan (€23.70, three hours five minutes), Rome, Innsbruck (two hours) and Munich (Germany). You can also catch a train from Bolzano to Brunico (1½ hours) and San Candido (two hours) in Val Pusteria; change trains in Fortezza.

Bolzano is well served by the A22 (the Brennero autostrada), which leads to the Brennero Pass and northern Europe.

CASTELROTTO (KASTELRUTH)
☎ 0471 / pop 6000

A large village of eye-catching onion-domed churches and pastoral backdrops, Castelrotto is a popular but laid-back tourist centre and a good base for excursions up onto the Alpe di Siusi and Monte Sciliar.

Information

The local **Associazione Turistica Sciliar Castelrotto** (☎ 70 63 33; www.castelrotto.com; Piazza Kraus 1) has regional and local information, as well as hotel lists and prices. The ski and climbing school **Dolomiten** (☎ 70 53 43; www.dolomiten-alpin.com; Via Dolomitenstr.) offers guided, seven-day treks and *via ferrata* excursions.

Sleeping & Eating

Hotel Alla Torre/Gasthof Zum Turm (☎ 70 63 49; www.zumturm.com; Kofelgasse 8, Castelrotto; s/d €42/88) with two names hints at a split personality, but this place within bell-ringing distance of Castelrotto's onion-domed church is anything but schizophrenic. With its neat rooms, apple strudel–friendly garden café and eclectic Tyrolean artefacts, your biggest dilemma will probably be choosing which superlatives to write in the guestbook when you leave.

Another place that garners regular praise is **Haus Silbernagl** (☎ 70 66 99; www.garni-silbernagl.com; per person €45) has an indoor pool and spa.

Silbernagl (☎ 70 62 22; Via Oswald Von Wolkenstein 10) is also the name of a well-stocked supermarket. For a quiet restaurant with open-air tables and a play area for kids, try **Liftstuberl** (☎ 70 68 04; Via Marinzen 35).

DOLOMITES

Getting There & Away

Castelrotto is accessible by **SAD** (www.sad.it) bus from Bolzano (€2.80, 50 minutues, every hour daily, less on Sunday), the Val Gardena (25 minutes to Ortisei) and Bressanone.

By car, exit the Brenner motorway (A22) at Bolzano Nord or Chiusa.

CORTINA D'AMPEZZO
☎ 0436 / pop 6090

Cortina is the Alps' ice-cool supermodel, a high-class ski resort where James Bond movies have been filmed and celebrity visitors sit down over après-ski cocktails to debate the merits of Gucci over Gortex. Underneath the glitz, Cortina is also unashamedly Dolomiten, shoehorned into one of northern Italy's five Ladin valleys and surrounded by imposing mountains.

Information

The Cortina **APT office** (☎ 32 31; www.apt -dolomiti-cortina.it; Piazzetta San Francesco 8) provides information. The Parco Naturale delle Dolomiti d'Ampezzo is operated by the **Comunanza delle Regole d'Ampezzo** (☎ 22 06; www.regole.it; Via del Parco 1), an ancient consortium of families dating back to the first Celtic/Roman settlements in the valley. The summer **information office** (Jun-Sep) is at the Fiames entrance to the park.

Supplies & Equipment

A central shopping centre, **La Cooperativa** (Corso Italia 40), includes a grocery shop. For high-quality equipment try **K2 Sport** (☎ 86 37 06; www.k2sport.com; Via Cesare Battisti 2).

Sleeping & Eating

About 3.5km north of Cortina at Fiames, **International Camping Olympia** (☎ 50 57; per person €4.50-8, per tent €7-9) is served by local buses (see Getting to/from the Walk, p172). Bungalows are also available.

Hotel Fiames (☎ 23 66; www.albergo fiames.it; Fiames 13; half-board per person €36-70), 150m north of the shuttle bus stop, is as cheap and basic as it gets.

In ritzy Cortina, reasonably priced accommodation is tougher to find. The best deal is **Hotel Montana** (☎ 86 04 98; www .cortina-hotel.com; per person €40-80) of 1920s vintage right in the centre of town.

For a good meal or a pizza, try **Ariston** (☎ 86 67 05, via Marconi 10; full meal €18.50), in front of the bus station.

Getting There & Away

Cortina's bus station is in Via Marconi. **SAD** (☎ 800 846047) buses leave Cortina at 8.10am, 10.10am, 1.15pm, 3.10pm, 5.10pm and 7.10pm for Fiames, Passo Cimabanche, Carbonin, Dobbiaco (change for Brunico and Bolzano), Braies or San Candido. **Dolomitibus** (☎ 0435 321 55) travels west to Passo Falzarego or southeast to Calalzo, where you can catch a FS train for Belluno-Venezia.

LA VILLA (STERN)
☎ 0471 / pop 260

Situated at the southern end of Val Badia, La Villa is a stronghold of the ancient Ladin culture and an excellent place to reacquaint yourself with 'civilisation', including some top-notch food.

Information

The **tourist office** (☎ 84 70 37; www.alta badia.org; Via Colz 75; 8am-noon & 3-7pm Mon-Sat, 10am-noon & 4-6pm Sun) provides information.

Sleeping & Eating

The nearest camping ground is **Sass Dlacia** (☎ 84 95 27; www.campingsassdlacia.it; Via Sciarè 11; person/tent with car €5.50/6.50), 4km from San Cassiano on the southeast road to Passo Falzarego.

Renovated in 2006, **Hotel La Villa** (☎ 84 70 35; www.hotel-lavilla.it; Boscdaplan 176, La Villa; d €70-130) sports larch wood furniture and a cosy Ladin ambience. There's a wellness centre, kids' playroom and on-site restaurant serving traditional Ladin cuisine.

For an expensive treat, dine at **St Hubertus** (☎ 84 95 00; www.rosalpina .it; Strada Micura de Ru 20, San Cassiano; set menus from €80, mains €27-35; dinner Wed-Mon) in the super luxurious **Rosa Alpina Hotel & Spa**, a two-Michelin-star joint that offers the kind of 'event' meal that you've been scrimping your whole trip to afford. Try the local beef wrapped in mountain hay.

For self-caterers there is a central supermarket, **Sport Tony** (Strada Colz 56).

Getting There & Away

La Villa is easily accessible from Bolzano (2½ hours) and Brunico (1¼ hours) on hourly **SAD** (☎ 800-846-047; www.sad.it) buses. Buses run less frequently outside of the summer season.

ORTISEI (ST ULRICH)

☎ 0471 / pop 4490

Culturally rich Ortisei is a picturesque Alpine town that boasts a pedestrian-only central area with an extensive system of escalators and moving walkways. It is in the heart of Val Gardena, one of five Ladin valleys that has managed to preserve its ancient traditions despite a modern influx of skiers. The valley's other claim to fame is its woodcarving artisans, known for their statues, figurines and toys.

Information

Try the Ortisei **tourist office** (☎ 77 76 00; Via Rezia 1; 8.30am-12.30pm & 2.30-6.30pm Mon-Sat, 8.30am or 10am-noon & 5-6.30pm Sun). Information about this area can be found at www.valgardena.it.

Sleeping & Eating

Ortisei, a winter ski resort, has over 5000 rooms, so you shouldn't be short of a bed. **Hotel am Stetteneck** (☎ 79 65 63; www.stette neck.com; Via Rezia 14, Ortisei; d from €78) dates from 1913. During WWI Italian troops were bivouacked here and in WWII it served as a military hospital. These days it presents a more benign face with cheery rooms, big bay windows, a swimming pool, and a Tyrol-meets-Mediterranean restaurant.

Another option is the spotless **Hotel Maria** (☎ 79 70 47; www.hotelmaria.cc; Via Rezia 49; d half-board from €78) in the main pedestrianised street.

Ristorante Concordia (☎ 79 62 76; Via Roma 41, Ortisei; meals €20-24) is the real deal: pasta made by hand, along with home-made breads, including olive, vegetable and nut varieties; the ham is also smoked on the premises. The wines come from the surrounding vineyards.

Getting There & Away

The Val Gardena is accessible from Bolzano and Bressonone by regular **SAD** (www.sad .it) buses year-round, and the neighbouring valleys in summer. The direct Bolzano–Ortisei run takes just over an hour and tickets start at €4. They run around every hour from 7.30am to 7pm.

If you're driving, take the A22 north from Bolzano, turning right into Val Gardena after 30km. Continue east along this road to Ortisei.

SAN CANDIDO (INNICHEN)

☎ 0474 / pop 3110

At the eastern end of the verdant Val Pusteria lie the Dolomiti di Sesto, Tre Cime di Lavaredo and the primarily German-speaking resort town of San Candido. This settlement is also famous for its Romanesque Collegiata, a church built in AD 769.

Information

The **tourist office** (☎ 91 31 49; www.alta pusteria.net; Piazza Magistrato 1) can help with information on the valley.

Sleeping & Eating

The nearest camp ground is **Caravan Park Sexten** (☎ 71 04 44; www.caravanparksex ten.it; Via San Giuseppe 54, Sesto; sites €11), southeast of Sesto on the road to Passo Monte Croce. There are also apartments from €94 per night, restaurant and car hire from €45 per day.

In San Candido itself, try **Villa Wald-heim** (☎ 91 31 87; Via Pascolo 1; per person from €52). A supermarket, **Despar Schafer** (Piazza San Michele 8), is centrally located.

Getting There & Away

SAD (www.sad.it) buses travel to Brunico (45 minutes, hourly) and Cortina D'Ampezzo (one hour 10 minutes, five daily) from San Candido. From Bolzano, there are buses to and from Merano, Val Badia, San Vigilio di Marebbe and Val Gardena (on the Innsbruck bus). From either town sporadic buses and trains go to Dobbiaco, from where buses run to Lago di Braies.

To get to Rifugio Auronzo (p170) at the Tre Cime di Lavaredo, catch the bus from San Candido (departures 8am, 8.30am and 10.30am). By car, San Candido is easily accessible from the A22 via Bressanone and from Cortina on the S51.

The whole Val Pusteria is connected by spanking new trains. Change at Fortezza for Bolzano (40 minutes from Fortezza).

Julian & Carnic Alps

HIGHLIGHTS

- Winding forest paths and soaring alpine rock walls on the **Fusine–Mangart Loop** (p181)
- The rich flora and stark, stony landscape of high limestone plateaus on the **Slovenian Two-Step** (p182)
- Rifugio Corsi, in a spectacular natural amphitheatre at the foot of mighty **Jôf Fuart** (p185)
- Wide, open spaces and airy ridge-tops around **Monte Carnizza** (p187)

Signature food: *Jota* soup	Celebrated native: Julius Kugy (mountaineer and writer)	Famous for... Solitude

Ignoring the porous and historically interchangeable borders of Central Europe, the Julian and Carnic Alps sit like a forgotten apostrophe at the end Europe's grandest mountain range.

Encased in the semi-autonomous region of Friuli-Venezia Giulia, the area has long been a melting pot for a culturally ambiguous mix of Celts, Lombards, Romans and Venetians. Today, the Carnics straddle the post-1919 border with Austria while large tracts of the Julians spill into neighbouring Slovenia. While Germanic and Slavic influences are rife, the main cultural identity is Friulian, a distinctive northeastern spin on Italian traditionalism.

To the walker, the historical background lends an intriguing, if sometimes sobering, air to a visit here. You're bound to notice traces of two world wars, even in improbably high, remote corners but, these days, the mood is anything but antagonistic. On trails in the Carnic Alps it's as common to be greeted with the German *'Grüss Gott'* as the Italian *'Salve'*, and in parts of the Julian Alps you'll hear the occasional Slovene *'Dober dan'*.

Greetings in any language, though, are far from frequent. Once away from places where walkers' paths converge – trailheads, passes and some of the more popular *rifugi* (mountain huts) – seeing any person is like spotting a rare bird.

Heavily forested and mostly free of large-scale development (though a new ski lift has ominously just straddled the Slovenian border), the Julian Alps are protected by Slovenia's Triglavski Narodni National Park, a factor that has helped to safeguard the region's environmental integrity. No less appealing or important are the lush uplands of the Carnic Alps, along the Austrian border, which host a great variety of wildflowers and offer walking in a rounded, rolling uplands that contrast majestically with their more rugged eastern cousins.

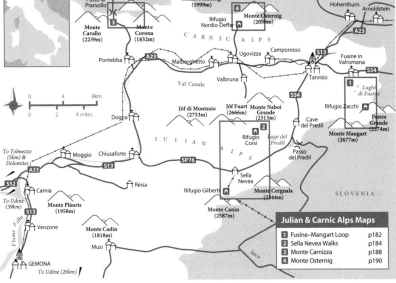

JULIAN & CARNIC ALPS

Julian & Carnic Alps Maps	
1 Fusine–Mangart Loop	p182
2 Sella Nevea Walks	p184
3 Monte Carnizza	p188
4 Monte Osternig	p190

CLIMATE

An Alpine climate prevails across the region. Summers are cool and rainy, though fine spells are not uncommon. Winters can be bitterly cold – pre-Alps to the south block warmer air currents from the Mediterranean – and snowfall is abundant. Snow depths reach 2m in Tarvisio, at less than 800m altitude, and snow banks may lie across higher trails well into the summer. Avalanches are common in spring. Conditions vary markedly between the warmer, more sheltered valley floors and the exposed tops, and between sunnier slopes with a southerly aspect and colder, north-facing ones. A couple of glaciers cling to existence on the northern slopes of Monte Canìn and Jôf di Montasio in the Julian Alps.

PLANNING
Maps

Many maps are good for planning and access information, including the 1:250,000 *Friuli-Venezia Giulia: carta turistico-stradale*, distributed free by tourist offices in Udine and elsewhere. The Tabacco 1:150,000 *Friuli-Venezia Giulia* map is more detailed and accurate.

Books

Wild Italy (2005), by Tim Jepson, has an enticing couple of pages on the area's natural history. There are numerous publications in Italian, including a comprehensive Club Alpino Italiano (CAI) guide to the marked trails. Free from the APT in Tarvisio, and particularly strong on geology, is the *Discover Nature* series of leaflets describing short walks in the Julian and Carnic Alps – including some of those described in this chapter.

Weather Information

There's a telephone **weather service** (☎ 800 860377) for all of Friuli-Venezia Giulia. The tourist office in Tarvisio posts up-to-date local weather bulletins – most days.

Emergency

The **national mountain rescue service** (☎ 118) can be contacted 24 hours a day. Outside populated areas, making a telephone call will generally mean using a mobile or reaching a *rifugio*.

GETTING THERE & AROUND

The gateway town of Udine is on the main Venice–Trieste train and bus lines, and easily accessed from the rest of Italy. From here you'll have to forge north by bus or train to Tarvisio. Thanks to their relative isolation, access to a couple of the walks in this chapter by public transport can be difficult verging on the impossible, and you may have to revert to a hire car or taxi.

GATEWAY

Udine (p191), the spiritual capital of Friulian culture, sits within sight of the purple-hued Julian and Carnic peaks and makes a viable and historically attractive gateway for these walks.

JULIAN ALPS

The Julian (*Giulie* in Italian) Alps are dramatic limestone monoliths that bear more than a passing resemblance to their more famous Dolomiti cousins. Though undergoing some recent development (including a cross-border ski lift), the area is still relatively pristine and retains a wildness feel often lacking further west. Forests along the Slovenian border are dense and ancient, the lakes deep and scenic, and the rivers refreshingly clear. Picturesque towns and villages nestle in valleys, their bell towers visible above the trees before anything else comes into view. So where are all the people?

The bulk of the tourists get ambushed by the more obvious beauty of the Dolomites and head west. Of the ones that remain, most congregate in Tarvisio (population 5100; elevation 754m), an alpine walking and skiing resort wedged into the Val Canale between the Julian and Eastern Carnic Alps 7km short of the Austrian border and 11km from Slovenia. The town is famous for its Saturday market that has long attracted day-trippers from Austria and Slovenia, but is also increasingly touted for its skiing; this is the snowiest (and coldest) pocket in the whole Alpine region.

Out of town, one or two easily accessible, scenic spots, such as the Laghi di Fusine, draw crowds on a fine day. Certain *rifugi* are also well visited by the *via ferrata* (iron way) set. Elsewhere, trails are quiet and the walking is a joy amid marvellous, wild scenery.

PLANNING

When to Walk

This region becomes a skiing destination in winter. The summer walking season extends, roughly, from early June to the end of September. That's when *rifugi* are open and SAF buses run to a summer schedule.

Maps

The Tabacco 1:25,000 map No 19 *Alpi Giulie Occidentali Tarvisiano* is the map of choice

---

LOCAL HERO

Spend time in the Julian Alps, and you're bound to come across the name, the likeness and the words of Julius Kugy. There's a street named after him in Tarvisio, while in Valbruna his sayings are recorded on stone plaques and the main piazza bears his name – you can even drop in for an espresso at Bar Julius Kugy.

Born in Gorizia in 1858, Kugy is said to have been captivated by mountains from childhood, and during his years as a law student devoted much time and energy to climbing in the Julian Alps with a couple of close friends – a fine tradition still upheld in universities everywhere. It's not clear what became of his legal career, but his course through life as a mountaineer was now set.

In the decades before WWI, Kugy explored the Julian Alps in the company of local herdsmen and hunters. These men of the mountains were his guides and, when war came, some of them were recruited to serve beside him as Alpine guides to the Austrian army. Kugy honoured their exploits, as well as the beauty of the mountains, in books such as *Anton Oitzinger, vita di una Guida Alpina*. At least one title has been translated into English, but they're hard to track down. It's easier if you read Italian – bookshops in the region carry recent editions of some of his works.

A humble museum, just off Piazza Julius Kugy in Valbruna, houses exhibits from Kugy's life, mostly from the time of the war.

for all the Julian Alps walks. It's available in bookshops in Udine and Tarvisio.

PLACE NAMES

The Julian Alps extend well into Slovenia as the Julijske Alpe, and dual naming in Italian and Slovene is widespread along the international border. In this section preference has been given to the Italian names.

The highest peak in the Italian part of the range, Jôf di Montasio, is one of a handful labelled with the term 'jôf' (meaning 'peak' or 'mountain'). Some people say it's a Friulian word; others, that it came south from German-speaking lands.

Books

Now in its twelfth year, the *Sulle orme di Julius Kugy* (In the Footsteps of Julius Kugy) programme offers all levels of guided walks in the Julian Alps that honour the legacy of local hero, Kugy, and his band of mountain guides (see p180). Trips run from late June to mid-September and cost between €3.50 for a simple nature trail to €50 for a guided *via ferrata*. The tourist offices in Udine and Tarvisio produce a colourful booklet with itineraries, prices and background information.

Emergency

The national **mountain rescue service** (☎ 118) operates in the Julian Alps but local emergency services **Cave del Predil** (☎ 0335 741 36 21) and **Sella Nevea** (☎ 0443 540 25) can also be contacted directly.

FUSINE–MANGART LOOP

Duration 3–4 hours
Distance 11km
Difficulty moderate
Start/Finish Lago Superiore di Fusine
Nearest Town Tarvisio (p190)
Transport bus

Summary Fine tracks wind through delightful forests and natural rock gardens, from a pair of picturesque lakes to the foot of an imposing alpine wall.

Picture yourself in the pages of a favourite bedtime story of a certain genre – enchanted forest, winding path – and you're ready for the climb from Lago Superiore di Fusine to Rifugio Zacchi. As CAI Track No 512 winds

upward through the forest, it would come as no surprise to meet Snow White and friends marching the other way. Beyond the *rifugio* the going is more rugged, crossing the base of huge scree slopes below the towering north face of Monte Mangart, before a wonderful, serpentine descent through more forest leads back to the valley floor. The walk begins and ends at a height of 930m, and reaches 1475m before descending.

The lakes themselves are very picturesque and are protected by the tiny Parco Naturale di Fusine. They are also very popular with day-trippers. Pleasant, easy trails (not described here) lead around both lakes – the northern shore of Lago Inferiore, in particular, gives pretty views of the Mangart group.

Monte Mangart and the crest west of Rifugio Zacchi are surmounted by several *vie ferrate*. The *rifugio* makes a suitable base for anyone with the inclination, experience and equipment to attempt them.

GETTING TO/FROM THE WALK

From early June to late September, **SAF** (☎ 0428 21 34) buses go from Tarvisio Città to the Laghi di Fusine (€1.50, 25 minutes, three a day). The first leaves Tarvisio at 8.50am, and the last returns from the Lago Superiore car park at 6pm. Apart from these times, five buses a day stop at Fusine in Valromana, 3.4km from the start.

By car, take the S54 east towards Slovenia for just over 6km, through Fusine in Valromana, then turn right onto the sealed road for 3.4km to park beside Lago Superiore.

THE WALK

Track No 512 leaves the Lago Superiore car park heading southwest, past Bar Ai Sette Nani, where drinks and snacks are sold. At this stage it's a comfortable, gravelled road and already there are fine views of Monte Mangart to the south. Once you're past a boom gate and heading south, red-and-white CAI track markers appear. Within 10 minutes a signpost indicates Track No 517a (initially Track No 513) to the right, which you'll descend later in the day. Continue along Track No 512, which soon narrows and begins a sometimes steep ascent. After a couple of minor, signposted junctions, it settles down to climb steadily through beautiful forest, and within about an hour

FUSINE–MANGART LOOP

pioneer vegetation. A final, short climb over a spur covered in dense, low plants leads to a big boulder where markers point back towards Rifugio Zacchi and up towards Bivacco Nogara. It's 40 minutes or so to here from the start of Track No 517.

The Laghi di Fusine nestle in the valley to the north, and Track No 517a leads down the spur in the same direction. It enters forest, and winds improbably and steeply down to emerge into the open again, rejoining Track No 513, at Alpe Tamer, about half an hour from the boulder. Continue northward across the clearing and bear right at the first fork. This soon merges with a road on the right that descends from Capanna Ghezzi and Rifugio Zacchi. Within half an hour from Alpe Tamer you will arrive back at the car park by Lago Superiore.

SLOVENIAN TWO-STEP

Duration 4–5½ hours
Distance 12km
Difficulty moderate
Start/Finish Funivia Canìn car park
Nearest Town Tarvisio (p190)
Transport bus

Summary A cable car gives easy access to a karst plateau rich in wildflowers, where scenic tracks lead to two passes on the Slovenian border, then back to the leafy valley floor.

gains a road. Beside this, at a height of 1380m and with great views of the cliffs, sits **Rifugio Zacchi** (☎ 0428 611 95; dm €17-20; Jun-Sep).

Continue south along the road. Within 10 minutes, at a well-signposted junction, Track No 513 leaves the road and goes left. Follow it, ignoring a climbers' route to the east towards Sella Strugova on the Slovenian border, through forest to the Alpe Vecchia, an area populated by dwarf vegetation at the foot of scree slopes. Another climbing route, the Via della Vita, soon goes left in the direction of a CAI *bivacco* (shelter) high on the ridge above, while Track No 513 swings west and remains reasonably level before a signposted junction with Track No 517 on the left, half an hour or so from the road. Track No 513 continues easily back to the lake from here.

Faint at first, Track No 517 winds and climbs through forest and shortly emerges near the base of large cliffs. Cairns and red-paint markers now persist even when the track itself is hard to make out. It heads west and crosses patches of bare scree alternating with areas being reclaimed by

Sella Nevea is a popular but compact ski resort. Lift lines rise on both the north and south sides of the valley, running west from the geographical *sella* (saddle). The Funivia Canìn cable car takes the sting out of the start of this walk, from Sella Nevea to the base of Piano del Prevala, which is in a spectacular setting below the imposing cliffs of Bila Pec ('White Rock' in Slovene).

You then continue climbing on foot to Sella Prevala, along what was once the most convenient route from Sella Nevea to Bovec (Slovenia). From Sella Prevala the trail crosses a broad plateau devoid of surface water but rich in low Alpine flora thanks to plentiful precipitation. Taller growth is limited by the quantity of snow and the frequency of spring avalanches. The plateau and the mountains above are composed of whitish-grey limestone, much shaped by glaciation and erosion. Caves in the area have been surveyed to depths of 560m. A second pass into Slovenia, Sella Robon, marks the start of a long descent back to the mixed coniferous and broad-leaved forest of the lower valleys.

Thanks to the Funivia Canìn, the day's walk involves 489m of ascent and 1198m of descent. The 'Canìn' in the name of the cable car is Monte Canìn (2587m), on the Slovenian border west of Sella Prevala. Its summit is accessible by a number of challenging routes – most directly, from Rifugio Gilberti along Track No 632 and the Ferrata Julia, established by Julius Kugy in 1903.

PLANNING
When to Walk
The *funivia* at the start of this walk doesn't open until 1 July meaning this walk is best tackled from July to September when the terrain should also be snow-free.

What to Bring
Carry plenty of water as you're unlikely to find any along the route.

GETTING TO/FROM THE WALK
If you are using public transport you'll need to get up early. There's an **SAF** (☎ 0428 21 34; www.saf.ud.it) bus to Udine that leaves Tarvisio Città at 6.05am and reaches Chiusaforte at 6.46am (€2.70), then one that leaves Chiusaforte at 7.15am and arrives in Sella Nevea at 7.50am (€1.85). For the fleet of foot, another combination leaves Tarvisio at noon and Chiusaforte at 1.45pm, reaching Sella Nevea at 2.20pm.

Returning, the last bus out of Sella Nevea leaves at 5.05pm and arrives in Tarvisio at 7.03pm with a change in Chiusaforte.

By car, take S54 south from Tarvisio for 11km through Cave del Predil, then turn right onto SP76 and continue another 11km to Sella Nevea. Park at the base of the Funivia Canìn cable car (signposted).

THE WALK
The **Funivia Canìn** (☎ 0433 540 26; opens 1 Jul) does most of the day's climbing – from Sella Nevea (1122m) to a height of 1831m, just below Rifugio Gilberti – in just a few minutes. In summer, cars go every 20 minutes from 9am to 12.30pm and 1.30pm to 4.45pm Monday to Saturday, and until

6pm Sunday. The one-way adult/concession fare is €6.50/5.50.

From the top station of the cable car it's only a short distance (signposted) to **Rifugio Gilberti** (☎ 0433 5 40 15; dm €12-24; 15 Jun-30 Sep) at 1850m, past a small **chapel** in memory of members of the Italian Alpine regiments who fought here during WWI. Track No 636 skirts behind and below the *rifugio*, and heads east, down into the wide, open **Piano del Prevala**. Until relatively recent times there was a glacier here, and there may be snow, even groomed ski trails, well into summer.

It's a straightforward but substantial climb, first on the north side of the valley and then the south, up bare slopes to **Sella Prevala** (2067m), about an hour from the top of the cable car and the first chance to step over into Slovenia.

Track No 636 turns briefly northward and sidles below **ruined barracks** to a minor, higher **col** (2109m) with more fine views. It then cruises downhill to the northeast, through a harsh but lush landscape (if that's possible) of green growth and colourful flowers against a glaring, whitish-grey backdrop of weathered limestone. Deep holes and weird rock formations abound.

The steep south face of Monte Poviz looms ahead. At a three-way junction, half an hour from the minor col, Track No 636 descends northwest towards Sella Nevea. Continue on to Sella Robon, turning sharply back to the east onto Track No 637. This heads across an even lusher karst plateau with fine views north to the Montasio and Fuart mountain groups across the upper Val Rio del Lago.

About 45 minutes from the junction, after traversing extensive scree slopes below Monte Cergnala, the track drops into a gravelly bowl, where signs point left (northwest) towards Sella Nevea. Continue east, climbing briefly through a series of switchbacks to **Sella Robon** (1865m). To the east are the peaks of Slovenia's Triglavski Narodni Park. Having come this far, you might want to explore nearby Monte Robon (see Side Trip, p185).

To descend to Sella Nevea, retrace your steps and find Track No 637 as it heads northwest, through the gravelly bowl, past a prominent '637' on a boulder and down

SELLA NEVEA WALKS

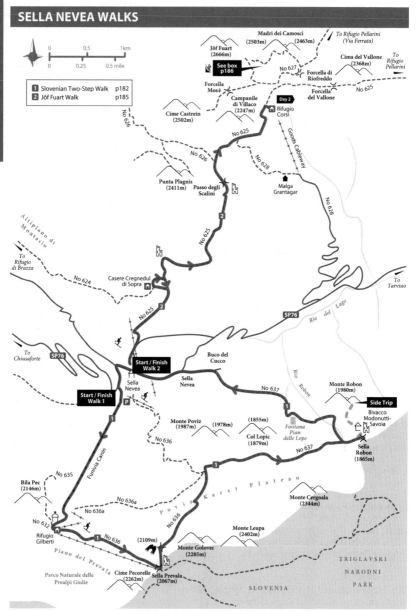

the rocky bed of Rio Robon for a short way. When the stream bed drops away steeply, the track swings to the true right side of the

gully, below cliffs on the west face of Monte Robon, then back to the west to recross Rio Robon.

The track is easier to follow now, although sometimes slippery as the terrain becomes damper and more densely vegetated, especially in the soggy hollow of **Fontana Pian delle Lope**, where water seeps from rock walls. About 90 minutes from Sella Robon the steady descent becomes briefly steep and loose, as the track drops to an unsealed road, which leads west for 500m to join SP76.

Continue west along the road; it's 1.5km through **Sella Nevea** to the car park at the base of the Funivia Canìn.

SIDE TRIP: MONTE ROBON MIDDLE PEAK
35 minutes, 1.5km, 77m ascent

From Sella Robon, a track leads north along the west side of the ridge past the ruins of a tiny WWI outpost and a cavers' shelter, **Bivacco Modonutti-Savoia**, in a small saddle. It sticks to the vegetated west side of the ridge for a bit further, then climbs a staircase (literally!) through a cleft onto the rocky top. A devious route marked with cairns and red paint continues, more or less on the west side, until it swings east round a big chasm to reach Monte Robon's second-highest summit (1942m) and some spectacular views. The main summit (1980m) is visible from here, just to the west looking back the way you've come, but is guarded by steep ground. Retrace your steps carefully to Sella Robon.

JÔF FUART

Duration	2 days
Distance	12km
Difficulty	moderate
Start/Finish	Sella Nevea
Nearest Town	Tarvisio (p190)
Transport	bus
Summary	A relaxed trip to a *rifugio* in the spectacular heart of the rugged Julian Alps.

Along with Montasio, Mangart and Canìn, Jôf Fuart is a peak emblematic of the Italian Julian Alps. The ascent of its northeast face, from Rifugio Pellarini, is a 'real climb', and even the normal route to the summit, above Rifugio Corsi, holds difficulties that demand specialist equipment and put it beyond reach for most walkers.

This walk offers a close-up look at Jôf Fuart without technical requirements, rounding a couple of ridges in unlikely fashion to enter the spectacular valley below the mountain's southeastern faces. Along the way, wartime fortifications, once impregnable but now decaying by natural causes, recall the area's not-so-distant past as fiercely contested ground.

It's possible to visit Rifugio Corsi, have a good look around and return to Sella Nevea in a day but, in a region rich with fine day walks and challenging routes, it is an excellent opportunity to stay a night in one of those grand locations that inspire people to build *rifugi*. The *gestore* (manager) and staff at Rifugio Corsi are a fount of knowledge regarding routes in the area – provided you can muster some Italian.

PLANNING
When to Walk

The ideal time to walk is when Rifugio Corsi is open, from the start of June until the end of September.

What to Bring

Provided you phone ahead and arrange to eat and sleep at Rifugio Corsi, all you need to bring is lunch and snacks. To include any *vie ferrate* in your itinerary, you'll need a helmet and the other equipment described in the Via Ferrata section (p46).

GETTING TO/FROM THE WALK

See Getting to/from Slovenian Two-Step (p182). The later bus combination leaves ample time to reach the *rifugio* if staying overnight, but not much time to look around and return the same day. With your own car, park near the start of the walk, just behind the Guardia di Finanza building, on about the only minor road on the north side of SP76, or at the foot of the nearby ski lift.

THE WALK
Day 1: Sella Nevea to Rifugio Corsi
2½–3 hours, 6km, 795m ascent, 96m descent

Track No 625 begins near the Guardia di Finanza building. Within a minute the track takes a sharp right (north) up a steep hill. Be warned, signposts are sometimes obscured by tree branches. A ski lift starts up the hill, just to the east, and the track crosses the lift line after only 100m or so. After 15 minutes or so, the red markers lead left, up the hill.

LEDGE OF THE GODS

The Sentiero Anita Goitan is a favourite among the many *vie ferrate* that link passes, peaks and ledges in the mountains around Rifugio Corsi. It begins at Forcella Lavinal dell'Orso as a track ascending a grassy hillside, but it's a narrow track and a steep hillside, and you wouldn't want to tackle even this without sure feet and a steady head. Once it gains the crest of Cime Castrein, and especially once it approaches the precipitous Forcella Mosè, Sentiero Goitan is no longer a mere walk.

Nor, however, is it a technically demanding climb. The protected sections around Forcella Mosè aren't difficult or long, and they lead to a straightforward traverse of the southeastern slopes of Jôf Fuart. Once there, the side trip to the 2666m summit is almost irresistible – little more than a plod, but with terrific views and real mountain atmosphere.

Then comes the Cengia degli Dei (Ledge of the Gods). On this traverse around the towers known as the Madri dei Camosci, on a ledge of variable width (from 2m to practically nothing) and through precipitous clefts between the pinnacles, most people will think seriously about using the equipment nearly every *via ferrata* enthusiast carries.

Many will connect themselves to the extensive safety cables here; others won't feel the need, or will argue that the security the cables offer is illusory – a view supported by the occasional eye-bolt that dangles loose on the end of a cable, pulled free of the rock it had been fixed to.

Nearly all, though, will don a helmet, for protection from falling rocks or should they themselves fall. Rocks can be dislodged unwittingly by people above – including your own companions – or by ibex and chamois as they bound about without concern for your safety. And sometimes, of course, rocks simply fall.

Partway along this imposing ledge (once you're completely committed to it), a metal box houses a logbook to record your passing. It's a nice touch, the equivalent of a summit log for a route with no summit.

On returning to Rifugio Corsi, it's fun to look up and try to trace where you've just been. Then look in a special Julian Alps issue of the Italian mountain magazine *Alp*, kept in the *rifugio*, for photographs from the first, and to date only, traverse of the Cengia degli Dei in winter.

The track markers and 'Giro delle Malghe' signs continue through forest, until the tree cover begins to thin allowing views of the cliffs above. About 40 minutes from the start, there is a large clear Track No 624 signpost on your left to **Casere Cregnedul di Sopra**. Follow this briefly west to emerge from the trees into a steep meadow. Ascend northwards following the red markers to some buildings. These buildings were once summer quarters for shepherds. The uppermost one is open to walkers for use as a shelter; you are allowed to stay overnight but there is no telephone and no *gestore*. There's water inside.

Head roughly east (still on Track No 624) avoiding the road, through a gate, and after 100m or so a sign at a three-way junction shows you've rejoined Track No 625. Continue north up the valley to some **ruins**, then follow the track as it swings east. After half an hour of sidling and a brief flurry of switchbacks, the track rounds a spur and emerges from the trees onto a wide, open

slope that faces southeast. About 1km to the north is a rocky crest, which is crossed, after another burst of zigzags, at **Passo degli Scalini** (1970m). Jôf Fuart, Rifugio Corsi and the unlikely looking track to the *rifugio* now come into view – a view that's even better from a short distance east along the crest.

The track ahead is milder than it appears – with a little help from wartime engineering. It passes turn-offs on the left (Track No 626 to Forcella Lavinal dell'Orso) and right (Track No 628 to Malga Grantagar) before skirting below a rocky tower, Campanile di Villaco, and dropping to **Rifugio Corsi** (☎ 0428 6 81 13; dm €17-20; 15 Jun-30 Sep). The *rifugio* (1874m) is perched in a valley ringed by rugged limestone peaks.

Day 2: Rifugio Corsi to Sella Nevea

1½–2 hours, 6km, 96m ascent, 795m descent

Retrace your steps via Passo degli Scalini to Sella Nevea. The detour to Casere Cregnedul di Sopra is optional.

CARNIC ALPS

The region known as Carnia is intrinsically Friulian (the language is widely spoken here) and named for its original Celtic inhabitants – the Carnics. Geographically, it contains the western and central parts of the Carnic Alps and presents wild and beautiful walking country flecked with curious villages.

Greener, less jagged and rounder than the Julian Alps, and at a slightly lower overall altitude, the mountains offer less resistance to walkers and are hence popular with locals. The Carnic's sedimentary rock yields many fossils and has been extensively shaped by glaciers.

Set upon what has been a long-standing cultural melting pot, the range forms the watershed between Austria's Black Sea catchment to the north and that of the Adriatic, on Italian territory to the south. The border between the two countries follows their crest – walking tracks and the frontier sometimes share the same markers. Until WWI the border was further south, but after 1919 much Austrian territory was ceded to Italy. On the two walks described here, there is a sense that you could be in Austria even when you're not.

The walks described here are quite short but take in some of the most scenic country easily accessible (by car, at any rate) from Tarvisio. There's plenty more walking further west, beyond the scope of this book. If you're looking for a longer alternative, the walks described share ground with the Traversata Carnica, a long-distance track which takes about seven days to walk. It begins in Sesto in the Dolomites, strays on to both sides of the international border, and has both an Italian and an Austrian finish, in Tarvisio and just over the border in Unterthörl, respectively.

PLANNING
When to Walk
The summer walking season extends, roughly, from early June to the end of September. Outside that time, bring your skis.

PLACE NAMES
Dual naming of geographical features, in German and Italian, is widespread along the border between Italy and Austria. We have given preference to the Italian names in this section.

MONTE CARNIZZA

Duration 3–4 hours
Distance 9km
Difficulty moderate
Start/Finish Passo di Pramollo
Nearest Town Tarvisio (p190)
Transport private

Summary Warm up on rustic roads, then climb above pastures to the Austrian border and take an airy ridge-top route with a foot in each country and views in all directions.

This pleasant ramble (and a bit of a scramble) on the Italy–Austria border takes advantage of the sealed road that connects Val Canale with the Gail valley in Austria across Passo di Pramollo (1530m) – or Nassfeld Pass, to give it its Austrian name. In both languages the name refers to the wet, marshy environs of the pass. Stausee, the small lake at the pass, has only been there since 1962, when an earthen dam was built.

The walk sets out along an unsealed road – part of the long-distance Traversata Carnica – through pastures where cattle still graze in summer. Once it climbs to the border, ski lifts on the Austrian side are a constant presence. But the ridge-top traverse to Monte Carnizza is thoroughly enjoyable, and the views on a good day extend from the Dolomites to the Julian Alps.

The area around Passo di Pramollo, on both sides of the border, is renowned for its wildflowers, and especially for a rare figwort, *Wulfenia carinthiaca*, which grows only here and in the mountains between Albania and Yugoslavia. There is plenty of mixed coniferous forest around, but for much of its distance the walk passes through pastures or follows a ridge largely clear of trees.

Rocks in the area are rich with fossils that date from the range's origins, hundreds of millions of years ago, as a stretch of tropical coast. Along the narrow crest of Monte Carnizza, several different rock types, including limestone and quartz conglomerates, can be found in the space of a few hundred metres.

The route ascends and descends 720m, with the option of an additional 40m up and down Monte Auernig.

PLANNING
Maps
The recommended map is the Tabacco 1:25,000 map No 18 *Alpi Carniche Orientali Canal del Ferro*. It's sold in bookshops in Udine and Tarvisio.

GETTING TO/FROM THE WALK
There's no bus to Passo di Pramollo from the Italian side. You could conceivably take a taxi from Tarvisio though a rental car is generally more economical. From Tarvisio take the S13 west to Pontebba (21km), then follow signs north up the valley of the Rio Bombaso. Park beside the road near the hotels, which are right by Stausee and just before the pass itself. Right at the start of the walk, both **Albergo Ristorante Wulfenia** (☎ 0428 9 05 06) and **Ristorante Hotel Al Gallo Forcello** (☎ 0428 900 14; www .forcello.com; s €40-89, d €60-158) serve meals all day from 11.30am. There is also a telephone here, should you need one.

THE WALK
From the north side of Ristorante Hotel Gallo Forcello, take the road that leads east past a barrier. It climbs briefly, then levels

out and soon comes to **Casera Auernig** and a junction on the north side with Track No 501. This is the way you'll descend later from Monte Auernig.

Continuing east it's a straightforward and pleasant walk along the road, gradually losing some height, with views towards Monte Malvueric to the south. After about 3km from the pass, the path bends roughly southeast. Follow for approximately 500m to a signposted junction on your left – Route No 501 – uphill to a small group of *malghe* (herders' summer huts) at Casera For.

Beyond here the track wanders east, then swings north and climbs through low vegetation to a meadow just below the top of Monte Corona (1832m). Even Daisy the cow has conquered Monte Corona but its quaint, flat summit gives good views. Just below the summit, at a T-junction (marked with a painted 'T' on a rock), the ridge-top traverse west to Monte Carnizza begins.

First the track drops into grassy **Sella Carnizza**. From here a trail heads south to Casera For and another – recently built up into a small road – descends on the Austrian side to Garnitzenalm. Continuing west, a narrow but distinct and well-marked track stays close to the crest (and the international boundary) as it climbs above the top station of an Austrian ski lift. By this point the crest

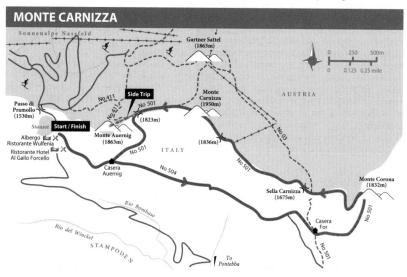

MONTE CARNIZZA

is narrow, and it narrows and steepens further as it drops into a saddle (1836m) before the final scramble to the airy top of **Monte Carnizza** (1950m). If the weather is kind, you'll have great views in all directions – into Austria, with the ski lifts around Gartner Sattel (1863m) and Gartnerkofel (2195m) close at hand, west past Monte Cavallo (2239m) towards the Dolomites, and southeast to the peaks of the Julian Alps.

Heading west from Monte Carnizza, the ridge is less precipitous, and tracks lead off on the Austrian side. After half an hour, at a signpost in a second, broad, saddle (1823m), Track No 501 heads down to the south towards 'Auernig Alm' (Casera Auernig). Monte Auernig is not far away (see Side Trip, below).

From the saddle it's an easy enough 15-minute descent on Track No 501 to Casera Auernig and the road west back to **Passo di Pramollo**.

SIDE TRIP: MONTE AUERNIG
25 minutes, 600m, 40m ascent

After Monte Carnizza, Monte Auernig doesn't present much of a challenge – but, on a nice day, why not stay high a little longer? The summit gives a good view over Passo di Pramollo, which has remained hidden hitherto. There's also an interesting variation on the usual summit marker! From the second saddle west of Monte Carnizza, where Track No 501 begins its descent to Casera Auernig, Austrian Track No 411 leads along the broad, scrubby ridge to Auernig's modest summit (1863m) – and then, when you're done, back again.

MONTE OSTERNIG

Duration	3–3½ hours
Distance	11km
Difficulty	easy–moderate
Start/Finish	Rifugio Nordio-Deffar
Nearest Town	Tarvisio (p190)
Transport	private
Summary	A steep climb leads to open pastures and a high point on the Austrian border.

Not unduly strenuous, this walk takes you to the wide, open spaces above the tree line and some fabulous views. Like some other summits in the Carnic Alps, Monte Osternig's rounded bulk brings to mind – of all places – the Australian Alps.

The Austrian influence is strong. Trail signs sponsored by competing breweries lure you towards *Gasthäuser* ('guesthouses' or 'inns' in German) just over the border in Austria. It wouldn't happen on the French border!

The route is easy to follow and not long. It might be graded 'easy' if it wasn't for the height gained and lost (872m) and the sometimes steep gradients. You could avoid more than a third of the climbing, although not the steepest sections (they're right at the start), by going no higher than Sella Bistrizza.

PLANNING
Maps
The Tabacco 1:25,000 map No 19 *Alpi Giulie Occidentali Tarvisiano* is recommended for this walk.

GETTING TO/FROM THE WALK
There are no buses to the start of this walk. You could conceivably take a taxi from Tarvisio but a rental car is a more convenient option. By car, take the S13 west from Tarvisio to Ugovizza (9km). At the sign to 'CAI Rifugio Fratelli Nordio', turn right onto Via Uqua, which leads through the village and up the valley of the Torrente Uqua. Continue to follow the narrow, sealed road and signs to the Rifugio Nordio-Deffar. After passing some farm buildings on your left and crossing a river, the surface road ends at an opening with ample room to park. Rifugio Nordio-Deffar, at the start of the walk, was severely damaged by a landslide in 2003 and has never re-opened. However, it is still signposted and marked on Tabacco maps.

THE WALK
From the car park, the unsealed road continues steeply northwards up the valley until a fork, where one way continues north to Sella di Lom. Swing east towards Osternig Alm (Feistritzer Alm) and climb steadily, with many switchbacks, up the north side of a valley. Forty-five minutes or so from the start of the walk, the track emerges from the trees and, in another 10 minutes, you arrive at bustling **Sella Bistrizza**, where the

JULIAN & CARNIC ALPS

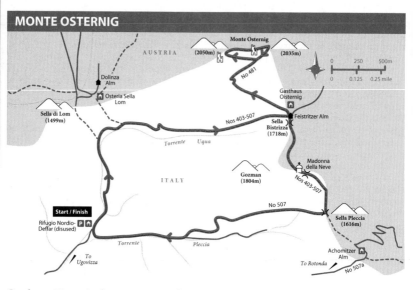

MONTE OSTERNIG

Gasthaus Oisternig does a roaring trade in meals and beer.

Track No 481 (northwest) to the summit of Monte Osternig is unmistakeable. It leads steadily up, through a couple of major zigzags, until some ruined fortifications appear on the right (north) side of the track. Head north here, following painted arrows, up the final slopes to the summit (2050m), about 40 minutes above Sella Bistrizza. The views include the Dolomites to the west beyond Monte Cavallo and Gartnerkofel, the Julian Alps to the south, and snowy Austrian peaks to the north. It's a pleasant wander east along the ridge to the lower summit (2035m), marked by a prominent cross, then down to the southwest to rejoin the main route near another wartime ruin.

Once back in Sella Bistrizza, a track leads south along the Austrian side of the ridge and, in just five to 10 minutes, reaches a saddle and the tiny chapel of **Madonna della Neve**, with poignant memorials inside to members of an ill-starred local family. Back on the Italian side, the route drops quite steeply but straightforwardly for another five to 10 minutes into Sella Pleccia.

From here follow Track No 507 west down the valley of Torrente Pleccia to Rifugio Nordio-Deffar.

TOWNS & FACILITIES

TARVISIO
☎ 0428 / pop 5100

Picturesquely positioned in Val Canale between the eastern Carnic Alps and the western Julian Alps, Tarvisio is fairly well provided with accommodation and transport options. It makes a logical base for walks in both ranges.

Through traffic (to/from Austria and Slovenia) can jam the narrow roads leading east out of town.

Information
The **APT office** (☎ 23 92; www.tarvisiano .org; Via Roma 14), is easy to find in the centre of town and has plenty of useful information, including SAF bus timetables and a simple town map. It posts local meteorological bulletins on a board outside – most days. The bookshop opposite sells Tabacco and other maps, as well as some guidebooks.

Supplies & Equipment
If you've forgotten, lost or run out of anything vital, **Lussari Sport** (☎ 4 04 74; Via Alpi Giulie 44), on the right on the way

into Tarvisio from Udine, stocks gear and clothing for skiing and cycling. In case of late-season snow you can also hire snow shoes (*racchetta da neve*) here.

For general needs, there's a **Supercoop supermarket** (Via Vittorio Veneto 184) and numerous general stores, often labelled '*Alimentari/Lebensmittel*'.

Sleeping & Eating

Within walking distance from Tarvisio's main bus stop, at the less congested, western end of town, are several perfectly adequate places to stay, such as **Albergo Regina** (☎ 20 15; Via Diaz 2; s/d without private bath €23/44).

Nearby is **Albergo 2000** (☎ 64 42 23; Via Parini 4; s/d with bath €45/60).

Slap bang in the centre is **Hotel Haberl** (☎ 23 12; Via Kugy 1; s/d with bath €50/70) with a large outside restaurant-bar-terrace – perfect for people-watching. There are other options in and around the heart of town – the APT office has details.

Ristorante Adriatico (☎ 26 37; Via Roma 59) is typical of Tarvisio's economical eating joints with a set two-course meat/fish menu including wine for less than €20.

Don't miss **Tizio e Caio** (Via Roma 53) in the centre of town for its outside terrace and many flavours of ice cream.

Getting There & Away

Tarvisio Boscoverde station, 2km east of town, is on the train line from Udine (€9.50; one hour 15 minutes) to Vienna (Austria).

SAF (☎ 21 34) buses serve Tarvisio from Udine with a change at Carnia or Gemona. Some SAF buses also make the complete journey. Buses come and go from Tarvisio Città, the bus stop on Piazza Unità in the middle of town. Bar Commercio, opposite the bus stop in Tarvisio, sells bus tickets. The trip takes about 1¾ hours.

By car, Tarvisio is just off the A23 to Villach (Austria), which connects south of Udine with the A4 between Venice and Trieste.

UDINE

☎ 0432 / pop 95,100

Few people outside Italy have heard of Udine, an enviably rich provincial city shoehorned into the country's little visited

northeastern corner less than 15km from the border with Slovenia.

The spiritual capital of Friulian culture, Udine gives little away in its utilitarian Italian suburbs. But, encased inside the peripheral ring road lies an infinitely grander medieval centre; a dramatic melange of Venetian arches, Grecian statues, and Roman columns.

Information

The **tourist office** (☎ 29 59 72; www.udine -turismo.it; Piazza I Maggio 7; 8.30am-6.30pm Mon-Sat, 10am-4pm Sun) has detailed information on accommodation in Tarvisio, and some general information on walks in the Julian and Carnic Alps.

Supplies & Equipment

A couple of bookshops in the old centre sell Tabacco maps and have a better range of Italian-language guidebooks than you may find in Tarvisio.

Sleeping & Eating

Hotel Europa (☎ 50 87 31; www.hotel europa.ud.it; Viale Europa Unita 17; s/d €58/92) is a standard close-to-the-station hotel, economical, although a little musty, but close enough to negotiate with a heavy suitcase and no sense of direction (meaning you'll save on taxi fares). The rooms are large and the service polite, but no-frills. If it's full, try the similarly priced **Hotel Principe** (☎ 50 60 00; Viale Europa Unita) next door.

For farmhouse accommodation around Udine, contact **Agriturismo del Friuli-Venezia Giulia** (☎ 20 26 46; www.agri turismofvg.com; Via Gorghi 27).

Several open-air cafés and restaurants are dotted around Piazza Matteotti and the surrounding pedestrian streets. Via Paolo Sarpi and surrounding streets are lined with lively restaurants and bars.

Sbarco dei Pirati (☎ 2 13 30; Riva Bartolini 12; meals €20) is embellished with pots, pans, saws, clogs, saddles and other assorted junk hanging from the ceiling. Meat-based Friulian fare fills the brief menu, popular with students and those on a student budget.

Trattoria ai Frati (☎ 50 69 26; Piazzetta Antonini 5; meals €25; Mon-Sat) is a delightful old-style eatery on a cobbled cul-de-sac; local specialities include *frico* (a thick, succulent cheese-and-potato omelette) and San Daniele ham.

Getting There & Away

From the **bus station** (☎ 50 69 41; Viale Europa Unita 31), services operated by **SAF** (☎ 0432 60 81 11; www.saf.ud.it) go to and from Trieste (€5.10, 1¼ hours, hourly) and Tarvisio (€7.40, two to 2½ hours, most require a change in Carnia). Buses also link Udine and Friuli-Venezia Giulia airport (€3.55, one hour, hourly).

If travelling to/from the Dolomites, a combination of trains and buses, with changes at Conegliano and Calalzo, connects Udine

with Cortina d'Ampezzo (€9.45, four hours depending on connections). There's also a daily SAF in each direction between San Candido and Trieste, which stops at Udine (€12.05, three hours 50 minutes). It leaves San Candido at 3.15pm and, in the other direction, leaves Udine at 8am.

From Udine's train station (Viale Europa Unita), services run to Trieste (€6-7, one hour and 10 minutes), Venice (€8, 1¾ to 2½ hours, several daily) and Gorizia (€3.25, 25-40 minutes, hourly) on the Slovenian border.

If travelling by car from Venice, take the A4 northeast for about 90km, then the A23 heading north towards Austria.

Tuscany

HIGHLIGHTS

- Finding solitude and getting lost (yes lost) in the insanely popular confines of internationally lauded **Chianti-shire** (p196)
- Spying the towers of San Gimignano from six different angles on the **Medieval Towns** walk (p201)
- Enjoying a spare day or three between hikes at a traditional Tuscan *agriturismo* (p200)
- Stumbling upon marble quarries – but no ski resorts – in the scarred but beautiful **Apuan Alps** (p207)

Signature food: *Bistecca alla fiorentina*	Celebrated native: Leonardo da Vinci	Famous for... Tourists

Benvenuti a Toscana; land of tall, slender cypress trees and turreted medieval towns; home of da Vinci, Boccaccio, and vacationing British prime ministers; the font of humanism, mannerism, the Uffizi, and a thousand and one Italian clichés – most of which are true.

For many people, Tuscany is Italy personified – an intoxicating dose of everything a food-loving, culture-embracing Italia-phile might dream about. A quick flick back through history does little to refute the legend. It was Tuscany that invented the Italian language, Tuscany that bred the peninsula's first organised civilisation (the Etruscans), and Tuscany that inspired the greatest cultural rebirth in modern history – the glittering Renaissance.

But, while the urban centres of Florence and Siena never cease to raise the collective pulse, Tuscany's less spectacular but no less engaging countryside is just as credit-worthy.

Hiking-wise, Tuscany offers everything the great art cities can't; peace, solitude, decent prices and a refreshing dose of rustic realism. Wedged between Italy's spinal mountains and the Mediterranean, the landscape here ranges from pretty pastoral to downright weird. In the north, the battlement-shaped Apuan Alps, with their huge, centuries-old marble quarries look like displaced, battle-scarred relics of the Apennines. Further south, the rolling hills of Chianti-shire and the San Gimignano region could almost pass for rural France on a clear day save for the Renaissance architecture and the odd stray Fiat 500.

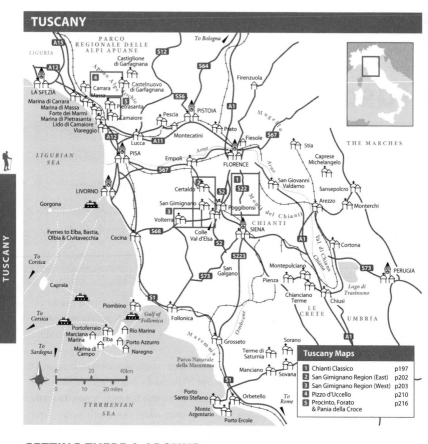

Tuscany Maps

1	Chianti Classico	p197
2	San Gimignano Region (East)	p202
3	San Gimignano Region (West)	p203
4	Pizzo d'Uccello	p210
5	Procinto, Forato & Pania della Croce	p216

GETTING THERE & AROUND

With such iconic tourist magnets as Florence, Siena and Lucca, Tuscany has excellent bus and train connections with the rest of the country. This service is replicated in the countryside where comfortable and punctual local buses reach all but the tiniest villages.

GATEWAY

The danger of staying in Florence (p218) is that you may never make it outside the city limits – there's simply too much to captivate, intrigue and distract you. But the illustrious capital of the Renaissance, with its close proximty to the Chianti countryside along with excellent bus and train connections, remains the region's most convenient and accessible gateway.

CHIANTI

Despite Chianti's pre-eminence in the book of breathless Italian clichés, its trails and footpaths remain surprisingly empty. For hikers, it's a mystery as perplexing as the Turin Shroud – but one that's worth jealously guarding. Jostling for elbow room in the more urbanised areas, the bulk of Tuscan tourists prefer to uncover the region's sublime secrets in less energetic ways; be it dining in San Gimignano, wine-tasting in charming Radda, or lolling by the swimming pool in their all-comforts-included *agriturismo*.

What they're missing is hard to capture and even harder to quantify. Wilderness-wise, Chianti is certainly no Alaska. Instead, this undulating slice of pastoral Italy offers one of the planet's most scenic and ecologically harmonious 'man-made' environments; a colourful cornucopia of striped vineyards and sun-flecked medieval villages punctuated by over 2000 years of bucolic history. Ah, words simply cannot describe the simplicity of it all.

HISTORY

Etruscan civilisation blossomed in these valleys from the 8th century BC until the area was absorbed by the expansion of Rome. In medieval times, the Chianti area was on the main route, called the Via Francigena, from northern Europe to Siena and Rome. Later, as Florence and Siena grew in size, the two cities faced off in Chianti, building castles on every hilltop they could find. In 1384, the Lega del Chianti (Chianti League) was formed for defence purposes by Radda, Castellina and Gaiole. Finally, in 1550, Florence defeated Siena and the great dukedom of Tuscany was established. The area then lost its strategic importance and the people were able to dedicate themselves entirely to agriculture. Chianti was already exporting wine to England in the 16th century. The aristocratic families, who owned entire districts, built countless luxurious country villas, many of which have now been reborn as wineries.

ENVIRONMENT

The Chianti ridge is a system of harmonious wooded hills between Florence and Siena, bordered by Val d'Arno to the east and Val d'Elsa and Val di Pesa to the west. To the west of Certaldo and Val d'Elsa are San Gimignano and Volterra, situated in an area known as the Medieval Hills, and featuring extensive woods and fields of grain.

The Chianti and the San Gimignano areas are composed predominantly of sandstone or clay-type sedimentary rock, and of layers of sand and gravel. In fact, 200 million years ago the area was covered by a sea. Starting in the Miocene epoch (20 million years ago), the pressure of the African plate on the Euroasiatic plate began to push up the land, forming hills where, in some areas, you can still find marine fossils. Where the sea was shallow, near present-day Volterra, the evaporating water left gypsum crystals, one variety of which is the alabaster now mined in the area.

The woods are dominated by four species of oak tree, including the holm oak. There are also maples, chestnuts, hazelnuts, alders, stone pines, cluster pines and black pines. In the areas of Mediterranean scrub, there are the typical gum tree, strawberry tree and myrtle associated with the holm oak. Elegant rows of cypresses, noble grape vines and olive trees complete the picture.

The largest mammal in the forests of Chianti is the wild pig, stalked intensively by its only dangerous predator – people. The Tuscan hunter is also fond of the resident pheasant, hare, fox, badger, weasel, beech-marten, squirrel and the bizarre porcupine, which was imported from Africa by the ancient Romans. Among the birds there are woodpidgeons, jays, blackbirds, hoopoes, kestrels, buzzards, crows and tits. Among reptiles there is the lizard and the innocuous water snake. In rocky areas you can run into poisonous vipers.

CLIMATE

The climate of Chianti and of the Val d'Elsa is mild and temperate. The average annual temperature is around 15°C, with peaks of 35°C in summer and the rare sub-zero winter day. Snow and fog occur only in exceptional cases.

PLANNING
When to Walk

In spring (Mar–May) and autumn (Sep–Nov) the climate is sunny and mild, and the palettes of seasonal colours are wonderful. At the beginning of October there is the *vendemmia* (grape harvest). In January and February, Chianti virtually closes down; summer is the least suitable for walking due to the sultry heat.

Emergency

For urgent medical assistance in the Chianti region, contact the **national emergency number** (☎ 118).

ACCESS TOWNS

San Gimignano (p220) is the best base for the Medieval Towns and Tuscan Hill Crests hikes. Greve in Chianti (p218) is handily located for the Chianti Classico. Siena (p221) is a viable and attractive base for both.

CHIANTI CLASSICO

Duration 3 days
Distance 52km
Difficulty easy
Start San Fabiano
Finish Vagliagli
Nearest Towns Florence (p218), Siena (p221)
Transport bus

Summary A pleasant walk, mainly on country roads, past vineyards, olive groves, *borghi* (ancient villages) and evocative forests. Enchanting, panoramic views of Badia a Passignano and the Chianti hills.

Subtle, with an interesting blend of complementary flavours, the Chianti Classico hike isn't a million miles from its namesake wine in terms of nuances and traditional Italian character. Not quite as downright gorgeous as the terrain around San Gimignano, the Chianti hills still glimmer romantically in sultry Tuscan sunsets and, while the vine-striped fields are an obvious highlight, there are plenty of other sights to spark the imagination.

Most of the hike is on dirt roads; indeed, it is negotiable on a mountain bike if you can get to grips with the small sections of single track punctuated with overgrown brambles. Day 1 is a little detached from the rest of the route. The gap between the two can be efficiently plugged by the local country bus service (see Getting to/from the Walk, below).

PLANNING
Maps
The SELCA 1:70,000 map *Il Chianti, terra del vino* is detailed enough for this walk. Multigraphic's 1:25,000 map No 512 *Chianti Classico, Val di Pesa, Val d'Elsa* does not, unfortunately, cover the very beginning of the walk.

GETTING TO/FROM THE WALK
San Fabiano (start)
To get to the start of the walk at San Fabiano, take the **SITA** (☎ 800 37 37 60) bus from the terminal in Via Santa Caterina da Siena, which you'll find near the main train station in Florence (€2.50, one hour, eight a day Mon-Sat, three a day Sun and public holidays).

From Greve (Piazza Trento) to Pieve di Panzano, the starting point of Day 2 of the walk, take the SITA bus for Lucarelli and get off 2km south of Panzano at Pieve di Panzano (15 minutes, three a day at 7.55am, 1.15pm and 5.55pm Mon-Fri, daily Sat). Be sure to take the right bus because most terminate at Panzano (17 buses a day). On Sunday, from Greve or Florence, it is possible to get only as far as Panzano (seven a day from 8.15am to 9.15pm).

Vagliagli (finish)
Getting there and away from the town piazza in Vagliagli, **Tra-in** (☎ 0577 20 42 45) bus No 34 goes to Piazza Gramsci in Siena (€1.40, 40 minutes, six a day including 1.50pm, 2.25pm, 4.10pm and 7.15pm Mon-Sat, 2.45pm and 7.45pm Sun). You can buy tickets at the bar in the piazza.

THE WALK
Day 1: San Fabiano to Greve in Chianti
4–5 hours, 16km, 350m ascent
San Fabiano is a tiny *borgo* (small town) featuring a Romanesque façade, which is all that remains of the local church. From San Fabiano head back downhill towards Florence along the surfaced road. After about 250m, turn left into Via Fornace Casavecchia, a dirt road that passes through picturesque olive groves with a panoramic view to the hills across the Val di Pesa. Below, to the right, is the **Castello il Palagio**, a small, medieval castle, and further ahead you can see the bell tower of the **Pieve di Santo Stefano a Campoli**.

In about 10 minutes you'll reach an ancient kiln. Follow the dirt road straight uphill (south) into the trees, and skirt a fine *casale* (farmhouse) and fountain. After another 10 minutes you reach a shrine at the corner of the buildings of **La Cava**. Here follow the road to the right through the yards of two *casali* and, in five minutes, you'll reach the Romanesque **Pieve di Santo Stefano a Campoli** (337m). The grassy churchyard, surrounded by stands of cypresses, provides a pleasant setting for repose and the contemplation of this ancient country church, built in the 10th century AD. Turn left (south) and follow the made road. Fortunately there is little traffic and in about 30 minutes you'll

CHIANTI CLASSICO

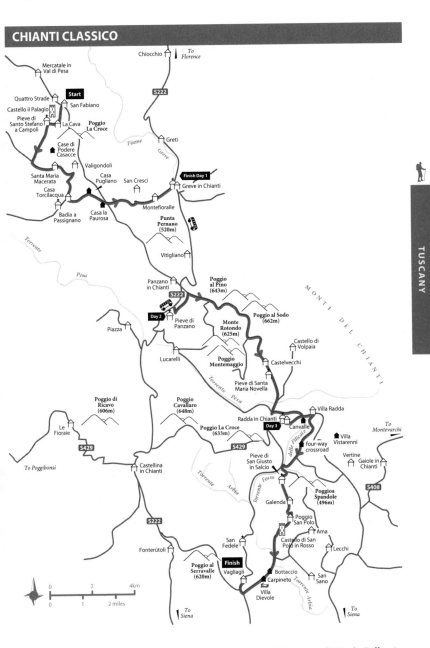

reach a large intersection, where you turn left. Passing between rows of vineyards and *casali*, in another 15 minutes you'll reach **Santa Maria Macerata** (363m). Following the gradually descending road you'll reach a triple junction with a cemetery and a shrine among the cypresses that marks the place where the asphalt turns into dirt road (350m).

Follow the dirt road down to the right and then make the steep ascent to the turn-off to the left for Valigondoli (443m) marked by an oak tree. Take the right fork; the road soon begins to descend, affording a view of the **Badia a Passignano**. The abbey is among the most beautiful in Tuscany, majestic and evocative with its two crenellated towers defended by a ring of lush cypresses. Continue past the tower-house called Tracolle and you'll reach the paved road near the abbey at **Casa Torcilacqua** (354m).

From Casa Torcilacqua, take the ascending road to the left for Greve in Chianti, which offers further excellent views. After passing the **Casa Pugliano** you reach **Casa la Paurosa** (496m) and the paved road that links the town of Mercatale with Panzano; turn to the right and after 200m turn left and head downhill on the recently paved road towards Greve (5km). There are panoramic views of the Chianti hills. The ancient, small town below you is Montefioralle.

Day 2: Pieve di Panzano to Radda in Chianti (p220)
4–5 hours, 16km, 344m ascent, 279m descent

On the opposite side of the road to the bus stop, there's a small paved street that leads up to the *borgo*, then continues up to the 10th-century **Pieve di Panzano** (457m) and 16th-century colonnade. Inside there is a 12th-century painting of the *Madonna Enthroned* and a 14th-century triptych by the Master of Panzano. Outside, enjoy the splendid panoramic view of the Val di Pesa, then visit the evocative 14th-century cloister.

Go back to the *borgo* and take the fork heading slightly uphill to the right; pass Hotel Villa Barone and continue on past a cemetery until you come to a T-junction. Turn right towards Montemaggio along a dirt road with a wide panorama looking south. After about 800m you pass a shrine on the right and, going down towards some cypresses, wonderful vistas open up to the north as well. Shortly afterwards is a triple fork where you take the central, uphill road towards Montemaggio-Castelvecchi. The road snakes off into the woods, passing

the large iron gate of the Cennatoio farm on the right.

You soon reach a meadow and continue comfortably along level ground, with extensive views south, until you come to a fork among the fields and oak trees of Poggio al Sodo (662m), featuring a sign for Radda. Turn to the right and begin the descent into the woods towards Montemaggio, following the dirt road marked 'SP114 Traversa del Chianti'. After 300m, at another fork (659m), follow the signs to Radda in Chianti as you continue to descend, keeping to the right.

Here the road narrows and after about 800m you'll come to the Montemaggio turn-off (625m); continue descending to the left, keeping to the main road. After 2.4km the pine wood is interrupted by some cypresses and then thins out into some beautiful meadows and cultivated fields, arriving at the romantic *borgo* of **Castelvecchi**. You can see Castello di Volpaia off to the left, built into the slope at the edge of the wood. From here the road was recently paved, and twists down among olive groves and vineyards to the charming **Pieve di Santa Maria Novella** (478m), which retains its original Romanesque structure of three apses.

The descent gets steeper here and reaches a fork in the road. Go right towards Radda, cross the bridge (351m) over Torrente Pesa, and head uphill to the road for Lucarelli and Panzano, then go left towards Radda in Chianti. You'll need to walk 1.7km on this busy road until you come to an unusual red-brick bridge. Pass under it, then immediately turn off to the left and swing back over the bridge towards **Radda**, which is now 1km away. The village of Villa Radda lies straight ahead along the road.

For overnight accommodation and transport details see p220. If you want to abort the walk here, **SITA** (☎ 800 37 37 60) buses run from Radda to Florence (twice daily), while **Tra-in** (☎ 0577 20 42 45) buses serve both Florence (once daily) and Siena (five daily).

Day 3: Radda in Chianti to Vagliagli
5–6 hours, 20km, 500m ascent

Retrace your steps downhill and continue east (left) on the busy paved road to **Villa Radda**, 1km east of Radda. Find the

ITALIAN LANDSCAPES IN LITERATURE

Throughout the 18th and 19th centuries, well-to-do members of the British aristocracy began to embark on what would become known as the 'Grand Tour', an expensive sojourn around the art cities of southern Europe financed by a weighty family inheritance. Decamping in Paris, Geneva, Turin and Rome, these stinking-rich pioneers of the modern-day 'gap year' made a beeline for Italy, and it wasn't long before the peninsula's distinctive landscapes and infectious *joie de vivre* were being immortalised – and romanticised – in countless works of English literature.

Lord Byron was one of the earliest adherents, moving semi-permanently to Venice in 1816 where he settled down to write *Don Juan*. Other admirers followed, including Charles Dickens who penned the travelogue *Pictures of Italy* in 1846, and Anglo-American novelist Henry James who gushed nostalgically about the 'luxury of loving Italy' in the exhaustive *Italian Hours* published in 1909.

One of the pre-war era's most celebrated Italia-philes was EM Forster who painted an indelibly romantic picture of Tuscany in his two early-20th-century classics, *Where Angels Fear to Tread* and *A Room with a View*. Forster balanced his rather scant knowledge of Italian culture with an innate ability to juxtapose drab Edwardian stuffiness against the raw passion of the Mediterranean. This successful formula made his books read like recruitment ads for the burgeoning Italian tourist industry and ably complemented the nascent Baedeker travel guides.

Forster's contemporary, DH Lawrence, visited Italy regularly in the 1920s during what became known as his 'savage pilgrimage', a thinly veiled effort to escape the derision and censorship he suffered in England. Impressed by Italy's perceived permissiveness and cultural freedoms, Lawrence spent an idyllic summer in 1927 travelling around the Tuscan countryside accompanied by his friend, Earl Brewster, comparing the glory of Etruscan culture with the brash modernism of Mussolini. His musings appear in the book *DH Lawrence and Italy*.

All of the aforementioned books add colour and poignancy to a modern Italian hiking trip and you'll quickly discover that, more often than not, few of the timeless landscapes that the 19th-century English romantics so eloquently described have changed.

red-and-white sign painted on the left corner of the hotel Villa Miranda, marking Trail No 68 for San Giusto, and turn off here.

Trail No 68 is actually a pleasant, little country road that heads south into a small, cultivated valley. Following the red-and-white signs, you'll pass the ancient tower of **Canvalle** on the right as you head up the other side of the valley. After a few metres, the paved road descends to the right at a junction, marked by a cypress with a sign for an *agriturismo*; instead, you continue straight on a stony track heading up into the forest. In a few minutes you reach a ridge and a three-pronged fork near the Casa Beretuzzo; go right, then straight on and more or less level, passing a wooden cross encircled by cypresses. Take care to stick to the marked trail and avoid deviations. After a few metres you can enjoy the view over the territory of Radda to the right and, to the left (southeast), the towers of Vertine and the 16th-century Villa Vistarenni.

Continue through a wide, grassy clearing with a four-way crossroads (530m). Go straight ahead here, following the main dirt road downhill (it curves slightly to the right) until you reach a T-junction (485m) where you'll turn right downhill in the direction of San Giusto in Salcio. Shortly afterwards, you'll see the elegant Romanesque bell tower of Pieve di San Giusto in Salcio peeping out of the trees on the other side of the valley. The road now descends in steep curves through fields and cypresses, veering right at a Y-junction, crossing a little bridge over a stream, and leading to the paved road at the valley bottom, where you will turn left (378m).

About 100m along the road there's a turn-off for Vagliagli–San Fedele on the right. Ignore it and continue on the paved road: you'll cross a bridge over Torrente Fosso delle Filicaie and, after walking another 200m, turn right (signposted Poggio Antinora) onto the cypress-lined dirt road to reach **Pieve di San Giusto in**

AGRITURISMI

With a landscape dotted with small traditional farmhouses, and a food tradition that screams out the words fresh, simple, local and home-grown; central Italy was surely invented with the concept of *agriturismi* in mind. In the circumstances, it's no small wonder that these historic working farms–cum–modern guesthouses are as popular as a steaming plate of *spaghetti al ragú* in downtown Florence.

For virgin agri-tourists, the idea is a simple one: ditch your heaving city hotel, learn a few words of passable Italian, and home in on an idyllic rural haven where a good portion of the food you eat is grown on the premises. Beyond that, no two *agriturismi* are the same. Some produce olive oil, others raise cattle, still more offer tempting additional extras such as swimming pools and cookery classes. The only given is the underlying philosophy: Italy offered as only the Italians can offer it – congenial, traditional, and blissfully romantic.

For aspiring hikers, there's an additional bonus: most *agriturismi* are situated on, or close to, major trails. However, due to their burgeoning popularity, it's advisable to book in advance rather than just turn up. For more information and/or reservations try www.agriturismo.com.

Salcio (419m). This 11th-century, triple-apsed church is marvellously positioned among ancient farmhouses, grassy courtyards and centuries-old trees. Continue past the church and walk uphill until you meet up with a dirt road, marked by a red-and-white sign on a tree, where you turn left.

After 20m you'll reach a three-pronged fork with two parallel dirt roads in front of you (480m); follow the right one for Galenda-Ama. The path follows the course of an ancient stone wall on your right. When the wall runs out, the path swerves left downhill before crossing a shallow stream. It then proceeds uphill to **Galenda** (485m), a delightful rural *borgo* where you can make a pleasant rest stop among the cypresses.

Leave the *borgo* through the vaulted passageway between the houses and, heading south, follow the narrow grassy path that traverses the side of the slope among the fields. Note the small shrine on your right. Walk downhill to the bottom of the small valley, cross the stream (450m) and continue to follow the path uphill (southeast) with olive groves to your right. Go through one iron gate and then another, all the time keeping the olive trees on your right until you reach a paved road where you turn right. Within five minutes you will be among the lovely houses of **Poggio San Polo** (527m). Of interest is the ancient *parata* (a kind of vaulted garage for housing farm equipment), which has been transformed into an elegant country home. There is a good restaurant here, **Il Poggio**

(☎ 0577 74 61 35; closed Mon Jan-Feb; meals without wine around €25).

Continue your descent on the asphalt road towards Castello di San Polo in Rosso, now following Club Alpino Italiano (CAI) Route No 66 instead of Route No 68. The road becomes a pleasant cypress-lined dirt road, which passes through a forest and leads to a small cemetery. There is a splendid view of San Polo in Rosso and the Sienese Chianti.

Pass an elegant *casale* with a portico surmounted by a rustic, double-arched window. You then reach the ancient **Castello di San Polo in Rosso** (456m), founded in AD 1000 as a *pieve* (parish church), fortified in the 13th century and later embellished with a Renaissance loggia. Unfortunately, the castle is closed to visitors.

Take the dirt road that heads downhill beside the parking area, passing a house with a lovely staircase supported by a column. The dirt road veers to the left and then winds down into the forest, affording a view of the *pieve* from the south. The dirt road continues its long descent through the forest towards Torrente Arbia and you'll begin to notice the rich birdlife. As the road approaches the bottom of the valley, it crosses a little grassy bridge spanning a secondary stream, and continues among the poplars maintaining a distance from the true left of the river. In a few minutes you'll come to a junction marked with a small shrine, where turning right you'll soon come to a small clearing. Here the dirt road turns into a trail, which veers to the right through boggy ground.

Heading back into the trees, the path tracks left and uphill; this old road, used by vehicles until 30 years ago, is now regularly consumed by rain water. It ascends into the forest in steep, sharp curves. When you reach a great oak tree at a fork, veer left and continue uphill a few metres to a dirt road and the beautiful, restored *casale* of **Bottaccio** (392m) with a double *parata* next to the entrance. From here you can enjoy the panorama with San Sano nestled among the vineyards.

Continue ascending and at a fork in the path, marked by a tree, go right. After passing a wall turn sharp left up some steps and under a passageway to reach the courtyard and Renaissance chapel of the tiny *borgo* of **Carpineto** (413m). As you continue uphill on the road you now have a view of the remarkably beautiful Crete Senese.

Follow the road on the ridge, ignoring the first deviation to the left, and after a few metres you'll reach a semicircle of cypresses. Here you can take the dirt road to the left, descending to the elegant manor house of **Villa Dievole** (420m), adorned with a little 17th-century chapel as elegant as it is tiny.

To continue to Vagliagli, follow the dirt road uphill to the asphalt road and turn right. **Vagliagli** is 1.8km from the semicircle of cypresses.

MEDIEVAL TOWNS

Duration 2 days
Distance 40km
Difficulty easy
Start Certaldo
Finish Volterra
Nearest Town San Gimignano (p220)
Transport train, bus

Summary A peaceful and panoramic walk, taking in medieval villages, solitary country churches and the abandoned fortress of Castelvecchio.

You've read the history books; now it's time to take part in the visceral experience. The Medieval Towns hike is a two-stage monastic romp through the Middle Ages with some quintessential Tuscan scenery thrown in for good measure. As a hike, it can be done as a two-day point-to-point with an overnight in San Gimignano, or be split into separate day hikes using the walled town as a base. Both options are made easy by decent local bus services. Day 2, with its pastoral views and sleepy *borghi*, is the more interesting and scenic.

PLANNING
Maps
The SELCA 1:50,000 *Dolce Campagna Antiche Mura* map is ideal for this walk.

GIOVANNI BOCCACCIO – ERUDITE TUSCAN SON

Day 1 of the Medieval Towns hike starts in Piazza Boccaccio in Certaldo, named after Giovanni Boccaccio, the great Italian author and poet who is popularly regarded as one of Tuscany's most famous literary sons. Whether Boccaccio was actually born in Certaldo is a matter of historical debate – some claim he hailed originally from Paris. What is more certain is that his birth was registered in the year 1313, by his father, Boccaccio di Chellino, a wealthy Certaldo merchant.

By 1332, the young Bocaccio had abandoned a short-lived career in business and law, and settled permanently in Paris where he pursued his lifelong interest in literature. His literary awakening came in 1334 when he was exposed for the first time to the poetry of fellow Italian humanist Francesco Petrarch.

It wasn't until 1350 that Boccaccio actually met Petrarch, and the two men quickly cemented a lifelong friendship from which they drew mutual inspiration. Boccaccio wrote his most famous work soon after, the seminal *The Decameron*, a collection of 100 bawdy fables about love in all its incarnations. For literary scholars, *The Decameron* came to define vernacular Italian in the same way that Chaucer's *Canterbury Tales* would ultimately define Old English (the young Chaucer is said to have been inspired after reading the Italian's book). Indeed today Boccaccio, along with Petrarch and Dante, is considered to be one of the three founding fathers of the modern Italian language.

Multigraphic's 1:25,000 map No 513 *S Gimignano, Volterra* does not, unfortunately, cover the start.

GETTING TO/FROM THE WALK
Certaldo (start)

Certaldo is easily accessible by train from both Florence (€4.20, one hour, 20 a day Mon-Sat, 12 a day Sun) and Siena (€3, 35 minutes, 15 a day Mon-Sat, 12 a day Sun).

If travelling from San Gimignano, catch the SITA bus to Poggibonsi and take the short train ride to Certaldo (€1.80, 10 minutes).

The S429, which runs along the Val d'Elsa, connects Poggibonsi with Empoli, passing by Certaldo.

Volterra (finish)

Buses operated by **CPT** (☎ 0588 8 61 86) connect Volterra to San Gimignano, Florence and Siena, via Colle Val d'Elsa (€3, one hour, four a day Mon-Sat).

THE WALK
Day 1: Certaldo to San Gimignano

3–4 hours, 14km, 380m ascent, 130m descent

Standing facing the Municipio building in the Piazza Boccaccio in central Certaldo, take the road on the left: Via XX Settembre. Turn left at the T-junction onto Via Giacomo Matteotti and then right onto Via Trieste following signs for San Gimignano. Cross a railway track, a bridge, a roundabout and a second bridge before turning left onto Viale del Platani. After less than 1km you'll come to an ERG petrol distributor, the hotel/restaurant Latini and a paved road on the right, with a blue sign indicating Pancole and Fattoria del Monte (Villa del Monte). The walk follows this road, rising gently southeast among new houses, then vineyards and olive groves, and immediately affords a beautiful view of Certaldo to the northeast and San Gimignano to the south. After about 3km of climbing on the road, you reach the little church of **Canonica**, where a double row of cypress trees lines the road up to the majestic **Villa del Monte** (202m), from where you can enjoy a wide panorama east over Val d'Elsa and the hills of Chianti.

The undulating road continues for 2.5km, past the *borgo* of **La Piazzetta** (222m), before entering the quaint *borgo* of **Pancole**

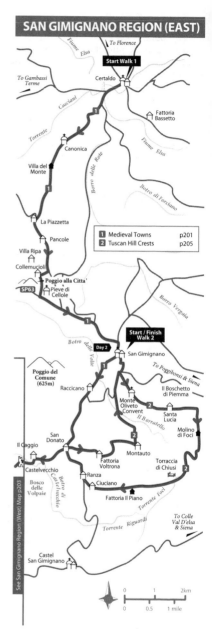

SAN GIMIGNANO REGION (EAST)

| | Medieval Towns | p201 |
| 2 | Tuscan Hill Crests | p205 |

(272m). Here there are two accommodation options, **Fratelli Vagnoni** (☎ 0577 95 50 77; www.fratellivagnoni.com;

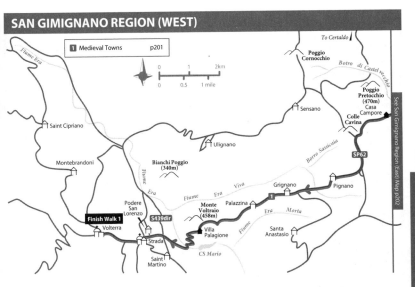

SAN GIMIGNANO REGION (WEST)

1 Medieval Towns p201

Pancole 82; d with bathroom from €45) and **Hotel Le Renaie** (☎ 0577 95 50 44; Pancole 10b; s/d €75/110), where you can also get a good meal in the restaurant from €25. The 17th-century sanctuary on the far side of Pancole was originally built in 1670, but was destroyed by the Germans in WWII. The existing arch, which spans the road, was rebuilt in 1949.

About 1km past the sanctuary, turn right at a bus stop onto a dirt track signposted Collemucioli. Take the next fork to the left and follow the path up in front of a house and through an olive grove and garden. At a T-junction turn left and, following a Via Francigena sign, veer right and uphill. Here you will pass through a recently restored *borgo* with a lovely tower. Continue along this road, passing under an archway and heading uphill – at this point there is a beautiful view of San Gimignano. You then come to a wide clearing across from the splendid **Pieve di Cellole** (385m), about 45 minutes from Pancole. The little church, unfortunately open only on Sunday and holidays from 10am to noon, has rows of cypresses in front of its elegant 13th-century façade. Descend south on the now paved road that, after 300m meets up with provincial road 63, where you turn left. This road can be busy and there are some blind bends so proceed with extreme caution. At

a roundabout, follow signs for San Gimignano and make use of the pavement for the last couple of kilometres. Just before you reach town, veer right onto Via Niccolo Cannicci which takes you up to the San Matteo gate.

Day 2: San Gimignano to Volterra

7–8 hours, 26km, 844m ascent , 383m descent

Turn right outside San Gimignano's Porta San Giovanni (324m), the city's main gate on the southern wall. Take the lane to the left of the car park just off the main plaza, signposted Santa Margherita. After about 500m, take the first turning to the left onto a dirt track by two mature cypress trees. Loop around the back of a farmhouse, head uphill and join a paved road lined with houses. At a T-junction turn left, and enjoy some magnificent views back over San Gimignano. Keep left at the fork and pass through the tiny *borgo* of **Raccicano**. The trattoria is open for lunch and dinner every day except Wednesday. The minor road joins the main road on a bend. Follow the road – which has some wide verges – for 1.5km before turning left into the village of **San Donato**. A section of this tiny, medieval village operates as **Fattoria San Donato** (☎ 0577 94 16 16; www.sando nato.it; d from €110). Breakfast is included

THE ETRUSCANS

'The Etruscans, as everyone knows, were the people who occupied the middle of Italy in early Roman days, and whom the Romans, in their usual neighborly fashion, wiped out to make room for Rome with a very big R.'

So wrote DH Lawrence in *Etruscan Places*, a posthumously published collection of essays that highlighted both his love of Etruscan culture and his evident disdain for the Romans.

Lawrence, in common with many 20th-century romantics, considered the Etruscans to be one of Europe's great 'forgotten' civilisations, their legacy stamped out by the Romans, and their artistic achievements undervalued by subjective history.

In many ways, he was right. Even today, the roots of ancient Etruria remain murky. While historians have traced the culture back to the 7th century BC, soon after the trail goes cold. Anthropological evidence suggests that the Etruscans migrated west from Asia Minor sometime before the founding of Rome in 709 BC and settled in present-day Tuscany (to which they ultimately lent their name). But, both the exact nature of their origins, and the details of their eventual assimilation into the Roman Empire around 100 BC are cloudy. Part of the problem is the indecipherability of the Etruscan language (which was not related to any other Indo-European language). Another is the absence of any written Etruscan history; indeed, most of our current knowledge about Etruscan culture comes from the colourfully inscribed *necropolisis* located in Tuscany.

Sophisticated Etruscan culture reached its zenith in the 5th and 6th centuries BC when its exuberant art emulated that of the Greeks and its benign kings ruled over Rome. But, the glory days were numbered. With the ascendancy of the Roman republic in the 2nd century BC, Etruscan influences were rapidly shunted sideways. Historically speaking, their sudden disappearance was almost as mysterious as their arrival. Indeed, one of the most perplexing riddles concerning the Etruscans is why the Romans, who readily aped so much of their art, architecture, and engineering techniques (including sewers, road-building, and irrigation know-how), subsequently chose to airbrush them out of history.

The best Etruscan museum in Italy today is located in Volterra in Tuscany. Volterra began life as a prosperous Etruscan city-state named Velathri in the 8th century BC. The exhaustive **Museo Etrusco Guarnacci** (☎ 0588 8 63 47; Via Don Minzoni 15; adult/student €8/5; 9am-7pm mid-Mar–Oct, 8.30am-1.45pm Nov–mid-Mar) and the adjacent archeological park both make good resting points at the end of the Medieval Towns hike.

and other meals are available for a cost. The *fattoria* (farm) produces its own wine, olives and saffron.

From San Donato's elegant little Romanesque church, head southwest to reach the provincial road – where you will notice a lamp post marked with a trail marker. Turn right onto the road and, after about 30m, turn left and ascend a steep dirt road signposted 'Il Caggio'. When the dirt road emerges onto a rocky crest, you can see the ruins of Castelvecchio beyond the narrow, wooded valley. Shortly after, the dirt road descends steeply and then goes uphill to a clearing in the woods in front of the farm of Il Caggio (390m), about 30 minutes from San Donato. From here descend southeast on the steep and sharply curv-

ing trail (No 18) to reach a ford (285m) over Botro di Castelvecchio. Once on the other side, continue west along the trail. After a fairly brief but tiring climb, you come to a clearing where there is a dirt road closed with a chain. If you want to visit the interesting ruins of **Castelvecchio** (379m), turn left (east) and hop over the chain. The ruins are about 600m away and you'll probably need about 30 minutes for a decent exploration.

If you don't want to visit the ruins, turn right (west) at the clearing and ascend on the dirt road. Cross through woods, ignoring all turn-offs, until you reach a plain. The road then passes under some high-tension wires, veers left and gradually descends until it reaches the intersection with the access road for the farmhouse of Casa Campore (440m) on your right. Follow the main dirt road to the left (west) and after a little more than 1.5km you'll reach SP53 (520m), locally known as di Poggio Cornocchio. Turn left (south) and walk along the road (which has some light traffic) on a panoramic crest for 1.1km. Here you'll find a dirt road on the right (west), marked with two stone wayside posts. Descend among the trees and you will soon meet another dirt road, where you head right again. Follow this lovely, cypress-lined walk up to the stupendous *borgo* of **Pignano** (502m), with its lovely 12th-century church, Romanesque **Pieve of San Bartolomeo Apostolo**, with a double access ramp, adorned with a palm and a cherry tree.

Follow the main dirt road, which descends sharply southwest, to a small bridge (370m), offering a panorama over the wooded territory south of Volterra. The route continues ascending west and then descends slightly along the ridge to the buildings of **Grignano**. Continuing southwest, in 1.3km you arrive at **Palazzina** with its abandoned 12th-century San Lorenzo chapel. A little more than 2km further on you reach the Medici-style villa of Villa Palagione (two hours from Pignano). Built in 1598 right under the rocky hump of Monte Voltraio, **Villa Palagione** (☎ 0588 3 90 14; www.villa-palagione.org) is a cosy and well-organised holiday centre offering various courses including Italian, cooking and art history (see website for details). It's 15km from San Donato and 7km from Volterra.

If you have the energy, you might like to climb the termite mound–shaped **Monte Voltraio** (458m). There is a path just across the road from the entrance to Villa Palagione (50 minutes return).

From Villa Palagione continue on the dirt road, which descends in steep, sharp curves southward. Cross a bridge (205m) over the Fiume Era Morta, continuing northwest until you reach S439dir, with signs for Pontedera to the right and Saline di Volterra to the left. Turn left onto the winding state road and, after just 20m, look for trail markers on the guard rail and on a tree, indicating Trail No 21 to the right. The trail is actually a bit difficult to see because it is hidden by the undergrowth. Ascend

through the thick vegetation and annoying, prickly bushes for about 300m, until you reach a junction with a narrow, paved road. If you go right, it will lead you to the *agriturismo* **Podere San Lorenzo** (☎ 0588 3 90 80; www.agriturismo-volterra.it; d with bathroom €95). The elegant villa offers a swimming pool, cooking classes and meals (€28 with wine) in a 12th-century Franciscan chapel.

To continue to Volterra, go straight on and ascend among the fields until you reach an intersection with another narrow, paved road. Turn left and, in a few metres, you'll be on the S68 at **Strada**. If you are tired of walking, from Strada there is a **CPT** (☎ 0588 8 61 86) bus for Volterra (four a day at 7.20am, 10.10am, 3.15pm and 6.50pm). Otherwise, turn right and continue along the road. In about 2km you'll reach **Volterra**. Turn right onto a path just past an Esso garage, ascend the steps and emerge beside an arch that takes you underneath the old Medici fortress and into the medieval town.

TUSCAN HILL CRESTS

Duration 7 hours
Distance 20km
Difficulty easy
Start/Finish San Gimignano (p220)
Transport bus

Summary A pretty pastoral meander through the Tuscany of legend, along hill crests and through ancient *borghi* barely changed since feuding fiefdoms faced off against each other in the Middle Ages.

Low rolling hills, fields full of barley, elegant cypresses and silvery green olives, vines ripening in the late summer sun, an old ruined monastery, a priest careering downhill in a rusty Fiat 500, potted geraniums, cyclists in multi-coloured jerseys, a rustic farmhouse reborn as an *agriturismo*…

Take an archetypal image of the Tuscan countryside, multiply it by 10, and suddenly you're there – romping enthusiastically through the wonderfully timeless landscapes that characterise this riveting rural walk.

Starting one small step outside the walls of San Gimignano, but one giant leap from the gelato-toting tour groups for which the town is famous, this medium-length pastoral hike through the soothing shades of the province's bucolic hinterland ought to be on every big-city therapist's prescription list.

That's the underlying power of the Tuscan spell; the subtle simplicity, the refreshing lack of pretension. Like all true beauty, it doesn't need to be glorified or made up. Just reserve a free afternoon, take a large-scale map and book a table at your favourite San Gimignano restaurant for when you return.

PLANNING
Maps
Multigraphic's 1:25,000 No 513 *San Gimignano, Volterra* is recommended for this walk.

GETTING TO/FROM THE WALK
For information on getting to/from San Gimignano, see p221.

THE WALK
Starting at San Gimignano's Porta San Giovanni, head around the Piazzale dei Martiri di Montemaggio to where a flight of steps cuts down to the road below (signposted 'Checkpoint Bus Turistici'). Turn right into Via Baccanella following the Via Francigena sign. At the roundabout, take the Volterra exit (straight ahead) and, within 50m, turn left onto a road signposted 'Santa Lucia 2.3 km'. This pleasant lane has a pedestrian pavement for the first kilometre or so and takes you past the Agriturismo Monte Oliveto, followed by the imposing **Monte Oliveto Convent** on the right. Continue straight ahead where Trail No 19 is signposted off to the right and you'll soon arrive on the edge of the village of **Santa Lucia**. Fork left just past the town sign into a narrow lane which leads you into the main street. Turn right in front of the church and then left at a T-junction. The road leaves the village and enters an olive grove (highlighted by a yellow 'Via Francigena' sign). Soon this narrow road leads sharply downhill and eventually arrives at a T-junction with a dirt road (80 minutes from San Gimignano). Turn right, and you will soon pass the Molino di Foci B&B on the left. The dirt road now tracks uphill through a number of switchbacks to

a junction on the crest where you fork left, signposted 'Torraccia di Chiusi 1.9 km'.

You're now on a magnificent hill crest with quintessential Tuscan views over towards San Gimignano to the north. At **Torraccia di Chiusi** (☎ 0577 94 19 72; www.torracciadichiusi.it) – a tempting *agriturismo* – ignore the Via Francigena sign to the left and continue straight past the house. Veer right on the other side by a pylon and branch out on an overgrown grassy track through an olive grove. Enter a wood briefly and then track along the side of another olive grove until you reach the dirt track that leads to the **Fattoria Il Piano**. Cross this track and the next one and you will soon merge with another dirt track that leads to the small *borgo* of **Ciuciano** with its engaging chapel. At a T-junction of dirt roads at the bottom of a short downhill section, go right and head towards **Ranza**, visible in the distance. Continue straight on a fainter track as the main track bends to the left and you will pass through the small *borgo* and arrive at the main road to San Gimignano on the other side. Cross this road and ascend on a narrow overgrown path on the opposite side. This then joins a dirt road that veers back down towards the main road. Bear left and within a few minutes you will reach the turn-off for San Donato on the right.

From **San Donato** turn right at the far end of the village on a dirt road signposted 'Voltrona'. This dirt road with fine views of San Gimignano bends left and right a couple of times before arriving at the **Fattoria Voltrona** (☎ 0577 94 31 52; www.voltrona.com; Montauto 50; s/d with breakfast €45/70), near a small lake. Soon after the *fattoria* the track ends by a lone house and a small wooden 'San Gimignano' sign points down a muddy path that leads along a dried up riverbed before emerging on the edge of a vineyard. Keep left and follow a tractor track up the slope towards a cluster of houses just beyond the crest. Pick up the dirt road here and you will soon arrive on the edge of the *borgo* of **Montauto** where the road becomes paved. Turn left before entering the *borgo* onto another paved lane signposted 'Trail 18'. This pleasant road weaves its way back towards San Gimignano, visible in the distance. After approximately 2km it joins the main

STAYING IN ITALIAN MONASTERIES

There was a time when Italian monasteries were out of bounds to the general public, the sole preserve of pious monks reverently muttering dark Gregorian chants. But somewhere between the Middle Ages and the invention of the internet, the ground rules were quietly updated – at least in terms of accommodation.

Shedding their image as bastions of anti-social religious hermits, many Italian monasteries have started to open their doors to discerning travellers in search of an economical sleepover. Equipped with all the tools of a standard hostel (and a bit more besides), visitors are welcomed into the monastic fold with plenty of traditional hospitality and accommodated in simple but comfortable rooms that belie the monkish cells of yore (most have private bathrooms). Some monasteries also offer breakfast, dinner and/or a packed lunch.

Monasteries easily emulate – and sometimes trump – hotels and guesthouses in terms of price, tranquillity and historical authenticity. Thanks to their location close to ancient pilgrim's routes, they are also often ideally placed for popular hikes.

For a decent overview of Italian Monastery, stays check out the website www.monastery stays.com.

Volterra road. Turn right and within 1km you with be delivered back to the main roundabout from where you can retrace your steps back to the San Giovanni gate.

APUAN ALPS

Many of the world's greatest works of sculpture – including Michelangelo's *David* – started life in the Apuan Alps (Alpi Alpuane) as huge chunks of marble embedded into the mountainsides. Situated in the far northwestern corner of Tuscany, this deceptively named range of mountains is not actually part of the Alps at all; rather it is a subrange of the Apennines chain. While the walks here might not be as well known as the trails around Chianti and San Gimignano, the brilliant white marble mines of Carrara and Massa that are visible from almost every angle have been providing the raw material for grand monuments and buildings since Roman times. Michelangelo is said to have travelled to the quarries behind Carrara personally to select the blocks of stone from which he carved many of his finest works.

The Apuan is also a range of real natural beauty. It forms a continuous ridge approximately 30km in length, but the ridge divides here and there and wanders from its main axis. It also includes almost disconnected peaks such as Monte Pisanino, the highest in the range at 1947m. The peaks are often described as 'dolomitic' in appearance and are separated in many cases by deep valleys.

One of the greatest challenges for the administration of the 543-sq-km Parco Regionale delle Alpi Apuane (established in 1985 in response to growing disquiet about the impact of human activity on the mountains) has been to balance environmental values with the ongoing economic health of the region. Around 22,000 people live within the borders of the park, many of them reliant to some degree on the marble industry. In an attempt to clarify the park's priorities, three levels of protection have been established, in which scenic, economic and natural values, take precedence. An area of 124 sq km has also been set aside for special protection in a series of *riserve naturali* (natural reserves). Walkers will quickly become aware, however, that protection of the park's natural, and even scenic, resources is frustratingly difficult to ensure.

Two longish walks, known as Apuane Trekking and Garfagnana Trekking, cover much of the best ground in the Apuan Alps. The latter also explores the Garfagnana valley, east of the Apuan Alps, and the Orecchiella mountains further inland. Both trails link a series of *rifugi* (mountain huts) and other cheap places to stay.

Two shorter walks, of two and three days respectively, are described in this section. They incorporate the precipitous Pizzo d'Uccello (1781m) in the north of the park, and the spectacular formations of Monte

Procinto and Monte Forato and the grand summit of Pania della Croce (1858m) in the south.

ENVIRONMENT

More than anything else, it is the geology of the Apuan Alps that has made them famous. The raw materials of today's marble, limestone and sandstone were laid down on the sea bed over hundreds of millions of years, and underwent severe compression and folding during the Tertiary period (beginning about 60 million years ago). At one time covered by a layer of sedimentary rock known as the Falda Toscana (Tuscan Layer), the Apuan Alps, now metamorphosed, were pushed up and the Falda Toscana slid off and became the Appennino Tosco-Emiliano range. The elements, principally water in the form of rain and then ice (during the last glacial period, which ended about 10,000 years ago), carved the new range into something like its current shape.

This modelling went on, and still goes on, below ground as well as above. Under the Apuan Alps is the largest cave system in Italy, and one of the largest in the world. It contains a number of deep, predominantly vertical *abissi* (abysses) – one of these, Abisso Olivifer, is the deepest cave in the country at 1215m. There is also the extensive complex of Antro del Corchia (with more than 60km of tunnels) and many caverns rich in beautiful formations. Some of the finest examples are accessible to the general public in the Grotta del Vento, near Fornovalasco.

One peculiarity of the geology of the Apuan Alps is that the predominantly calcareous rock quickly absorbs most of the plentiful rain that falls, feeding it into underground watercourses. This leaves the surface comparatively arid and almost without permanent running water. This has practical implications for walkers, who must as a rule carry all the water they will need during a day's walk.

Because of the range's geological diversity (and its dramatic rise from the Ligurian Sea to a height of nearly 2000m in less than 20km), there is a great variety of plant communities. Species of the Mediterranean *macchia* (scrub) give way over a relatively short distance to alpine varieties. Vegetation types also change, quite discernibly to the experienced eye, at the boundaries between different geological zones. On top of this, human activities (aside from quarrying for marble) have over the centuries had a significant impact on the original vegetation.

In the lower valleys, up to an altitude of about 800m, the sweet chestnut tends to dominate. While originally a naturally occurring species, the chestnut was spread during centuries of cultivation by local people, who depended on it for sustenance and income. Although cultivation has all but ceased since WWII and the number of trees has been reduced by disease, chestnut forests now cover something like 20% of the Apuan Alps. On seaward slopes at these altitudes, the cluster pine is more common.

The most common tree of the higher slopes, from 800m to 1700m or so, is the

---

CARRARA MARBLE

View a satellite image of northern Italy on *Google Earth* and you'll see the world famous Carrara marble quarries long before you spot Turin, Venice or even Milan. Etched like angry white scars onto the Apuan Mountains, these gargantuan quarries have been around since Roman times and have supplied the prized stone for everything from London's Marble Arch to Michelangelo's *David*.

But, while there's no doubting the flawless beauty of *David* and his ilk, the prettiness of the landscape that the mining has left behind is a matter of some debate.

The area around the town of Carrara contains an estimated 300 marble quarries that dig out approximately one million tonnes of the stone every year. You can get a bird's-eye view of the landscape on the Pizzo d'Uccello hike (p211), but for a more comprehensive look visit Carrara's **Museo del Marmo** (☎ 0585 84 57 46; Viale XX Settembre; admission free; 10am-6pm Mon-Sat May-Jun & Sep, 10am-8pm Mon-Sat Jul-Aug, 9am-5pm Oct-Apr) or sign up for a **guided quarry tour** (☎ 339 765 74 70; adult/child €6/3; 25-minute tour 3.30-7pm Mon-Fri, 10.30am-7pm Sat).

beech. This is despite the beech being exploited for firewood and now covering less of the Apuan Alps than it once did. Birch and oak are also found in this altitude band. Grasses and other low-growing species, a number of them endemic to the Apuan Alps, occupy the highest slopes and cling to cracks in the cliffs.

In spring and summer, the forest floors and upper slopes support magnificent displays of wildflowers, including jonquils, crocuses, anemones, gentians and a number of orchid species, and, late in summer, pink cyclamens.

Badgers, martens, foxes and other small mammals live in the Apuan forests, but are seldom seen. A variety of small forest birds also live here, and above the tree line walkers may see choughs in large colonies, falcons and the occasional, majestic golden eagle.

CLIMATE

The Apuan Alps are among the wettest places in Italy, with an annual rainfall in some areas of more than 3000mm. The two sides of the range, however, receive very different weather. The southwestern slopes enjoy mild, humid Mediterranean conditions, with warm summers and mild winters, and an annual average temperature of roughly 15°C. On the northeastern side of the range, summers are hot and winters are cold, with significant snowfalls. On the highest peaks and internal ridges of the mountain range, winter can extend to more than four or five months of the year, with average temperatures falling below 7°C.

PLANNING
When to Walk

Rifugi and some other accommodation options remain open from mid-June until mid-September, and bus companies operate to an expanded summer timetable for roughly the same period, making this the most convenient period to walk. During winter, snow cover and prohibitive mountain weather make walking impractical.

What to Bring

Always pack wet- and warm-weather clothing, no matter how clear the forecast, as the weather in the Apuan Alps can change dramatically with little warning.

Maps

To help with planning and to give you a good overall picture of the layout of the Apuan Alps, pick up a copy of the Touring Club Italiano 1:200,000 map *Toscana*, widely available in Italian bookshops.

The most detailed map of walking tracks and *rifugi* is the Edizioni Multigraphic 1:25,000 map No 101/102 *Alpi Apuane* in the Carta dei Sentieri e Rifugi series. Edizioni Multigraphic's 1:50,000 *Carta Turistica e dei Sentieri map Parco delle Alpi Apuane* is less detailed, but the fact that the entire range is displayed on one sheet makes it easier to use. The maps have some discrepancies in mountain heights and some track inaccuracies, but nothing that should affect navigation. Both list *rifugi* details and are available from bookshops in the major towns in the area.

Books

There are few books published in English on the Apuan Alps but many in Italian. The *Guida all'Alta Via del Parco delle Alpi Apuane* (2005) by Angelo Nerli provides a guide to all the high-altitude trails in the park and was produced in collaboration with the CAI. It comes in English translation. Another book that contains handy background information, if your Italian is up to it, is *Alpi Apuane: Guida al territorio del Parco*, by Frederick Bradley and Enrico Medda.

Information Sources

The Parco Regionale delle Alpi Apuane has three main **visitor centres** (☎ 0584 7 58 21, Via Corrado del Greco 11, Seravezza; ☎ 0585 75 61 44, Viale Stazione 82, Massa; ☎ 0583 64 42 42, Piazza delle Erbe 1, Castelnuovo di Garfagnana). The official website of **Parco delle Alpi Apuane** (www.parks.it/parco.alpi.apuane/Eindex .html) provides a brief English-language introduction to the park, listing places to stay in the area along with publications available for purchase from the park's administration by mail order.

Emergency

If you strike trouble in the mountains (and can get to a telephone), contact the *carabinieri* (police) on the **national emergency**

PIZZO D'UCCELLO

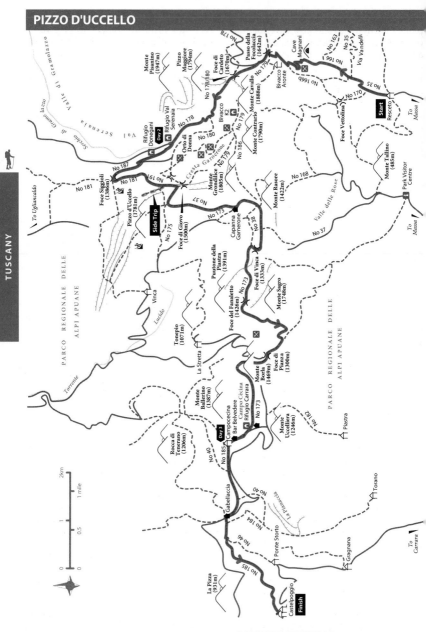

number (☎ 112) or for medical assistance call the **national ambulance** number
(☎ 118).

ACCESS TOWNS

For ultimate convenience walkers can
stay in the nondescript towns of Massa or

Pietrasanta. But the lure of nearby Lucca (p219) is hard to resist. For this reason (along with some good rail links), it makes a viable base for the following two walks.

PIZZO D'UCCELLO

Duration 3 days
Distance 29.5km
Difficulty moderate
Start Resceto
Finish Castelpoggio
Nearest Town Lucca (p219)
Transport bus
Summary Traverse of the northern Apuan Alps, with the full gamut of park experiences from marble quarries to shady beech wood, and a breathtaking ridge walk past the spectacular, sheer face of Pizzo d'Uccello.

At just 1781m, Pizzo d'Uccello is not the highest peak in the Apuan Alps, but its isolated position at the northwestern end of the range and the steepness of its faces and ridges make it one of the most imposing. Pizzo d'Uccello's north face, which drops approximately 700m from the summit, appeared in the records of English mountaineer Francis Fox Tuckett in 1883. He considered it one of the most impressive rock walls in the Apuan Alps, but at least four decades were to pass before it was first climbed. Opinion differs on whether the honour went to two Genovesi (from Genoa) in 1927 or two Milanesi (from Milan) in 1940. Today the face sports many alpine rock climbing routes. Among them are some of Italy's hardest, and repeat ascents are few.

This walk views the north face of Pizzo d'Uccello from close range and includes the option of a side trip to its airy summit by the easiest route. This calls for a steady head but no special skills as a rock athlete. Val Serenaia, into which the walk descends on the first day, is one of the most extensive glacial valleys in the Apuan Alps and is enclosed by the major peaks of the northern Apuan: Pizzo d'Uccello, Monte Pisanino (1947m), Monte Cavallo (1888m), Monte Contrario (1790m) and Monte Grondilice (1805m). Its upper reaches, in particular the area covered in beech forest known as

Orto di Donna (Lady's Garden), are rich in plant species. The trail also skirts areas devastated by the scourge of the Apuan Alps environment, the marble extraction industry, at Passo della Focolaccia, on the Cresta Garnerone and at Foce di Pianza. However, it also provides many of the glorious views, both mountainous and coastal, for which the Apuan Alps are, in their own small way, justly famous.

As described, the walk is in three stages; however, Day 3 is short and allows you to be in Carrara or Massa by lunchtime. The walk could be extended and made into a circumambulation of Pizzo d'Uccello with additional overnight stops in Ugliancaldo and Vinca. Alternatively, it could be extended south past Monte Tambura to link up with the southern part of the Apuane Trekking route and the Procinto, Forato & Pania della Croce walk (p215).

GETTING TO/FROM THE WALK
Resceto (start)
Resceto, at the start of the walk, is accessible by **CAT** (☎ 0585 8 52 11; www.cat spa.it) bus from Massa (€1.70, 30 min). Unfortunately, the only bus convenient for an early start leaves Massa at the enthusiasm-dampening time of 6.35am, Monday to Saturday from outside the ticket office on Largo Matteotti, just off Viale Chiesa. The second bus leaves at 1.20pm, still leaving you just enough time to complete Day 1 before dusk in summer.

By car, Resceto is only a short drive north (10km) of Massa up into the valley of the Torrente di Renana.

Castelpoggio (finish)
At the end of the walk, frequent CAT buses leave from opposite Bar Liviana on Castelpoggio's main street, traveling to Carrara (€1.20, 30 minutes, 10 buses Mon-Sat, four buses Sun and public holidays); you can buy your ticket on the bus. The first bus departs at 6.55am (10am Sun and public holidays).

Castelpoggio is roughly 5km north of Carrara along the S446d. Massa is another 5km southeast of Carrara along the S1 (Via Aurelia), with frequent CAT buses (leaving from the Piazza Allende bus terminal) connecting the two.

TUSCANY

THE WALK
Day 1: Resceto to Rifugio Val Serenaia
4–5 hours, 9.5km, 1185m ascent, 520m descent

From the car park just above Resceto, where the bus from Massa turns around, an unsealed road continues up the valley of Canale di Resceto. Red-and-white paint markers label it as Track No 35. Follow the road north, past a junction (left) where Track No 170 heads towards Foce Vettolina. After 10 minutes or so, at a small quarry, the road gives way to a narrower but still impressively steep track, once a *via di lizza* down which marble blocks were lowered from the quarry above. A few hundred metres further on is another track junction, 1km from Resceto. Here Track No 35, the remarkable Via Vandelli, crosses Canale Pianone to the east and begins its tortuous zigzag ascent of nearly 1000m to Passo della Tambura.

Continue up the west side of the valley on Track No 166, past yet another impeccably signposted track junction, this time where Track No 166b departs on a higher route to Passo della Focolaccia. After another half-hour of slow climbing, Track No 163 heads off to the east at a clearly marked junction. Stay on Track No 166, which heads left here and up some grassy slopes, then begins to negotiate gullies full

---

THE SPECKS ON THE MAP

Pruno, Pignano, Pancole, Grignano and Galenda – Tuscany is scattered with small rural hamlets that show up as little more than tiny specks on large-scale local maps. Sometimes the settlements are embellished with a church or a monastery; at others, you'll find little more than a villa, or a homey *agriturismo*.

The Italians call these small clusters of buildings *borghi* (plural of *borgo* which translates roughly as burg or 'town') and you'll encounter many bucolic examples on your picturesque rural walks. Connected by rough dirt roads or thin, winding ribbons of asphalt, the settlements retain the soporific air of quiet medieval villages and make excellent stops for picnics, wine-quaffing, or quiet contemplations of nature.

---

of marble 'scree'. A short scramble past cairns and painted markers, and along the occasional stretch of well-engineered track, leads to the lower edge of **Cave Magnani**, a functioning marble quarry. The western slopes of Monte Tambura (1895m) loom across the valley to the east.

The final climb to the pass follows the zigzagging road through the quarry – interesting if unattractive – past some buildings on the right and then a junction where Track No 166b rejoins the route. **Bivacco Aronte**, the oldest walkers' shelter in the Apuan Alps, appears a short distance off to the left, just below the pass, and is equipped with a wood stove and sleeping platforms for emergencies. (Note that the location of this shelter is not marked accurately on the *Carta dei Sentieri e Rifugi* map). The rocky crest just west of Bivacco Aronte, including the elegant needle of Punta Carina, sports a number of classic rock climbs.

Although approaching it through a quarry is good mental preparation, **Passo della Focolaccia** (1642m) still comes as a shock. The original pass has disappeared, engulfed by a huge pit from which slabs of the precious white stone are probably being carved out and carried away before your eyes. At the time of writing, the walking trail descended to the right, smooth and white underfoot, along the road round the main pit (the red trail markers may be difficult to spot in overcast weather) and down to the bottom of the quarry. Above the quarry to the southeast, Monte Tambura wears a somewhat forlorn look.

Track No 179 leaves the road only a short distance beyond Passo della Focolaccia and contours to the northwest, joining up with Track No 178 on its way to Foce di Cardeto. The start of the track (where it leaves the road) is not clearly marked, and if you suspect you've missed it – in particular, if you reach the point where the road switches back to the south, downhill – head uphill from the road to regain the track and follow it to **Foce di Cardeto** (1670m). The lush Val Serenaia now lies ahead to the northwest, and towering beyond the valley is Pizzo d'Uccello. All along the western side of the valley, reaching up to the rugged Cresta Garnerone, the effects of marble extraction are plain to see.

A hundred metres from the pass, Track No 179 splits off left towards Foce di Giovo.

Continue along Track No 180, the more northerly of the two options, following a sign to Rifugio Donegani. It descends to the northwest, staying above a couple of gullies, then heads down a spur to enter the beautiful beech forest of Orto di Donna. Although well marked and mostly well defined, the track takes a devious route through the forest, and it pays to be watchful. The descent, over exposed rock outcrops, can be quite slow.

About 1km below Foce di Cardeto, at a clearly marked three-way junction, Track No 180 goes left (west) across a gully system, then continues in a roughly northerly direction, while Track No 178 continues north down the spur. Either path is feasible, although Track No 178 is the more direct route to Rifugio Val Serenaia, the end of the day. Continuing its leafy descent, it eventually emerges from the forest after another 1km (one to 1½ hours from the pass), passes a small stone house and continues next to a gravel nature trail to the road. On the left is a fenced camping enclosure. Take the lower (eastern) arm of the road to **Rifugio Val Serenaia** (☎ 0583 61 00 85; www .rifugialpiapuane.it; camping per person/ tent €3.50/5, dm with breakfast €25; Apr-Oct), 100m away. The privately run *rifugio* also has primitive camping facilities. Bookings are essential as the owners do not always stay overnight at the *rifugio*.

Day 2: Rifugio Val Serenaia to Campocecina

5–6 hours, 15km, 825m ascent, 655m descent

From Rifugio Val Serenaia follow the road back (southeast) to the hairpin bend and then round and upwards to Rifugio Donegani. Continue north beyond the *rifugio* for 500m to a second sharp bend in the road, past a sign marking the boundary of the *cava di marmo* (marble quarry). A short distance on, markers on rocks indicate the start of Track No 187, on the right which heads back towards the north at an acute angle from the road. A sign, 'Pericoloso, Sentiero Altrezzato', warns of the occasionally airy sections to come along this trail. Passing first through lovely beech forest, then angling up more open slopes with views to the right across the Alta Garfagnana, the track comes to **Foce Siggioli** (1386m), 40 minutes and 300 vertical metres from

Rifugio Donegani. The uninterrupted view of the sheer north face of Pizzo d'Uccello, makes it seem just a stone's throw away. A few metres north along the Cresta di Capradosso ridge is the top of a *via ferrata* (iron way), which offers those with the necessary equipment and experience a strenuous but spectacular route up from the valley floor more than 500m below.

The well-marked Track No 181 leads south along the picturesque ridge top for two minutes, then leaves the crest and traverses steep hillsides, where beech forest alternates with rocky, open spurs and gullies. A few short sections of the track are somewhat exposed and are equipped with metal cables – a kind of miniature *via ferrata* – but in good weather should not present problems to moderately experienced walkers; no special equipment or technical skill is required. About 30 minutes from Foce Siggioli the track regains the ridge top at a small saddle (1497m), where Track No 191 heads down to the west and an unnumbered route leads north towards the summit of Pizzo d'Uccello. If it's a fine day and you have a good head for heights, you'll probably be tempted to make the Side Trip (p214) to the top.

To continue towards Campocecina, head south for an easy 500m to **Foce di Giovo** (1500m), the main weakness in the Cresta Garnerone ridge connecting Pizzo d'Uccello with Monte Grondilice. A descent of less than 10 minutes to the northwest brings you to a track junction above a group of ruined buildings marked on some maps as 'Capanne del Giovo'. Ignore Track No 175, which continues towards Vinca. Instead take Track No 37 on a long, descending traverse to the south. After nearly 2km in the open below the rocky Cresta Garnerone, the track enters mixed forest. Only a few minutes into the forest is the locked metal bulk of the **Capanna Garnerone**, 45 minutes from the Foce di Giovo. Just below the hut is a reliable source of piped water.

Track No 37 is now joined by Track No 173 from Vinca and continues through a forest now dominated by introduced pines. After 15 minutes, Track No 38 heads downhill on the right. To enjoy the scenic crest that connects Monte Rasore and Monte Sagro, continue uphill for another five minutes to the ridge top and a junction

TUSCANY

with Track Nos 168 and 186. Follow Track No 37/173 west along the north side of the ridge, past a narrow gap where Track No 37 peels away to the south, then touching the crest at another low point, before reaching **Foce di Vinca** (1333m), roughly 30 minutes from Capanna Garnerone.

From here make your way attentively down to the north, bearing left at every opportunity, still on Track No 173. This heads generally west, becoming more clearly marked and with spectacular views of Pizzo d'Uccello, crossing scree slopes and encountering abandoned machinery in a gully. A climb up this gully, steep and criss-crossed with fixed cables towards the top, leads to a ridge and a patch of eerie forest. The track swings to the west below the cliffs of Monte Sagro and 1km from the top of the gully, after several sections equipped with fixed cables, emerges at the **Foce del Fanaletto** (1426m). The scene to the west is one of monumental destruction – or of busy production, depending on your point of view.

It is now necessary to skirt round the south side of the quarry that fills the intervening valley. Markers lead south at first, round the steep western slopes of Monte Sagro, then across the head of the valley, up onto a spur and along it, with excavations below on both sides, to meet the road through **Foce di Pianza** (1300m).

The final 30 minutes from Foce di Pianza is a pleasant coda to the day's exertions as the trail leaves the rumble of heavy machinery behind. From the pass, cross the road and follow Track No 173, north at first, up and around the eastern flank of Monte Borla. Signs are faint to begin with but lead quickly into a beech wood and along a clearly marked path to the broad, open slopes of **Campo Cècina**. The track crosses the open pasture and descends gently to the scattered buildings of **Campocecina** village. Just above the road is **Rifugio Carrara** (☎ 0585 84 19 72, 339 460 57 96; half-board €35; open year-round) with 18 beds.

SIDE TRIP: PIZZO D'UCCELLO SUMMIT
1¼–1¾ hours, 290m ascent, 290m descent

Painted markers on rocks lead all the way up the south ridge of Pizzo d'Uccello from the saddle at 1497m. The gradient is gentle at first. As it steepens, the route seeks out the line of least difficulty and becomes

less direct. The ridge is increasingly airy, and it is necessary to use your hands on the steepest sections and look carefully where you place your feet, but there is no great climbing skill required. The markers continue, so if faced with an impossibly sheer-looking stretch of rock, look about you for a splash of red paint. After an unhurried 45 minutes from the saddle, the summit cross appears ahead on a knoll. After a final clamber down into a dip and up the other side, you are there.

On a clear day, the summit of **Pizzo d'Uccello** or 'Bird's Peak', is a spectacular eyrie, with views of the snow-capped Alps away to the north and northwest, the Gulf of La Spezia to the west and, closer at hand, the rest of the Apuan Alps, including the highest point, Monte Pisanino, just across the valley to the east. With the benefit of familiarity, the descent to the saddle takes little more than half the time it took to get up there – but take your time and take care.

Day 3: Campocecina to Castelpoggio
1½ hours, 5km, 770m descent

This short, straightforward, downhill amble is a pleasant way to finish the walk. Follow the track from the front of Rifugio Carrara downhill to the northwest to meet the road opposite a car park. Continue past **Bar Belvedere**, then, just before a little bridge, |follow red-and-white markers down the hill to the west. The track winds between fields, fences, caravans and buildings for a few minutes, then proceeds down the side of a ridge. Track No 40 joins from the north, then a few minutes later departs to the south at a grotto. Follow Track No 185, which swings north down a spur among interesting rock formations, including an archway that may be partly natural, before it meets a sealed road and the intersection of several walking tracks at Gabellaccia.

Cross the road and continue downhill to the west on Track No 185. Track No 184 soon branches off south towards La Pianaccia and Gragnana, followed by Track No 46 towards Ponte Storto. After a gently descending traverse of 2km, Track No 185 rounds a spur and passes beneath power lines, then merges with an unsealed vehicle track and makes its way into **Castelpoggio**, perched picturesquely on a spur.

PROCINTO, FORATO & PANIA DELLA CROCE

Duration 2 days
Distance 26km
Difficulty moderate
Start Stazzema
Finish Ponte Stazzemese
Nearest Town Lucca (p219)
Transport bus
Summary Glorious ridge-top walking past the spectacular formations of Monte Procinto and Monte Forato to the summit of the 'queen' of the Apuan Alps, with an overnight stop in a cosy *rifugio*.

Despite the three peaks in the title, this hike is more of a ridge walk than an out-and-back mountain expedition. The saw-toothed crest between Procinto and Pania della Croce is a stunner that requires some steep ascents and a couple of rocky scrambles. A highlight – though you'll see it better from the valley below – is the famous 'Mountain with a hole', the local name given to surreally shaped Monte Forato. The high point is 1858m Pania della Croce whose summit (crowned by a huge cross) is reached via a short side trip.

Although the first few kilometres are relatively gentle, the hike has its arduous moments – hand chains over exposed sections – while the wildness of the terrain enables you to feel a degree of poetic isolation. But, surrounded on all sides by marble quarries, clustered Apuan villages and cosy *rifugi*, civilisation is never far away.

The super-fit might want to try squeezing these 26km into a single-day hike. For the less bombastic, buses can pick up passengers from Pruno or Cardoso, further up the valley, if the prospect of a final leg along a sealed road does not appeal.

It is possible during summer to fill in the gaps between this walk and the Pizzo d'Uccello walk (p211), combining the two into a long traverse of the entire Apuan Alps closely following the marked Apuane Trekking route from Pietrasanta to Carrara.

GETTING TO/FROM THE WALK

Stazzema (start)
Hourly **CLAP** (☎ 0584 701 36) buses connect Pietrasanta with Seravezza (€1.10, 10

minutes), departing from the bus station on the other side of the railway line from the train station and accessible by a pedestrian underpass. From here three buses a day head for Stazzema (8.10am, 11.10am, 12.50pm). The second two options require changing again in Ponte Stazzemese.

Ponte Stazzemese is a short, if circuitous, drive from Pietrasanta up into the foothills of the Apuan Alps via the town of Seravezza. Stazzema is another 3km uphill from Ponte Stazzemese along a sealed road. Pietrasanta is accessible by train from Lucca (€3, 45 minutes).

Ponte Stazzemese (finish)
Returning to Pietrasanta from the end of the walk, afternoon buses leave from the main piazza in Ponte Stazzemese (five a day at 6.55am, 8.25am, 12.15pm, 3.15pm, and 8pm Mon-Sat, three a day at 7.45am, 2.30pm, 2.55pm Sun & public holidays), near the turn-off up the hill to Stazzema. There are also several afternoon buses from Pruno (not Sun) and Cardoso, 4km and 2km respectively along the walk trail from Ponte Stazzemese.

THE WALK

Day 1: Stazzema to Rifugio Enrico Rossi
4½–5½ hours, 13.5km, 1300m ascent, 90m descent
Follow first a road and then a path up through the village of Stazzema. Veer left onto another road on the far side of the village and follow up as the road bends sharply to the right. Pass a house on the right and, within 100m, a path turns off to the right, signposted Trail Nos 5 and 6. Monte Procinto (1147m) rises prominently above to the northeast.

A few hundred metres after it leaves the road, the walking track divides. Track No 6 goes left and is the more direct route to Monte Forato. However, it is worth going right to visit the picturesque Rifugio Forte dei Marmi. Follow Track No 5 for a further 45 minutes to meet Track No 121. At the track junction is a stone shelter and water fills a stone tank nearby. Two hundred metres to the right (southeast) from here, with a dramatic view of Monte Procinto, is the welcoming **Rifugio Forte dei Marmi** (☎ 0584 77 70 51; daily 15 Jun-15 Sep, Sat & Sun only rest of year), with bar, restaurant and 52 beds.

PROCINTO, FORATO & PANIA DELLA CROCE

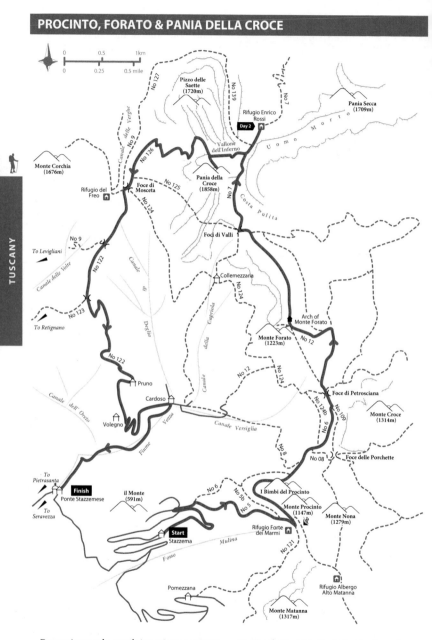

Returning to the track junction continue straight (with stone tank on your right) for 30m and then turn sharp left uphill on Track No 121 (look for trail marker on tree). This passes below the cliffs of Monte Procinto and round the western end of a group of smaller towers known as I Bimbi del Procinto. Monte Forato (1223m) and Pania della Croce (1858m) now dominate the view across the valley to the north. A couple of faint tracks come in from below, followed by Track No 6 (marked) and Track No 8 from Cardoso (at the opposite angle to that shown on Multigraphic maps of the area); the latter soon splits off and climbs to Foce delle Porchette. Continue along Track No 6, ignoring first Track No 124b on the left, then Track No 109 on the right and Track No 124 on the left, to **Foce di Petrosciana** (931m). Plans to build a road through this pass, connecting the Versilia region to the south with the Garfagnana to the north, have never been realised.

Take the path confusingly signposted Trail No 110 (it's actually 131) through the trees. It starts flat and goes slightly downhill until you reach the junction with Track No 12 (labelled on a rock). Turn left here and progress steeply uphill to a ridge emerging just above the tree line. A few feet before the ridge top turn right at a T-junction below the two summits and famous **arch of Monte Forato** (1209m), 'the mountain with a hole'. This faint track which traverses a spectacular saw-toothed ridge is marked by a mixture of blue, and more distinct red and white markers. Grassy and open rocky sections are interspersed with patches of dwarf beech forest. There are lovely views back beyond Monte Forato's two summits to Monte Nona, and ahead to the huge, open southeastern slope of Pania della Croce, known as 'Costa Pulita'. The track leads down through **Foci di Valli** at the base of the Costa Pulita and a four-way track junction. Follow Track No 7 as it climbs steeply up a grassy slope marked by small wooden poles adorned with red and white markers. As the path steepens it crosses the Costa Pulita to the eastern shoulder of Pania della Croce, an ascent of 400m.

From here the trail descends roughly north and crosses a couple of exposed rocky sections where chains have been drilled into the rocks for extra hand support. Pass the indistinct junction with Track No 126 (tomorrow's route) and then Track No 139 (signposted). After a further five minutes of relatively level walking some solar panels on the left announce the cosy **Rifugio**

Enrico Rossi (☎ 0583 71 03 86; www .rifugiorossi.it; dm incl half-board €20-26; daily 20 Jun-10 Sep, Sat & Sun only rest of year) at 1609m. It has a bar, restaurant and 22 bunks. *Panini* (bread rolls) and chocolate bars can be provided for lunch on the trail.

Day 2: Rifugio Enrico Rossi to Ponte Stazzemese

3½–4 hours, 12.5km, 250m ascent, 1700m descent

Retrace your steps southwest for 500m, past the signed start of Track No 139, to the point where Track No 126 branches right (look carefully for a sign on a rock). Follow it steeply up through the tumbled rock landscape of the evocatively named Vallone dell'Inferno (Valley of Hell) to the ridge top. Except perhaps on the windiest of days, you should reward yourself with a straightforward detour to the summit of Pania della Croce (1858m) and its massive cross, just 200m south (actually, a few degrees east of south) along the crest of the ridge. On a good day, this is an exhilarating viewpoint with the sea just 15km away to the southwest and the Apuan Alps stretching in both directions parallel to the coast.

Back on the narrow ridge follow Trail No 126 west, signposted Foce di Mosceta. The path drops off the ridge and zigzags down across open ground eventually arriving at the saddle of **Foce di Mosceta** where Track No 125 comes in on the left. A few minutes on, where a stone shelter stands beside the track, No 127 goes right (north) and Track No 122 heads left (south). Straight ahead across a little gully you will see the large and comfortable **Rifugio del Freo** (☎ 0584 77 80 07; www.rifugiodelfreo.it; half-board €35; daily 15 Jun-15 Sep, Sat & Sun only rest of year). Relatively accessible by road, the *rifugio* is a popular weekend getaway.

Turn south on the well-defined Track No 122. To the northwest is Monte Corchia (1676m), beneath which is the deepest and most extensive limestone cave system in Italy, known as Antro del Corchia. In a small saddle 1km from Foce di Mosceta, Track No 9 drops steeply off the ridge to the west, heading for the village of Levigliani, and after a little over 500m, in another small saddle, Track No 122 drops south towards Pruno while Track No 123, not as defined but more clearly marked than

Track No 122, continues to the southwest towards Retignano.

Leave the ridge on Track No 122, dropping past some small clusters of decrepit buildings, and one or two well-maintained ones. Track markers are infrequent but the walking is easy. Half an hour from the ridge top the track joins a steep, winding, sealed road, but after only a couple of minutes leaves it again at a red-and-white marker painted on the corner of a building on the left (it looks like a private path, but it's not). A further 15 minutes, mostly spent on a venerable stone-paved mule track, brings you to **Pruno**, where Track No 122 descends a flight of concrete steps to meet the asphalt at a car park and a park information board.

From Pruno it's sealed road all the way. In clear conditions Monte Forato is seen to good advantage above and to the east. Once on the valley bottom, which you reach at the lower end of **Cardoso** (30 minutes from Pruno), the last 2km are relatively flat along a road that was badly damaged by flooding in 1996. Before you know it, you're in the pretty settlement of **Ponte Stazzemese** where a bus will whisk you back to Pietrasanta.

TOWNS & FACILITIES

GREVE IN CHIANTI
☎ 055 / pop 22,700
Greve in Chianti at the end of Day 1 on the Chianti Classico hike (p196) is about 20km south of Florence on the S222 in the heart of the Chianti hills. With its quintessential Tuscan scenery and good transport links it makes an ideal base for this and other walks.

Information
The **tourist office** (☎ 854 62 87; Piazza Matteotti 11; 9am-1pm & 2-6pm Mon-Fri, Mon-Sat May-Sep) stocks a mine of electronic info on wineries to visit and trails to cycle or stroll.

Sleeping & Eating
The 10-room **Albergo Giovanni da Verrazzano** (☎ 85 31 89; www.ristorantever razzano.it; Piazza Matteotti 28; s/d €68/90 with bathroom €86/105) has a restaurant with a beautiful terrace overlooking the piazza.

Albergo del Chianti (☎ 85 37 63; www .albergodelchianti.it; Piazza Matteotti 86; s/d from €65/80), has a pool and a garden.

The town is surrounded by countless rural eating/sleeping havens including the exquisite **Fattoria di Rignana** (☎ 85 20 65; www.rignana.it; Val di Rignana 15, Rignana; d €95-105), an old farmstead/villa with a restaurant, 3.8km off the Chinati Classico walking route near Badia di Passignano.

Getting There & Away
Greve in Chianti is connected by frequent **SITA** (☎ 800 373760) buses to/from Florence (€3, one hour, 23 a day). Buses also connect with Panzano for the start of Day 2 of the Chianti Classico walk. By road the scenic SS222 bisects the Chianti region north–south between Florence and Siena passing through Strada in Chianti, Greve in Chianti and Castellina in Chianti.

FLORENCE
☎ 055 / pop 352,200
Yes, there are thousands of tourists; but, given the surroundings, who really cares? Florence is the cradle of the Renaissance and one of the most beguiling cities on the planet. It's also rather strategically positioned for bucolic sorties into the equally intoxicating Chianti countryside.

Information
APT Florence (www.firenzeturismo.it) has offices in **Piazza Beccaria** (☎ 2 33 20; Via Manzoni 16; 9am-1pm Mon-Fri); **San Lorenzo** (☎ 29 08 32; Via Cavour 1r; 8.30am-6.30pm Mon-Sat, 8.30am-1.30pm Sun); and **Amerigo Vespucci Airport** (☎ 31 58 74; 8.30am-8.30pm).

Supplies & Equipment
A well-stocked outdoor shop is **Climb** (☎ 324 50 74; www.climbfirenze.com; Via Marigliano 149/151). If you are looking for maps or books, **Libreria Stella Alpina** (☎ 41 16 88; www.stella-alpina.com; Via Corridoni 14B/r) specialises in Italian-language maps, travel books and guides.

Sleeping
Academy Hostel & Lodge House (☎ 239 86 65; www.academyhostel.eu; Via Ricasoli

9; dm €35-42, tw with bathroom €72-86) A relatively new hostel on the first floor of a 17th-century *palazzo* near the Duomo that gets excellent reviews, cheapness at the Academy doesn't compromise on comfort. Three-to six-bed dorms are bright and well set up.

Hotel Dalí (☎ 234 07 06; www.hoteldali .com; Via dell' Oriuolo 17; s without bathroom €34-40 , d without bathroom €56-65, d with bathroom €68-80) Offering a great price for its central location, this spruce, simple hotel is run energetically by its owners. Rooms overlooking the leafy inner courtyard are serene; those facing the street can be noisy.

Hotel Morandi alla Crocetta (☎ 234 47 47; www.hotelmorandi.it; Via Laura 50; s €70-90, d €90-170) Upping the price and style is this medieval convent-turned-hotel away from the madding crowds in the San Marco district. Refined rooms are decked out with authentic period furnishings and paintings. Some come with tiny gardens and one is a frescoed former chapel.

Eating

To eat cheaply in central Florence hit the glorified sandwich joints including '**Ino** (☎ 21 92 08; Via dei Georgofili 3r-7r; *panini* €5-8; 11am-8pm Mon-Sat, noon-5pm Sun) where *panino* prices include a shot of the house wine, and **Cantinetta dei Verrazzano** (☎ 26 85 90; Via dei Tavolini 18-20; platters €4.50-12, focaccia €3-3.50, *panini* €1.70-3.90; noon-9pm Mon-Sat), a *forno* (baker's oven) and *cantinetta* (small cellar) where topped focaccia fresh from the oven also come with a Chianti accompaniment.

For something more substantial try the classic **La Canova di Gustavino** (☎ 239 98 06; Via della Condotta 29r; meals €24; noon-midnight) serving full meals or simple cheese and meat platters near the Duomo, or the regularly lauded, if a little touristy, **Trattoria Mario** (☎ 21 85 50; www .trattoriamario.com; Via Rosina 2; meals €22; noon-3.30pm Mon-Sat, closed three weeks in Aug) which has been knocking out soulful Tuscan treats since 1953.

Getting There & Away

From the **SITA bus station** (☎ 800 373760; www.sitabus.it; Via Santa Caterina da Siena 17r), just west of Piazza della Stazione, there are *corse rapide* (express services) to/from

Siena (€6.80, 1¼ hours, at least hourly). To get to San Gimignano (€6) you need to go to Poggibonsi (50 minutes, at least hourly) and catch a connecting service. Direct buses also serve Castellina in Chianti, Greve in Chianti and other smaller cities throughout Tuscany.

Vaibus (☎ 21 51 55; www.vaibus.it) runs frequent buses to/from Lucca (€5.10, 1½ hours).

Florence is on the Rome–Milan rail line. There are regular trains to/from Rome (€16-40 1¾ hours to 4¼ hours), Milan (€22.50-45, 2¼ to 3½ hours) and Venice (€19-54, 2¾ to 4½ hours). Frequent regional trains run to Lucca (€5, 1½ hours, half-hourly).

Florence is connected by road to the A1 northwards to Bologna and Milan, and southwards to Rome and Naples. The Auto-strada del Mare (A11) links Florence with Prato, Lucca, Pisa and the coast.

LUCCA
☎ 0583 / pop 81,900

Lucca would be the best attraction in any other region, but in relic-stuffed Tuscany it is usually relegated down the list to third (after Florence and Siena). But what a third! Surrounded by thick walkable walls, and populated by perfectly coiffed *ragazzi* (guys) and *ragazze* (girls) who float around the historic centre on bicycles without sweating, this dazzling Renaissance diamond is perfectly poised for excursions into the Apuan Alps (p207).

Information

APT Lucca (www.luccatourist.it) operates offices at **Piazza Napoleone** (☎ 91 99 41; 10am-1pm & 2-6pm Mon-Sat) and **Piazza Santa Maria** (☎ 91 99 31; 9am-8pm Apr-Oct, 9am-12.30pm & 3-6.30pm mid-Nov–mid-Dec, 9am-12.30pm & 3-6.30pm Mon-Sat mid-Dec–Mar). The Piazza Santa Maria office offers pricey internet access (€5 per 30 minutes)

Sleeping & Eating

Ostello San Frediano (☎ 46 99 57; www .ostellolucca.it; Via della Cavallerizza 12; dm with/without bathroom €20/18, d/tr/q with bathroom €55/75/100) Even the youth hostels are regal in Lucca where this historic, atmospheric and frankly magnificent hostel offers top-notch comfort and service

TUSCANY

with 141 beds in voluminous rooms. The grandiose dining room serves breakfast/lunch/two-course dinner for €3/11/11.

Tango Hotel (☎ 340 498 24 95; www .tangohotellucca.com; Via della Formica 390; d from €99) Mixing the intimacy of a B&B with the professionalism of a hotel, Tango, situated outside the city walls but within walking distance of the train station, is well worth the extra hike. Beautifully decorated rooms are complemented by generous hosts and a top-notch modern-meets-medieval decor.

San Frediano Guest House (☎ 46 96 30; www.sanfrediano.com; Via degli Angeli 19; s with shared bathroom €38-65, d €48-80, s with bathroom €50-90, d €65-110) If you want to reside inside the walls, gravitate towards this comfortable 17th-century townhouse just off Via Fillungo in the centre. Less expensive rooms share a bathroom. If full, ask about its sister guesthouse.

Trattoria da Leo (☎ 49 22 36; Via Tegrimi 1; meals €17; Mon-Sat) Ask a local to recommend a lunch spot, and you'll probably end up here in the kind of bustling salt-of-the-earth trattoria for which Italy is famous. The food ranges from acceptable to delicious, with stand-out dishes including the *vitello tonnato* (cold veal with a tuna and caper sauce) and *torta di fichi e noci* (fig and walnut tart).

Caffè Di Simo (☎ 49 62 34; Via Fillungo 58; 9am-8pm & 8.30pm-1am) An atmospheric art-nouveau café-bar-restaurant where Puccini once filled in on piano, these days the locals stand at the bar for coffee and sit down for €10 lunch buffets.

Getting There & Away

From the bus stops around Piazzale Verdi, Vaibus runs services throughout the region. It also runs buses to/from Florence (€5.10, 1½ hours, hourly), Pisa and Pisa Airport (€2.80, 45 minutes to one hour, 30 daily) and Viareggio (€3.20, 50 minutes, five daily).

The train station is south of the city walls. Regional train services connect Lucca with surrounding cities and towns. Destinations include Florence (€5, 1¼ to 1¾ hours, hourly), and Pisa (€2.40, 30 minutes, every 30 minutes). Catch the train to Pietrasanta (€3, 35 minutes, hourly) and Massa (€3.60, 45 minutes, hourly) where you can connect with buses to access the Apuan Alps walks.

The A11 runs westwards to Pisa and Viareggio and eastwards to Florence. To access the Garfagnana, take the SS12 and continue on the SS445.

RADDA IN CHIANTI
☎ 0577 / pop 1700

About 10km east of Castellina and 17km south of Panzano in Chianti, Radda is an old village and a good base from which to reach some of the best spots in Chianti.

Information

The volunteer-staffed **Pro Loco tourist office** (☎ 73 84 94; Piazza Castello 6; 10am-1pm & 3-7pm Mon-Sat, 10.30am-1pm Sun mid-Apr–mid-Oct, 10.30am-12.30pm & 3.30-6.30pm Mon-Sat mid-Oct–mid-Apr) supplies tourist information, including information on walking in the area.

For free expert advice, check out www .chiantinet.it for information on hotels, residences, wine-tasting and travel tips.

Sleeping & Eating

One of the most economical options is **La Bottega di Giovannino** (☎ 73 80 56; Via Roma 6-8; d €70) a renovated B&B in the centre of Radda run by a couple of congenial wine experts who also own a deli next door. There are plenty more delightful old farmhouses in the area; check at the tourist office or on the Chianti website above.

Getting There & Away

SITA (☎ 800 373760) buses run from Radda to Florence (twice daily). **Tra-in** (☎ 20 42 45) buses serve both Florence (once daily) and Siena (five daily).

SAN GIMIGNANO
☎ 0577 / pop 7100

Originally an Etruscan village, San Gimignano had morphed into a wealthy fiefdom by the beginning of the 11th century. Flaunting their wealth, the city's powerful families built 72 towers before the plague passed through in 1348 decimating the town's population and leaving all but 14 of the towers in ruins. But the historic legacy was not lost. Today San Gimignano is one of the best-preserved medieval cities in Europe and sits on one of Tuscany's most beautiful perches. In summer and at weekends year-round it is crowded with tourists.

Information

The **Pro Loco tourist office** (☎ 94 00 08; www.sangimignano.com; Piazza Duomo 1; 9am-1pm & 3-7pm Mar-Oct, 9am-1pm & 2-6pm Nov-Feb) is in the main square and offers extensive information on accommodation, public transport, car and bicycle rentals and many other services.

Sleeping & Eating

Camping Boschetto di Piemma (☎ 94 03 52; www.boschettodipiemma.it; per person €7-10, tent €5-9, car €1.50-3; Easter-Oct) is 2km south of San Gimignano's southern gate, towards Santa Lucia, on the Tuscan Hill Crests walk, making it very handy.

Foresteria Monastereo di San Girolamo (☎ 94 05 73; www.monasterosangirolamo .it; Via Folgore da San Gimignano 26-32; per person €27) is an excellent budget choice. Run by friendly nuns, it has basic but spacious, comfortable rooms with attached bathrooms, sleeping two to five people. Ring ahead as it is perpetually booked.

Hotel Leon Bianco (☎ 94 12 94; www .leonbianco.com; Piazza della Cisterna 13; s €65-80, d €85-135) This smoothly run hotel occupies a 14th-century building and is welcoming and friendly with a ground-floor abundance of plants, a pretty inner courtyard, a breakfast patio, a billiard table and a fitness room.

Of San Gimignano's many eating joints there are two notables.

Gelateria di Piazza (Piazza della Cisterna 4; Mar–mid-Nov) is where well-known Tuscan holidaymaker Tony Blair used to go for his afternoon gelato, as a signed letter on the wall attests. Not surprisingly, it knocks out ice cream fit for a prime minister.

Il Pino (☎ 94 04 15; Via Cellolese 8-10; meals €40; Fri-Wed) is a non-budget place but it's well worth the investment, especially if you've just hiked copious kilometres. The seasonal menu includes massive pasta plates and several truffle-based specialities.

Getting There & Away

San Gimignano has no train station. Buses depart from Piazzale Martiri di Montemaggio, outside the city's southern wall gate, Porta San Giovanni. **SAP** (☎ 93 81 15) runs regular buses to Poggibonsi (€1.80, 30 minutes, frequent) 11km to the east where you can connect with train services to Certaldo, Siena and Florence. There are direct/indirect bus services to Florence (€6, 1¼ hours, over 30 daily) and Siena (€5.30, one to 1½ hours, 10 daily). For Volterra (€4.30, 1½ hours, four daily except Sun), change in Colle di Val d'Elsa, and (sometimes also) Poggibonsi.

By road from Florence or Siena, take the SS2 to Poggibonsi, then the SS429 and finally the SP63. From Volterra, take the SS68 east and follow the turn-off signs north to San Gimignano. There's a car park below Porta San Giovanni.

SIENA

☎ 0577 / pop 48,000

Lesser than Florence in size, but (arguably) greater in beauty, Siena is little bothered by the superior pulling power of its more illustrious northern rival. There's culture and art aplenty here, along with the unique spectacle of Il Palio, a frenetic medieval horse race still celebrated every July and August in the Piazza del Campo.

Information

The **tourist office** (☎ 28 05 51; www.terre siena.it; Piazza del Campo 56; 9am-7pm) can reserve accommodation.

Book Shop (☎ 22 65 94; www.book shopsiena.com; Via San Pietro 19) and **Libreria Senese** (☎ 28 08 45; Via di Città 62-6) sell books, maps and international newspapers. **Internet Train** (Via di Città 121; Via di Pantaneto 57; per hr €4; 10am-10pm Sun-Fri) is a popular café with cables for laptop hook-ups.

Supplies & Equipment

At the **Sport Center** (☎ 4 61 23; Viale Sclavo 210), 500m from the train station, you'll find a limited range of outdoor equipment and clothing.

Sleeping & Eating

Ostello Guidoriccio (☎ 5 22 12; www .ostelloguidoriccio.com; Via Fiorentina 89, Località Stellino; per person €20) A rare treat – all rooms are doubles at Siena's HI-affiliated youth hostel, about 2km northwest of the city centre. Take bus 10 or 15 from Piazza Gramsci, or bus 77 from the train station.

TUSCANY

Among the city's budget options are **Albergo Bernini** (☎ 28 90 47; www.albergo bernini.com; Via della Sapienza 15; s €50, d with shared bathroom €30-65, d with bathroom €45-85), a family-run hotel with a tiny terrace sporting views across to the cathedral and the Chiesa di San Domenico, and **Hotel La Perla** (☎ 22 62 80; www .hotellaperlasiena.com; Piazza Indipendenza 25; s €40-60, d €70-85), a friendly and well-run place whose slightly musty rooms are compensated by an excellent location, seconds from Piazza del Campo.

Hit the *osterias* for good midrange food including the no-nonsense **L'Osteria** (☎ 28 75 92; Via dei Rossi 79-81; meals €27) whose locally lauded food reflects the simplicity of its name, and **Osteria Boccon del Prete** (☎ 28 03 88; Via San Pietro 17; meals €30), which is small and hectic, but typically Sienese.

Getting There & Away

Siena is not on a major train line. If you're coming from Rome, change at Chiusi, or from Florence change at Empoli.

There are direct bus services from Rome to Siena (€20, three hours, eight a day) run by **SENA** (☎ 800 930960) departing from Piazzale Tiburtino in Rome, accessible from Termini, the main train station, on the Metro Linea B (get off at Stazione Tiburtina). **Tra-in** (☎ 20 42 45) and **SITA** (☎ 800 373760) run more than 10 direct buses daily between Florence and Siena's Piazza Gramsci, where Tra-in buses also depart for Castellina, Gaiole and Radda in Chianti.

Central Apennines

HIGHLIGHTS

- Crossing a long, airy ridge and several panoramic peaks on the **Sibillini Traverse** (p227)
- Taking a step back to marvel at the monolithic beauty of the Gran Sasso and Corno Grande range from the expansive **Campo Imperatore plateau** (p233)
- Walking in the footsteps of escaped POWs in the **Parco Nazionale della Majella** (p235)
- Keeping an eye out for one of a handful of bears in **Parco Nazionale d'Abruzzo** (p238)

Signature food: *Maccheroni alla chitarra*	Celebrated native: Ovid (Roman poet)	Famous for... Earthquakes

How's this for an oversight. Italy's symbolic spinal mountains, the Apennines, are also its least crowded. Indeed, at times, a visit here feels like a trip back to the 1950s; a world of wheezing trains and buzzing Vespas (motor scooters); a landscape of ruined farmhouses and fields splashed with blood-red poppies. All this is good news for prospective hikers who share the region's ample trails with sheep dogs, mountain goats, abundant birdlife and the odd – rarely sighted – human being.

While the Apennines proper stretch from the Maritimes on the French border down to the plain of Sibari in Italy's metaphoric toe, the highest and most imposing part of the range is crowded into a compact central stretch that straddles the borders of Umbria, Le Marche and Abruzzo.

These loftier peaks are characterised by their abundant beech woods, lonely plateaus and quiescent lightly populated valleys, all of which have resisted the modern interferences of tourism. While smaller than the Alps, the range's crowning pinnacle, Corno Grande, just northeast of L'Aquila, is no dwarf; it is a hulking limestone peak whose slopes protect the expansive Campo Imperatore plateau and the southernmost glacier in Europe.

A major national park building effort in the 1990s has created an almost unbroken swathe of protected land across the Apennines that runs from Monti Sibillini in the north to Abruzzo in the south.

CENTRAL APENNINES

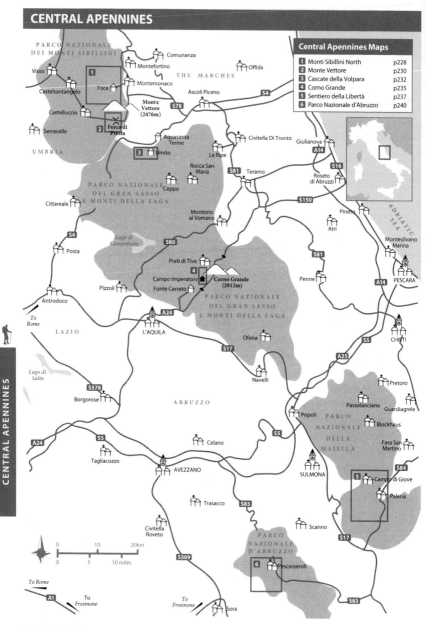

CENTRAL APENNINES

Central Apennines Maps

1	Monti Sibillini North	p228
2	Monte Vettore	p230
3	Cascate della Volpara	p232
4	Corno Grande	p235
5	Sentiero della Libertà	p237
6	Parco Nazionale d'Abruzzo	p240

CLIMATE

The Apennines offer an interesting mix of alpine and Mediterranean climate. Summers are warm and dry, with daytime temperatures in the valleys and slopes normally in the mid-20s°C. Temperatures are lower on the summits but the strength of the sun may still make it feel hot, especially with so little shade available. Snow may fall on the higher ground from October to June, with the eastern side of the range receiving the lion's share. Maximum daytime temperatures during the winter can be as low as 3°C in the highest inhabited areas; such cold weather has enabled Europe's most southerly glacier to survive beneath the northeast face of Corno Grande.

PLANNING
When to Walk
Fickle weather in the Apennines can bring both early and late season snow – although the region enjoys a slightly longer walking season than the Alps. It's best not to attempt the higher mountains of Monte Vettore, Monti Sibillini and Corno Grande before mid-June. The first snows often arrive in late September. Lower level trails are generally good from mid-May to early October.

Maps
Touring Club Italiano's 1:200,000 maps *Umbria e Marche and Abruzzo e Molise* are ideal for general orientation. See the Planning section of individual walks for specific map requirements.

Books
Stephen Fox's *Central Apennines of Italy: Walks, Scrambles & Climbs*, published in the UK by Cicerone, suggests a range of day walks within the Sibillini and Gran Sasso-Laga national parks.

Emergencies
For medical assistance contact the **national emergency** number (☎ 118). In Abruzzo there is also the **mountain rescue service** (☎ 167 258239). Carry a mobile phone.

GETTING THERE & AROUND
While public transport within the Central Apennines can sometimes be challenging, initial access to the area is easy thanks to its proximity to Rome and various international airports, train stations and bus termini.

GATEWAY
The walks in this section are spread out over a wide area. Though no one town serves as a gateway for all of them, the historic

---

WARNING
On April 6th 2009, Italy suffered its most devastating earthquake since 1980. The quake, which measured 6.3 on the Richter scale, was centred on the medieval city of L'Aquila in Abruzzo. It killed 307 people, injured over 1000 and made 50,000 homeless. At the time of writing, the region was still picking itself up after the disaster and much of L'Aquila was out of bounds. As a result, some of the information in this chapter, particularly with regard to L'Aquila (p243) and Parco Nazionale del Gran Sasso e Monti della Laga (p231), could be liable to change.

---

city of L'Aquila (p243) with its proximity to Rome and good transport connections comes closest.

PARCO NAZIONALE DEI MONTI SIBILLINI

In the southwest corner of the Marches, the Parco Nazionale dei Monti Sibillini covers almost 710 sq km and encompasses more than 20 peaks over 2000m in height. The highest point of the Monti Sibillini range is the summit of Monte Vettore (King's Mountain; 2476m). The park was established in 1993, and over 16,000 people live in small, traditional communities within its boundaries.

ENVIRONMENT
The park is home to 1800 species of plants, 50 species of mammals and 150 species of birds. Wolves, porcupines, wildcats and martens roam the area, while snow voles have survived here since the last ice age. The chamois (a cross between a goat and an antelope) is a recent reintroduction. Among the more charismatic bird species here are golden eagles (also successfully reintroduced), sparrowhawks and eagle owls. The park also marks the northernmost habitat in Italy of Orsini's viper. The lower slopes are characterised by forests of oak and beech, with the tree line generally around 1750m.

THE FIAT CINQUECENTO

You hear it before you see it: the metallic purr of the 479cc rear-fitted engine, the tinny rattle of the curvaceous 2.97m-long frame. And then suddenly, there it is, hurtling towards you like a runaway horse along a rough rural track barely wide enough to accommodate two passing cyclists. And you thought this was a 'hiking' trail.

It's hard to think of a more quintessential image of postwar Italy than the diminutive Fiat 500 (or *cinquecento* as it's affectionately known), a car once voted the 'sexiest automobile on the planet' by the readers of BBC's *Top Gear* magazine.

First unveiled in 1957 with its distinctive grille-less front and cute bubble-like exterior, the *cinquecento* quickly established itself as a durable and unpretentious cultural icon that rivalled the British Mini for its fly-weight capabilities. Encapsulating its understated appeal, *Top Gear*–presenter James May once described it as a vehicle that 'advertises nothing about its owner except that it's someone who doesn't need to try' – an interesting concept, especially in normally fashion-conscious Italy.

In 2007, the *cinquecento* was reincarnated as the Nuova 500 on the 50th anniversary of the car's original launch. Sleeker, bolder and slightly larger in size, the Nuova was an instant success selling out of its entire initial production stock of 58,000 in just three weeks. But, for purists, the beauty – and nostalgia value – will always lie with the original. Just keep a lookout on those trails!

PLANNING
When to Walk
The park's walks are generally accessible from May to October with a slightly shorter season on the higher ground. Check weather forecasts and try to avoid mountain ridges during high winds.

Maps
The Club Alpino Italiano (CAI) *Parco Nazionale dei Monti Sibillini*, and Edizioni Multigraphic's *Parco Nazionale dei Sibillini* both cover the park at 1:25,000, and are suitable for walking. There's also the Kompass 1:50,000 map No 666 *Monti Sibillini*.

Books
Italy's Sibillini National Park by Gillian Price published by Cicerone Press lists over 20 walks in the park and outlines the long-distance Grand Anello dei Monti Sibillini.

Information Sources
For further information contact the **park headquarters** (Ente Parco Nazionale dei Monti Sibillini; ☎ 0737 97 27 11; www .sibillini.net; Piazza del Forno 1, 62039 Visso).

GETTING THERE & AROUND
Sibillini is one of Italy's more isolated regions and not particularly well served by public transport. The nearest train stop is in Ascoli Piceno to the east of the park, from where regular buses depart for Montemonaco. There's also a daily bus from Rome. While there is no public transport to the start of the two walks, both are walkable (5–6km) from Montemonaco.

ACCESS TOWNS
The small hill town of Montemonaco (p243) on the eastern side of the national park is 5km to 6km from the start of both walks and hence the best place to use as a base.

LA GOLA DELL'INFERNACCIO

Duration 3 hours
Distance 8.5km
Difficulty easy
Start/Finish L'Infernaccio trailhead
Nearest Town Montemonaco (p243)
Transport private

Summary An easy and justifiably popular walk through a deep and twisted limestone gorge. Continuing to the head of the valley provides escape from the sightseers and offers good mountain views.

La Gola dell'Infernaccio is probably the most impressive gorge in the Apennine Range. The start of the walk is a short drive from Montemonaco, and the most dramatic part of the gorge is only a few minutes' walk from the parking area. Such easy access attracts plenty of people and the early stages of the walk are marred by the poor toilet habits of some visitors! Overlooking this, the continuation of the path leads gently up through pleasant beech forest, crossing the rushing stream several times to arrive at an open meadow at the head of the valley. For an easy half-day walk involving 350m of ascent, simply return along the same route. If you prefer more of a challenge take up one of the options given for extending this walk.

PLANNING
When to Walk
The walk will be at its most impressive during the thaw from May to late June, when the stream is full, although any time between May and October is possible. To escape the worst crowds avoid weekends and walk early or late in the day.

What to Bring
Bring water, as the stream should not be trusted without filtering.

Maps
Although it isn't strictly necessary to carry a map unless you plan to go beyond the head of the valley, the best map for the walk is the CAI 1:25,000 *Parco Nazionale dei Monti Sibillini*.

GETTING TO/FROM THE WALK
Public transport will take you only as far as Montemonaco (p243), 6km from the start. From there follow signposts for the village of Isola S Biagio, and then for L'Infernaccio itself. Stalwarts may want to shift the start by walking to Montemonaco thus making it a 20km hike – though the hike along the road is none too exciting. The final 2km to the trailhead is along a gravel road; there's a parking area at the end.

THE WALK
Follow the wide track as it descends steeply beneath the limestone cliffs. After 10 or 15 minutes you reach a bridge crossing the Fosso Tenna at the mouth of the gorge. Drips from the overhanging limestone walls on the left provide a refreshing shower even in late summer. Cross the stream and climb steeply into the **gorge**, descending to a second bridge between rock walls only a few metres apart. The stream cuts a virtual tunnel through the rock here, and the path

detours around to the left to recross the stream via a third bridge (particularly impressive and noisy if there is a lot of water).

From this bridge the path is forced away from the stream and climbs around a house-size boulder, while the water passes through a narrow defile to its left. Climb past a fourth and fifth bridge to where the gorge widens out and shady beech forest takes hold. A side path climbs through the trees to the right, signposted for the natural springs at San Leonardo. This path also leads to the high-level route that traverses the slopes above the north walls of the gorge.

On the main trail, the gorge soon begins to close in once again. On the left, **two tributaries** flow down from spectacular gorges cut into the southern walls. Cross again to the right (north) side of the Fosso Tenna and climb more steeply through attractive woodland reaching the meadows of Cerasa, 1½ to two hours from the start. An obvious hill with a **small ruin** on the left gives splendid views back down L'Infernaccio and also across the slopes of the surrounding mountains.

Retrace your steps to the start, or more ambitious walkers can extend the route from the meadow along several different trails. One option is to return to the start by climbing up to either of the trails traversing the steep slopes on the north and south side of the gorge (allow four to five hours). Alternatively, by climbing higher still on the south side, walkers can join up with the Sibillini Traverse and enjoy several kilometres of airy ridge walking, returning to either the start of La Gola dell'Infernaccio, or to Montemonaco (allow five to seven hours for each option).

SIBILLINI TRAVERSE

Duration 6 hours
Distance 18km
Difficulty moderate–demanding
Start/Finish Rifugio Sibilla
Nearest Town Montemonaco (p243)
Transport private

Summary A long, narrow ridge crosses the Sibillini Range, offering great views and very memorable walking.

This route traverses the roadless heart of the Parco Nazionale dei Monti Sibillini, offering vistas across most of its peaks and

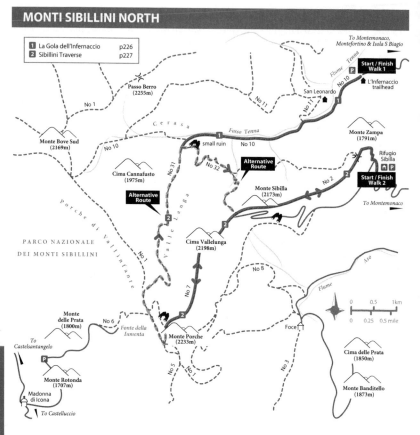

MONTI SIBILLINI NORTH

1 La Gola dell'Infernaccio	p226
2 Sibillini Traverse	p227

giving a wonderful overview of the area. However, the views will often take second place to what is going on underfoot; the main ridge section of the route stretches for over 4km along a continuously narrow spine of rock. Though not dangerously exposed, there are three short rock steps that require the use of hands and perhaps deserve a 'demanding' grading, around the peak of Monte Sibilla. The ridge crosses three major summits and nine peaks over 2000m, with the final peak, Monte Porche, providing the highest point at 2233m.

PLANNING
When to Walk
The ridge is exposed to the elements and has few escape routes; avoid walking in high winds or stormy weather (with risk of lightning). Wet weather will also lessen the friction of the rock, making it slippery. June to October is the ideal walking season.

What to Bring
No water is available en route – make sure you carry plenty.

Maps
The best map for the walk is the CAI 1:25,000 *Parco Nazionale dei Monti Sibillini*.

GETTING TO/FROM THE WALK
Rifugio Sibilla (☎ 0736 85 64 22; www .rifugiosibilla1540.com; per person €20-26) is 5km from Montemonaco (for Getting There & Away see p244). There is no regular public transport, but the *rifugio* staff will sometimes arrange a pick-up bus if you stay

overnight. Contact the *rifugio* for details. Otherwise you can hire a car/taxi, or walk the initial 5km from Montemonaco.

THE WALK

Take the wider path uphill from the *rifugio* (1540m) as it zigzags across the hillside past another disused *rifugio* and towards a ridge. To the northwest lies the hulk of Monte Zampa (1791m). On reaching the crest a less distinguishable path swings southwest descending to a **saddle**. From here it contours around the southern slopes of an unnamed peak before rejoining the ridge and ascending across a grassy slope. Marked by blue and red markers, the path heads towards the summit of Monte Sibilla. A few hundred metres below the summit is a rock step. Hands will be called on to negotiate this; a short metal cable provides assistance. A black memorial cross marks the summit of **Monte Sibilla** (2173m), undoubtedly the most visually impressive summit on the ridge.

Drink in the stupendous view before tackling the narrow fin of pink rock that links Monte Sibilla, Cima Vallelunga and Monte Porche. The ridge can appear intimidating on the approach, but it's easier than it looks, although hands will be called on for one or two short sections of easy scrambling as you descend and ascend again in a southwesterly direction. The terrain is generally rocky underfoot as the ridge undulates towards and past **Cima Vallelunga** (2198m). The path is obvious throughout. Intermittent red-paint splashes and old signposts mark the way, and views down into the valleys on either side are continually impressive.

Soon you will veer off the ridge and ascend a small rise to the summit of **Monte Porche** (2233m). An incredible panorama of the Sibillini Range awaits at the summit cairn, including an impressive view of the ridge you have just traversed. Retrace your steps back to the start.

ALTERNATIVE ROUTE: VALLE LANGA
2½ hours, 9km

For a more interesting walking circuit, descend the south side of Monte Porche over steep open terrain with no fixed path down to the col (2090m) that divides it from Monte Argentella. Turn sharp right here off the ridge onto Trail No 1. Ignore the turn left (Trail 6) at a cairn on a shoulder and stay on path for another 500m. Branch right onto Trail No 31 and return back to the Valle Langa to the turnaround point in the La Gola dell'Infernaccio walk (p226). From here you cut up Trail No 32 back to join the Sibillini ridge just west of Monte Sibilla or follow the La Gola dell'Infernaccio walk back to the start point (4km) and on to Montemonaco.

MONTE VETTORE

Duration 4–4½ hours
Distance 10km
Difficulty easy–moderate
Start/Finish Forca di Presta
Nearest Town Montemonaco (p243)
Transport private
Summary The highest mountain in the Sibillini Range, Monte Vettore can be climbed in a few hours by a strenuous path rising from the Forca di Presta.

Sitting on the border of Le Marche and Umbria, Vettore is another Apennine mountain doused in legend and at 2476m it is no dwarf. Local walkers would probably not consider the 10km (942m ascent) route from the Forca di Presta to be the connoisseur's approach, since the longer and harder route from the Valle Lago di Pilato is less crowded and more scenic. However, the Forca di Presta route has much to offer. The well-formed trail and relatively high starting point mean that it is the easiest and most straightforward option, and it does give fantastic views south across the Monti della Laga. Once on the shoulder at the basic and unstaffed Rifugio Tito Zilioli there are also great views down the Valle Lago di Pilato. The ascent is steep and unrelenting and plenty of water should be carried, especially on a hot day when the south-facing slopes can become really hot. This popular route can be crowded on summer weekends.

PLANNING
When to Walk

Choose fine weather between June and October for this walk and try to avoid windy days. You should also avoid days when the cloud is down and when there is a chance of electrical storms.

What to Bring

Bring plenty of water as there is none on the route.

Maps

The best map is the CAI 1:25,000 *Parco Nazionale dei Monti Sibillini.*

GETTING TO/FROM THE WALK

There is no public transport to the start of the walk. You'll need to read your map carefully if you're approaching by car from Montemonaco (p243). Navigate south on SP83 to Montegallo where you connect with SS89. Look out for a right turn at a junction 7km from Montegallo that will take you up to the Forca di Presta on SP34. The route starts opposite the signpost for the Rifugio degli Alpini and there is plenty of roadside parking.

To bag an early start you can stay over in the fully serviced **Rifugio degli Alpini** (☎ 0736 80 92 78; www.rifugiomontisibillini.it; dm/half-board €16.50/35), well positioned on a hillside overlooking the Forca di Presta at the beginning of the walk.

The total journey from Montemonaco to Forca di Presta is 30km making a taxi journey very pricey.

THE WALK

Follow the obvious trail onto the grassy slopes above the **Forca di Presta**. The gradient is moderate at first but soon steepens. In places the trail is littered with loose stones, and progress can be tiring. After ascending for 45 minutes to an hour, the gradient eases and the trail sides around the southeastern slopes for a few hundred metres, leading to a small saddle where a rest can be taken.

From this saddle the trail climbs steeply and passes beneath Monte Vettoretto (2052m) before climbing into a small **saddle** just to the north of that summit. From here you can walk the short distance (two minutes) out onto the summit, which is really no more than a bump on the ridge, but from where there are great **views** across to the Monti della Laga.

Again the trail steepens as you climb diagonally across steep slopes. The **Rifugio Tito Zilioli** is just visible on the skyline, but you must negotiate a very steep and eroded section of trail and an awkward outcrop of rock before reaching it, 1½ to two hours from the start. The *rifugio* has

sleeping platforms but is otherwise a fairly unappealing shelter.

If you have the time and the inclination, from here you can make a worthwhile detour to Cima del Lago (see Side Trip, below).

On the main trail, head northeast from the *rifugio*, enjoying the fantastic view down into the Valle Lago di Pilato. After a few hundred metres the slopes steepen and the trail begins to make large switchbacks as you near the summit of **Monte Vettore** (2476m), which is 2¼ to three hours from the start. From here the great bald summits and ridges of the northern Sibillini are revealed, and on a clear day you should also be able to make out the Adriatic coast.

Retrace your steps down to the Forca di Presta.

SIDE TRIP: CIMA DEL LAGO
40–50 minutes, 1.6km

This fine, rocky and at times narrow ridge gives airy views and adds a little excitement to the main route.

From Rifugio Tito Zilioli head west on Trail No 1, eventually swinging around to the northwest and Cima del Lago.

PARCO NAZIONALE DEL GRAN SASSO E MONTI DELLA LAGA

Welcome to one of Italy's most underappreciated and least crowded upland zones. This huge park established in 1993 incorporates two separate, geologically distinct mountain ranges. The remote Monti della Laga in the north is comprised of harsh and rugged terrain that juxtaposes deep wooded gorges with smooth rounded peaks. South of the park bisecting Vomano Valley lies the imposing Gran Sasso massif that rises like a noble Notre Dame above the blustery pastures of Campo Imperatore. Gran Sasso is the domain of the highest summit in the Apennines, (Corno Grande; 2912m), Europe's most southerly glacier (Ghiacciaio del Calderone) and one of the most biodiverse regions on the continent. It is also endowed with copious flora and fauna and characterised by roaming herds of sheep that are watched over by huge Maremma guard dogs. The area earned historical noteriety in 1943 when an imprisoned Mussolini was dramatically 'kidnapped' by Nazi commandos from a Campo Imperatore hotel (see boxed text p234).

ENVIRONMENT

The Gran Sasso Range consists of limestone and dolomite, with peaks and high vertical walls gouged out over time by both water erosion (creating numerous karstic features) and ancient glaciation. Europe's southernmost glacier still survives on the northern slopes of Corno Grande. The more rounded peaks and deeply incised valleys of the Monti della Laga owe their form to a sandstone-marl rock base, which keeps water flowing on the surface. Beech is the most common tree on the lower slopes of both areas, often interspersed with holly and yew (relics of a warmer, wetter climatic period). Woodland typically covers the valleys up to a height of 1800m.

Of the fauna in the park, the Abruzzo chamois has perhaps the most interesting story to tell. A rare species of chamois exclusive to the Apennines, Gran Sasso was once the centre of its territory, until it was hunted to extinction in the area towards the end of the 19th century. Around a century later it was reintroduced, and there are currently around 50 chamois in the region. This is also an important habitat for Orsini's viper, an insect-preying snake that lives in greater numbers here than in any other part of Italy.

PLANNING
Maps

Selca publish a two-map set entitled *Parco Nazionale del Gran Sasso e Monti della Laga*, which covers the park at a scale of 1:50,000. Much better for walking in the Gran Sasso area is the CAI 1:25,000 *Gran Sasso d'Italia*. For general orientation there's the Kompass 1:50,000 map No 669 *Gran Sasso d'Italia – L'Aquila*.

Books

Gran Sasso: Le Piú Belle Escursioni (1996), by Alberico Alesi, Maurizio Calibani and Antonio Palermi, details a wide variety of walks within the park. An English supplement is available.

Information Sources

For further information contact the **park headquarters** (Ente Parco Nazionale del Gran Sasso e Monti della Laga; ☎ 0862 6 05 21; www.gransassolagapark.it; Via del Convento 1) in Assergi.

GETTING THERE & AROUND

Thanks to its proximity to L'Aquila, Gran Sasso has speedy links to Rome. Buses traverse the last section out to Fonte Cerreto. The peninsula-bisecting A24 motorway cuts right through the middle of the park via the Traforo del Gran Sasso (Gran Sasso tunnel).

ACCESS TOWNS

This Corno Grande walk can be done as a long day trip from the medieval city of L'Aquila (p243) that sits flanked by the Gran Sasso Mountains to the west of the park.

The Cascate della Volpara hike is best tackled from the north with Montemonaco (p243) acting as a viable base if you have your own wheels.

CASCATE DELLA VOLPARA

Duration 3½–4½ hours
Distance 8km
Difficulty moderate
Start/Finish Umito
Nearest Town Montemonaco (p243)
Transport private

Summary A small path leads through beautiful beech woodland to two of central Italy's most picturesque waterfalls.

The Cascate della Volpara is among the highest and most spectacular of the many waterfalls in the Monti della Laga range. On the way to the fall, this route also explores a section of pristine beech woodland, which is as beautiful as any forested slope in the Apennines. The day's ascent is 512m.

PLANNING
When to Walk
The waterfall is at its best during spring or as early as possible in summer. Avoid walking after rain when the ground can become very slippery.

What to Bring
Although the route to the cascade is not long, the ground covered, particularly towards the waterfall itself, is sometimes steep and rough; good boots are essential.

MAPS
The northern sheet of Selca's 1:50,000 *Parco Nazionale del Gran Sasso e Monti della Laga* covers the area, though waterfalls are incorrectly positioned and the path isn't marked.

GETTING TO/FROM THE WALK
The Volpara hike is best tackled with your own wheels and can be easily incorporated with the three Parco Nazionale dei Monti Sibillini hikes (p225) using Montemonaco (p243), 40km to the north, as a base.

Public transport will get you as far as Acquasanta Terme, 10km from the start/finish where you can attempt to organise your own transport. The town has several hotels. Try **Albergo Terme** (☎ 0736 80 12 63; Piazza Terme 20; d from €60) alongside the main road. Acquasanta is served by **START** (www.startspa.it) buses that run four times a day between Rome (2¾ hours) and Ascoli

Piceno (20 minutes) where you can change for Montemonaco.

From Acquasanta Terme, take the road to Umito that leads south from the eastern edge of town, and continue for 9km. Just before the turning circle at the end of the road in Umito, is a narrow gravel track on the right, signed to Volpara. Follow this for 1km and park beside a footbridge.

THE WALK
Continue up the gravel track from the parking area, climbing to a small white building after 2km. The track ends here and a mud path continues, quickly entering thick beech woodland. The path is immediately attractive, skirting beneath small rock escarpments amid the trees. The climb is sustained, with switchbacks in places, though the beauty of the plants and flowers of the forest floor, set against the lime green leaves of the beech, offers plenty of distraction. At times it is necessary to step over or duck under fallen branches.

Around 1km into the wood the trail passes a grotto beneath a large boulder. Within another few hundred metres there is a second **grotto**, with entrance wall, doorway, window, and interior oven all virtually intact. These caves served as shelters for local woodsmen until relatively recently. Soon after the grottoes, cross a patch of waist-high vegetation and a stream before reaching the picturesque **Cascata della Prata**.

The route then joins the Volpara stream, and follows up its east bank into more mature beech woodland. The ground underfoot is sometimes rough and steep. An alternative trail joins the main path from the left, and a short climb leads out of the beech trees and into thicker vegetation. You are now close to

CASCATE DELLA VOLPARA

the Volpara falls, but the path degenerates into a maze and can be difficult to navigate. The best advice is to watch for forks diligently, and keep right at every occasion. Two streams are crossed, and there is a good view of the entire height of the **Cascate della Volpara** from the second. Following this, a steep, rocky section of path leads to a fallen tree. Turn right here (the main path continues as steep switchbacks into more beech woodland) to reach the base of a rock slab 50m high that forms the lower falls, about two to 2½ hours from the start.

Retrace your steps to the starting point.

CORNO GRANDE

Duration 5–6 hours
Distance 9km
Difficulty moderate–demanding
Start/Finish Campo Imperatore
Nearest Town L'Aquila (p243)
Transport cable car

Summary An impressive and surprisingly straightforward route to the summit of the highest peak in the Apennines.

As the highest peak in the Apennines, Corno Grande (2912m) receives a lot of attention from walkers, especially since it is so readily accessible from high-altitude starting points at either Campo Imperatore or Prati di Tivo. It even attracts its fair share of nonwalkers, some of whom find the steep ground more than they bargained for. The impressive rock peak has extremely steep faces and from most viewpoints looks like the preserve of climbers.

The *via normale* (normal route) provides a relatively straightforward, well-marked, out-and-back route. It is graded moderate–demanding because of the steep slopes (the day's ascent is 812m) towards the top. As long as care is taken these should present no problem for most walkers, and the physical demands are really more on a par with a walk of a moderate grade.

For a more challenging option, see the West Ridge Alternative Route (p235).

PLANNING
When to Walk
Depending on the previous winter's snowfall, the route should be largely free of snow from early June. The first snows of autumn can be expected in late September or early October, after which the mountain is best left to alpinists. Even in midsummer, conditions can turn nasty, so pick a fine, clear day with light winds. Also consider making an early start to avoid both the crowds and the strong sun, which can reflect quite intensely from the limestone.

What to Bring
There are no reliable water sources on this route, so bring plenty.

Maps
Use the CAI 1:25,000 map *Gran Sasso d'Italia*.

GETTING TO/FROM THE WALK
Campo Imperatore is accessible by **cable car** (☎ 0862 40 00 07; Tue & Thu €9, Mon, Wed & Fri €11, Sat & Sun €13) from the resort town of Fonte Cerreto. The service runs every 30 minutes from 8.30am to 5pm year-round except for maintenance closures in May and October. Check ahead at these times. Campo Imperatore is also accessible by driving 25km east from Fonte Cerreto.

To reach Fonte Cerreto from L'Aquila, take **ARPA** (☎ 0862 41 28 08) bus No 76 from the bus station to Piazza Santa Maria Paganica (€0.90, 20 minutes). Change here onto bus M6 to Fonte Cerreto (€0.90, 20 minutes). There's a camping ground in Fonte Cerreto and a hostel at Campo Imperatore if you need a cheap place to stay.

By car, Fonte Cerreto is 124km east of Rome via the A24, and around 90km west of Pescara via the A14 and the A24.

THE WALK
Leave the Campo Imperatore main parking area and walk north, passing to the left of the observatory. Follow the obvious stony track up the steep slope towards the Rifugio Duca degli Abruzzi, which is just visible. About a third of the way to the *rifugio*, turn right at a signposted junction and follow a narrow path traversing steep slopes to the northeast. The path climbs around a shoulder, and then climbs through steep switchbacks to a ridge at the Sella di Monte Aquila (45 minutes to one hour from the start). Turn right along the ridge and then left at a signposted junction a little further

CENTRAL APENNINES

THE GRAN SASSO RAID

Of all Hitler's wartime gambles, the snatching of Mussolini from under the noses of his Italian captors at Campo Imperatore in September 1943 was perhaps the most audacious.

Following his dismissal by King Victor Emmanuel III on 24 July 1943, Italy's 'Sawdust Caesar' was subsequently arrested by the *carabinieri* (police) and bundled away in secret to the island of Ponza, a one-time penal colony in the Tyrrhenian Sea.

In the weeks that followed, Mussolini was kept constantly on the move in a bid to deter attempts to rescue him. At the same time, a new Italian government, under Pietro Badoglio, secretly brokered an armistice with the Allies; a deal which was officially signed on 3 September 1943.

By this point Mussolini was interred in a hotel called Campo Imperatore in the Apennines Mountains, a peacetime ski resort known to Italians as 'Little Tibet' for its hostile terrain and heavy winter snowfalls.

The mission to rescue him – known officially as Operation Eiche or the Gran Sasso Raid – was headed up by Otto Skorzeny, a stealthy commander in the Waffen SS handpicked by Hitler himself. Skorzeny had learnt of Mussolini's whereabouts by intercepting a coded Italian radio message while working undercover in Rome. Arriving in the Apennines, he organised for a team of crack German paratroopers to fly in a dozen gliders over Gran Sasso Mountain before landing on the high plateau adjacent to the hotel where Mussolini was being held.

In the event, the ill-equipped gliders crash-landed into the side of the mountain but, undeterred by the setback, the paratroopers regrouped and, led by Skorzeny, recklessly stormed the hotel. By his own testimony, Skorzeny was first inside where he lost no time in disabling the radio operator with his jackboot and the radio with his pistol butt. Within 10 minutes, the flabbergasted Mussolini had been freed without a shot being fired.

The rescue of Mussolini was a huge propaganda coup for Hitler at a time when the war was rapidly turning against Germany. Not only did it temporarily stall Allied advances in Italy, it also allowed the Italian dictator to return briefly to power as a German puppet in the short-lived Italian Social Republic.

Hero of the hour, Otto Skorzeny subsequently became something of a Nazi celebrity and briefly earned the title 'the most dangerous man in Europe'. After the war he was de-Nazified *in absentia* by an Allied court and later worked undercover for governments in Spain, Argentina and Egypt.

---

along. The right fork leads to the direct route up Corno Grande's south face, which is a challenging scramble, best left to walkers with climbing experience.

Follow the delightful trail across grassy slopes at the head of Valle Maone, continuing straight ahead at a junction. Prominent cliffs and scree rise beneath the west ridge of Corno Grande (snow may persist here into early summer), where the trail steepens and climbs to the foot of the west ridge (1½ to two hours from the start). There are great views from here out across Campo Pericoli to Pizzo Cefalone (2533m). Follow the paint splashes up the ridge for a short distance (be careful not to follow the slightly lower trail signposted to the Rifugio Garibaldi), and then climb around the stoney northwest flanks of the mountain. The trail soon steepens and zigzags up into a large flat area at the base of the deep bowl

forming the northwestern side of Corno Grande. To the north the steep buttresses of Corno Picolo (2655m) dominate the view. The *via normale* continues across a small depression and onto the scree slopes sweeping down from the summit.

The change in gradient is quite abrupt and soon you'll find yourself picking a way back and forth up the steep, loose ground. Not far from the summit ridge the ground steepens further and you'll need to use your hands for balance in places. After 30 to 40 minutes of effort you should reach a **prominent notch** on the summit ridge, where the rocks frame a fantastic view across the remains of the Calderone Glacier to the pinnacles on Corno Grande's central summit. Turn right along the ridge and follow the paint splashes to the **summit**, where there is a small metal cross and a visitors book (10 or 15 minutes from the notch). The view is spectacular, even in

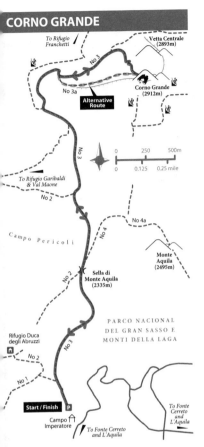

CORNO GRANDE

To Rifugio Franchetti

Vetta Centrale (2893m)

No 3

No 3a

Alternative Route

Corno Grande (2912m)

No 3

0   250   500m
0   0.125   0.25 mile

To Rifugio Garibaldi & Val Maone

No 2

No 4a

Campo Pericoli

No 4

Monte Aquila (2495m)

No 2

Sella di Monte Aquila (2335m)

PARCO NACIONAL DEL GRAN SASSO E MONTI DELLA LAGA

Rifugio Duca degli Abruzzi

No 3

No 2

No 1

Start / Finish   P

Campo Imperatore

To Fonte Cerreto and L'Aquila

To Fonte Cerreto and L'Aquila

be desirable, the use of ropes is not necessary and the route is suitable for confident walkers with a reasonable head for heights.

PARCO NAZIONALE DELLA MAJELLA

Founded in 1993, the Parco Nazionale della Majella encompasses an 860-sq-km area of the Majella mountain chain, an offshoot of the main Apennine Range. There are 30 summits over 2000m in height clustered within the park's borders. However, the area is renowned for its alpine plateaux and rounded mountain tops rather than for sharp peaks. Monte Amaro (2795m) marks the highest point of the park. Once the mythological home of the goddess Maja, the region became a centre of prayer and retreat for religious hermits during the Middle Ages. Many of the numerous abbeys and hermitages around the lower mountain slopes date from this time.

ENVIRONMENT

Below 900m the slopes of the Majella Range are forested with oak and maple, while beech predominates above this. Around and above the tree line, at around 1700m, only stunted mountain pines grow. Almost everywhere is the yellow laburnum, and theory has it that the old local term for this plant, *majo*, is the basis of today's name Majella. The range's location between the two distinct habitats of the Apennines and Adriatic also means that a huge variety of plant life can be found here. In total the park is home to around a third of all Italian plant species, including flora from Mediterranean, alpine, Balkan and arctic species.

The park's wildlife includes wolves, Marsican brown bears, chamois and 130 species of bird, including the dotterel, which nests only here in all of Italy. Also special in the park is the rare apollo butterfly, a large butterfly with black and red spots on otherwise transparent wings.

PLANNING
Maps

The CAI 1:25,000 *Gruppo della Majella* is the best walking map for the area.

late summer when haze blurs the distant horizons. All around, the mountain seems to drop away in impossibly steep rock walls, leaving most walkers with a great sense of achievement at having reached the summit of such an apparently improbable peak.

Retrace your steps to return to Campo Imperatore, taking care when descending the steep ground from the summit ridge.

ALTERNATIVE ROUTE: THE WEST RIDGE
45 minutes–1 hour, 1km

The ascent can be spiced up by climbing the *cresta ouest* on the way up, and then descending on the *via normale*. This option requires some scrambling (use of hands for balance) across a moderately exposed rock ridge. Although previous climbing experience would

Also handy for this area is the park-produced 1:50,000 *Carta Turistica* with the Sentiero della Libertà clearly marked in blue.

PLACE NAMES
The park's name Majella is sometimes seen written as Maiella.

Information Sources
For further information contact the **park headquarters** (Ente Parco Nazionale della Majella; ☎ 0871 8 03 71; www.parks.it/parco .nazionale.majella; Palazzo di Sciascio, Via Occidentale 6, Guardiagrele).

GETTING THERE & AWAY
Sulmona is an important transport nexus with regular train services to Rome, Naples, L'Aquila and Pescara. The local ARPA buses also run between many other locations in the Apennines and can shunt you over to Parco Nazionale d'Abruzzo.

ACCESS TOWN
Lying to the west of the park and accessible by a convenient train line, the sizeable town of Sulmona (p244) is the best base for walkers undertaking this hike.

SENTIERO DELLA LIBERTÀ

Duration 8 hours
Distance 21km
Difficulty moderate
Start Campo di Giove
Finish Stazione di Palena
Nearest Town Sulmona (p244)
Transport train

Summary A one-time great escape route bisects through a national park, incorporating lonely passes and sleepy villages before finishing at one of Italy's tiniest train stations.

Mixing the call of the wild with the call of freedom, this pioneering, isolated trail along part of the historic Sentiero della

LONG WALK TO FREEDOM

Compared to the well-documented breakouts from Colditz and Alcatraz, the escape from Sulmona has a slightly less cinematic appeal. But for the proud residents of Abruzzo, its historical resonance is just as important.

During WWII, with the Allies advancing swiftly through southern Italy, inmates in the Italian POW camp, Fonte d'Amore – or Campo 78 – 5km east of Sulmona began to sniff freedom. But as their lackadaisical Italian guards surrendered to the advancing Anglo-American army, a more officious group of well-trained Nazis quickly stepped into their shoes.

Preparing for a heavy Allied onslaught, the Germans abruptly decided to abandon Campo 78 in September 1943 and marched its beleaguered inmates north; but not before many of them had escaped.

With the help of sympathetic local partisans, the ex-prisoners fled east across the Apennines Mountains to Casoli on the Sangro River forging a new trail as they went. Casoli had been liberated by Allied soldiers a few months previously and, throughout the winter of 1943/44, as the Allied advance was temporarily halted by German troops along the 'Gustav Line', it became the hallowed end point of the so-called Sentiero della Libertá, an escape route that led east from German-occupied Sulmona to freedom.

The Sentiero's most celebrated escapee was future Italian president, Carlos Azeglio Ciampi (president 1999–2006), then an army lieutenant and active member of the Italian Resistance. But, with its well-guarded checkpoints and mountainous terrain, others weren't so lucky. On a windswept pass known as Guado di Coccia halfway between Campo di Giove and Palena, a stone monument stands in memoriam to Ettore De Corti, an Italian partisan captured and executed by the Germans in September 1943 – an enduring symbol of the underground resistance.

Today the Sentiero della Libertá is a popular long-distance hiking trail that cuts east through the mountainous Parco Nazionale della Majella. Stops along the way include Sulmona, Campo di Giove, Taranta Peligna, Lama and Casoli. For a thought-provoking walk through history, walkers can partake in the Sentiero della Libertá hike here.

Libertà is big on solitude and heavy with memories of one of WWII's lesser known great escapes (see boxed text Long Walk to Freedom, p236). The understated joys of the Apennines – steeped in tradition and invariably bereft of other hikers – are apparent as soon as you get off the train in Campo di Giove.

Due to the point-to-point nature of this hike, you'll need to double-check the return train times from Stazione di Palena before you start (the times are available in Campo di Giove). Miss the last train and you'll be stuck in the middle of nowhere a good 10km from Palena village. Though it's possible to skirt the edge of Palena as you descend from Guado di Coccia, the village has a pleasant atmosphere, and a couple of spirit-reviving bars and restaurants are worth the diversion.

GETTING TO/FROM THE WALK
Campo di Giove (start)
At least two daily trains connect Sulmona with Campo di Giove (€2.70, 25 minutes). There are also approximately four daily buses from Sulmona (€2.20) with Autolinee **ARPA** (☎ 0871 4 24 31)

Stazione di Palena (finish)
Palena station – situated quite literally in the middle of nowhere – is only 15 minutes east of the starting point at Campo di Giove by train. Three daily trains connect Stazione di Palena with Sulmona (€3.10, 40 minutes). The last (and best option for hikers) is at 7.38pm. Make sure you catch it, or you'll be stranded.

THE WALK
From outside the information centre in the central square in Campo di Giove (1064m), follow the road east past the post office. Soon after passing the last buildings in town, branch left off the paved road and onto a path marked with a red, white and green Italian flag motif denoting the Sentiero della Libertá. Head uphill, cross a wider track and follow the path as it continues southeast ascending diagonally across the mountainside towards the pass. At a V-junction, fork left on the higher path (the lower path leads to a small chapel and soon dead-ends). Within 15 minutes you'll join a wider track at the top end of a chairlift that will take you up to the ski station and **rifugio** at the Guado di Coccia (1674m). Keeping the dark mass of Monte Porrara on

SENTIERO DELLA LIBERTÀ

your right, follow the Sentiero della Libertà straight over the col and down the other side. The Sentiero is now a good dirt track that progresses downhill through open grassy terrain. After about 15 minutes the main track swings right and crosses a small river in a gulley. Follow it as it zigzags down with the river on your left. The track briefly joins a paved road by a hut at the bottom of a **ski lift**; 200m further on you leave the road via another track on the left and head downhill towards the village of Palena below. The track joins and immediately leaves another road before finally joining it again by the outlying houses of **Palena**. If you want to divert into the village for refreshments, veer left off the road onto a lane that doubles back towards the centre.

To continue, stay on the main road a few moments longer. Path No 12 branches off to the right just behind the **Museo dell'Orso Marsicano** (☎ 0872 91 89 51; 2 Vico II Gradoni) on the southwestern edge of Palena. A narrow track – sometimes overgrown – bisects pastoral fields above the road below. After a couple of kilometres the path descends close to the road and cuts around the back of a small factory complex. Just before a junction with the main road on the other side of the factory, veer right up a small incline on a dirt track, go past a house and enter a scrubby pasture. The path parallels the road for approximately one kilometre before joining

it by a national-park noticeboard. Turn right on the road and follow it for about 300m to a bend where park No 12 veers off to the right (signposted). The path now climbs continuously for several kilometres through thick woods to reach the small **chapel of Madonna dell'Altare** (1278m; a popular pilgrimage site in the summer). From the chapel, a paved road now winds its way gently downhill through trees to join up with the main valley road again. At the junction turn right and follow the road around to the left where it hits a T-junction. A right turn here will lead you over a small crest, beyond which you will see the **Stazione di Palena** perched on the edge of the verdant Riserva Orientata Quarto di Santa Chiara below. Veer right at the small roundabout to reach the platform.

PARCO NAZIONALE D'ABRUZZO

Italy's second-oldest national park is also one of its most ecologically rich. Established by royal decree in 1923, the Parco Nazionale d'Abruzzo began as a 5-sq-km reserve that ultimately morphed into the 440-sq-km protected area it is today. The evolution wasn't easy. Indeed, the park was abolished

MARSICAN BROWN BEAR

Bear paranoia can put the frighteners on the most idyllic of wilderness hikes – as plenty of bell-brandishing, spray-welding North American travellers will testify. But nervous visitors to the Italian peninsula can take comfort; Italy is bear-free – well almost.

The Marsican brown bear is one of the most critically endangered species on the planet. At last count, there were estimated to be 40 remaining in the wild, nearly all of them concentrated in the Parco Nazionale d'Abruzzo, Lazio e Molise in central Italy. According to recent environmental reports, the numbers could soon drop further. In 2007–08 at least three bears were found dead from poisoning in the Abruzzo region, the result of ongoing battle between conservation groups on one hand and locals who feel that their crops and livestock have been put at risk on the other.

Driven towards urban areas due to natural habitat loss, bears have been forced into closer contact with humans in a desperate bid to survive. But, despite the Marsican Brown being one of the most innocuous members in the bear family (there is little history of aggression towards humans), the misguided poisoning and poaching continues.

The Marsican is a subspecies of the brown bear and a relative of the North American grizzly. The small Italian population also shares a handful of Western European cousins in tiny enclaves in the Pyrenees and Cantabrian Mountains in France and Spain.

altogether in 1933 by the Mussolini government and returned to the fold in 1950 only to face further encroachment from housing construction, road building and ski tracks. Always at the forefront of the conservation movement in Italy (though particularly in the last 35 years), Abruzzo has frequently encountered hostility from political, bureaucratic and hunting interests. Nonetheless it has managed to successfully initiate a host of campaigns to reintroduce and protect animals such as the Abruzzo chamois, Apennine wolf, lynx, deer and, most notably, Italy's largest surviving enclave of Marsican bears. Plant life is similarly rich with over 2000 species, most famously, the thick beech woods that cover 60% of the park's total area. Today Abruzzo's 440 sq km extends over 22 municipalities and three provinces (the park's official name is actually Parco Nazionale d'Abruzzo, Lazio e Molise). Thanks to its longer history, it receives more visitors than most of the other parks in the area – around two million each year. The visitor services are equally spiffy.

ENVIRONMENT

The limestone hills and deep valleys of the Parco Nazionale d'Abruzzo are covered by thick forests of beech, black pine and maple. It is these forests that have offered sanctuary to the recovering populations of protected animals. In 1969 there were an estimated 60 bears, seven wolves, 150 chamois, and no trace of lynx in the park. Today there are thought to be around 40+ bears, 60 wolves, 600 chamois and 10 lynx living wild within the park. Numerous other animals have also spread into neighbouring parks and reserves.

PLANNING
Maps

The park-produced 1:25,000 *Monti Marsicani* is the best walking map for the area.

Books

Stefano Ardito's *A Piedi Nel Parco D'Abruzzo* (available in Italian only) details over 30 walks of varying difficulty within the park.

Information Sources

For further information contact the **park headquarters** (Ente Parco Nazionale d'Abruzzo; ☎ 0863 9 11 31; www.parco abruzzo.it; Viale Santa Lucia, 67032 Pescasseroli).

Permits & Regulations

To protect the environment, it is forbidden to leave marked paths within the park. Picking flowers, damaging vegetation, dropping litter or making excessive noise are also forbidden. Camping and campfires are permitted in designated areas only.

Rifugi

The *rifugi* in the park are locked; contact the **park office** (☎ 0863 9 19 55) to obtain access to park-controlled huts. Facilities are minimal.

ACCESS TOWN

Slap bang in the middle of the park, the small town of Pescasseroli (p244) has plenty of decent sleeping and eating options and acts as the official park headquarters.

ABOVE PESCASSEROLI

Duration 2½–3 hours
Distance 8km
Difficulty easy–moderate
Start/Finish Pescasseroli (p244)
Transport bus
Summary A easy stroll around and above the town of Pescasseroli, through pasture and woodland, to the remains of an 11th-century castle.

A good practice run for the Rocca Ridge hike, or a soft initiation to the Abruzzo area for the less athletically inclined; this short circuit above the national-park hub of Pescasseroli visits a ruined castle and provides excellent views over the town and the surrounding countryside.

There are a couple of ups and downs – as should be expected in a mountainous region – but no major obstacles, and you should have plenty of time to explore the streets of the small town afterwards.

PLANNING
When to Walk

Keeping to the lower hills around Pescasseroli this walk is usually good from May to October.

Maps

Use the park-produced 1:25,000 *Monti Mariscani*.

GETTING TO/FROM THE WALK

The hike starts from the centre of Pescasseroli. For getting there and away details see p244.

THE WALK

From the main square in Pescasseroli follow Via della Chiesa north. After kinking to the left, the street straightens out, heading northeast. Just before you reach the impressive **Chiesa Parrocchiale** (worth a quick detour) turn sharp left up a small alley with steps labelled 'Salita Dott. Ciolli'. The alley almost immediately joins a paved road; turn left here and then right into Via Castello. Follow the paved road out of town

as it bends around to the left. Various **Stations of the Cross** are on the right, with terracotta rooftops of Pescasseroli materialise on the left. After passing a walled cemetery, the road dead-ends. Go through a gate in the fence and cut diagonally down a steep bank to join a track below next to a cattle trough. Follow this track west, away from the town. Within five minutes, bear right off the main track on a fainter path marked by a fence on its right. When the fence runs out after about 100m so does the path, and you'll need to cut diagonally across a sloping pasture to pick it up again in front of some trees on the opposite side.

Once found, the path is clear and marked by orange paint splashed onto rocks and trees. Progressing uphill, the path parallels the edge of the meadow before turning right at a junction just before a river

PARCO NAZIONALE D' ABRUZZO

| 1 | Above Pescasseroli | p239 |
| 2 | Rocca Ridge | p241 |

CENTRAL APENNINES

gulley and bridge (don't cross the bridge). The path now steepens and plunges into the forest, zigzagging up the slope. At the first fork, veer left and continue uphill. At the second, turn right and start to traverse the slope on a straighter, narrower path. Within 500m this path joins a much wider one; turn right and enjoy the flatter terrain and splendid views of Pescasseroli and the Abruzzo Park below. Before long you'll reach the splayed castle ruins spread over a surprisingly large area. The **Castel Mancino** was built in the 10th and 11th centuries during the Logobard era in an almost impregnable position on the crags above town. After falling into disuse, it was pillaged for stone in the mid-19th century. Pines that had grown up around the castle were cut down in the 1920s resulting in some weather-inflicted damage, but the spooky remains are still strangely evocative. A fairly clear path zigzags down steeply through the ruins before re-entering the forest and emerging by the Stations of the Cross on the Via Castelo just above Pescasseroli. Turn left here, and retrace your steps to the main square.

ROCCA RIDGE

Duration 6–7 hours
Distance 19.5km
Difficulty moderate
Start/Finish Pescasseroli (p244)
Transport bus

Summary Pristine beech woodland and a limestone-studded mountain ridge offer a flavour of the typical landscape of this beautiful national park.

Rocca Ridge dominates the skyline as you look west from Pescasseroli, with the summit of La Rocca (1924m) providing the highest point. The ridge is very accessible from the town, and offers one of the most beautiful and convenient walks in the park. This circuit passes through fine beech woodland on its way to the limestone heights (775m ascent), although the descent leads down through ski runs and lacks the same wilderness atmosphere. Views from the ridge are wonderful, and it is worth keeping an eye open for bears in the forested valleys below.

PLANNING
When to Walk

The area should be clear of snow between June and October. The ridge section of the walk is exposed to the elements and has few escape routes; avoid walking in high winds or if lightning is a possibility.

What to Bring

Water is available from the spring below the Rifugio della Difesa, but not anywhere else on the walk; make sure to bring enough.

Maps

Use the park-produced 1:25,000 *Monti Mariscani*.

GETTING TO/FROM THE WALK

See Getting There and Away details for Pescasseroli, p244.

THE WALK

From the town hall in the centre of Pescasseroli, walk south along the Viale S Lucia and continue over a crossroads onto the Via Fonte Fracassi. This leads to a fork in the road at a prominent hotel – follow the road to the right. The pavement soon ends and the road becomes a gravel track, leading to a spring below the park-owned **Rifugio della Difesa**. This is the official start of the route, around 3km from the town centre.

A painted sign indicates the start of path C3, which leads left off the track at the spring and climbs past the *rifugio*. The route is well marked with red and white paint splashes as it climbs up the Valle Mancina. After approximately 45 minutes the path mounts a steep, rocky section and meets the gravel track again. Cross the track, passing a roofed plaque in a clearing, before plunging back into the trees.

The gravel track is crossed several more times before steeper terrain forces the path into a series of tight switchbacks. These lead to the edge of the forest, where the picturesque **Santa Maria di Monte Tranquillo church** (1600m) stands on a bluff. This is the end of the gravel road, but a faint farm track continues up open hillside ahead. Follow this and climb beneath the northern slopes of Monte Tranquillo. Pass **Rifugio di Monte Tranquillo**, a privately owned hut in a hollow, and continue up the rocky slope to join the ridge itself.

CENTRAL APENNINES

The ridge marks a junction of paths; turn right (northeast) to follow path C5 along the ridge line. A variety of paint colours are apparent on the rocks – a black 'A' on a yellow background prominent among them. The route soon drops down to the east to skirt around a small copse before returning to the ridge at a saddle. The ridge line is now followed for 5km. If you lose the path among the limestone outcrops, return to the ridge and continue uphill, and you will soon pick it up.

The first cairn, around 1km onto the ridge, marks the summit of **Monte Pietroso** (1876m) From here the path continues to climb to the large pile of stones at the top of **La Rocca** (1924m), reached around three hours from the start. The views from here are panoramic – craggy ridges and forested valleys fall steeply on either side, with Pescasseroli visible far below to the east.

The ridge narrows to the north of La Rocca but the path is better defined, and the terrain is largely level as the path either follows the ridge top or contours just below it. The **Rifugio di Lorio** soon becomes visible on the ridge to the north, and is reached around an hour from La Rocca. Continue along the ridge past this *rifugio* for around 150m, before dropping down to the right (east) on a stone path that zigzags down to the forest below. Turn right beside a painted rock in a clearing, and a red B4 on a tree trunk will soon confirm that you are on the right descent route.

Around 1km later the forest path joins a vehicle track (B1); turn right here and descend past two ski tows. A gate that may be closed across the track can easily be skirted on the left, and it is then a straightforward (if not overly scenic) descent to join the paved road just north of Camping La Panoramica. Turn right along the road and follow it to a roundabout, taking the second left along the Viale Colli dell'Oro. This will lead back to the Viale S Lucia and the centre of Pescasseroli.

MORE WALKS

PARCO NAZIONALE DEI MONTI SIBILLINI
Valle Lago di Pilato
This route follows a long and beautiful valley to the Lago di Pilato, a picturesque lake

in the basin beneath Monte Vettore, the highest mountain in the range. It can be walked as a 5½ hour, 12km, out-and-back excursion from the village of Foce (the path begins where the road ends, around 7km southwest of Montemonaco). This option involves 995m of ascent but is well worth it. Alternatively the valley walk can be linked with the Monte Vettore walk (p229). Begin at Foce and continue south from the Lago di Pilato to join up with the Monte Vettore route at Rifugio Tita Zilioli. This option lends itself to a two-day excursion with an overnight stay at the *rifugio*. Use the CAI's 1:25,000 *Parco Nazionale dei Monti Sibillini*.

PARCO NAZIONALE DEL GRAN SASSO E MONTI DELLA LAGA
Salinello Gorges
In the northeastern corner of the Gran Sasso-Laga national park, the Salinello Gorges are one of its most spectacular areas, and a designated nature reserve. The walk starts and finishes at the enchanting little monastery of Grotte Sant'Angelo, a shrine in a cave that has been used for various religious purposes since prehistoric times. Access the monastery parking area via a signed gravel road from Le Ripe (around 7km southwest of Civitella del Tronto). This is an out-and-back route along a marked path, and you can turn round at any stage. Make sure you walk as far as the ruins of Castel Manfrino for a wonderful viewpoint over the gorges. The northern sheet of Selca's 1:50,000 *Parco Nazionale del Gran Sasso e Monti della Laga* covers the area, though is not strictly necessary in order to complete the walk.

Vallone delle Cornacchie & Rifugio Franchetti
This route offers two options for walkers of varying abilities. Both begin from Piano del Laghetto, 4km east of Prati di Tivo at the end of the paved road. An easy excursion leads to the spectacularly situated **Rifugio Franchetti** (☎ 0861 95 46 34; dm €20). Head south along the ridge-line path, pass the cable car-station (closed since 1997), and keep to the left to pass through the rocky Vallone delle Cornacchie (Crow's Valley) to reach the *rifugio*. Allow five hours for the return trip, which involves 800m of ascent. A longer A-to-B excursion suitable for those with basic scrambling experience

is also possible. Continue south from the *rifugio*, keeping left then right at trail junctions, to join up with the path described in the Corno Grande walk (p233). The end of this walk will be Campo Imperatore. Use the CAI's 1:25,000 *Gran Sasso d'Italia*.

PARCO NAZIONALE DELLA MAJELLA
Valle di Santo Spirito Gorge
The most dramatic gorge accessible to walkers in the Majella chain, a trip up the Santo Spirito Valley can also be the first part of an extended mountain circuit. A parking area at the south of Fara San Martino (around 36km south of Pretoro, on the eastern edge of the national park) is the start and finish for both walk options. The 8.5km round trip from the parking area to the path junction at the top of the gorge involves around 600m of ascent and takes around 2½ hours. A more adventurous alternative to retracing your steps from the top of the gorge is to turn right at the trail junction and climb the ridge to the north, returning along the ridge line to Fara San Martino (4½ to five hours). Use the CAI's 1:25,000 *Gruppo della Majella*.

TOWNS & FACILITIES

L'AQUILA
☎ 0862 / pop 68,500
Picking itself up after the devastating April 2009 earthquake (see box, p225), L'Aquila may or may not be fully operational when you visit. Check ahead.

Information
The main **tourist office** (☎ 2 23 06; Via XX Settembre 8; 9am-1pm & 3-6pm Mon-Sat, 9am-1pm Sun) can provide good regional information.

Sleeping & Eating
Residence Azzurro (☎ 3 48 21; Via G di Vincenzo cnr Via Corrado; d/ste €80/110) is a little bit out of the centre, but is near the train station and has some excellent rooms and apartments, plus its own restaurant.
   Hotel San Michele (☎ 42 02 60; www .stmichelehotel.it; Via del Giardini 6; s/d €55/75) is another option.

Try elegant **Pasticceria Fratelli Nurzia** (☎ 2 10 02; Piazza del Duomo 74) for a coffee and snack.
   La Matriciana (☎ 2 60 65; Via Arcivescovado 5a; meals €20; Mon-Sat) is a no-frills trattoria with robust red wines and *al dente* pasta.

Getting There & Away
ARPA (☎ 199 166 952; www.arpaonline.it) buses run regular services to Rome's Stazione Tiburtina (€9.10, 1¾ hours, 19 daily) and Sulmona (€4.50, 1½ hours, nine daily). For Pescasseroli, change buses in Avezzano.
   By car, L'Aquila is 110km from Rome along the A24 autostrada. The SS17 connects with Sulmona.

MONTEMONACO
☎ 0736 / pop 700
On the eastern boundary of the Parco Nazionale dei Monti Sibillini, Montemonaco (1080m) is a picturesque hilltop village that receives a surprising number of visitors during the summer.

Information
The **park office** (☎ 85 64 62; Via Roma) is in the centre of the village, while maps and guidebooks for the area are available from both the general store and the *alimentari* in the main square. The nearest petrol station is 8km to the north in Montefortino.

Sleeping & Eating
In the centre of the village is **Albergo Sibilla** (☎ 85 61 44; Via Roma 52; r from €40.) The **Albergo Carlini** (☎ 85 61 27; Via Roma 18; r from €50) is nearby. Both include breakfast.
   About 4km north of Montemonaco towards Montefortino (along the road signed to Amandola) is **Camping Montespino** (☎ 85 92 38; adult/tent (€4.15/6.50). The bus service from Rome to Amandola (see p244) passes this camping ground.
   The CAI-run **Rifugio Sibilla** (☎ 85 64 22; dm €20) is around 5km northwest of town, up a steep gravel road, just off the road to Isola S Biagio.
   Almost all the hotels in Montemonaco have restaurants offering evening meals including **La Scampagnata** (☎ 85 63 92; www.lascampagnata.it; Via Don Settimio Vallorano) with *tagliatelle alla Mussolini* and wild-boar casserole.

Getting There & Away

Montemonaco is reasonably well served by buses. **START** (☎ 0734 22 99 03) buses run from Rome to Amandola via Montemonaco (four hours and 10 minutes, two a day). **Mazzuca** (☎ 40 22 67; www.mazzuca .it) buses travel to Ascoli Piceno (five a day), from where there are train connections to Rome (€20-40, 5½ hours), L'Aquila (€10.50, 4½ hours) and Pescara (€4.60, 1½ hours) on the east coast.

PESCASSEROLI

☎ 0863 / pop 2100

Right in the centre of the Parco Nazionale d'Abruzzo, the red-roofed town of Pescasseroli has the open, airy feel of a large village. Narrow streets and medieval churches suggest a rich history, but the lure of the wilderness is never far away.

Information

The **tourist office** (☎ 91 04 61; Via Principe di Napoli; 9am-1pm & 4-7pm in summer) is friendly and helpful, while the **Centro di Visita** (☎ 911 32 21; Viale Colli d'Oro; 10am-7.30pm) has a small museum and zoo.

Supplies & Equipment

There are plenty of *alimentari* and general stores in the town centre, though walking and camping supplies are limited.

Sleeping & Eating

There are five camping grounds near Pescasseroli. **Campeggio dell'Orso** (☎ 919 55; two people with tent €11.35), 1km along the road to Opi, is the cheapest. Someone comes to collect the fees each evening.

Pensione Al Castello (☎ 91 07 57; www .pensionecastello.it; Viale D'Annunzio 1; r €46-60, half-board per person €40-60) just off the main square is one of the cheapest of the numerous hotels in town.

Pizzeria San Francisco (☎ 91 06 50; Via Isonzo 1) is recommended locally for the treats that appear from its traditional wood oven.

Getting There & Away

Pescasseroli is well served by buses. **ARPA** (☎ 2 65 61) runs to and from Avezzano (€4.70, 1¼ hours, six a day), from where there are frequent bus and train connections to Rome, L'Aquila and Pescara. Buses to Castel di Sangro (€3.60, 1¼ hours) connect to Sulmona (see below).

By car, Pescasseroli is 142km from Pescara and 160km from Rome via the A24/ A25 and then the S83 south.

SULMONA

☎ 0864 / pop 25,300

Birthplace of Roman poet Ovid (43 BC–AD 18), Sulmona's historic centre retains more vestiges from the Middle Ages than the era of Caligula and Julius Caesar. Complementing its beguiling history are the Apennines mountains brooding in the east overlaid by the expansive Parco Nazionale della Majella.

Information

The **tourist office** (☎ 5 32 76; www.abruzzo turismo.it; Corso Ovidio 208; 9am-1pm & 4-7pm Mon-Fri, 9am-1pm Sun) has all the local information and some facts on Parco Nazionale della Majella.

Sleeping & Eating

B&B Case Bonomini (☎ 5 23 08; www.bed andbreakfastcasebonomini.com; Via Quatrario 71; s €25-30, d €50-70) Down a back street in the city centre, this mini-apartment is a modest place with pleasant decor and a fully equipped kitchen.

Albergo Ristorante Stella (☎ 5 26 53; www.hasr.it; Via Panfilo Mazara 18; s €40-50, d €70-80) A modern three-star in the town centre that boasts a smart ground-floor wine bar–restaurant (lunch €14) and can organise bike and car hire.

For eating try **La Cantina di Biffi** (☎ 3 20 25; Via Barbato 1; meals €20; closed Sun afternoon and Mon), just off Corso Ovidio with homemade food and local wine.

Getting There & Away

ARPA (☎ 199 166952; www.arpaonline.it) buses go to/from L'Aquila (€5.50, 1½ hours, nine daily), and Pescara on the east coast (€5.50, one hour, nine daily); SATAM buses go directly to Naples (€15, 2½ hours).

Trains link with L'Aquila (€3.90, one hour, 11 daily), Pescara (€3.90, 1¼ hours, 17 daily), Rome (€8.80, 2½ hours, seven daily) and Campo di Giove (€2.70, 25 minutes).

By car, Sulmona is just off the A25 autostrada. From L'Aquila follow the SS17 south.

Campania

HIGHLIGHTS

- Climbing to the top of volatile **Vesuvius** (p247) and looking down into its dangerously silent crater
- Feeling like Jupiter above the Amalfi rooftops as you tackle the magnificent **Sentiero degli Dei** (Path of the Gods, p253)
- Watching the evening sun slant obliquely through the cypress trees in the wonderfully peaceful **Valle delle Ferriere** (p256)
- Gazing in the exotic shores of the island of Capri from the grass-coasted tip of the **Sorrento peninsula** (p258)

Signature food: Pizza margherita	Celebrated native: Enrico Caruso (opera singer)	Famous for... Vespas

Looked at through the prism of its often-frenetic tourist industry, Italy's most densely populated region can sometimes feel more like a human zoo than a temple to history and art. But the outward mayhem belies a curious inner calm. Away from the gelato-toting tourists, Campania hides a parallel universe of ancient footpaths and deserted trails glimmering like a Botticelli masterpiece across a not-too-distant horizon.

The Amalfi coast is Campania's crowning glory, an irresistible melange of jaw-dropping vistas and steep cliffside trails that will raise your pulse in more ways than one. A Unesco World Heritage site of ancient coastal communities, the region is eerily reminiscent of Cinque Terre in Liguria, but with the temperature turned up 5°C and an even higher quota of fashionistas and sports cars.

To the west lies the glittering Sorrento peninsula where dandy aristocrats once traded poetic stanzas over post-dinner glasses of *limoncello*, while to the east legendary SITA coaches carry passengers on white-knuckle bus rides between the splayed cliffside towns. Omnipresent in almost every Neapolitan view is the volatile hulk of Mt Vesuvius, the glowering volcano that buried Roman Pompeii and still threatens to wreak significant damage to the blemished but beautiful city of Naples.

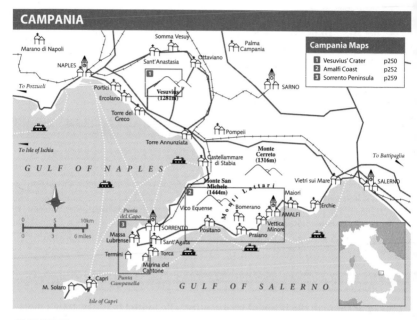

CLIMATE

Hot, dry summers and cool, damp winters define Campania's Mediterranean climate, a pattern produced mainly by the movement of Atlantic weather fronts. In summer, the few fronts that approach the western Mediterranean are pushed north and south by a subtropical anticyclone anchored near the Azores.

Rainfall between June and September is minimal. Long hours of sunshine are the norm and temperatures are high (25°C upwards). The sirocco, a hot wind from North Africa, can make life uncomfortable by bringing humid and overcast conditions to already very warm days.

From September to November, lurking Atlantic depressions bring changeable and cloudy, though still mild (around 10°C) weather. Rainfall comes in short sharp showers. The year's rainfall is confined to about 100 days, with a total fall of 1000mm along the coast and up to 1500mm inland.

PLANNING
When to Walk

September to mid-May is the ideal time, when the area is relatively uncrowded and cooler weather makes walking less like a sojourn through the Sahara; from early March until May the displays of wildflowers are superb. From mid-June to the end of August, the area is overflowing with visitors and getting about becomes something of an endurance test.

What to Bring

Sunscreen and a shady hat are absolutely essential from April onwards. A 1.5L water bottle is indispensable; surface water is virtually nonexistent away from the towns and villages, where you'll find fountains and bars. If you're planning to camp, bring plenty of fuel for your stove; there are no reliable local sources.

Maps

Touring Club Italiano's (TCI's) 1:200,000 *Campania–Basilicata* map is ideal for helping you find your way about. See Planning for each walk for details of specific map requirements.

Emergency

In Campania's mountainous areas contact the **mountain rescue service** (☎ 081 551 59 50). For medical assistance call the **national emergency** number (☎ 118).

GETTING THERE & AROUND

With Naples as its gateway, Campania has excellent connections with the rest of Italy, be it by bus, train or road. Inside the region itself trains will get you to Vesuvius, Sorrento and Salerno, while the famous SITA buses connect along the winding Amalfi coastline.

GATEWAY

The best gateway for these walks is regional capital and Italy's third-largest city, Naples (see p262)

VESUVIUS

Of all the volcanoes on the planet, Vesuvius (1281m) is probably the best known. It made history when it erupted in AD 79 and in two days wiped out the Roman settlements of Pompeii, Herculaneum, Stabia and Oplontis. Today it sits amid one of the most densely populated urban sprawls in Italy. About 600,000 people live within a 10km radius of the crater, and that doesn't include the population of the city of Naples.

In the midst of this teeming Mediterranean chaos, the only oases of nature left intact are the slopes of the volcano itself and those of the adjacent Monte Somma (1132m). Between these two peaks is the enchanting Valle del Gigante (Valley of the Giant), where the pioneer vegetation has to recolonise the fertile volcanic ash after every eruption.

In 1995, the Parco Nazionale del Vesuvio was created, partly to protect against illegal building and poaching. Access to the remotest southern parts of the protected area, the Riserva Tirone-Alto Vesuvio, is restricted.

HISTORY

Europe was astonished when, by chance, the first traces of the buried city of Pompeii were uncovered. In 1748, the king of Naples, Charles of Bourbon, began the excavations which, even today, continue to yield surprises. The terrible eruption took place on 24 August AD 79, obliterating Pompeii, Herculaneum, Stabia and Oplontis under a 5m-thick layer of ash and stone. It is believed that 2000 people died in Pompeii and Herculaneum.

The most illustrious victim was Pliny the Elder, commander of the Roman fleet stationed at Porto Miseno. Pliny was a passionate naturalist and it is said that, while

---

VESUVIUS & POMPEII

In AD 79, 24 August was a perfectly normal day for the citizens of Pompeii – or so it seemed. People went about their daily business in their usual carefree manner: a visit to the market; a rendezvous at the local baths, morning prayers in the temple. In the hours before the explosion, few had an inkling of the chaos to come. And then what began as a distant rumble on brooding Mt Vesuvius grew into a frightening roar; and then, quite suddenly, all hell broke loose.

The eruption of Vesuvius in that engulfed the settlement of Pompeii (and its near neighbour, Herculaneum) left the city – quite literally – frozen in time. But, what was a catastrophe for the unfortunate citizens of a thriving Roman settlement has provided modern generations with an almost perfect snapshot of everyday Italian life in the years immediately after the life of Christ.

Covered in mountains of ash 12 layers thick; Pompeii lay buried and forgotten for almost 17 centuries. It wasn't until 1748 that the first serious excavations began under the auspices of Swiss architect Karl Weber.

In the two millennia since, the destructive power of Vesuvius has unleashed itself on numerous occasions. The most recent activity was in 1944 when a sizeable eruption buried 88 US B-25 bombers based near Allied-occupied Naples during WWII.

Vesuvius, along with Mt Etna, has been designated a Decade Volcano by the UN, a group of 16 volatile volcanoes worldwide that are subject to special study by scientists due to their destructive capabilities and proximity to dense population centres. One in a trio of active Italian volcanoes (the other two are Etna and Stromboli in the south), Vesuvius is also considered to be one of the world's most dangerous, due to the proximity of over three million Neapolitans who live precariously in its fall-out zone.

carrying out rescue operations along the coast, his curiosity took him too close to the cataclysm.

After a long period of dormancy, another powerful eruption let loose on 16 December 1631. Massa, Somma and Bosco were destroyed. The event reverberated throughout Europe, and Vesuvius, with its smoking peak, became the hallmark of the Neapolitan landscape in prints and paintings of the era. In the second half of the 18th century, Naples, Vesuvius and Pompeii were obligatory destinations on the Italian Grand Tour.

From that day to this, the list of illustrious visitors has grown. To name a few: Montesquieu, Casanova, Mozart, Goethe, Shelley, Hans Christian Andersen, Dickens, Mark Twain, Anton Chekhov and Walter Benjamin. The most well-to-do visitors went up with guides and porters on mules or horseback to the Atrio del Cavallo, from where they continued on foot. The laziest were carried up on sedans to the edge of the crater. Those who found the courage climbed down inside the crater, which is no longer permitted. In 1848, King Ferdinand II had the Osservatorio Vesuviano (Vesuvius Observatory), the first vulcanological observatory in the world, built.

ENVIRONMENT

Vesuvius began to form about 300,000 years ago. The great crater of Monte Somma formed first – ending its activity in ancient times with the collapse of its summit caldera. Inside the depression created by the collapse, Vesuvius began to grow, with its startling crater 500m in diameter and 230m deep. Vesuvius is part of a vast volcanic area that includes the Campi Flegrei (Phlegraean Fields) west of Naples with the adjacent crater lakes of Averno, Fusaro and Miseno, and beyond, the islands of Ischia, Procida and Vivara.

Vesuvius last erupted in 1944, as Naples struggled to recover from the devastation of WWII. A relatively modest eruption generated lava flow in the Atrio del Cavallo, visible from the road that comes up from Ercolano.

Eruptions have destroyed the vegetation on Vesuvius more than once. Regeneration begins immediately after the lava cools with a silvery-grey lichen, which gives colour to the dark, gloomy lava. After a few decades come robust small Mediterranean plants, among them dock and poppies. Then the *ginestre* (broom) arrives, with its brilliant yellow June flowers. Growing in the midst of the broom are artemesia, helychrisum and red valerian, and in the late spring they all bloom together in a riotous perfumed technicolour mix.

Reforestation in this century has accelerated the comeback of the wooded areas. There are holm oaks, cluster pines, aleppo pines and, in the Valle del Gigante, clusters of locust trees and silver birch.

Groups of harmless stray dogs hang around the parking area at 1000m. In the park there are foxes, weasels and martens, which probably find food in the outskirts of the towns since only the little dormouse and its relatives the *topo quercino* and *moscardino* remain. Many bird species pass through during migration, including buzzards, kestrels, owls, turtledoves, quails, cuckoos, whippoorwills, golden orioles and many others. A colony of ravens is stationed on Monte Somma where red woodpeckers nest as well, along with tawny owls, wrynecks, tomtits and robin redbreasts.

Among reptiles are two innocuous serpents: the black coluber on the warm slopes of Vesuvius and the robust cervone on Monte Somma. Poisonous vipers may also be encountered in the rocky areas of Valle del Gigante.

PLANNING
When to Walk

The hottest months, July and August, are to be avoided. In spring there is the added spectacle of the wildflowers. In winter Vesuvius is less crowded, and offers frequent sunny days; and the special clearness of the winter skies allows great views.

What to Bring

A compass and altimeter are a good idea in case of fog. At the crater (approximately 1200m), temperatures are lower than at the base of the mountain and there can be strong winds, so bring the appropriate gear. Bring your own supply of water (although a kiosk sells drinks at the summit).

Maps

The walk is very straightforward and barely needs a map for orientation. You can get a good overview of the mountain with the Freytag & Berndt 1:50,000 *Bay of Naples*. The information point on the road leading to the Quota 1000 car park from Ercolano sells a schematic map of the park at 1:20,000 that shows the main trails.

Information Sources

The **Ente Parco Nazionale del Vesuvio** (☎ 081 771 09 11; www.parks.it/parco .nazionale.vesuvio; Via Palazzo del Principe, Ottaviano; Mon-Fri) is a good source of park information. More information is available on www.parconazionaledelvesuvio .it. There is also an information point along the road that heads up to the Quota 1000 car park from Ercolano.

ACCESS TOWN

Vesuvius is easily done as a day trip from the regional gateway of Naples (p262).

VESUVIUS' CRATER

Duration 2 hours
Distance 3km
Difficulty easy–moderate
Start/Finish Quota 1000 car park
Nearest Town Naples (p262)
Transport bus, taxi
Summary An well-trodden loop around the crater's summit slopes with unforgettable views into the volcanic abyss on one side and over the enchanting Gulf of Naples on the other.

Anti-social walkers beware. The climb up Vesuvio is the busiest and most commercialised hike in Italy. Fortunately, the magnitude of what you witness just about makes up for the aggravation of squeezing past hordes of panting, sweating, flip-flop-wearing humanity, some of whom clearly assumed that their car would take them all the way to the top. It nearly does. The Quota 1000 car park at 1000m is only 281m below Vesuvius' modern summit necessitating a 860m steep and stony dash to the rim of the gaping crater. These days the trail is enclosed by wooden fences and enterprising locals will rent you a walking stick at the base. There are the predictable cache of tourist huts on the rim but, my word, the view!

WARNING

Vesuvius is under constant monitoring by seismologists at the **Osservatorio Vesuviano** (Vesuvius Observatory; ☎ 081 610 84 83; www.ov.ingv.it; Via Diocleziano 328), a few kilometres west of the crater. Sooner or later there will be another memorable eruption. You climb Vesuvius at your own risk, particularly if you plan to go to the crater. Those who wish to be reassured personally by vulcanologists may contact the Osservatorio.

Also watch out for vipers and, on a lighter note, illegal taxi drivers.

GETTING TO/FROM THE WALK

The easiest way to get from central Naples to Vesuvius is by train. **Circumvesuviana** (☎ 081 772 24 44; www.vesuviana.it) runs trains connecting Naples and Sorrento (every 20 minutes). They leave from the station on Corso Garibaldi which is interconnected with the Stazione Centrale (take the underpass). You can disembark at Ercolano or Pompeii.

From Ercolano there are only two buses, departing from Via Panoramica (about 50m from the train station) at 8.25am and 12.45pm and returning at 2.40pm and 5.25pm. Return tickets, available on board, cost €7.80 for the 90-minute round trip. Avoid the so-called minibuses outside the station. They offer poor customer service and only wait 90 minutes at the Quota 1000 car park.

From Pompeii up to the crater car park, **Vesuviana Mobilità** (☎ 081 963 44 20) operates eight (10 in summer) return-trip buses daily from Piazza Anfiteatro. Journey time is one hour each way and return tickets cost €8.90.

By car, exit the A3 at Ercolano Portico and follow signs for the Parco Nazionale del Vesuvio.

THE WALK

Ascend in a southwesterly direction from the Quota 1000 car park. The path switchbacks after a couple of hundred metres and then climbs steadily at an average gradient of 14% towards the crater rim (860m; 15 to 25 minutes from the start). The going underfoot is stony but not difficult (you

CAMPANIA

VESUVIUS' CRATER

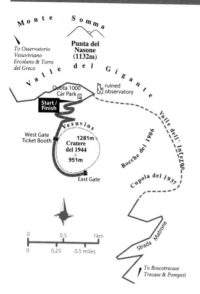

can usually hire a walking stick at the bottom) and the path itself is well marked and heavily trafficked all day long. There are a handful of wooden structures on the crater rim selling overpriced drinks and tourist tattle. At the time of writing you could only follow the crater path for half of its circumference, up to the East Gate where a barrier prevents further access. Take your time up here to soak up the enormity of what lies beneath you. If the clouds part, the views are stupendous. Descend by the same route you came up. Entrance to the crater rim costs adult/child €6.50/4.50. The whole area is a bit of a tourist trap; to avoid rip-offs it's better to carry your own drinks.

AMALFI COAST

Great beauty rarely goes unnoticed; hence the Amalfi coast's ranking as one of the premier glamour spots in Italy's much fêted gallery of must-sees. Throughout history, everyone from inspiration-seeking writers to romantic honeymooners has flocked to these exotic shores, lured by a combination of dramatic scenery and stylish Italian pizzazz. As a result, the Amalfi's narrow coastal strip can sometimes seem more like a crowded football stadium than a charming retreat. Clamouring for elbow room in the region's small medieval towns, casual day-trippers chomp on gelati while big spenders with fat wallets parade their sports cars through streets more renowned for their traffic jams than their tranquility.

For aspiring hikers, the best way to escape the mayhem is to rise above it – quite literally – into the colourful hills that tower over the tightly packed coastal settlements of Ravello and Positano. Access to this hallowed terrain is gained via a series of steep interconnecting staircases which, while physically taxing, are well worth the energy expenditure. Perched 400 vertical metres above sea level, it's not just the vistas that are amplified – there's more breathing space too. For every 100 people you bump into in Amalfi town there are mere handfuls up here, hiking on well-marked, ancient paths that criss-cross the seemingly impregnable hillsides.

Bathed in balmy Mediterranean sunlight, the bird's-eye views from the assorted *sentieri* (paths) are astounding. Steep farmed terraces cascade down towards small somnolent village piazzas that glow like great works of art in the late evening sun. Listen carefully and you'll catch a faintly audible accompanying soundtrack: goats braying, the distant clang of a church bell, and the omnipresent breeze rustling gently through the elegant cypresses and gnarly olive trees.

ENVIRONMENT

From the coast between Amalfi and Atrani deep valleys cut back towards the spine of the Monti Lattari Range. Here the small Riserva Statale Valle delle Ferriere protects plants usually found in Africa and South America. Everywhere lush woodlands and dense vegetation of the valleys, especially the beautiful, slender Italian cypresses, contrast with the open, sparsely vegetated slopes above.

Massed pink and white rock roses are the most colourful of the wildflowers, and orchids are plentiful.

PLANNING

When to Walk

With its mild winter temperatures, walking is possible in the Amalfi year-round. To avoid stifling heat and heaving crowds (in the towns at least) you may want to avoid the peak summer months of June, July and August.

Maps

The Kompass 1:50,000 map No 682 *Penisola Sorrentina* is helpful for planning purposes only. It includes town maps plus notes about the area's attractions in English, French, German and Italian. The Club Alpino Italiano (CAI) 1:30,000 *Monti Lattari* map is far more useful than the Kompass map, but keep in mind that path numbering differs from what you'll find on the ground. The tourist offices give out some limited free maps (not always to scale).

Books

Julian Tippett's *Sorrento, Amalfi Coast and Capri* (2008) describes 20 (mostly short) walks in the area and is invaluable.

The best local source of maps and books is **Libreria** (Corso Repubbliche Marinare), a bookshop in Amalfi, not far from the bus station.

Information Sources

The Amalfi **AAST office** (☎ 089 87 11 07; www.amalfitouristoffice.it; Corso delle Repubbliche Marinare 33; 8.30am-1.30pm & 3-5.15pm Mon-Fri, 8.30am-noon Sat, to 7.15pm Mon-Fri Jul & Aug) has limited facilities – an accommodation guide is of some use.

The helpful Positano AST (p263) issues a local accommodation list and town map.

GETTING THERE & AROUND

A convenient way to get around the region is by bus (see p255). A less congested but more expensive mode of transport is ferry, worth sampling just once for the views. Regular summer ferries run between Salerno, Amalfi, Positano and Sorrento (see Positano p263). There are no train lines on the coast itself.

ACCESS TOWN

For most people, Positano (p263) is love at first sight making it the obvious choice as an access town for this region's walks.

POSITANO CIRCUIT

Duration 4–5 hours
Distance 7km
Difficulty moderate
Start/Finish Positano (p263)
Transport bus
Summary A short hike that you'll want to linger over thanks to the continually stunning vistas of the Amalfi's most celebrated town nestled on the coast below.

It's easy to while away a sedative morning in Postiano, people-watching in a restful café while the shadows shorten around your coffee table. And then, suddenly it's midday and you're on to your third cappuccino, still no closer to starting that ridiculously ambitious hike that was supposed to shake you abruptly out of your early morning reverie.

The Positano circuit is a half-day hike for procrastinating culture vultures in need of some boisterous afternoon exercise. The hike's 'moderate' tag comes on account of the stone steps – of which there are many – that take you high above the picturesque Amalfi town for bird's-eye views that will linger long on your retinas. If you manage to catch an early start you may want to extend the walk east on the Sentiero degli Dei walk (p253) by turning left rather than right when you reach the Nocelle Road (p252).

GETTING TO/FROM THE WALK

For getting there and away information for Positano, see p263. To avoid the climb up to the Bar Internazionale and the start of this walk, catch the town shuttle bus from the Piazza dei Mulini.

THE WALK

From the coast road at **Bar Internazionale** (☎ 089 87 54 34; Via G Marconi 306) high on the western side of Positano, go up Via Chiesa Nuova; cross the piazza in front of the church and continue along an alley before turning right up steps to a road. Cross it and ascend the steps just to the left. Thus starts a long, but increasingly scenic grind up numerous flights of steps to the Santa Maria del Castello chapel. About 45 minutes in you'll see a hut and a pylon to the right of the zigzagging path. Twenty minutes further on the path delivers you to the foot of towering cliffs and then up to the edge of the plateau above. Near a small plateau on the right, the path swings left through grass and towards a house. Bear right beside another pylon to a minor road and follow it straight on (following a CAI sign) to a crossroads and turn right. About 200m along you reach a minor road on the right leading to church of **Santa Maria del Castello** (1¼ hours from Positano).

Turn left along the main road, soon passing a bar on the right (a good refreshment stop). Follow the road for 450m from Santa Maria to a concrete road on the right, with signs to the Sentiero degli Dei, Path No 29 and CAI's Path No 00. This short road leads to a path passing above gardens and into beautiful Italian cypress groves, then winding spectacularly around the mountainside. At a fork veer right, and then right again just above an old stone building known as the **Caserma Forestale** (one hour from Santa Maria). Facing south in front of the building, head east (to the left) down hundreds of steps

through cypresses, across the slope then head straight down to the Montepertuso–Nocelle road (45 minutes from Caserma Forestale).

If you want to combine this walk with the Sentiero degli Dei, turn left here and follow the route described on p253. Otherwise, turn right and walk down to **Montepertuso**. In the small piazza on the right, just past the soccer pitch, there are a bar and gelateria (nearly an hour from the Caserma Forestale). From the piazza, cross the main road and bear right down a pedestrian street (Via Pestella) keeping the large church above you. After several hundred metres, turn right at a T-junction. Turn right at the next two T-junctions and descend down steps through olive groves to a minor road on the edge of **Positano**. Follow this road around a switchback and you will quickly join the main coast road on the eastern edge of Positano. The Sponda bus stop (on the Amalfi–Sorrento bus route) is about 250m to the left (45 minutes from Montepertuso). For the town itself, cut down the stairway on the opposite side of the road and keep walking downhill.

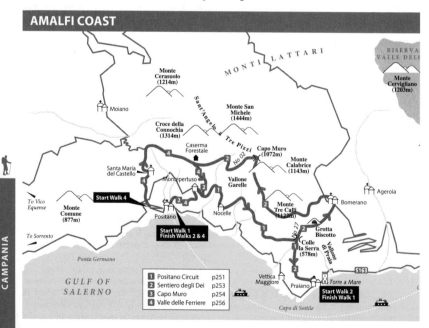

SENTIERO DEGLI DEI

Duration 5 hours
Distance 10km
Difficulty moderate
Start Positano (p263)
Finish Praiano
Transport bus

Summary One of the classic walks on the peninsula: superb paths clinging to near-vertical mountainsides with panoramic views and beautiful groves of Italian cypresses.

Sentiero degli Dei translates as 'Path of the Gods' – and this high-level coastal hike certainly has a celestial quality. The elongated variation described here veers slightly off the 'classic' route in places, but the spectacular cliffside traverse still follows the ancient path east–west from Nocelle to Colle La Serra. The excursion can be further lengthened by adding the first two-thirds of the Positano Circuit onto the start before turning left on the Nocelle road after the descent from Caserma Forestale. In this way, the walk becomes a more strenuous all-day outing.

GETTING TO/FROM THE WALK
Positano (start)

For getting there and away information for Positano, see p263.

Praiano (finish)

Praiano is served by regular SITA buses from both Positano (€1.20) and Amalfi (€1.40). They will drop you on the main road a few hundred metres below the *alimentari* and the start of this walk.

Praiano is 54km from Naples via the A3 to the Castellammare di Stabia exit, the S145 to Piano di Sorrento and the S163. From the south and east, exit from the A3 just west of Salerno and follow the S163 (37km from Salerno).

THE WALK

From Piazza dei Mulini in Positano walk east along the road to Amalfi (Via Cristoforo Colombo) for about 200m before turning left and taking a short stairway up to the main coast road (SS163). Turn left here and in 30m fork right at a sign indicating a cemetery. Go immediately right again and follow a narrower road up to a junction where you fork left. A stairway now carries you up to the vista-laden village of **Montepertuso**. Ignore another stairway going off to the left and within about 15 to 20 minutes you should reach the outer houses of the village. Turn left and proceed along the widening street (Via Pestella) with a church to your right. At the junction with the paved road, turn right and follow it up past the football pitch towards the village of Nocelle. You'll pass the Trattoria La Tagliata and soon after cross a bridge. Just past a bridge, diverge right down to a path signposted to **Nocelle**. This takes you to a lane between houses and up to Via Nocelle where you turn left. Soon you reach **Santa Croce** (☎ 089 87 53 19), a bar-trattoria where the view from the light, airy dining room makes a stop worthwhile even before you've taken a sip (30 minutes after reaching the road).

Continue along Via Nocelle to a crossroads and turn left up steps by a small shrine. Take the first right turn along a minor road which soon becomes a path. The Sentiero degli Dei stretches ahead, in places defying normal expectations of where a path can go, beneath soaring cliffs. Eventually the route passes through old

CAMPANIA

terraces (where waymarkers are scarce) and goes up past a house on the left to a wider path where there's a tap over a large water barrel (1¼ hours from Nocelle). **Colle la Serra** is about 100m up to the left.

To reach Praiano, continue downhill from the barrel, soon passing above a terrace, then continuing left across the slope (sparse markers) to long flights of steps. At a large concrete structure follow Via Colle della Serra along the base of the cliffs and across a spur – and there's **Praiano** below. Continue for another 200m then descend steps on the right, cross a road and descend more steps to a T-junction. Take a few steps left and go down Via Oratorio; swing round behind the parish museum to Piazza San Luca, where there's a bar (45 minutes from the coll). To reach the coast road, walk away from the church through a short tunnel and continue to steps on the left (Via Antica Seggio) just past a large lookout; descend to Via Umberto I. Follow this to the left, down past the *alimentari* and 20m further on go left down steps (Via San Giovanni) to a T-junction and bear left. Follow this lane around and down to steps on the right almost opposite a small shrine; these steps lead down to the coast road close to Hotel Continentale and a **bus stop**.

CAPO MURO

Duration 6½–7 hours
Distance 14km
Difficulty demanding
Start Praiano
Finish Positano (p263)
Transport bus

Summary Escape on the real high-route amid the wild limestone cliffs that rise above the teeming tourists of Positano and the more ubiquitous trekkers that frequent the Sentiero degli Dei.

The biggest physical challenge on the Amalfi coast is this non-technical high-level hike that takes you up above the more popular paths to where tourists are scant and the views resemble zoomed-out images on *Google Earth* – well almost. Despite its name, the path doesn't ascend a definitive peak, but rather a saddle on a spur known as Capo Muro. The path is relatively well marked – though pay attention

in the higher sections around the Capo – and regular SITA buses allow you to start at either end and get a lift back at the finish. The attractive town of Bomerano with its myriad cafés and bakeries makes an excellent lunch stop.

PLANNING
What to Bring
Carry enough water for the duration. Refreshments are available in Bomerano; the next watering place is Montepertuso, a few hours away.

GETTING TO/FROM THE WALK
Praiano (start)
Praiano is served by regular SITA buses from both Positano (€1.20) and Amalfi (€1.40). They will drop you on the main road a few hundred metres below the *alimentari* and the start of this walk.

Praiano is 54km from Naples via the A3 to the Castellammare di Stabia exit, the S145 to Piano di Sorrento and the S163. From the south and east, exit from the A3 just west of Salerno and follow the S163 (37km from Salerno).

Positano (finish)
For getting there and away information for Positano see p263.

THE WALK
From the Tutt Tutti *alimentari* in Praiano on a bend in Via Umberto I, walk west for a few hundred metres. Twenty-five metres past Hotel Margherita turn right up steps (Via Antica Seggio) and climb to a road. Turn right and continue to Piazza San Luca. Go round behind the large building to the left of the church, then bear left up Via Oratorio to a T-junction. Take a few steps left; then go right, up more steps. Cross a road, go under a passageway beneath some houses and climb another flight of steps. At a T-junction turn left and follow a path past a hut on the right. The path soon swings right and heads uphill with more steps. Within 15 minutes you'll skirt a garden in front of an isolated house. Beyond here turn left at a junction and climb up to another house and path intersection. Turn right up some final steps to reach **Colle la Serra** (about an hour from Praiano).

Follow the path leading north (initially left and then straight, heading slightly downhill

INCHES FROM THE ABYSS

Saucers rattle, dust flies, and a lone priest breakfasting outside an Amalfi café mutters a hurried *Hail Mary* as a bus whizzes around the corner and passes just inches from his tilted cappuccino. There's a screech on the brakes, a hoot of the horn, and then all is silent save for a scurrying cat and the breeze lilting through the bougainvillea.

Thanks to its precipitous topography, Amalfi has never benefited from a train line. Instead train passengers offloaded in Salerno in the east, or Sorrento in the west, must take their life into their hands and hire a car, or – slightly less risky – put their life into someone else's hands and hop onto one of the region's famous blue SITA buses.

For most day-trippers there's no contest. The dexterous SITA bus drivers who ply the winding roads that wrap their way around the Amalfi coast are a breed apart. Job qualifications are light on academia, but notoriously hard to master: wrought-iron nerves, an air of pervading nonchalance, and the peripheral vision of a hard-tackling Serie A footballer. Think Cristiano Ronaldo crossed with Michael Schumacher without the €50,000 weekly pay cheque.

Ten minutes into your first journey and you quickly get a preview of the cabaret to come. A coach hurtles around the corner from the opposite direction, your driver jams sharply on the brakes and suddenly, there you are, hanging just inches from the abyss, gazing nervously down at the suddenly uninviting sight of the turquoise Mediterranean, glistening 200 vertical metres below.

But nervous types needn't worry. SITA buses have an excellent safety record and experiencing the coast road's adrenalin rush on a bus rather than a car has become something of an Amalfi rite of passage. It's certainly the most efficient way of getting to and from this chapter's hikes.

---

at first) past a ruin on the left. The path contours the upper reaches of Vallone di Praia to **Grotta Biscotto**, a huge overhang sheltering disused cliff houses. Continue to a bitumen road and follow it for about 500m to rough concrete steps on the right, almost opposite a two-storey white house. Follow the steps down to a track, cross a bridge and bear left up a path which leads into the piazza in **Bomerano** (45 minutes from Colle la Serra). Here you'll find a bar-gelateria (ice-cream parlour) several *alimentari* and a bus stop for the SITA service to Amalfi.

From the piazza go along the road to the right as you face the church, then turn left along Via Iovieno. Take the first turn left, then go straight through a crossroads (now with Route No 41) and continue for about 200m as the road bends 90° to the left. Almost immediately go right off the road (no sign) on a path, tracking up some steps between gardens and terraces. Cross a minor road and up rougher steps, with trees on the right, to a second road where you turn left. There are now great views over the red roofs of Bomerano. About 800m further, faint yellow markers indicate a short cut up rough steps and rocks, across a spur and down through some rough undergrowth to rejoin the road opposite a stone building on

the left. The bitumen ends about 300m further on and a rough vehicle track continues through chestnut woodland. At a distinct fork about 10 minutes further on, turn right uphill and, following the blue (and some red-and-white) waymarkers, climb a rough path up an open, rosemary-scented spur to **Capo Muro**, a distinct saddle abutting the towering, tiered cliffs above (about 1¾ hours from Bomerano).

From the saddle, continue westwards on a better path (No 02) contouring the steep slope above Vallone Grarelle. After about 700m the path swings away from the valley and begins to descend with a wooden handrail on the left. About 500m further on, the path swings into a wide, deep valley and resumes contouring, with superb views across Positano and the awesome cliffs of Sant'Angelo a Tre Pizzi above. In places along here, dense bushes screen the rather long, steep drop to the left. Eventually you reach **Caserma Forestale**, a large stone forestry barracks (1½ hours from Capo Muro). Turn left off the main track and descend to the building.

Facing south in front of the *caserma*, head east (left) down through cypresses on hundreds of steps, then straight down to the Montepertuso–Nocelle road. Turn right and walk down to **Montepertuso**. In the small piazza on the right, just past the soccer pitch, there are a bar and gelateria (nearly one hour from the Caserma Forestale). From the piazza, cross the main road and bear right down a pedestrian street (Via Pestella), below and to the right of a large church. After several hundred metres, turn right at a T-junction. With houses on both sides, turn right at another T-junction and right again at the next. Descend through olive groves and houses to a minor road which you follow around a switchback to another road. This is the main coast road on the eastern edge of **Positano**. The Sponda bus stop (on the Amalfi to Sorrento bus route) is about 250m to the left (45 minutes from Montepertuso). For the boat or a decent cappuccino cut down the stairway opposite into the town centre.

VALLE DELLE FERRIERE

Duration 4½–5 hours
Distance 12km
Difficulty moderate
Start/Finish Atrani
Nearest Town Positano (p263)
Transport bus

Summary Traditional villages, spectacular limestone cliffs, cool oak and chestnut woodlands, waterfalls, superb coastal views, and plenty of opportunities for refreshment.

If you could stuff the most alluring aspects of the Amalfi coast into a succinct four-hour box, the stunning Valle delle Ferriere hike would surely be it. Clinging to the rugged cliffs behind the region's eponymous port town, its myriad ingredients are scenically superb. Impossibly positioned vine terraces, Eden-like vegetable gardens, blooming bougainvillea and unexpected peek-a-box glances of Byzantium churches through the clefts in the hills. Starting and finishing in Atrani (Amalfi's smaller and quieter maritime cousin) this circuitous hike can be tackled in either direction, although progressing clockwise and descending from the hills above Atrani in early evening is particularly transfixing.

ENVIRONMENT

The 455-hectare Riserva Statale Valle delle Ferriere contains vegetation and landforms that have adapted to the variations in the local microclimate. The depths of the steep-sided valley shelter a mixed woodland and on the slopes above are typical Mediterranean scrub, adapted to dry conditions and relatively poor soils. Though you'd be lucky to see them, wild boars, hares, wolves and badgers have been recorded in the area.

PLANNING
What to Bring

Although you pass watering places in Pogerola and Pontone and, perhaps, flowing streams in Valle delle Ferriere, it's wise to carry some drinking water.

GETTING TO/FROM THE WALK

Just east of Amalfi, Atrani is on the **SITA** (☎ 081 552 21 76; www.sitabus.it) bus route with a bus stop on the main road just above the main square (take the steps down). Regular buses head east (to Salerno and train connections) and west to Amalfi, Positano and Sorrento. If you're staying in Amalfi, Atrani is a 15-minute walk to the east.

THE WALK

From Piazza Umberto I in Atrani, walk along Via Campo, the narrow passage by the red post box. Turn left at a T-junction and head up the steps; turn left at house No 18, then head up more steps between houses and continue generally ahead between and under houses to a scenic path which then winds down to the main road in **Amalfi** (15 minutes from Atrani). Bear right and then first right, through one small piazza then another, from where a passage in the far left corner leads to Piazza Duomo. Leave this piazza from the left-hand side (with the Banco di Napoli on the right) and walk along Via Lorenzo d'Amalfi for 500m; pass under a long arch beneath houses and go on for 50m, then left up Via Casamare and around a bend. Soon the road ends and a steep climb up steps leads up to the piazza in **Pogerola** (where the bus stops; 40 minutes from Amalfi). Here you'll find a cocktail bar–tea room–gelateria, **Bar Sport** – a good place for drinks, and **La Capannina** a *ristorante-pizzeria*.

To continue, go back to the last few metres of the approach to the piazza and turn right along a lane (with La Capannina on the right) and go past Osteria Rispoli (a bar) on the left, following Route No 59 with

DUE CAPPUCCINI, PER FAVORE

After a week or two of savouring strong, aromatic cappuccinos (or *cappuccini*, to be linguistically correct) in the bars and cafés of Italy, you might start to wonder why American-style coffee chains ever became a global phenomenon. It's almost as if the whole country functions as an unofficial finishing school for near faultless coffee confection. From the tiniest bar at the end of the most obscure, out-of-the-way hike, to the biggest, most grandiose piazza in Rome, Italy's array of rich, warm, velvety *caffè* is guaranteed to jolt even the most reluctant of walkers out of their early morning reverie.

While the coffee plant is indigenous to Ethiopia, the method of confecting the beans has long been an Italian forte. The Espresso machine was first patented by Italian Luigi Bezzera in 1901 and, making use of the strange new contraption, the industrious Italians lost no time in creating a whole menu of delicious caffeine-derived drinks.

The proverbial coffee bar *crème de la crème* – the indulgent cappuccino – first became an Italian staple soon after WWII as an antidote to weaker, milkier café lattes. Traditionally served in a small porcelain cup to retain the heat, the drink consists of an espresso topped with warm steamy milk and sprinkled with powdered cocoa.

In contrast to the bucket-like measures you get in America, Italian cappuccinos only come in one size – small – and, although the milk is tepid, it is never served piping hot. Italians invariably drink their cappuccinos at breakfast accompanied by a sweet pastry and you'll quickly be outed as a 'tourist' if you're seen sinking one after 10am. The concept of coffee 'to go' is similarly rare. Even in busy train stations, stalwart coffee traditionalists prefer to stand three deep at the bar with one eye on the departure board than risk the ignominy of upsetting their frothy milk in a mad dash for the train.

red-and-white markers. About 150m along, fork left up steps and continue, gaining a little height and ignoring sharp turns to the left. About 10 minutes from Pogerola you merge with a rough path, which leads into woodland; soon there's a longish flight of steps to climb which brings you to a stream bed (30 minutes from Pogerola). Walk upstream a short distance to more steps; about 150m further on from the steps, the path leads through cultivated terraces then past an old stone building on the right. Swing left here into chestnut woodland, and follow the path straight (ignore any turn-offs) into the heart of Valle delle Ferriere. About 15 minutes further on, cross a stream near a waterfall. Walk up sloping rocks and back into woodland. Then descend to another stream and, further on, cross the main stream, which, with luck, will be cascading into inviting pools (an hour from Pogerola and the point where you head back south). You soon pass an old sign marking the boundary of the Valle delle Ferriere reserve and emerge into more open country.

About 45 minutes from the main stream crossing, continue ahead at a prominent path junction, along a path at the base of the cliffs, with fantastic views down to Pogerola and Amalfi. Just 15 minutes from the last junction go through a short tunnel on the far side of which the path is flanked by stone walls. Soon it crosses a spur, descends through terraces then houses and goes steeply down to the right to reach the Minuta–Scala road just below a tight bend. The bus stop is 1km north along the road.

To continue, go down to the right to **Minuta's** small piazza, continue right, past a fountain, for about 200m then bear left at a fork beneath an archway and go on to the piazza in **Pontone** where **Bar Luca** is waiting to tempt you (10 minutes from Minuta). Go through the arch left of the church and turn right down a narrow road. Descend to cross a road diagonally in the direction of a sign to Torre dello Ziro and go down past a house. About 150m from the road, turn left down steps (the path can be a little overgrown here). At a T-junction turn left, then cross a bridge, from which steps and paths lead to another junction. Go right and down, then right again on a bend; cross a small piazza in front of Ristorante Le Palme to the main road in **Atrani** – Piazza Umberto is about 250m to the left (50 minutes from Pontone).

SORRENTO PENINSULA

The relatively gentle contours of this populous peninsula contrast strikingly with the steep mountains of the Amalfi Coast. A variety of walks link the beautiful coastline with a rural hinterland of villages, terraces and olive groves. The island of Capri is omnipresent on the horizon. Convenient bus services make it easy to enjoy these walks from any one of several possible bases: Termini, Nerano or coastal Marina del Cantone (Marina).

ENVIRONMENT

A line of cliffs extending southeast from Punta Gradelle on the Gulf of Naples to Punta Germano on the Gulf of Salerno forms a clear divide between the mountains above the Amalfi Coast and the gentle hills of the Sorrento Peninsula. The highest point on the gently undulating ridge extending southwest to Punta Campanella, the peninsula's spine, is Monte Tore (528m) near Sant'Agata. Surface water is sparse, though stream courses cut deep into the limestone rock.

On the intensively cultivated peninsula, only pockets of the once widespread oak and chestnut woodlands survive. In uncultivated areas maquis thrives – a grouping of small evergreen trees and shrubs adapted to poor rocky soil and the long summer drought. Formerly cultivated ground eventually reverts to a type of vegetation known as garrigue, with many colourful dwarf shrubs, among which the pink and white rock roses stand out.

Wildlife of any kind is, sadly, very scarce on the peninsula – shotgun cartridges scattered around tell the story. However, in warm weather you are likely to come across small black snakes, which seem more interested in escaping than in investigating you more closely.

An extensive stretch of this magnificent coast, from Punta del Capo west of Sorrento all the way round to a point just west of Positano is protected, in varying degrees, within the Area Marina Protetta di Punta Campanella. A zoning scheme controls fishing, diving and boat access, guards natural and historical features, and ensures that recreation and fishing can coexist.

PLANNING
Maps

The Sorrento AAST office (p264) usually hands out the free 1:14,000 *Terra del mito di Ulisse dimora delle Sirene Passegiate*. It has a reliable topographical map showing the numerous waymarked walks in the area as far east as Torca, and a great deal of background information.

The Kompass 1:50,000 map No 682 *Penisola Sorrentina* is helpful for planning purposes only.

The CAI 1:30,000 map *Monti Lattari* usefully supplements the local and Kompass sheets, but paths may be numbered differently on the ground than on the map.

PLACE NAMES

The Kompass map and Tippett's book both use the spelling Marine di Cantone. The local maps and the official village sign use Marina del Cantone, which is the spelling adopted here.

Books

Julian Tippett's *Sorrento, Amalfi Coast and Capri* (2008) describes numerous, mainly short walks and is invaluable.

ACCESS TOWN

Some claim it has 'sold out' to the populist tourist hordes, but charming Sorrento (p264) still knows how to wine and dine the *glitterati*, and makes an excellent base for these two walks

PUNTA PENNA

Duration 3–3½ hours
Distance 7km
Difficulty easy–moderate
Start/Finish Marina del Cantone
Nearest Town Sorrento (p264)
Transport bus
Summary A scenic walk to a spectacular headland with superb views of the Isle of Capri.

This walk provides an excellent introduction to the Sorrento Peninsula, with fine sea and mountain views, typical limestone formations in the sheer cliffs and smaller crags, as well as extensive remains of olive groves. The Punta Penna headland bounds the eastern side of the very beautiful Bay of Ieranto and overlooks the Gulf of Salerno to the east.

The route is easy to follow and is way-marked throughout, with red-and-white, and blue-and-green markers from Marina and blue-and-green only from Nerano onwards. The total ascent is about 350m.

When the walk was surveyed, an extensive restoration project was in full swing around Bay of Ieranto, involving stabilisation and some reconstruction of several old buildings including the crumbling Torre di Montalto, stone-wall building and path construction.

The walk starts and finishes in Marina; alternatively, you could start and finish at Nerano (on the Sorrento–Marina bus route), thus reducing the distance by 1km and the time by 20 to 30 minutes.

PLANNING
What to Bring
Be sure to carry water for this walk – there are no refreshments available beyond Nerano.

Maps
Use the *Terra del mito di Ulisse* map (see Maps, p317) or one of the free walking trails maps given out at the tourist office (p264).

GETTING TO/FROM THE WALK
SITA (www.sitabus.it) buses from Sorrento to Marina (called Nerano Cantone on the timetable) go via Sant'Agata and Termini or via Massa Lubrense and Termini (€1.50, one hour, 10 daily). In Marina, you can buy tickets from the bar next to the bus terminus.

By road from Sorrento or the Amalfi Coast, reach Sant'Agata, then continue southwest for about 3.5km to the turn-off for Marina, a further 3.4km.

THE WALK
The path up to Nerano starts from the northwestern (uphill) corner of the large car park behind the hotels and bars in Marina. Follow it between houses and gardens and up to the main road. Cross it, and further up bear left along Via Cantone and follow it to the road beside the large church of San Salvatore in Nerano. There are an *alimentari* and two other shops close by. Continue left (south) along Via Amerigo Vespucci for about 50m then

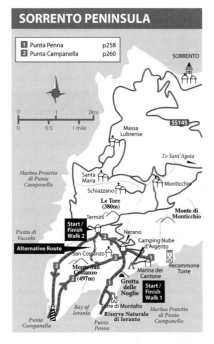

bear right along Via Ieranto. Further along, the wide path leads through a red archway and passes the flower-decked shrine at the small **Grotta delle Noglie** (Cave of the Cats) where skinny, long-legged cats are fed by the locals.

Soon you're out in open grassland with scattered, long-deserted terraces; Capri floats on the horizon ahead. Just past a house and garden on the left is a path junction; bear left for Montalto and Punta Penna. Descend the rocky path; at the entrance to the **Riserva Naturale di Ieranto** on the right, follow the path beside a superbly built stone wall. At the corner of the wall, about 150m along, you may be able to diverge along a path up to the 15th-century **Torre di Montalto**, depending on its current stability.

Continue southwest along the path through olive groves; it angles up slightly to the left to a gap between the two high points of the headland. Follow a path, or make your own way up to the seaward side of the highest point for the best views (one to 1½ hours from Marina).

Retrace your steps up to the path junction near the house and with luck you'll

CAMPANIA

be able to go down the long flight of steps to the shore of **Bay of Ieranto**, a popular destination with the many yachts and small cruisers that frequent these waters.

Return to Marina by the paths followed on the outward journey.

PUNTA CAMPANELLA

Duration 4–4½ hours
Distance 8km
Difficulty moderate
Start/Finish Termini
Nearest Town Sorrento (p264)
Transport bus

Summary Panoramic views from the historic southwest tip of the Sorrento Peninsula and from the chapel on Monte San Costanzo, perched high above Marina del Cantone.

Sorrento has seduced many an enamoured North European visitor and this hike on an open, grassy peninsula with spectacular views across the Bay of Naples to the island of Capri will do little to sully its lofty reputation. The first half of the walk to the *punta* is easy enough and could make a decent half-day family outing (out and back). The grunt to the top of the ridge is a little more taxing (but safe) while the steepish descent back down to Nerano is broken by a welcome flight of steps.

This being in the vicinity of Sorrento, the hike – or variations of it – is rather popular, so expect some company, especially in the early sections out to Punta Campanella.

PLANNING
Maps
The best map is the local *Terra del mito di Ulisse* (see Maps, p317). Carry plenty of water from Termini.

GETTING TO/FROM THE WALK
The Sorrento–Nerano–Cantone **SITA** (www.sitabus.it) bus leaves from outside the train station and stops in Termini (40 minutes, 10 daily). The service runs between 8am to 9pm.

THE WALK
From the Piazza San Croce in Termini, follow Via Campanella to the left (south) for about 200m then turn right downhill along a minor road. Go round a sharp right-hand bend following a sign to Punta Campanella and continue past the turn-off to Mitigliano (which forks to the right). About 600m further on, beyond a small wayside shrine, the minor road leads across the open rocky hillside and becomes a wide track. **Punta Campanella** (an hour from Termini) makes a spectacular end-point for the peninsula with magnificent views of Capri westwards and across Bay of Ieranto to the mountains beyond. The modern light beacon stands close to the crumbling (and dangerous) ruins of a *torre* (tower) about 250m beyond the one and only fork in the path (where you keep right).

Walk back along the track to the junction, now on your right and distinguished by a red-and-white marker with the figures 00. Follow this stone path up and across the steep slope to the ridge crest. Here you turn sharp left (no sign, so look for marks on rocks) onto an indistinct but relatively well-marked path that ascends steeply close to the ridge, through thick, low scrub and rock outcrops. Piles of stones and the remains of small stone shelters are clues to long-gone settlements in this exposed place.

The building at the summit of **Monte San Costanzo** (497m; 1¼ hours from Punta Campanella) is not a mirage of a five-star hotel but a fenced-off military installation. The path skirts the southwestern (right) side of the compound just shy of the summit and then descends to a minor road; turn right. About 50m along the road at a small parking bay on the right, turn off and follow the red-and-white waymarkers, keeping to the widest path through a pine grove. From the far (eastern) edge of the pines (the Alternative Route to Termini, p261, diverges here), go up steps to the plain white chapel of **San Costanzo**, another superb viewpoint. Retrace your steps from the chapel (200m) and go down to the left at the edge of the pine grove on a faint path diagonally across a grassy slope. The sight of a large clump of cacti and an olive grove below should confirm you're on the right course. Contour the slope past a vegetable garden and a stone hut on the right. Then swing left to pass a deep cleft on the right and almost immediately, at the corner of a stone wall, turn diagonally right along a path and descend (hands required) through woodland. Eventually, two flights of steps take you down to the cobbled Punta Penna path; turn left to reach Nerano (one hour from the chapel).

From the Via Fontana di Nerano in Nerano go up beside the *alimentari* and pass between houses and olive groves. Bear left at a fork and follow a steep concrete-paved road labelled with yellow markers up to Piazza San Croce in Termini.

ALTERNATIVE ROUTE: SAN COSTANZO TO TERMINI
30–45 minutes, 1km

On the edge of the pine grove 100m west of San Costanzo chapel, an obscure red-and-green marker indicates a turn northwards down through scattered pines to a road. Turn right for only 10m then go left down a path, cross a road and continue downhill to meet the road again. Turn right; 20m along, head left along a path with a stone wall on the right, with red-and-green markers. Then cross the road again and descend a many-stepped path to a road which leads into Termini.

MORE WALKS

AMALFI COAST
Croce della Conocchia
This is the westernmost peak (1314m) on the long, dramatically rugged chain of huge lumps of limestone called Sant'Angelo a Tre Pizzi – the highest part of the Monti Lattari Range. Unlike the main summits, it's easily accessible from the coast. A path, waymarked with the CAI's red-and-white stripes, ascends north from Caserma Forestale (see p252) through woodland and into open ground with stunning views of cliffs and the coast. The crucifix-topped summit is easily gained, although the waymarked path bypasses it to the left in hazel woodland. The view embraces the sprawling city of Naples, Vesuvius, the isles of Ischia and Capri and mountains to the northwest.

It is an 8km return walk from the Caserma; allow about two hours uphill (550m ascent) and slightly less down. The CAI 1:30,000 *Monti Lattari* map shows part of the route.

Vallone di Praia
This deep, steep-sided valley just northeast of Praiano displays a great array of terraces and some fine high cliffs. It's easily accessible from Praiano. Having traversed the valley, you can then walk up to the small town of Bomerano with several bars and cafés, quite different from the coastal cliff-hanging villages and towns. Return by the same route, or via Colle la Serra (see p254 for a route description in reverse). Alternatively there's a regular daily SITA bus service to Amalfi.

Allow roughly two hours from Praiano to Bomerano (about 640m ascent) and another 1½ to two hours back to Praiano via Colle la Serra, a total of 9km. The Vallone walk is included in Tippett's book (see Maps, p317). Use the CAI 1:30,000 map *Monti Lattari*.

Atrani–Ravello–Maiori
Ravello is a beautiful old town, clustered on a narrow plateau rising steeply between Atrani and the coastal town of Maiori. It can provide the focus for an easy day out from Atrani or can be one of the highlights in a moderate walk from Atrani, up to Ravello, then down to the coast at Minori (the site of an ancient Roman coastal resort) and on to Maiori. The 6km route follows old paths and laneways through olive and citrus groves and quiet villages with extensive coast and mountain vistas.

Allow one to 1½ hours for the walk up to Ravello which includes 300m ascent; from there to Minori via the village of Torello, it's nearly all downhill (40 minutes to an hour). From Minori to Maiori, there's about 260m ascent, for which allow 50 minutes to an hour. You could make a nearly circular walk of it by returning to Minori then following a route back to Atrani via Torello, bypassing Ravello. This involves about 480m of ascent and should take about three hours. The CAI and Kompass maps show the lie of the land; you'll need Tippett's book for precise directions (see p251).

There are hourly SITA buses between Amalfi and Ravello, and between Amalfi and Salerno via Maiori and Minori.

Monte dell'Avvocata
This prominent peak at the eastern end of the Monti Lattari Range is clearly in view

from Atrani and the nearby mountainsides. From its summit (1014m) the magnificent panoramic view takes in Naples, Vesuvius, and mountains to the west and south. A one-time monastery stands just below and southwest of the summit and can be identified from the coast.

The mountain can be approached from the coast road (S163) near the village of Erchie. This involves 940m of ascent, 8km and about six hours of walking, essentially up the western side of a long valley, across its stream to a spur which leads to the main ridge, then along it to the summit. Much of the ascent follows rough paths and flights of steps; the section between the stream crossing and the main ridge had been burnt not very long before the walk was surveyed in May 2001 and the path was very difficult to follow. Elsewhere, either the path is clear, or red-and-white waymarkers indicate the route. From the top, descend the well-used path to Maiori. To reach the start, catch the Amalfi–Salerno SITA bus to the stop above Erchie – ask the driver to let you know when the bus reaches the stop for 'Sentiero all'Avvocata'.

The CAI 1:30,000 *Monti Lattari* map is useful for general orientation only. The walk is described in Tippett's book (see Books, p251).

SORRENTO PENINSULA
Marina del Cantone to Sorrento via Torca
The CAI's Alta Via dei Lattari (waymarked 00 with the usual red-and-white stripes) is a challenging long-distance route linking Termini and Punta Campanella with Corpo di Cava in the east (6km northwest of Maiori on the Amalfi Coast), a distance of 90km. Sparseness of accommodation would make a full, continuous traverse difficult and camping isn't a realistic option in the absence of adequate water sources. The westernmost section is covered in the Punta Campanella walk (p260).

From Marina, it's not difficult to follow the Alta Via's outstandingly scenic route to Fontanelle, involving about 7km, 5½ to six hours and 550m ascent. From here you can take a moderately amenable route (1¾ hours) down to Sorrento, described in Tippett's book. Between Recommone and Torca is it possible to detour to the

ancient settlement of Crapolla. The local map *Terra del Mito di Ulisse* is useful as far east as Monticello. The CAI *Monti Lattari* map covers the whole walk; the route near Malacoccola has changed since it was published. For details of these publications see p258.

The walk could be spread over two days by breaking off at Torca and following a waymarked route to Sant'Agata on the Sorrento–Marina del Cantone bus route.

TOWNS & FACILITIES

NAPLES
☎ 081 / pop 989,000
Some love it; some hate it; few are indifferent. Famous for its uncollected garbage, Camorra Mafia, flapping lines of washing, and buzzing Vespas; Italy's third-largest city hits first-time visitors like a sharp slap around the face. But hidden in the shadow of volatile Vesuvius lies a Unesco World Heritage site, dozens of authentic pizzerias, and street after street of irresistible Neapolitan madness.

Information
Naples has several tourist offices, including at the **Mergellina train station** (☎ 761 21 02) and Via San Carlo 9 (☎ 40 23 94). There's a particularly helpful **AAST office** (☎ 552 33 28; Piazza del Gesù Nuovo 7; 9am-7pm Mon-Sat, 9am-2pm Sun) southeast of Piazza Dante. Also useful is the **City of Naples Tourist Board's website** (www .inaples.it). The **Feltrinelli book store** has branches in Chiaia (☎ 240 54 11; Piazza dei Martiri) and Toledo (☎ 552 14 36; Via San Tommaso d'Aquino 15) with a good selection of maps, fiction, nonfiction and Lonely Planet titles in English.

Sleeping & Eating
Hostel of the Sun (HOTS; ☎ 420 63 93; www.hostelnapoli.com; Via Melisurgo 15; s €40-50, d €50-70, dm without bathroom €16-20) is an ultra-friendly hostel on the 7th floor of an uninspiring *palazzo* near the port. It's a bright, sociable and recently renovated. Five floors down, there's a series of hotel-standard private rooms. Show

your Lonely Planet guidebook for a 10% discount.

Hotel Ideal (☎ 26 92 37; www.albergo ideal.it; Piazza Garibaldi 99; s €34-50, d €39-60), a short stagger from the train station, is convenient and welcoming with salmon tones and polished wood furniture.

6 Small Rooms (☎ 790 13 78; www.at6 smallrooms.com; Via Diodata Lioy 18; dm/ s/d €18/35/45) is near Spaccanapoli and includes breakfast in its rates. A kitchen is available for self-caterers.

Spaccanapoli and Stazione Centrale areas have an array of grocery stores, pizzerias and a couple of spots for seafood. Good economical bets include the dingy **Da Michele** (☎ 553 92 04; Via Cesare Sersale 1; Mon-Sat) with its legendary Neapolitan pizza (two flavours only: margherita and marinara from €4.50), and **Trattoria da Carmine** (☎ 29 43 83; Via dei Tribunali 330; meals €18) a tranquil haven of homely, Neapolitan cooking in the midst of the tumultuous *centro storico*.

Getting There & Away

About 8km northeast of the city centre **Capodichino Airport** (☎ 789 62 59, 848 88 87 77) is southern Italy's main airport, linking Naples with most Italian and several major European cities.

Most buses for Italian and some European cities leave from Piazza Garibaldi in front of Stazione Centrale. Check destinations carefully or ask around because there are no signs. The exception is local company **SITA** (☎ 552 21 76; www.sitabus.it). You can buy tickets and catch SITA buses at the **main office** (Via Pisanelli), near Piazza Municipio, or Via G Ferraris, near Stazione Centrale. SITA runs buses to Pompeii, Ercolano, Sorrento, other towns on the Amalfi Coast and Salerno (by motorway). See also the boxed text, Inches from the Abyss, (p255).

Many trains originating in the north pass through Rome and terminate in Naples; you can call for **information** (☎ 848 88 08 88). Trains arrive and depart from **Stazione Centrale** (☎ 554 31 88) or **Stazione Garibaldi** (on the lower level). There are up to 30 trains daily to/from Rome. Circumvesuviana trains to Ercolano, Pompeii and Sorrento depart from Corso Garibaldi, about 400m southwest of Stazione Centrale.

Naples is on the major north to south Autostrada del Sole, numbered A1 (north to Rome and Milan) and A3 (south to Salerno and Reggio di Calabria. The A30 rings Naples to the northeast, while the A16 heads northeast to Bari.

POSITANO
☎ 089 / pop 3900

Positano suffers from the curse of beauty. Just as modern Hollywood stars are plagued by the paparazzi, this stunning ancient Amalfi village is inundated with tourists. Yet, somehow, none of it detracts from its dazzling Mediterranean sheen. Up on the trails, meanwhile, you'll discover another Amalfi, little altered since the High Middle Ages.

Information

The **tourist office** (☎ 87 50 67; www.azienda turismopositano.it; Via del Saracino 4; 8am-2pm & 3.30-8pm Mon-Sat Apr-Oct, 9am-3pm Mon-Fri Nov-Mar) gives out basic information and is good for bus and ferry timetables. **Positano.com** (www .positano.com) is a slick website with hotel and restaurant listings, itineraries and transport information.

Sleeping & Eating

Hostel Brikette (☎ 87 58 57; www.brikette .com; Via Guglielmo Marconi 358; dm €23-25, d €65-85, apt €115-180; late Mar-Nov) not far from the Bar Internazionale (start of the Positano Circuit walk) is a bright and cheerful hostel offering the cheapest accommodation in town. Options include six- to eight-person dorms (single sex and mixed), double rooms and apartments for two to five people. There's also laundry, free wi-fi and left-luggage facilities.

Another splendid budget choice is **Pensione Maria Luisa** (☎ 87 50 23; www.pen sionemarialuisa.com; Via Fornillo 42; s €50, d €70-80) where recently renovated rooms shine with fresh new blue tiles and private terraces. There are magnificent bay views.

Da Costantino (☎ 87 57 38; Via Montepertuso; pizzas from €4, meals €20; closed Wed) 300m above the coast road is a slog worth making for one of the few authentic places in town. Expect honest, down-to-earth Italian grub, including excellent pizzas and delicious *scialatielli* (ribboned pasta).

CAMPANIA

Il **Saraceno d'Oro** (☎ 81 20 50; Viale Pasitea 254; pizzas from €5, meals €25; Mar-Oct) blends cheery service, uncomplicated food and reasonable prices. The pizzas are good and the desserts are sticky and sweet. Stick around for a complimentary glass of *limoncello*.

Getting There & Away

SITA (☎ 081 552 21 76; www.sitabus.it) runs frequent buses to/from Amalfi (€1.40) and Sorrento (€1.40). Buses drop you off at one of two main bus stops: coming from Sorrento and the west, opposite Bar Internazionale; arriving from Amalfi and the east, at the top of Via Cristoforo Colombo. When departing, buy bus tickets at Bar Internazionale or, if headed eastwards, from the tobacconist at the bottom of Via Cristoforo Colombo.

Between April and October, daily ferries link Positano with Amalfi (€6, six daily), Sorrento (€9, five daily), Salerno (€8.50, five daily), Naples (€14, four daily) and Capri (€15.50, five daily).

There is no train line along the Amalfi. To connect with train services take the bus/boat to Sorrento or Salerno.

SORRENTO

☎ 081 / pop 16,500

Sorrento has been gripping travellers – in particular, the British – for nearly 150 years. Attracted by the balmy climate and invigorated by shots of the locally made *limoncello*, 19th-century aesthetes congregated here to admire the sheer cliffs and relive the fortunes of the mythical sirens who, according to the Greek legend, lured sailors to their doom with their beautiful songs.

Information

The **AAST office** (☎ 807 40 33; Via Luigi De Maio 35; 8.45am-6.15pm Mon-Sat, plus 8.45am-12.45pm Sun in Aug) in the Circolo dei Forestieri (Foreigners' Club) has plenty of useful printed material and a hotel reservation service. **La Capsa bookshop** (Corso Italia), a short distance east of the side road leading to the train station, has a good stock of local maps and guides.

Supplies & Equipment

For self-catering, remember that shops are closed on Thursday afternoon. There

is a supermarket opposite the hostel and a **Standa supermarket** (Corso Italia) between Piazza Tasso and Piazza A Lauro.

Sleeping

Less than 15 minutes' walk from the town centre, beside the road to Massa Lubrense is **Camping Nube d'Argento** (☎ 878 13 44; www.nubedargento.com; Via Capo 21; camping per person €11, two-person bungalow €50-85; Mar-Dec). It offers camping on terraced pitches with pretty good sea views. The site has its own pizzeria, bar and swimming pool.

Situated five minutes from the train station, **Hostel Le Sirene** (☎ 807 29 25; www.hostellesirene.com; Via degli Aranci 160; dm/d €16/22.50) has cramped four- and six-bed dorms, each with a tiny bathroom. The tariff includes sheets and a light breakfast. You can leave luggage here and access the internet. **Hotel Linda** (☎ 878 29 16; Via degli Aranci 125; s/d €50/75) is a clean friendly place where you can have relative peace and quiet, and some space.

Eating

The choice of places to eat is vast. **Angelina Lauro** (☎ 807 40 97; Piazza Angelina Lauro 39-40; self-service meal €12; daily Jul-Aug, Wed-Mon Sep-Jun) belies its college canteen look with some filling, inexpensive lunch options. At **Ristorante Giardinello** (☎ 877 12 00; Via Accademica 7; meals €18; Tue-Sun) you can eat well at garden tables from an extensive menu that includes ravioli, and pizzas from €3.50. In **Bufalito** (☎ 338 163 29 21; Via Fuoro 21; meals €25; closed Nov-Feb) is a sanctioned Slow Food mozzarella bar-restaurant with sterling local produce such as Sorrento-style cheese fondue, and *salsiccia* (local sausage) with broccoli.

Getting There & Away

Sorrento is well served by public transport, land and sea.

Alilauro (☎ 878 14 30; www.alilauro.it) runs up to seven hydrofoils daily between Naples and Sorrento (€9, 35 minutes). Slower **Metrò del Mare** (☎ 199 60 07 00; www.metrodelmare.com) covers the same route (€6.50, one hour, four daily).

There are daily SITA (☎ 089 386 67 11; www.sitabus.it) bus services to

Sorrento from Naples (Via Pisanelli) and from Salerno (Piazza della Concordia) via the Amalfi coast including the towns of Amalfi (€2.50, 1½ hours) and Positano (€1.50, 50 minutes). In Sorrento, buses depart from outside the Circumvesuviana station and tickets are sold at the adjacent newsagent and bar. **Curreri Viaggi** (☎ 801 54 20; www.curreriviaggi.it) operates a service between Sorrento (Piazza Tasso) and Naples' Capodichino airport (€10, one hour, six a day).

The privately run **Circumvesuviana** (☎ 772 24 44; www.vesuviana.it) provides a service from the station in Naples at Corso Garibaldi (about 400m southwest of Stazione Centrale) to Sorrento (€3.20, 30 per day).

From Naples, take the A3 and leave it at the Castellammare exit near Pompeii and follow the S145 to Sorrento (48km from Naples). From the south and east, take the Vietri sul Mare turn-off from the A3 (just west of Salerno) to join the S163 which snakes along the coast to Colli San Pietro, 8km west of Positano. Here it meets the S145 which leads to Sorrento (50km from Salerno).

Sicily

- Viewing the smoking gun of **Mt Etna** (p269) from various angles on the long march through its western foothills
- Peering into the abyss of the **Grotta del Gelo** (p276), a lava-sculpted ice cave that retains ice year-round on Etna's northern slopes
- Looking out at the Aeolian Islands from the rim of Vulcano's gently steaming **Gran Cratere** (p279)
- Staying overnight in an old hunting lodge, surrounded by age-old beech woods on the **Nebrodi Lake Circuit** (p281)

Signature food: *Pasta con le sarde*	Celebrated native: Giuseppe Tomasi di Lampedusa (novelist)	Famous for... Volcanoes

Images of Sicily loom large on any Mediterranean horizon, beckoning modern travellers like they once lured Greek warriors and trade-hungry Phoenicians. There's fiery Mt Etna and temperamental Stromboli; ripe red tomatoes and salty, green olives; Troisi in *Il Postino* and Pacino in *The Godfather*; Papa in the piazza and Mamma on a Vespa. One image you curiously won't see is that of people hiking. Sicily isn't exactly over-endowed with weekend rambling associations. Aside from the arid tramp up Mt Etna – generally done with the aid of jeeps and a cable car – the walking culture here usually begins and ends with a short (yet sweet) stroll to the gelataria.

Protected in a handful of fledgling regional parks – including the omnipresent Parco dell'Etna – lightly trafficked paths do exist, even if legible signposts don't, and negotiating them is a perfect under-the-radar way of discovering the little-heralded 'island within an island' that is inland Sicily.

Despite its semi-autonomous regional status and unique Greek, Arabic and Norman history, Sicily has long stood for everything that is quintessential about Italy. What is arguably the nation's greatest novel (*Il Gattopardo*) was set and written here, while Sicily's exquisite yet earthy food is conceived, concocted and served out of what gastronomes reverently refer to as 'God's Kitchen'.

Two hikes cover the greener and quieter slopes of Sicily's insomniac volcano, while a third tackles the less menacing terrain of Vulcano in the Aeolian Islands to the north. A wild card is the 18km stroll through the Parco dei Nebrodi, a strangely un-Sicilian melange of ancient beech woods and pastoral lakes that shimmer like dislodged vistas from a sepia-toned northern postcard.

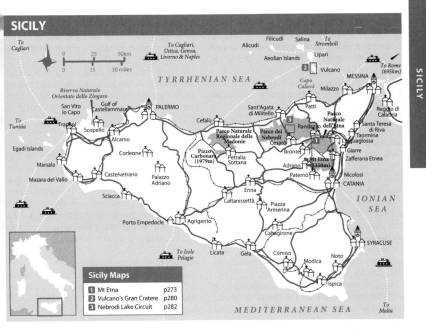

SICILY

Sicily Maps

1	Mt Etna	p273
2	Vulcano's Gran Cratere	p280
3	Nebrodi Lake Circuit	p282

HISTORY

Paying a sometimes heavy price for its strategic location in the heart of the Mediterranean, Sicily has, since prehistory, been an attractive territorial prize, bringing a succession of colonisers and settlers to its shores. It is believed the earliest settlers were the Sicanians, Elymians and Siculians, arriving from various points around the southern Mediterranean. They were later followed by the Phoenicians. Greek colonisation began in the 8th century BC with the foundation of Naxos. By 210 BC Sicily was under Roman control, with power eventually passing to the Byzantines and then to the Arabs, who had settled in by AD 903.

Norman conquest of the island began in 1060, when Roger I of Hauteville captured Messina. Mastery of Sicily subsequently passed to the Swabians and the Holy Roman Emperor Frederick II, known as Stupor Mundi (Wonder of the World). In the 13th century the French Angevins provided a period of misrule that ended in 1282 with the revolt known as the Sicilian Vespers. The island was ceded to the Spanish Aragón family and, in 1503, to the Spanish crown. After short periods of Savoy and Austrian rule in the 18th century, Sicily again came under the control of the Spanish Bourbons of Naples in 1734, who united the island with southern Italy in the Kingdom of the Two Sicilies.

On 11 May 1860 Giuseppe Garibaldi landed at Marsala with his 'one thousand' and began the conquest that set the seal on unification. Life did not greatly improve on Sicily, and between 1871 and 1914 more than one million Sicilians emigrated, mainly to the US.

In 1943 some 140,000 Allied troops, under General Dwight Eisenhower, landed on southeastern Sicily. Initially blocked by dogged Italian and German resistance, Eisenhower's field commanders entered Messina within six weeks, after heavy fighting had devastated many parts of the island. The Allied occupation lasted until early 1944. In 1948 Sicily became a semiautonomous region and, unlike other such regions in Italy, it has its own parliament and legislative powers.

ENVIRONMENT

Extending over 25,708 sq km, triangular-shaped Sicily is the largest island in the Mediterranean. Physically the largely

SICILY

mountainous island (83% of the total surface can be described as either hilly or mountainous) straddles two continental shelves: the northern and eastern half is considered to be an extension of the Calabrian Apennines, while the southern and western half is topographically similar to the Atlas mountains of North Africa.

The topography of the island is a combination of mountain, plateau and fertile coastal plain. In the northeast, the mountains are made up of three distinct ranges: the Nebrodi and Madonie ranges, which skirt virtually the entire length of the Tyrrhenian coast up to Palermo; and the Peloritani, which rise above the length of the eastern coast. The interior is mostly hills and plateaus, which extend and slope downwards to the southern coast. The coasts are an alternating panorama of rugged cliffs and low, sandy shores, making up some of the island's most beautiful scenery.

Sicily is renowned for its volcanic activity and the eastern half of the island is dominated by the imposing cone of Mt Etna (3350m), Europe's largest active volcano. Sicily's two other active volcanoes are to the north of the island in the Aeolian archipelago: Vulcano and Stromboli.

CLIMATE

Sicily enjoys a temperate Mediterranean climate with mild winters and long, relentlessly hot summers fanned by the *scirocco* (sirocco), blowing from the deserts of northern Africa. During summer, average daily temperatures on the coast are over 30°C. Mountainous areas remain several degrees cooler. Winter temperatures average between 10°C and 14°C. Rainfall is low and occurs almost exclusively during late autumn and winter, when downpours can be sudden and heavy.

PLANNING
When to Walk

Sicilian hikers have more year-round options than most, thanks to the milder seasons and less invasive snowfall, though don't underestimate the potential chill of a Sicilian winter especially in the Nebrodi region or on the higher reaches of Mt Etna. Spring and autumn are the most pleasant times to walk. July and August can be stiflingly hot.

What to Bring

Always walk with at least 2L of water on your person; Sicily's *sorgenti* (natural springs) are far from ubiquitous. Pack warm clothes if you're climbing high on Mt Etna, even in the summer. If you're not up to navigating the island's sometimes patchy bus system, carry your driver's license as you may elect to hire a car.

Maps

Available free from visitor centres in Catania (p285), the Touring Club Italiano (TCI) 1:175,000 *Province of Catania* map is a useful tool for planning. If supplies have run out, the same map can also be found in city bookshops. Alternatively, the TCI 1:200,000 *Sicilia* map, covering the whole island, is also perfectly adequate.

Books

Lonely Planet's *Sicily* guide gives in-depth coverage to the island. More general information is provided in the current edition of Lonely Planet's *Italy* country guide.

An excellent English-language walking guide to Sicily, with more than 40 short tours to the island's most renowned tourist sites, as well as to some wonderfully undiscovered parts, is *Sunflower Landscapes Sicily* (2006), by Peter Amann. It concentrates on walks that fit neatly with car tours around the island – a convenient companion for walkers with their own wheels. Another useful read is *Walking in Sicily: Short and Long Distance Walks* (2006) by Gillian Price, published by Cicerone.

Emergency

For search and rescue assistance in the mountains of Sicily, contact **Soccorso Alpino** (☎ 095 91 41 41). For urgent medical assistance, contact the **national emergency** number (☎ 118). See also Emergency (p272) for local contacts while on Mt Etna.

GETTING THERE & AROUND

Sicily is easily accessed from other European cities via a growing list of cheap airlines that use Palermo and Catania as hubs. Direct train connections from Rome, Milan, Naples and Florence on the mainland link with Catania and Palermo through the northeastern city of Messina. Ferries cross the narrow straits to Reggio di Calabria or venture further afield to Naples, Genoa, Cagliari (Sardinia), Malta and Tunisia.

Sicily's bus system is comprehensive on the coast but more limited the further you penetrate inland. Check schedules in advance.

GATEWAY

The best gateway for all of these walks is Catania (p285), Sicily's second city, a crowded but exuberant urban centre that lies in the shadow of smoking Mt Etna.

MT ETNA

Dominating the landscape in eastern Sicily between Taormina and Catania and visible from the moon (apparently), the majestic Mt Etna (3350m; known to Sicilians as Mongibello) is Europe's largest live volcano and one of the world's most active. Coated in snow for much of the year, this almost perfectly cone-shaped mountain remains one of Sicily's most enduring and fascinating icons. For volcano lovers, frequent eruptions offer a rare opportunity to glimpse, at a safe distance, something of the massive forces at work beneath the earth's fragile crust. The most devastating eruption of the modern era was in 1669 and wiped out a good part of Catania taking 12,000 lives. In recent years eruptions have been frequent; a 2002 lava flow destroyed buildings in the Rifugio Sapienza complex and in September 2007 Catania's Fontanarossa airport was temporarily closed as a precautionary measure after Etna started spewing lava 400m into the air.

Since 1987 the volcano and its slopes have been part of a national park covering 590 sq km in a territory that includes 20 communities. The park encompasses a fascinatingly varied natural environment, from the severe, almost surreal summit area, with its breathtaking panoramas, to the deserts of lava encrusting the volcano's sides.

HISTORY

In ancient times Etna's summit was frequently lit up by spectacular pyrotechnic displays. The volcano was visible for hundreds of kilometres out to sea and acted as a night beacon for the ancient navigators of the Mediterranean.

Not surprisingly, the spectacularly eruptive Etna features in some very early writings. The classical world saw the volcano in mythological terms as the home of the god Pluto and of the Titans who had rebelled against Zeus. In the 18th century BC, Homer mentioned Etna in the episode of Ulysses and the Cyclops. In the 5th century BC, the historian Thucydides referred to the incredible eruptive activity of Etna. Aeschylus, who was at Syracuse in 472 BC, cited a 16th-century BC legend in his *Prometheus*, in which Etna is described as a 'column holding up the sky', with the giant Tifone (Typhoon) at its base, shaking his 100 heads and making the whole world tremble.

The first documented visitor to Etna was Pietro Bembo in 1493, who wrote the Latin work *De Aetna*, telling of his adventures. This encouraged an influx of English, German, French, Dutch and Danish travellers. English physicist Patrick Brydone is considered the founder of the Sicilian 'Grand Tour'. In 1773 he published his *Tour Through Sicily and Malta*, which was translated into French and German. His lyrical and dreamy descriptions of the ascent to the crater inspired many aristocrats to visit Etna.

With local guides, it was a two-day mule ride to make the round trip from Nicolosi to see the sunrise at Etna's main crater. Among those who made the trip were Dumas, De Dolomieu and the French landscape painter Jean Hovel. By the 19th century, Etna had a strong local economy founded on the presence of these travellers.

ENVIRONMENT

Triggered by a combination of volcanic and regional tectonic activity more than half a million years ago, a number of eruptive centres appeared off the east coast of Sicily and began to deposit material. Over the next several hundred thousand years, a series of overlapping volcanic cones built up and then collapsed to form giant calderas. The most recent phase of volcanism, about 35,000 years ago, created the present-day stratovolcano, known as Etna.

With a circumference of 165km and covering an area of 1260 sq km, Etna is the largest active volcano in Europe and one of the few large wild areas of Sicily. Rising directly out of the sea, it reaches roughly 3350m, although this figure varies after eruptions and as lava accumulates around the summit craters. Belying the simplicity of its conical shape, the volcano is made up of a complex network of channels and fractures. The central conduit, which leads to the present four summit craters, is surrounded by more than 200 major and secondary cones dotting the volcano's flanks. During an eruption, magma forces its way upwards through any number of these escape valves from a reservoir 20km beneath the surface. Measuring roughly 7km by 5km, the Valle del Bove, a depression on the eastern side of Etna, is a caldera formed after a cone collapsed several thousand years ago.

There is evidence to suggest that volcanic activity was once far more violent than the frequent, relatively low-key eruptions that take place on Etna today. The volcano's most notorious eruption occurred in 1669 and lasted 122 days. A huge river of lava poured down its southern slope, destroying 16 towns and engulfing a good part of Catania, dramatically altering the landscape. Twenty-thousand people were killed by the accompanying earthquake. Recent eruptions have been restricted to periodic lava flows that, while newsworthy, generally haven't threatened the local population. Flows (at a sizzling 1100°C) rarely cover more than 10km, travelling at anywhere between several tens of metres per second (near the source) and a more leisurely few metres per hour. The few who have lost their lives on the volcano were surprised by eruptions while visiting the craters – a risky business at the best of times. In 1979, nine people died in an explosion at the Cratere Sud-Est (southeast crater) and eight years later another two were killed at the same crater.

Plants

Once covered by huge forests, the fertile volcanic soils on the lower flanks of Etna now support very productive vineyards and groves of olive, almond, pistachio, hazelnut, chestnut and fruit trees. Beyond the agricultural fringe, in steeper terrain and between solidified lava flows, patches of holm and deciduous oak survive. Also on the damper eastern slopes, manna ash, hornbeam and maple trees are concentrated. Several species of broom also thrive below the tree line.

Between 1000m and 1800m the larch pine performs an important role as a pioneer plant, recolonising lava flows. Higher up, on the cold northwest slopes up to 2000m, copper beech grows – this is the southernmost point in Europe at which the beech is found. A dwarf version can be found up to 2250m in the Punta Lucia area. Etna's birch grows up to 2100m and is considered an endemic species, like the beech, left over from the last ice age.

The most surprising vegetation is found at high altitudes beyond the forested areas. These are surreal, pillow-shaped tussocks of milk-vetch, another of Etna's endemic species that survives to 2450m. Inside, under its trusty thorns, the sweetly scented chrysanthemum nestles, protected from the wind. Above 2500m even the thorntree disappears and the only vegetation are *Rumex* (docks and sorrels) and the odd Sicilian soapwort, with its delicate pink flowers.

Animals

Etna's forested slopes were once home to wolves, wild boars, roebucks, otters, martens and griffon. However, unable to adapt to human encroachment on the mountain and hunted to extinction, these larger carnivores have long since died out. Only three carnivores remain in the Parco dell'Etna: foxes, weasels and wild cats. These hunt smaller mammals, such as rabbits, hares, mice and hedgehogs. The porcupine is found along the trail and is the largest wild animal on Etna. There are at least eight species of bat that inhabit the ravines and caves created by the lava, including the rare *molosso del cestoni*.

Among the birds of Etna, the royal eagle has recently returned to nest in the park. You'll also see sparrowhawks, buzzards, kestrels, peregrine falcons and nocturnal predators: the only Sicilian colonies of common owls, tawny owls and barn owls. In the woods and high mountain areas there are many species of woodpecker, as well as ravens, doves, crows, rare rock partridges and an infinite number of small birds.

There are numerous innocuous reptiles, but watch out for the viper, a poisonous snake found throughout Italy.

CLIMATE

The climate on Etna varies with altitude. At higher altitudes there is a mountain climate, becoming colder towards the summit area (above 2000m), which is exposed to strong, freezing winds. Snowfall is common from November to April, but can occur year-round. Further down the mountain, the climate becomes gradually more typical of the mild Mediterranean conditions that characterise Sicily – expect cloudless, hot summer days.

PLANNING
When to Walk
The best periods for walking on Etna are spring and autumn, between April and May, and September and October, when the weather is mild and the vegetation puts on a magnificent display of colour. During the height of summer, trekking across lava fields under an unforgiving Mediterranean sun can be an uncomfortably hot experience.

What to Bring
Unlike many of the CAI-run *rifugi* (mountain huts) of northern Italy, the huts around Mt Etna are not serviced, although they are clean and stocked with supplies of firewood. Walkers on the circuit will need to bring a sleeping mat to lay out on the stone benches, a sleeping bag, fire-lighting equipment and a torch (flashlight). All food and water for the three days should also be carried, along with cooking gear. The water supplies at the *rifugi* are limited and local advice is that the water is not drinkable. Bring purification tablets and/or your own supply.

A hat is handy during the hotter months, while at night, when the temperature drops considerably, you will need warm clothing.

If you are planning on a trip up to the craters, take all the trappings of a high-altitude excursion: warm clothes, a wind jacket, warm headgear and gloves. It is also advisable to carry a compass, as banks of fog can develop, making orientation difficult. Mobile phones are an excellent safety precaution, but be aware that they won't work everywhere on the mountain.

Maps
For navigational purposes, the best option is Selca's 1:25,000 *Mt Etna* map. Alternatively there's the smaller scale TCI 1:50,000 *Mt Etna* map. The Istituto Geografico Militare (IGM) maps of the area at 1:25,000 are more than 40 years old, ancient history on a mountain where lava remoulds the landscape two or three times a decade.

Information Sources
The office of the **Parco dell'Etna** (☎ 095 82 11 11; Via Etnea 107/a, Nicolosi) is on the southern slopes of Etna above Catania. More convenient for the Mt Etna hikes, however, is the provincial visitor centre in Catania (p285), which has friendly English-speaking staff and numerous useful publications.

If not passing through Catania, there is a good Pro Loco **tourist office** (☎ 095 64 30 94; www.prolocolinguaglossa.it; Piazza Annunziata 5) on the north side of Etna at Linguaglossa, and a decent visitors' centre in Randazzo (p287).

At the end of the walk (Rifugio Sapienza), there's the **Etna Sud APT office** (☎ 095 91 63 56; open daily).

The park's official website www.parco etna.ct.it is in Italian only. More comprehensive are the pages on the official Italian parks portal at www.parks.it.

Guided Walks
There are several groups that organise tours towards the craters and elsewhere on the mountain, involving both trekking and 4WD tours with a volcanologist or alpine guide. Most cater for groups rather than individuals, so unless you can find space on a tour, the cost to hire a guide between one or two people can be prohibitively expensive. Bear in mind that not all the guides speak English.

Volcano Trek (☎ 333 209 66 04; www .volcanotrek.com; Via Minicucca 16, San Giovanni La Punta) is run by expert geologists. Several tour options are available; see the website.

Siciltrek (☎ 095 96 88 82; www.sicili trek.it; Via Marconi 27, Sant'Alfio) runs group tours up Etna, including the cable car and bus trip to 2900m. Andrea Ercolani of Siciltrek also organises and leads excellent private tours throughout the region.

Gruppo Guide Alpine Etna Sud (☎ 095 791 47 55; Via Etnea 49, Nicolosi) is the official guide service on the mountain's southern flank, running one-day or multi-day guided itineraries from their hut below Rifugio Sapienza.

Gruppo Guide Alpine Etna Nord (☎ 095 64 78 33; Piazza Santa Caterina 24, Linguaglossa) runs a similar tour service to Etna Sud, taking in the north side of the volcano.

Emergency

In case of emergency, ring either the **Soccorso Alpino Etna Nord** (☎ 0337 902 82 36) or **Soccorso Alpino Etna Sud** (☎ 0330 36 81 52).

ETNA'S WESTERN FOOTHILLS

Duration 2 days
Distance 36km
Difficulty moderate
Start Rifugio Sapienza
Finish Randazzo
Nearest Town Catania (p285), Randazzo (p287)
Transport bus

Summary A superbly scenic walk around the lava-scarred western foothills of Europe's most active volcano, crossing rocky moonscapes and dense woods.

Hiking up Mt Etna can be a bit of a human traffic jam replete with purring jeeps and busy tour groups who forfeit a significant portion of elevation by taking the *funivia* (cable car). However, hiking around the mountain – especially along its western flanks – is a different story, an ethereal mix of harsh lava moonscapes and improbable beech and larch forest dominated by the ever-present sight of Sicily's fiery giant brooding like a smoking gun on your right-hand side.

A trail, known as the *altomontana* (high mountain), closed to traffic and well maintained by the Guardia Forestale (forestry department), plies a long, semicircular route from Rifugio Sapienza all the way to Rifugio Brunek in the park's northeast corner. It is a beautiful route that traverses the wooded slopes of the volcano at altitudes between 1300m and 1800m, and crosses many time-worn lava flows. There are several unstaffed, ranger-maintained *rifugi* along the way that function similarly to the *bivacchi* (emergency shelters) of the Alps. They are always open and are an OK place to spend a night wrapped in a sleeping bag.

The walk described here follows a large section of this trail as far as Rifugio Monte Spagnola from where you visit the lava-sculpted town of Randazzo. You can spend three days virtually isolated from the rest of civilisation up here, but you'll need to carry all your food and water. At the beginning

there's a comfortable, alpine-style staffed *rifugi* offering food and accommodation. Trips up to the craters can be organised from here.

ACCESS TOWN

If you're planning to do this walk as mapped out below then you best base is the soulful Sicilian city of Catania (p285). If you would prefer to do it in reverse, the small town of Randazzo (p287) is the ideal starting point.

GETTING TO/FROM THE WALK

Rifugio Sapienza (start)

Despite its position as the main tourist nexus on Mt Etna, public transport to the **Rifugio Sapienza** (☎ 095 91 63 56; Piazzale Funivia; s/d €65/100) is relatively poor. One **AST** (☎ 095 723 05 11; www.azienda sicilianatrasporti.it) bus a day (including Sundays) leaves from outside Catania train station at 8.15am for the *rifugio*. It takes about 1¾ hours and stops off in Nicolosi.

If you wish, you can overnight in the *rifugio* in order to have an early start on this hike the following morning. There is a decent restaurant and a café on the premises.

Another accommodation option is **Hotel Corsaro** (☎ 095 780 99 02; B&B s/d €50/100, half-board s/d €70/140), 100m to the west that offers year-round accommodation in a stark environment of rock and hardened lava flows.

Randazzo (finish)

See p287 for getting there and away information on Randazzo.

THE WALK

Day 1: Rifugio Sapienza to Rifugio Monte Scavo

4–5 hours, 14.5km

From Rifugio Sapienza descend on the main provincial road SP92 towards Nicolosi for 2km. The road bends in both directions to counter the mountain slope, but has wide verges and is not dangerous for walkers. At the first major junction, turn right on a minor paved road towards the **Osservatorio Astrofisico** (Astrophysics Observatory). The road passes the tree-covered volcanic cone of Monte Vetore (1821m) and a sign for the Osservatorio both off to your left. After 1.5km you reach a path junction close to another diminutive volcanic cone, that of

MT ETNA

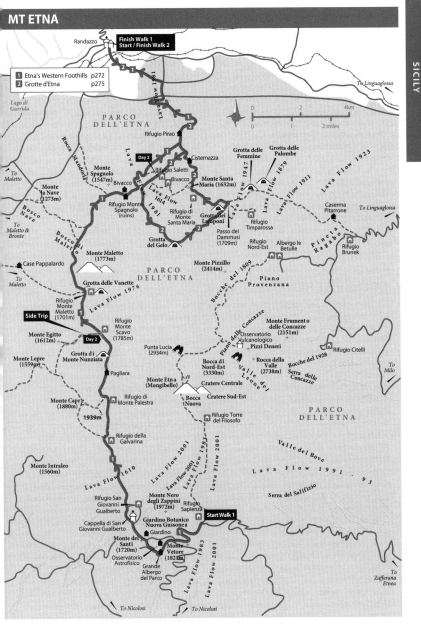

Randazzo

**Finish Walk 1
Start / Finish Walk 2**

1 Etna's Western Foothills p272
2 Grotte d'Etna p275

To Linguaglossa

Lago di
Gurrida

P A R C O
D E L L ' E T N A

Rifugio Pirao

Cisternazza

Grotta delle
Femmine

Grotta delle
Palombe

To
Maletto

Monte
Spagnolo
(1547m)

Day 2

Rifugio Saletti

Bivacco

Bivacco

Monte Santa
Maria (1632m)

Caserma
Pitarrone

To Linguaglossa

To
Maletto

Monte
la Nave
(1273m)

Rifugio Monte
Spagnolo
(ruins)

Lava Flow 1614

Rifugio di
Monte
Santa Maria

Grotta dei
Lamponi

Rifugio
Timparossa

To
Maletto &
Bronte

Passo dei
Dammusi
(1709m)

Rifugio
Nord-Est

Albergo le
Betulle

Rifugio
Brunek

Grotta
del Gelo

Monte Maletto
(1773m)

Case Pappalardo

Grotta delle Vanette

P A R C O
D E L L ' E T N A

Monte Pizzillo
(2414m)

P i a n o
P r o v e n z a n a

To
Maletto

Rifugio
Monte
Maletto
(1701m)

Side Trip

Rifugio
Monte
Scavo
(1785m)

Monte Egitto
(1612m)

Day 2

Grotta di
Monte Nunziata

Punta Lucia
(2934m)

Monte Frumento
delle Concazze
(2151m)

Osservatorio
Vulcanologico

Rifugio Citelli

Monte Lepre
(1559m)

Pagliara

Bocca di
Nord-Est
(3330m)

Pizzi Deneri

To
Milo

Rocca della
Valle
(2738m)

Bocche del 1928

Monte Etna
(Mongibello)

Cratere Centrale

Monte Capre
(1880m)

1939m

Rifugio di
Monte Palestra

Bocca
Nuova

Cratere Sud-Est

P A R C O
D E L L ' E T N A

Rifugio della
Galvarina

Rifugio Torre
del Filosofo

Valle del Bove

Monte Intraleo
(1560m)

Lava Flow 1610

Lava Flow 2001

Lava Flow 1983

Lava Flow 2001

Lava Flow 1991 - 93

Serra del Salifizio

Rifugio San
Giovanni
Gualberto

Monte Nero
degli Zappini
(1972m)

Rifugio
Sapienza

Start Walk 1

Cappella di San
Giovanni Gualberto

Giardino Botanico
Nuova Gussonea

Giardino

Monte dei
Santi
(1720m)

Monte
Vetore
(1811m)

To
Zafferana
Etnea

Osservatorio
Astrofisico

Grande
Albergo
del Parco

To Nicolosi

To Nicolosi

Monte dei Santi (1720m). Fork right here
and in approximately 400m take another
sharper turning to the right on a paved road

that passes around some (usually closed)
green metal gates. Continue straight past
the entrance to the **Giardino Botanico**

SICILY

Nuova Gussonea (botanical garden) on the right. If open, the garden (admission free) is worth a brief stopover as it recreates on a small scale the main environments and botanical species found on Etna. A short distance further on you'll come to the **Cappella di San Giovanni Gualberto** on the right, basically a large wayside shrine regularly embellished with fresh flowers.

A road forks to the right here to the **Rifugio San Giovanni Gualberto**. Keep left and follow the paved road as it veers sharply to the right. Almost immediately a less distinct dirt track heads off to the left – the *alto-montana* (high mountain road). This is your path for the next 20km as you traverse Etna's western foothills with few deviations.

The track alternates between lush larch wood and semi-exposed lava flows dating from the 17th to the 19th centuries. Ignore the minor, lateral roads and keep going

until you reach the basic unstaffed **Rifugio della Galvarina** 4km from the Capella. To the left of the *rifugio* is another trail, which connects with a trail for the volcanic cones of Monte Capre, Monte Lepre and Monte Intraleo. Two more kilometres of walking will bring you to the diminutive **Rifugio di Monte Palestra** (1917m) where another left-turning leads off to the aforementioned volcanic cones. Keeping on the main dirt track you'll soon pass a **pagliara**, a typical conical shelter for workers producing charcoal, built with tree branches and earth and – 1km further on – the gaping **Grotta di Monte Nunziata** used in the past by the people of Bronte who filled this depression with snow in winter, so that they could have ice in summer.

Continue north ignoring a track that heads off to the right. Within 10 minutes of leaving the *grotta* you'll arrive at the **Rifugio Monte**

GOD'S KITCHEN

Pull up a chair in any simple Sicilian trattoria and you'll quickly end up thinking you've died and gone to heaven. Welcome to God's kitchen, where gastronomic cultures collide and tasty food is left to marinate for centuries in a mish-mash of exotic Mediterranean flavours stirred up every 500 years or so by the odd conquering emir or passing Phoenician. Thanks to its history, Sicilian gastronomic customs are proudly singular. The natives of Palermo and Messina happily suck on ice cream for breakfast and spread anchovies on their pizza for lunch. Spurning the typically northern Italian penchant for risotto, they roll their rice up into little balls and stick them in a deep fryer to produce *anancini siciliani* (croquettes), signature Sicilian street food.

While the north argues over cheese recipes, Sicilians scream tomatoes; not just any old tomatoes, but big red, ripe, juicy things that will rank among the best you've ever tasted. Then there are the olives – salty, green and doused in herbs – and impossibly shiny courgettes and aubergines that look like they've been plucked opportunistically from some erstwhile Garden of Eden. Dine here for a day or two and you'll rapidly start to understand why that quintessential Sicilian-American movie *The Godfather* contained not one, but 61 scenes of people eating.

Unlike the Sardinians, the Sicilians have always looked towards the sea to fill their dinner plates with rich harvests of swordfish, tuna and clams arriving ripe on Catania's rustic restaurant tables. Try *spaghetti alla vongole veraci* (spaghetti and clams in a white wine and garlic sauce) or *pasta con le sarde* (pasta and sardines), both regional signature dishes, or get a load of raw anchovies in Catania's bustling fish market. Rather like their Iberian cousins to the west, 500 years of Arab colonisation has led to the enhancement of Sicily's raw materials with a cache of exotic spices including saffron, nutmeg, cinnamon and sinful sugar cane. Such flavours are reflected in dishes such as Trapani's *couscous al pesce* (couscous with fish) and the island-wide penchant for desserts and sweets.

Plenty of discussions about Sicilian gastronomy skip the main course altogether and head directly for the *dolci* (desserts). Sicily has gifted the world's sugar addicts with three dangerously sweet treats: *cannoli*, sheep's milk ricotta squeezed into a fried pastry tube; *granita* a semi-frozen sorbet-like mix of water, sugar and flavourings served with a brioche for breakfast; and cassata, an Arabic melange of plain white cake filled with ricotta and topped with icing and sugared fruit.

Hit the trails, work up an appetite, and come back down in time to sample a few more surprises from God's kitchen.

Scavo. This basic unstaffed *rifugio* (which is normally left unlocked in peak season) is one of the more popular sleepovers on the Etna circuit. It is equipped with firewood/ fireplace, a wooden table and chairs, and a stone ledge on which to set your sleeping mats. There's a water pump across the path which may or may not be working. It is best to come prepared for the latter scenario.

SIDE TRIP: MONTE EGITTO
2 hours
If you still have some energy, walk to Monte Egitto through an immense, dramatic desert of lava formations. The path leaves from next to the water pump and heads due west. It is signposted with yellow trail markers. Be careful of vipers in this area.

Day 2: Rifugio Monte Scavo to Randazzo
6–7 hours, 21.5km
Leaving the *rifugio* on the dirt track and heading north–northwest you soon get to the lowest extent of a more recent 1976 **lava flow**. A path goes off to the left here which you ignore. Two kilometres further on another track goes off to the right for **Rifugio Monte Maletto** (1701m). Immersed in a thick and isolated forest a little more than 1km from the turn-off, this charming *rifugio* is among the least frequented on Mt Etna. Stocked with firewood and with a good supply of water, this could be an alternative point at which to end the day should the Rifugio Monte Scavo be full.

Still heading north, circumnavigate the western slopes of Monte Maletto (1773m) another moon-like lava cone. Ignore the path going off to the right and plunge instead into the Bosco di Maletto, a haven of larch trees, birds and welcome shade.

A turn-off to the left leads to Bosco Nave and the town of Maletto, 8km distant and a viable 'alternative finish' if time or energy are lacking. The view north now reveals the town of Randazzo nestled in a broad valley in front of you but, don't get too excited, it's further away than it looks.

The road continues west, through an area reafforested with cedar pines, to the south of the little Monte Spagnolo volcano (1547m). You'll pass a path going off to the left on the near side of the volcano; ignore it and continue east past the ruined Rifugio Monte

Spagnolo (1440m) and badly maintained *bivacco* opposite, useful only as an emergency shelter. Take the next turning to the left and cut down from the old *altomontana* (high mountain road) onto a lower road that provides an easier crossing of the still coal-black **1981 lava flow**. Almost 30 years ago, this lava flow reached the town of Randazzo, eventually flowing into the Fiume Alcántara.

The road continues to gradually descend past startling vents thrown up by the eruption until it reaches a grassier area from where the rust-coloured lookout tower of the **Rifugio Pirao** can be seen above a clump of trees. Traverse the slope until you reach the gates of the *rifugio* (closed to the public) on your left. From here a stony vehicle track continues through a red and white barrier to a paved road. Turn left on the road and follow it downhill towards Randazzo and the valley below. The road passes stone terraces, a ruined house, and a couple of small residences as it swings from east to west in broad curves down Etna northern slopes. Eventually you will reach a main road at the bottom. Turn left here and then fork immediately right onto another minor paved road that descends to the valley floor with the barren 1981 lava flow reappearing on the left. At a crossroads, turn left and follow the road west into Randazzo visible approximately 1km away. On entering the town, the road becomes Via Galiano and, soon after passing under the railway line, delivers you in central Piazza Lareto just steps from Hotel Scrivano.

GROTTE D'ETNA

Duration 2 days
Distance 31km
Difficulty moderate
Start/Finish Randazzo (p287)
Transport train
Summary This is a walk across the dozing volcano's northern flanks to two partially obscured lava tubes filled with shade, shadows and ice.

Away from the hullabaloo of Etna's southern slopes, the mountain's northern flanks are an entirely different proposition; a caustic juxtaposition of dense beech woods and rocky lava flows that provide graphic testimony to the cycles of destruction and rejuvenation that characterise the mountain's ongoing lava wars. Hidden at an altitude of between 1500m and 2000m are a number of gaping holes (over 200 in total), essentially lava tubes posing as caves that provide an interesting insight into the intricacies of volcanism and its dark, mysterious, ice-filled creations.

The following walk is a triangular loop above the Rifugio Pirao that skirts Etna's *altomontana* (vehicle-width mountain road) before breaking out over tougher, rockier terrain to the Grotta del Gelo. Getting to Rifguio Pirao requires an 8km hike on paved roads from Randazzo at the beginning and end of the walk; there is a further 3km climb to Rifugio Sapetti at the end of Day 1. To avoid doing this section twice, the walk can be combined with the Etna's Western Foothills hike (p272).

PLANNING
What to Bring

This is a long hike over hot, dry terrain. Beyond Randazzo there are no reliable water sources. It is recommended you carry a minimum of 3L of water if embarking on this walk. Bring water purification tablets if you want to use the tap at Rifugio Sapetti.

As you will be staying in an unstaffed *rifugio* you will need a sleeping bag, mat, food, and plenty of warm clothing outside of the high summer season.

Maps

The Selca 1:25,000 *Mt Etna* map covers the path above Rifugio Pirao in sufficient detail. For the first part of the walk from Randazzo use the TCI 1:50,000 *Mt Etna* map

ACCESS TOWN

Randazzo (p287) nestled in Etna's northern shadow is the best base for this hike.

GETTING TO/FROM THE WALK

For information on getting from Randazzo see p287. You can shorten this walk significantly if you hire a car in Randazzo and drive to Rifugio Pirao.

THE WALK
Day 1: Randazzo to Rifugio Saletti
4 hours, 11km

From Piazza Loreto, in central Randazzo (adjacent to the Hotel Scrivano), take Via Galiano heading southeast. Follow the street past a Spar supermarket and veer left at the train station crossing underneath the train line by means of a small tunnel. Stay on Via Galiano as it starts to swing east leaving the town and heading towards the near fatal – and still eerily evident – lava flow spewed out by Etna in 1981. At the first major crossroads turn right onto another paved road signposted 'Mille Quota'. The road climbs quite steeply up alongside the coal-black **lava flow** (on your right) and rounds a couple of bends before meeting a trunk road at a T-junction. Turn left here and then after 150m turn right, back onto another narrow asphalt road signposted 'Rifugio Pirao'. This road climbs for approximately 3km in long, gradual curves up the lower northern flanks of Mt Etna, past terraced agricultural plots, ruined farmhouses and the odd isolated residence.

You'll see the *rifugio*, evident by its distinctive rust-coloured watchtower poking above the trees, 10 minutes before you reach it. As you near the top of the paved road, turn right onto a stony track next to a blue Corpo Forestale sign. This fenced track traverses the grassy slope for 400m, passes through a red and white barrier, and leads to the gates of the rustic **Rifugio Pirao** (1100m; closed to the general public) on the right. Turn left just before the gates onto a grassy vehicle-width track that disappears uphill. After rounding a couple of gentle curves, you'll quickly reach the point where the asphalt road ends. Walkers, picnicking families and romantic sunset-seekers often park their cars here. Stay on the grassy track as it continues uphill. At a track divide turn right (the incoming path on your the left is your return route tomorrow) and turn right again at a T-junction 300m further on. Pretty soon you'll reach the unstaffed **Rifugio Saletti** on your left set in a shady wood with a tempting water tap outside which, frustratingly, dispenses non-potable water (bring purification tablets if you need a drink).

Day 2: Rifugio Saletti to Randazzo via Grotta del Gelo
7 hours, 20km

Ignore the incoming track on your right and continue straight ahead. You'll cross an old lava flow (1614) and plunge back into the woods for five minutes before the well-formed track disintegrates into a rocky path to cross the newer tree-less **1981 lava flow**. Re-enter the beech wood on the vehicle-width *altomontana* on the far side of the lava flow and, within 200m, you'll spot a fainter, narrower path, marked by a couple of erect sticks propped up by stones, going off to the left. Take this path as it forges south and uphill through a thick beech wood carpeted with dead brown leaves. The path is marked by faint red and white markers painted on the trees, but you'll have to keep your eyes peeled at certain points to ensure efficient navigation. The climb, which begins gently, gets progressively steeper gaining 600 vertical metres over 3km. While initially under tree cover, the path soon starts to alternate between beech forest and open rocky sections before ultimately leaving the wood altogether for the final 800m of steep climbing up the lava flow to the **Grotta del Gelo** (look out carefully for small cairns and white markers on the now indistinct path).

You can access the *grotta* via a steep entry path, but come equipped with a headlamp, good shoes and warm clothing if you plan to make a full exploration – temperatures stay well below freezing inside even in high summer. One of over 200 caves and lava tubes on Etna, the Grotta del Gelo (ice cave) is situated at a height of 2043m with its opening uphill, meaning snow and ice that accumulates here in winter lingers year-road. This has led some observers to dub it the most southerly 'glacier' in Europe.

From the *grotta* a clearer and better marked path towards the Grotta del Lamponi heads east and then northeast across more uncompromising black lava. The descent is gradual with some flatter sections and you'll see the distinct *altomontana* that originates at the Rifugio Brunek long before you join it. Just before the path junction you'll fall upon the smaller equally well-camouflaged **Grotta dei Lamponi**.

To find the cave entrance, follow the cairned trail across the lava. Once inside, head south along the tunnel for about 100m – you'll pass two lovely pools of light framed by delicate grasses at points where the roof

of the cave has collapsed. At the end of the cave is a tongue-shaped strip of lava.

Go back the way you came. Just before the cave entrance, you'll find a small tunnel on the left. A bit narrow at first, it then widens and opens onto the main tunnel. Go in and descend for about 300m, passing carefully over a large landslide, to reach the cave exit. The tunnel actually continues its descent underground to the north, but there is a danger of cave-ins and continuing is not recommended.

From the *grotta* descend to a dirt road (the *altomontana*) at **Passo dei Dammusi** (1709m), where three different paths converge. Turn left (west) enjoying the now easy hike as the dirt road meanders around the mountain offering sporadic stretches of welcome shade. Just after passing the **Rifugio di Monte Santa Maria** on the left (the *rifugio* has a fireplace but is otherwise bare and without a water supply), turn right off the main dirt road and proceed through a gate on the eastern side of the vegetation-covered volcanic cone of **Monte Santa Maria**. A narrow path circumnavigates the small peak, but you'll only need to follow it halfway. On the north side of the Monte, a mess of small barely distinguishable mule tracks drop down for 200m onto a more distinct track below. Pick any one of them and fight your way down through the brambles and you'll soon hit the wider track that zigzags down to eventually meet the dirt track you ascended yesterday about 1.5km east of Rifugio Sapetti. Turn right and retrace your steps down to **Rifugio Pirao**. From here it's a straightforward return on paved roads back to **Randazzo** (a direct reversal of yesterday's route).

VULCANO

A world away from Italy's urban chaos, Vulcano is in the starkly beautiful volcanic Aeolian archipelago (Isole Eolie). Visible from the mainland of northeastern Sicily, the seven islands appear adrift on the sea haze. Approaching Vulcano by boat, the mythological grandeur of the landscape is even more striking – a rugged volcanic cone rising abruptly out of the sea, smoking fissures and steaming sulphur-yellow rocks. This is a land where, according to legend, the gods of wind and fire once conjured up the elements, and where, amid the rotten-egg stench of volcanic fumes, the medieval popes decreed the mouth of Hell lay. While today the island attracts a somewhat more prosaic crowd of summer tourists, the Vulcano experience has lost little of its primal appeal.

One of two still-active volcanic islands in the archipelago, the 21-sq-km Vulcano is formed by the vast high plain of Vulcano Piano. The island is dominated to the south by Monte Aria (500m); to the north by the promontory of Vulcanello (123m), with its three, small inactive craters; and by the large active central cone called the Fossa, which looms over Porto di Levante. Although steep, Fossa is a relatively small volcano, measuring 391m at its highest point. Its lower slopes are covered by a mantle of shrubbery that, when flowering in late spring, sweetens the landscape with beautiful yellow flowers and an intense perfume. From the rim of the Gran Cratere, as Fossa's crater is called, are superb panoramic views of the island, the Sicilian mainland and the rest of the archipelago.

HISTORY

The Aeolian Islands were already inhabited in the 4th millennium BC by people who prospered from mining and trading obsidian, a sharp, black, lustrous and valuable volcanic glass that can still be found on Lipari. In the Bronze Age, around the 18th century BC, the islands were colonised by people of Mycenaean Greece who gave the archipelago its name, linking it with the myth of the wind god, Aeolus (Eolo). Thucydides, in the 5th century BC, reported a tremendous eruption on Vulcano.

With their strategic position in the Mediterranean, the Aeolian Islands were coveted by the Sicilian city-states of Magna Grecia, and later by Carthage and Rome. Since ancient times, the caves of Vulcano have yielded alum, a mineral salt used as a powerful caustic, and in the days of the Roman Empire, Cicero praised the island's excellent thermal waters. In the Middle Ages, the Fossa crater was believed to be the mouth of Hell.

In 1083 the Aeolians were conquered by the Normans. In 1544 the islands' population was decimated when Lipari, less than 1km from Vulcano, was sacked by the Moslem pirate Ariadeno Barbarossa, and all the inhabitants were taken into slavery. In the 1550s, Lipari was repopulated by Charles V of Spain, and from that time on the history of the archipelago has followed that of Sicily and the Kingdom of Naples. During the years of economic hardship before and after WWII, many of the islands' residents were forced to emigrate. Most went to Australia, which is often referred to as the 'eighth Aeolian island'.

ENVIRONMENT

The Aeolian archipelago is found in the lower Tyrrhenian Sea, from 20km to 40km north of Sicily, and is made up of seven originally volcanic islands. During the Pliocene Age, as tectonic plate movements created the shelves of the Tyrrhenian Sea, magma escaped through fissures up to 1000m deep in the sea floor, gradually creating an underwater mountain chain. Emerging from the sea at different times during the last 300,000 years, the visible tips of these mountains form the islands. Wind and rain erosion have consumed and compacted the exposed landscape, leaving it low and flattened.

The youngest of the islands, Vulcano and Stromboli (100,000 and 40,000 years old, respectively) are the only ones still active today. Vulcanello (123m), a small, inactive peninsula on Vulcano, was created suddenly in an underwater eruption in 183 BC, recorded in eyewitness accounts of the time.

After a century of only minor 'secondary' activity, limited to gas emissions from fumaroles, there is evidence that pressure may again be building up within the volcano. It may be comforting (or not) to know that the area has been placed under observation by the Ministry of Civil Protection.

CLIMATE

Mild temperatures in winter and not-too-high temperatures in summer, combined with scarce rain, make for a very pleasant climate year-round in the Aeolian Islands. Average temperatures vary from 13°C in January to 27°C in July. Only 500mm to 600mm of rain falls annually, with the wettest months in January and December. Summers are dry. Winds are predominantly from the northwest (the *maestrale*) or from the southeast (the *scirocco*).

PLANNING
When to Walk
The warm season is from April to October. The best months to walk are April and May (when the wildflowers are blooming), and September and October (when it is still possible to swim in the warm sea). Dawn and sunset are the optimum times to head towards the crater, escaping the worst of the heat and avoiding any crowds. Prices are lower from November to March (not including Easter), but during this time most of the hotels and restaurants close, transport to the island is irregular and Porto di Levante reverts to being a sleepy island village.

What to Bring
There is absolutely no shade around the crater of Vulcano and the sun becomes searingly hot as the day progresses, so bring adequate sun protection and plenty of water. If you find the sulphurous smell that seeps out of the crater offensive (although for brief periods of exposure the fumes are not dangerous), it's not a bad idea to take along a cotton scarf to filter out the worst emissions. Running shoes (trainers) are quite adequate if you don't have good walking shoes.

Maps
The path up to the Gran Cratere is self-evident and few people bother to take a map with them, although it's useful for identifying the surrounding islands and Vulcano landmarks visible from the crater's rim. There are several widely available maps that use an old IGM 1:25,000 map as their base, covering all the islands of the archipelago. If intending only to visit Vulcano, pick up a copy of the easy-to-read Rebus Edizioni 1:25,000 map *Vulcano* sold in shops around the island.

Emergency
For medical assistance in an emergency, contact the **Guardia Medica** (☎ 090 985 22 20).

ACCESS TOWN
The most pleasant base for this walk is in Porto di Levante (p287) on the island itself.

VULCANO'S GRAN CRATERE

Duration 2½–3 hours
Distance 11km
Difficulty easy
Start/Finish Porto di Levante (p287)
Transport ferry

Summary A short but steep climb up to the steaming rim of a still-active island crater, with magnificent views across to the other islands in the Aeolian archipelago.

The Gran Cratere is an easy half-day excursion, suitable for the whole family. The walk provides a rare (and safe) opportunity to get a close look at a still-active, if geriatric, volcano and the classic 'Vulcanian' landforms it has created. With only the gentle seeping of gases from fumaroles on the cone's rim to remind visitors there is life in the old girl yet, it is hard to imagine that only a century ago the volcano's last explosion wiped out a settlement and the burgeoning alum extraction business of a Scottish tycoon. The more adventurous may like to continue on to the nearby island of Stromboli, where eruptions are continuous and an immense expanse of volcanic waste, the Sciara del Fuoco, edges its way down to the sea.

THE WALK
From the waterfront in Porto di Levante, follow the narrow, sealed road that leads southwest towards Vulcano Piano, past the rooftop terrace restaurant of Al Cratere, on the right. The massive body of the crater rises before you.

After a 10-minute walk along the road, and 50m beyond a boat storage facility on the left, take an unmarked trail that heads steeply uphill to the left through stands of brushwood; this is a short cut that, in two minutes, links up with the main trail. (The main path begins on the left, another 200m up the road.) When you reach the main trail, continue left (east) until you come to a sharp curve to the right, where a sign in four languages announces the dangers of the crater. If you proceed (which everyone does) you won't have any problems with officialdom, but you do need to be aware that Fossa is only sleeping, and *is* an active volcano.

Several minutes later, the trail turns left again. The soil underfoot, which until now

VULCANO'S GRAN CRATERE

(Map labels: Bocche di Vulcano; To Isola di Lipari; Punta Samossà; Spiaggia Sabbia Nera; Vulcanello (123m); Porto di Ponente; Capo Grosso; Laghetto di Fanghi; Porto di Levante; To Milazzo (Sicily); Punta del Monaco; Start/Finish; boat storage facility; Punta Lùccia; Testa Grossa; Fossa di Vulcano (391m); Gran Cratere (208m); TYRRHENIAN SEA; Monte Rosso (328m); Monte Sareceno (481m); Cappo Secco; Vulcano Piano; Punta del Mortaro; 0 2 4km; 0 1 2 miles)

has been made up of a small, dark volcanic gravel, changes to a sandy colour. The trail takes on the impressive look of a deep erosion furrow where the path has been worn into a grooved shelf cutting obliquely across the slope. At the end of this shelf you reach a wide, flat clearing of lava pebbles. Ascend again to the left (southeast), following the main trail. In three minutes you'll arrive at the lowest point of the crater's edge (290m, 45 minutes to 1 hour from the start).

To your left, the inside wall of the crater is full of countless fissures, covered in splendid yellow-orange crystals, that let off columns of sulphurous gases. The bottom of the volcano is clearly visible less than 50m below, formed by two 'cold' (inactive) calderas – two perfectly circular and level intersecting spaces covered by a layer of solid, sun-dried mud. A steep trail descends to the bottom in three minutes. Many go down for an unconventional walk along the hard crater floor.

Once on the crater's rim, walk clockwise round the crest of the crater, with stunning 360-degree views of the Aeolian Islands lined up to the north. From left to

right they are Alicudi, Filicudi, and Salina peeking out from behind Lipari (beyond the little crater of Vulcanello), then to the northeast Panarea, and the dark and distant smoking cone of Stromboli. To the south, from east to west, you can see the province of Calabria with its Aspromonte (1437m) and, on clear days, a long piece of the Sicilian coast dominated by the imposing bulk of Etna. Depending on the direction of the wind, fumes from the fumaroles will be wafting over some sections of the trail; it is a good idea to pass these sections quickly, avoid walking too close to any of the vents as the temperature of the escaping gas can be searing.

It's the changing panorama that makes this part of the walk interesting. You can get to the highest point of the **crest** (391m) in about 20 to 25 minutes, from where you can see to the Sicilian coast and over the part of the island called Vulcano Piano. To the west you will note that the crest of the cliff is no more than a section of the great ancient volcano, eroded by the millennia, inside which the present crater was formed.

Returning back down the volcano, take the same trail. Deviations are not recommended down the very steep slope, with its unstable, crumbly soil. In any case, it is best to keep to the main trail to avoid damaging the rare plants that are attempting to grow in this inhospitable land of lava.

PARCO DEI NEBRODI

A short detour inland from Sicily's crowded north coast resorts takes you up into Parco dei Nebrodi and the cool, leafy respite of the largest beech forest in Europe. The soft, rolling peaks of Nebrodi form part of the Sicilian extension of the Apennines. With Nebrodi's highest point (Monte Soro) a modest 1847m, the thickly wooded slopes and green meadows are a far cry from the harsh, scorched landscape characteristic of much of the island. This is not a pristine natural environment (there is very little of that left in Sicily) but since its creation in 1993, the 850-sq-km park has become a valuable ecological haven – an island within an island. Around 25% of Sicily's forest lies inside the park's boundaries and, despite the ever-present human factor, shelters a rich array of animal and plant life.

CLIMATE

Nebrodi's climate varies considerably across the region, influenced by altitude and coastal proximity. Near the coast, average annual temperatures range from 17°C to 18°C; further inland and up into the hills, the thermometer drops to between 10°C and 13°C. The coldest days are in January and February, with minimum average temperatures of around -1°C. Autumn and winter are the wettest months. Snow begins to fall in November and can remain until well into March.

PLANNING
What to Bring

There is only one reliable water source along the trail, so bring supplies with you.

When to Walk

Like elsewhere on the island, spring and autumn are the best times for exploring the mountains. In spring (Mar–May) wildflowers turn the mountain pastures into a heady riot of colour, while the woods in autumn (Sep–Nov) are transformed into blazing orange. Do not rule out walking in summer, however, when the cool mountain breezes provide a welcome relief from the sweltering heat on the coast below.

Maps

The only map with sufficient detail on the park is the TCI 1:50,000 *Il Parco dei Nebrodi*, produced in cooperation with the park's administration. Be warned, however, that tracks have been marked inaccurately in a number of places, and the map leaves out quite a few of the smaller forestry tracks found on the ground – potentially confusing. For the section of the walk described here between Monte Soro and Lago di Biviere, refer closely to the walk description and use the 1:50,000 map in conjunction with the one in this book.

Books

The park's administration has produced a number of Italian-language publications on the region, including *Parco dei Nebrodi*, by Francesco Alaimo, which describes in detail a number of possible (read 'unmarked') walk itineraries in the park.

Information Sources

Tracking down information on Parco dei Nebrodi is frustratingly difficult. Few of Sicily's general tourist offices keep tourist material on the area, while the park's visitor centres are relatively inaccessible for walkers dependent on public transport. The most useful centre, if you can get there, is the **Cesarò park office** (☎ 095 69 60 08; Strada Nazionale, 98033), which has very enthusiastic staff and publications for sale, including the TCI *Il Parco dei Nebrodi* map. Alternatively try the park office in Randazzo (p287).

For a list of publications and other information, see the website of **Parco dei Nebrodi** (www.parks.it/parco.nebrodi).

ACCESS TOWNS

Take your pick between Sant'Agata di Militello (p288), 33km to the north, and Randazzo (p287), 46km to the southeast.

NEBRODI LAKE CIRCUIT

Duration 5–5½ hours
Distance 18km
Difficulty easy–moderate
Start/Finish Villa Miraglia
Nearest Towns Sant'Agata di Militello (p288), Randazzo (p287)
Transport bus
Summary A circuit walk into the heart of the Nebrodi, climbing to near the summit of Monte Soro, before descending along shady tracks to Lago di Biviere, a wetland haven for migrating birds.

The described walk is a full-day circuit into the central Nebrodi area, climbing the flank of Monte Soro and then descending through beech wood to skirt the edge of the Lago di Biviere. Set against a serene natural backdrop of forest and open meadows, the lake is the jewel in the Nebrodi crown, considered Sicily's most ecologically valuable mountain wet area.

The return route along an unsealed road used by grazing livestock provides a delightful rural idyll, passing stone farmhouses on

SICILY

the northern edge of the Contrada Sollazzo Verde forest and skirting Lago di Maulazzo. Herds of wild Sanfrettelano horses, introduced by the Normans during the Middle Ages, keep a watchful eye on the passing human traffic.

It's good to remember before setting out that recreational walking has never been a part of the Sicilian tradition and the park's foray into the world of ecotourism is only a very recent phenomenon. Trails are poorly marked, if marked at all, and there is little or no walking infrastructure. If you stray off the trail, you may well end up on private property.

GETTING TO/FROM THE WALK

There *is* an **ISEA** (☎ 095 53 68 94) bus, but it's limited and it requires some tenacity to make the 5am departure from Sant'Agata di Militello (€3, one hour, one daily). An alternative would be to catch the 2pm bus from Catania (€10.50, 2½ hours, one daily) and stay overnight at the highly pleasant **Villa Miraglia** (☎ 095 69 73 97; S289; half-/full board per person €55/70). This lovely old, stone *albergo*, once a hunting

lodge, is set in the middle of the Nebrodi beech wood 300m beneath Portella Femmina Morta. Now owned and managed by the province of Messina, it is stuffed full of fabulous collectibles: quirky ceramics, colourfully painted cart panels, old paintings and an absorbing collection of Italian detective novels. With good, simple food, this is a rural retreat to savour. You will need to book ahead on weekends and in the height of summer.

If you're driving, the Villa Miraglia lies between Sant'Agata di Militello (33km) and Cesarò (18km) on the S289, one of three main routes traversing the park. Cesarò is easily accessible from Randazzo which lies 28km to the east.

THE WALK

Head north along the road (S289) from Villa Miraglia to Portella Femmina Morta (1524m), 300m away. Just before the pass, turn right onto an unsealed forestry track that heads east. (Note that this is not the main paved road into Monte Soro.) The track winds through wood and meadow (with tantalising glimpses of Mt Etna

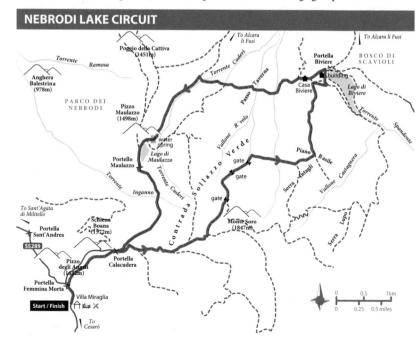

NEBRODI LAKE CIRCUIT

smoking in the distance), climbing gently to meet the main road at Portella Calacudera (1562m), a little over 1km later.

Here the main road divides. The unsealed left fork heads down towards Lago Maulazzo (your return route). Follow, instead, the sign to 'Monte Soro' along the sealed road (right fork), which climbs its way up through a hunting reserve. Higher up are long views back to the hilltop towns of Troina and Enna.

About 1km before the summit (one hour from the start of the walk), just as the road begins a tight curve to the south, turn off left along an unsignposted leafy track. The summit, crammed with telecommunications equipment, doesn't really warrant a detour. The track passes through a wooden gate (50m from the turn-off), then a second, 10 to 15 minutes later, as it descends steadily north then east through a thick beech wood. Stay on the main track, ignoring any rough-looking turn-offs, as it crosses two often-dried-up streams in quick succession and then negotiates a third gate. The trail switches to the north again as the wood opens out into a small, green meadow, then swings back east to cross another stream with a paved crossing. Shortly afterwards (40 to 45 minutes from the road) the trail forks. Take the left, descending track, which opens out onto another magnificent view of Mt Etna. Five minutes later you arrive at the meadow of the **Piano Basile**. To the north on a fine day you can see the distinctive outline of Rocche del Crasto, standing sentinel over the village of Alcara li Fusi.

Continue to the end of the meadow and a T-intersection with a north–south cart track. Follow this track left (north), descending steeply through more woodland for 2km to the shores of **Lago di Biviere**. As it nears the lake, the trail opens out onto a grassy slope and swings left descending down to a track by a locked gate and building where you have to turn right. Continue along this track past another small tile-roofed building, then fork almost immediately left along a track that leads to the lake's edge (2½ hours from the beginning of the walk). This is a perfect spot

IL GATTOPARDO (THE LEOPARD)

'If you want things to stay as they are, things have to change'.

Thus spoke Tancredi Falconeri, pivotal character in the literary classic, *Il Gattopardo* (The Leopard), by Giuseppe di Lampedusa, popularly considered to be Italy's greatest novel. Profound yet ambiguous, the quote – in which Tancredi urges his aristocratic uncle, Don Fabrizio, to take action in order to ensure his Sicilian family's survival amid the tumult of the Risorgimento – has become one of the most immortal lines in Italian literature.

Set in the 1860s in a Sicily wracked by the upheavals of Italian reunification, *Il Gattopardo* chronicles the life and times of the aristocratic yet world-weary Don Fabrizio Cobrera, heir to the House of Salina and last in a long line of illustrious Sicilian princes.

With Sicily's two fledgling kingdoms crumbling and Garibaldi's 'red-shirts' laying siege to Palermo, Don Fabrizio faces a classic existential crisis: how to survive in a world where the old order of class and privilege is being rapidly superseded by a nascent new Italian nation.

Sweeping in scope and packed with a cast of complex characters, the book's rather odd title offers a subtle hint at Don Fabrizio's messy quandary. A 'Gattopardo' is an African serval, a small leopard-like wild cat hunted to the verge of extinction in southern Italy during the 19th century. If Don Fabrizio ignores the metaphoric writing on the wall and fails to adapt to the new political realities, the beleaguered House of Salina faces the same shabby predicament.

Though written in the 1950s, nearly a century after Italy's political map had been redrawn, Di Lampedusa's novel is loaded with autobiographical references. Himself, the descendent of a Lampedusa prince, the author's privileged life largely parallels that of the cynical Don Fabrizio's, albeit in a different era.

Di Lampedusa's lengthy manuscript was repeatedly rejected during his lifetime; it finally found a publisher a year after his death in 1958. In the ensuing decades it has become a publishing phenomenon, spawning an award-winning movie starring Burt Lancaster and shifting more copies than any Italian book before or since.

to kick off your shoes and crack open the *panini* (bread rolls) though you may be sharing space with a few resident cows. A bank of trees lines the shore to the south, while to the north the lake is bounded by a gentle, grassy slope. Before beginning the walk back to Villa Miraglia, you could continue on the trail that heads southeast along the water's edge (a full circuit takes 20 minutes).

From the western end of the lake, cross the fence via a foot ladder next to the lake track and walk across the small field to the glorified cart track that follows the northern edge of Lago di Biviere (accessed by another foot ladder). Turn left for Lago Maulazzo (5km, 1 hour). This is probably the least attractive, but still very enjoyable, section of the walk, sticking to the stony road as it negotiates several small streams and winds its way west through farming country along the woodland border. The Rocche del Crasto dominates views to the north.

Roughly 30 minutes from the Lago di Biviere, the road reaches a junction at Passo Taverna. A sign pointing north indicates the way to Alcara li Fusi (20km). To the left, the road climbs gently up the Torrente Cuderi valley to **Lago di Maulazza**. Just before the lower dam wall of the artificial lake is a fountain with deliciously drinkable water. Ascend up to the right-hand side of the dam and follow the track along the side of the lake which is often, lamentably, scarred by uncollected litter. At a road junction on the near edge of the lake, a sign indicates the road back to 'Portella Femmina Morta' (4.1km) curving round the western shore of the lake. Ignore a right turn to Militello Rosamarino and cross the upper dam wall. From here, the road rises steadily back to **Portella Calacudera**, an easy climb of 100 vertical metres. Retrace your steps to the beginning of the walk (20 minutes away).

MORE WALKS

PARCO NATURALE DELL'ETNA

Parco Naturale dell'Etna offers some wonderful walking opportunities against the scenic backdrop of Etna's summit craters. Walkers can either base themselves at Rifugio Sapienza (p272), on the southern side of the volcano, or on the less-visited

northern slopes, at Rifugio Brunek. The Selca 1:25,000 *Mt Etna* map is the best available for navigation.

ETNA SUMMIT

Most climbs up Etna start from where the AST bus from Catania drops you off at the Rifugio Sapienza (1923m). From here the **Funivia dell'Etna** (☎ 095 91 41 41; www .funiviaetna.com; cable car one-way/return €14.50/27, incl bus & guide €60; 9am-4.30pm) runs a cable car up the mountain to 2500m.

Once out of the cable car you can attempt the long walk (3½ to four hours return) up the winding track to the authorised crater zone (2920m). If you plan to do this, make sure you leave yourself enough time to get up *and* down before the last cable car leaves at 4.45pm. Otherwise hop on one of the Mercedes Benz trucks (with obligatory guide; €21).

On a clear day, the landscape above the cable-car station is stunning – the black cone of the Cratere Sud-Est against a bright blue sky. The guided tour takes you on a 45-minute walk around the Bocca Nuova. On the eastern edge of the volcano, the Valle del Bove falls away in a 1000m drop. Smoke billows up from its depths, enveloping you on the ridge above.

You can also make an ascent on the northern flank of the volcano from the Piano Provenzano (1800m) an area severely damaged by the 2002 eruptions. There are similar 4WD excursions to the summit from here (around €40 per person), but you will need a car to get here. The nearest public transport terminates at Linguaglossa, 16km away.

If you're interested in other Mt Etna area hikes, pick up a copy of the excellent free *Nature Paths Guide booklet* from tourist offices throughout the region; it details 24 mapped hikes of varying difficulty.

VULCANO

The north coast of Vulcanello, the little volcanic promontory to the north of the island, offers short walks to admire the splendid panorama over the *faraglioni* (rock stacks) of Lipari. You can also visit the little craters of Vulcanello (one hour).

If you want to spend another half-day exploring the island, go back to the sealed road at the beginning of the trail to Vulcano's crater. Go to the left towards Vulcano Piano and get lost in the countless little country roads beneath Monte Aria (500m), the highest point on the island. And to top it all off, follow the road that descends from the Piano to the extreme south of the island to reach the lighthouse at Gelso, from where there are views across to Sicily (three to four hours). There are frequent buses back to Portro di Levante from here.

PARCO NATURALE REGIONALE DELLE MADONIE

Established in 1989, Parco Naturale Regionale delle Madonie covers 400 sq km of the Madonie mountains, west of the Nebrodi range in northern Sicily. Thickly wooded and crowned with limestone cliffs, the park is botanically the richest region in the Mediterranean; half of Sicily's plant species grow here. Like Nebrodi, this is not an untouched wilderness, but a glimpse of traditional rural Sicily, complete with hamlets, farms and grazing livestock. Walkers will find trails are still in the process of being marked, while public transport access is limited. The 1:50,000 *Madonie/Carta dei Sentieri e del Paesaggio* map can be obtained from the Palermo Tourist Office (Piazza Castelnuovo). For more information, contact the **park headquarters** (☎ 0921 68 02 01; Petralia Sottana).

RISERVA NATURALE ORIENTATO DELLO ZINGARO

After a successful grass-roots protest against the construction of a coastal road, a large tract of the Zingaro region in the northwest of Sicily was declared a nature reserve in 1980; the island's first. This stunning coastal landscape of limestone mountains overlooking the turquoise-blue Gulf of Castellammare lies within easy distance of either Palermo or Trapani, and makes for an ideal day trip by car. There is public transport as far as the small town of Scopello (with accommodation), 2km south of the park. A visitor centre at the park's southern entrance has copies of the 1:25,000 park map.

GULF OF CASTELLAMMARE

Starting from the southern park entrance, a 15km circuit climbs inland and north along a well-maintained nature trail, passing between the peaks of Pizzo del Corvo (403m) and Pizzo Passo del Lupo (615m), and eventually reaching the isolated hamlet of the Baglio Cosenza. The return route curves back south along a cliffside path that provides superb views over the gulf, with some easy detours down to sheltered, sandy coves. Graded moderate, with 600m of ascent, the whole circuit takes between four and five hours. There is little shade along the route, so take plenty of water.

TOWNS & FACILITIES

CATANIA

☎ 095 / pop 313,000

With all the edgy chaos, traffic congestion and general decay you'd expect of Sicily's second-largest city, Catania sounds like an unsavoury prospect; fortunately someone forgot to tell this to the locals. A glance below the grit and grime reveals a sophisticated and vibrant city, with a rich history and a kicking summer night-life.

Information

The **Municipal tourist office** (☎ 742 55 73; bureau.turismo@comune.catania.it; Via Vittorio Emanuele 172; 8.15am-7.15pm Mon-Fri, 8.15am-12.15pm Sat) is the central nexus of information. **Etna Convention Bureau** has taken over **airport** (☎ 093 70 24; 9am-3pm Mon-Sat) and **train station** (☎ 093 70 23; 9am-9pm) tourist information posts formerly operated by Catania's provincial tourism board.

Supplies & Equipment

The best place to buy maps is **Librerie Cavallotto** (Corso Sicilia 91) – an excellent bookshop if you're hunting generally for books on Catania and Sicily. There are a number of bookshops along Via Etnea that also sell Etna maps; try **Libreria Editrice** (Via Etnea 390) or **La Paglia** (Via Etnea 393). Luggage can be left at the train station for a small fee for up to 12 hours.

Sleeping

Camping Jonio (☎ 49 11 39; www.jonio eventi.it; Via Villini a Mare 2; camping per person/tent €9/9, bungalow per person €40)

Close to a beautiful rocky beach, this campsite is about 5km north of the city. There are is a variety of bungalows, caravans and small houses for up to six people. To get there, catch buses No 534, 535 or 448 from downtown Catania.

Agorà Hostel (☎ 723 30 10; www.agorahostel.com; Piazza Currò 6; dm €18-21, s €25-30, d €50-55) In one of the most interesting parts of the old city behind Piazza del Duomo, this is the best option for travellers on a rock-bottom budget.

Hotel Rubens (☎ 31 70 73; www.hotelrubenscatania.com; Via Etnea 196; s/d/tr €45/75/95) Tucked away in a small courtyard off Via Etnea, this place with its seven rooms is central, comfortable and well priced. It also has an affable English-speaking owner.

Hotel del Duomo (☎ 250 31 77; www.hoteldelduomo.it; Via Etnea 28; s €50-65, d €75-95) Armed with a devastating mix of cheap prices and central location, this crusty old dame sandwiched between Piazza del Duomo and Piazza dell'Università occupies an entire wing of an ancient *palazzo*. The rooms have a faded charm and big bathrooms and many offer romantic views over the floodlit piazza at night.

Eating

You could plan a holiday around Catania's food. All manner of fresh produce can be bought from the city's excellent and central markets, open every day except Sunday. **La Fiera** (Piazza Carlo Alberto) has bread, fresh fruit, cheese and numerous odds and ends, while **La Pescheria** (Piazza del Duomo) is the place to buy fish.

Eating out can be pleasant and inexpensive in Catania, with innumerable stalls and bars serving delicious Sicilian snacks and savoury titbits. Don't miss the wide selection of delectable sweet and savoury pastries in Via Etnea and the gelatarias in Piazza Bellini.

Authentic Sicilian home cooking abounds in the following places:

Osteria Antica Marina (☎ 34 81 97; Via Pardo 29; meals €30-35; closed Wed) This salt-of-the-earth trattoria behind the fish market is the place to come for fresh seafood, including the local speciality: raw anchovy salad. Decor-wise we're talking solid wooden tables and rough stone walls. Reservations are essential.

Trattoria La Paglia (☎ 34 68 38; Via Pardo 23; meals €15-25; closed Sun) Situated just behind Piazza del Duomo in the heart of the *pescheria* (fish market), this is one of Catania's best traditional seafood restaurants. Freshness is guaranteed.

Metrò (☎ 32 20 98; Via Crociferi 76; meals €25-35; closed Sun) The north comes south with this Slow Food eatery giving a bit of extra style and innovative to traditional Sicilian specialities. Their *tonno in cipuddata* (tuna steak smothered in caramelized onions) is more than delicious, as is the *dialogo fra il cioccolato e il pistacchio* (dense chocolate cake topped with cream and a dome of pistachio flan).

Getting There & Away

Catania's airport, Fontanarossa, is 7km southwest of the city centre and services domestic and European flights. A number of cheap airlines such as easyJet and Ryanair land here. Take the special Alibus No 457 (€1, 20 minutes) from outside the train station or in Via Etnea.

Intercity buses terminate in the area around Piazza Giovanni XXIII, in front of the train station. **SAIS** (☎ 53 61 68; Via d'Amico 185) serves Syracuse, Palermo (€13, 2½ hours) and Messina (€7, 1½ hours). It also has services to Naples (€32, 8¾ hours) and Rome (€45, 10½ hours).

AST (☎ 746 10 96; Via Luigi Sturzo 232) also services these destinations and many smaller provincial towns around Catania, including Nicolosi, the cable car on Mt Etna and Noto. **Interbus Etna Trasporti** (☎ 095 53 27 16; Via d'Amico 185) runs buses to Piazza Armerina, Taormina, Messina, Enna, Ragusa, Gela, Syracuse and Rome.

Frequent trains connect Catania with Messina and Syracuse (€7, 1½ hours for both) and there are less frequent services to Palermo (€12, 3¼ hours) and Enna (€6, 1¾ hours). The private **Ferrovie Circumetnea** (☎ 095 54 12 50; www.circumetnea.it) train line circles Mt Etna, stopping at the towns and villages around the volcano's base including Randazzo (€4.70, two hours). The station is a 10-minute metro ride from Catania's main station.

Catania is easily reached from Messina on the A18 and from Palermo on the A19. From the A18, signs for the centre of Catania will bring you to Via Etnea.

PORTO DI LEVANTE
☎ 090 / pop 9200

A bit of a tourist trap, Porto di Levante on the northern end of the island of Vulcano makes a viable base for a hike up the eponymous volcano, if you can stand the all-pervading stench of sulphur. Resort facilities are concentrated on the narrow strip of land between Porto di Levante and Porto di Ponente, which boasts the Spiaggia Sabbia Nera (Black Sand Beach), the only sandy – if soot-black – beach on the islands.

Information
The summer-only **visitor centre** (☎ 985 20 28; 8am-2pm Jun-Oct) is housed in a dome-like building on the main street, 50m from the boat dock. The centre provides basic information on the island's accommodation and tourist services. Many of the shops lining the main street in the port sell maps and books on the archipelago, along with the usual collection of tourist paraphernalia.

A number of companies on the main street offer day trips to the volcanic island of Stomboli. Boats take tourists to the base of the Sciara del Fuoco, an immense expanse of volcanic waste that descends towards the sea. Alternatively, you can take a guided walk up 918m to a vantage point above the crater, with sunset views of the eruptions below.

Sleeping & Eating
On the black-sand beach of Porto di Ponente is **Camping Togo Togo** (☎ 985 23 03; www.campingvulcano.it; campsites per person €10-12, bungalows two/four person €60/100; Apr-Sep).

A pleasantly low-key place on the way to the crater is **Pensione La Giara** (☎ 985 22 29; Via Provinciale 40; s €31-59, d €62-102; Apr–mid-Oct), offering rooms with bathroom and air-con. **Hotel Conti** (☎ 985 20 12; www.contivulcano.it; Porto Ponente; s €50-71, d €84-126) is an older hotel with an attached restaurant and sprawling terrace overlooking Spiaggia Sabbia Nera.

La Forgia Maurizio (☎ 339 137 91 07; Via Provinciale 45) is one of the smartest, if overpriced, restaurants in Porto di Levante with dishes with an Indian tinge. Otherwise, there are a number of cheaper restaurants, cafés and pizzerias along the main street.

There is a supermarket and bakery on the road to Vulcano Piano, Via Provinciale.

Getting There & Away
Both **Ustica Lines** (www.usticalines.it) and **Siremar** (☎ 928 32 42) run hydrofoils from Milazzo to the Aeolian Islands. From 1 June to 30 September hydrofoils depart almost hourly (from around 7am-7pm) to Lipari, stopping en route at Vulcano (€15, 45 minutes). **SNAV** (☎ 928 78 21; www.snavali .com) runs daily ferries to Vulcano from Naples. Siremar car ferries to Vulcano are slower and less frequent than the hydrofoils but cost about half.

In Milazzo, the ticket offices are in or around the port, while in Messina the office is halfway up Via Vittorio Emanuele II. Peak season is from June to September with winter services much reduced and sometimes cancelled due to heavy seas.

RANDAZZO
☎ 095 / pop 11,300

Like a cat whose nine lives have nearly been extinguished, Randazzo's dicey fate rests in the hands of smouldering Mt Etna. An unpretentious and proudly traditional Sicilian town, this diminutive settlement (the nearest to Etna's summit) has so far been spared the fall-out of a major eruption, though the 1981 explosion came dangerously close. Randazzo is a good nexus for the Etna's Western Foothills and Grotte d'Etna hikes and an ideal place to stick your finger on Sicily's fast-beating pulse.

Information
Randazzo has an excellent **Centro Visite Parco dei Parchi** (☎ 799 16 11; Corso Umberto 197) covering both Parco dei Nebrodi and Parco Naturale d'Etna.

Supplies & Equipment
Good local maps – including the Selca 1:25,000 *Mt Etna* map - can be procured in **La Sicilia** (Via Umberto 40) a newsagent-cum-bookshop.

If you want to hire a car in order to shorten the Grotte d'Etna hike or get to the start of the Parco dei Nebrodi walk, try **Auto Grasso** (☎ 92 13 27; Via Giunta 1). Prices hover at around €50 per day for a small Fiat.

Sleeping & Eating
For sleeping, look no further that the friendly, family-run **Hotel Scrivano** (☎ 92 11 26;

www.hotelscrivano.com; Via Bonaventura; s/d €50/90) which boasts an on-site restaurant, roof terrace and downstairs bar (with wi-fi connection). It's stuck rather incongruously behind a petrol station, but don't let the oily mechanics put you off; the interior's clean and modern. If it's full, they'll probably point you in the direction of the nearby **B&B Edelweiss** (☎ 347 626 28 21; Via Duca degli Abruzzi 233; d €60).

The town's best restaurant is the sublime **Trattoria San Giorgio e il Drago** (☎ 92 39 72; Piazza San Giorgio 28; meals €20) in the equally sublime square where you get good honest Sicilian food in a dreamy setting. Bag an alfresco seat and try the shared antipasto plate.

Getting There & Away

Randazzo is on the **Ferrovie Circumetnea** (☎ 095 54 12 50; www.circumetnea.it) railway line. Trains to Catania (€4.70, two hours) via Maletto and Bronte leave every couple of hours.

Interbus SPA (☎ 0935 50 31 41; www.interbus.it) has a couple of early morning buses to Catania (€4.50, 1½ hours) at 6.15am and 7.55am. They also run direct buses to Messina. For the Nebrodi Lake Circuit walk (p281), buses will only take you as far as Cesarò, 18km from Villa Miraglia (p282).

SANT'AGATA DI MILITELLO

☎ 0941 / pop 13,100

This businesslike seaside town is the easiest base on the north coast from which to access the Parco dei Nebrodi. Worth a quick browse before heading up into the hills is the **Museo Etno-Antropologico dei Nebrodi** (Via Cosenz 70; admission free), near the train station.

Information

The *comune* (town council) **tourist office** (☎ 7 22 02; 8.30am-12.30pm), in the

Castello dei Gallego, is a fairly basic outfit. There's also a park **visitors centre** (☎ 70 59 43; Via Corsenz 149).

Sleeping & Eating

There are only two hotels in town: **Roma Palace Hotel** (☎ 70 35 16; hotelroma@tiscalinet.it; Via Medici 443; s/d €36/67) and **Hotel Parimar** (☎ 70 18 88; Via Medici 1; s/d €35/55). Both offer reasonable, if unexceptional, accommodation.

There are several restaurants and pizzerias along Via Cosenz, just below Castello dei Gallego. **Ristorante Carletto** (☎ 70 31 57; Via Cosenz 151) is where diners can choose from a sumptuous array of Sicilian antipasti.

Getting There & Away

Sant'Agata di Militello is on the main train line between Messina and Palermo, with frequent services daily.

ISEA (☎ 095 53 68 94) runs one bus a day bus to Catania (€10.55; 2½ hours) leaving at an anti-social 5am. This bus is only of interest to people wishing to complete the Nebrodi Lake Circuit hike, as it stops at the Villa Miraglia at the beginning of the walk (about one hour from Sant'Agata di Militello). A return bus leaves Catania at 2pm and arrives in Sant'Agata di Militello at around 4.30pm (it also passes the Villa Miraglia). The bus stop in Sant'Agata can be hard to find. From the tourist office walk up Via Medici from the eastern edge of the piazza. When the street veers left, continue ahead up Via Generale Aurelio Iotta for 100m before turning right into Via Cernaia. The bus stop is another 50m on the left in a parking bay.

Sant'Agata di Militello is on the A20 connecting towns along the north coast. At the time of writing, the autostrada was yet to be completed all the way to Palermo, and the section between Sant'Agata di Militello and Cefalù was serviced by the S113.

Sardinia

HIGHLIGHTS

- Stumbling like an archaeological pioneer upon the hidden Nuraghic village of **Tiscali** (p296) obscured in a hard-to-reach sinkhole above the Valle del Lanaittu
- Exploring the mountainous area of Barbagia, including **Gola di Gorropu** (p294)
- Wandering along the secluded coastline of the **Golfo di Orosei** (p299) and wondering where all the other hikers are

Signature food: *Porcheddu* (roast suckling pig)	Celebrated native: Grazia Deledda (author)	Famous for... Centenarians

And now for something completely different...

Sardinia is Italy's time-warped pre-Roman relic, a rugged, often misunderstood region once famous for its brutal kidnappings but now more revered for its unspoiled coastline and – for those in the know – barely charted hikes. An island of roaming shepherds and barren, bushy wilderness, this strangely untapped Mediterranean enclave evades the standard Italian stereotypes of high fashion and high-brow culture, and instead throws up some esoteric inventions of its own. While Sicilians have traditionally hogged the coast, the Sardinians have burrowed resourcefully inland hiding behind the giant limestone slabs of the Supramonte where they fashioned independent tight-knit mountain settlements that raised goats, sheep and pigs.

Sardinia's separation from what locals refer to as *il continente* (mainland Italy) has its roots in Palaeolithic times when Nuraghic villages were built on barely pregnable ridges, mounds and karstic sinkholes. The Romans arrived in 238 BC. In the early 14th century the Spanish came, and their 400-year occupation diluted Sardinian culture with Iberian traditions, customs and linguistic peculiarities.

Harsh and sparsely populated, contemporary Sardinia harbours some of Italy's most challenging hiking terrain and is bereft of any real discernable trail network. Signposting and path markings in the complicated puzzle of valleys and gorges are often deliberately vague – a feature that, while initially confusing, can sometimes be a blessing in disguise (read: fewer people).

This chapter offers two grand walking epics in the rugged heart of eastern Nuoro province that will test the stamina and navigational skills of adventurous hikers in search of solitude, mysterious *nuraghe* ruins, and Europe's own mini Grand Canyon.

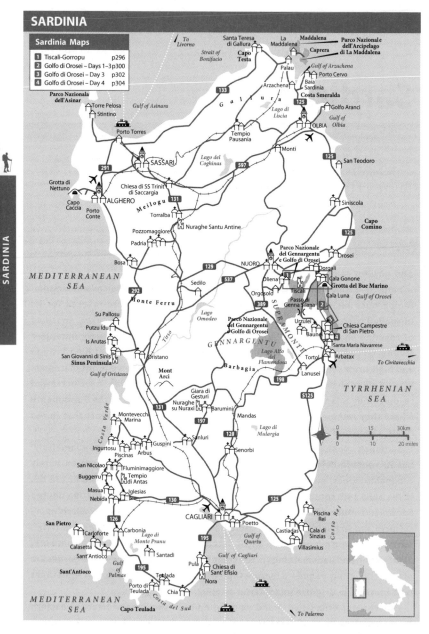

SARDINIA

Sardinia Maps

1. Tiscali-Gorropu   p296
2. Golfo di Orosei – Days 1–3 p300
3. Golfo di Orosei – Day 3   p302
4. Golfo di Orosei – Day 4   p304

HISTORY

Sardinia is dotted with thousands of *nur-aghi*, cone-shaped megalithic fortresses that are the only remnants of the island's first in-habitants – the Nuraghic people (see p291). In the years immediately before Christ,

Sardinia's coast was often visited by Greeks and Phoenicians, who came first as traders and later as invaders, before the island was eventually colonised by the Romans.

The Romans, in turn, were followed by the Pisans, Genovese, Spanish, Austrians and, finally, the Savoy royal family, whose possessions became the Kingdom of Sardinia and were eventually incorporated into the newly united Kingdom of Italy in 1861. The countryside is flecked with a full kaleidoscope of historical artefacts including imposing Nuraghic royal fortresses (such as at Barumini), Carthaginian towns (such as Nora and Tharros on the west coast) and isolated Pisan-style Romanesque churches (in the province of Sassari).

ENVIRONMENT

Sardinia is in the middle of the western Mediterranean, about 190km from the coast of Africa and 180km from the Italian peninsula. The island is separated from Corsica, to the north, by an 11km stretch of sea, known as the Straight of Bonifacio. The island has a population of about 1.7 million, which equals an average of 68 people per sq km – making it a very sparsely inhabited region compared with the Italian average (190 per sq km). The island is 68% mountainous, with plains making up only 18% of the territory. The Gennargentu, in Barbagia, is the highest area, reaching 1834m at Punta La Marmora. On the east coast there are long, sandy beaches between San Teodoro and Capo Comino, between Santa Maria Navarrese and Arbatax, and at Poetto beach at Cagliari. The rest of the eastern Sardinian coastline is mainly rocky. The west and south coasts of Sardinia retain a rich heritage of brackish lagoons – ideal habitat for many birds,

SARDINIA

NURAGHIC CULTURE

If you thought Italy's mainland Etruscan civilisation was hard to penetrate, try blowing the dust off Sardinia's little-documented Nuraghic culture, a nebulous melange of sculpted metal figurines and strange megalithic stone towers that is about as murky as the frigid surface of Mars.

For historical scholars, the facts are scant and hard to pin down. Nuraghic culture is thought to have evolved around 1600 BC during the transition from ancient to middle Bronze Age, before mysteriously fizzling out just over a millennium later in 500 BC with the permanent arrival of Phoenician traders from the Levant. Its final trouncing came with the arrival of the Romans in Sardinia in 238 BC.

Over the course of nearly two millennia, the Nuraghic people evolved from Bronze Age farmers living in haphazard patriarchal communities into skilled metallurgists and traders whose upland settlements were characterised by distinctive conical towers, known as *nuraghi*. So sturdy and well-built were these iconic towers that over 7000 of them still remain. In more recent times their unmistakable form has become a defining cultural symbol of modern Sardinia. The name *nuraghe* supposedly derives from the Sardinian word *nurra*, which means 'heap' or 'mound'.

Despite the ubiquity of *nuraghi*, their use and function is still heavily debated. Some claim the towers served a military function (they are nearly always found in upland areas), while others promote their possible role as temples, farm-stores, sanctuaries or even castles for feudal elites. What is more certain is that *nuraghi* exhibited a style of architecture way ahead of its time; rounded walls were constructed out of heavy, rough-cut slabs of basalt scavenged from extinct volcanoes and piled together without the use of adhesive or cement.

The Nuraghic people were also advanced metallurgists who fashioned human-like statuettes – known as *bronzetti* – from locally produced bronze. To date, over 500 bronze figurines have been uncovered across the island. It is thought that these and other metal objects may have been important trading tools between Nuraghic people and societies in the Balearics, Greece, Crete and Sicily. However, unlike their more transparent Mediterranean neighbours, the Nuraghic people left no written word, meaning the details of their history is less clear.

Examples of Nuraghic culture in this chapter's hikes include the 'lost' settlements of Tiscali and Sos Carros, and a number of stony ruins that scatter the Golgo plain between Cala Sisine and Rifugio Golgo.

SARDINIA

PARCO NAZIONALE DEL GENNARGENTU E GOLFO DI OROSEI

The largest of Sardinia's three national parks, 74,000-hectare Parco Nazionale del Gennargentu e Golfo di Orosei has faced multiple threats to its existence in recent years including an ongoing dispute over animal pastures and local land rights that has left its special park status hanging in the balance.

Situated in the island's wild east, the park ostensibly protects Sardinia's highest mountain range – the Gennargentu – the barren Supramonte massif, and one of the most pristine tracts of coastline in the Mediterranean, the glittering Golfo di Orosei. Encased inside the park's boundaries lie a cache of other interesting sites, including brooding Punta la Marmora (at 1833m, the island's loftiest peak), Sardinia's only ski lift (on the adjacent Bruncu Spina), the Nuraghic village of Tiscali, and the vertiginous Gola di Gorropu – Europe's deepest gorge. Oak trees once covered these harsh limestone mountains that are flecked with hidden caves, gorges and sinkholes, but they were cut down in medieval times to burn for charcoal. These days the most fertile land is given over to pasture watched over by an ever diminishing band of traditional shepherds (albeit ones that drive sports utility vehicles/SUVs); the rest is a retreat for mouflons, deer, high-flying eagles and opportunistic vultures, plus a handful of rare Sardinian foxes and wild cats.

including the pink flamingo, and a strategic point for migratory species using the island as a stopover between Africa and northern Europe.

Millions of years ago Sardinia and Corsica broke off the southern coast of France, leaving behind the Côte d'Azur. Ancient volcanic activity, extinct for centuries, has left distinct traces in Monte Ferru, Meilogu and Monte Arci along the west coast; in the evocative granite formations of the Gallura to the north; and in flat, basalt high plains such as the Giara di Gesturi, inland from the Gulf of Oristano. The vast central-east limestone high plains that form the Supramonte of Orgosolo and Oliena are, on the other hand, originally sedimentary and contain numerous grottoes, underground streams and deep gorges.

Sardinia's rich flora is shaped by the Mediterranean climate, and the generally arid and rocky terrain. Numerous species endemic to Sardinia and Corsica have evolved in this hard, dry environment, restricted at times to particular areas in the Gennargentu and Supramonte mountain ranges.

There are three prevalent landscape types: coastal, plain-hillside and mountain. On the east coast the typical low Mediterranean scrub of cistus (rockrose), myrtle and gum trees, often found together, make a splendid, multicoloured and perfumed floral spectacle in spring and summer. Also found here, heather, euphorbia, rosemary and broom are often associated with trees such as the holm oak, juniper, oleander and tamarisk. In the grassy vegetation you'll see many flowers including the violet, the blue of the periwinkle and lavender, and the colourful mix of irises and many species of orchid. On the Supramonte, the elegant rose-pink bloom of the peonies is justifiably famous.

Although hunters and poachers have traditionally been active in Sardinia, some wildlife remains. The list includes the ever-present wild boar, the mouflon with its great curved horns, the endemic Sardinian wild cat and the Sardinian deer. Fox, weasel, marten, hare and dormouse complete the list of wild terrestrial animals. The Mediterranean monk seal was recently declared extinct in the area.

Sardinia is a paradise for birdwatchers. There are many species, some of which are really spectacular – such as the flamingos in the salt ponds near Cagliari and Oristano, and the colony of griffon vultures on the west coast near Bosa. Among birds of prey, the golden eagle is easy to find throughout Barbagia, while the smaller Bonelli's eagle nests in the coastal area of the Supramonte, and Eleanora's falcon along the rocky shores of the Golgo area.

You can see kestrels, peregrine and swamp falcons, buzzards, goshawks, sparrowhawks and Sardinian owls. Besides the Barbary partridge, crow, jay, hoopoe and wood pigeon, there are many species to be found in the ponds. These include the rare purple gallinule and waders such as the grey heron, white egret, purple heron, night heron, water rail, little egret, curlew, avocet and other migratory species of duck and goose.

Sardinia is the only region of Italy where there are no poisonous vipers. You might meet harmless species of snake like the natrix viper (similar in appearance to the poisonous adder), the Sardinian coluber and the endemic Sardinian lizard. Interesting among amphibians is the cave-dwelling Sardinian newt.

CLIMATE

High average temperatures and little rain mean that Sardinia has at least seven months of good weather each year. Average daily maximum temperatures along the coast are 19°C in autumn, 10°C in winter, 12°C in spring and 22°C in summer. On the east coast, winds from the north create clear skies and a cool airflow, while winds from the south or east bring occasional rain, which rarely lasts long. However, there can be strong winds which last for several days.

PLANNING
When to Walk

The best period for walking is from March to June, when the days are beginning to lengthen and the wildflowers are in bloom. In addition there are frequent patron saint feast days in the local towns and villages. On these occasions, the young women and men dress in their traditional costumes with beautiful, coloured embroidery and perform traditional folk dances. Autumn is also a pleasant time to walk. Winter is too cold, and summer is far too hot for walking, with the beaches packed with tourists.

What to Bring

Natural springs aren't ubiquitous in dry, dusty Sardinia meaning you should always be aware of the location of your next water source when walking, and always travel carrying at least 2L. Insect repellent is also useful, as are good lightweight boots and long leggings to counter the sometimes spiny vegetation on the rocky Supramonte.

If you are going to follow the Golfo di Orosei hike over three to four days without interruptions, you will need camping equipment – tent, sleeping bag, cooking equipment, fuel and food (see also the equipment Checklist, p333).

Maps

The Touring Club Italiano's (TCI) 1:200,000 *Sardegna* map (available outside the island) is ideal for route planning and general orientation. You can find other regional maps at newsstands and in bookshops.

PLACE NAMES

Place names on the IGM maps and on signs throughout the island are sometimes in local dialects, and may differ slightly from those used in this book.

Books

DH Lawrence (1885–1930), the English novelist and poet, was one of Sardinia's earliest cheerleaders though he only visited the island on a one-week winter excursion from Sicily in the early 1920s. The result of his trip was the remarkably observant *Sea and Sardinia*.

The Sunflower guide, *Landscapes of Sardinia* (2004), by Andreas Stieglitz, covers 37 long- and short-day walks; both are useful if you would like to explore more of Sardinia.

Guided Walks

The **Società Gorropu** (☎ 0782 64 92 82; www.gorropu.com; Via Sa Preda Lada 2, Urzulei) is an organisation of young, competent and environmentally motivated guides. There is a variety of guided one-, five- and six-day walks, including the descent of the Codula di Luna to the sea, climbing from the depths of the Gola di Gorropu, and the six-day 'Selvaggio Blu' climbing-walk (p298). Guides can also take you to explore fascinating caves crossed by underground rivers.

The **Cooperativa Goloritzè** (☎ 0782 61 05 99, 368 702 89 80; www.coopgoloritze .com) has a base in the Golgo high plain, 9km north of Baunei, and offers guided treks in the area – on foot, horseback or, if you prefer, donkey. The programme includes day trips on horseback exploring the Golgo high plain, two-day excursions from Golgo to Cala Sisine and the six-day Selvaggio Blu (p298) climbing-walk from Pedra Longa (Baunei) to Cala Luna.

The **Cooperativa Ghivine** (☎ 0784 9 67 21, 338 8341618; www.ghivine.com; Via La Marmora 69E, Dorgali) organises nature walks, and archaeological, caving and scuba excursions in the Dorgali area.

Barbagia Insolita (☎ 0784 28 60 05; www.barbagiainsolita.it; Corso Vittorio Emanuele 48, Oliena) has guided tours to out-of-the-way areas by 4WD and on foot. You can choose between demanding treks and relaxing walks to places including Tiscali, the Gola di Gorropu and Monte Corrasi.

Atlantikà (☎ 328 972 97 19; www.atlant ika.it; Via Lamarmora 195) is a Dorgali-based consortium of local guides who run trekking, canyoning and diving trips. They also hire out mountain bikes (from €20 per day) and canoes (€24 per day).

Information Sources

Italy's biggest hiking organisation, the **Club Alpino Italiano** (CAI), has two branches in Sardinia – one in Cagliari (☎ 070 66 78 77) and one in Nuoro (☎ 0784 3 49 26).

Emergency

For urgent assistance while walking in Sardinia, contact the **mountain rescue service** (☎ 070 28 62 00) or the **national emergency** number (☎ 118).

GETTING THERE & AROUND

Sardinia is easily accessed by a variety of budget airlines flying from either inside Italy or from other major cities in Europe. Sea connections run from numerous mainland Italian ports as well as Palermo in Sicily. Ferries also make the short hop north to the French administered island of Corsica. Sardinia has a basic rail network and a more extensive and reliable system of buses which penetrate almost every corner of the island.

GATEWAY

With its busy east-coast ferry terminal and small but efficient airport served by numerous cheap European airlines, the bland but well-organised city of Olbia (p306) serves as the best gateway to the hikes in this chapter.

TISCALI-GORROPU

Duration 4 days
Distance 53km
Difficulty easy
Start Oliena (p307)
Finish Dorgali (p305)
Transport bus
Summary A walk through Sardinia's prehistory taking in two hard-to-reach Nuraghic villages and Europe's deepest gorge.

Sardinia's past, human and natural, is jealously guarded in the remote Valle del Lanaittu. This walk provides a unique opportunity to explore these secrets, sifting through the ruins of the ancient Nuraghic sites of Sos Carros and Tiscali, and admiring the spectacular chasm of Gola di Gorropu. As much as you'll sometimes curse the lack of signposts (and they are comically lacking; at others you'll relish the solitude their absence has ensured.

If you arrive in Oliena with half a day to spare before starting the walk, you can head up to Scala è Pradu (p304) to admire the panoramic and enchanting view. Note you can continue from Scala è Pradu to Rifugio Budurrai (the end of Day 1); however, this route presents serious navigational difficulties and is suitable for experts only. Walkers who fancy this option are advised to employ a local guide (see p293).

Camping at the Gola di Gorropu at the end of Day 2 is a grey area that provokes different reactions from locals. If you're not up for it you can abort the walk by hiking directly from Ponte Sa Barva to Dorgali (a long day, but doable, if you start early). With a car or lift from Dorgali to the Ponte Sa Barva, Gorropu can easily be done as a separate day walk (16km return). Alternatively, you can partake in a guided trip (with transport) offered by numerous businesses in Dorgali and Oliena.

If you want take a chunk out of the walk at the start, you can cut the first 6km of road walking by catching a local bus (every two hours in summer) from Oliena to the Su Gologone junction on the Dorgali road.

To extend this walk, it can be linked with the three-day coastal Golfo di Orosei walk (p299), which starts in Cala Gonone (9km from Dorgali).

PLANNING
Maps
This walk is covered by two IGM 1:25,000 maps, No 500 III *Oliena* and No 500 II *Dorgali,* both available from bookshops in Dorgali. Unfortunately, the southernmost section of the route, the entrance to the Gola di Gorropu, lies on the border between IGM 1:25,000 No 517 IV *Funtana Bona* and No 517 I *Cantoniera Genna Silana.* It isn't worth buying them just for this section as it presents no serious navigational problems.

ACCESS TOWN
The mountain town of Dorgali (p305) situated at the end of this walk serves as the best access town.

THE WALK
Day 1: Oliena to Rifugio Budurrai
4 hours, 17km, 103m ascent, 268m descent

Take the asphalt road from Oliena heading towards Dorgali. This road carries a fair bit of traffic but there is a pavement-width verge for some of the way. To avoid the speeding cars you can divert right after 3km and follow the minor asphalt road to the **Chiesa di Nostra Signora di Montserrato** before looping back left onto the main road approximately 1km before the Hotel Su Gologone turn-off. The Su Gologone turn-off forks to the right about 6km from Oliena and is clearly signposted. Hikers with less time can jump on the local Oliena–Dorgali bus which passes this junction every two hours during the summer. Heading east on another minor asphalt road, the entrance to **Hotel Su Gologone** (p307) appears on the right after 2km. Go past the entrance ramp of the hotel and, shortly afterwards, turn right onto a road that climbs a little valley. Thirsty hikers can divert 300m straight ahead here to reach the **Sorgente di Su Gologone**, an underground spring which gushes out in a strong jet from the mountain, then flows into **Fiume Cedrino**. Entry to the spring now costs €2, while a bottle of water from the restaurant concession in the car park costs €1. Take your pick. On the rock above the *sorgente* fissure is the little church of **Nostra Signora della Pietà**.

Back on the paved road, which climbs the little valley, you will gain altitude and round a rocky shoulder to enter the fresh green Valle del Lanaittu, crowned by imposing limestone peaks as high as 1400m. Just before the entrance to the valley there is another (free) ice-cold spring on the right followed by third one 1km down the road on the left.

The road now descends towards Rio Sa Oche where it becomes a dirt track and runs alongside the river until it divides into two, one straight and to the left crossing a plateau of abandoned fields, and one to the right at mid-slope cutting through the vegetation. Both reach the speleologists' shelter of Rifugio Sa Oche (145m). Follow the road to the left, which passes through some gateposts and proceeds along a straight tree-lined road to the white-walled **Rifugio Budurrai** (closed at the time of research, this place was due to open to the public in the spring of 2010).

SIDE TRIP: SOS CARROS
45 minutes, 2km

After exiting the *rifugio* via another tree-lined track you will arrive at a three-way track junction. Here you turn right to get to the **Rifugio Sa Oche** and the imposing entrance to **Grotta Sa Oche** (Cave of the Voice), which is named after the sound made by the large amounts of water which pour out of it when flooded. The *rifugio* has no accommodation but sells drinks and ice cream, and often has a spit-roasted pig cooking on a barbecue out back.

WARNING

As you'll be walking in some very isolated areas, it's a good idea to notify someone of your route and destination before setting out. A mobile telephone could solve a lot of problems.

Never underestimate the difficulty of navigation in Sardinia's wilderness areas! You might also encounter problems crossing the limestone terrain of the Supramonte – it is full of deep holes and channels covered by vegetation, and therefore it is not a good idea to leave the trail. If you do lose the trail, the best idea is to retrace your steps to find it. If you would like to explore the area, but doubt your orienteering abilities, hire a local guide for an initial exploration of the area.

TISCALI-GORROPU

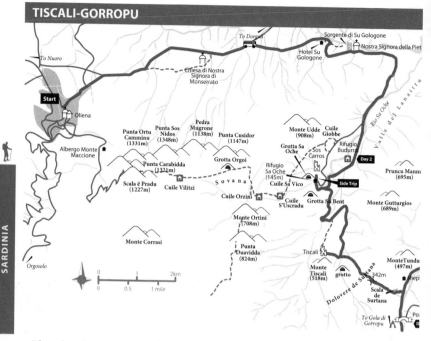

Three hundred metres north of Rifugio Sa Oche, on the wooded slope overlooking the bridge, is an important archaeological site with the remains of the Nuraghic village of **Sos Carros** (adult/child €4/2; 9.30am-6.30pm). The area is fenced in but you can ask the guard, who is also the shepherd of the adjacent sheepfold, to let you in. You can see the remains of a small area where a family would have gathered together at an unusual circular stone seat, perhaps to perform some ancient ritual.

Day 2: Rifugio Budurrai to Ponte Sa Barva via Tiscali

8 hours, 8km, 460m ascent, 262m descent

After leaving the *rifugio*; head south on the dirt road passing the turn-off on the right to Rifugio Sa Oche. You'll soon pass a couple of minor track forks. Veer left at the first fork, signposted 'Grotto Elihes Atras', and left again at the second. The third fork is marked by a small metal bar – once a signpost – sticking out of the ground. Take another left here and follow the dirt road as it doubles back and starts to head north and slightly uphill. After

approximately 300m you'll pass a track going off to the right which offers a harder and less-well-signposted access path to Tiscali (in summer cars sometimes park here).

Ignore this track and continue left on the main track which emerges from the trees and heads northeast for another 600m where it rounds the end of a mountain ridge. Here the route almost doubles back on itself and starts to head south up a narrow river valley. The track quickly disintegrates into a narrow path marked with faded white paint and small cairns as it travels alongside a dried-up riverbed in and out of the trees. After approximately 1km following the river you'll reach a signposted path junction in a small clearing. Veer right here following the wooden sign towards Tiscali. The path begins to climb and passes a grotto in a rock wall. Soon after, another path goes off to the left towards Dorone and Campu Donanigoro. Continue climbing upwards following the signs for Tiscali now only 15 minutes above you. The path steepens as you draw closer to the archaeological site and a bit of rock-hopping is required to negotiate the last few

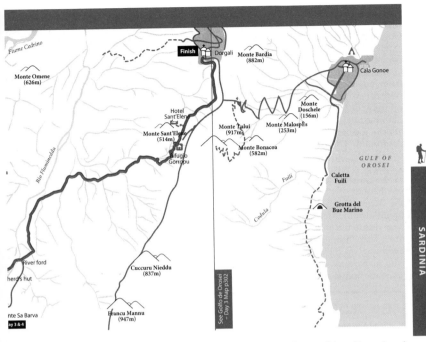

See Golfo de Orosei – Day 3 Map p302

SARDINIA

hundred metres. Once inside the amazing *dolina* (sinkhole) where Tiscali is located, the trusty guardian (normally a cheerful, loquacious fellow) will relieve you of €5 and allow you to follow the short circuit around the collapsed cave.

The natural karst environment of the enormous *dolina*, formed by a collapse of the limestone rock on a mountain crest, appears to have been utilised by the Nuraghic inhabitants of Sos Carros as a hiding place from invading enemies. Sited on a crest within the actual sinkhole, **Tiscali** offered various possibilities for escape and received a constant supply of water, which dripped from the roof of the cave overhanging the settlement.

Exit Tiscali the same way you came in and retrace your steps by climbing down the steep slope, past the first path junction and the grotto, to a small clearing that you passed earlier where a sign points southeast to Surtana. This route ascends gently through trees on a forest path that becomes rockier as you climb further up the shady valley known as the Dolovere di Surtana. About 25 minutes from the junction in the clearing you emerge over a saddle (342m)

and see the Rio Flumineddu valley splayed out below you. To reach it you have to descend steeply down a narrow rocky gorge known as the **Scala de Surtana**. At the bottom join a dirt track and turn right towards **Ponte Sa Barva**.

Unless you're skipping the Gola di Gorropu section and heading straight back to Dorgali (Day 4), you'll want to overnight here. Camping is generally 'allowed' (this being Italy, the rules are ambiguous) near the bridge or about 1km further south at a grassy clearing between the dirt road and the river. From here you can enjoy an evening stroll along the river.

Day 3: Gola di Gorropu
4 hours, 15km return

To reach the Gola di Gorropu, a natural spectacle with 400m of sheer rock walls so close together they almost touch, head southwards on the dirt road to the west of Ponte Sa Barva (damaged and being rebuilt at the time of research although the river is easily fordable in various places).

Follow the river along the undulating dirt road, leading to the very short and steep little path that takes you right down into the silent northern entrance of **Gola di Gorropu**, a magical place that deserves an extended stopover (343m, 1½ to two hours from the bridge).

Strangely, the noise of the water comes from outside the gorge. East of the entrance, beyond the enormous boulders and a lovely, little limestone clearing, the Rio Flumineddu gushes back out into the open after a journey of several kilometres underground. The clearing is an ideal place to enjoy the sun and a snack, alongside the gurgling, crystal-clear water. To the right of the clearing, looking downhill, you can see the start of a tough trail that ascends to the Genna Silana pass on the S125 (650m uphill, two to three hours).

A visit to the gorge is not complete without a walk through the narrow passageway overhung by high walls that are clogged with giant blocks of fallen rock shaped by water erosion. It's an exciting and humbling experience to climb among the deep channels of a river that isn't there, among huge rocks in perennial shadow, being hit now and then by mysterious drips. Those who are able to get through the tricky (mountaineering Grade III) passages can ascend the gorge as far as an impassable 20m gap.

Very few plants survive under these conditions; however, there are ferns and mosses taking advantage of the dampness and lack of light, and rare endemic insects, which spend their whole existence in this vast underground system. During long periods of rain the water table rises and the gorge floods, a phenomenon that we recommend you avoid. Check with the Società Gorropu in Urzulei (see p293) about the status of the gorge before setting out.

After visiting the gorge, re-trace your steps to the Ponte Sa Barva. Here you can either camp out another night or – if you've got the energy – head directly back to Dorgali (see p305).

THE SELVAGGIO BLU – ITALY'S TOUGHEST TRAIL?

It may not be Italy's longest hike or its most vertiginous, but Sardinia's seven-day Selvaggio Blu (the name translates rather ominously as 'savage blue') is a definite contender for the nation's toughest trail. First conceived in 1989 as the brainchild of former Baunei mayor, Pasquale Zucca, the 'Blu' set out to preserve a precious network of old charcoal burners and shepherds' paths that criss-crossed the cliffs above the isolated Golfo di Orosei.

Measuring 42km between its starting point in Santa Maria Naveresse to its scenic finish in Cala Fuili just south of Cala Gonone, this sinuous and uncompromising collection of rough trails pulls no punches and rarely seeks to pamper to the whims of the average middle-of-the-pack hiker. Remote and with little road access, the paths track as close as possible to the azure Mediterranean, with caves, grottoes, weird rock formations, staggering viewpoints and drop-offs that teeter between adrenalin-tinged and terrifying. Vertigo sufferers need not apply. While the first three days as far as Cala Goloritzè are relatively straightforward, days four and five require 45m abseils, UIAA Grade IV climbs, and nerves of steel.

While the Selvaggio Blu can be undertaken independently, many hikers do it as part of an organised trip. Aside from the necessary climbing skills (this is no fixed protection *via ferrata*), the primary issue for go-it-aloners is the lack of available water en route; with only one natural water source, travellers must either carry their own supply or pre-arrange to have provisions brought in by boat to various beaches on the way. The other issue is that old Sardinian chestnut of signposting – or lack of it. Though ostensibly marked with splashes of blue spray-paint on rocks, the Blu's directional arrows are patchy and you'll need to keep a close eye on your IGM map.

The seven stages run between Pedro Longa, Cuile Despiggius, Porto Cuao, Cala Goloritzè, Bacu Mudaloru, Cuile Mancosu, Cala Sisine and Cala Fuili. Overall, you can bank on moving at an average pace of 1km per hour. Independent hikers will need to equip themselves with a climbing harness, rope, insect repellent, light boots, a tent, sleeping bag and adequate provisions. For group excursions contact Cooperative Goloritzè (p293).

An excellent guide to the trail (in Italian) is Corrado Conca's *Il Sentiero Selvaggio Blu* (2007), available in bookshops in Dorgali.

Day 4: Ponte Sa Barva to Dorgali
3 hours, 13km

Follow the western bank of the river for 1km past Ponte Sa Barva. You'll soon reach a friendly **shepherd's hut** where you can buy cold drinks, cheese and local wine about 400m past the path turn-off for the Scala de Surtana (where you descended yesterday). Continue north past the hut along the west bank of the river to a **ford** where you can cross the river on stepping stones. Join the paved road on the other side and turn left. From here it is approximately 11km through vineyards and farmland to Dorgali. When you arrive near the Hotel Sant'Elene, join the busier secondary road for the final section.

GOLFO DI OROSEI

Duration 4 days
Distance 45km
Difficulty moderate
Start Cala Gonone
Finish Baunei
Nearest Town Dorgali (p305)
Transport bus

Summary A multifarious coastal walk notable for its isolation that mixes snippets of hedonistic Sardinian beach life with spectacular sections of the precipitous Golfo di Orosei littoral.

In a country not short on spectacular coastal hikes (think Cinque Terre and the shimmering Amalfi), the Golfo di Orosei adds a new dimension. This is the Mediterranean as you rarely see it; wild, lonely and wonderfully unblemished. In a land of no roads, the only fellow beings you're likely to come into contact with are sheep, eagles, adventurous hikers and the armies of finely chiselled sun-worshippers who get ferried in to lie on (and rarely leave) a trio of magnificently secluded beaches.

Hiking along this precipitous stretch of the Sardinian littoral, you will encounter both beautiful and demanding sections. It is a largely self-sufficient route that many locals in the tourist offices and information centres will tell you to avoid attempting alone. Don't believe them. Armed with a good map, plenty of water and a healthy sense of adventure, this hike will rank among the highlights of any outdoor Sardinian sojourn.

The walk starts and ends with 4km and 8km of road-walking respectively. These can be eliminated by using local ferry services or organising 4WD transport (see Getting to/from the Walk, below). There are also some alternative finish options: Urzulei via Codula di Luna and Santa Maria Navarrese via Pedra Longa. For accommodation on Days 1 and 2, you're looking at camping – a murky subject in Sardinia – but an activity that is popular with numerous Italian travellers. At the end of Day 3 you can take advantage of the hospitality and the extracurricular activities at the popular Rifugio Golgo.

This coastal walk can also be linked with the four-day Tiscali-Gorropu hike (p294), which ends in Dorgali (9km from Cala Gonone and linked by regular buses).

PLANNING
Maps

This walk is covered by four IGM 1:25,000 maps, No 500 *II Dorgali*, No 517 I *Cantoniera Genna Silana*, No 518 III *Capo di Monte Santu* and No 518 IV *Punta è Lattone*. No 500 and No 517 are essential. The other two aren't really necessary if you follow the walk instructions below carefully.

GETTING TO/FROM THE WALK
Cala Gonone (start)

Cala Gonone is 9km east from Dorgali; regular **ARST** (☎ 0784 29 08 00; www.arst .sardegna.it) buses ply the route (€1, 20 minutes, 11 daily) between 6.20am and 8pm.

You can shorten the start of the walk by taking a boat. From Cala Gonone, **Nuova Consorzio Trasporti Marittimi** (☎ 0784 9 33 05; www.calagononecrociere.it) operates large boats along the coast, several times a day from the end of March to mid-November. The boats go to the Grotto del Bue Marino (€16.50 return), which includes a guided visit to the caves where a colony of the now-extinct monk seal once lived, Cala Luna (€15 return) and Cala Sisine (€19 return). The first boat from Cala Gonone to Cala Luna (the overnight stop on Day 1 of the walk) departs at 9am (11am low season) and the last boat from Cala Luna to Cala Gonone leaves at 5.30 or 3.30pm, depending on the season.

SARDINIA

Baunei (finish)

There are only two **ARST** (☎ 0784 29 08 00; www.arst.sardegna.it) buses a day between Baunei and Dorgali at an unsociable 5.55am and at a more doable 4.10pm. The spectacular journey through dramatic mountain scenery costs €5.50 and takes just over an hour.

It is usually possible to organise transport between Rifugio Golgo and Baunei (9km) if you are staying at the *rifugio* or if you contact them in advance. Cooperativa Goloritzè (see p293), which operates the *rifugio*, offers car transfers for a small fee. You could also use the co-op's transport to get from Cala Sisine to Baunei, thus shortening the route by 24km.

Another option is to walk, from the *rifugio*, to Cala Goloritzè (see Side Trip, p303) and catch a boat to Santa Maria Navarrese.

THE WALK
Day 1: Cala Gonone to Cala Luna
3 hours, 11 km, 274m ascent/descent

Head south for about 4km along Viale del Bue Marino, following the asphalt coast road. You could consider asking your hotel for a lift along this section. You'll reach the deep fissure of the **Codula Fuili**, where the road ends at a turnaround, after one hour. The trail descends via a staircase to cross the *codula*, a long gorge formed by water erosion. From here you can spend some time exploring the gorge; alternatively a few metres to your left (east) is the pleasant beach of Cala Fuili.

The main trail continues south, climbing the opposite side of the gorge and following a route marked sporadically by green arrows painted on the rocks (another lesser trail heads off to the left down to the Grotto del Blu Marino). While sometimes stony underfoot, the path is always clear, cutting through high bushes and low trees with occasional peek-a-boo glimpses of the sea. Ignore any turn-offs and stay on the well-marked trail heading south; you'll soon pass the highest point of the day – a relatively modest 131m – one hour from Codula Fuili. The trail then begins to descend, reaching the rocky entrance of the Oddoana cave and passing **Codula Oddoana** a short distance from the beach.

From the gorge, the trail ascends again to the south and passes the hill known as Fruncu Nieddu (120m), crossing its eastern

slope at about 100m altitude with a great view of the sea. The trail then begins a steep descent, with sharp turns, to the gravel

GOLFO DI OROSEI – DAYS 1–3

riverbed of the magically beautiful **Codula di Luna** (see Side Trip, below). Follow this canyon to the left (east), cross the riverbed and reach the low building of **Ristorante Su Neulagi** (☎ 0784 9 33 92; Apr-Oct), one hour from the high point. The restaurant serves drinks, coffee and full-blown meals. Though a caretaker lives here all year round, out of season only mineral water is sold. There's no official campground, but some people pitch their tents near the mouth of the *codula*.

You are now separated from the sea by only a narrow strip of oleanders, full of colourful flowers in summer, and the low dunes of the beach, which sometimes hold the water of the *codula* to form lovely little freshwater ponds. The beach stretches beyond the cliffs and rocky outcrops to the north towards a series of strange caves that look like great garages for resting whales.

In July and August the beach is crowded with day-trippers from Cala Gonone. Most of them will leave with the last boat, so you could consider spending a romantic night nearby under the stars.

SIDE TRIP: CODULA DI LUNA
2 hours, 4km return

From the beach of Cala Luna, follow the dry riverbed of the gorge inland (west). This is a real riverbed made up of large, rounded river stones, so the walking can be difficult. You can enjoy a short walk along this majestic limestone canyon and then return to the beach.

Day 2: Cala Luna to Cala Sisine
4 hours, 12km, 630m ascent/descent

Tourist offices and some locals will tell you that this section of the walk is notoriously poorly signposted and warn you off it. Don't be cowed. Aside from one vague path junction halfway through, the hike from Cala Luna to Cala Sisine is along clear, well-made paths that are both scenic and easy to follow. It is, however, useful to carry two IGM 1:25,000 maps: No 500 *II Dorgali*, and No 517 I *Cantoniera Genna Silana* to ensure efficient navigation.

From behind the restaurant, where the toilets are, ascend south along easy curves on a 2m-wide stony track. After 20 minutes you come to a level section, at about 100m altitude where there's a marvellous

panorama of the coast to the south. From here, the track descends into the striking gorge called **Badde de Lupiru** and then ascends again in a south–southwesterly direction. Continue to ascend gradually along the wide, gravelly track (it seems almost purpose-built), passing an imposing rock arch called **S'Architieddu Lupiru** (365m) on the left after one hour where you can stop for some excellent photo opportunities.

Ascending on a well-made path with some shade, you'll soon reach a section where the track veers south and enters a stonier environment. It develops into a level track at mid-slope along the eastern face of Punta Onamarra until it crosses over a bare ridge (600m) where there are exciting views over the coastline and the deep incision of the Codula di Luna. The track now descends gradually for a short distance, ascends, descends and ascends again contouring the slopes of the various coastal hills. At this point you will need to be vigilant and keep an eye out for a hidden turning on the left (the only real turning on this section of the walk). The turning comes approximately one hour after the S'Architieddu Lupiru and 15 minutes after passing a sign for Cala Luna inscribed on a rock pointing back the way you have come. During a scrubby, bushy section, look out for an isolated, 2.5m-high fillirea (similar to a holm oak) on the right (west) side of the trail, with a 4m-high juniper on the left (east) side. Just after these two trees there is a small cairn on the left (east), at about 630m elevation, marking a fainter yet discernable path turning off to the left (marked on the IGM map).

The new path, marked with faded red and white paint stripes and small cairns, swings left after 200m and then back to the right as it starts to descend towards the coast. Follow the most direct and obvious route past a grassy coal-merchant's clearing surrounded by stones to until you reach a peculiar, circular threshing-floor made of flat stones. Pass along the right of the circle to a junction close by, turn left, and in few metres you'll reach the distinctive **Cuile Sacedderano** (531m), an abandoned, cone-shaped shed made of juniper logs, with a goat pen alongside. This takes 30 minutes from the turn-off. Baunei's shepherds call this Cuile Girove Longu.

SARDINIA

Descend to the right (south), pass a juniper tree leaning south, then zigzag down a short, steep scree slope towards the bottom of the valley (called Girove Longu on the IGM map), where a dense wood begins. Note a triangular, white mountain face in front of you. Enter the wood and zigzag east descending down the sporadically marked trail (actually a dry riverbed). Walk for about 30 minutes and you'll pass the base of a big, white rock. Five minutes later, the trail begins to veer right along the rocky shoulder to the southeast. The trail then leaves the valley floor, rising gradually until it emerges from the woods with breathtaking views of the northern coast and Cala Gonone. Continuing on, cross over the rocky shoulder to reveal a view to the south of the imposing cliff of **Cala Sisine**.

Now the more obvious trail re-enters a forest, descending in sharp curves among invasive vegetation. Open sections across rocks alternate with sections through woods. The trail descends diagonally towards the inside of Codula Sisine, then at a junction it curves sharply to the left towards the beach (1½ hours from Cuile Saccederano), which you can reach by a steep descent near a small ruin.

The bottom of the path opens into a shady area often used by tent campers. Turn left here for the beach or right along the gravel riverbed for the **Ristorante Su Coile** (☎ 0784 9 32 71; May-Sep). The restaurant has a snack bar, large outside seating area along with a full-blown dining room. You can unofficially camp here (free) all year, but there is no fresh water. When the restaurant is open, it is advisable to camp on the south side of the beach, which is secluded and often downwind. During the rest of the year, when the restaurant is closed, it is possible to set up your bivouac overnight on its external cement skirting block, which is protected from the wind and the relatively innocuous wild cows that live in the *codula*.

Day 3: Cala Sisine to Golgo
4–5 hours, 13km, 450m ascent
From the restaurant ascend into the *codula* following the vehicle-wide stony track. This soon curves left at a junction with **Codula Bacu Arala** and leads south into Codula Sisine. After 30 minutes, you'll reach a dirt

clearing that acts as a kind of makeshift car park for beach-bound travellers. The track, now a reasonable dirt road traversed by everything from Land Rovers to small Fiats goes up into the *codula*. During winter/spring it is often washed out by floods. Meander through the *codula* past a collection of bizarre rock formations modelled by the wind. These structures, sheltered by thick vegetation, are inhabited by many species of small birds.

One hour from the start of the dirt road you will reach another dirt road ascending steeply to the right. This road was built in 1996 and is not marked on the IGM map. Ignore it and continue on the main dirt road within the *codula*. After another 30 minutes of walking, another track shoots off to the right. Ignore this also and follow the main track (which is briefly cobbled) as it swings to the left and leaves the *codula*. After ascending further around some steepish, sharp curves you'll pass a **small picnic area** on the right and emerge at a junction (270m) on a wide crest which is actually the start of the high **Plain of Golgo**. Here a road leads to the left (north) towards **Cuile**

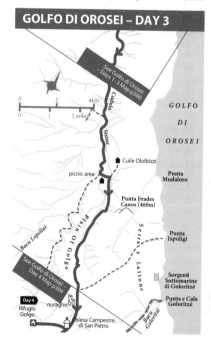

GOLFO DI OROSEI – DAY 3

See Golfo di Orosei
Days 1–3 Map p300

0   2   4km
0   1   2 miles

Codula

GOLFO
DI
OROSEI

Sisine

■ Cuile Ololbizzi

picnic area

Punta
Mudaloro

Punta Frades
Canos (460m)

Bacu Lopellai

See Golfo di Orosei
Day 4 Map p304

P l a i n o f G o l g o

S e r r a   L a t t o n e

Punta
Ispuligi

Sorgenti
Sottomarine
di Goloritzé

Day 4
Rifugio
Golgo

nuraghe

Punta e Cala
Goloritzé

Bacu Goloritzé

▲ Chiesa Campestre
di San Pietro

Ololbizzi. Ignore this and continue south on the dirt road that, after a while, starts to descend, passing a couple of turn-offs to the right (which you shouldn't take). The dirt road ascends and descends relatively gently across the plain until you reach another turn-off to the right to a *nuraghe*. One to 1½ hours from the road to Cuile Ololbizzi, you'll see a major turn-off to the left – the road to Ispuligi – and a signpost marked Cala Sisine pointing back the way you have come.

Go straight on. You will know that you are nearing your destination when you spot the distinctive gabled roof of the **Chiesa Campestre di San Pietro** (385m), above and to the right of the track, soon after the Ispuligi turn-off. The church is still deceptively distant, but you should reach it within 20 minutes of spotting it. You'll need to deviate slightly off the main track here, turning right at the signpost and right again to enter the enclosed churchyard, which is dominated by an enormous, centuries-old tree. In front of the church entrance is an ancient *nuraghic betile*, a monolith of dark stone with the outlines of female attributes – a symbol of fertility. The wall that encircles the church contains shelters used by pilgrims who have been gathering here for centuries for the annual feast of San Pietro on 28 and 29 June.

Turn right on exiting the church and follow the dirt road through clusters of feeding cattle and donkeys. The scenery here resembles the Mexican *altiplano* (high plain). One almost expects to see Pancho Villa riding out of the dust. The low, fenced buildings of the popular Cooperativa Goloritzè – **Rifugio Golgo** (☎ 0782 61 05 99, 368 702 89 80; www.coopgoloritze.com; s/d with bathroom & breakfast €30/45; Apr-Oct) are situated about 500m west of the church. It is worth spending a couple of nights here, allowing time to explore this fascinating area, including a walk to the magnificent beach of **Cala Goloritzè** (see Side Trip, p303). Staff at the *rifugio* can also organise short guided walks in the area, including horse-riding or a dinner at a shepherd's *pinnetta*. Alternatively, you can use the *rifugio* as a brief pit-stop and a chance to fuel up with food and drink before the final leg.

Continuing south towards Baunei you soon reach a crossroads with signs pointing to the left (east) for Su Sterru and *piscinas*, and to the right (west) for Il Golgo restaurant. About 300m away, on the hilltop (430m), **Ristorante Il Golgo** (☎ 337 81 18 28; meals from €25) is renowned for its local dishes. You can sometimes arrange to pitch a tent outside the restaurant in the camping ground. Check ahead.

SIDE TRIP: CALA GOLORITZÈ
3½ hours, 9km, 521m ascent/descent
About 300m east of the crossroads, downhill from Il Golgo restaurant, is the impressive natural chasm of **Su Sterru**, a huge opening covered over with a net. It's a 280m sheer drop. A short distance to the south of the chasm are the *piscinas*, atmospheric archaic tubs, where animals come to drink.

To get to the beach from the crossroads, take the dirt road heading east towards and beyond the *piscinas* and, after crossing the dry Bacu e Sterru riverbed, continue northeast until you come to a parking area near a sheep pen. From here take the trail that ascends diagonally to the left among the rocks

---

ONE HUNDRED YEARS & COUNTING
Want to enjoy enduring good health and live until you're 100? Then waste no time and move to Sardinia! Despite its rugged geography and historical isolation, Sardinia has been classified – along with parts of Japan and California – as a 'Blue Zone', a human longevity hot spot that protects one of the world's oldest demographics. People regularly live into their 90s here and the island purportedly supports more male centenarians than anywhere else on the planet. The secret is a topic of some debate, though certain generic lifestyle practices innate to Sardinia have been singled out by scientific study groups.

The key – if you want to blow out the candles on your 100th birthday cake – is don't smoke, maintain strong family ties, be socially interactive, eat vegetables, partake in consistent exercise and, most importantly, spend plenty of time in Sardinia – preferably hiking on the east coast.

up to a level saddle (471m). Crossing over the saddle, you then enter the evocative Bacu Goloritzè gorge, which descends rapidly to the sea. The atmosphere is truly fairy-tale-like, with centuries-old oaks and rocky ravines where shepherds have built their unusual huts, evoking images of Homer's Odyssey. Still descending, you arrive at the beach with its imposing, 143m-high rocky spire, well-known among free-climbers. There are no springs here so you will need to bring drinking water with you.

Day 4: Golgo to Baunei
2 hours, 9km, 430m descent

The road to Baunei is now paved, but is lightly trafficked and provides for a not unpleasant walk. Take the dirt road from the *rifugio* through the grazing cows and curious donkeys and veer right when you reach the asphalt. The road ascends gently for approximately 7km leaving the Golgo plain and skirting the edge of a leafier wood. Ascending again along a couple of switchbacks you reach a bushier high-level pass before dropping dramatically via a series of steep switchbacks (10% gradient) into **Baunei**.

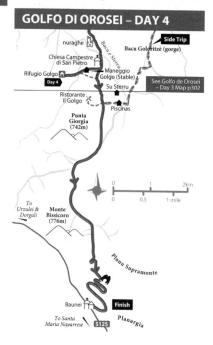

GOLFO DI OROSEI – DAY 4

The views over the last 2kms are stupendous. In Baunei the buses leave from the bus stop in front of the town hall, almost opposite the church. Tickets can be brought from the *tabacchi* 100m up the road.

The staff at Rifugio Golgo can usually arrange 4WD transport to Baunei, which gives you the option of finishing the walk in the high plain and avoiding a long walk on the road. They can also organise a guided walk to Pedra Longa (three hours), where you can be picked up by 4WD and taken to Santa Maria Navarrese. This is an excellent way to end the walk, but is recommended for walkers with mountaineering experience only. It has an exposed section along a spectacular, high ledge.

MORE WALKS

CAPO TESTA

The seaside resort of Santa Teresa di Gallura on the north coast is a very pleasant spot for a relaxing walk, particularly if the magnificent granite rock pools of Capo Testa, 5km west of Santa Teresa, appeal to you. The best time to walk is from March to October, apart from August when the area becomes extremely crowded. The central **tourist office** (☎ 0789 75 41 27; www.comunesant teresagallura.it; Piazza Vittorio Emanuele 24; 9am-midnight daily Jun-Sep, 9am-1pm Mon-Fri & 4-6pm Tue & Wed Oct-May) has loads of useful information and distributes a rough walking map. At Capo Testa is the basic **Albergo Bocche di Bonifacio** (☎ 0789 75 42 02; www.bocchebonifacio .it; half-board €75). From the lighthouse, at the end of the asphalt road, turn left (southwest) following the coast, through easy passages, to enchanting coves. Follow the coast until you reach a wide valley, called Valle della Luna, from where you ascend to the left (south) until you reach the road. During the tourist season, frequent local buses depart for Capo Testa from Via Eleonora d'Arborea in Santa Teresa di Gallura.

SCALA È PRADU

This is a good option for anyone who arrives in Oliena with half a day to spare before starting the Tiscali-Gorropu walk (p294). Although only about 3km, it takes about three hours to climb to the pass with a tough

77m of ascent. However, the view from Scala è Pradu is panoramic and enchanting. From the centre of Oliena, follow the signs for Orgosolo, but before leaving the town take the road that ascends to the left at a sign that reads 'Coop Turistica ENIS – Monte Maccione'. The road ascends and turns left again, then, at an intersection, continues to the right, climbing in narrow switchbacks along the slope of the mountain under the majestic limestone face of Punta Carabidda, up to Albergo Monte Maccione (one hour). From the turn-off for the hotel, continue at mid-slope on the now unsealed road to the right, which begins a very demanding ascent. Avoid the deviation to the right for Fonte Daddana and keep going up the dirt road that climbs the practically vertical wall along horrible, scalloped curves that become narrower and narrower. You will leave the forest behind to arrive at Scala è Pradu (1227m, two hours from Albergo Monte Maccione). To the southeast of the pass you can take in the immense wilderness of the Supramonte, separating you from the sea; and to the northwest is Nuoro, with its ugly, spaceship-like hospital right in the worst possible spot. A bit further south, the summit of Monte Corrasi (1463m), the highest point of the Supramonte, should be visible. Use the IGM 1:25,000 map No 500 III *Oliena*.

TOWNS & FACILITIES

DORGALI
☎ 0784 / pop 8200

Despite its proximity to the coast, Dorgali is a typical Sardinian mountain town and makes an excellent base for all of the walks in this chapter. Splayed on the lower slopes of rocky Monte Bardia and armed with some cheap and friendly places to stay and eat, you'll still spy ladies in traditional black dresses here along with clusters of spry octogenarians advertising the island's human longevity credentials.

Information

At the Pro Loco **tourist office** (☎ 9 62 43; Via La Marmora) you can pick up information about accommodation and trails in the area. Some of the staff speak English. Hook up to the internet with a cappuccino at **Blues Bar** (☎ 9 52 17; Via La Marmora 154) for €2 per half-hour.

Supplies & Equipment

The bookshop **La Scolastica** (☎ 9 48 01; Via la Marmora 69) sells local IGM maps as does **Libreria Cartotecnica** (Corso Umberto 118; 7.30am-1pm & 5-8.30pm).

Sleeping

Camping Cala Gonone (☎ 9 31 65; Via Collodi 1; camping per person €18, bungalows 2/4 people €85/140) The nearest campsite is 9km distant in Cala Gonone, handily placed right at the start of the Golfo di Orosei walk. This is a good place to test out your tent before you hit the *codulas* and beaches. There's a good bar/restaurant on-site as well as a mini-market.

Rifugio Gorropu (☎ 9 48 97; www.rifugiogorropu.it; B&B/half-board €35/55; Easter–mid-Nov) Favoured by climbers, this place is 300m south from the junction for the Hotel Sant'Elene, 3km from Dorgali. Accommodation is very basic though there's astounding views from the terrace. There is also a camping ground (with own tent/tent hire €8/13). Guided trips can be easily arranged here.

Hotel S'Adde (☎ 9 44 12; www.hotelsadde.it; Via Concordia; s/d €70/110) Not at all 'sad(de)', Dorgali's best hotel by far is a friendly, family-run place that also hosts one of the town's best restaurants. Rooms are bright and breezy and the hotel is quietly situated just steps from the town centre. Breakfast is €5 extra and is taken on a pleasant roof terrace.

Hotel Sant'Elene (☎ 9 45 72; www.hotelsantelene.it; d €70, with half-board €120) Set in a panoramic position 3km south of Dorgali at Monte Sant'Elene, the Sant'Elene makes a welcome sight on Day 3 of the Tiscali-Gorropu hike. Aside from eight spiffy rooms with fine views, it has an excellent restaurant with a reasonably priced tourist menu.

Eating

Both the Sant'Elene and S'Adde hotels (above) have excellent restaurants that could easily compete with the two stalwarts overleaf.

Ristorante S'Udulu (☎ 9 52 39; Corso Umberto 20) Upstairs above a daytime coffee bar, the S'Udulu, offers tasty, filling Italian cusine that goes down like nectar after a day or two of hot, arduous hiking. Service is slick and quick and the ambience is local and family orientated, if you don't mind the odd screaming child.

Ristorante Colibrì (☎ 9 60 54; Via Gramsci 14; meals €30; Mon-Sat) Signposted all over town the Colobrì is tucked away in an incongruous residential area and might appear as something of an anticlimax with its dull location and drab decor. But this place is 'the bee's knees' for meat eaters keen to sniff out classic Sardinian specialities such as *cinghiale al rosmarino* (wild boar with rosemary) and *porcheddu* (suckling pig). The pasta is also excellent.

Getting There & Away

ARST (☎ 070 409 83 24; www.arst.sardegna .it) buses serve Nuoro (€2.50, 45 minutes, six daily) for connections to Cagliari, Olbia (€7.50, 2¾ hours, two daily) and Oliena (€1.50, 20 minutes, nine daily). Private company **Deplano** (☎ 29 50 30; www.deplanobus.it) offer four more daily services to Olbia (€15, two to 2½ hours) via Orosei. Up to six daily services shuttle back and forth between Dorgali and Cala Gonone (€1, 20 minutes).

There is one bus a day from Arbatax to Dorgali (via Tortolì), leaving the port following the arrival of the ferry (5am Mon-Sat). The bus arrives in Dorgali at 7.10am, then continues to Oliena and Nuoro.

OLBIA

☎ 0789 / pop 45,500

The major port for ferries from Civitavecchia, Genoa and Livorno and a busy industrial centre, Olbia is not particularly pleasant but is convenient as a first port of call in Sardinia. Take advantage of the efficient airport and good transport connection and head quickly for the hills.

Information

The **tourist office** (☎ 55 77 32; www.olbia turismo.it; Via Nanni 39; 8am-2pm Mon-Fri & 3-6pm Mon-Thu) is near the causeway that leads to the port. The staff speak English, and are very keen to help and advise on places to stay and eat. They can also provide information about accommodatio and places to visit elsewhere on the island.

Supplies & Equipment

As well as selling outdoor equipmen (including fuel for portable stoves), **Medi terraneo** (☎ 2 17 59; Centro Martini, Vi D'Annunzio 45) organises guided tours an walks.

Sleeping & Eating

Hotel Cavour (☎ 20 40 33; www.cavou hotel.it; Via Cavour 22; s €50-65, d €75 90) An inviting hotel in Olbia's old towr Rooms are simple white affairs with unfuss furniture, pastel fabrics and double-glaze windows – a necessity given the noise fron the lively streets below.

Hotel Terranova (☎ 2 23 95; www.hote terranova.it; Via Garibaldi 3; s €40-80, d €70 130) On a narrow lane in the heart of the ac tion, this is a friendly, family-run three-sta with small, cosy rooms and a highly-rate restaurant, **Ristorante Da Gesuino** (mea €35-40), specialising in seafood.

Antica Trattoria (☎ 2 40 53; Via Pal 4; fixed menus €15-25, meals €23; Mon Sat) Welcome to antipasto heaven. Tray of marinated anchovies, vegetables in oliv oil, creamy potato salad and a whole lo more, just sits there waiting to be eater There's also excellent pizza, pastas and fai safe meat dishes.

La Lanterna (☎ 2 30 82; Via Olbi 13; pizzas €8, meals €30; Thu-Tu winter, daily summer) The Lanterna dis tinguishes itself with its cosy subterranea setting and beautifully fresh food. Start of with sweet and sour sardines and move o to almond-crusted bream served with celery and pepper sauce.

Getting There & Away

Olbia's **Aeroporto Olbia Costa Smerald** (OLB; ☎ 56 34 44; www.geasar.it) is abou 5km southeast of the centre and handle flights from most mainland Italian airpor and Sicily, as well as international flight from a number of European cities.

Buses run from Olbia to Santa Teresa d Gallura (€4.50, 1½ hours, five daily), Nuor (€7.50, 2½ hours, five daily), and Dorgal (€7.50, 2¾ hours, two daily). Get ticket from **Café Adel** (Corso Vittorio Veneto 2) just over the road from the main bus stops

More expensive is to Dorgali (€15, two to 2½ hours) and Cala Gonone (€15, 2¼ to 2¾ hours) with private bus company **Deplano** (☎ 0784 29 50 30; www.deplanobus. it). They run four buses daily in both directions stopping at both the airport and the port terminal.

Local bus No 2 (€0.80, or €1.30 if ticket is bought onboard) runs half-hourly between 7.30am and 8pm between the airport and Via Goffredo Mameli in the centre.

Tirrenia (☎ 199 12 31 99; www.tirrenia .it) ferries connect the port of Olbia (Isola Bianca) with Genoa (€59, with car €108, 13 hours) and Civitavecchia (€43, with car €102, eight hours). Tirrenia runs a fast, summer-only service between Olbia and Genoa (six hours) or Civitavecchia (four hours).

Moby Lines (☎ 199 30 30 40; www.moby lines.it) runs ferries between Olbia and Genoa, Livorno or Civitavecchia, and offers special fares for daytime passages in low season. **Sardinia Ferries** (☎ 199 40 05 00; www.sardiniaferries.com) runs ferries between Golfo Aranci and Livorno or Civitavecchia. Both Moby Lines and Sardinia Ferries also run services between Sardinia and Corsica. **Grandi Navi Veloci** (www .gnv.it) runs ferries, summer only, between Olbia and Genoa.

OLIENA
☎ 0784 / pop 7600

From Nuoro you can see the pastel-shaded rooftops of noble Oliena nestled in the shelter of rocky Monte Corrasi. Quainter and more atmospheric than Dorgali, the old grey-stone town centre has echoes of more quintessential mainland settlements. Founded by the Romans in a truly magnificent setting, Oliena today is famous for its blood-red Cannonau wine and traditional Easter celebrations.

Information
The small but helpful **tourist office** (☎ 28 60 78; Via Grazia Deledda 32) is in the centre of town.

Sleeping & Eating
In the centre of Oliena, **Hotel Ci Kappa** (☎ 28 87 33, 28 80 24; Corso Martin Luther King 2; s/d €40/60) is simple but comfortable and the modest restaurant/pizzeria delivers.

Albergo Monte Maccione (☎ 28 83 63; www.coopenis.it; s €37-46, d €62-76), run by the Cooperativa Turistica Enis is deep in the woods 4km from Oliena. You can pitch a tent in the grounds for €15. You can arrange a 4WD ride up to Scala è Pradu from the hotel for around €9 per person for a minimum of five people.

The luxurious **Hotel Su Gologone** (☎ 28 75 12; www.sugologone.it; s €115-180, d €140-240) is on the way to Valle del Lanaittu, 8km east of Oliena on Day 1 of the walk. In a lovely setting, this elegant hotel is a good option for people wanting to enjoy easy exploration of the area; the hotel organises guided tours and walks. The restaurant is justifiably renowned throughout the island.

Getting There & Away
Up to nine **ARST** (☎ 070 409 83 24; www .arst.sardegna.it) buses daily connect Oliena with Dorgali (€1.50, 20 minutes) and Cala Gonone (€2.50, 40 minutes). A similar number of buses head in the opposite direction for Nuoro (€1.50, 25 minutes) for connections to Cagliari.

Connections for Olbia go through Nuoro or Dorgali.

From Arbatax there is one daily ARST bus to Dorgali at 7.10am, with a connection to Oliena (7.30am) and on to Nuoro.

SARDINIA

Walkers Directory

ACCOMMODATION

Throughout this book, places to stay (and eat) at the end of each stage of a walk, or which could serve as a base for day walks, are specifically noted. Wherever possible at least two places are covered, although on extended walks there may be only one option, such as on a *rifugio*-to-*rifugio* walk in the mountains.

Many places offer half-board (dinner, bed and breakfast) and full board (bed and all meals) which is handy if there are few or no other restaurants in the village.

Local tourist offices can provide detailed lists of camping grounds, serviced accommodation and self-catering establishments in their area.

If you arrive at a large town with no bookings and after the tourist office has closed, you may find an after-hours accommodation service nearby – a video screen with a map and details of establishments, and a telephone which you can use to make free calls to the place of your choice.

If you are undertaking a multiday hike in the summer (particularly in August) it is always wise to book ahead and reserve a space in a *rifugi* (mountain hut). If it is full, you may find yourself dragging your tired legs at dusk onto the next mountain hut or – even worse – sleeping on the hard floor.

As this is a hiking guide, the accommodation options listed are usually towards the budget end of the scale. A more comprehensive range of prices can be found in the current edition of Lonely Planet's *Italy*, or any of the more detailed regional guides.

Prices can fluctuate enormously depending on the season, with Easter, summer and the Christmas/New Year period being the typical peak tourist times. There are many variables. Summer is high season on the coast, but in the parched cities it can equal low season. In August especially, many city hotels charge as little as half-price. It is always worth considering booking ahead in high season (although in the urban centres you can usually find something if you trust to luck).

If you're planning on undertaking early- or late-season hiking in mountainous areas, bear in mind that many winter ski resorts virtually shut down for the months of April and October, meaning accommodation in these places at these times will be limited.

Camping & Caravan Parks

Many *campeggi* (camping grounds) in Italy are large, landscaped complexes with a swimming pool, restaurant and bar, shop, laundry – and places to park campervans, cars and caravans, and even pitch tents. Most also have a collection of small bungalows (cabins, chalets) and some static (on-site, fixed) caravans. Like hotels, they are graded according to a star system to indicate the facilities available.

At most places the tariff comprises a fee for each person (€6 to €10) plus a fee for the pitch/tent (€8 to €12); you may have to pay extra if you have a car. It's not unknown to have to pay a small fee for a hot shower. This could end up costing more

han a night in a hostel but less than a room
n a one-star hotel.

Locations are usually attractive – with sea
views on the coast or of mountains in the
Alps. They're very sociable places and great
for meeting people from all over the world,
especially Europe. At busy times though,
ampeggi can become almost oppressively
crowded.

The Italy-wide website www.camping.it
gives detailed information on camping
grounds throughout the country. An Eng-
ish version is available.

CAMPING ON THE WALK
Wild camping is generally not permitted in
Italy and you might be disturbed during the
night by the police. Out of the main tourist
season, if you choose a spot out of sight of
the nearest road, and don't light a fire and
generally keep a low profile, you shouldn't
have any trouble. Always seek permission
from the landowner if you want to camp on
private property close to a house.

Camping is prohibited in national parks
and nature reserves, except in recognised
camping areas – and there are very few
of these.

Guesthouses & B&Bs
B&B options in Italy can range from seaside
bungalows to restored buildings in historic
cities. Tariffs per person cover a wide range
from around €25 to €75. For more information, contact **Bed & Breakfast Italia** (☎ 06
687 86 18; www.bbitalia.it; Corso Vittorio
Emanuele 282, 00186 Rome).

Other peculiarly Italian accommodation options include *agriturismi* (farm-stay
accommodation) and monasteries, both
particularly popular in Tuscany. For more
information on these places see the boxed
texts in the Tuscany chapter (p200).

Hostels
These are called *ostelli per la gioventù* and
most are run by the Associazione Italiana
Alberghi per la Gioventù (AIG), which is
affiliated to Hostelling International (HI).
You don't have to have an HI card to stay
at a hostel but it does simplify things. Membership cards can be purchased at major
hostels, AIG offices and from HI offices in
your home country.

Nightly tariffs range from €14 to €20,
which may include breakfast; if not, it's an
extra €2. Some hostels levy a fee for use
of hot water and for heating in the cooler
months, usually around €1. Evening meals
are often provided, from €9.50.

Accommodation is in segregated dormi-
tories; some hostels have family rooms, at
a higher rate per person. Many hostels are
in interesting and historic buildings (villas

PRACTICALITIES

o Use the metric system for weights and measures.

o Plugs have two or three round pins. The electric current is 220V, 50Hz, but older buildings may still use 125V.

o If your Italian's up to it, try the following newspapers: *Corriere della Sera,* the country's leading daily; *Il Messaggero,* a popular Rome-based broadsheet; or *La Repubblica,* a centre-left daily with a flow of Mafia conspiracies and Vatican scoops. For the Church's view, try the *Osservatore Romano.*

o Tune into **Vatican Radio** (www.radiovaticana.org; 93.3 FM and 105 FM in the Rome area) for a rundown on what the Pope is up to (in Italian, English and other languages); or state-owned Italian **RAI-1**, **RAI-2** and **RAI-3** (www.rai.it), which broadcast all over the country and abroad. Commercial stations such as Rome's **Radio Centro Suono** (www.radiocentrosuono.it) and **Radio Città Futura** (www.radiocittafutura.it), **Naples' Radio Kiss Kiss** (www.kisskissnapoli.it) and Milan-based left-wing **Radio Popolare** (www.radiopopolare.it) are all good for contempo-rary music.

o Switch on the TV to watch state-run **RAI-1**, **RAI-2** and **RAI-3** (www.rai.it) and the main commercial stations (mostly run by Silvio Berlusconi's Mediaset company): **Canale 5** (www.canale5.mediaset.it), **Italia 1** (www.italia1.mediaset.it), **Rete 4** (www.rete4.mediaset.it) and **La 7** (www.la7.it).

and small castles) and in scenic locations (overlooking lakes or the sea).

Some hostels close from 9am to 3.30pm, others at different times or not at all; check-in and curfew times vary from place to place.

Accommodation at the country's 85 hostels can be booked via the head office of the **AIG** (☎ 06 487 11 52; Via Cavour 44, 00184 Rome), which also has an informative booklet about Italian hostels. Some can be booked via the London office of the **International Youth Hostels Federation** (www.iyhf.org).

Independent hostels are virtually unknown in Italy outside Rome.

Hotels

Usually there isn't any obvious difference between a *pensione* and an *albergo* (hotel); in fact, some hotels use both titles. They are graded according to a system of one to five stars, indicating the range of facilities – from basic rooms with shared facilities to luxury establishments with everything that opens and shuts.

Meublé alberghi (furnished hotels) either have rooms with self-catering facilities or simply provide B&B; most hotels have their own dining room. *Locande* (inns) and *alloggi* or *affittacamere* (flats/apartments)

may be cheaper, but are not always given star gradings.

A *camera singola* (single room) or single occupancy of a double/twin room is relatively inexpensive – expect to pay a minimum of €25 in a one-star place to at least €40 in a three-star hotel. Some hoteliers will charge you the full room rate. A *camera doppia* (double room with twin beds) and a *camera matrimoniale* (double room with double bed) range from €40 to €80. Half-board is a popular choice especially in the mountainous regions in the north of the country. Prices are relative bargains – from single/double (s/d) €45/70 for dinner, bed and breakfast at a three-star hotel. Half-and full board prices are nearly always quoted 'per person'.

Rifugi

There's an excellent network of *rifugi* in the Alps, pre-Alps (hinterland of the Lake District), northern Apennines and Apuan Alps. There are fewer in the Maritime Alps and almost none in the south of the country, Sicily or Sardinia. *Rifugi* are marked on the topographical maps covering walking areas.

If you are counting on staying overnight at a *rifugio*, always phone ahead to make sure the place is open and has room, and

---

NO CAMPING PLEASE, WE'RE ITALIAN

Repelled by the thought of freeze-dried pot noodles and chilly mud-splattered tents, the Italians have never been the world's most enthusiastic backcountry campers. Preferring thick walls over thin canvas, they'd much rather do their 'camping' indoors in a cozy, stone, mountain hut known locally as a *rifugio*.

To satisfy the national need, the hiking trails of Italy are sprinkled with a rustic yet welcoming clutch of sturdy *rifugi* most of which are within an easy day's walk of each other.

The earliest *rifugi,* date from the late 18th century when gold miners in the Alps constructed basic shelters on the slopes of Monte Rosa to protect them from the inclement weather. With the birth of the Club Alpino Italiano (CAI) in 1863 and the ensuing 'golden age of alpinism', several more *rifugi* were built to accommodate the pioneering mountaineers who were gradually working their way through a long list of unclimbed alpine summits. The Dolomites gained its first *rifugio* in 1877 and, with the inauguration of Italy's first national park, Gran Paradiso, in 1922; old lodges formerly used by hunters were gradually upgraded into hostel-style accommodation.

Today Italy maintains 761 *rifugi*, most of which are scattered around its northern mountains. Some are managed by the CAI while others remain in private hands. All *rifugi* provide a bare minimum of services, including accommodation, heating and running water. A typical night involves a deck of cards, a bottle of grappa and plenty of exuberant multilingual conversation long into the night.

o let the staff know approximately when you expect to arrive. *Rifugi* fill up quickly n midsummer, and occasionally one closes or repairs or burns down. *Rifugi* are also he first point of inquiry if someone goes missing in the mountains and staff are genuinely concerned for walkers' safety. Technically, *rifugi* may not refuse to provide shelter; however, they are also obliged o heed regulations, which state they cannot accommodate more people than there are beds. If full and there is enough time for you to reach the next *rifugio* before dark, you will be sent on. If it's too late, you'll be allocated a space on the floor.

Some *rifugi* are privately run, many others are owned and run by the CAI (see boxed text, p310). The CAI *rifugi* are usually cheaper and more likely to have mixed dormitory accommodation, either in largish rooms with long platforms on which a dozen or more bodies lie tightly packed, or in smaller rooms with individual bunks. Blankets are provided; you'll need a sleeping sheet and pillow case, although some *rifugi* have them for hire. A torch (flashlight) will probably come in handy – night-time lighting is minimal. Don't expect a hot shower at the end of the day – some *rifugi* provide only basins with cold water in the communal washrooms. Private *rifugi* may have smaller rooms with conventional beds. The average tariff per person (non-CAI member) for bed and breakfast ranges from €20 to €26.

Meals are always served – expect to pay €12 to €18. The meal usually consists of pasta or soup, a *secondo* (second or main course), which is almost always a meat dish with vegetables, and then *dolce* (dessert) or cheese. Vegetarians should let the *gestore* (manager) know their requirements on arrival – you'll most likely be given an omelette instead of the meat dish. Drinks cost extra and are relatively expensive because of the cost of getting them there (helicopters, and sometimes mules, horses and people). Breakfast is simple: bread, butter, jam and coffee. You can usually obtain hot water if you want to fill a flask for hot drinks during the day; packed lunches may be available if ordered the night before.

Most *rifugi* are open full-time only from mid-June to late September. Those at lower altitudes or close to roads may also open on

weekends from Easter until mid-October. Additional information, including contact details, can be obtained from local tourist offices and the **CAI's website** (www.cai.it).

You could consider taking advantage of the reciprocal rights scheme (or Reciprocity Fund) that operates at CAI *rifugi*. By joining your national alpine or mountaineering club or association and obtaining a reciprocal-rights card, you are entitled to pay CAI members' rates. The overnight tariff is just half that for nonmembers, and food and drink prices are between 60% and 75% of the full rate. In Britain, contact the **British Mountaineering Council** (☎ 0161 445 61 61; www.thebmc.co.uk; 177-179 Burton Rd, Manchester M20 2BB).

As well as the *rifugi*, there are *bivacchi* (mountain huts) in more remote and often higher locations. A *bivacco* is a more basic shelter and not staffed by a *gestore*. Some are always open; for others it's necessary to arrange by telephone to collect a key before you head into the wilderness. Contact the nearest tourist office for details.

BUSINESS HOURS

As a general rule shops open 9am to 1pm and 3.30pm to 7.30pm Monday to Saturday. Pharmacies keep similar hours but usually close on Saturday afternoon. Bigger shops and supermarkets tend to forgo the siesta and remain open all day. Bank hours are more limited: 8.30am to 1.30pm and 3.30pm to 4.30pm Monday to Friday. Money exchanges in big cities stay open at weekends. Central post offices open 8.30am to 6.30pm Monday to Saturday; smaller branches usually close on Friday.

Standard bars and cafés stay open from breakfast until dinner – 8am to 8pm is typical. Bars with a late-night crowd carry on till the small hours, perhaps 1am or 2am. Restaurants have more limited hours than northern Europe or North America: noon to 3pm and 7.30pm to 11pm is the standard, meaning it is difficult to have your usual 6pm dinner.

Most museums, galleries and archeological sites shut on Mondays.

CHILDREN

Many Italian families enjoy walking together. Some carry babies in specially designed backpacks and it's not unusual to see children as young as six walking happily at high levels. However, it you have never taken your child walking before, don't expect the introduction to be trouble-free. It may take some time and demand lots of patience to 'train' a child to go on walks of any duration. If you're bringing along inexperienced youngsters, choose areas where it's easy to find short walks, such as Tuscany, Liguria, the Amalfi-Sorrento area and parts of the Lake District.

Cable cars and chair lifts provide easy access to higher altitudes and, if you plan carefully, you could cover sections of some walks in the Dolomites (for example) without stretching your children unduly. Beware of narrow and exposed sections on walks that are not always marked on maps.

For further general information see Lonely Planet's *Travel with Children*.

Eating out with kids in Italy is made easy by the plethora of family restaurants. Even ostensibly upmarket places often welcome kids. Though children's menus aren't common, most places will be able to whip out a quick plate of pasta *al ragù* to satisfy your hungry offspring.

CLIMATE

Italy's diverse climate can be divided into three major zones, each with its own local variations.

Starting in the north, the alpine zone is warmer and drier at its western end than in the east. This is best summed up by the difference in the height of the snow lines: in Valle d'Aosta it's 3060m and to the east in the Julian Alps it's down at 2505m. A typical annual rainfall reading in the west is 660mm and in the east 1050mm. Rainfall is greatest in summer, and you can expect

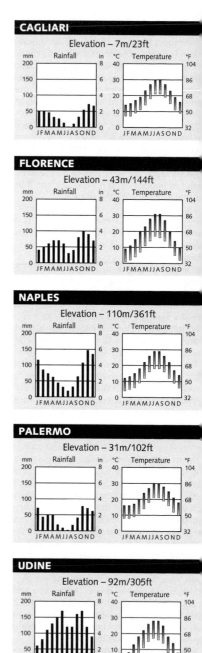

thunderstorms between May and October. Snow can fall at any time, but the heaviest falls are concentrated in the winter months (Dec-Mar). The foothills of the Alps, or the pre-Alps, including the Lakes, enjoy sunnier and warmer conditions during summer than the mountainous areas, and the winters are milder. In these foothills you may experience the föhn, a strong southerly wind.

Abutting the pre-Alps are the flat, low-lying Po valley and northern plains – all the way from Turin (Torino) to Venice and south to Ravenna, Bologna and Genoa. Summers are generally sunny and hot; the average summer temperature at Turin is 23°C. Winters are cold with plenty of frost, fog and snow; Turin's winter average is 0.3°C. Thunderstorms bring much of the summer and autumn rain, but the area is still fairly dry; Venice's average annual rainfall is 750mm.

Peninsular Italy can be subdivided into the mostly mountainous interior and the coast. In the Apennines temperatures are much lower (an annual average of around 13°C) and rainfall higher than along the coast, where hot, mainly dry summers are the rule. The highest temperatures are experienced in the south, where rainfall is minimal. The prevailing winds along the northwestern coast around Liguria are from the southwest; the area is protected from cold northerly winds by the Apennines. Sicily and Sardinia have mild winters and hot, dry summers; during July and August the maximum averages around 28°C but it can reach 40°C.

Weather Information

Forecasts in the press and on TV are fairly generalised, but do give a basic idea of overall trends. Contacts for some local telephone forecast services are given in walks chapters. Some tourist offices and national park visitor centres display forecasts, which may not always be up to date. Useful Italian-language websites:

Nimbus (www.nimbus.it) Good forecasts for all the mountain regions, plus Tuscany, and reasonably detailed information for southern areas. For the mountains you get a detailed forecast including wind, rain and phenomena such as fog.

Meteo (www.meteo.it) Has a Europe-wide isobar chart, but only generalised forecasts. **Meteo Italia** (www.meteoitalia.it) The regional forecasts might be useful in lowland areas such as Tuscany and Campania, or in Sicily and Sardinia.

CUSTOMS

Goods purchased in one EU country and taken from there to another incur no additional taxes, provided duty has been paid somewhere within the EU and the goods are for personal consumption.

Travellers coming into Italy from outside the EU can import, duty free, 200 cigarettes, 1L of spirits (or 2L of wine), 50g of perfume, 250mL of eau de toilette and other goods up to a value of €175. Anything over this limit must be declared on arrival and the appropriate duty paid; carry all receipts.

DANGERS & ANNOYANCES

Italy is a generally safe country and only normal precautions apply with regard to money, valuables and theft. The cities can sometimes be polluted, but if you're spending most of your time hiking this shouldn't be an issue. Traffic rules are more volatile in Italy and pedestrians fall lower down the pecking order than in say the UK or Canada. Don't expect drivers to politely yield for pedestrians and be extra wary on crossings.

Out on the trails, take the usual hiking precautions and be sure to carry the essentials (see Don't Leave Home Without…p22). Weather in the northern mountains can be fickle and unforgiving – be prepared. Take similar care on high altitude walks where occasional exposed sections across potentially dangerous terrain may require some deft footwork (especially when wet).

Italy has no dangerous fauna (its few bears are rarely seen and almost never encountered). Even the dogs are gentle here (especially compared to other Mediterranean countries), though keep an eye open in the Central Apennines for the sometimes over-zealous Maremma sheepdogs.

The country's lack of true wilderness credentials mean that you're never far from the bold mark of civilisation. However, to minimise the risk of lengthy and invariably expensive rescue operations, always carry a mobile phone.

DISCOUNT CARDS

Seniors, students and sometimes families will be entitled to various discounts in museums and other sightseeing spots. Be sure to carry your relevant documentation. An **International Student Identity Card** (www.isic.org) should also win you some discounts for transport, entertainment, hotels and restaurants. Check the website for details. A valid **Hostelling International** (HI; www.iyhf.org) card will save you money when staying in hostels and *rifugi* (see p310). Obtain this in your home country by becoming a member of your national Youth Hostel Association (YHA) or you can join in Italy. The national youth hostel association is called the **Associazione Italiana Alberghi per la Gioventù** (AIG; ☎ 06 4 87 11 52; www.aighostels.com; Via Cavour 44, Rome). Membership entitles you to various discounts in Italy, including on train travel and car hire, and at some bookshops. Check out the AIG website for more discounts.

EMBASSIES & CONSULATES

For foreign embassies and consulates in Italy not listed here, look under 'Ambasciate' or 'Consolati' in the telephone directory. In addition to the following, some countries run honorary consulates in other cities.

Australia Rome (☎ 06 85 27 21, emergencies 800 877790; www.italy.embassy.gov.au; Via Antonio Bosio 5, 00161); Milan (☎ 02 7770 4217; www.austrade.it; Via Borgogna 2, 20122)

Austria (☎ 06 844 01 41; www.bmaa.gv.at; Via Pergolesi 3, Rome, 00198)

Canada (☎ 06 85 44 41; www.dfait-maeci .gc.ca/canadaeuropa/italy; Via Zara 30, Rome, 00198)

France Rome (☎ 06 68 60 11; www.france -italia.it; Piazza Farnese 67, 00186); Milan (☎ 02 655 91 41; Via della Moscova 12, 20121); Naples (☎ 081 598 07 11; Via Francesco Crispi 86, 80121); Turin (☎ 011 573 23 11; Via Roma 366, 10121); Venice (☎ 041 522 43 19; Palazzo Morosini, Castello 6140, 30123)

Germany Rome (☎ 06 49 21 31; www.rom .diplo.de; Via San Martino della Battaglia 4, 00185); Milan (☎ 02 623 11 01; www.mai land.diplo.de; Via Solferino 40, 20121);

Naples (☎ 081 248 85 11; www.neapel.diplo .de; Via Francesco Crispi 69, 80121)

Ireland (☎ 06 697 91 21; www.ambasciata -irlanda.it; Piazza Campitelli 3, Rome, 00186)

Japan Rome (☎ 06 48 79 91; www.it.emb -japan.go.jp; Via Quintino Sella 60, 00187); Milan (☎ 02 624 11 41; Via Cesare Mangili 2/4, 20121)

Netherlands Rome (☎ 06 3228 6001; www .olanda.it; Via Michele Mercati 8, 00197); Milan (☎ 02 485 58 41; Via San Vittore 45, 20123); Naples (☎ 081 551 30 03; Via Agostino Depretis 114, 80133); Palermo (☎ 091 58 15 21; Via Enrico Amari 8, 90139)

New Zealand Rome (☎ 06 853 75 01; www .nzembassy.com; Via Clitunno 44, 00198); Milan (☎ 02 7217 0001; Via Terraggio 17, 20123)

Switzerland Rome (☎ 06 80 95 71; www .eda.admin.ch/roma; Via Barnarba Oriani 61, 00197); Milan (☎ 02 777 91 61; www.eda.admin.ch/milano; Via Palestro 2, 20121); Naples (☎ 081 734 11 32; vertre-tung@nap.rep.admin.ch; Centro Direzion ale, Isola B3, 80143)

UK Rome (☎ 06 4220 0001; www.british embassy.gov.uk; Via XX Settembre 80a, 00187); Florence (☎ 055 28 41 33; Lungarno Corsini 2, 50123); Milan (☎ 02 72 30 01; Via San Paolo 7, 20121); Naples (☎ 081 423 89 11; Via dei Mille 40, 80121)

USA Rome (☎ 06 4 67 41; http://rome .usembassy.gov; Via Vittorio Veneto 119a, 00187); Florence (☎ 055 26 69 51; Lungarno Amerigo Vespucci 38, 50123); Milan (☎ 02 29 03 51; Via Principe Amedeo 2/10, 20121); Naples (☎ 081 583 81 11; Piazza della Repubblica, 80122)

FOOD

In Italy, food is an alternative religion and with such an abundance of culinary excellence, you shouldn't go hungry, even after the most taxing of hikes.

Italian meals are generally split into *antipasto* (appetiser) *primo*, *secondo* and *dolce*. A *contorni* is a side dish often consisting of vegetables (which aren't usually included in the main). Fresh bread is always brought to the table first and is included in the cover charge. Restaurants don't normally serve tap water, but will bring you the bottled variety (with or without gas) for a small charge. Most

Italians drink wine rather than beer with their meals.

You are by no means obliged to order every course. Many travellers get by on just a *primo* and a *contorni*. Hungry hikers will invariably need more. Italians, more often than not, order the full spread and spend hours eating it.

Regional Food

What the world regards as Italian cooking is really a collection of regional cuisines; cooking styles vary markedly from region to region and significantly between the north and south.

Among the country's best-known dishes are lasagne and *tagliatelle al ragù* (also known as spaghetti bolognese), both from Emilia Romagna. In Trentino-Alto Adige, the Austrian influence is strong and you'll find *canederli* (dumplings) made with stale bread, cheese and, perhaps, liver. Polenta (corn meal) with all kinds of sauces, and/or with *fontina* (cheese) is very popular in Valle d'Aosta. Two Ligurian specialities are pesto (sauce or paste of fresh basil, garlic, oil, pine nuts and sharp cheese) and focaccia (flat bread). In Tuscany the locals use plenty of olive oil and herbs, and regional dishes are noted for their simplicity, fine flavour and use of fresh produce. Among the staples of Tuscan cuisine are small white cannellini (beans).

As you go further south the food becomes spicier, and the cakes and pastries sweeter and richer. A pizza in or near Naples (where it was created), and local fish around Amalfi and Sorrento shouldn't be missed.

In Sicily try the *pesce spada* (swordfish); *melanzane* (eggplant) is popular here, in pasta sauces or filled with olives, anchovies, capers and tomatoes. Sardinia's treats include *carte musica* (thin crisp bread), eaten warm with oil and salt, and *pecorino* (aged sheep's cheese) sprinkled on pasta.

For more on regional food, see the relevant boxed texts in the Liguria (p56), Maritime Alps (p85), and Sicily (p274) chapters.

On the Walk

For economy and safety it's a good idea to carry some of your own food on walks. Always carry emergency supplies; light, high-energy items include nuts, dried fruits and chocolate. Electrolyte drinks and energy snacks or gels can also provide an energy jolt when you're depleted. On many – but not all – walks you'll pass through a town or village during the day where you can stock up or have a light meal. In the mountains, *rifugi* are open during the day for snacks and drinks and a hearty lunch (see Rifugi, p310).

BUYING FOOD

Snack foods, cheese, sliced meat, pâté, bread, vegetables and fruit can be purchased at supermarkets, *alimentari* (delicatessen/grocery store), and speciality fruit and vegetable shops and, if you're in the right place at the right time, open-air fresh-produce markets. For fresh bread, look for *panetteria*/*panificio* (bakery) or *pasticceria* (pastry shop).

COOKING

You can, of course, bring your own stove and cook meals at camping grounds and, perhaps, at *rifugi*, although this isn't a common practice and probably not very popular with the warden or other guests. Inexpensive places to eat and superb fresh produce make the weight of a stove superfluous and the bother of buying fuel an unnecessary complication.

WHERE TO EAT

In towns and villages there's usually a choice of places to eat. A *tavola calda* is a self-service

---

AUTHOR'S CHOICE

- Best wine – Barbaresco and Barolo in Piedmont/Maritime Alps

- Best breakfasts – Bolzano, Dolomites

- Best pasta dish – *pesto al genovese*, Liguria

- Best seafood – Catania, Sicily

- Best ice cream – San Gimignano, Tuscany

- Best cafés - Positano on the Amalfi Coast, Campania

- Best liqueur – the *limoncello* in Sorrento, Campania

- Best slow food – Cuneo, Piedmont/ Maritime Alps

WALKERS DIRECTORY

eatery, offering inexpensive instant meat, pasta and vegetable dishes, and doesn't charge extra for you to sit down. A *rosticceria* usually offers cooked meats and other takeaway food. A pizzeria will, of course, serve pizza and usually has a full menu of pasta, fish and meat dishes; the best pizzas are *al forno* – cooked in a wood-fired oven. An *osteria* is the classic place to eat in Italy, usually a bar offering a choice from a small simple menu emphasising local food. A trattoria is essentially a more homely, less expensive version of a *ristorante* which, in turn, has more professional service and a greater range of dishes, although not necessarily of a higher standard than you'll find at a trattoria.

Menus are usually posted outside so you can check prices, as well as the *pane e coperta* (cover charge), which is usually around €2, and perhaps a service charge (around 15%). For opening hours see Business Hours (p311).

Vegetarians will have no problems eating in Italy. Specialist vegetarian restaurants are fairly rare, but vegetables, pasta, rice and pulses are staples of the Italian diet. Most eating places have a good selection of *contorni* (vegetable dishes) and *insalate* (salads), as well as meat-free antipasti (appetisers), soup, rice and pasta dishes and pizzas.

You can buy sandwiches at bars or have them made in *alimentari* or a *panificio/panetteria*. A *pasticceria* is the place to go for the accompanying cake or pastry. *Pizza a taglio* (pizza by the slice or massive slab) is sold in takeaway places. *Gelaterie* (gelati

---

WATER

Water from *sorgenti* (fountains) in towns and villages, and from taps over troughs in the countryside is safe to drink, unless a sign stating '*acqua non potabile*' tells you that it isn't. There are mineral springs all over the place, usually easily identified by people filling bottles and containers. Water from streams and rivers will almost certainly be polluted. In the mountains it's tempting to drink from streams, but you can't be certain that there aren't animals – dead or alive – upstream. See Water Purification (p340) for advice on water-purification methods.

---

shops) are plentiful everywhere; look out for those displaying a sign with the word *artigianale* (home-made), which should mean it is made on the premises and contains fresh ingredients.

HOLIDAYS

Many businesses and shops close for at least part of August, when most Italians take their annual holidays, particularly during the week around Ferragosto (Feast of the Assumption) on 15 August.

National public holidays:

○ Epiphany	6 January
○ Easter Monday	March/April
○ Liberation Day	25 April
○ Labour Day	1 May
○ Feast of the Assumption	15 August
○ All Saints' Day	1 November
○ Feast of the Immaculate Conception	8 December
○ Christmas Day	25 December
○ Feast of Santo Stefano	26 December

Individual towns have public holidays to celebrate the feasts of their patron saints. Religious festivals are particularly numerous in Sicily and Sardinia.

INSURANCE

Buy a policy that generously covers you for medical expenses, theft or loss of luggage and tickets, and for cancellation of and delays in your travel arrangements. It may be worth taking out cover for mountaineering activities and the cost of rescue. Check your policy doesn't exclude walking, particularly on *vie ferrate* (iron ways), as a dangerous activity.

Buy travel insurance as early as possible to ensure you'll be compensated for any unforseen accidents or delays. If items are lost or stolen get a police report immediately – otherwise your insurer might not pay up.

INTERNET ACCESS

If you plan to carry your notebook or palmtop computer with you, carry a universal AC adaptor for your appliance (most appliances are sold with these). Do not rely on finding wi-fi whenever you want it, as hot spots remain few and far between and often require payment. Another option is to buy a card pack with one of the Italian mobile-phone operators, which gives wireless access through the mobile-telephone network. These are usually pre-pay services that you can top up as you go.

Most travellers make constant use of internet cafés and free web-based email such as Yahoo, Hotmail or Gmail. Internet cafés and centres are present, if not always abundant, in all cities and most main towns (don't forget your incoming mail server name, account name and password). Prices hover at around €5 to €8 per hour. By law, you must present photo ID (such as passport or driver's licence) to use internet points in Italy.

LEGAL MATTERS

For many Italians, finding ways to get around the law is a way of life. This is partly because bureaucracy has long been seen by most (with some justification) as a suffocating clamp on just about all areas of human activity.

The average tourist will only have a brush with the law if robbed by a bag-snatcher or pickpocket.

Alcohol & Drugs

Italy's drug laws were toughened in 2006 and possession of any controlled substances, including cannabis or marijuana, can get you into hot water. Those caught in possession of 5g of cannabis can be considered traffickers and prosecuted as such. The same applies to tiny amounts of other drugs. Those caught with amounts below this threshold can be subject to minor penalties.

The legal limit for blood-alcohol level is 0.05% and random breath tests do occur.

Police

If you run into trouble in Italy, you are likely to end up dealing with the police – either the *polizia statale* (state police) or the *carabinieri* (military police).

The *polizia* deal with thefts, visa extensions and permits (among other things). They wear powder-blue trousers with a fuchsia stripe and a navy-blue jacket. Details of police stations, or *questure,* are given throughout this book.

The *carabinieri* deal with general crime, public order and drug enforcement (often

---

> ## LEGAL AGE
>
> - The right to vote: 18 years old
> - Age of consent: 14 years old (both heterosexual and homosexual, but there are some exceptions to the general rules)
> - Driving: 18 years old

---

overlapping with the *polizia*). They wear a black uniform with a red stripe and drive night-blue cars with a red stripe. They are based in a *caserma* (barracks), a reflection of their past military status (they came under the jurisdiction of the Ministry of Defence).

One of the big differences between the *polizia* and *carabinieri* is the latter's reach – even many villages have a *carabinieri* post.

Other police include the *vigili urbani,* basically local traffic police. You will have to deal with them if you get a parking ticket or your car is towed away. The *guardia di finanza* are responsible for fighting tax evasion and drug smuggling. The *guardia forestale,* aka *corpo forestale,* are responsible for enforcing laws concerning forests and the environment in general.

For national emergency numbers, refer to the Planning section of each region.

Your Rights

Italy still has antiterrorism laws that could make life difficult if you are detained. You should be given verbal and written notice of the charges laid against you within 24 hours by arresting officers. You have no right to a phone call upon arrest. The prosecutor must apply to a magistrate for you to be held in preventive custody awaiting trial (depending on the seriousness of the offence) within 48 hours of arrest. You have the right not to respond to questions without the presence of a lawyer. If the magistrate orders preventive custody, you have the right to then contest this within the following 10 days.

MAPS
Buying Maps

The best places to buy maps in Italy are newsagents, bookshops and *tabaccherie* (tobacconists; all-purpose shops where bus tickets and, often, phone cards are sold)

MAPS IN THIS BOOK

The maps in this book are based on the best available references, sometimes combined with GPS data collected in the field. They are intended to show the general routes of the hikes we describe. They are primarily to help locate the route within the surrounding area. They are not detailed enough in themselves for route finding or navigation. You will still need a properly surveyed map at an adequate scale – specific maps are recommended in the Planning section for each hike. Most chapters also have a regional map showing the gateway towns or cities, principal transport routes and other major features. Map symbols are interpreted in the legend on the inside front cover of this book.

On the maps in this book, natural features such as river confluences and mountain peaks are in their true position, but sometimes the location of villages and routes are not always so. This may be because a village is spread over a hillside, or the size of the map does not allow for detail of the path's twists and turns. However, by using several basic route-finding techniques (see p336), you will have few problems following our descriptions.

in the towns and villages in walking areas. Major city bookshops (such as Feltrinelli) have map sections but the range is usually limited. Prices range from €6 to €10.

You can order maps online at two excellent websites: www.stanfords.co.uk, the site of the famous London-based travel book/map store, and www.omnimap.com, which is run out of the US.

Large-scale Maps

Maps of walking trails in the Alps and Apennines are available at all major bookshops in Italy, but the best are the TCI (Touring Club Italiano) bookshops.

The best walking maps are the 1:25,000 scale series; they contain an enormous amount of detailed information, including waymarked paths, although the numbering may not be entirely accurate or up to date. Different publishers specialise in different parts of the country.

Kompass publishes 1:25,000 and 1:50,000 series for most areas, many with a separate booklet of background information (usually in Italian and German, or Italian and French). However, Kompass' depiction of walking routes is often fanciful, and needs to be treated with caution and supplemented by other sources.

Tabacco produces a superb 1:25,000 series covering the Dolomites, Parco Nazionale dello Stelvio and the Julian and Carnic Alps. Edizioni Multigraphic produces a series of maps concentrating on Tuscany and the Apennines. Istituto Geografico Centrale publishes two series – 1:25,000 and 1:50,000 – for the Western Alps,

Maritime Alps and Liguria. CAI maps are also quite common, particularly in the central Apennines and the Amalfi-Sorrento area.

In Sardinia it may be necessary to use the 1:25,000 Istituto Geografico Militare (IGM) maps, in the absence of any commercial publications. Most local newsagents and bookshops stock these maps or you can contact **IGM** (☎ 055 48 06 72; Viale Filippo Strozzi 10, 50122 Florence).

The series of *Guide dei Monti d'Italia*, 22 grey hardback volumes published by the TCI and CAI, are an exhaustive collection of walking guides with maps.

PLACE NAMES

In Italy's northern mountains, where ancient linguistic boundaries pay little attention to modern international borders, many settlements and places have two or sometimes three different names. This is particularly prevalent in the Dolomites and Stelvio National Park where Italian, German and, to a lesser extent, Ladin are still in everyday usage. In this book we have generally favoured the more common place names and highlighted any local alternatives under the 'maps' subhead in the individual chapters. We have also highlighted dual-name towns/villages/places of interest confusingly marked on maps in just one language.

A similar situation occurs in the Valle d'Aosta, though this time the linguistic mix is Italian, French and Valdôtain.

Small-scale Maps

Michelin has a series of good fold-out country maps. No 735 covers the whole country on a scale of 1:1,000,000. You could also consider the series of six area maps at 1:400,000. TCI publishes a decent map of Italy at 1:800,000, and a series of 15 regional maps at 1:200,000 (€7).

MONEY

The euro (€) is the currency of cash transactions in Italy, along with 11 other EU countries. The euro comprises 100 cents. Coin denominations are one, two, five, 10, 20 and 50 cents, €1 and €2. The notes are €5, €10, €20, €50, €100, €200 and €500. Exchange rates are displayed on the inside back cover of this book. For the latest rates check out www.xe.com.

ATMs

The quickest and most flexible source of cash are ATMs (Automatic Teller Machines). Look for the sign 'Bancomat'. You'll find them in the wall of most banks and at major train stations. It's not uncommon for Italian ATMs to reject foreign cards – if that happens try a few more ATMs at major banks (where your card's logo is displayed) before assuming that your card is the problem and not the local system.

Cash

There is little advantage in bringing foreign cash into Italy. True, exchange commissions are often lower than for travellers cheques, but the danger of losing the lot far outweighs such gains.

Credit Cards

Credit and debit cards (Visa and MasterCard) for withdrawing cash and for general purchases are accepted in most places in large towns and cities, but much less commonly in small towns, and rarely in villages. American Express cards aren't widely recognised.

Moneychangers

At airports and train stations in large cities and at tourist offices, exchange offices (look for the 'Cambio' sign) are much faster, open longer hours and easier to deal with than banks. However, banks are generally more reliable and tend to offer the best rates. You can also exchange money at post offices. Keep a close eye on the commission charged and, if it seems absurdly high, ask for your money back.

On the Walk

Generally the safest way to travel is with a moderate amount of cash, to be topped up regularly via a credit card, and supplemented by some travellers cheques. On longer walks when you won't be passing through any towns, ensure that you have enough cash to last several days.

Receipts

Laws to tighten controls on payment of taxes place the onus on the buyer to ask for and keep receipts for all goods and services. Although it rarely happens, you could be asked by an officer of the *guardia di finanza* (fiscal police) to produce the receipt immediately after you leave a shop or restaurant. If you don't have it, you may have to pay a very hefty fine.

Tipping

You are not expected to tip on top of restaurant service charges but it is common practice to leave a small amount. In the absence of a service charge, you might consider leaving a 10% tip, but this certainly isn't obligatory. In bars, Italians often leave any small change as a tip, even only €0.05 or €0.10.

Bargaining in shops is not acceptable, though you might wrangle small discounts on large purchases or if you're staying in a *pensione* for more than a few days.

Travellers Cheques

Banks, post offices and exchange offices may give a better rate for travellers cheques than for cash, but banks usually exact a hefty commission. Largely outmoded by plastic these days, travellers cheques are perhaps best employed as a safe back-up money supply.

PERMITS & FEES

There are no national park fees in Italy. The only two walks that will cost you money are the Sentiero Azzurro in Cinque Terre where you will need to first purchase a Cinque Terre card (see boxed text, p57) and the

Vesuvius Crater in Campania that currently costs adult/child €6.50/€4.50.

TELEPHONE
Mobile Phones
Mobile Phones Italy has very good mobile-phone coverage, although reception can be variable in the mountains and in more isolated areas such as the Supramonte in Sardinia. Mobiles will usually receive at open, high points, but might not receive in isolated mountain valleys.

Italy uses the GSM 900/1800 cellular phone system, compatible with phones sold in the UK, Australia and most of Asia, but not those from North America or Japan. Check with your service provider before you leave home that they have a roaming agreement with a local counterpart.

It is possible to purchase another SIM card for your handset to use while in Italy (first check with your home service provider that your phone is compatible). It can cost as little as €10 to activate a local pre-paid SIM, often with €10 worth of calls on the card.

Payphones
Telecom Italia's public payphones are plentiful. The older orange models, some of which are very temperamental if you ask them to make too many toll-free or international calls, are slowly being replaced by sleek grey models, which are infinitely more friendly and efficient. Although the oldest machines accept coins and *carte/schede telefoniche* (phonecards), coin machines are in the minority.

Peak times for domestic calls are from 8am to 6.30pm Monday to Friday and from 8am to 1pm Saturday. Cheap rates apply outside these times and public holidays. Different times apply for international calls. You can make cheap calls to the UK from 10pm to 8am Monday to Saturday and all Sunday, to the US and Canada from 7pm to 2pm Monday to Friday and all weekend, and to Australia from 11pm to 8am Monday to Saturday and all Sunday.

A *comunicazione urbana* (local call) from a public phone to a landline costs €0.10 per 70 seconds. Rates for a *comunicazione interurbana* (long-distance call within Italy) cost €0.10 when it's answered and €0.10 for every 57 seconds thereafter.

A three-minute call to Australia will cost around €2.90 from a public phone; to Europe and North American, approximately €0.90 for three minutes. Calls to mobiles are more expensive.

Phone Codes
Area codes of up to four digits (all beginning with 0) are an integral part of the phone number for all calls – even if calling within a single zone. They are followed by anything from four to eight more digits. Mobile-phone numbers in Italy begin with a three digit prefix, such as ☎ 330, ☎ 335 or ☎ 347. *Numeri verdi* (freephone or toll-free numbers) begin with ☎ 800. For national directory inquiries, phone ☎ 12.

The country code for Italy is ☎ 39; you must always include the initial 0 in area codes.

Direct international calls can be made from most public telephones by using a phonecard. Dial ☎ 00 to get out of Italy, then the relevant country and area codes, followed by the telephone number.

Phonecards
These are available at post offices, *tabaccherie*, newspaper stands and from vending machines in Telecom offices. They are usually sold for €2.50 or €5. They can be used for both local and long-distance/international calls. You must break off the top left-hand corner of the card before you use it. Most phonecards have an expiry date.

Telecom Italia also issues international call cards for either Europe, the US and Canada, or for other parts of the world), which give up to three hours' call time – provided you're ringing off-peak and to a nearby country.

TIME
Italy operates on the 24-hour clock. The country is one hour ahead of GMT/UTC and in the same time zone as neighbouring countries. When it's noon in Rome, it's 3am in San Francisco, 6am in New York and Toronto, 11am in London, 9pm in Sydney and 11pm in Auckland.

Daylight-saving time starts on the last Sunday in March, when clocks are put forward one hour. Clocks are put back an hour on the last Sunday in October.

WALKING CLUBS

Italy's ultimate walking club is the **Club Alpino Italiano** (CAI; www.cai.it), a highly inclusive organisation split into regional chapters across the country that currently boasts over 300,000 members. Membership has numerous benefits including cut-price deals at *rifugi* and other accommodation.

For more details on the CAI see the boxed text p310.

TOURIST INFORMATION

There are three tiers of tourist office in Italy: regional, provincial and local. Regional offices, which focus on promotion, budget and other esoteric concerns, are of no use to the average visitor.

Provincial offices are called either the Ente Provinciale per il Turismo (EPT) or, more commonly, Azienda di Promozione Turistica (APT). They usually have information about their province and the town in which they're located, especially accommodation, and can be particularly helpful with details of transport between the province and major cities; many have an exchange office.

Local offices have two common names, Informazioni e Assistenza ai Turisti (IAT) and Azienda Autonoma di Soggiorno e Turismo (AAST), and you'll occasionally come across a Pro Loco office. These concentrate on their town. You can obtain information about local accommodation (including *rifugi* or mountain huts), transport, walking routes, organised walks and mountain guides. Some sell maps and guidebooks, notably where walking is popular – the Alps and Tuscany (Toscana).

English is usually spoken at offices in larger towns and major tourist areas, but isn't widely spoken in small towns and villages. It's much more likely that staff will speak French and/or German in addition to Italian. Printed information is generally provided in several languages. Tourist offices are generally open from 9am to 12.30 pm or 1pm, and from 3pm to around 7pm Monday to Friday, and on Saturday morning. During summer, many offices open daily, or at least extend to all day Saturday and part of Sunday.

Small information offices at most major train stations keep similar hours, but some only open during summer. Many will help you find a hotel.

Tourist Offices Abroad

Ente Nazionale Italiano per il Turismo (ENIT; www.enit.it), the Italian State Tourist Board has offices in several countries:

Australia (☎ 02 9262 1666, italia@italian tourismcom; Level 4, 46 Market St, Sydney 2000)
Canada (☎ 416 925 4882, www.italiantour ism.com; Suite 907 South Tower, 17 Bloor St East, Toronto M4W 3R8)
UK (☎ 020 7355 1557, italy@italiantourist board.co.uk; 1 Princess St, London W1R 9AY 1)
US (☎ 212 245 4822, www.italiantourism .com; Suite 1565, 630 Fifth Ave, New York 10111)

VISAS

Italy signed the Schengen Convention whereby various European countries abolished checks at common borders. There are currently 25 states in the Schengen area: the whole of the EU (minus the UK, Ireland, Cyprus, Romania and Bulgaria) plus Iceland, Norway and Switzerland. Citizens of Schengen states can travel to Italy with their ID cards alone; people from countries that do not issue ID cards, including the UK, must carry a valid passport. Nationals from all other countries must also have a valid passport and (if necessary) a visa.

Citizens of several non-Schengen countries, including Canada, the US, New Zealand, Australia, Israel, Japan and Brazil, do not need visas (but require passports) for tourist visits of up to 90 days. Citizens of other countries should contact an Italian consulate to discuss specific visa requirements.

Several walks in this book briefly pass through neighbouring countries, including France, Austria and Slovenia, but there are no border-crossing formalities.

Transport

CONTENTS

GETTING THERE & AWAY

For travel between Italy and other parts of Europe, including the UK, buses are the cheapest but most tiring type of transport, although discount rail tickets are competitive and budget flights can be good value.

There are plenty of rail and bus connections, especially with northern Italy. Car and passenger ferries operate to ports in Albania, Corsica, Croatia, Greece, Malta, Spain, Tunisia and Turkey.

Flights, tours and rail tickets can be booked online at www.lonelyplanet.com/travel_services.

ENTERING THE COUNTRY

Citizens of the 27 European Union (EU) member states and Switzerland can travel to Italy with their national identity card alone. If such countries do not issue ID cards – as in the UK – travellers must carry a full valid passport. All other nationalities must have a full valid passport.

If applying for a visa (see p321), check that your passport's expiry date is at least six months away. If not an EU citizen, you may be required to fill out a landing card (at airports).

By law you are supposed to have your passport or ID card with you at all times. It doesn't happen often, but it could be embarrassing if you are asked by the police to produce a document and you don't have it with you. You will need one of these documents for police registration when you take a hotel room.

In theory, there are no passport checks at land crossings from neighbouring countries, as all are members of the Schengen zone (in which border controls have been eliminated). However, random customs controls still take place when crossing between Italy and Switzerland. Airport security is tighter than ever. Check the latest restrictions on what can and cannot be carried on flights as handheld luggage. At the time of writing, for example, people flying from EU airports could only carry liquids in quantities of 100mL or less in transparent bottles sealed in plastic bags.

AIR
Airports & Airlines

Italy's main intercontinental gateway is Rome's **Leonardo da Vinci airport** (☎ 06 6 59 51; www.adr.it), also known as Fiumicino. International flights also operate in and out of many other airports including Milan's **Malpensa** (☎ 02 748 52 20) and **Naples** (☎ 081 789 62 59). The major airports are linked to their nearby cities

THINGS CHANGE...

The information in this chapter is particularly vulnerable to change. Check directly with the airline or a travel agent to make sure you understand how a fare (and ticket you may buy) works and be aware of the security requirements for international travel. Shop carefully. The details given in this chapter should be regarded as pointers and are not a substitute for your own careful, up-to-date research.

BAGGAGE RESTRICTIONS

Airlines impose tight restrictions on carry-on baggage. No sharp implements of any kind are allowed onto the plane, so pack items such as pocket knives, camping cutlery and first-aid kits into your checked luggage.

If you're carrying a camping stove you should remember that airlines also ban liquid fuels and gas cartridges from all baggage, both check-through and carry-on. Empty all fuel bottles and buy what you need at your destination.

by regular bus (and in some cases train) services.

Airlines operating to Italy:

Air Canada (AC; ☎ 06 6501 1462; www .aircanada.com)
Air Dolomiti (EN; ☎ 045 288 61 40; www .airdolomiti.it)
Air France (AF; ☎ 848 884466; www.air france.com)
Air Transat (TS; ☎ 800 873233; www.air transat.it)
Alitalia (AZ; ☎ 06 22 22; www.alitalia .com)
American Airlines (AA; ☎ 06 6605 3169; www.aa.com)
BMI (BD; ☎ 0044 1332 64 8181; www .flybmi.com)
British Airways (BA; ☎ 199 712266; www .britishairways.com)
Brussels Airlines (SN; ☎ 899 800903; www.flysn.com)
easyJet (U2; ☎ 899 676789; www.easyjet .com)
Emirates Airlines (EK; ☎ 06 4520 6070; www.emirates.com)
Eurofly (GJ; ☎ 800 4590581; www.eurofly .it)
KLM (KL; ☎ 199 414207; www.klm.com)
Lufthansa (LH; ☎ 199 400044; www.luft hansa.com)
Meridiana (IG; ☎ 892928; www.meridi ana.it)
Qantas (QF; ☎ 848 350010; www.qantas .com.au)
Ryanair (FR; ☎ 899 678910; www.ryanair .com)
Swiss (LX; ☎ 848 868120; www.swiss.com)

Singapore Airlines (SQ; ☎ 02 777 29 21; www.singaporeair.com)
Thai Airways International (TG; ☎ 02 890 03 51; www.thaiair.com)
United Airlines (UA; ☎ 02 6963 3707; www.united.com)
US Airways (US; ☎ 848 813177; www.us airways.com)

Tickets
The internet is increasingly the easiest way of locating and booking reasonably priced seats. This is especially so for flights from around Europe, regardless of whether you are flying with major carriers, like Alitalia, or low-cost airlines.

Full-time students and those under 26 sometimes have access to discounted fares, especially on longer haul flights from beyond Europe. You have to show a document proving your date of birth or a valid International Student Identity Card (ISIC) when buying your ticket. Other cheap deals include the discounted tickets released to travel agents and specialist discount agencies.

There is no shortage of online agents:

○ www.cheapflights.com
○ www.ebookers.com
○ www.expedia.com
○ www.flightline.co.uk
○ www.flynow.com
○ www.kayak.com
○ www.lastminute.com
○ www.opodo.com
○ www.orbitz.com
○ www.planesimple.co.uk
○ www.priceline.com
○ www.skyscanner.net
○ www.travelocity.co.uk
○ www.tripadvisor.com

UK
The cheapest way to fly between the UK or Ireland and Italy is, generally, the no-frills way. **EasyJet** (www.easyjet.com), flies to Milan, Naples, Palermo, Pisa, Rome and Venice. Irish **Ryanair** (www.ryanair.com) has numerous destinations connecting various airports in the UK (especially London Stansted) and Ireland (and elsewhere in Europe) with Italian destinations including Alghero, Ancona, Bergamo, Bologna, Brescia, Brindisi, Bari, Cagliari, Cuneo, Genoa, Lamezia (Calabria), Milan, Olbia,

---

DEPARTURE TAX

The departure tax, payable when you leave Italy by air, is included in your airline ticket.

Palermo, Parma, Perugia, Pescara, Pisa, Rimini, Rome, Trapani, Trieste, Turin and Venice. Some of these routes are seasonal. **BMI Baby** (www.bmibaby.com) flies from Birmingham to Bergamo and Rome. Prices vary wildly according to season and depend on how far in advance you book.

The two national airlines linking the UK and Italy are British Airways and Alitalia, both operating regular flights to Rome, Milan, Venice, Florence, Naples, Palermo, Turin and Pisa.

Continental Europe

All national European carriers offer services to Italy. The largest, Air France, Lufthansa and KLM, have offices in all major European cities. Italy's national carrier, Alitalia, has a huge range of offers on many European destinations. Check out the low-cost airlines too (see Airports & Airlines, p322).

USA & Canada

The North Atlantic is the world's busiest long-haul air corridor and the flight options are bewildering. Several airlines fly direct to Italy, landing at either Rome or Milan. These include Alitalia, Lufthansa, Air France and Delta Air Lines. If your trip will not be confined to Italy, check for cheaper flights to other European cities.

There are direct flights to Milan and Rome from Toronto and Montreal in Canada.

Australia & New Zealand

Cheap flights from Australia and New Zealand to Europe generally go via South-East Asian capitals, involving a stopover at Kuala Lumpur, Bangkok or Singapore. If a long stopover between connections is necessary, transit accommodation is sometimes included in the price of a ticket. If the transit accommodation is at your own expense, it may be worth considering a more expensive but direct ticket.

Qantas and Alitalia offer occasional direct flights from Australia; if you are looking for a bargain airfare you will probably end up with another airline.

LAND

Not quite all roads lead to Rome, but there's a good choice of routes into Italy by train, bus or car. Bus travel is generally cheaper, but with less frequent and much less comfortable services than those offered by trains.

If you're travelling to Italy overland, check whether you need visas to the countries you'll pass through en route.

Border Crossings

The main points of entry to Italy are the Mont Blanc tunnel from Chamonix in France, which leads to the A5 for Turin and Milan; the Grand St Bernard tunnel from Switzerland, which also connects with the A5; the Simplon tunnel which connects to the SS33 to Lago Maggiore; the St Gottard tunnel from Ticino in Switzerland which takes the N2 south into Italy; and the Brenner pass from Austria, which links with the A22 to Bologna. Other routes, via high-altitude mountain passes, such as Grand St Bernard and Little St Bernard into Valle d'Aosta, are generally open only from mid-June to mid-September but do provide a much more scenic approach.

Bus

The main long-distance bus company in Europe is **Eurolines** (in UK ☎ 08705 14 32 19, 1582-40 45 11; www.eurolines.com; 52 Grosvenor Gardens, London SW1W 0AU, UK). The Eurolines Pass is good for those planning to do a lot of bus travel. It's valid for unlimited travel to 40 cities in 26 countries for 15 days (adult/under 26 & over 60, €199/169) or 30 days (€299/229). Fares increase in the peak summer season (Jun-Sep). Italian cities on the network include Milan, Florence, Venice, Rome and Siena.

Car & Motorcycle

You can take your car or motorcycle from the UK to France by ferry or via the Channel Tunnel on the **Eurotunnel** (in UK ☎ 08705 35 35 35; www.eurotunnel.com) car train. Operating between Folkestone and Calais, trains run around the clock with up to four crossings (35 minutes) per hour in July and

August. You only pay for the vehicle, and fares vary according to season and time of day. The most expensive fares are between May and September; it costs more if you depart during the day Friday to Sunday. Motorcyclists rarely have to book ahead for ferries.

When driving in Europe, always carry proof of ownership of a private vehicle and evidence of third-party insurance. If driving a vehicle registered and insured in an EU country, your home country insurance is sufficient. Theoretically, the International Insurance Certificate, also known as the Carta Verde (Green Card), is no longer required for EU-registered cars. Unfortunately, in case of an accident, police may still ask for it!

Ask your insurer for a European Accident Statement (EAS) form, which can simplify matters in the event of an accident.

Every vehicle travelling across an international border should display a nationality plate of its country of registration (unless it has the standard EU number plates with the blue strip and country ID).

Train

In common with the much of Europe, Italy has an extensive and well-run rail network. Furthermore, travelling on it is generally a comfortable, fast, economical and relatively hassle-free experience. It is also infinitely greener – especially when compared to flying. With future expansion plans and blueprints for more efficient high-speed trains in the works, the network is only likely to improve in the coming years.

Regular EuroCity (EC) services connect European countries with Italy along eight lines: from southern France you can reach Genoa; other lines go from Paris and Barcelona to Turin and beyond; there are trains to Milan from Swiss, German and French stations; and from Eastern Europe, Austria and Germany services go to Rome via Verona. High-speed Cisalpino trains operate between Milan and Switzerland and southern Germany.

If coming from the UK, the **Eurostar** (☎ 08705 18 61 86, 02079 28 51 63; www .eurostar.com; Eurostar House, Waterloo Station, London SE1 8SE) passenger train service links London Waterloo and Paris Nord via the Channel Tunnel. Alternatively,

you could buy a train ticket that includes the Channel crossing by ferry, SeaCat or hovercraft, to Calais and other ports, then onwards by train.

Thomas Cook's *European Rail Timetable* has a complete listing of train schedules. The timetable is updated monthly and available from **Thomas Cook** offices worldwide and online (www.thomascookpublishing.com) for around UK£14. It is always advisable, and sometimes compulsory, to book seats on international trains to/from Italy. Some of the main international services include transport for private cars. Consider taking long journeys overnight as the €20 or so extra for a sleeper costs substantially less than Italian hotels.

Several discount passes and cards are available for train travel to/from Italy:

Eurail Pass (www.eurail.com) This is for people who live outside Europe and should be purchased before arriving in Europe. The passes are good for travel in 20 European countries (not including the UK), and are valid for 15 or 21 days or for one, two or three months. Eurail passes are expensive (you need to cover more than 2400km within two weeks to get value for money), so look at the options before committing yourself. There are two price brackets; one for those over 26 years of age, and one for those under. Children aged four to 11 go half-price. Children three and under go free. For more information and up-to-the-minute prices, check the website.

InterRail Pass (www.interrail.net) This pass is designed for people who have lived in Europe for six months or more and are aged under 26, but there is a more expensive version for older people, the InterRail 26+. A Global pass encompassing 30 countries comes in four versions, ranging from five days' travel in 10 days to a full month's travel.

Regional & National Passes Eurail also offers an Italy national pass and several two-country regional passes (France–Italy, Spain–Italy and Greece–Italy). You can choose from three to 10 days' train travel in a two-month period for any of these passes. As with all Eurail passes, you want to be sure you will be covering a lot of ground to make these worthwhile. Check some sample prices in euros of where you intend to travel on the **Trenitalia** (www.trenitalia .com) website to compare.

SEA

Dozens of ferry companies connect Italy with virtually every other Mediterranean country. The helpful search engine **Traghetti online** (www.traghettionline.com) covers all the ferry companies in the Mediterranean; you can also book online. Tickets are most expensive in summer, and many routes are only operated in summer. Prices for vehicles usually vary according to their size.

Ferry companies and their destinations:

Agoudimos Lines (☎ 0831 52 14 08; www .agoudimos.it; Via Giannelli 23) Brindisi to Vlore (Valona in Italian, Albania) and Corfu, Igoumenitsa, Paxos (Greece), Bari to Albania (Durrës) and Cephalonia, Igoumenitsa, Patras (Greece).

Blue Star Ferries (www.bluestarferries .com) Bari and Ancona to Patras and Igoumenitsa (Greece).

Grandi Navi Veloci (☎ 010 209 45 91; www1.gnv.it) Genoa to Tangiers (Morocco) via Barcelona (Spain), and Tunis (Tunisia).

Grimaldi Ferries (☎ 081 49 64 44; www .grimaldi-ferries.com) Plies the Mediterranean from Civitavecchia, Livorno, Salerno and Palermo to Tunis (Tunisia), Porto Vecchio (Corsica), Toulon (France) and Barcelona (Spain).

Jadrolinija (in Croatia ☎ 00385 51 666 111; www.jadrolinija.hr) From Ancona to destinations along the Croatian coast, including Split and Zadar and from Bari to Dubrovnik.

Marmara Lines (☎ 071 207 61 65; www .marmaralines.com; Corso Garibaldi 19) Ancona to Cesme (Turkey).

Minoan Lines (in Greece ☎ 0030 2810 399800; www.minoan.gr) Venice and Ancona to Igoumenitsa, Corfu or Patras (Greece).

Montenegro Lines (☎ 080 578 98 11; www.morfimare.it) Reservations via Morfimare Travel Agency; Bari and Ancona to Bar (Montenegro).

Tirrenia Navigazione (☎ 892123; www .tirrenia.it) Bari to Durrës (Albania) and Genoa to Tunis (Tunisia).

Virtu Ferries (☎ 095 53 57 11; www .virtuferries.com) Catania and Pozzallo to Malta.

GETTING AROUND

AIR

The main airports are in Rome, Pisa, Milan, Naples, Palermo and Cagliari; the many smaller airports include Aosta, Florence, Trieste, Venice, Verona and Turin.

Airlines in Italy

Domestic airlines:

AirAlps (☎ 06 22 22; www.airalps.at)
Alitalia (☎ 848 86 56 41, www.alitalia.it)
easyjet (☎ 0870 600 00 00, www.easyjet .com)
Meridiana (☎ 199 11 13 33, www.meridiana.it)

Domestic air passes are unknown in Italy. Barring special deals, a one-way fare is generally half the cost of the return fare.

BICYCLE

Cycling is a national pastime in Italy; its annual Giro d'Italia is second only to the Tour de France. There are no special road rules for cyclists. Helmets and lights are not obligatory, but you would be wise to equip yourself with both. You cannot take bikes onto the autostrade.

Bikes can be taken on all trains displaying a bike logo, but you'll need to pay for an extra bike ticket: €3.50, or €5 to €12 on Intercity and Eurostar services. Dismantled bikes go free. Bikes can also be transported free on ferries to Sicily and Sardinia.

You can hire bikes in most Italian towns, and many places have both city and mountain bikes available. An increasing number of towns and cities have metro-bike schemes whereby you can borrow a bike for no charge or a small payment. Inquire at individual tourist offices.

Look out for Lonely Planet's *Cycling Italy* (2009), packed with cyclist-friendly information and tours throughout the country.

LOCAL TRANSPORT TO & FROM THE WALKS

Of the dozens of walks in this book, all but a small handful can be reached by public transport. Given the excellent network of relatively cheap bus and train services in Italy, this is a great, stress-free way of traversing (and seeing) the country – and of being part of the great Italian travelling public.

Bus travel is less expensive than train travel, and is more useful in getting you to isolated walk starts. Train travel, on the other hand, is better for negotiating the longer distances between different regions or key cities. Other forms of transport you will encounter on your travels are passenger ferries, cable cars and perhaps the occasional taxi.

The whole of this revised edition of *Hiking in Italy* was researched without a car. On the rare occasions when there was no public transport available, the author bridged the gaps with taxis, a bicycle, or – on more than one occasion – his own two feet.

BOAT

Navi (large ferries) service the islands of Sicily and Sardinia; all vessels carry vehicles. Ferries and hydrofoils ply the waters of the three big lakes in the Lake District, and offer a relaxing alternative to buses or cars as you move around the area. There are also popular passenger ferries serving towns on the Amalfi coast and the Ligurian coast and providing access to many of this book's walks.

For a comprehensive guide to all ferry services into and out of Italy, check out **Traghettionline** (www.traghettionline .com, in Italian). The website lists every route and includes links to ferry companies, where you can buy tickets or search for deals.

BUS

Within Italy, bus services are provided by numerous companies and range from local routes linking small villages to fast, reliable intercity connections, making it possible to reach just about any location throughout the country. Buses can be a cheaper and faster way to get around if your destination is not on a main train line. Buses almost always leave on time.

Bus timetables for the provincial and intercity services are usually available from local tourist offices. In larger cities, most of the main intercity bus companies have ticket offices or operate through agencies. In some smaller towns and villages, tickets are sold in bars – ask for *biglietti per il pullman* – or on the bus. Most cities offer 24-hour or daily tourist tickets, which can represent big savings. You must always buy tickets before you board and validate them.

If you get caught with an unvalidated ticket, you will be fined on the spot.

It is not usually necessary to reserve a seat, although it is advisable in July and August for longer journeys.

CAR & MOTORCYCLE

Italian roads are generally good and there is an excellent network of autostrade, for which tolls apply. Contact **Società Autostrade** (☎06 4 36 31; www.autostrade.it) for details.

Strade statali (state roads) can be multilane dual carriageways (divided roads) and are toll-free. They are represented on maps and road signs as 'S' or 'SS'. The *strade regionali* (regional roads) and *strade provinciali* (provincial roads) are sometimes little more than country lanes, linking the many small towns and villages. They are represented as 'SR' and 'SP' on maps and signs.

See Driving Licence (p328) for details of paperwork needed when driving in Italy.

Automobile Associations

The ever-handy **Automobile Club d'Italia** (ACI; www.aci.it; Via Colombo 261, Rome) is a driver's best resource in Italy. To reach the ACI in a roadside emergency, dial ☎803116 from a landline or ☎800 116800 from a mobile phone. Foreigners do not have to join, but instead pay a per-incident fee. The numbers operate 24 hours a day.

Bring Your Own Vehicle

Cars entering Italy from abroad need a valid national licence plate and an accompanying registration card. A car imported from a country that does not use the Latin alphabet will need to have its registration card translated at the nearest Italian consulate before entering the country.

If you plan to ship your car, be aware that you must have less than a quarter of a tank of petrol. Unfortunately, you can't use your vehicle as a double for luggage storage; it's supposed to be empty apart from any necessary car-related items. All vehicles must be equipped with any necessary adjustments for the Italian market; for example, left-side drive cars will need to have their headlamps adjusted.

Driving Licence

If you want to drive a car or motorcycle in Italy, you will need your national driving licence. All EU member states' driving licences are fully recognised throughout Europe. Non-EU licence holders are also supposed to obtain an International Driving Permit (IDP) to accompany their national licence. In practice you will probably be OK with national licences from countries such as Australia, Canada and the USA. The IDP is available from your national automobile association and is valid for 12 months; it must be kept with your national licence.

Fuel & Spare Parts

Italy is covered by a good network of petrol stations. Prices are among the highest in Europe and vary from one service station (*benzinaio, stazione di servizio*) to another. Lead-free fuel (*senza piombo;* 95 octane) costs up to €1.11/L. A 98-octane variant costs as much as €1.20/L. Diesel (*gasolio*) comes in at €1.06/L. Prices fluctuate with world oil prices.

For spare parts, you could call 24-hour **ACI motorist assistance**, ☎ 80 31 16, although it may be easier to seek out a garage.

Hire

It is cheaper to arrange car rental before leaving your own country, ideally through a fly/drive deal offered by one of the major car-hire firms. In Italy, most tourist offices can provide information about car or motorcycle rental; otherwise, look in the local Pagine Gialle (Yellow Pages) under *autonoleggio*.

You have to be aged 25 or over to hire a car in Italy and you have to have a credit card. Most firms will accept your standard licence, sometimes with an Italian translation (which can usually be provided by the agencies themselves).

Multinational car-rental agencies: **Avis** (☎ 199 10 01 33; www.avisautonoleggio .it), **Budget** (☎ 199 30 73 73; www.budget autonoleggio.it), **Europcar** (☎ 199 30 70 30; www.europcar.com) and **Hertz** (☎ 0870 8 44 88 44; www.hertz.it).

You'll have no trouble hiring a small motorcycle such as a scooter (Vespa) or moped. There are numerous rental agencies in cities and tourist destinations, where you'll also usually be able to hire larger motorcycles for touring. Most agencies will not rent motorcycles to people aged under 18. Many places require a sizable deposit; you could be responsible for reimbursing part of the cost of the bike if it is stolen.

Road Rules

In Italy, drive on the right side of the road and overtake on the left. Unless otherwise indicated, you must always give way to cars coming from the right. Random breath tests now take place across the country; the blood-alcohol limit is 0.05%. Speed limits, unless otherwise indicated, are 130km/h on autostrade (the speed limit is reduced for small cars and motorcycles, cars towing caravans or trailers, and on weekends and holiday periods); 110km/h on all main, nonurban highways; 90km/h on secondary, nonurban highways; and 50km/h in built-up areas.

It is compulsory to wear seatbelts if fitted to the car. If you are caught not wearing a seatbelt, you will be required to pay an on-the-spot fine. To ride a motorcycle or scooter up to 125cc, you must be aged 16 or over and be licensed (a car licence will do). For motorcycles over 125cc you do need a motorcycle licence. Helmets are compulsory for all types of motorcycle.

To get **roadside assistance** call ☎ 116. *Motoring in Europe*, published in the UK by the RAC, summarises road regulations in each European country, including parking rules. Motoring organisations in other countries have similar publications.

HITCHING

Hitching is never safe in any country and we don't recommend it. Women

BUS & TRAIN TICKETS – SOME TIPS

If you're going to be spending a significant amount of time hiking in Italy, it's likely that you will be using lots of buses and trains to get you to and from the trailheads. While Italy's public transport system is relatively easy to negotiate, there are a few pointers that are useful to know about in advance.

○ Local bus tickets are generally purchased at *tabacchi* (tobacconists) or newspaper sellers. The ticket seller is normally the shop nearest to your embarkation point and will advertise the fact in their front window. On some of the more isolated routes, the driver sells tickets on board the bus. If you are in a rush and have no time to buy a ticket, the driver may allow you to purchase the fare at your destination. Check before boarding.

○ Bus tickets are validated on the bus in an automatic machine that prints both the time and date of your journey. Hop-on inspectors make regular checks of bus tickets and will fine anyone without one.

○ Train tickets are normally sold from the *bilighetteria* (station ticket office) or, in smaller stations, at an adjacent bar/*tabacchi*. Tickets must also be validated in one of the small yellow machines that are situated at all Italian train stations. Failure to validate your ticket will result in, at best, a ticking off from the conductor or, at worst, a fine.

○ All Italian train stations display clear and up-to-date posters containing information on *partenze* (departures) and *arrivi* (arrivals). Alternatively you can plan your route using the excellent Trenitalia website www.trenitalia.it.

○ Local bus information is usually displayed on a placard at the bus stop. For longer routes ask at the nearest visitor information office.

travelling alone should be extremely cautious about hitching anywhere. Hitchhiking is not a major pastime in Italy, but Italians are friendly people and you will generally find a lift.

It is illegal to hitchhike on Italy's autostrade, but acceptable to stand near the entrance to the toll booths. It is sometimes possible to arrange lifts in advance – ask around at youth hostels.

TAXI

Taxis are expensive – €10 to €15 for a short city journey – and it is better to catch a bus.

You can usually find a taxi in ranks at train and bus stations – the only realistic place from which to catch one. Taxis will rarely stop when hailed on the street as, strictly speaking, it's illegal for them to do so and, generally, they will not respond to telephone bookings if you are calling from a public phone.

Watch out also for taxi drivers who take advantage of new arrivals and stretch out the length of the trip, and consequently the size of the fare.

TRAIN

Trains in Italy are relatively cheap compared with other European countries and the better categories of train are fast and comfortable.

Trenitalia (☎ 89 20 21 in Italian; www.trenitalia.com, www.ferroviedellostato.it) is the partially privatised, state train system that runs most services. Other private Italian train lines are noted throughout this book.

There are several types of trains. Some stop at all or most stations, such as *regionale* or *interregionale* trains. Intercity (IC) trains are fast services that operate between major cities. Eurocity (EC) trains are the international version. High-speed *pendolini* and other fast services are collectively known as Eurostar Italia (ES), and some make fewer stops than others.

Quicker still, the Alta Velocità (High Speed) services (variously known as AV and ESA) that began operation on the new Turin–Milan–Bologna–Florence–Rome–Naples–Salerno line in late 2009 have revolutionised train travel on that route. Non-stop trains between Milan and Rome take three hours, at least 2½ hours less than any other standard service (an Intercity train takes 6¼ hours)! With stops in Bologna and Florence, the time is 3½ hours. Already in early 2009, fast trains using standard track had cut traditional travel times (3½ and four hours respectively on the Milan–Rome route). Prices vary according to the time of travel and how far in advance you book.

All tickets (except those purchased outside Italy) must be validated before boarding your train by punching them in the yellow machines at the entrance to all train platforms. If you don't, you risk a large fine.

Classes
There are 1st- and 2nd-class sections on nearly all Italian trains; on Eurostar trains, 2nd class is about as good as 1st class on other trains. A 1st-class ticket costs a bit less than double the price of a 2nd-class one.

Costs
To travel on Intercity, Eurocity and Eurostar Italia trains you have to pay a *supplemento* (supplement), an additional charge determined by the distance you are travelling. Always check what type of train you are about to catch and pay the appropriate supplement before you get on (otherwise you pay extra on the train). CIS trains (jointly operated by Italian and Swiss rail companies) have their own ticketing system.

On overnight trips within Italy, it can be worth paying extra for a *cuccetta* – a sleeping berth (commonly known as a *couchette*) in a four-bed compartment.

Rail Passes
It is not worth buying a Eurail or InterRail pass if you are going to travel only in Italy, since train fares are reasonably cheap.

Trenitalia offers various discount passes. The one-year Carta Verde (Green Card, €40) is for people between the ages of 12 and 26 and the Carta d'Argento (Silver Card, €30) is for seniors over 60. They attract discounts of between 10% and 15% on most trains and up to 25% off standard fares on international journeys beginning or ending in Italy. They can be worth considering if you are staying in Italy for a while and planning to cover a fair amount of ground. Apply at train stations and most travel agents.

Other discount possibilities include the Amica and Familia options. The former can get you up to 20% certain trips that are booked ahead, while the latter offers discounts for families of three to five people, of whom at least one must be an adult and one a child under 12. Ask at stations. For information on various rail passes you can acquire before arrival in Italy, see p325).

Reservations
It's worth reserving a seat on a long train trip – particularly if you're travelling at the weekend or during holiday periods. Reservations are obligatory for Eurostar and other fast trains. There are special booking offices for Eurostar trains at the relevant stations. Allow plenty of time as long queues are the norm.

Clothing & Equipment

You don't need to spend a fortune on gear to enjoy walking, but you do need to think carefully about what you pack to make sure you're comfortable and prepared for an emergency. Taking the right clothing and equipment on a walk can make the difference between an enjoyable day out or a cold and miserable one; in extreme situations, it can even mean the difference between life and death.

The gear you need will depend on the type of walking you plan to do. For day walks, clothing, footwear and a backpack are the major items; you might get away with runners, a hat, shorts, shirt and a warm pullover. For longer walks or those in alpine regions, especially if you're camping, the list becomes longer.

We recommend spending as much as you can afford on decent footwear, a waterproof jacket and a sweater or fleece jacket. These are likely to be your most expensive items but are a sound investment, as they should last for years.

The following section is not exhaustive; for more advice visit outdoor stores, talk to fellow walkers and read product reviews in outdoor magazines.

CLOTHING
Layering
A secret of comfortable walking is to wear several layers of light clothing, which you can easily take off or put on as you warm up or cool down. Most walkers use three main layers: a base layer next to the skin, an insulating layer, and an outer, shell layer for protection from wind, rain and snow.

For the upper body, the base layer is typically a shirt of synthetic material such as polypropylene, with its ability to wick moisture away from the body and reduce chilling. The insulating layer retains heat next to your body, and is often a windproof synthetic fleece or down jacket. The outer shell consists of a waterproof jacket that also protects against cold wind.

For the lower body, the layers generally consist of either shorts or loose-fitting trousers, polypropylene 'long-john' underwear and waterproof overtrousers.

Waterproof Shells
The ideal specifications are a breathable, waterproof fabric, a hood which is roomy enough to cover headwear but still allows peripheral vision, a capacious map pocket and a good-quality, heavy-gauge zip protected by a storm flap. Make sure the sleeves are large enough to cover warm clothes underneath and that the overall length of the garment allows you to sit down on it.

Waterproof overtrousers, though restrictive, are essential if you're walking in wet and cold conditions. As the name suggests, they are worn over your trousers. Choose a model with slits for pocket access and long ankle zips so that you can pull them on and off over your boots.

Footwear
Your footwear will be your friend or your enemy, so choose carefully. The first decision you will make is between boots and shoes. Runners or walking shoes are fine over easy terrain but, for more difficult trails and across rocks and scree, most walkers consider that the ankle support offered by boots is invaluable. If you'll be using crampons, or walking in snow, you need a rigid-soled walking boot.

Buy boots in warm conditions or go for a walk before trying them on, so your feet can expand slightly, as they would on a walk. Make sure you have 'test-walked' your boots/shoes/runners thoroughly before embarking on your trip. Hikers who 'christen' their footwear out in the field often end up with multiple blisters.

Most walkers carry a pair of thongs or sandals. These will relieve your feet from the heavy boots at night or during rest stops. Sandals are also useful when fording waterways.

GAITERS
If you will be walking through snow, deep mud or scratchy vegetation, consider using gaiters to protect your legs and keep your socks dry. The best are made of strong fabric with a robust zip protected by a flap and an easy-to-undo method around the foot.

SOCKS
The best walkers' socks are made of a hard-wearing mix of wool (70-80%) and a synthetic (30-20%), free of ridged seams in the wrong places (toes and heels). Socks with a high proportion of wool are more comfortable when worn for several successive days without washing. Spare socks are equally valuable, especially in wet walking conditions.

EQUIPMENT
You should always carry emergency food, a torch and a whistle on walks of more than a few hours.

Many Italian walkers also carry an umbrella, which may not be as silly as it seems, provided it isn't windy. You can see where you're going much more easily than if you're imprisoned inside a jacket hood and won't run the risk of overheating on a long ascent.

Backpack
For day walks, a day-pack of 30L or less will usually suffice, but for multiday walks you will need a backpack of 45L and up. Deciding whether to go for a smaller or a bigger pack can depend on where you will be walking, and whether you plan to camp or stay in *rifugi* etc. In Italy, with its dearth of backcountry camping, you'll probably end up erring smaller. Your pack should be large enough that you don't need to strap bits and pieces to the outside, where they can become damaged or lost or, like foam mats, leave unsightly souvenirs in trackside bushes. However, if you buy a bigger pack than you really need there's the temptation to fill it simply because the space is there; its weight will increase and your enjoyment decrease.

A good backpack should:

o be made of strong fabric such as canvas, Cordura or similar heavy-duty woven synthetic, with high-quality stitching, straps and buckles, a lightweight internal or external frame, and resilient and smoothly working zips

o have an adjustable, well-padded harness that evenly distributes weight

o be equipped with a small number of internal and external pockets to provide easy access to frequently used items such as snacks and maps.

Even if the manufacturer claims your pack is waterproof, use heavy-duty liners (garden refuse bags are ideal; custom-made sacks are available).

Tent
A three-season tent will fulfil the requirements of most walkers. The floor and the outer shell, or fly, should have taped or sealed seams and covered zips to stop water leaking inside. Weight will be a major issue if you're carrying your own gear so a roomy tent may not be an option; most walkers find tents of around 2kg to 3kg (that will sleep two or three people) a comfortable carrying weight. Popular shapes include dome and tunnel, which are better able to handle windy conditions than flat-sided tents.

Check you know how to pitch your tent before taking it away, and always check that your poles and pegs are packed.

Sleeping Bag & Mat
You'll need a sleeping bag or an inner sheet for overnight stops in *rifugi*, which only supply blankets (see also Rifugi, p310). Inner sheets are also compulsory in some youth hostels.

When buying a sleeping bag, choose between down and synthetic fillings and mummy and rectangular shapes. Down is warmer than synthetic for the same weight and bulk but, unlike synthetic fillings, does not retain warmth when wet. Mummy bags are best for weight and warmth, but can be claustrophobic. Sleeping bags are rated by temperature; the given figure (-5°C for instance) is the coldest temperature at which a person should feel comfortable in the bag. However, the ratings are notoriously unreliable. Work out the coldest temperature at which you

CHECKLIST

This list is a general guide to the things you might take on a hike. Your list will vary depending on the kind of hiking you want to do, whether you're camping or planning on staying in hostels or B&Bs, and on the terrain, weather conditions and time of year.

CLOTHING

- boots and spare laces
- gaiters
- hat (warm), scarf and gloves
- jacket (waterproof)
- overtrousers (waterproof)
- runners (training shoes), sandals or thongs (flip flops)
- shorts and trousers or skirt
- socks and underwear
- sunhat
- sweater or fleece jacket
- thermal underwear
- T-shirt and long-sleeved shirt with collar

EQUIPMENT

- backpack with liner (waterproof)
- first-aid kit*
- food and snacks (high energy) and one day's emergency supplies
- insect repellent
- map, compass and guidebook
- map case or clip-seal plastic bags
- pocket knife
- sunglasses
- sunscreen and lip balm
- survival bag or blanket
- toilet paper and trowel
- torch (flashlight) or headlamp, spare batteries and globe (bulb)
- water container
- whistle

OVERNIGHT HIKES

- cooking, eating and drinking utensils
- dishwashing items
- matches and lighter
- sewing/repair kit
- sleeping bag and bag liner/inner sheet
- sleeping mat
- spare cord
- stove and fuel
- tent, pegs, poles and guy ropes
- toiletries
- towel
- water-purification tablets, iodine or filter

OPTIONAL ITEMS

- altimeter
- backpack cover (waterproof, slip-on)
- binoculars
- camera, film and batteries
- candle
- emergency distress beacon
- GPS receiver
- groundsheet
- mobile phone**
- mosquito net
- notebook and pen
- swimming costume
- walking/hiking/trekking poles
- watch

* see the First-Aid Check List (p338)
** see Mobile Phones (p320)

anticipate sleeping, assess whether you're a warm or a cold sleeper, then choose a bag accordingly.

An inner sheet will help to keep your sleeping bag clean, as well as adding an insulating layer. Silk 'inners' are the lightest, but inners also come in cotton or polypropylene.

Self-inflating sleeping mats are popular and work like a thin air cushion between you and the ground; they also insulate from the cold and are essential if sleeping on snow. Foam mats are a low-cost but less comfortable alternative.

Stove

As a general guideline, the stove you choose needs to be stable when sitting on the ground and to have a good wind shield. Fuel stoves fall roughly into three categories: multifuel, methylated spirits (ethyl alcohol) and butane gas.

Multifuel stoves are small, efficient and ideal for places where a reliable fuel supply is hard to find. However, they tend to be noisy and sooty, and require frequent maintenance.

Stoves running on methylated spirits are slower and less efficient, but are safe, clean and easy to use.

Butane gas stoves, although clean and reliable, can be slow, and the gas canisters can be awkward to carry and a potential litter problem. They are also more wasteful of resources than liquid fuel.

Fuel

Super-refined petrol for stoves, known as Coleman fuel (Shellite in some countries; in Italy it's known as Coleman fuel or, less frequently, *benzina* Coleman) is available from outdoor shops; Coleman fuel costs from €7 for 500mL. Alternatively, *senza piombo* (unleaded petrol or gasoline) can be bought from any filling station.

Alcool denaturato (methylated spirits) is pink-coloured and widely available in supermarkets, hardware and outdoor shops; it costs around €1 for a 750mL bottle.

Gas or *cherosene* (kerosene) might be obtainable from shops that sell gear for Italy's abundant hunters and anglers. They usually have signs outside that include the words *caccia* (hunting) and *pesca* (fishing). As a guide, a 250mL canister costs €5 and a 500mL one €8.

Carry your fuel in a clearly labelled and sturdy plastic or aluminium bottle. Note that fuel cannot be carried on aeroplanes.

Technical Equipment

The specialist equipment you'll need for tackling *vie ferrate* (iron ways) is discussed in the Via Ferrata section (p46).

An ice axe, and possibly crampons, may be essential for crossing high mountain passes in late spring. It's essential to have had some experience in using them before you embark on high-altitude walks in Italy.

BUYING & HIRING LOCALLY

Some brands of Italian walking boots enjoy an excellent international reputation and it may be worth considering a purchase once you're in Italy. Prices are competitive, no matter where you come from.

Addresses of gear shops in towns near the walks described are given in the walk chapters. A useful source of addresses of outdoors shops is www.outdooritalia.it, although few are readily accessible from areas covered in this book.

Apart from crampons, ice axes and *via ferrata* gear, hiring is virtually unknown.

NAVIGATION EQUIPMENT
Maps & Compass

You should always carry a good map of the area you are hiking in (see Maps, p317) and know how to read it. Before setting off on your trek, ensure that you understand the contours and the map symbols plus the main ridge and river systems in the area. Also familiarise yourself with the true north–south directions and the general direction in which you are heading. On the trail, try to identify major landforms such as mountain ranges and gorges, and locate them on your map. This will give you a better understanding of the region's geography.

Buy a compass and learn how to use it. The attraction of magnetic north varies in different parts of the world, so compasses need to be balanced accordingly. Compass manufacturers have divided the world into five zones. Make sure your compass is balanced for your destination zone. There are also 'universal' compasses on the market that can be used anywhere in the world.

Global Positioning System (GPS)

Originally developed by the US Department of Defense, the Global Positioning System (GPS) is a network of more than 20 earth-orbiting satellites that continually beam encoded signals back to earth. Small, computer-driven devices (GPS receivers) can decode these signals to give users an extremely accurate reading of their location – to within 30m, anywhere on the planet, at any time of day, in almost any weather.

The cheapest hand-held GPS receivers now cost less than US$100 (although these may not have a built-in averaging system that minimises signal errors). Other important factors to consider when buying a GPS receiver are its weight and battery life.

Remember that a GPS receiver is of little use to hikers unless used with an accurate topographical map. The receiver simply gives your position, which you must

HOW TO USE A COMPASS

This is a very basic introduction to using a compass and will only be of assistance if you are proficient in map reading. For simplicity, it doesn't take magnetic variation into account. Before using a compass we recommend you obtain further instruction.

1. Reading a Compass
Hold the compass flat in the palm of your hand. Rotate the **bezel** so the **red end** of the **needle** points to the **N** on the bezel. The bearing is read from the dash under the bezel.

2. Orienting the Map
To orient the map so that it aligns with the ground, place the compass flat on the map. Rotate the map until the **needle** is parallel with the map's north–south grid lines and the **red end** is pointing to north on the map. You can now identify features around you by aligning them with labelled features on the map.

3. Taking a Bearing from the Map
Draw a line on the map between your starting point and your destination. Place the edge of the compass on this line with the **direction of travel arrow** pointing towards your destination. Rotate the **bezel** until the **meridian lines** are parallel with the north–south grid lines on the map and the **N** points to north on the map. Read the bearing from the dash.

4. Following a Bearing
Rotate the **bezel** so that the intended bearing is in line with the **dash**. Place the compass flat in the palm of your hand and rotate the **base plate** until the **red end** points to **N** on the bezel. The **direction of travel arrow** will now point in the direction you need to walk.

5. Determining your Bearing
Rotate the **bezel** so the **red end** points to the **N**. Place the compass flat in the palm of your hand and rotate the **base plate** until the **direction of travel arrow** points in the direction in which you have been hiking. Read your bearing from the **dash**.

1	Base plate
2	Direction of travel arrow
3	Dash
4	Bezel
5	Meridian lines
6	Needle
7	Red end
8	N (north point)

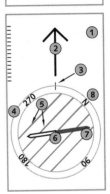

then locate on the local map. GPS receivers will only work properly in the open. The signals from a crucial satellite may be blocked (or bounce off rock or water) directly below high cliffs, near large bodies of water or in dense tree cover and give inaccurate readings.

GPS receivers are more vulnerable to breakdowns (including dead batteries) than the humble magnetic compass – a low-tech device that has served navigators faithfully for centuries – so don't rely entirely on a GPS.

Altimeter
Altimeters determine altitude by measuring air pressure. Because pressure is affected by temperature, altimeters are calibrated to

take lower temperatures at higher altitudes into account. However, discrepancies can still occur, especially in unsettled weather, so it's wise to take a few precautions when using your altimeter:

- Reset your altimeter regularly at known elevations such as spot heights and passes. Do not take spot heights from villages where there may be a large difference in elevation from one end of the settlement to another.
- Use your altimeter in conjunction with other navigation techniques to fix your position. For instance, taking a back bearing to a known peak or river confluence, determining the general direction of the track and obtaining your elevation

will usually give you a pretty good fix on your position.

Altimeters are also barometers and are useful for indicating changing weather conditions. If the altimeter shows increasing elevation while you are not climbing, it means the air pressure is dropping and a low-pressure weather system may be approaching.

Route Finding

While accurate, our maps are not perfect. Inaccuracies in altitudes are commonly caused by air-temperature anomalies. Natural features such as river confluences and mountain peaks are in their true position, but sometimes the location of villages and trails is not so. This may be because a village is spread over a hillside, or the size of the map does not allow for detail of the trail's twists and turns. However, by using several basic route-finding techniques you will have few problems following our descriptions:

1. Be aware of whether the trail should be climbing or descending.
2. Check the north-point arrow on the map and determine the general direction of the trail.
3. Time your progress over a known distance and calculate the speed at which you travel in the given terrain. From then on, you can determine with reasonable accuracy how far you have travelled.
4. Watch the path – look for boot prints and other signs of previous passage.

Health & Safety

CONTENTS

Keeping healthy on your walks and travels depends on your predeparture preparations, your daily health care while travelling and how you handle any medical problems that develop. While the potential problems can seem quite frightening, and few travellers actually experience anything more than an upset stomach, as with other aspects of travel, the better informed and equipped you are before you leave, the better your experince will generally be. The following sections aren't meant to alarm but are recommended reading before you go.

BEFORE YOU GO

FIRST AID

It's a good idea to know the appropriate responses for a major accident or illness, especially if you are intending to walk for some time in a remote area. Consider learning basic first aid on a recognised course before you go, or taking a first-aid manual in your first-aid kit. Although detailed first-aid instruction is outside the scope of this book, some basic points are listed under Traumatic Injuries (p343). Preventing accidents and illness is vitally important – read Safety on the Walk (p345) for more advice. You should also know how to summon help should a major accident or illness befall you or someone with you – see Rescue and Evacuation (p346).

HEALTH INSURANCE

Make sure that you have adequate health insurance; Italy's private hospitals and clinics are good but expensive without insurance, and some treatments in public hospitals have to be paid for and can be expensive. See Insurance (p316).

IMMUNISATIONS

No immunisations are required for Italy, but before leaving home it's worth ensuring that you're up to date with routine vaccinations such as diphtheria, polio and tetanus. It's particularly important that tetanus is up to date – the initial course of three injections, usually given in childhood, is followed by boosters every 10 years.

MEDICAL COVER

Citizens of European Union (EU) countries are covered for emergency medical care upon presentation of an E111 form, which you need to get before you travel. In Britain, it's available free at any post office. In other EU countries, obtain information from your doctor or local health service. Although the form entitles you to free treatment in government clinics and hospitals, you will have to pay for dental treatment,

FIRST-AID CHECK LIST

This is a list of items you should consider including in your medical kit – consult a pharmacist for brands available in your country.

ESSENTIALS

- adhesive tape
- bandages and safety pins
- elasticised support bandage – for knees, ankles etc
- gauze swabs
- nonadhesive dressings
- paper stitches
- scissors (small)
- sterile alcohol wipes
- sticking plasters (Band-Aids, blister plasters)
- sutures
- thermometer (note that mercury thermometers are prohibited by airlines)
- tweezers

MEDICATIONS

- antidiarrhoea and antinausea drugs
- antifungal cream or powder – for fungal infections and thrush
- antihistamines – for allergies, eg, hay fever; to ease the itch from insect bites or stings; and to prevent motion sickness
- antiseptic (such as povidone-iodine) – for cuts and grazes
- cold and flu tablets, throat lozenges and nasal decongestant
- painkillers – eg, aspirin or paracetamol (acetaminophen in the USA) – for pain and fever

MISCELLANEOUS

- calamine lotion, sting relief spray or aloe vera – to ease irritation from sunburn, and insect bites or stings
- eye drops
- rehydration mixture – to prevent dehydration, eg, due to severe diarrhoea; particularly important when travelling with children

any medicines bought from pharmacies (even if a doctor has prescribed them) and possibly for tests. At home, you may be able to recover some or all of these costs from your national health service.

Australia (Medicare) has a reciprocal arrangement with Italy; you are entitled to subsidised health care for up to six months from the date of arrival. However, treatment in private hospitals is not covered, and charges are also likely for medication, nonurgent dental work and secondary examinations, including x-rays and laboratory tests. Medicare publishes a brochure with the details and it is advisable to carry your Medicare card.

PHYSICAL PREPARATION

Some of the walks in this book are physically demanding and most require a reasonable level of fitness. Even if you're tackling the easy or easy–moderate walks, it pays to be relatively fit rather than launch into them after months of fairly sedentary living. Fitness is essential for the demanding walks (see Level of Difficulty, p21).

Unless you're a regular walker, start your get-fit campaign at least a month before your visit. Take a vigorous walk of about an hour, two or three times per week, and gradually extend the duration of your outings as the departure date nears. If you plan to carry a full backpack on any walk, carry a loaded pack on some of your training jaunts. Walkers with little previous experience should have a medical check-up beforehand.

OTHER PREPARATIONS

If you have any known medical problems or are concerned about your health in any way, it's a good idea to have a full check-up before you go. It's far better to have any problems recognised and treated at home than to find out about them half way up a mountain. It's also sensible to have had a recent dental check-up since toothache on the *sentiero* (track) with solace a couple of days or more away can be a miserable experience. If you wear glasses, take a spare pair and your prescription.

If you need a particular medicine, take enough with you to last the trip. In case you do need more, take part of the packaging showing the generic name, rather than the brand, as this will make getting replacements easier. It's also a good idea to have a legible prescription or letter from your doctor to prove that you legally use the medication to avoid any problems at customs.

STAYING HEALTHY

COMMON AILMENTS
Blisters
This problem can be avoided. Make sure your walking boots or shoes are well worn in before your visit. At the very least, wear them on a few short walks before tackling longer outings. Your boots should fit comfortably with enough room to move your toes; boots that are too big or too small will cause blisters.

Similarly for socks – be sure they fit properly, are specifically made for walkers and there are no seams across the widest part of your foot. Wet and muddy socks can also cause blisters, so, even on a day walk, pack a spare pair of socks. Keep your toenails clipped but not too short.

If you do feel a blister coming on, stop and apply a simple sticking plaster or, preferably, one of the special blister plasters, which act as a second skin; follow the maker's instructions for replacement.

Fatigue
A simple statistic: more injuries of whatever nature happen towards the end of the day than earlier, when you're fresher. Although tiredness can simply be a nuisance on an easy walk, it can be life-threatening on narrow, exposed ridges or in bad weather. You should never set out on a walk beyond your capabilities on the day. If you feel below par, have a day off. To reduce the risk, don't push yourself too hard – take rests every hour or two, and have a half-hour lunch break. Towards the end of the day, slacken the pace and try to increase your concentration. You should also eat sensibly throughout the day; nuts, dried fruit and chocolate are good energy-giving snack foods.

Knee Strain
Many walkers feel the strain on long, steep descents. It can be reduced but never eliminated by taking shorter steps with your legs slightly bent, ensuring that your heel hits the ground before the rest of your foot. Some walkers find tubular bandages help (although these could be uncomfortable in hot weather), while others use hi-tech, strap-on supports. Walking poles are very effective in taking some of the weight off the knees.

FOOD
The stringent food hygiene regulations imposed by the EU are in force in Italy, so you should feel confident the food you eat in restaurants is safe.

HYGIENE
To reduce the chances of contracting an illness you should wash your hands frequently, especially before preparing or eating food.

Take particular care to thoroughly dispose of all toilet waste when you are on a walk (see Human Waste Disposal, p37).

INTERNET RESOURCES
There is a wealth of travel health advice to be found on the internet. For further information, **Lonely Planet** (www.lonelyplanet.com) is a good place to start. The **WHO** (World Health Organization; www.who.int/ith) publishes a superb book called *International Travel and Health*, which is revised annually and is available online at no cost. Another website of general interest is **MD Travel Health** (www.mdtravelhealth.com), which provides complete travel health recommendations for every country and is updated daily.

It's usually a good idea to consult your government's travel health website before departure, if one is available:

Australia (www.dfat.gov.au/travel)
Canada (www.travelhealth.gc.ca)
UK (www.dh.gov.uk/en/healthcare/health advicefortravellers)
USA (wwwn.cdc.gov/travel)

WATER
In Italy, tap water is generally safe to drink. Water from *sorgenti* (fountains) in towns

and villages, and from taps over troughs in the countryside is safe to drink, unless a sign stating *acqua non potabile* tells you that it isn't. There are mineral springs all over the place, usually easily identified by people filling bottles and containers. Water from streams and rivers will almost certainly be polluted. In the mountains it's a temptation to drink from streams, but you can't be certain that there aren't animals – dead or alive – upstream.

Water Purification
If you have any doubts about the water, the simplest way to purify it is to boil thoroughly. Vigorous boiling should be satisfactory, otherwise you can use a chemical agent. Chlorine and iodine are usually used, in powder, tablet or liquid form, available from outdoor equipment suppliers and pharmacies. Follow the recommended dosages and allow the water to stand for the correct length of time. Chlorine tablets will kill many pathogens, but not some parasites like Giardia and amoebic cysts. Iodine is more effective in purifying water. Follow the directions carefully and remember that too much iodine can be harmful.

FURTHER READING
Travel with Children, from Lonely Planet, includes advice on travel health for younger children. Other recommended references include *Traveller's Health* by Dr Richard Dawood (Oxford University Press) and *International Travel Health Guide* by Stuart R Rose, MD (Travel Medicine Inc).

MEDICAL PROBLEMS & TREATMENT

BITES & STINGS
Bees & Wasps
These are usually painful rather than dangerous. However, people who are allergic to them may experience severe breathing difficulties, and urgent medical care is required. Calamine lotion or a commercial sting relief spray will ease discomfort, and ice packs will reduce the pain and swelling.

Snakes
To minimise your chances of being bitten, always wear boots, socks and long trousers when walking through undergrowth where snakes may be present. Don't put your hands into holes and crevices.

A bite by any of the adders or vipers found in Italy is unlikely to be fatal. Even so, immediately wrap the bitten limb tightly, as you would for a sprained ankle, then attach a splint to immobilise it. Keep the victim still and seek medical assistance; it will help if you can describe the offending reptile. Tourniquets and sucking out the poison are now totally discredited treatments.

Ticks
Always check all over your body if you have been walking through a potentially tick-infested area as ticks can cause skin infections and other more serious diseases. Ticks are most active from spring to autumn, especially where there are plenty of sheep. They usually lurk in overhanging vegetation, so avoid pushing through tall bushes if possible.

If a tick is found attached to the skin, press down around the head with tweezers, grab the head and gently pull upwards. Avoid pulling the rear of the body as this may squeeze the tick's gut contents through its mouth into your skin, increasing the risk of infection and disease. Smearing chemicals on the tick will not make it let go and is not recommended.

ENVIRONMENTAL HAZARDS
Walkers are at more risk than most groups from environmental hazards. The risk, however, can be significantly reduced by applying common sense – and reading the following section.

Altitude
Lack of oxygen at high altitudes (over 2500m) affects most people to some extent. The effect may be mild or severe, and occurs because the air pressure is reduced, and the heart and lungs must work harder to oxygenate the body. In addition, fluid can build up in the lungs and brain causing extreme breathlessness – the person ultimately drowns in this fluid if he or she doesn't descend. Although the highest altitude reached on walks described in this book is 3292m (Col Lauson on the

Valnontey – Rhêmes Notre Dame walk, p94) and the likelihood of suffering any significant effects is slight, it is still important to take precautions. Take a couple of days to acclimatise yourself to altitudes above 2500m if you're planning to cross the higher passes in the Western and Maritime Alps or Parco Nazionale dello Stelvio; do not ascend until your body has adjusted to the higher altitude. If symptoms, including breathlessness, headaches, nausea, dizziness, difficulty sleeping and loss of appetite, persist or are severe, it is essential to descend immediately.

Cold

Too much cold can be just as dangerous as too much heat!

HYPOTHERMIA

This occurs when the body loses heat faster than it can produce it and the core temperature of the body falls.

It is frighteningly easy to deteriorate from very cold to dangerously cold due to a combination of wind, wet clothing, fatigue and hunger, even if the air temperature is above freezing. If the weather deteriorates, put on extra layers of warm clothing: a wind- and/or waterproof jacket, plus wool or fleece hat and gloves are all essential. Have something energy-giving to eat and ensure that everyone in your group is fit, feeling well and alert.

Symptoms of hypothermia are exhaustion, numb skin (particularly toes and fingers), shivering, slurred speech, irrational or violent behaviour, lethargy, stumbling, dizzy spells, muscle cramps and violent bursts of energy. Irrationality may take the form of sufferers claiming they are warm and trying to take off their clothes.

To treat mild hypothermia, first get the person out of the wind and/or rain, remove any wet clothing and replace it with dry, warm clothing. Give hot liquids – not alcohol – and some high-kilojoule, easily digestible food. Do not rub victims; instead, allow them to slowly warm themselves – it helps to put them between companions. This should be enough to treat the early stages of hypothermia. The early recognition and treatment of mild hypothermia is the only way to prevent severe hypothermia, a critical condition.

> # WARNING
>
> Self-diagnosis and treatment can be risky, so you should always seek medical help. For emergency treatment, go straight to the *pronto soccorso* (casualty) section of a public hospital, where you can also get emergency dental treatment. Sometimes hospitals are listed in the phone book under Aziende Ospedaliere. The local tourist office or your accommodation host can usually recommend a local doctor or clinic.
>
> We have used generic rather than brand names for drugs throughout this section – check with a pharmacist for locally available brands.

Snow Blindness

This is a temporary, painful condition resulting from sunburn of the surface of the eye (cornea). It usually occurs when someone walks on snow or ice without sunglasses. Treatment is to relieve the pain – cold cloths on closed eyelids may help. Antibiotic and anaesthetic eye drops are not necessary. The condition usually resolves itself within a few days and there are no long-term consequences.

Heat

Treat heat with respect! Take time to acclimatise to high temperatures, drink sufficient liquids and don't do anything physically demanding until you are acclimatised.

PRICKLY HEAT

This is an itchy rash caused by excessive perspiration trapped under the skin. It usually strikes people who have just arrived in a hot climate. Keeping cool, bathing often, drying the skin and using a mild talcum or prickly-heat powder may help. Fungal infections of the skin also occur more commonly in hot, humid conditions – for more details, see Fungal Infections (p343).

DEHYDRATION & HEAT EXHAUSTION

Dehydration is a potentially dangerous and generally preventable condition caused by excessive fluid loss. Sweating combined with inadequate fluid intake is a common cause among walkers, but other important causes are diarrhoea, vomiting and high

EVERYDAY HEALTH

Normal body temperature is up to 37°C (98.6°F); more than 2°C (4°F) higher indicates a high fever. The normal adult pulse rate is 60 to 100 per minute (children 80 to 100, babies 100 to 140). As a general rule the pulse increases about 20 beats per minute for each 1°C (2°F) rise in fever.

Respiration (breathing) rate is also an indicator of illness. Count the number of breaths per minute: between 12 and 20 is normal for adults and older children (up to 30 for younger children, 40 for babies). People with a high fever or serious respiratory illness breathe more quickly than normal. More than 40 shallow breaths per minute may indicate pneumonia.

fever – see Diarrhoea (next column) for appropriate treatment.

The first symptoms are weakness, thirst and passing small amounts of very concentrated urine. This may progress to drowsiness, dizziness or fainting on standing up and, finally, coma.

It's easy to forget how much fluid you are losing via perspiration while you're walking, particularly if a breeze is drying your skin. Always maintain a steady fluid intake – the minimum recommended is 3L per day.

Dehydration and salt deficiency can cause heat exhaustion. Salt deficiency is characterised by fatigue, lethargy, headaches, giddiness and muscle cramps. Salt tablets are unnecessary; it's probably sufficient to add extra salt to your food.

HEATSTROKE
This is a serious, occasionally fatal, condition that occurs if the body's heat-regulating mechanism breaks down and the body temperature rises to a dangerous level. Long, continuous periods of exposure to high temperatures and insufficient fluids can make you vulnerable to heatstroke.

The symptoms are feeling unwell, sweating little or not at all, and a high body temperature (39°C to 41°C). When sweating has ceased, the skin becomes flushed and red. Severe, throbbing headaches and lack of coordination will also occur, and the sufferer may be confused or aggressive.

Eventually the victim will become delirious or convulse. Hospitalisation is essential; meantime get the victim out of the sun, remove clothing, cover with a wet sheet or towel, and fan continuously. Give fluids if the person is conscious.

Sun
Protection against the sun should always be taken seriously; in the rarefied air and deceptive coolness of the mountains, sunburn develops rapidly. Slap on the sunscreen and a barrier cream for your nose and lips, wear a broad-brimmed hat, even on partly sunny days, and protect your eyes with good quality sunglasses with UV lenses, particularly when walking near water, sand or snow. If, despite these precautions, you get burnt, calamine lotion, aloe vera or other commercial sunburn relief preparations will soothe.

HAY FEVER
If you suffer from hay fever, bring your usual treatment, as the pollen count in most areas covered by this book (except high in the mountains) is very high from May to July.

INFECTIOUS DISEASES
Diarrhoea
Simple things like a change of water, food or climate can all cause a mild bout of diarrhoea, but a few rushed toilet trips with no other symptoms are not indicative of a major problem. More serious diarrhoea is caused by infectious agents transmitted by faecal contamination of food or water, by using contaminated utensils or directly from one person's hand to another. Paying particular attention to personal hygiene, drinking clean water and taking care with what you eat are important in avoiding diarrhoea.

Dehydration is the main danger with any diarrhoea, particularly in children or the elderly as dehydration can occur quite quickly. Fluid replacement (at least equal to the volume being lost) is the most important thing to remember. Weak black tea with a little sugar, soda water, or soft drinks allowed to go flat and diluted 80% with water are all good. With severe diarrhoea a rehydrating solution is preferable to replace minerals and salts lost. Commercially available oral rehydration salts (ORS) are very useful; add them to water. In an emergency you can make up a solution of six teaspoons of sugar and a half tea-spoon of salt to a litre of water. You need to drink at least the same volume of fluid that you are losing in bowel movements and vomiting. Urine is the best guide to the adequacy of replacement – if you pass small amounts of concentrated urine, you need to drink more. Keep drinking small amounts often. Stick to a bland diet as you recover.

Gut-paralysing drugs such as diphenoxy-late or loperamide can be used to bring relief from the symptoms, although they don't cure the problem. Only use these drugs if you do not have access to toilets, eg, if you must travel. These drugs are not recommended for children under 12 years, or if you have a high fever or are severely dehydrated.

Seek medical advice if you pass blood or mucus, are feverish, or suffer persistent or severe diarrhoea.

Fungal Infections

Sweating liberally, probably washing less than usual, and going longer without a change of clothes mean that long-distance walkers risk picking up a fungal infec-tion, which, while an unpleasant irritant, presents no danger.

Fungal infections are encouraged by moisture, so wear loose, comfortable clothes, wash when you can and dry your-self thoroughly. Try to expose the infected area to air or sunlight as much as possible, and apply an antifungal cream or powder like tolnaftate.

Tetanus

This disease is caused by a germ, which lives in soil and in the faeces of horses and other animals. It enters the body via breaks in the skin. The first symptom may be dis-comfort in swallowing, or stiffening of the jaw and neck; this is followed by painful convulsions of the jaw and whole body. The disease can be fatal. It can be prevented by vaccination, so make sure your shots are up to date before you leave.

INSECT-BORNE DISEASES
Lyme Disease

This is a tick-transmitted infection. The ill-ness usually begins with a spreading rash at the site of the tick bite and is accompanied by fever, headache, extreme fatigue, aching joints and muscles, and mild neck stiffness. If untreated, these symptoms usually resolve over several weeks, but over subsequent weeks or months disorders of the nervous system, heart and joints may develop. Treat-ment works best early in the illness. Medical help should be sought.

TRAUMATIC INJURIES
Burns

Immerse the burnt area in cold water as soon as possible, then cover it with a clean, dry, sterile dressing. Keep this in place with plasters for a day or so in the case of a small, mild burn, longer for more extensive injuries. Seek medical help for severe and extensive burns.

Cuts & Scratches

Even small cuts and grazes should be washed well and treated with an antiseptic such as povidone-iodine. Dry wounds heal more quickly, so where possible avoid bandages and dressing strips, which can keep wounds wet. Infection in a wound is indicated by red, painful and swollen skin margins. Se-rious infection can cause swelling of the whole limb and of the lymph glands, and a fever may develop; seek medical attention immediately.

Fractures

Indications of a fracture (broken bone) are pain, swelling and discoloration, loss of function or deformity of a limb. Unless you know what you are doing, you shouldn't try to straighten an obviously displaced broken bone. To protect from further in-jury, immobilise a nondisplaced fracture by splinting it; for fractures of the thigh bone, strap it to the good leg to hold it in place. Check the splinted limb fre-quently to ensure the splint hasn't cut off circulation.

Fractures associated with open wounds (compound fractures) require urgent treatment as there is a risk of infection. Dislocations, where the bone has come out of the joint, are very painful, and should be set as soon as possible by a doctor.

Broken ribs are painful but usually heal by themselves and do not need splinting. If breathing difficulties occur or the person coughs up blood, medical attention should be sought urgently, as it may indicate a punctured lung.

Internal Injuries

Internal injuries are more difficult to detect, and cannot usually be treated outdoors. Watch for shock, which is a specific medical condition associated with a failure to maintain circulating blood volume. Signs include a rapid pulse and cold, clammy extremities. To manage shock, raise the person's legs above heart level (unless their legs are fractured), loosen tight clothing and keep the patient warm. A person in shock requires urgent medical attention.

Major Accidents

Falling or having something fall on you, resulting in head injuries or fractures, is always possible when walking, especially if you are crossing steep slopes or unstable terrain. Following is some basic advice on what to do if a major accident does occur; detailed first-aid instruction is outside the scope of this book (see First Aid, p337, for information sources). If a person suffers a major fall:

1. make sure you and other people with you are not in danger
2. assess the injured person's condition
3. stabilise any injuries, such as bleeding wounds or broken bones
4. seek medical attention – see Rescue & Evacuation (p346)

If the person is unconscious, immediately check for breathing – clear the airway if it is blocked; and check for a pulse – feel the side of the neck rather than the wrist. If the person is not breathing but has a pulse, you should start mouth-to-mouth resuscitation immediately. It is best to move the victim as little as possible in case the neck or back is broken. Keep the person warm by covering them with a sleeping bag or dry clothing; insulate them from the ground if possible.

Check for wounds and broken bones; if the victim is conscious, ask where pain is felt. Otherwise gently inspect all over (including the back, and back of the head), moving the body as little as possible. Control any bleeding by applying firm pressure to the wound. Bleeding from the nose or ear may indicate a fractured skull. Don't give the person anything by mouth, especially if they are unconscious.

Most cases of brief unconsciousness are not associated with serious brain damage. Nevertheless, anyone who has been knocked unconscious should be watched closely. Carefully note any signs of deterioration (eg, change in breathing patterns) to report to the rescuers/doctor.

Sprains

Ankle and knee sprains are common injuries among walkers, particularly when walking over rugged terrain. To help prevent ankle sprains in these circumstances, you should wear an all-leather boot that has adequate ankle support. If you do suffer a sprain, immobilise the joint with a firm bandage, and, if feasible, immerse the foot in cold water. Distribute the contents of your pack among your companions. Once you reach shelter, relieve pain and swelling by keeping the joint elevated for the first 24 hours and, where possible, by putting ice on the swollen joint. Take simple painkillers to ease the discomfort. If the sprain is mild, you may be able to continue your walk after a couple of days. For more severe sprains, seek medical attention as an x-ray may be needed to find out whether a bone has been broken.

WOMEN'S HEALTH

Walking is not particularly hazardous to your health; however, women's health issues can be a bit trickier to cope with when you are on a long walk.

Menstruation

A change in diet, routine and environment, as well as intensive exercise can all lead to irregularities in the menstrual cycle. This, in itself, is not a huge issue and your cycle should return to normal when you return to your normal routine. It is particularly important during the menstrual cycle to maintain good personal hygiene, and regularly change sanitary napkins or tampons (for disposal options, see Human Waste Disposal, p37). Antibacterial hand gel or pre-moistened wipes can be useful if you don't have access to soap and water. You can also use applicator tampons to minimise the risk of contamination, although these are quite bulky. Because of hygiene concerns and for ease while on an extended trip, some women prefer to temporarily stop menstruation. You should discuss your options with a doctor before you go. It is also important to note that failure to menstruate could indicate pregnancy! If concerned about irregularities seek medical advice.

Pregnancy

If you are pregnant, see your doctor before you travel. Even normal pregnancies can make a woman feel nauseated and tired. In the third trimester, the size of the baby can make walking difficult or uncomfortable.

Thrush (Vaginal Candidiasis)

Antibiotic use, synthetic underwear, tight trousers, sweating, contraceptive pills and unprotected sex can each lead to fungal vaginal infections, especially when travelling in hot, humid climates. The most common is thrush (vaginal candidiasis). Symptoms include itching and discomfort in the genital area, often in association with a thick white discharge. The best prevention is to keep the vaginal area cool and dry, and to wear cotton rather than synthetic underwear and loose clothes. Thrush can be treated by clotrimazole pessaries or vaginal cream.

Urinary Tract Infection

Dehydration and 'hanging on' can result in urinary tract infection and the symptoms of cystitis, which can be particularly distressing and an inconvenient problem when out walking. Symptoms include burning when urinating, and having to urinate frequently and urgently. Blood can sometimes be passed in the urine. Drink plenty of fluids and empty your bladder regularly. If symptoms persist, seek medical attention because a simple infection can spread to the kidneys, causing a more severe illness.

SAFETY ON THE WALK

You can significantly reduce the chance of getting into difficulties by taking a few simple precautions. These are listed in the boxed text Walk Safety – Basic Rules. A list of the clothes and equipment you should take appears in the Clothing & Equipment chapter (see p331).

CROSSING RIVERS

Sudden downpours are common in the mountains and can speedily turn a gentle stream into a raging torrent. If you're in any doubt about the safety of a crossing, look for a safer passage upstream or wait. If the rain is short-lived, it should subside quickly.

If you decide it's essential to cross (late in the day, for example), look for a wide, relatively shallow stretch of the stream rather than a bend. Take off your trousers and socks, but keep your boots on to prevent injury. Put dry, warm clothes and a towel in a plastic bag near the top of your pack. Before stepping out from the bank, unclip your chest strap and belt buckle; this makes it easier to slip out of your backpack and swim to safety if you lose your balance and are swept downstream. Use a walking pole, grasped in both hands, on the upstream side as a third leg, or go

---

WALK SAFETY – BASIC RULES

- Allow plenty of time to accomplish a walk before dark, particularly when daylight hours are shorter.

- Don't overestimate your capabilities. Study the route carefully before setting out, noting the possible escape routes and the point of no return (where it's quicker to continue than to turn back). Monitor your progress during the day against the time estimated for the walk, and keep an eye on the weather.

- It's wise not to walk alone. Always leave details of your intended route, number of people in your group, and expected return time with someone responsible before you set off; let that person know when you return.

- Before setting off, make sure you have the relevant map and a compass – a GPS receiver should not be relied upon in remote areas. You should also make sure you know the weather forecast for the area for the next 24 hours.

arm in arm with a companion, clasping at the wrist, and cross side-on to the flow, taking short steps.

CROSSING SNOW

High in the mountains, even in midsummer, you may find a stretch of late-lying snow. If it's soft and not too steeply angled, you should be able to march across, still taking care to ensure your feet are firmly placed with each step and using poles to keep your balance. However, if the snow is hard and icy, even if thinly decorated with a fresh fall, and the slope is steep, you need two or more of an ice axe, a rope, crampons, companions, a clear head and good balance. Walking poles are no substitute for an ice axe on hard snow. Remember that once you start the crossing, it's awkward to reverse if the going gets too difficult. It may be possible to descend the slope to a narrower, gentler crossing – provided you can safely regain the path on the far side.

DOGS

During walks in settled and farming areas of Italy, you're likely to encounter barking dogs – tethered or running free. Regard any dog as a potential attacker and be prepared to take evasive action: even just crossing the road can take you out of its territory and into safety. A walking pole may be useful, though use it as a last resort, especially if the owner is in sight. Knowing your tetanus immunisation is up to date is reassuring.

LIGHTNING

If a storm brews, avoid exposed areas. Lightning has a penchant for crests, lone trees, small depressions, gullies, caves and cabin entrances, as well as wet ground. If you are caught out in the open, try to curl up as tightly as possible with your feet together and keep a layer of insulation between you and the ground. Place metal objects such as metal-frame backpacks and walking poles away from you.

ROCKFALL

Even a small falling rock could shatter your hand or crack your skull, so always be alert to the danger of rockfall. Trail sections most obviously exposed to rockfall lead below cliffs fringed by large fields of raw talus (rocks that have broken away, ie scree) – don't hang around in such areas. If you accidentally let loose a rock, loudly warn other walkers below.

RESCUE & EVACUATION

If someone in your group is injured or falls ill and can't move, leave somebody with them while another one (or more) goes for help. They should take clear written details of the location and condition of the victim, and of helicopter landing conditions. If there are only two of you, leave the injured person with as much warm clothing, food and water as it's sensible to spare, plus the whistle and torch. Mark the position with something conspicuous – an orange bivvy bag, or perhaps a large stone cross on the ground. Remember, the rescue effort may be slow, perhaps taking more than a day to remove the injured person.

Emergency Communications

There are different emergency telephone numbers for different emergency services, all available nationally (see the boxed text Emergency Numbers, p347). There are also regional search and rescue numbers for mountainous areas (see Search & Rescue Organisations, below). In the mountains, telephones are available at most *rifugi*. For details on payphones and mobile-phone coverage, see Telephones (p320). Only call out a rescue team in a genuine emergency – not for a relatively minor discomfort such as a lightly sprained ankle.

If no other emergency communications are available, use the international distress signal. Give six short signals, such as a whistle, a shout or the flash of a light, at 10-second intervals, followed by a minute's rest. Repeat the sequence until you get a response. If the responder knows the signals, this will be three signals at 20-second intervals, followed by a minute's pause and a repetition of the sequence.

Be ready to give information on where an accident occurred, how many people are injured and the injuries sustained, and, if a helicopter needs to come in, what the terrain and weather conditions are like at the place of the accident.

Search & Rescue Organisations

The **Corpo Nazionale Soccorso Alpino e**

Speleologico (CNSAS; ☎ 02 2953 0433, www.cnsas.it; Via E Petrella 19, 20124 Milan)) is, by law, entrusted with the responsibility of search, rescue and saving of lives in the mountains. It is organised regionally with specific telephone numbers for several regions. For all other regions you should ring the **national emergency number** (☎ 118).

The regional numbers may change, so you should check with CNSAS or local tourist offices for up-to-date numbers.

REGION	EMERGENCY NUMBER
Abruzzo	☎ 167 25 82 39
Alto Adige	☎ 0471 79 71 71
Campania	☎ 081 551 59 50
Emilia Romagna	☎ 800 848088
Friuli–Venezia Giulia	☎ 118
Liguria	☎ 0336 68 93 16
Lombardy	☎ 118
The Marches	☎ 118
Piedmont	☎ 118
Sardinia	☎ 070 28 62 00
Sicily	☎ 095 91 41 41
Trentino	☎ 118
Tuscany	☎ 0348 352 04 08
Umbria	☎ 075 584 70 70
Valle d'Aosta	☎ 0165 23 02 53
Veneto	☎ 118

EMERGENCY NUMBERS

Wherever you are in Italy, these are the numbers to ring in an emergency:

Ambulance (Ambulanza)	☎ 118
Fire Brigade (Vigili del Fuoco)	☎ 115
Highway Rescue (Soccorso Stradale)	☎ 116
Police (Carabinieri)	☎ 112
Police (Polizia)	☎ 113

Helicopter Rescue & Evacuation

If a helicopter arrives on the scene, there are a couple of conventions you should be familiar with. Standing face on to the chopper:

o Arms up in the shape of a letter 'V' means 'I/We need help'.
o Arms in a straight diagonal line (like one line of a letter X) means 'All OK'.

In order for the helicopter to land, there must be a cleared space of 25m x 25m, with a flat landing pad area of 6m x 6m. The helicopter will fly into the wind when landing. In cases of extreme emergency, where no landing area is available, a person or harness might be lowered. Take extreme care to avoid the rotors when approaching a landed helicopter.

Language

CONTENTS

Italian is a Romance language related to French, Spanish, Portuguese and Romanian, all directly descended from Latin. The Romance languages belong to the large Indo-European group of languages, which includes English. As English and Italian have common roots in Latin, English speakers will recognise many Italian words.

Many older Italians still expect to be addressed in the third person formal (*lei* instead of *tu*). What's more, it's not considered polite to use the greeting *ciao* when adressing strangers, unless they use it first; it's better to say *buongiorno* (or *buona sera* as the case may be) and *arrivederci* (or the more polite form, *arrivederla*). We have used the formal address for most of the phrases in this guide; use of the informal address is indicated by 'inf' in brackets. Italian has both masculine and feminine forms, usually ending in 'o' and 'a' respectively. Where both forms are included, they are separated by a slash, with the masculine first.

For a more comprehensive guide to the language, get a copy of Lonely Planet's *Italian Phrasebook*.

PRONUNCIATION

Italian isn't difficult to pronounce once you have learnt a few basic rules. Some of the more clipped vowels and stress on double letters require a bit of practice for English speakers.

Vowels

a	as in 'art'
e	as in 'tell'
i	as in 'pit'
o	as in 'dot', eg *donna* (woman); as in 'port', eg *dormire* (to sleep)
u	as in 'put'

Consonants

The pronunciation of many Italian consonants is similar to those of English, but depends on certain rules:

c	as 'k' before **a**, **o** and **u**; as the 'ch' in 'choose' before **e** and **i**
ch	as the 'k' in 'kit'
g	as in 'get' before **a**, **o**, **u** and **h**; as the 'j' in 'job' before **e** and **i**
gli	as the 'lli' in 'million'
gn	as the 'ny' in 'canyon'
h	always silent (ie not pronounced)
r	a rolled 'rr' sound
sc	as 'sk' before **a**, **o**, **u** and **h**; as the 'sh' in 'sheep' before **e** and **i**
z	as the 'ts' in 'lights', except at the beginning of a word, when it's like the 'ds' in 'beds'

Note that when **ci**, **gi** and **sci** are followed by **a**, **o** or **u**, the 'i' is not pronounced unless the accent falls on the 'i'. Thus the name 'Giovanni' is pronounced 'joh-*vahn*-nee'. Double consonants are pronounced as a longer, often more forceful sound than a single consonant.

Word Stress

Stress often falls on the second-last syllable, as in spa-*ghet*-ti. When a word has an accent, the stress falls on that syllable, as in cit-*tà* (city).

GREETINGS & CIVILITIES

Hello.	*Buongiorno.*
	Ciao./Salve. (inf)
Goodbye.	*Arrivederci.*
	Ciao. (inf)

LANGUAGE

Yes./No.	*Sì./No.*
Please.	*Per favore./Per piacere.*
Thank you.	*Grazie.*
That's fine.	*Prego.*
You're welcome.	
Excuse me.	*Mi scusi./Scusami.*
Sorry. (forgive me)	*Mi scusi./Mi perdoni.*

SMALL TALK

What's your name?
Come si chiama?/Come ti chiami? (pol/inf)
My name is ...
Mi chiamo ...
Where are you from?
Di dov'è?/Di dove sei? (pol/inf)
I'm from ...
Sono di ...
How are you?
Come sta?/Come stai? (pol/inf)

LANGUAGE DIFFICULTIES

I (don't) understand.
(Non) Capisco.
Do you speak English?
Parla inglese?
Please write it down.
Può scriverlo, per favore.

GETTING AROUND

What time does ...	*A che ora parte/*
leave/arrive?	*arriva ...?*
bus (city)	*l'autobus*
bus (intercity)	*il pullman*
ferry	*il traghetto/la nave*
plane	*l'aereo*
train	*il treno*

I want to go to ...	*Voglio andare a ...*

I'd like a ... ticket.	*Vorrei un biglietto ...*
one-way	*di solo andata*
return	*di andata e ritorno*
1st-class	*di prima classe*
2nd-class	*di seconda classe*

Do I have to change trains/platforms?
Devo cambiare treno/binario?
The train has been cancelled/delayed.
Il treno è soppresso/in ritardo.

the first	*il primo*
the last	*l'ultimo*
left luggage office	*deposito bagagli*
platform number	*binario numero*
station	*stazione*

SIGNS

Entrata	Entrance
Uscita	Exit
Completo	No Vacancies
Informazioni	Information
Aperto/Chiuso	Open/Closed
Vietato	Prohibited
Camere Libere	Rooms Available
Gabinetti	Toilets
Uomini	Men
Donne	Women

ticket office	*biglietteria*
timetable	*orario*

I'd like to hire ...	*Vorrei noleggiare ...*
a bicycle	*una bicicletta*
a car	*una macchina*

DIRECTIONS

Where is ... ?	*Dov'è ...?*
Go straight ahead.	*Si va sempre diritto.*
Turn left.	*Gira a sinistra.*
Turn right.	*Gira a destra.*
at the next corner	*al prossimo angolo*
at the traffic lights	*al semaforo*
behind	*dietro*
in front of	*davanti*
opposite	*di fronte a*

AROUND TOWN

I'm looking for ...	*Cerco ...*
a bank	*un banco*
the police station	*la questura*
the post office	*la posta*
a public toilet	*un gabinetto/bagno pubblico*
the tourist office	*l'ufficio di turismo*

What is the address?
Cos'è l'indirizzo?
I'd like to make a telephone call.
Vorrei telefonare.

I want to change ...	*Voglio cambiare ...*
money	*denaro*
travellers cheques	*degli assegni per viaggiatori*

ACCOMMODATION

I'm looking for ...	*Cerco ...*
a camping ground	*un campeggio*
a guesthouse	*una pensione*
a hotel	*un albergo*
a youth hostel	*un ostello per la gioventù*

LANGUAGE

Do you have any rooms available?
Ha camere libere?/C'è una camera libera?

I'd like ...	*Vorrei ...*
a bed	*un letto*
a single room	*una camera singola*
a double room	*una camera matrimoniale*
a room with two beds	*una camera doppia*
a room with a bathroom	*una camera con bagno*
to share a dorm	*un letto in dormitorio*

How much is it ... ?	*Quanto costa ...?*
per night	*per la notte*
per person	*per ciascuno*

| May I see it? | *Posso vederla?* |

Do you accept ...?	*Accettate ...?*
credit cards	*carte di credito*
travellers cheques	*assegni per viaggiatori*

I'm staying for ...	*Resto per ...*
one day	*un giorno*
two days	*due giorni*

SHOPPING

bookshop	*libreria*
chemist/pharmacy	*farmacia*
newsstand	*edicola*
stationers	*cartolaio*
supermarket	*supermercato*

I'd like to buy ...	*Vorrei comprare ...*
How much is it?	*Quanto costa?*
I'm just looking.	*Sto solo guardando.*
I'll take it.	*Lo/La compro.*
more/less	*più/meno*

HEALTH

I'm ill.	*Mi sento male.*
It hurts here.	*Mi fa male qui.*
I need a doctor.	*Ho bisogno di un dottore/medico.*

I'm ...	*Sono ...*
asthmatic	*asmatico/a*
diabetic	*diabetico/a*
epileptic	*epilettico/a*

I'm allergic ...	*Sono allergico/a ...*
to antibiotics	*agli antibiotici*
to penicillin	*alla penicillina*

EMERGENCIES

Help!	*Aiuto!*
Call a doctor!	*Chiami un medico!*
Call the police!	*Chiami la polizia!*
Careful!	*Attenzione!*
I'm lost.	*Mi sono perso/a.*
Go away!	*Vai via!*

antiseptic	*antisettico*
aspirin	*aspirina*
blister	*vescica*
condoms	*preservativi*
contraceptive	*anticoncezionale*
diarrhoea	*diarrea*
medicine	*medicina*
nausea	*nausea*
sunblock cream	*crema/latte solare (per protezione)*
tampons	*tamponi*

TIME & DATES

What time is it?	*Che ora è?/Che ore sono?*
It's (8 o'clock).	*Sono (le otto).*
When?	*Quando?*

in the morning	*di mattina*
in the afternoon	*di pomeriggio*
in the evening	*di sera*
today	*oggi*
tomorrow	*domani*
yesterday	*ieri*

Monday	*lunedì*
Tuesday	*martedì*
Wednesday	*mercoledì*
Thursday	*giovedì*
Friday	*venerdì*
Saturday	*sabato*
Sunday	*domenica*

January	*gennaio*
February	*febbraio*
March	*marzo*
April	*aprile*
May	*maggio*
June	*guigno*
July	*luglio*
August	*agosto*
September	*settembre*
October	*ottobre*
November	*novembre*
December	*dicembre*

NUMBERS

0	*zero*
1	*uno*
2	*due*
3	*tre*
4	*quattro*
5	*cinque*
6	*sei*
7	*sette*
8	*otto*
9	*nove*
10	*dieci*
11	*undici*
12	*dodici*
13	*tredici*
14	*quattordici*
15	*quindici*
16	*sedici*
17	*diciasette*
18	*diciotto*
19	*diciannove*
20	*venti*
21	*ventuno*
22	*ventidue*
30	*trenta*
40	*quaranta*
50	*cinquanta*
60	*sessanta*
70	*settanta*
80	*ottanta*
90	*novanta*
100	*cento*
1000	*mille*
2000	*due mila*
one million	*un milione*

quarter	*un quarto*
half	*un mezzo*

FOOD
Basics

breakfast	*prima colazione*
lunch	*pranzo*
dinner	*cena*

What is this?	*(Che) Cos'è?*
I'm a vegetarian.	*Sono vegetariano/a.*
I'd like the set menu.	*Vorrei il menù turistico.*
bill/cheque	*il conto*
cover charge	*coperto*
service charge	*servizio*

bottle	*bottiglia*
cup	*tazza*
fork	*forchetta*
glass	*bicchiere*
knife	*coltello*
plate	*piatto*
spoon	*cucchiaio*
teaspoon	*cucchiaino*

Common Food & Drink

bread	*pane*
butter	*burro*
cheese	*formaggio*
coffee	*caffè*
eggs	*uova*
fruit juice	*succo di frutta*
jam	*marmellata*
milk	*latte*
mineral water	*acqua minerale*
oil	*olio*
pepper	*pepe*
rice	*riso*
salt	*sale*
sugar	*zucchero*
tea	*tè*
vinegar	*aceto*
wine	*vino*

Self-Catering

baker	*fornaio/panetteria*
delicatessen	*salumeria*
greengrocer	*fruttivendolo*
grocer	*alimentari*
pastry shop	*pasticceria*
supermarket	*supermercato*

a portion of ...	*un etto di ...*
a slice of ...	*una fetta di...*

Menu Decoder
FISH & SEAFOOD

acciughe	*anchovies*
aragosta	*lobster*
calamari	*squid*
cozze	*mussels*
gamberi	*prawns*
pesce spada	*swordfish*
sarde	*sardines*
tonno	*tuna*
vongole	*clams*

FRUIT & NUTS

albicocce	*apricots*
arance	*oranges*
arachide	*peanuts*
banane	*bananas*
castagne	*chestnuts*
ciliegie	*cherries*

LANGUAGE

fragole	*strawberries*
lamponi	*raspberries*
mandorle	*almonds*
mele	*apples*
noci	*walnuts*
noccioli	*hazelnuts*
pere	*pears*
pesche	*peaches*
pompelmi	*grapefruit*
uva	*grapes*

MEAT & POULTRY

agnello	*lamb*
bistecca	*steak*
maiale	*pork*
manzo	*beef*
pollo	*chicken*
prosciutto	*cooked/cured*
cotto/crudo	*ham*
salsiccia	*sausage*
vitello	*veal*

VEGETABLES

aglio	*garlic*
cipolle	*onions*
fagiolini	*string beans*
finocchio	*fennel*
funghi	*mushrooms*
melanzane	*aubergines/eggplant*
patate	*potatoes*
pomodori	*tomatoes*
sedano	*celery*

ON THE WALK
Clothing & Equipment

backpack	*zaino*
battery	*pila*
(walking) boots	*scarpone*
camera	*macchina fotografica*
compass	*bussola*
crampons	*ramponi/grappette*
film	*pellicola*
fleece jacket	*giubbotto di pile*
gloves	*guanti*
ice axe	*piccozza da alpinisti*
lighter	*accendino*
(walking) map	*carta*
matches	*fiammiferi*
pocket knife	*temperino*
rain jacket	*impermeabile*
sleeping bag	*sacco a pelo*
socks	*calzini*
sunglasses	*occhiali da sole*
tent	*tenda*
toilet paper	*carta igienica*

torch/flashlight	*torcia elettrica*
walking pole	*bastone da passeggio*
warm hat	*cappello di stoffa calda*
water bottle	*borraccia*

Directions & Trail Terms

How many more hours to ...?
Restano quante ore a ...?
We're walking from ... to ...
Andiamo da ... a ...
Does this path go to ...?
Questo sentiero arriva a ...?
Can you show me on the map?
Può mostrarmi sulla carta?
Where have you come from?
Da dove è venuto/a?
How long does it take?
Ci vuole quanto tempo?
How much snow is there on the pass?
Quanta neve c'è sul passo?
Can the river be crossed?
Si può attraversare il fiume?

Go straight ahead.	*Si va sempre diritto.*
Turn left/right.	*Gira a sinistra/destra.*
the first left/right	*il primo a sinistra/destra*
direction	*direzione*
round trip	*(viaggio di) andata e ritorno*
turnoff	*bivio*

ahead	*avanti/davanti*
behind	*dietro*
above	*sopra*
below	*sotto*
before	*prima di/davanti a*
after	*dopo*
beginning	*inizio*
end	*fine*
downstream	*a valle*
upstream	*a monte*
flat	*piatto*
steep	*ripido*
high	*alto*
low	*basso*
near	*vicino*
far	*lontanto*
beside	*accanto a*
between	*tra*
level with	*alla pari di*
opposite	*di fronte*
north	*nord*
south	*sud*
east	*est*
west	*ovest*

SPEAK A LITTLE GERMAN

In South Tyrol and the Carnic Alps the first language of many locals is German and you're more likely to be greeted in (Austrian) German than Italian. While Italian will suffice, it certainly won't hurt to know a few greetings and trail words in German, and it may help with map references.

BASICS
Hello.
Grüss Gott.
Bye.
Tschüss.
Yes./No.
Ja./Nein.
Please.
Bitte.
Thank you (very much).
Danke (schön).

What is your name?
Wie heissen Sie?
My name is …
Ich heisse …
Where are you from?
Woher kommen Sie?
I'm from …
Ich komme aus …
I have a reservation for the refuge/inn.
Ich habe eine Reservierung für die Hütte/Gusthof.
How much is it per night?
Wieviel kostet es pro Nach?

WALKING TALK
Is this the trail/road to …?
Ist das der Weg/die Strasse nach …?
Which trail goes to …?
Welcher Weg führt nach …?
How many kilometres to …?
Wieviele Kilometer sind es bis …?
Where are you going?
Wohin gehen Sie?
Is the trail safe?
Ist der Weg sicher?
Can you show me (on the map)?
Können Sie mir (auf der Karte) zeigen?
I'm looking for …
Ich suche …
Go straight ahead.
Gehen Sie geradeaus.

Turn left/right.
Biegen Sie links/rechts ab.
near/far
nahe/weit

alp hut	*Alphütte*
alp track	*Alpweg*
avalanche	*Lawine*
backpack	*Rucksack*
bridge	*Brücke*
cable car	*Luftseilbahn*
cairn	*Steinmännchen*
crampons	*Steigeisen*
crossing	*Übergang*
direction	*Richtung*
east	*Ost*
food/meal	*Speise*
gap	*Furgge/Scharte*
glacier	*Gletscher*
gorge/ravine	*Schlucht*
hut	*Hütte*
lake	*See*
map	*Landkarte*
mountain guide	*Bergführer*
north	*Nord*
path/trail	*Pfad/Wanderweg*
peak/summit	*Gipfel*
reservoir	*Stausee*
ridge	*Grat*
river	*Ufer*
rockfall	*Steinschlag*
saddle	*Joch/Sattel*
scree/talus	*Geröll*
signpost	*Wegweiser*
snow	*Schnee*
south	*Süd*
stream	*Bach*
thunderstorm	*Gewitter*
valley	*Tal*
walking map	*Wanderkarte*
waterfall	*Wasserfall*
west	*Wes*

Weather
What's the forecast?
Come sono le previsioni?
Tomorrow it will be …
Domani sarà …

good weather	*bel tempo*
bad weather	*brutto tempo*
cloudy	*nuvoloso*
cold	*freddo*
flood	*alluvione*
fog/mist	*nebbia*
hot	*caldo*
ice (it's icy)	*ghiaccio (è ghiacciato)*
lightning	*fulmine*
rain (it's raining)	*pioggia (piove)*

LANGUAGE

snow (it's snowing)	neve (nevica)
storm	tempesta
sunny	soleggiato
thunderstorm	temporale
wind (it's windy)	vento (c'è vento)

Features

bend (in road)	curva
bridge	ponte
cable car	funivia
cairn	tumolo (di peitre)
farm	fattoria
fence	recinto
footbridge	passerella
ford	guado
forest	foresta/bosco
house/building	casa/edificio
hut	rifugio
path	sentiero
quarry	cava
road	strada
shelter	bivacco
signpost	cartello indicatore
spring (of water)	sorgente
town	città
tree	albero
village	frazione/paese/villagio
way marker	segnale

Landforms

avalanche	valanga
bay	baia
bog/swamp	palude

cape/headland	capo
cave	caverna/grotta
cliff	scogliera scoscesa/rupe
coast	costa
crater	cratere
gap	passo/valico
glacier	ghiacciaio
gorge	gorge
hill	collina/colle
island	isola
junction (in river or stream)	confluenza
lake	lago
landslide	frana
moraine	morena
mountain	montagna
mud	fango
pass	passo/forcella
peninsula	peninsola
plateau	altipiano
ridge	cresta
river	fiume/rio/torrente
riverbank	riva
rockfall	caduta di pietra/caduta massi
saddle	sella
scree/talus	ghiaione
slope	versanto
snowfield	nevaio
stream	ruscello/torrente
summit/peak	cima/sommità
valley	valle/val/vallone
volcano	vulcano
waterfall	cascata

Also available from Lonely Planet:
Italian Phrasebook

Glossary

A

AAST – Azienda Automona di Soggiorno e Turismo; local tourist office

agriturismo – farm-stay, tourist accommodation on a working farm

AIG – Associazione Italiana Alberghi per la Gioventù; Italy's youth hostel association

albergo (s), **alberghi** (pl) – hotel, guesthouse

alimentari – all-purpose shop for groceries and fresh food

alluvione – flood

alm – summer grazing pastures and associated buildings

alp, **alpe**, **alpeggio** – summer base in mountain pastures for making dairy products

alpinismo – mountaineering, requiring technical skills

alta via – high level walking route

APT – Azienda di Promozione Turistica; tourist office (usually regional)

AST – Azienda Soggiorno e Turismo; local tourist office

B

bach – stream

baia – bay (maritime)

baita – building providing shelter, open to all, usually not a high altitudes

becca – mountain peak with pointed profile

berg – mountain

berghütte – mountain hut (see *rifugio*)

bivacco (s), **bivacchi** (pl) – remote, high mountain shelter, which may or may not be locked

bocca – mouth, entrance

bocchetta – pass, saddle, low point on a ridge

borgo (s), **borghi** (pl) – ancient town or village

bosco – woodland, forest

bussola – compass

C

caccia – hunting (of animals)

caduta massi – falling rocks (a common sign beside roads and some paths)

CAI – Club Alpino Italiano; Italian Alpine Club

cairn – mound of stones

cala – bay

campeggio (s), **campeggi** (pl) – camping ground with facilities

campo – field

canale, **canalone** – rocky alpine gorge, valley

capo – cape (coastal)

cappella – chapel

carabinieri – police with military and civil duties

carreggiabile – accessible by vehicle

carta, **cartina** – map

caserma – barracks

cascata – waterfall

castello – castle

cattivo – bad (as in bad weather)

caverna – cave

chiesa – church

cima – mountain peak, summit

codula – geo or gorge (Sardinia)

colle – hill, pass

comune – town council; the local government area for which it is responsible

conca – hollow, valley

corno – mountain peak, usually steep-sided

cresta, **crinale** – mountain ridge, the divide between streams

curva di livello – contour line

D

discesa – descent

dislivello – gradient; difference in altitude between two places

divieto d'accesso – keep out

divieto di sosta – no parking or stopping

doccia – shower (bathing)

dora – river (similar to a *fiume*)

dosso – rise

E

ENIT – Ente Nazionale Italiano per il Turismo; Italian state tourist office

EPT – Ente Provinciale per il Turismo; provincial tourist office

escursione – walk, hike, tramp

est – east

F

fermata – bus stop

ferrovia – train station

finestra – narrow gap or pass on a mountain ridge
fiore selvatico – wild flower
fiume – major river (larger than a *torrente*)
fonte – spring (water source)
forcella – col, saddle, low point on a ridge
frana – landslide
frazione – village
FS – Ferrovie dello Stato; Italian state railway
fulmine – lightning
fumarole – vent in a volcano from which hot gases are emitted
funivia – cable car

G

galleria – tunnel
GEA – Grande Escursione Appenninica; long distance route in the Apennines
gestore – manager of a *rifugio*
gettone – token, occasionally needed to operate shower at a *campeggio* or *rifugio*
ghiacciaio – glacier
gias – herders' camp (Maritime Alps)
golfo – gulf
grotta – cave
guardia forestale – forest ranger
GTA – Grande Traversata delli Alpi; long distance route through foothills of the Alps

I

IAT – Informazioni e Assistenza ai Turisti; local tourist office
itinerario – route rather than a formed path

J

joch – mountain ridge, pass from one valley to another
jôf – peak (Julian Alps)

L

laghetto – small lake
lago – lake
lama – very narrow mountain ridge
letto – bed
LIPU – Lega Italiana Protezione Uccelli; Italian League for the Protection of Birds
locanda – country inn, smaller than a p*ensione*

M

malga (s), **malghe** (pl) – herder's summer hut
marcellaria – butcher's shop
meridione – south

mezza pensione – half pension, half-board (dinner, bed and breakfast)
montagna – mountain
monte – mount
mouflon – mountain sheep
mulattiera – path originally used by mules, along which mules were led

N

nebbia – fog, mist
névé – mass of porous ice, formed from snow, that has not yet become a glacier
nord – north
nuraghe (s), **nuraghi** (pl) – cone-shaped megalithic stone fortresses (Sardinia)
nuvoloso – cloudy (weather)

O

occidentale – western
oratorio – wayside shrine
oriente – east
ospizi – hospices, inns
ostello per la gioventù – youth hostel
ovest – west

P

paese – village, small town
panetteria, pasticceria – baker, cake shop
parco nazionale – national park
parco naturale regionale – regional natural (nature) park
parete (di rocccia) – rockface
passerella – footbridge
passo – pass, crossing between two valleys
pensione – small hotel
pericolosissimo – very dangerous
percorso – route
pericoloso – dangerous
pian, piano – plain, fairly level area
piazza – town square
pieve – parish church
pineta – pine forest
pioggia – rain
piovoso – wet (weather)
ponte – bridge
posto tappa – place to stay at the end of a day's walk, especially on a long-distance path
prato – meadow, flat grassy area
previsioni del tempo – weather forecast
Pro Loco – small local tourist office
proprietà privata – private property
punta – mountain peak

Q

quota – altitude, height above sea level

R

ramponi – crampons, spiked metal frames strapped to boots for walking or climbing on ice or snow

ricovero – fairly basic shelter in mountain areas

rifugio (s), **rifugi** (pl) – mountain hut, similar to a simple hotel, often with bunkrooms

rio – river (smaller than a *fiume*, similar to a *torrente*)

riva – river bank

rovina, rudere – ruin(s) of a building

S

salita – climb, ascent

scarpone – walking/hiking/mountain boots

scharte – gap, low point on ridge

scorciatoia – short cut

scree – accumulated rock fragments at the foot of a cliff or across a mountainside

seggiovia – chairlift

segnale, segnaletica – signposting

sentiero (s), **sentieri** (pl) – footpath or defined walking route on formed path

settentrionale – northern

SI – Sentiero Italia; long-distance route through Italy

soccorso – help, assistance

soccorso alpino – mountain rescue

sopra – upper

sorgente – spring, often of mineral water

sotto – lower

spitze – mountain peak with pointed profile

strada – street, road

sud – south

T

tabaccheria – tobacconist, all-purpose shop where bus tickets and, often, phonecards are sold

TCI – Touring Club Italiano

tempesta – storm

tempo – weather

tempo di percorrenza – time needed to complete a walk

temporale – thunderstorm

tenda – tent

terme – thermal baths

testa – mountain resembling a head in shape or position

tetti – small group of houses, hamlet

torre – tower, fortified towerlike building

torrente – small river, stream

trattoria – cheap restaurant

U

UIT – Ufficio Informazioni Turistiche

Unesco – United Nations Educational, Scientific & Cultural Organisation

V

val, valle – valley

valanga – avalanche

Valdostane – particular to Valle d'Aosta

vallone – deep or large valley

vedretta – hanging glacier

vento – wind

vetta – mountain peak

via – street, road

via ferrata (s), **vie ferrate** (pl) – very steep route over rock equipped with fixed cables, ladders, bridges and/or metal rungs

via normale – normal route

W

wald – forest

Z

zaino – rucksack

GLOSSARY

Behind the Scenes

THIS BOOK

This guidebook was commissioned in Lonely Planet's Melbourne office, and produced by the following:

Publisher Chris Rennie
Associate Publisher Ben Handicott
Commissioning Editors Bridget Blair, Janine Eberle
Language Content Laura Crawford
Cover Designer Brendan Dempsey
Cover Image Research Naomi Parker
Internal Image Research Jane Hart
Project Manager Jane Atkin
Thanks to Andy Lewis, Graham Imeson, Mik Ruf
Production [recapture]

THANKS
FROM THE AUTHOR

Many thanks to all the untold train guards, bus drivers, national park rangers, restaurateurs and innocent bystanders who helped me during my research. Particular thanks to Bridget Blair for offering me the gig in the first place, Janine Eberle for softening the blows en route, and to Louise McKee who did a fantastic job researching and making notes for the Julian and Carnic Alps chapter. Special thanks also to fellow walkers and companions in Italy including my sister Theresa, nephews Matt and Jamie, parents Connie and Brian, Andy McKee and – as always – my stalwart wife Liz and my three-year-old son Kieran.

OUR READERS

Many thanks to the travellers who used the last edition and wrote to us with helpful hints, useful advice and interesting anecdotes:

Kyle Barbour, Fernando Condal, C Dalton, Maureen Downes, Andrea Harchar, Dick Hazelwood, Marianne Mueller, Keith Tapp

ACKNOWLEDGMENTS

Internal photographs p6 (#5) Vito Arcomano/Alamy; p11 (#3) Gareth McCormack/Alamy; p8 (#4) Photoshot Holdings Ltd/Alamy; p9 (#2) Gillian Price/Alamy. All other photographs by Lonely Planet Images, and by Glenn Beanland p2 (#1); Alan Benson p4 (#5); Bethune Carmichael p5 (#4); Guylain Doyle p4 (#1); John Elk III p2 (#2), p11 (#1); Ionas Kaltenbach p8 (#5); Holger Leue p3 (#3); Diana Mayfield p10 (#2); Andrew Peacock p3 (#5), p7 (#2); Giorgio Perbellini p6 (#3); Damien Simonis p10 (#4); Witold Skrypczak p12; Philip & Karen Smith p4 (#2), p6 (#4); Dallas Stribley p8 (#1).

THE LONELY PLANET STORY

Fresh from an epic journey across Europe, Asia and Australia in 1972, Tony and Maureen Wheeler sat at their kitchen table stapling together notes. The first Lonely Planet guidebook, *Across Asia on the Cheap*, was born.

Travellers snapped up the guides. Inspired by their success, the Wheelers began publishing books to Southeast Asia, India and beyond. Demand was prodigious, and the Wheelers expanded the business rapidly to keep up. Over the years, Lonely Planet extended its coverage to every country and into the virtual world via lonelyplanet.com and the Thorn Tree message board.

As Lonely Planet became a globally loved brand, Tony and Maureen received several offers for the company. But it wasn't until 2007 that they found a partner whom they trusted to remain true to the company's principles of travelling widely, treading lightly and giving sustainably. In October of that year, BBC Worldwide acquired a 75% share in the company, pledging to uphold Lonely Planet's commitment to independent travel, trustworthy advice and editorial independence.

Today, Lonely Planet has offices in Melbourne, London and Oakland, with over 500 staff members and 300 authors. Tony and Maureen are still actively involved with Lonely Planet. They're travelling more often than ever, and they're devoting their spare time to charitable projects. And the company is still driven by the philosophy of *Across Asia on the Cheap*: 'All you've got to do is decide to go and the hardest part is over. So go!'

Index

000 Map pages
000 Photograph pages

INDEX

000 Map pages
000 Photograph pages

INDEX

INDEX

LONELY PLANET OFFICES

Australia
Head Office
Locked Bag 1, Footscray, Victoria 3011
☎ 03 8379 8000, fax 03 8379 8111
talk2us@lonelyplanet.com.au

USA
150 Linden St, Oakland, CA 94607
☎ 510 893 8556, toll free 800 275 8555
fax 510 893 8572
info@lonelyplanet.com

UK
2nd fl, 186 City Rd,
London EC1V 2NT
☎ 020 7106 2100, fax 020 7106 2101
go@lonelyplanet.co.uk

PUBLISHED BY LONELY PLANET PUBLICATIONS PTY LTD

ABN 36 005 607 983

© Lonely Planet Publications Pty Ltd 2010

© photographers as indicated 2010

Cover photograph: Suedtirol, Italien, Dolomiten, Berge, Drei Zinnen, Bildagentur RM. Many of the images in this guide are available for licensing from Lonely Planet Images: www .lonelyplanetimages.com.

Printed by Fabulous Printers Pte Ltd
Printed in Singapore

Mixed Sources
Product group from well-managed forests and other controlled sources
www.fsc.org Cert no. SGS-COC-005002
© 1996 Forest Stewardship Council
FSC